AF605932

Tradition and Transformation

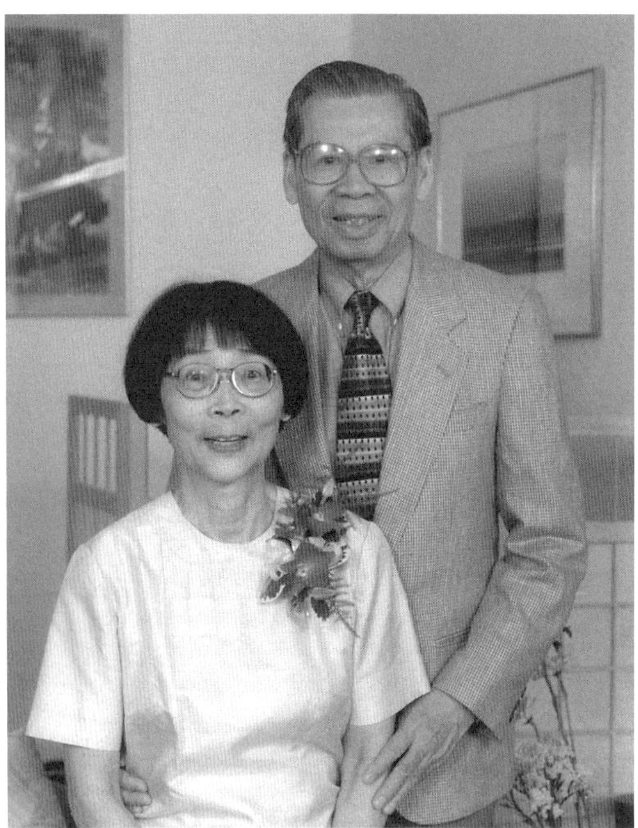

Dr. Chu-tsing Li and Yao-wen Li, 1998

Tradition and Transformation

STUDIES IN CHINESE ART IN HONOR OF CHU-TSING LI

Edited by Judith G. Smith

Spencer Museum of Art, The University of Kansas
in association with The University of Washington Press, Seattle and London

CONTENTS

AN APPRECIATION OF CHU-TSING LI

This volume of essays presented to Chu-tsing Li by friends and former students attests to the important role he played as a teacher and chair of the Department of the History of Art at the University of Kansas.

Chu-tsing Li, born and educated in China, came to the University of Kansas in 1966 after first teaching at the University of Iowa, where he earned his Ph.D. in 1955. He arrived with a clear mission: he wanted to establish the University of Kansas as the leader in the Midwest, and eventually one of the major centers in the nation, for the study of Asian art. Some would have thought he was a dreamer, for when he joined the Department of the History of Art, no one had ever taught Chinese art at the university. Dr. Li at once set about creating not a course or even a series of courses, but an entire program that culminated in the doctoral degree. By the end of his teaching career, in 1990, this program had produced specialists in both Chinese and Japanese art and had trained and inspired an impressive number of doctoral students.

A key element in the teaching and research program at the University of Kansas was the liaison that Dr. Li established with the Nelson-Atkins Museum of Art in Kansas City, Missouri. He convinced the great museum director and scholar of Chinese art, Lawrence Sickman, a man who had never taught, to offer courses in connoisseurship and in Chinese art. Until his death in 1988, Mr. Sickman was a major figure in the study of Asian art at Kansas, making available to university students his vast knowledge and insight and the riches and resources of the Nelson-Atkins Museum.

Having created a thriving teaching and research program at home, Dr. Li turned his attention abroad. He established successful personal and institutional relations with Taiwan, later with Hong Kong, and finally with the People's Republic of China, in the process enabling Kansas students to study and carry out research projects.

In 1978 Dr. Li was honored by being appointed the first Judith Harris Murphy Distinguished Professor of Art History. His prodigious work as a scholar and as a collector of modern Chinese art is a noteworthy achievement, as demonstrated by the bibliography of published research that is included here. Dr. Li fostered the appreciation of contemporary Chinese art when few people in the United States were aware of the work being done by artists in China or from that part of the world. The achievements of painters and printmakers, many of whom are now collected and exhibited in Western as well as Asian museums, were brought to public and critical attention by Dr. Li.

Formerly a dedicated teacher, Dr. Li remains one of those rare individuals who is still available to friends and students. He seems to have no need for the rest and relaxation enjoyed by most of us. Furthermore, he and his late wife, Yao-wen Li, provided a home away from home for foreign students as well as that invaluable mentoring which assists the transition from new student to mature professional. He has been, without doubt, among the greatest teachers of Asian art in the United States and a formidable influence on all who have been fortunate to know him and to call him their friend.

Marilyn Stokstad
Judith Harris Murphy Distinguished
Professor of Art History Emerita
University of Kansas

A PERSONAL VIEW

It was late December of 1978 that I traveled for the first time across the Pacific Ocean, from Taipei to Lawrence, Kansas. For me, a young foreign student from subtropical Taiwan, the snowy landscape of the Midwest was truly like a Christmas card come to life. After my arrival at the dormitory for international students, even before I began my studies, I received an invitation to Dr. and Mrs. Chu-tsing Li's New Year's Eve party. As I discovered, the Lis opened and shared their house with many friends, colleagues, and students, and for students like myself it became a home away from home for many years to come. Even today, I can recall the warm reception I received as a stranger in a wintry land nearly three decades ago.

Dr. Li developed connections with China rather early. In 1979, soon after the establishment of diplomatic relations between the United States and the People's Republic of China, he was among the first group of exchange professors, one of five scholars who were invited to visit and travel in China by the Ministry of Culture. In the early summer of 1982, he led the Henan Archaeological Tour, comprised of thirty-three participants, including members of the University of Kansas faculty and staff, students, alumni, and friends. We were able to travel extensively in China. Dr. Li was especially generous in sharing with his students his personal and professional connections abroad for their research projects. Because of his open-mindedness concerning their research, his students were always allowed to follow their hearts in selecting these projects. His students majored not only in the arts of China, but also in those of Japan and Korea. They ranged over the fields of painting, archaeology, Buddhist art, ceramics, and furniture, from ancient to contemporary times. As their professor and mentor, Dr. Li was gentle in his advice and generous in making himself available. As his students, we all benefited from his selflessness. Among Dr. Li's former students, many are now museum directors, curators, university professors, or other art or art history-related professionals, both in the U.S. and abroad.

It was not only students from different parts of the world who came to study at the University of Kansas. Scholars from China, Hong Kong, and Taiwan were invited to co-teach with Dr. Li, and thus enriched the Asian art program immensely. This festschrift, containing contributions from Dr. Li's colleagues and students, again from both the U.S. and abroad, is evidence of the international range of his scholarship and influence of his personality. From the heartland of the United States he has made an unsurpassed contribution to the field of Chinese art history over the last four decades.

Joseph Chang
Associate Curator of Chinese Art
Freer Gallery of Art and
Arthur M. Sackler Gallery
Smithsonian Institution,
Washington, D.C.

ACKNOWLEDGMENTS

This publication has benefited from the collaboration and commitment of many people. Chief among them are the authors, who have responded with extraordinary patience to editorial inquiries, usually on a very demanding schedule. Also essential to the success of this publication has been the assistance of the Spencer Museum of Art, the University of Kansas. In particular, we are indebted to three individuals for guidance in the final stages of production: Saralyn Reece Hardy, Director; Carolyn Chinn Lewis, Assistant Director; and Stephen Goddard, Professor of Art History and Senior Curator of Prints and Drawings. Maud Humphrey, Department of the History of Art at Kansas, was crucial in facilitating administrative matters in connection with the publication.

We are especially grateful to Raymond Furse and Elizabeth Powers for their invaluable assistance in editing and proofreading; Angela Darling for typing the edited papers; Lynn Huang for her help in preparing the Glossary; Chen (Cynthia) Liu and Chun-yi Lee for their assistance in compiling the Bibliography; and David W. Goodrich of Birdtrack Press for typesetting the Chinese essays and the Glossary. The existence of this elegant volume is due in no small part to the exceptionally talented partnership of Joseph Cho and Stefanie Lew of Binocular, who were responsible for the book's design and production.

Last, but by no means least, we gratefully acknowledge the generous financial support of J.S. Lee and Kuo-sung and Mo-hua Liu. Other contributors include Janet Baker, The Bei Shan Tang Foundation, Heather Berger, Claudia Brown, Margaret Carney, Janet Carpenter, Joseph Chang, Richard Edwards, Charles and Jane Eldredge, Wen C. Fong, Marilyn Gridley, The Kress Foundation Department of Art History, Lin-hwei Lee, Dorothy Leidig, Choonsang and Chingchia Leong, Li He, Lin-I Liu, Lin-shih Liu, Robert Mowry, Hsio-Yen Shih, Spencer Museum of Art, Marilyn Stokstad, The University of Kansas Endowment Association, Wan Qingli, Jean Wetzel, and Donald Wood. Without their generosity, this publication would not have been possible.

Judith G. Smith
Editor

CONTRIBUTORS

ALAN G. ATKINSON
Adjunct Instructor of History and Art, University of Oklahoma

JANET BAKER
Curator of Asian Art, Phoenix Art Museum

SARAH BLICK
Assistant Professor of Art History, Kenyon College, Ohio

CLAUDIA BROWN
Director, Center for Asian Studies, College of Liberal Arts and Sciences; Associate Professor of Art History, Herberger College of Fine Arts, Arizona State University

JANET LOUISE CARPENTER
Lecturer, Art Department, City College of San Francisco

JU-HSI CHOU
Professor Emeritus, School of Art, Arizona State University; Former Curator of Chinese Art, The Cleveland Museum of Art

TSENG YUHO ECKE
Former Professor, University of Hawaii; Former Adjunct Curator of Chinese Art, Honolulu Academy of Arts

RICHARD EDWARDS
Professor Emeritus, History of Art Department, University of Michigan

WEN C. FONG
Professor Emeritus, Princeton University

MARILYN GRIDLEY
Research Associate, Center for East Asian Studies, University of Kansas

JUNGHEE HAN
Professor of Art History, Hongik University, Seoul

JIN WEINUO
Chairman Emeritus, Department of Art History, Central Academy of Fine Arts, Beijing

JANE C. JU
Associate Professor, Department of History, National Chengchi University, Taipei

THOMAS LAWTON
Director Emeritus, Freer Gallery of Art and Arthur M. Sackler Gallery, Smithsonian Institution, Washington, D.C.

AN-YI PAN
Associate Professor,
Department of the History of Art,
Cornell University

RAO ZONGYI
Distinguished Professor Emeritus,
Chinese University of Hong Kong

HSIO-YEN SHIH
Honorary Professor of Fine Arts,
The University of Hong Kong

HSING-LI TSAI
Independent Scholar

WAN QINGLI
Professor of Chinese Art History,
The University of Hong Kong

ANKENEY WEITZ
Associate Professor of Art,
Colby College

JEAN WETZEL
Associate Professor of Art History,
California Polytechnic State
University, San Luis Obispo

RICHARD L. WILSON
Professor of Asian Art and
Archaeology and Chair, Graduate
School, Division of Comparative
Culture, International Christian
University, Tokyo

DONALD A. WOOD
Chief Curator and the Virginia
and William M. Spencer III
Curator of Asian Art, Birmingham
Museum of Art, Alabama

PHILIP C.J. WU
Assistant Professor, Department
of Fine Arts, Tunghai University,
Taiwan

XUE YONGNIAN
Chairman Emeritus, Department
of Art History, Central Academy of
Fine Arts, Beijing

SILIANG YANG
Regional Vice President,
PROS Revenue Management,
Houston, Texas

YANG XIN
Deputy Director Emeritus,
Palace Museum, Beijing

SELECTED BIBLIOGRAPHY OF CHU-TSING LI

BOOKS AND EXHIBITION CATALOGUES

Que Hua qiuse: Zhao Mengfu de shengping yu huayi (The Autumn Colors on the Que and Hua Mountains: The Life and Art of Zhao Mengfu). Taipei: Shitou chuban gufen youxian gongsi, 2003.

Zhongguo xiandai huihua shi: Dangdai zhi bu, 1950–2000 (A History of Modern Chinese Painting: Contemporary Period, 1950–2000), with Wan Qingli. Taipei: Shitou chuban gufen youxian gongsi, 2003.

Zhongguo xiandai huihua shi: Min chu zhi bu, 1912–1949 (A History of Modern Chinese Painting: Republican Period, 1912–1949), with Wan Qingli. Taipei: Shitou chuban gufen youxian gongsi, 2001.

Zhongguo xiandai huihua shi: Wan Qing zhi bu, 1840–1911 (A History of Modern Chinese Painting: Late Qing, 1840–1911), with Wan Qingli. Taipei: Shitou chuban gufen youxian gongsi, 1998.

Artists and Patrons: Some Social and Economic Aspects of Chinese Painting, ed. Lawrence, Kansas: Kress Foundation Department of Art History, the University of Kansas, and The Nelson-Atkins Museum of Art, Kansas City, in cooperation with University of Washington Press, 1989.

The Chinese Scholar's Studio: Artistic Life in the Late Ming Period, ed. with James C.Y. Watt. New York: Thames and Hudson in association with The Asia Society Galleries, 1987.

Modern Chinese Art, ed. *Register of the Spencer Museum of Art* 6, no. 3 (1986).

China Omnibus, with D. Shankel and Chae-jin Lee. Lawrence, Kansas: Center for East Asian Studies, 1983.

Jade and Silk of Han China: Xia Nai, trans. and ed. Lawrence, Kansas: Spencer Museum of Art, the University of Kansas, 1983.

Catalogue of the Oriental Collection, ed. with Stephen Addiss. Lawrence, Kansas: Spencer Museum of Art, the University of Kansas, 1980.

Trends in Modern Chinese Painting: The C.A. Drenowatz Collection. Ascona, Switzerland: Artibus Asiae, 1979.

Rocks, Trees, Clouds and Water: The Art of Hung Hsien. Lawrence, Kansas: Spencer Museum of Art, the University of Kansas, 1978.

A Thousand Peaks and Myriad Ravines: Chinese Paintings in the Charles A. Drenowatz Collection. Ascona, Switzerland: Artibus Asiae, 1974.

Landscape Paintings by Kwangtung Masters during the Ming and Ch'ing Periods. Hong Kong: Chinese University of Hong Kong, 1973.

Chinese Fan Paintings from the Collection of Chan Yee-pong. Lawrence, Kansas: The University of Kansas Museum of Art, 1970.

New Directions in Chinese Painting. Lawrence, Kansas: The University of Kansas Museum of Art, 1970.

Liu Kuo-sung: The Development of a Modern Chinese Artist. Taipei: National Gallery of Art and Museum of History, 1969.

The New Chinese Landscape: Six Contemporary Chinese Artists, with Thomas Lawton. New York: The American Federation of Arts, 1966.

The Autumn Colors on the Ch'iao and Hua Mountains: A Landscape by Chao Meng-fu. Artibus Asiae Supplementum 21. Ascona, Switzerland: Artibus Asiae, 1965.

ESSAYS, ARTICLES, AND REVIEWS

Liu Guosong and Modern Chinese Ink Painting. In *Liu Guosong: A Universe of His Own.* Hong Kong: Hong Kong Museum of Art, 2004.

Chen Qikuan: An Outstanding Talent Who Bridges East and West. In *Xumi jiezi: Chen Qikuan bashi huigu zhan* (A Retrospective of Chen Qikuan at Eighty), ed. Ying Xiaowei. Beijing: China Fine Arts Museum, 2000. (In Chinese)

The Art of Annie Wong. In *The Paintings of Annie Wong Leung Kit Wah.* Bonn: Frauen-Museum, 1999.

Looking at Late Qing Painting with New Eyes. In *Art at the Close of China's Empire,* ed. Ju-hsi Chou. *Phoebus* 8 (1998).

The Abstract World of Chu Teh-Chun. In *Retrospective Exhibition of Chu Teh-Chun's Works,* ed. Fangling Tseng. Kao-hsiung, Taiwan: Kao-hsiung Municipal Art Museum, 1997.

Review of Maggie Bickford, *Ink Plum: The Making of a Chinese Scholar-Painting Genre. Ars Orientalis* 27 (1997).

The Art of Szeto Keung. In *Superreal.* Hong Kong: Hanart Gallery, 1996.

China und der Westen. In *Chinesische Tuschmalerei im 20. Jahrhundert.* Cologne: Museum für Ostasiatische Kunst, 1996.

Das innere Auge des Chen Chi-kwan. In *Chen Chi-kwan, geb. 1921: Chinesische Malerei,* with Uta Rahman-Steinert. Berlin: Museum für Ostasiatische Kunst, 1996.

A Merging of the Art of China and the West: On the Development of the Art of Liu Kuo-sung. In *Selected Essays on the Study of Liu Kuo-sung*, ed. Li Chun-yi. Taipei: National Museum of History, 1996. (In Chinese)

Art and Literature in the Family of Chao Meng-fu. In *Essays on Cultural Objects and Archaeology: Essays Commemorating the Thirtieth Anniversary of the Min Chiu Society, Hong Kong*. Hong Kong: Woods Publishing Co., 1995.

The Art of Yu Cheng-yao. In *Yu Cheng-yao: The Musical Landscape*. New York: Taipei Gallery, 1995.

Chao Meng-fu's *Red-Robed Luohan* Scroll in the Liaoning Museum. In *Liaoning sheng bowuguan cangbao lu* (Treasures of the Liaoning Museum), ed. Yang Renkai. Shanghai: Joint Publishing Co., 1995. (In Chinese)

Chinese Art Before 1280 (chap. 9) and Chinese Art After 1280 (chap. 10). In *Art History*, ed. Marilyn Stokstad. New York: Harry N. Abrams, 1995.

The Role of France in the Development of Modern Chinese Art. In *Images de la Chine: le contexte occidental de la sinologie naissante* (Actes du VIe Colloque international de sinologie de Chantilly, September 11–14, 1989), ed. Edward Malatesta and Yves Raguin. San Francisco: Ricci Institute for Chinese-Western Cultural History, 1995.

Tradition and Innovation. In *Twentieth-Century Chinese Painting: Tradition and Innovation*. Hong Kong: Hong Kong Museum of Art and Hong Kong Urban Council, 1995.

The Art of C.C. Wang. In *C.C. Wang: Landscapes and Calligraphy*. Hong Kong: Plum Blossoms International, 1994.

Ink Painting and Modern Ink Painting. *Journal of the Taiwan Museum of Art* (Taichung), no. 24 (April 1994).

Luo Ping and the Yangzhou School. In *The Jade Studio: Masterpieces of Ming and Qing Painting and Calligraphy from the Wong Nan-p'ing Collection*. New Haven: Yale University Art Gallery, 1994.

French Influence on Chinese Art in the Early Years of the Republic of China. *Unitas* (Taipei), no. 100 (February 1993).

The Period of "Nan-Chang and Pei-Pu" in Modern Chinese Art. *Hsiung Shih Art Monthly* (Taipei), no. 268 (June 1993). (In Chinese)

Recent Studies on Chao Meng-fu's Painting in China. *Artibus Asiae* 53, nos. 1 and 2 (1993).

Wang Meng's *Ko Hung Moving His Family* in the Palace Museum, Beijing. In *Qingzhu Rao Zongyi jiaoshou qishiwu sui lunwen ji* (Festschrift in Honor of Professor Rao Zongyi on the Occasion of His Seventy-Fifth

Birthday). Hong Kong: Institute of Chinese Studies, Chinese University of Hong Kong, 1993. (In Chinese)
Dong Qichang. *Orientations* 23, no. 3 (March 1992).
From Taiwan to the World: On the Development of Liao Shiou-ping's Art. In *The Art of Liao Shiou-ping*. Taichung: Taiwan Museum of Art, 1992. (In Chinese)
In His Life and Art, East Met West (on Zhang Daqian). *China Daily* (Beijing), February 13–14, 1992.
The Return to the Past and the Search for the New in Yüan Painting. In *Proceedings of the International Colloquium on Chinese Art History, 1991*. Taipei: National Palace Museum, Taipei, 1992.
Studies on the History of Modern Chinese Art since the Founding of the Republic of China. In *Mingguo yilai guoshi yanjiu de huigu yu zhanwang yantaohui lunwen ji* (Essays from the Symposium on Looking Back and Ahead in Chinese Historical Studies since the Founding of the Republic of China). Taipei: National Taiwan University, 1992. (In Chinese)
Tseng Yuho: Unusual Life, Unusual Art. In *Dsui Hua: Tseng Yuho*. Hong Kong and Taipei: Hanart Gallery, 1992.
Chen Chi-kwan: A Genius Who Fuses the Chinese and Western Artistic Traditions. *Han Mo* (Hong Kong), no. 20 (1991). (In Chinese)
The Chu-hsi Thatched Cottage by Chang Wu. *Liaohai wenwu xuekan* (Shenyang), no. 2 (1991).
Contemporary Art in Mainland China. In *Contemporary Art in the Pan-Pacific Region*. Taipei: National Central Library, 1991. (In Chinese)
Eighteenth Century Foundations in Modern Chinese Painting. In *Chinese Painting under the Qianlong Emperor*, ed. Ju-hsi Chou and Claudia Brown. *Phoebus* 6, no. 2 (1991).
Grooms and Horses by Three Members of the Chao Family. In *Words and Images: Chinese Poetry, Calligraphy, and Painting*, ed. Alfreda Murck and Wen C. Fong. New York: The Metropolitan Museum of Art, 1991.
Major Reforms in Painting in Early Republican China. In *China: Modernity and Art*. Taipei: Taipei Fine Arts Museum, 1991. (In Chinese)
Time, Space, and the Human World: On the Development of Chen Chi-kwan's Painting. In *Chen Chi-kwan: A Retrospective*. Taipei: Taipei Fine Arts Museum, 1991.
The Confluence of Chinese and Western Art: The Art Growth of the Painter Liu Kuo-sung. In *Paintings of Liu Kuo-sung*. Taipei: Taipei Fine Arts Museum, 1990.

The Bamboo Paintings of Jin Nong. In *Yangzhou Baguai pinglun ji* (Papers on the Eight Eccentrics of Yangzhou), ed. Zheng Ji and Huang Ticheng. Nanjing: Jiangsu meishu chubanshe, 1989. (In Chinese)

Li Chun-i: A New Star in Chinese Ink Painting. In *Exhibition of Li Chun-i's Ink Painting*. Taipei: Gallery Trifore, 1989.

The Meeting of the Ideal and Reality: The Art of Hsia I-fu. In *The Art of Hsia I-fu*. Taipei: Taipei Fine Arts Museum, 1989.

On the Study of Modern Chinese Art History since the Founding of the Republic of China. *Artist Monthly* (Taipei) 10, no. 173 (1989).

Wu Guanzhong's Biography and the Theoretical Foundations of His Art. In *Wu Guanzhong: A Contemporary Chinese Artist*, ed. Lucy Lim. San Francisco: Chinese Culture Foundation of San Francisco, 1989.

Chang Dai-chien and Western Art. *Contemporary Monthly* (Taipei), no. 25 (May 1988).

The Eternal Searcher: Wan Qingli. In *Wan Qingli: The Scholar-Artist in Modern China*. Wichita, Kansas: Wichita Art Museum, 1988.

From Craft to Painting: Hsia I-fu's Road to Art. *Artist* (Taipei), no. 158 (July 1988).

A Late Bloomer: Yu Cheng-yao. In *Majestic Mountains: Yu Cheng-yao at Ninety*. Taipei: Hanart Gallery, 1988.

Martin Cheng: A Searcher for Art. *Hsiung Shih Art Monthly* (Taipei), no. 207 (May 1988). (In Chinese)

On Yu Ch'eng-yao. In *The World of Yu Ch'eng-yao*. Taipei: Hsiung Shih Art Books, 1988. (In Chinese)

Paris and the Early Development of Western Painting in China. In *Paris: China*. Taipei: Taipei City Art Museum, 1988.

The Place of Chang Dai-chien in Modern Chinese Painting. In *Essays in Commemoration of Chang Dai-chien*. Taipei: National Museum of History, 1988.

Shih Tao's *Ku-gua-miao-ti* Album in The Nelson-Atkins Museum of Art. *Duo Yun* (Shanghai), no. 16 (1988).

Some Problems Connected with Sui Dynasty Narrative Paintings at Dunhuang. *Dunhuang Studies* (Lanzhou), no. 15 (1988).

Traditional Painting Development during the Early Twentieth Century. In *Twentieth-Century Chinese Painting*, ed. Mayching Kao. Hong Kong and New York: Oxford University Press, 1988.

Two Paintings of Mynah Birds by Bada Shanren in The Nelson-Atkins Museum of Art. In *Studies on Bada Shanren*. Nanchang: Jiangxi renmin

chubanshe, 1988. (In Chinese)
Li Rihua and His Literati Circle in the Late Ming Dynasty. *Orientations* 18, no. 8 (August 1987).
Narrative Paintings in the Sui Caves of Dunhuang. In *Dunhuang Grottoes International Symposium.* Dunhuang: Dunhuang Research Institute, 1987. (In Chinese)
The Strange Peaks by Xiao Yuncong and a Landscape Album by Hongren in The Nelson-Atkins Museum of Art. In *Papers on the Huangshan School of Painting*, ed. Anhui Institute of Literature and the Arts, Hefei. Shanghai: Renmin meishu chubanshe, 1987.
Venerable Friends by Xiang Shengmo and Zhang Qi in the Shanghai Museum. *Journal of the Shanghai Museum*, no. 4 (1987).
H.N. Han's Development as a Painter. In *Paintings of H.N. Han.* Taipei: Asiaworld Gallery, 1986.
The Meeting of East and West: The Art of Chuang Che and Wucius Wong. In *The Art of Chuang Che and Wucius Wong.* Beijing: Chinese Fine Art Gallery, 1986.
On the Painter Yu Cheng-yao. *Hsiung Shih Art Monthly* (Taipei), no. 189 (November 1986). (In Chinese)
Recent Studies of Yüan Painting. *National Palace Museum Research Quarterly* (Taipei) 6, no. 2 (Winter 1986). (In Chinese)
The Appeal of New York as a Modern Metropolis. In *C.J. Yao* (Overseas Chinese Artists Series). Guangzhou: Lingnan meishu chubanshe, 1985.
Shui Mo: The New Spirit of Chinese Tradition, an Introduction. In *Shui Mo.* Hong Kong: Hong Kong Art Center, 1985.
Expanding the Realm of Modern Chinese Painting: Notes on the Development of Chuang Che's Painting. *Hsiung Shih Art Monthly* (Taipei), no. 165 (1984). (In Chinese)
The Search for Art: An Exhibition of Six Taiwan Artists. In *Six Taiwan Artists.* Beijing: Chinese Fine Art Gallery, 1984. (In Chinese)
Bai Xueshi, with Yao-wen Li. *Orientations* 14, no. 3 (March 1983).
Bamboo Paintings by Three Members of Chao Meng-fu's Family. *New Asia Academic Journal* (Chinese University of Hong Kong) 4 (1983).
Liu Guosong: Creator of the New Ideal in Chinese Painting. In *Liu Guosong huazhan* (Exhibition of Liu Guosong's Paintings). Beijing: Chinese Fine Art Museum, 1983. (In Chinese)
The Place of Chang Dai-chien in Modern Chinese Painting. *Hsiung Shih Art Monthly* (Taipei), no. 147 (May 1983). (In Chinese)

Problems Concerning Chao Meng-fu's Serving Under the Yüan. In *Essays in Commemoration of the Golden Jubilee of the Fung Ping Shan Library (1932–1982)*, ed. Chan Ping-leung. Hong Kong: Hong Kong University Press, 1982.

Review of James Cahill, *An Index of Early Chinese Painters and Paintings. Journal of Asian Studies* 41, no. 2 (February 1982).

Studies on Chao Meng-fu: Part II, Chao Meng-fu's Teachers. *National Palace Museum Quarterly* 16, no. 3 (Spring 1982). (In Chinese)

The Role of Wu-hsing in Early Yüan Artistic Development under Mongol Rule. In *China Under Mongol Rule*, ed. John D. Langlois Jr. Princeton: Princeton University Press, 1981.

Studies on Chao Meng-fu: Part I, The Genealogy of Chao Meng-fu. *National Palace Museum Quarterly* 16, no. 2 (Winter 1981). (In Chinese)

The Visions of Chen Chi-kwan. In *Chen Chi-kwan Paintings, 1940–1980*. Taipei: Art Book Co., 1981.

Wang Chien and Chao Meng-fu: Notes on a Chinese Handscroll in the Helen Foresman Spencer Museum of Art. In *The Shape of the Past: Studies in Honor of Franklin D. Murphy*, ed. Giorgio Buccellati and Charles Speroni. Los Angeles: Institute of Archaeology and Office of the Chancellor, 1981.

A Hundred Days in China: An Art Historian's Research Experience. *China Exchange News* (Committee on Scholarly Communication with the People's Republic of China, National Academy of Sciences, Washington, D.C.) 8, nos. 3 and 4 (Summer 1980).

Review of "The Great Bronze Age of China: An Exhibition from the People's Republic of China." *Art Journal* 40, nos. 1 and 2 (September/December 1980).

Problems Concerning the Life of Wang Mien, Painter of Plum Blossoms. *Renditions* (Chinese University of Hong Kong), no. 6 (1977).

Hsiang Sheng-mo's Poetry and Painting on Eremitism. *Journal of the Institute of Chinese Studies of the Chinese University of Hong Kong* 8, no. 2 (December 1976).

The Uses of the Past in Yüan Landscape Painting. In *Artists and Traditions: Uses of the Past in Chinese Culture*, ed. Christian F. Murck. Princeton: The Art Museum, Princeton University, 1976.

Review of *Chinese Fans* (from the collection of Dr. and Mrs. Franco Vannotti of Lugano). *Artibus Asiae* 37 (1975).

Review of Osvald Sirén, *Chinese Painting: Leading Masters and Principles.*

Artibus Asiae 37 (1975).
The Bamboo Paintings of Chin Nung. *Archives of Asian Art* 27 (1973–74).
Review of Max Loehr, *Chinese Landscape Woodcuts: From an Imperial Commentary to the Tenth-Century Printed Edition of the Buddhist Canon*. *Art Bulletin* 55, no. 4 (1973).
The Development of Painting in Soochow during the Yüan Dynasty. In *Proceedings of the International Symposium on Chinese Painting*. Taipei: National Palace Museum, Taipei, 1972.
The Art of Hung Hsien. In *Hung Hsien*. Cincinnati: Contemporary Arts Center, 1971.
Bodhidharma Crossing the Yangtze River on a Reed: A Painting in the Charles A. Drenowatz Collection in Zurich. *Asiatische Studien* (Bern) 25 (1971).
Su Jen-shan (1814–1849): Rediscovery and Reevaluation. *Oriental Art* 16, no. 4 (Winter 1970).
Stages of Development in Yüan Landscape Painting. *National Palace Museum Bulletin* 4, no. 1 (May–June 1969) and no. 3 (July–August 1969). (In Chinese)
The Freer *Sheep and Goat* and Chao Meng-fu's Horse Paintings. *Artibus Asiae* 30, no. 4 (1968).
Chinese Paintings in the Charles A. Drenowatz Collection. *Asiatische Studien* (Bern) 21 (1967).
Fong Chung-ray: An Appreciation. In *The Paintings of Fong Chung-ray*. Taipei: National Taiwan Arts Center, 1967.
The World of Chen Ting-shih. In *The Paintings of Chen Ting-shih*. Taipei: National Taiwan Arts Center, 1967.
The Paintings of Chuang Che: Voices of an Intense Inner Life. In *The Paintings of Chuang Che*. Taipei: Hai-tien Gallery, 1966.
Tradition and Innovation. In *The Paintings of Liu Kuo-sung*. Taipei: National Historical Museum, 1965.
Review of F.W. Mote, *The Poet Kao Ch'i, 1336–1374*. *Artibus Asiae* 27, no. 3 (1964).
The Oberlin *Orchid* and the Problem of P'u-ming. *Archives of the Chinese Art Society of America* 16 (1962).
The Rocks and Trees and the Art of Ts'ao Chih-po. *Artibus Asiae* 23, nos. 3 and 4 (1961).
Recent History of the Palace Collection. *Archives of the Chinese Art Society of America* 12 (1958).

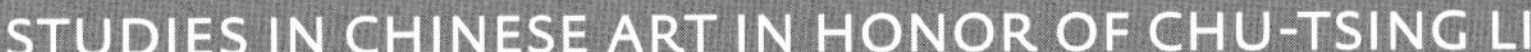

STUDIES IN CHINESE ART IN HONOR OF CHU-TSING LI

STUDIES IN HONOR OF CHU-TSING LI

Liao Painting and the Northern Grasslands School

MARILYN GRIDLEY

In Western histories of Chinese art the chapter on Liao painting is largely unwritten, not because the painters and paintings are unworthy but because their time and place have put them at a great disadvantage. The painters were active from the tenth through the early twelfth century in the territory ruled by the Liao dynasty (907–1125). Founded in 907 by Abaoji (d. 926), the leader of the Qidans, a semi-nomadic tribe of Manchuria, the Liao governed the north of China throughout the Five Dynasties (907–960) and Northern Song (960–1127) periods. The Song came to hold the Liao in high regard,[1] but history has relegated them to the category of a "barbarian dynasty," one outside the mainstream of Chinese dynastic succession. This division is mirrored in art-historical scholarship: the development of landscape painting in the Five Dynasties and Song periods has preoccupied many scholars, while Liao achievements have received only incidental attention. In 1980 Chen Zhaofu began to assess the Liao contributions as those of the Northern Grasslands school.[2] As Chen defines it, the school is not a landscape tradition as such; figure and animal paintings were the forte of the Liao painters. That is precisely why the name "Northern Grasslands school" is a good one: it draws attention to the little-recognized fact that the steppe *landscape* is a unique and integral part of the Liao painting tradition.

How did the Grasslands artists perceive and use their own landscape? How did they respond to the development of the landscape tradition to the south? In the search for answers to these questions, this study focuses on those Liao dynasty paintings that incorporate landscape elements. In tenth-century Liao paintings the grasslands serve as a distinctive backdrop for the portrayal of activities common to the northern steppe country: hunting, herding and grazing, scenes of encampments and encounters. Throughout the Liao period those subjects never lose their appeal, but in the late tenth and early eleventh centuries, historical events become a popular subject incorporated into a landscape setting. By the mid-eleventh century, the grasslands appear as a distinct subject in the murals of a Liao imperial mausoleum. Extant paintings reveal that from the mid-tenth century the Liao painters were also painting in the landscape styles of their Chinese contemporaries in the south.

Not only is Liao painting of landscape important in its own right, but a knowledge of it is critical for understanding Song, Yuan (1272–1368), and Ming (1368–1644) paintings of grasslands themes.[3] Moreover, any study that expands our knowledge of Liao culture is also relevant today; the terrain, ecology, and culture of the grasslands are unique, and the region is vitally important for the future of China's economy and its people. Studies of Liao paintings have focused mainly on the customs and culture those paintings reveal,[4] or on specific categories such as horse or bird-and-flower painting.[5] How Liao painters recorded and used landscape imagery—their own as well as their experience of landscape images from south of their border—has received little attention.

The major problem in studying extant Liao painting is that many of the tomb murals are published only in line drawings or poor reproductions. Some of the important scrolls are not reproduced in any form. My hope is that this study will create an interest in Liao painting and the Grasslands school that will prompt publication of the unpublished scrolls and better illustrations of previously reproduced paintings.

The most extensive and satisfying studies of landscape in Liao painting have focused on the murals of the *Four Seasons* (see figs. 4–6), dating to about 1031, discovered in the 1920s in the mausoleum of the Liao emperor Shengzong (r. 982–1031) at Qingling, in eastern Mongolia,[6] and the landscape scroll *A Chess Party in the Mountains* (see fig. 3), dated to about 936–83, discovered in 1974 in Tomb 7 at Yemaotai, Liaoning Province.[7] The famous pair of paintings *Deer in Autumn Forest* and *Deer in Red Maples* (hereafter referred to as *Deer in Autumn Forests*), in the National Palace Museum, Taipei, also have come under scrutiny, usually in conjunction with commentary on the *Four Seasons* murals.[8]

It is important to consider the historical and geographical context of the Grasslands school in order to understand why it nearly lost its identity as a distinct tradition. Alexander Soper's annotated translation of Guo Ruoxu's (active 11th century) *Tuhua qianwen zhi* (An Account of My Experiences in Painting)[9] and James Cahill's comments in his *Index of Early Chinese Painters and Paintings*[10] are excellent sources of information on certain Liao dynasty painters, but the painters are buried under the headings of Tang (618–907), Five Dynasties, and Song. In his *Chinese Painting: Leading Masters and Principles*, Osvald Sirén discusses the two most famous painters of the Grasslands school, Hu Gui (active early 10th century)[11] and Yelü Bei (Yelü Tuyu; 899–936), as Five Dynasties figure painters. He also analyzes the *Deer in Autumn Forests* as magnificent examples of Five Dynasties, not Liao, painting.[12] Yan Wanzhang's publication of the results of his research on twenty-one Liao dynasty painters, the majority of whom were Qidan, is a major contribution to the effort to restore the painters to their proper context.[13]

Hu Gui and Yelü Bei have often been classified as Five Dynasties painters because their lives are intimately tied up with the political and military maneuvers of the Liao in northern China during that period. In 926 when the Liao captured the territory of Bohai and renamed it Dongdan (east of the Qidan), Abaoji, the first emperor of the Liao (Taizu), made his eldest son, Yelü Bei, ruler of Bohai. When Taizu died only a few months later, his second son, Yelü De Guang, succeeded him as the Liao emperor Taizong (r. 927–47). In 930 Yelü Bei and forty followers, having recognized their threatened position, fled by sea to the Five Dynasties kingdom of Later (Hou) Tang, which controlled all of North China from 923 to 936. There Bei was warmly received by the emperor Mingzong (r. 926–34), who gave him the Chinese name Li Zanhua.[14] When in 934 an adopted son of Mingzong killed the emperor and assumed the throne, Bei "dispatched a memorial to the Liao emperor requesting an invasion of Later Tang territory."[15] As a consequence, he was killed by the Later Tang at the young age of thirty-eight.[16]

LIAO PAINTINGS BEFORE THE REIGN OF THE LIAO EMPEROR SHENGZONG (R. 982–1031)

Fifteen of Yelü Bei's paintings were in the imperial collection of the Song emperor Huizong (r. 1101–25).[17] The subjects—foreigners riding, hunting, and shooting—reveal that he was a specialist in painting horses and riders, probably Qidans. (The one exception is a painting of a thousand-horned deer.) None of the extant paintings now attributed to Bei incorporate landscape elements, but the title of one painting, *Riding in the Snow*, recorded in the twelfth-century *Xuanhe huapu* (Catalogue of the Imperial Painting Collection During the Xuanhe Era) is evidence that on occasion he provided such a setting. The best extant painting attributed to Yelü Bei is a large album leaf now in the National Palace Museum, Taipei.[18] With its fine, varied brushwork and careful composition of the motifs of a Qidan soldier standing in front of his horse, the painting is extremely important for tracing the development of horse painting from Han Gan (active ca. 742–56) in the Tang dynasty to Li Gonglin (ca. 1041–1106) in the Song and Zhao Yong (1289–after 1360) in the Yuan.[19] Each of these painters follows the Tang style of a plain ground with no landscape elements or other indications of a setting. It is Qiu Ying (ca. 1495–1552) of the Ming dynasty who provides Bei's horse with a grasslands setting; in the center foreground of Qiu's *Hunting on the Autumn Plain* is a fine version of Bei's horse and rider.[20]

Hu Gui is today considered the most famous painter of the Northern Grasslands school. Although most works on famous Chinese painters include him, the records do not agree on his period and native place. Surveying the literature, Yan Wanzhang finds that while the *Xuanhe huapu* lists Hu Gui as a man of Fanyang of the Tang period and Guo Ruoxu's *Tuhua qianwen zhi* adds that he lived at the end of Tang, the fourteenth chapter of the *Shiqu baoji chubian* (Catalogue of Painting and Calligraphy in the Qianlong Imperial Collection) describes him as a Five Dynasties painter from Waqiao.[21] The *Wudai minghua buyi* (Record of Famous Painters of the Five Dynasties) record of Later (Hou) Liang (907–923) painters lists him as a Qidan from Shanhou, and a native of Zhenzhou, of the Wusugu tribe. The *Shiqu baoji sanbian* lists him as a Later (Hou) Tang painter.[22]

Much of the confusion over Hu Gui's time and place rises out of the succession of dynasties that controlled these regions, all of which were located southwest of modern-day Beijing, during his lifetime. More than one record classifies him as a Tang painter, so he may have come to the area before the end of the Tang in 907. Some evidence suggests that "he settled in Hebei after the 905 alliance between the Qidans and the Shatuo Turkish leader Li Keyong."[23] He can also be called a Five Dynasties painter of the Later Liang because it had control of that region from the fall of the Tang until 923 when the Later Tang took over. After the period of intrigue in 935 and 938 when Yelü Bei lost his life, the region was given to the Liao as part of the famous Sixteen Prefectures.[24] Thus, Hu Gui can be classified as a painter of the Tang dynasty or of the Five Dynasties kingdoms of Later Liang or Later Tang, or as a painter of the Liao dynasty.

Because all the various place names associated with Hu Gui—Fanyang, Zhenzhou, Waqiao, Shanhou—can be pinpointed to the area between Fangshan and Zhouxian, just southwest of Beijing, Yan Wanzhang concludes that Hu Gui was not originally a Qidan but a Later Tang painter who, by virtue of the region's transfer to the Liao in 938, "became" a Qidan.[25] This conclusion is surprising given that the *Wudai minghua buyi*, as noted above, states that Hu Gui was of the Wusugu tribe, evidence that he was a Qidan by birth. Chen Zhaofu finds this tribe recorded in the *Jiu Tang shu* (Old History of the Tang) as from the area southwest of Hulun Lake in Inner Mongolia's Hulun Buir Meng.[26]

The most convincing evidence that Hu Gui was a Qidan, I believe, lies not in the historical records but in certain paintings attributed to him. They reveal a great affection for the northern grasslands and the life there. The landscape around Fangshan and Zhouxian is not that of the northern grasslands. While Hu Gui could have become familiar with the costumes and physical features of the Qidans without ever leaving the Beijing area, it seems more likely that his intimate knowledge of and clear sympathy for the nomadic life on the grasslands derived from his having been born to that life.

The *Xuanhe huapu* lists sixty-five paintings by Hu Gui in the imperial collection. The majority of his works, like those of Yelü Bei, are of horses and of tribesmen hunting, shooting birds, feeding camels and horses, and stealing horses. Images such as tribesmen riding out at dawn or stopping to rest at dusk suggest that Hu was interested in capturing the time of day. Certain subjects—tribesmen drinking from a spring, mounted tribesmen crossing small hills— indicate that the landscape was an important part of the composition. In these paintings, the landscape is a backdrop.

Perhaps the most famous scroll attributed to Hu Gui is *Zhuoxie tu* (literally "standing rest"; fig. 1),[27] in the Palace Museum, Beijing. The artist Zhang Zhao in 1713 gave the painting its current title.[28] Tsao Hsingyuan,

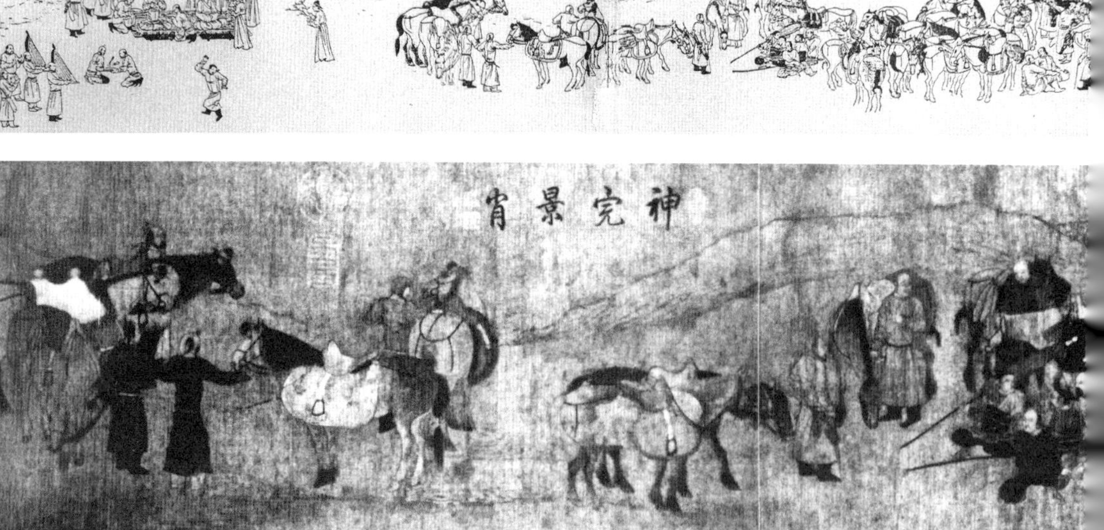

whose close inspection of the painting revealed two dead swans hanging on the sides of two of the horses, has made a convincing case that the actual subject of the scroll is the celebration of a successful spring hunt for swans, one of the "most important [Liao] rituals."[29] The painting is divided into three parts, each more spaciously composed than the one before (fig. 1). The first scene presents a dense complexity of pose and movement of twenty horses, in two clusters of ten, with their dismounted riders. This scene allows the artist to display his skill in painting horses and figures, from every angle and in a complex grouping. The second section (fig. 2) features only ten horses and a few men. Arranged in a semicircle, they stand as though unwinding from the tight circles of the two clusters in the preceding section. The relative calm of this scene leads into the repose of the final scene, which depicts figures but no horses. The chieftain and his wife sit cross-legged on a red, black, and tan patterned carpet. Four female servants, one of whom carries an exquisite ewer, attend the seated woman. Four men stand beside the chieftain, while two kneel to serve him. The wife glances toward the chieftain, who looks at a boy dancing in the foreground. To the left of the dancer, two other servants kneel preparing food. Five musicians, two playing the *konghou* (an ancient kind of lute) and three clapping, close the scroll at the lower left. The dancing boy and the "sound" of clapping and music enliven the restful scene.

In the painting, the steppe terrain unobtrusively but effectively emphasizes and weaves together the tripartite composition. The high horizon of rolling grasslands rises and falls to frame the three sections and to lead the viewer from one to the other. In the middle section, for instance, a grasslands hillock dips into a depression making an S-shaped curve, delimiting and reinforcing the "unwinding" arrangement of the men and horses. Lightly brushed *cun* (texture stroke patterns) and a delicately drawn single-line horizon sweep up and away from this middle section to the last scene; similar brushwork at the upper left, above the musicians, closes the scroll. In the foreground and in certain spots in the background, a subtle gray-green wash and clusters of tiny *dian* (dots) indicate sparse grasslands vegetation. This light staccato touch adds to the vibrancy of the colorful scene.

Deep greens and reds enhance the beauty of the painting and draw attention to certain details. The harpstrings, for instance, are red, as are the cylinders the Qidans used for binding horses' tails midway down and for dressing a tuft of the mane at the forehead. Only the royal couple's four

FIGURE 1
Drawing by Chen Zhaofu of Hu Gui (active early 10th century), *Resting at Midday*. Handscroll. Palace Museum, Beijing. From *Meishu yuekan* 3 (1980), 46–47

FIGURE 2
Hu Gui (active early 10th century). *Resting at Midday*. Detail. Handscroll. Palace Museum, Beijing

horses (two for riding and two spares) have their tails and manes dressed in this manner; one has red plumes at the front and back of the saddle. Sashes and saddle blankets in red are a counterpoint to those in green. The leopard-skin quivers and saddle blankets and the patterned carpet all add color and texture to the painting.

Aside from being a masterpiece of composition and color, the painting is valuable for what it reveals of Qidan customs. A boy dancing a similar dance and accompanied by a group of musicians appears in one of the better preserved Liao tomb murals.[30] The horses in the scroll are in groups of ten, consistent with the system of organizing steppe armies "according to a decimal system, with units of 10, 100, 1000, and 10,000."[31] All of these details as well as the overall composition point to Hu Gui as the painter of this scroll. Tsao Hsingyuan's discovery of the swans and her conclusion that the subject is the spring swan hunt ritual of the Liao would seem to support this attribution. Tsao, however, has pointed out several troubling details that lead her to the "preliminary conclusion ... that [the painting] must have been done by a Han Chinese artist, or by several [artists]."[32] For instance, the wine pot that the servant carries toward the seated couple has a spout like those on ethnic Han wine pots of the period, not the short spout characteristic of Liao pots. It could, of course, represent prized booty. Based on a careful examination of tomb murals, Tsao has found that the hairstyle of the horsemen in the scroll matches a Jurchen rather than a Qidan style. While these apparent discrepancies must be considered, the evidence from murals is limited. Few tenth-century Liao tombs with murals have been excavated, leaving whole regions of the Liao territory yet to be documented.

Chen Juzhong, a Southern Song academy painter active between 1201 and 1230, may well have seen this scroll. Perhaps it was one of the few that were not lost when the Jurchens took the Northern Song capital Kaifeng in 1126; two paintings by Hu Gui with the title *Resting at Midday* were in the Northern Song imperial collection, and one is listed in the Southern Song collection.[33] In the hanging scroll *Wenji's Return to China*, attributed to Chen Juzhong and now in the National Palace Museum, Taipei,[34] several passages—for example, the pose of the chieftain seated on the patterned carpet, the attendant leaning forward to pour him a drink from a ewer, and the poses and grouping of the laden horses in the foreground—are very close to those in *Resting at Midday*. The biggest difference, as might be expected, is in the profusion and complexity of landscape elements in the later painting. The terrain could still be rough grassland, but the trees could not.

Such paintings based on the legend of Lady Wenji (Cai Yan; active late 2nd–early 3rd century) of the Han dynasty have generated the most interest in Liao painting among scholars of Chinese art history. Wenji was captured in about 195 by the Xiongnu and lived with them for many years on the grasslands of Inner Mongolia before being ransomed and brought back to Henan. Based on representations of Qidan life in relief sculptures and murals of excavated Liao-period tombs, nearly all scholars agree that the representations of the Xiongnu of the Wenji scenes are after Qidan models.[35] Hu Gui's scroll has not received much notice as a possible source for some of the motifs, but several important details can be matched up. One of the most curious is the gear for the royal horses. In three scenes in The Metropolitan Museum of Art's fifteenth-century handscroll *Eighteen Songs of a Nomad Flute: The Story of Lady Wenji*[36]—*Departure from China*, *Encampment by a Stream*, and *Dawn*—the chieftain's saddle pad is white with a black design of the flaming jewel of Buddhism; to either side of the jewel is a scrolling pattern. This same pattern is discernible on the royal horse in the center section of *Resting at Midday*. The spare horse in that scene wears the same white saddle cover with two red plumes as the one in the *Departure* scene in the Metropolitan's painting.

Another work attributed to Hu Gui, also titled *Zhouxie tu*, is in the National Palace Museum, Taipei. Tsao Hsingyuan has recently published this painting and argued that it is by Hu Gui, while the Beijing scroll is not.[37] Clearly the two paintings cannot both be by Hu Gui. They are very different, especially in the rendition of the landscape. The landforms in the Taipei scroll figure much more prominently in the overall composition, at times almost swallowing up the assortment of tiny figures and animals, which are scattered throughout the composition. The vantage point is extremely high, looking down on the vast scene from above the geese. In that respect the work is more akin to a painting like *Tartar Horsemen Hunting* by Chen Juzhong.[38] The composition of the Taipei scroll is the reverse of the Beijing scroll, where the figures and horses dominate the scene, and the vantage point is close and only slightly raised. The expanse of gentle rolling hills that makes up the central portion of the Taipei scroll certainly represents the grasslands terrain, but the opening and closing landforms do not. Tsao writes that the opening section is like the landscapes found in the tomb of Wang Chuzhi (d. 924),[39] Hebei Province, which dates to the time and place in which Hu Gui was active. The quality of the reproduction of the Taipei scroll is poor and in the opening section also very dark, so any corroboration of the comparison must await a better reproduction. What appears to be a sheer cliff and an arbitrary rocky projection in the upper right at the beginning of the scroll and an incongruous Guo Xi-style formation bulging up out of the rolling hills at the end of the short scroll need to be carefully examined.

Two important album leaves, *Hunters with Greyhounds* and *Hunters with Falcons*, in the National Palace Museum, Taipei, are attributed to Hu Gui.[40] In the former, two mounted Qidans hold their greyhounds in front of them and face left toward a third rider. He is seen from the back, his elegant white hound sitting behind him on the rump of the horse. The three horses stand in a semicircle like several of the horses in *Resting at Midday*. In the latter album leaf, four mounted hunters holding falcons are bunched tightly together, apparently consulting about their next move. The figures and horses in both album leaves, however, are rather stiff and lack the lively air that permeates *Resting at Midday*. The hounds of the first leaf steal the show with their quizzical expressions, graceful bodies, and curled tails.

Like the undulating horizon in *Resting at Midday*, the background hills in the album leaves frame and emphasize the composition of the figure groupings. The landscape elements in each are appropriate for a grasslands setting but are more pronounced than in the scroll. In the album leaves, the painter uses many more *dian*, which are also bigger and blacker. He adds more calligraphic touches with the brambles on the tops of background hills. Shaded depressions mark the recession of ever larger hillocks toward the high horizon. The feathery grasses in the fore- and background are quite distinct. These pronounced landscape elements and the somewhat stiff horses and riders support the judgment that these album leaves are "fine Song paintings in the Liao tradition."[41]

The handscroll *The Parting of Su Wu and Li Ling*, now in the National Palace Museum, Taipei,[42] is important for the study of the Northern Grasslands school, but also fits, I believe, into the category of a Song painting in the Liao tradition. While never attributed to Hu Gui, the work has been assigned to the tenth century and the Liao period, and should be considered in the light of Hu Gui's painting style. The handscroll, in ink and color on silk, was, until recently, attributed to Zhou Wenju (active ca. 940–75), a native of Nanjing and a figure painter at the court of the Southern Tang dynasty (937–976); however, the authors of the catalogue for the 1961–62 exhibition *Chinese Art Treasures* believe it belongs in the Liao tradition because it is much closer in style and subject matter to paintings by Hu Gui than to paintings by Zhou Wenju.[43] Cahill lists it as a Song painting in the Liao–Jin tradition.[44] Linda Cooke Johnson makes the observation that Su Wu and Li Ling wear Liao costume, and that "the two servants holding the horses are dressed in Jurchen style."[45] Such dress would point to a Liao rather than a Jin artist simply because it seems unlikely that a Jin painter would present the Jurchens as servants to the Liao. Even so, the subject matter seems an unlikely choice for either a Liao or a Jin painter: the story praises Su Wu for his loyalty to the Han and criticizes Li Ling for serving the barbarian Xiongnu after he was captured. By the same token, the subject would surely appeal to a Song painter aware of many similar episodes of captured countrymen who did or did not serve the Liao court. The painter of this subject, then, like the painters of the Wenji legend, would have used the Northern Grasslands painting style for the setting and the costume. The artist lavishes attention on the landscape; the convoluted hills on the left, the profusion of grass, heavy sprinkling of *dian*, and the calligraphic brambles are an exaggerated version of these motifs in the two album leaves and even further removed from the subtle treatment of the grasslands setting in *Resting at Midday*.

Both Hu Gui and Yelü Bei passed on their talents to their sons. Hu Gui's son, Hu Qian, was a famous painter of horses. Forty-four of his paintings are listed in the *Xuanhe huapu*,[46] where we also learn that he had his father's skill and that it was hardly possible to tell their works apart. According to the *Xin Wudai shi* (New Standard History of the Five Dynasties), Yelü Bei's eldest son, Yelü Yuan (Wuyu; 918–951), who became the third Liao emperor, Shizong (r. 947–51), was a painter. Although nothing is known about his style or subject matter, it seems likely that Shizong would have been greatly influenced by his father.[47]

The two scrolls found in the tenth-century Liao tomb at Yemaotai may have been painted during Shizong's reign. Yang Renkai dates the paintings between 936 and 983.[48] The scrolls are incontrovertible evidence of the kind of painting Liao patrons treasured and admired in this period. One is a landscape (fig. 3), the other a scene of two rabbits eating plantain and three birds perched on stalks of bamboo. Wen Fong discusses the Yemaotai landscape and the *Four Seasons* murals as valuable evidence of the development of Chinese landscape painting in general, but not in

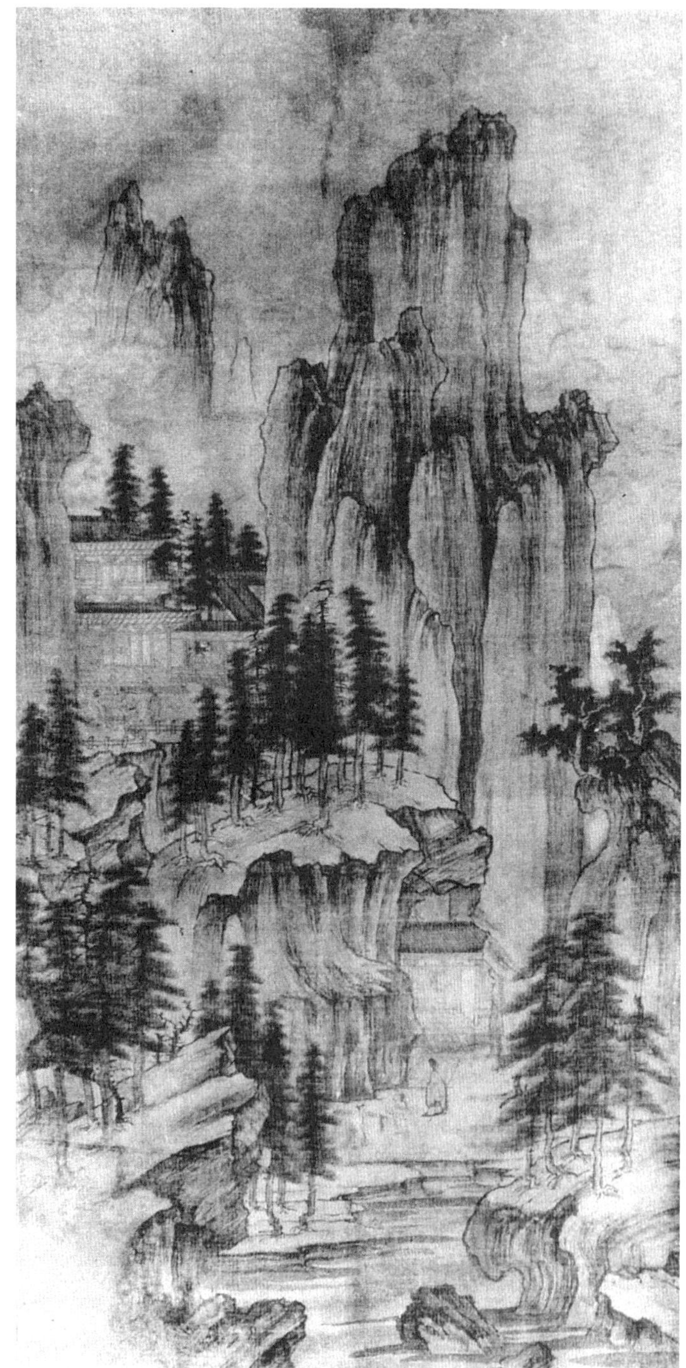

FIGURE 3
Unidentified artist (10th century). *A Chess Party in the Mountains*, ca. 936–83. Hanging scroll, ink and color on silk, 41 7/8 × 25 5/8 in. (106.5 × 65 cm). Liaoning Provincial Museum. From Smith and Fong 1999, 262

the context of Liao dynasty painting. He makes the important point that the Yemaotai landscape scroll "is the earliest indubitable tenth-century silk hanging scroll with a landscape subject."[49] James Cahill examines what the scroll reveals of the perception and treatment of space in tenth-century Chinese landscape painting.[50] Richard Vinograd explores the implications of the Yemaotai landscape for interpreting how landscape painting styles of the late Yuan period relate to earlier Chinese landscape painting traditions.[51]

The Yemaotai scrolls are invaluable for the study of early styles of paintings of the same themes. The birds, rabbits, and bamboo are an excellent resource, for example, for the study of the Northern Song Academy painter Cui Bo's (active ca. 1060–85) treatment of these motifs in *Magpies and Hares*, painted about a century later, in 1061.[52] Although the motifs in the earlier painting are all quite close to the picture plane, the fact that the upper third of the painting is empty sky gives a sense of space that points to a Grasslands artist.

While the Yemaotai landscape painting with its mountains and narrow valleys is in almost every way the polar opposite of its companion "feathers and fur" scroll, there are some common factors. Wai-kam Ho mentions the Daoist symbols in the scene of the rabbits eating young plaintain, and makes a strong case that the subject of the other scroll "may well be one of the thirty-six 'grotto-heavens' (*dongtian*), the mountain retreats of the Daoist immortals."[53] The artist(s) use the same blue-green color—the one for the distant mountains, the other for the plantain. The red painted pavilions tucked into valleys beside and beneath the central mountain call to mind the colorful pavilions of Tang paradise scenes.

James Cahill examines the landscape painting as the earliest datable evidence of a spatial organization more complex than the "additive space-cell mode."[54] The tall straight pines are in the tenth-century Dong Yuan–Juran tradition, while the ink-brushed central mountain composition and the gnarled pines clinging to the peak on the middle right are in the Li Cheng–Guo Xi tradition. The sophisticated rendering of that landscape tradition in the Liao scroll may at first seem surprising in light of the token reference to the tradition in the imperial mausoleum's *Four Seasons* murals painted at least fifty years later. The scroll is outside the mainstream of what has been preserved of Liao painting, but Yang Renkai believes that the scroll was done by an artist living in the Liao southern capital Beijing and well-versed in the traditions of Han Chinese culture, which continued to thrive there alongside those of the Qidan.[55] The Yemaotai landscape, along with its literati motifs of playing chess and the *qin*, makes it clear that Liao painters had access to tenth-century landscape traditions from areas south of their border.

PAINTINGS PRODUCED DURING AND AFTER THE REIGN OF THE LIAO EMPEROR SHENGZONG (R. 982–1031)

In the late tenth century and throughout the eleventh century, portrait painters and painters of historical scenes take center stage to record the emergence of the Liao kingdom as a major power successfully challenging the Song on all fronts, culturally and militarily. In 1018 Liao Shengzong summoned the Hanlin court painter (*yuan daizhao*) Chen Sheng to paint the Southern Victory (*Nan cheng desheng tu*) in the Wu Luan Hall at Shangjing.[56] From this commission we know that Chen Sheng (*zi* Jizhi, *hao* Zhupo) was active during the reign of Shengzong. A painting by Chen titled *Signing the Alliance at the Bian Bridge* (*Bian qiao huimeng tu*) is in the Palace Museum, Beijing.[57] It depicts the Tang emperor Taizong (r. 626–49) and the Tujue leader Xieli Kehan meeting at the Bian bridge outside Chang'an's city wall to sign an alliance. Almost ninety percent of *Bian Bridge* is taken up by mounted horsemen, with the scene of the two principal figures occupying only the remaining ten percent.[58] In August 1991 a copy of the final section of the scroll was on display in the Tang case in the Provincial Museum of Inner Mongolia, in Hohhot. The landscape had gnarled trees before the bridge, willows at the bridge, and became quite complex at the end. Because of the complexity, I do not think this version, at least, could be a Liao painting, but it is useful as an indicator of what the Liao original may have looked like. Although neither *Southern Victory* nor *Bian Bridge* would have been in a grasslands setting, Chen Sheng, like Hu Gui, used landscape elements as compositional devices in painting the grand murals and scrolls of historic events. The painting is signed, but the character that might help date the painting is illegible. I would speculate that the work was painted around 1005, the date of the signing of the Shanyuan Treaty, which ended the Liao war with the Song that had begun in 979. The treaty established a stable Song–Liao border and initiated a long period of peace between the Song and Liao empires.[59] During the course of that war, the Song had been reflecting on the parallels between Tang Taizong's relationship with Xieli Kehan and Song Taizong's (r. 976–

97) with Liao Shengzong.[60] The Liao, too, no doubt, had a strong interest in the parallels.

The magnificent *Four Seasons* wall murals found in the tomb of Liao Shengzong (figs. 4–6) provide the most reliable evidence of Liao dynasty landscape painting. Tamura Jitsuzō and Kobayashi Yukiō, who analyze all available evidence to arrive at the conclusion that the tomb is that of Shengzong,[61] write:

> If we are right in identifying the East Mausoleum with the tomb of Shengzong, the wall paintings ... must have been made in the early days of Xingzong's reign [1031–55] .... He is known as one of the greatest painters of the Liao dynasty. This fact seems to furnish a key to the problem [of] why we find such rich painting only in the East Mausoleum.[62]

These paintings are invaluable documents for the study of the landscape painting of the Northern Grasslands school in the second quarter of the eleventh century.

Tamura and Kobayashi have studied the content and technique of these paintings in great detail, but they have overlooked an important point, that is, how the paintings are bound together into a skillfully unified composition. Richard Barnhart notes that these murals "form a roughly continuous panorama if read left to right in the sequence *Spring*, *Summer*, *Fall*, *Winter*."[63] Tsao Hsingyuan likens them to a "gigantic horizontal scroll, interrupted only by the columns and doors." Tsao adds the perceptive political interpretation that "the deceased Shengzong was perpetuated in his role as emperor by the offering of these landscapes, the spatial extension of his nation, and the seasons, the temporal extension of his empire."[64]

Each of the four scenes can stand alone as a monumental painting, but when taken together as a single unified composition, they become even more impressive. The clumps of reeds[65] accenting the course of the streams, the rolling hills that slope abruptly into the streams, and the banks of clouds tinged with red and green are motifs common to each scene and unifying elements of the whole cycle.

Although we cannot today view them in their original setting,[66] we can get some sense of the unity of the paintings by illustrating them side by side (figs. 4, 5). On entering the central tomb chamber from the southeast, one would have looked across to the colorful *Autumn* scene on the west wall and the *Winter* scene on the north wall. The seasons succeed each other in a clockwise direction (fig. 6). The contours of the hills of *Autumn* continue smoothly into *Winter*. The long, low curve of the slope from lower left to middle right of *Winter* continues into the middle ground of the flatter, marshlike *Spring* landscape on the east wall. A meandering stream flows through the center of *Spring* from back- to foreground, angles off to the right, and continues across the foreground of *Summer* on the south wall. Xingzong must have considered the representation of each

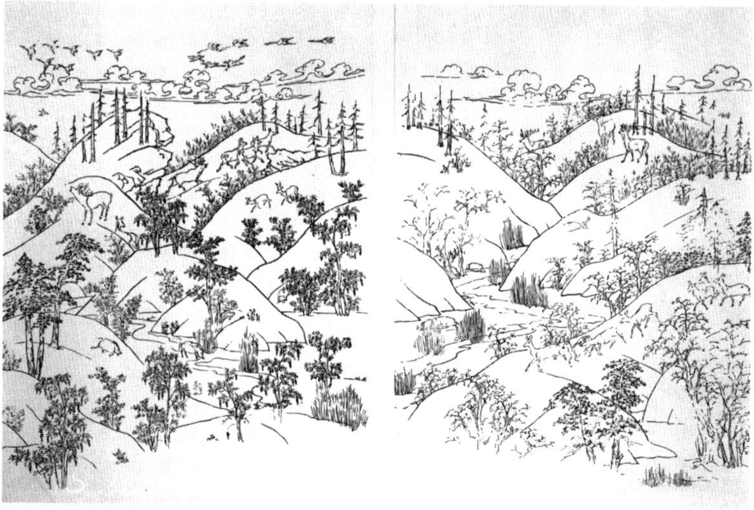

FIGURE 4
Drawings of the *Four Seasons*: *Autumn* (west wall) and *Winter* (north wall), ca. 1031. Mural paintings. Central chamber, East Mausoleum, Qingling, Inner Mongolia. From Tamura Jitsuzō and Kobayashi Yukiō 1953, vol. I, figs. 88, 89

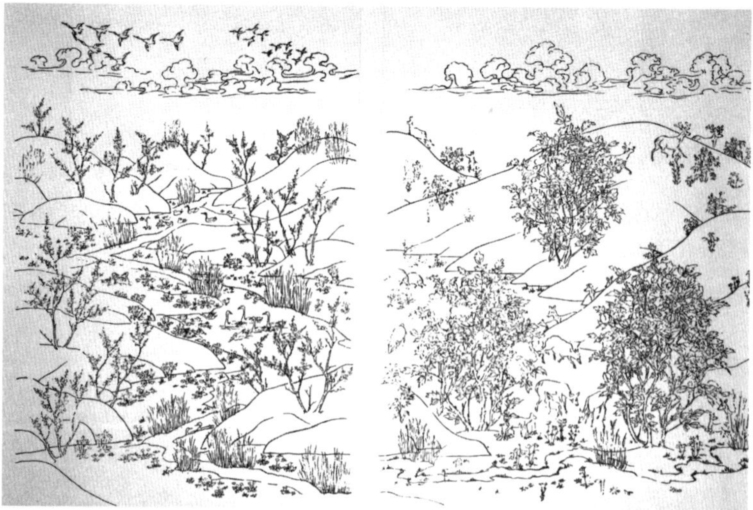

FIGURE 5
Drawings of the *Four Seasons*: *Spring* (east wall) and *Summer* (south wall), ca. 1031. Mural paintings. Central chamber, East Mausoleum, Qingling, Inner Mongolia. From Tamura Jitsuzō and Kobayashi Yukiō 1953, vol. I, figs. 86, 87

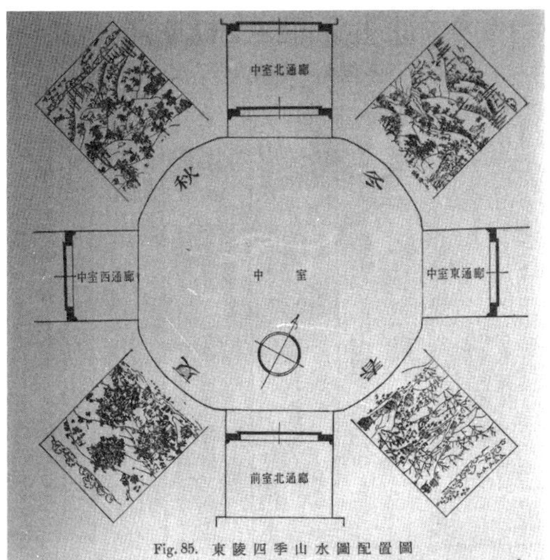

FIGURE 6
Plan of the central chamber showing the arrangement of the *Four Seasons* murals. East Mausoleum, Qing-ling, Inner Mongolia. From Tamura Jitsuzō and Kobayashi Yukiō 1953, vol. I, fig. 85

season on the grasslands to be a matter of the utmost importance in the final resting place of his father.

Beyond noting that these scenes represent "the seasons of the year [and] depict actual landscapes on and around Mt. Qingyun," Tamura and Kobayashi make the point that because the four seasons correspond to the four cardinal directions on the tomb walls, the scenes may incorporate the symbolism of the Guardian Kings of the Four Quarters found in tombs of the Six Dynasties period (220–589).[67] The emphasis on the cardinal directions permeates Liao culture, from their five capitals (Upper, East, South, West, and Central) to the mandala-governed orientation and ornamentation of their octagonal pagodas. This emphasis, though not unique to the Liao, is especially strong in their architecture. At the top of each of the *Four Seasons* paintings, above a painted gathered strip of cloth, is an architectural frame of brightly decorated simulated beams and bracketing. Such an architectural frame is evidence that murals were an integral part of the interior decorations of Liao palaces and halls as well as tombs.

Four Seasons is the fullest and most realistic depiction in Liao painting of grasslands topography, flora, and fauna. Unlike earlier extant examples of Liao painting, no human figures inhabit these scenes—only deer, a few wild boar, and a variety of birds. In *Autumn*, deer and boar find their place in the hills and along the streams, while above the clouds one flock of birds circles and another in V-formation heads south. In *Summer* and *Winter*, deer and boar have the hills and streams to themselves; in *Spring*, birds,

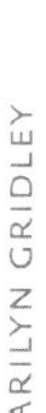

some of which head north above the bank of colorful clouds, monopolize the landscape. Wen Fong interprets the changing seasons, with the geese departing in winter and returning in spring, as "an elegiac theme for funerary wall decoration, [wherein the] landscapes symbolized the cyclical movement of nature from birth to growth to decline and death and rebirth."[68]

The artists of the murals depict with such precision the swans, ducks, and geese that Tamiji Kawamura has been able to identify their species.[69] Tamura and Kobayashi note that Qidan artists "seem to have been keener observers of animals than of plants, so that the plants ... are more difficult to identify."[70] Still, it is the plants that most prominently define each season. The flowering apricot trees and dandelions of *Spring* give way in *Summer* to enormous peony bushes, sweet william, asters, and lilies,[71] whose vividly colored blossoms vie with the bright green foliage of the trees. In the *Autumn* scene the few trees that still bear green leaves and a cluster of green-needled pines complement the dominant tones of reds and yellows. Purple grapelike clusters of fruit weigh down the branches of fore- and middle-ground trees. Tall, leafless larches are spiky vertical accents linking the background hills of *Autumn* and *Winter*.[72] In *Winter* a few yellow leaves cling to the scrub oaks, but the calligraphic silhouettes of winter trees are the most striking motif.

The variety of brush techniques and styles of the *Four Seasons* murals suggest several different artists at work. These artists were grounded in Tang traditions but apparently were aware of Five Dynasties and Song styles. *Autumn*'s most distinctive landscape features—the jagged cliff on the high horizon and a single rock in the upper right—are the only landforms in the whole cycle that are not softly rounded. Photographs of details of this scene[73] reveal masterful brushwork in the depiction of the rock and pine needles and one of the stags. The pine needles, rendered with curved black strokes radiating from the center, closely resemble the snow-white clusters on foreground trees in the painting *Travelers in Snow-Covered Mountains* by the Five Dynasties painter Jing Hao (ca. 870–ca. 930) in the Nelson-Atkins Museum of Art.[74] Tamura and Kobayashi note that the brushwork in *Autumn* is closer to that of landscapes of the Five Dynasties and Song while the *Summer* landscape "is derived from Tang ornamental landscapes."[75] Certain perspective devices in *Winter*, *Spring*, and *Autumn* are also based on Tang landscapes. The rivers, for instance, move in a zigzag pattern from fore- to background. In the succession of hills ranging from the front to the back, only the tops of trees growing in the valleys appear from behind the contours of the hills, a time-honored technique for indicating recession in space.

The *Autumn* scene of the *Four Seasons* tomb murals is one of the major pieces of evidence that scholars use to assign to the Liao period the pair of paintings *Deer in Autumn Forests*, in the National Palace Museum, Taipei. The subject of the paintings is the same: antlered stags,[76] doe, and the colorful foliage of autumn.

A major difference between the *Four Seasons* murals and the National Palace Museum hanging scrolls lies in their composition. In the murals, rolling hills fill the scenes, while in the scrolls, trees resplendent with autumn foliage dominate the composition. The effect is quite different; in the former, a sense of vast expanse replaces the almost claustrophobic crowding of trees in the latter. While this difference may mean only that the murals and scrolls are from a different time and place within the period and territory of the Liao, I believe the puzzle of the origin of the scrolls is still far from solved.

The *Deer in Autumn Forests* paintings might have been done by an artist such as Chang Siyan (1031–1100), who was famous for his paintings of forests. Chang, a commoner, who dwelt "amid the shadows of the North" in Beijing,[77] drew praise from Guo Ruoxu, who learned about him while escorting two Liao envoys in the year 1071. They told him that Chang "was so excellent a painter of landscapes, forests, and single trees that people came to court him in great numbers." In a note at the end of the passage, Guo comments:

> My humble opinion is this concerning Master Chang who undertook the practise of art while dwelling amid the shadows of the North, and was truly competent without ever having received the cultural influence of the Middle Kingdom; who could not be moved by force nor beguiled by profit: this was indeed a man![78]

This statement might have been added after 1074, when Guo was an envoy to the Liao court in Beijing (the southern capital of the Liao after 938), where he may have seen Chang's paintings.[79]

If the painter of the mid-tenth-century Yemaotai landscape scroll was, as Yang Renkai suggests, from the Liao southern capital, then that scroll gives some inkling of the tradition behind Chang's landscape paintings. It is logical that paintings done in the southern capital would reflect most closely the major developments in landscape and literati painting across the Liao-Song border, which lay just south of Beijing.

The Kulunqi Tomb 1, believed to date to 1088, provides evidence that Liao painters working near the eastern border of Inner Mongolia[80] were familiar with Han Chinese literati traditions by the late eleventh century. The tomb's figure paintings have received the most attention, but the paintings that are most relevant here are those from the north and south walls of the antechamber (fig. 7).[81] The motifs in the top three registers (figures comprise the bottom register) are drawn from nature, but not from the grasslands. The second register features four rocks, solid rectangular shapes each set neatly in the midst of the foliage and blossoms of peony bushes. Trailing cloud scrolls with three-lobed tips decorate the narrow third register. In the top register a pair of cranes on the north side and a single crane on the south stride through bamboo groves. The top panel on the south side has a rectangular extension depicting lotus and pussy willows in a pool of water. The world of nature portrayed in these paintings is seen almost completely through the eyes of Song painters. The rocks, bamboo, and cranes favored by Song literati-artists replace the rolling grasslands and swans of the Liao emperor Shengzong's tomb of a half century before.

The Kulunqi tomb was that of a member of the Xiao, a Uighur clan that gained high status in the Liao hierarchy by marriage into the Yelü (imperial) clan.[82] Two important Liao dynasty painters were members of the clan, and each was a literatus. The more famous one, Xiao Yong (active mid-11th century), served as a high official in the court during the reign of Xingzong (r. 1031–55). Records of Xiao Yong's landscapes document the strong influence the Tang tradition still exerted on the Grasslands school in the mid-eleventh century. Xiao Yong specialized in painting landscapes in the style of the Tang painter Pei Kuan (ca. 700–760) and birds in the style of the Tang painter Bian Luan (ca. 785–802).[83] A Ming dynasty painting with a Xiao Yong signature, *Pheasants on a Rock by a Stream*,[84] now in the National Palace Museum, Taipei, has ensured the artist's continuing reputation as a bird-and-flower painter. He was well-read and vitally interested in artistic achievements of the Song. His paintings, however, were not inspired by his contemporaries south of the border, but by Tang dynasty masters.

The other painter from the Xiao clan is the only recorded Liao dynasty woman painter. Her name is known from her epitaph as Qinjinguo fei

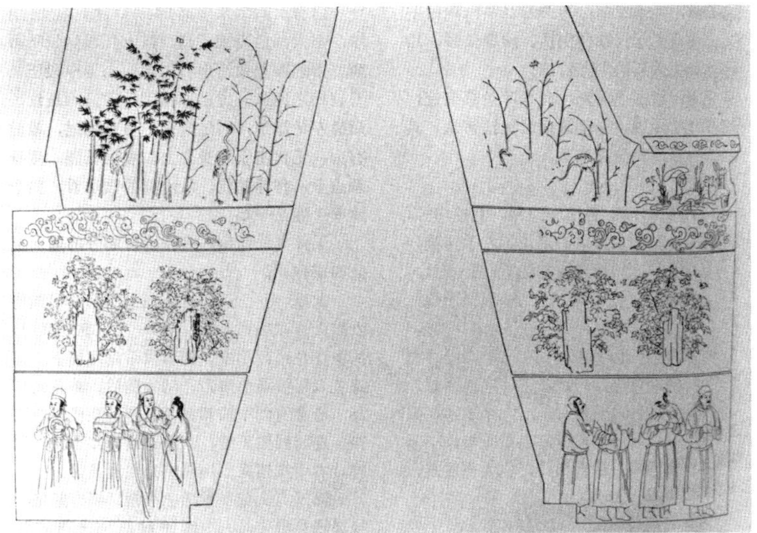

FIGURE 7
Drawing of the murals of donors and landscape motifs on the north and south walls of the air shaft. Kulunqi Tomb 1. From *Wenwu* 8 (1973), 10

Xiaoshi (1001–1069). Liao Jingzong (r. 969–82) was her grandfather. In 1016 she married Shengzong's younger brother, Yelü Longqinq, the powerful vice-regent of the southern capital.[85] Although no record remains of what she painted, she was especially fond of hunting and riding. It is plausible that she, like so many Liao painters, would have chosen to paint these activities, but she was also a literatus and a popular poet, and had an elegant mastery of "flying white" brushwork.[86]

The records of and surviving paintings by Liao painters make it clear that the emperors, princes, consorts, and nobility valued highly the art of painting and practiced it themselves. They were proud of their land and heritage and took these as subjects for their paintings. Liao painting did not develop in a vacuum or as an independent or even foreign tradition. It was solidly grounded in the Tang traditions of horse, figure, bird-and-flower, and landscape painting. By the mid- to late-tenth century, Liao painters had access to developments in landscape painting of the Five Dynasties and early Song periods. In the eleventh century, they combined certain of those developments with Tang traditions and transformed them into a style well suited to painting the landscape of the northern grasslands. Liao painting, in turn, influenced Song, Yuan, and Ming painters who chose to paint grasslands themes. The Grasslands school provided models when figure and animal paintings were popular but fell by the wayside when the "mountain and water" landscape tradition prevailed; that is, Liao painters

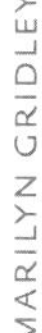

exerted considerable influence in the Northern and Southern Song periods and the Yuan, less in the Ming, and were almost entirely eclipsed in the Qing.

The land and the people of the border regions of China are once again popular subjects for Chinese painters. The most famous twentieth-century painter who took the grasslands as one of his major subjects was Wu Zuoren (1908–1997). The renewed interest in the grasslands, past and present, has resulted in a number of scholarly studies of Liao culture. These studies have revealed that the Song came to regard the Liao as a kingdom equal in many ways to their own, and that Liao painters enjoyed the high regard of Song emperors and critics, who admired and avidly collected their works. One hopes that scholars today can be as discriminating, and that the Northern Grasslands school of painting will be recognized as the important and influential tradition it was and still is in the history of Chinese painting.

NOTES

1. Tao Jing-shen 1988, 34–52. See also Wang Gungwu 1983, 47–65. I would like to acknowledge here the Committee for Scholarly Communication with the People's Republic of China and the National Endowment for the Humanities for their support from August 1987 to August 1988 in China. During that period I was able to collect much of the material used in the preparation of this article.

2. For the origin of this term, see Chen Zhaofu 1980.

3. Several scholars have made important contributions to the study of Liao painting in the course of their research on painters and paintings of other periods. Chu-tsing Li finds the *Parting of Su Wu and Li Ling* useful in tracing Zhao Mengfu's sources for his *Sheep and Goat* in the Freer Gallery. Thomas Lawton discusses at some length the Grasslands painter Yelü Bei, as two other paintings in the Freer Gallery are based on an original painting by him of a procession of foreigners on horseback (see n. 19 below). Studies of the representations of nomads in paintings of the Wenji story from the Song and later periods have provided much useful information about Liao scroll and tomb paintings. See Fontein and Wu 1973, 221–24 for bibliography up to 1973; Rorex and Fong 1974; Rorex 1984.

4. Luo Shiping 1999; Tsao 1996b; 1993, 42–44; 1995; Rorex 1984; Johnson 1983.

5. In Harrist 1997, Robert Harrist includes in his opening essay a section on

"Horses and the Non-Chinese World," in which he examines what the paintings reveal of the relations between the Song and the Liao. See also Liang 1994, 74–88; 1992.

6. These paintings were first published in Torii Ryūzō 1931, 272–80; no. 491, pp. 283–89; no. 492, pp. 313–17; no. 493, pp. 343–50. They are also published in Torii Ryūzō 1936. Additional photographs, with a detailed analysis of the subject matter and technique, are published in Tamura Jitsuzō and Kobayashi Yukiō 1953.

7. See Yang Renkai 1984; 1975, 37–39. The painting is now in the Liaoning Provincial Museum. It is dated to ca. 940–85 in Smith and Fong 1999, 263.

8. Tsao Hsingyuan has examined the relationship between the murals and the scrolls as a way to establish the original format and architectural context of the scrolls and discussed what the murals and scrolls reveal of the meaning of deer and deer hunting for the Liao. See Tsao 1996a; 1996b, 244–49. Laurence Sickman wrote of the similarities between the two scrolls *Deer in Autumn Forests* and the deer in the landscape murals of the *Four Seasons*; see Sickman and Soper 1956, 126 and pl. 97. See also Cahill 1960b, pls. 1, 2; 1960a, 67–68.

9. Soper 1951.

10. Cahill 1980.

11. Hu Gui is sometimes rendered Hu Huai.

12. Sirén 1956–58, vol. 1, pp. 175, 183; vol. 3, pls. 135, 142, 143.

13. Yan Wanzhang 1986.

14. In published compilations of painters, Bei is usually included in the Five Dynasties section under his Chinese name.

15. Wittfogel and Feng 1949, 577.

16. Soper 1951, n. 284; Wittfogel and Feng 1949, 577. Yan Wanzhang 1986, 86, gives Bei's age at death as thirty-eight; but, according to Chinese custom, which puts the age at birth as one year, he would have been thirty-nine.

17. These are listed under the name Li Zanhua in *Xuanhe huapu*, sec. 8.

18. Reproduced in color in Smith and Weng 1972, 154.

19. See Lawton 1973, 174, for Zhao Yong's *Horse and Groom*, and Li 1968, fig. 10, for Li Gonglin's *Five Horses*.

20. *Tang Song Yuan Ming Qing* 1963, pl. 50.

21. Yan Wanzhang 1986, 87.

22. Ibid.

23. Rogers 1980.

24. The Later Tang prefect, Shi Jingtang (892–942), asked for Liao Taizong's aid against the Later Tang emperor. The Liao emperor took the opportunity to personally lead armies through the Yanmen Pass south of Datong to defeat the Later Tang forces near Taiyuan. The supplicant prefect was then made emperor of the new kingdom of Later (Hou) Jin (936–949) by Taizong, who in return received in 938 the Sixteen Prefectures. These included a peninsula territory in Hebei Province that reached approximately 150 miles south of present-day Beijing to Hejian. The most important of these Sixteen Prefectures was Yu (Beijing). As soon as Taizong acquired Yu in 938, he named it the Southern Capital of the Liao Kingdom.

25. Yan Wanzhang 1986, 86.

26. Chen Zhaofu 1980, 45; *Jiu Tang shu: Shi shu chuan*.

27. The painting, in color on silk, measures 256 x 33 cm. The best reproduction is in color in *Zhongguo lidai huihua* 1978, 76–79. See also the color reproduction in Harrist 1997, fig. 11.

28. Tsao 1996b, 201.

29. Tsao 1996b, 205; 1993, 42–44.
30. Reproduced in *Wenwu* 8 (1975), color pl. 2.
31. Morgan 1986, 88–89.
32. Tsao 1996b, 210.
33. Ferguson 1968, 194–95.
34. Reproduced in *Chinese Art Treasures* 1961, 113.
35. See Shen Congwen 1959, 33–34, which argues that this is indeed a representation of the Wenji story but that the clothes are Jin and Song costumes, not Qidan. The tomb murals that have been discovered since 1959 document a great variety of styles worn by the Qidan, including those seen in *Resting at Midday*. See especially Neimenggu Kulunqi 1987, 74–84. The difficulty of basing dates on the costume is compounded by the fact that the Qidan officials, especially in the Southern Court, wore Chinese dress. See Wittfogel and Feng 1949, 228, n. 16.
36. See Fong 1992, 209–15, pls. 27a–d.
37. Tsao 1995; 1996b, 134–62. The hairstyles are consistent with those of figures in Qidan tomb murals.
38. Reproduced in Harrist 1997, fig. 13.
39. Hebei sheng 1998, color pls. 14, 18–20.
40. Ink and color on silk. See *Chinese Art Treasures* 1961, 42–43.
41. Cahill 1980, 34.
42. Reproduced in *Chinese Art Treasures* 1961, pl. 9. An excellent black-and-white reproduction appears in Li 1968, fig. 16. An excellent color detail of the two main figures appears in *Masterpieces of Chinese Figure Painting* 1973, pl. 7.
43. *Chinese Art Treasures* 1961, pl. 45.
44. Cahill 1980, 28.
45. Johnson 1983, 130, n. 66.
46. *Xuanhe huapu*, sec. 8.
47. Yan Wanzhang 1986, 90; *Xin Wudai shi*, *juan* 73.
48. Yang Renkai 1975, 38.
49. Fong 1984, 25.
50. Cahill 1985.
51. Vinograd 1981.
52. *Chinese Art Treasures* 1961, 71. For a discussion of this painting, see Laing 1994, 60–63.
53. Ho 1991, 381–82.
54. Cahill 1985.
55. Yang Renkai 1984; 1975, 37–39.
56. Yan Wanzhang 1986, 90. Chen's title, Hanlin *yuan daizhao*, raises the question of the nature of the Liao Hanlin *yuan* and how comparable it was to the Song Academy of Painting. Wai-kam Ho's examination of the complexities encompassed in the term "Hanlin *yuan*" as used by scholars for the Song Academy makes one realize how difficult, if not impossible, it is to determine the nature of the Liao Hanlin *yuan*. I am indebted to Susan Bush for alerting me to this problem and to Wai-kam Ho's discussion in Ho et al. 1980, xxv–xx.
57. Wang Bomin 1987, vol. 4, 135. The painting was written up in *Meishu* 12 (1955). I want to thank Susan Bush for calling my attention to this latter source.
58. Chen Zhaofu 1980, 46.
59. See Wang Gungwu 1983, 55.
60. Ibid., 52.
61. Tamura Jitsuzō and Kobayashi Yukiō 1953, vol. 2, pp. 55–59.
62. Ibid., 59.
63. Barnhart 1991, 246, n. 28.
64. Tsao 1996b, 270.
65. Tamura Jitsuzō and Kobayashi Yukiō identify these as leafless willows, but they must be reeds.
66. Johnson 1983,107, n. 1, laments the loss of the landscapes. At the International Academic Conference on North China's Ancient Culture held in Jifeng, Inner Mongolia, August 1993, Guo Zhizhong from the Hohhot wenwu yan-

jiusuo gave a report on the re-excavation of the eastern tomb and showed slides of the few remaining traces of the murals. The tomb has since been resealed.

67. Tamura Jitsuzō and Kobayashi Yukiō 1953, vol. 2, p. 26.

68. Fong 1992, 83.

69. Tamura Jitsuzō and Kobayashi Yukiō 1953, vol. 2, p. 18, n. 8.

70. Ibid., 19, n. 10.

71. For Torii Midori's copies, see Torii Ryūzō 1936, vol. 3, pls. 205–12.

72. The best photograph of the winter scene that I have seen is in Tamura Jitsuzō and Kobayashi Yukiō 1953, vol. 2, pl. 67.

73. Ibid., pls. 63, 64.

74. See Fong 1984, fig. 28a; and Tamura Jitsuzō and Kobayashi Yukiō 1953, vol. 2, pl. 64.

75. Tamura Jitsuzō and Kobayashi Yukiō 1953, vol. 2, p. 25.

76. The thousand-horned stag was a popular subject with court painters of the Liao period. In addition to the five scrolls of the subject by the Liao emperor Xingzong is the aforementioned record of an early-tenth-century painting of this subject by the first Liao emperor's son, Yelü Bei.

77. Soper 1951, 102.

78. Ibid.

79. The end date for material included in Guo's treatise is well after 1074. See Soper 1951, 105.

80. The area of Zhelimu meng Kulunqi has been incorporated at various times into Jilin Province or Inner Mongolia, so the location is given as one or the other depending on the date of the report.

81. Drawings of these important antechamber paintings are published in *Wenwu* 8 (1973), 10. See also Laing 1994, 74–88, fig. 11; Johnson 1983, 131–32; Wang Jianqun and Chen Xiangwei 1989, 19–22.

82. Wittfogel and Feng 1949, 239n.

83. Yan Wanzhang 1986, 91.

84. Wittfogel and Feng 1949, 498, fig. 39.

85. Ibid., 415.

86. Tsao 1996b, 130–33; Yan Wanzhang 1986, 91.

REFERENCES

Barnhart, Richard M. 1991. *Streams and Hills under Fresh Snow* Attributed to Kao K'o-ming. In *Words and Images: Chinese Poetry, Calligraphy, and Painting*, ed. Alfreda Murck and Wen C. Fong. New York: The Metropolitan Museum of Art.

Cahill, James. 1960a. *Chinese Painting*. Geneva: Skira.

———. 1960b. *Chinese Paintings XI–XIV Centuries*. New York: Crown Publisher, Inc.

———. 1980. *An Index of Early Chinese Painters and Paintings: T'ang, Sung, and Yüan*. Berkeley: University of California Press.

———. 1985. Levels of Meaning in a Tenth-Century Chinese Landscape Painting. Paper presented at the College Art Association annual conference, New York.

Chen Zhaofu 1980. Khitanzu huajia Hu Gui he beifang caoyuan huapai (The Khitan painter Hu Gui and the Northern Grasslands school of painting). *Meishu yuekan* 3: 45–48.

Chinese Art Treasures: A Selected Group of Objects from the Chinese National Palace Museum and the Chinese National Central Museum, Taichung, Taiwan. 1961. Geneva: Skira.

Ferguson, John C., comp. 1968. *Lidai zhulu huamu* (Index of paintings recorded in various dynasties). Taipei.

Fong, Wen C. 1984. Pictorial Representation in Chinese Landscape Painting. In *Images of the Mind: Selections from the Edward L. Elliott Family and John B. Elliott Collections of Chinese Calligraphy and Painting at The Art Museum, Princeton University*, by Wen C. Fong et al. Princeton: The Art Museum, Princeton University.

———. 1992. *Beyond Representation: Chinese Painting and Calligraphy 8th–14th Century*. New York: The Metropolitan Museum of Art.

Fontein, Jan and Tung Wu. 1973. *Unearthing China's Past*. Boston: The Museum of Fine Arts, Boston.

Harrist, Robert E. Jr. 1997. *Power and Virtue: The Horse in Chinese Art*. New York: China Institute.

Hebei sheng wenwu kaogu yanjiusuo. 1998. *Wudai Wang Chuzhi mu* (The Five Dynasties tomb of Wang Chuzhi). Beijing: Wenwu chubanshe.

Ho, Wai-kam, Sherman E. Lee, Laurence Sickman, and Marc F. Wilson. 1980. *Eight Dynasties of Chinese Painting: The Collections of the Nelson Gallery-Atkins Museum, Kansas City, and The Cleveland Museum of Art*. Cleveland: The Cleveland Museum of Art.

———. 1991. Picture-like ("Ju-hua") and Picture-Idea ("Hua-i"). In *Words and Images: Chinese Poetry, Calligraphy, and Painting*, ed. Alfreda Murck and Wen C. Fong. New York: The Metropolitan Museum of Art.

Johnson, Linda Cooke. 1983. The Wedding Ceremony for an Imperial Liao Princess. *Artibus Asiae* 44, no. 2/3: 107–36.

Laing, Ellen Johnston. 1992. Liao Dynasty (A.D. 907–1125) Bird-and-Flower Painting. Paper presented at the International Academic Conference of Archaeological Cultures of the Northern Chinese Ancient Nations, Hohhot, Inner Mongolia, August 11–18.

———. 1994. A Survey of Liao Dynasty Bird-and-Flower Painting. *Journal of Sung-Yuan Studies* 24: 57–99.

Lawton, Thomas. 1973. *Freer Gallery of Art Fiftieth Anniversary Exhibition, II: Chinese Figure Painting*. Washington, D.C.: Smithsonian Institution.

Li, Chu-tsing. 1968. The Freer *Sheep and Goat* and Chao Meng-fu's Horse Paintings. *Artibus Asiae* 30, no. 4.

Luo Shiping. 1999. Liao mu bihua shi tu (A reading and examination of Liao tomb murals). *Wenwu* 1: 76–85.

Masterpieces of Chinese Figure Painting in the National Palace Museum. 1973. Taipei: National Palace Museum.

Morgan, David. 1986. *The Mongols*. Oxford: Basil Blackwell Ltd.

Neimenggu Kulunqi qi ba hao Liao mu (Liao Tombs 7 and 8 at Kulunqi, Inner Mongolia). 1987. *Wenwu* 7: 74–84.

Rogers, Howard. 1980. Tartar Horseman Hunting. In *Eight Dynasties of Chinese Painting: The Collections of the Nelson Gallery-Atkins Museum, Kansas City, and The Cleveland Museum of Art*, by Wai-kam Ho et al. Cleveland: The Cleveland Museum of Art, 56.

Rorex, Robert A. 1984. Some Liao Tomb Murals and Images of Nomads in Chinese Paintings of the Wen-chi Story. *Artibus Asiae* 45, no. 2/3: 174–98.

Rorex, Robert A. and Wen C. Fong. 1974. *Eighteen Songs of a Nomad Flute: The Story of Lady Wen-chi*. New York: The Metropolitan Museum of Art.

Shen Congwen. 1959. Tan tan "Wenji gui Han tu" (Discussion of paintings of "Wenji's Return to Han"). *Wenwu* 6: 32–35.

Sickman, Laurence and Alexander C. Soper. 1956. *Art and Architecture in China*. Harmondsworth, England: Penguin Books Ltd.

Sirén, Osvald. 1956–58. *Chinese Painting: Leading Masters and Principles*. London: Lund Humphries.

Smith, Bradley and Wan-go Weng. 1972. *China: A History in Art*. New York: Doubleday and Co. Inc.

Smith, Judith G. and Wen C. Fong, eds. 1999. *Issues of Authenticity in Chinese Painting*. New York: The Metropolitan Museum of Art.

Soper, Alexander C., trans. and ann. 1951. *Kuo Jo-hsü's Experiences in Painting (T'u-hua chien-wen chih): An Eleventh Century History of Chinese Painting Together with the Chinese text in Facsimile*. Washington, D.C.: American Council of Learned Societies.

Tamura Jitsuzō and Kobayashi Yukiō. 1953. *Tombs and Mural Paintings of Ch'ing-ling Liao Imperial Mausoleums of Eleventh Century A.D. in Eastern Mongolia*, 2 vols. Kyoto: Kyoto daigaku bungakubu.

Tang Song Yuan Ming Qing huaxuan (Selected paintings of the Tang, Song, Yuan,

Ming and Qing dynasties). 1963. Guangzhou: Yishu hua baoshe.
Tao Jing-shen. 1988. *Two Sons of Heaven: Studies in Sung-Liao Relations*. Tucson: University of Arizona Press.
Torii Ryūzō. 1931. Ryōdai no hekiga ni tsuite (On the wall paintings of the Liao dynasty). *Kokka* 490 (September–December).
————. 1936. *Kōkogaku-jō yori mitaru Ryō no Bunka: Zufu* (Illustrations of archaeology), 4 vols. Tokyo: Tōhōbunka gakuin, Tokyo kenkyūjo.
Tsao, Hsingyuan. 1993. On the Subject of the *Zuoxie tu* or "Tartars Resting" Scroll Attributed to Hu Gui (in Chinese). *Songzhou xuekan* 11.
————. 1995. Chuan Hu Gui *Fanma tu* zuozhe kaolu (An investigation of the author of *Barbarian Horses*, attributed to Hu Gui). *Wenwu* 12: 80–89.
————. 1996a. Deer for the Palace: A Reconsideration of the *Deer in Autumn Forest* Paintings. In *Arts of the Song and Yüan*, ed. Maxwell K. Hearn and Judith G. Smith. New York: The Metropolitan Museum of Art.
————. 1996b. From Appropriation to Possession: A Study of the Cultural Identity of the Liao through their Pictorial Art. PhD diss., Stanford University.
Vinograd, Richard. 1981. New Light on Tenth-century Sources for Landscape Painting Styles of the Late Yüan Period. In *Suzuki Kei Sensei kanreki kinen: Chūgoku kaigashi ronshū* (Articles on Chinese painting history: In commemoration of Professor Suzuki Kei's sixtieth birthday). Tokyo: Yoshikawa Kōbunkan, 1–30.
Wang Bomin. 1987. *Zhongguo meishu tongshi* (History of Chinese art). Jinan: Shandong jiaoyu chuban.
Wang Gungwu. 1983. The Rhetoric of a Lesser Empire: Early Sung Relations with Its Neighbors. In *China among Equals: The Middle Kingdom and Its Neighbors, 10th–14th Centuries*, ed. Morris Rossabi. Berkeley: University of California Press.
Wang Jianqun and Chen Xiangwei. 1989. *Kulun Liaodai bihua mu* (Liao dynasty murals in the Kulun tombs). Beijing: Wenwu chubanshe.
Wittfogel, Karl and Chia-sheng Feng. 1949. History of Chinese Society: Liao. *Transactions of the American Philosophical Society* 36 (March).
Xin Wudai shi (New standard history of the Five Dynasties). Compiled by Ouyang Xiu (1007–1072). Beijing: Zhonghua shuji, 1974.
Xuanhe huapu (Catalogue of the imperial painting collection during the Xuanhe era; preface dated 1120). In *Yishu congbian*, comp. Yang Chia-lo. Taipei, 1962.
Yan Wanzhang. 1986. Liao dai huajia kao (Researches on Liao dynasty painters). *Liaodai wenwu xuekan* 2: 86–93.
Yang Renkai. 1975. Yemaotai Liao mu chutu guhua de shidai ji qita (Ancient paintings excavated from the Liao dynasty tomb at Yemaotai, their dates and other problems). *Wenwu* 12.
————. 1984. *Yemaotai di qi hao Liao mu chutu guhua kao* (Ancient paintings excavated from Liao tomb 7 at Yemaotai). Shanghai: Renmin yishu chubanshe.
Zhongguo lidai huihua: Gugong bowuyuan cang huaji (Chinese painting of successive dynasties: Selected paintings from the collection of the Palace Museum). 1978. Vol. 1, Eastern Jin through Five Dynasties. Beijing: Renmin meishu chubanshe.

The Search for Zhao Bosu

RICHARD EDWARDS

In an effort to define the art of the Southern Song (1127–1279) and especially that aspect of it associated with the so-called blue-green style, two names appear with tantalizing insistence, those of the brothers Zhao Boju (ca. 1120–1162) and Zhao Bosu (1124–1182). It is tantalizing because of the difficulty of discovering paintings that can with confidence be attributed to their hands. At the same time, as with so many painters of the period, we are given sparse assistance from literary sources. With Zhao Bosu, however, a path to understanding is at least partially opened by preservation of a biographical text, his memorial tablet or "divine way stele" (*shendao bei*), written in 1203 by his close contemporary, the scholar-statesman Zhou Bida (1126–1204). At the time of Zhao Bosu's death in 1182, Zhou Bida held the high position of Administrator of Military Affairs (*Zhi Shumi yuan shi*).[1] This memorial tablet is supplemented by the existence of a remarkable handscroll attributed to Zhao Bosu, *Palace in the Pines* (*Wansong jinque*; lit. "ten thousand pines and golden gates"), now in the collection of the Palace Museum, Beijing (see fig. 1). Finally, what is extremely rare for this period is the preservation of a statement by the artist indicating the theoretical premises of his art.

Zhao Bosu was just born at the fall of the Northern Song (960–1127) capital, Kaifeng, in 1126. A seventh-generation descendant of the first Song emperor (Taizu, r. 960–76), he could not have been much older than his late teens when, along with his surely more mature brother, he was introduced to the reestablished court at Hangzhou. He seems to have embraced many of the virtues and accomplishments praised in those who were of aristocratic background and held high positions of state. As Ellen Laing sums up his personality:

> He was a cautious person, clever and quick in nature, a man who had wide knowledge and experience and yet was reserved. He apparently enjoyed entertaining guests, but did not neglect the Confucian education of his family, which, upon the death of an older brother, extended to include the latter's children. Chao Po-su's interests spanned both civil and military accomplishments. He was a poet whose literary endeavors comprised twelve *juan* and Chou Pi-ta comments that he "amused himself with the arrangement of calligraphy, paintings, bows and swords."[2]

Zhou Bida's account lists a somewhat bewildering series of official appointments—titles both honorary and those bearing actual responsibilities.[3] Most influential for Zhao Bosu in the Shaoxing period (1131–62) was recommendation to the court by Han Xiaozhou of the Bureau of Military Affairs (*Shumi yuan*) who, according to Zhou, was a leading figure in his time. But he also received personal attention from Emperor Gaozong (r. 1127–62) himself. The emperor, a great admirer of Mi Fu's (1052–1107) calligraphy,[4] was delighted to receive Mi's original writing of an engraved tablet. Its contents drew Gaozong's comment that Zhao Bosu's grandfather, Zhao Lingjun, was a follower of Su Shi (1037–1101) and Huang Tingjian (1045–1105), and it was common knowledge among those in the palace that his descendants ("sons and nephews") all had Confucian training. This led the emperor to present Zhao Bosu with the honor of a "belt" and a dwelling place. His closeness to the emperor must have continued, for in 1164 he was promoted to the post of Deputy Director-General of Soldiers and Horses in the Principal Circuit and concurrently Presentation Director of Soldiers and Horses in the Deshou Palace (*Benlu bingma fudujian* and *Deshou gong jin bingma qianxia*). The Deshou Palace was where Gaozong had retired in 1162. In 1170 the prominent poet-official Fan Chengda (1126–1193) was appointed to lead a delegation to the Jin court in order to negotiate matters concerning the Song royal tombs in Henan and the ritual ceremony for "receiving documents" (*shoushu li*). Although the mission was generally unsuccessful, Zhou Bida—in his account of Zhao Bosu—suggests that there was "no stubborn resistance," and thus shortly afterward, the emperor (i.e., Xiaozong, r. 1162–89) sent a second envoy to congratulate the Jin ruler on his birthday. Zhao Bosu was the deputy or vice-ambassador on this latter mission, an appointment that inaugurated the practice of sending a member of the royal house to accompany such delegations to the north.[5] Zhao Bosu was especially acquainted with the Suzhou area, where he advised on the selection of a naval harbor as well as fortifications. He also drew what must have been a very accurate rendering of a Suzhou Daoist temple, Tianqing guan (Abbey to Celebrate the Heavens), which was later inscribed by Xiaozong with orders that the rendering be used to build a similar Daoist structure called Xuanmiao guan (Abbey of Mysterious Wonder). Zhao was buried in the hill area to the southwest of Suzhou at Zhixingshan. Clearly he did not just stay in the court.

Zhao Bosu fits the pattern of the well-placed scholar-official with unique access to the highest levels of society. As an artist he would have been free from any strictures the academy might have imposed. Like Mi

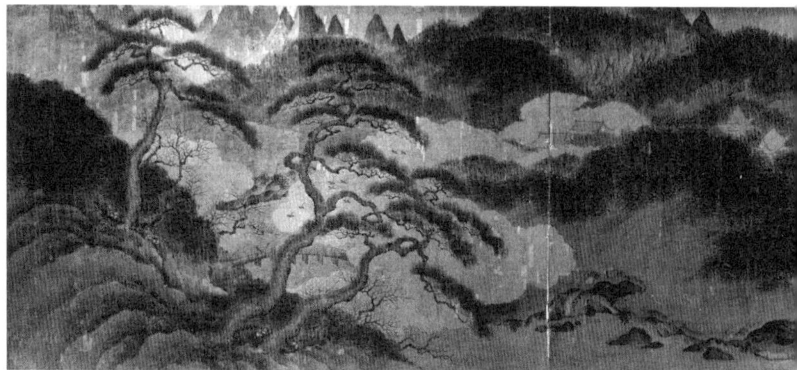

Youren (1074–1151) or Jiang Shen (ca. 1090–1138) of the previous generation, he would have been in a position to paint as he wished, using wide-ranging skills variously attributed to him: figures, birds and flowers, landscapes, wall painting, precise architectural drawing, and the use of color. He certainly could be looked upon by later admirers as fitting the scholarly mold. Indeed this seems to have been the case if we are to believe the single most promising surviving work connected with his name.

The handscroll *Palace in the Pines* (fig. 1)[6] has, in its present state, no title and no inscription written on it. However, mounted after the painting on separate paper are colophons written by Zhao Mengfu (1254–1322) and Ni Zan (1301–1374), both of whom used this title. Ni Zan's colophon (a poem) is dated to the year 1372, which was two years before his death. It is followed by a third colophon, undated, but one that may have been written not too far from this time since it is by an early Ming official, calligrapher, and painter of bamboo, Zhang Shen. Although coming from Jinan in Shandong Province, during the Hongwu reign era (1368–98) Zhang served as an official in Zhejiang where he held the position of Provincial Administration Commissioner (*Buzheng shi*), a post for disseminating government policies at the local level. Since the post was not created until 1376, we can assume that Zhang Shen was well along in his career before the turn of the century, increasing the possibility that his colophon was brushed not long after that of Ni Zan.[7] Zhao Mengfu's colophon records the earliest extant approval of the painting:

> When the Song moved to the south, there were of the royal house [Zhao] Boju, whose *zi* was Qianli, and his younger brother, Bosu, whose *zi* was Xiyuan. Both were good at painting with special

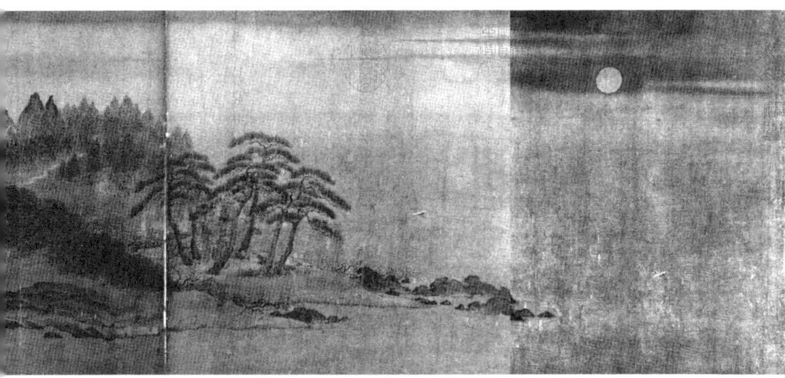

FIGURE 1
Attributed to Zhao Bosu (1124–1182). *Palace in the Pines.* Handscroll, ink and color on silk, 10⅞ × 53¼ in. (27.7 × 135.2 cm). Palace Museum, Beijing

> skills in applying colors. When Gaozong was emperor, he placed Bosu in the palace where he hastened to carry out imperial commands for whatever paintings were desired. This painting, *Ten-Thousand Pines and Golden Gates*, certainly is Xiyuan's work—pure richness, elegant beauty—a style of its own and a marvel for our time.

In his colophon, Zhao Mengfu confirms the close connection between emperor and painter. Further, the subject-title used by Zhao and in each of the other two colophons can readily be associated with this particular scroll. Emerging from the rounded hills of greenery, in the second half of the painting, are the golden roofs of what we can assume to be splendid architecture, lined along a single hill-valley axis that well might shelter palace gateways and great halls. That the covering on the swelling layers of hills may be readily interpreted as pine forest is a suggestion surely growing out of its deep, massed green coloring and the prominence of selected pines both at the beginning and the end of the scroll. A fourth colophon is worthy of mention. It was written by the poet Gao Qi (1336–1374). No longer extant, it is preserved in Gao's collected works. Using the same title for the painting, it is further confirmation of the significance of such a scroll in the fourteenth century. From its content the poem could well have been inspired by this scroll.[8]

Valuable as they are as historical evidence, the colophons were written long after the time of Zhao Bosu—Zhao Mengfu's at least one hundred years after the artist's death, if we postulate a writing in 1282 when Zhao was still in Wuxing, his native place, and as much as one hundred forty years if we stretch the time to the last year of his life. Ni Zan wrote one hundred ninety years after the death of the Song painter. As a work of Zhao Bosu, *Palace in the Pines* would already have been a painting of some antiquity when Yuan commentary was placed after it. Doubtless these early writers had more information than we—possibly a signature and certainly greater knowledge of the style of Zhao Bosu, especially as Zhao Mengfu came from the same royal family. Be that as it may, we do not have such benefit today. Our surest recourse is to look closely at the work itself and, since it is one of considerable refinement, to view it in detail.

Painted on silk, the scroll opens with a full yellow-pigmented moon on dark horizontal passages of a gray-ink sky that rides above a gently rising and falling water pattern—a weave of bowed parallel lines. These gradually fade from foreground into distance until they blend with the silk and the brooding darkness of the sky. There are small accents of two flying cranes, white wings trimmed with black, one over the water, one over the rocky point by which we now approach the land. Here are also the low, sharp crackling angles of plum trees and paired pines in a six-pine grove sheltering an empty slab of table on a rustic rocky base. There are two walking cranes—one with head lowered, one with head raised—a selective dualism expanding the theme of the flying pair. Here, too, is found a color pattern that is often the logic of a blue-green painting: rocks and rock surfaces essentially blue, level and more gentle land green with, for both, contrasting warm or umber tones for their bases, sides, and underparts. To suggest finer touches of detail, pine needles on neatly isolated branches point sharply upward; they are in ink backed by bluish lines. Green grasses sprout in selected groups on the green land. Still-preserved red dots affirm the crackling low trees as blossoming plums, thus anchoring season and mood—a dreamlike fragrant moonlit night in early spring.

Land now rises sharply. A foreground hillock masks yet points toward a wash-bordered empty path. The path disappears in a thick grove of evergreens. Above and slightly to the left are two more flying cranes, unobtrusive, continuing notes of immortality. But our entrance is reluctant. Land hangs like a suspended wall over the hollows of an eroded base that is continuously and restlessly undercut with shadows of umber and pocked passages of blue. It is further pressed from us by intervening lines of continuing water, the hovering of the hills, however, adding to the dream of a miraculous nighttime vision. Now water lines are clearer, the silk surface much better preserved (although careful, small rectangles of repair are evident here as earlier). Cool, fused brush-dots are spotted over the water, hanging plants answered by moss-dots on a few emerging blue rocks. Just above, the waterside erosion is flat gray-green. It is accented by a continuing bird theme, a rightward angling flight of white-winged water birds (essentially invisible in reproduction). Water, however, eventually leads us to the landscape by disappearing beneath low outlined clouds, then reappearing under a red-railed bridge close to the end of the scroll's brief length.

Throughout the painting, hill forms take the shape of repeated interlocking curves. They start as pale gray-green wash soon thickly covered by curving moist green brushstrokes of foliage—ink with a bluish tone—swelling tree-covered mounds that peak above cloud-framed golden roofs, only to be cut by the top edge of the scroll. Washlike strokes are ultimately touched with ink daubs—horizontal in the lower hills, vertical in the upper summits.

At the end of the scroll is the strongest motif of all: three extended pine trees leaning back into the painting with curving, occasionally looping, patterns of branches and horizontal cushions of pine needles (again the swelling curve) that sprout from restless flat twigs. Wet blue moss grows on bark surfaces. Hill shapes and clouds now act as echoing shapes, often framing the trees. The pines are a return to a familiar motif introduced at the scroll's beginning. So, too, are the crackling plums below them with dots, now of both red and white blossoms. The familiar lined water slips behind the forward trees and is seen as an inlet to be crossed by the already mentioned, gently arced red-rail bridge. The bridge is anchored at the left to a brief plateau, which also is edged with a red railing.

Clouds are a striking emptiness after so much massing of green-blue hill. They are the untouched silk rimmed by a light line and flat cool washes. Like the leaning trees, they are a major accent of return into the painting, embracing as well the leftmost palace roofs. Here, as at the beginning, are the accents of birds. Two are perched on the bridge, while a flock of eight water birds—strangely miniature for so apparently close a view—aim their long necks across clouds toward palace roofs. Dark against the light clouds, they echo the flight of the white-winged birds against darker land that we have just passed. Birds in this painting are significant inhabitants, consciously placed. The painting being devoid of human representation, we have only scattered symbols of human artifacts.

At this point the composition turns into a "typical" late-twelfth-to-thirteenth-century composition anchored in one corner, here the lower left with extension into space at the right. Returning through the scroll,

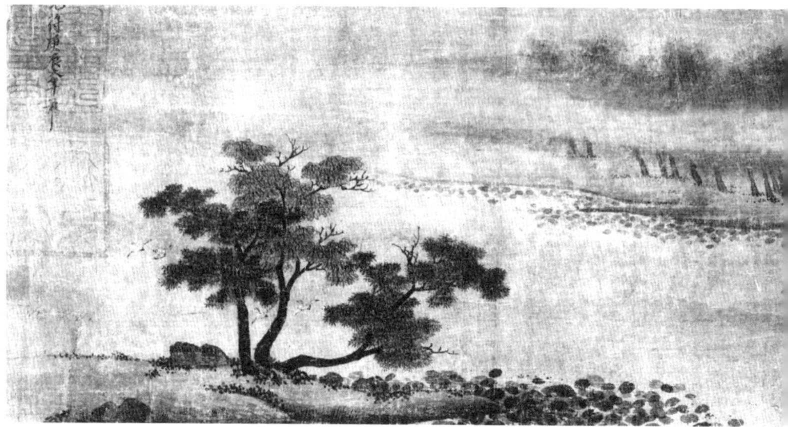

we go into the valleys that half conceal the palace, but we also see beyond the hillcrest to far peaks. They are visible above the nearer hills, not because we are forced to lift our point of view, but rather because in typical late Song fashion their pinnacles rise high enough to be visible from where we stand. Yet in their rich color and repetitious placement they tend to deny their distance and become a sharp pattern contrasting with hill curves. They are green-gray, blue, and two are warm amber. *Palace in the Pines* is a landscape quite unlike any other surviving Song painting. Yet it is one that leans obliquely toward Song vision.

The most important source must have been Zhao Danian (active ca. 1070–1100), who as a fifth-generation descendant of the imperial line had, in the late eleventh and early twelfth centuries, been in a social position similar to that of Zhao Bosu two generations later. Traditionally Zhao Danian was the originator of a special type of landscape presenting a direct, unassuming view of the world. Robert Maeda has illuminated the style, and in doing so calls our attention to Huizong's (r. 1101–25) *Xuanhe huapu* (Catalogue of the Imperial Painting Collection During the Xuanhe Era): "In his painting there are the charms of low embankments and lakes, shady groves, vaporous clouds, ducks and geese: they have an air of spaciousness and ease."[9]

These words are consistent with what we see in possibly the only authentic surviving painting from the hand of Zhao Danian, *River Village in Clear Summer* (*Jiangxiang qingxia*), an impeccably crafted handscroll now in the Museum of Fine Arts, Boston (fig. 2). It is signed by the artist and dated to the year 1100. While recognizing a shift in style, one can admit general parallels between it and *Palace in the Pines*. Both handscrolls

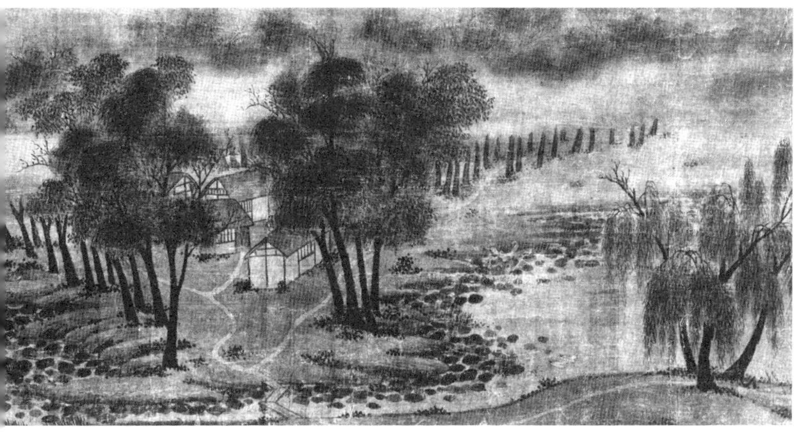

FIGURE 2
Zhao Danian (late 11th century–early 12th century). *River Village in Clear Summer*, dated 1100. Detail. Handscroll, ink and color on silk, 7½ × 64⅛ in. (19 × 163 cm). Museum of Fine Arts, Boston

are painted in ink and color on silk. Both begin and end with significant tree motifs. Both present a direct low-level view in which "embankments and lakes" play a significant role, rising, however, to a limiting screen of rounded hills in *Palace in the Pines*. In both is a conscious play of a mist-cloud motif. There are no human figures; architecture and empty paths are the only concessions to human activity. Birds fill active roles throughout. Aside from man's few artifacts, they are the sole inhabitants of a stilled, disarmingly compelling world.

Color is important to both, but with *Palace in the Pines* its striking use brings the landscape into the range of the blue-green mode. As Chu-tsing Li has clearly indicated, especially by referring to a comment by Zhao Xigu (ca. 1190), the manner had by this time assumed a traditional heritage reverting to Li Zhaodao (active ca. 670–730) in the eighth century, picked up by Wang Shen (ca. 1048–after 1104) and Zhao Danian in the late eleventh century, and continued by Zhao Boju (and presumably his younger brother) in the twelfth.[10] Now the mode itself was an automatic referent to antiquity. While the color in *River Village in Clear Summer* is more subdued, in his day Zhao Danian had a high reputation for his use of it, and that color was associated with the Tang period (618–907):

> Ta-nien used colors in rendering mountains, water, bamboo, trees, wild duck, wild geese, and the like, in the well modulated manner of the famous masters of the T'ang dynasty. The closest parallels that might be drawn to his work are the wonderful paintings by members of the imperial clan of the T'ang.[11]

The Tang link for Zhao Danian was more complete, however, for his small snow landscapes were connected to Wang Wei (700–761) both by Mi Fu and by Deng Chun (active ca. 1167).[12]

Finally, the theme of *Palace in the Pines* can be said to parallel the subjects undertaken by the earlier painter. Because of restrictions on travel by the royal family, the landscapes of Zhao Danian were said to be limited to the 500 *li* between Kaifeng (the capital) and Luoyang. This led to the witticism that when a new landscape was painted it must be the result of another visit to the imperial tombs, which were located to the east of the latter city near the Yi River in Gongxian.[13] The subject of the scroll attributed to Zhao Bosu is, in fact, of such an appropriate imperial nature. If the Yuan-period title is correct, we are looking at the golden roofs of the imperial palace at Hangzhou in the area reserved for high officials known as the Hill of the Ten Thousand Pines.[14]

A unique feature of *Palace in the Pines* is the repeated brush-daubing that defines the rich texture of the painting's curving hills. Again, in Zhao Bosu's time there was significant precedent. It rested in the painting of his older contemporary, Mi Youren. Mi's *Cloudy Mountains* (*Yunshan tu*; fig. 3), now in The Cleveland Museum of Art, is dated 1130, after he, like Zhao Bosu and his brother, had retreated to the south. Although the total effect—the style and its meaning—is markedly different, *Cloudy Mountains* offers a concrete datable precedent for the creation of rounded hills in a non-linear manner, the potential strength and expressiveness of stressing wash and repeated similar daubs of the brush. Nor did others in Zhao Bosu's time neglect this pointillist approach, for it can be found in an especially sensitive manner in the work of Ma Hezhi (active ca. 1130–ca. 1170): "Flecks of pale ink tones sprinkled over thin washes," as Robert Maeda has expressed it.[15]

While *Palace in the Pines* grows out of a definable tradition—the blue-green manner—and leans on the kind of painting suggested by the above masters—Zhao Danian, Mi Youren, Ma Hezhi—it presents these artistic impulses in a recognizably different fashion, not in imitation of any known previous painting.

Most significantly, while there may be areas suggesting recession, it is not a spacious picture. Even the opening section, with a peninsula probing waters of seemingly limitless extension into a brooding night, contradicts a sense of implied openness. There are streaks of ink-darkness in the upper sky. These and the insistent full moon painted in golden yel-

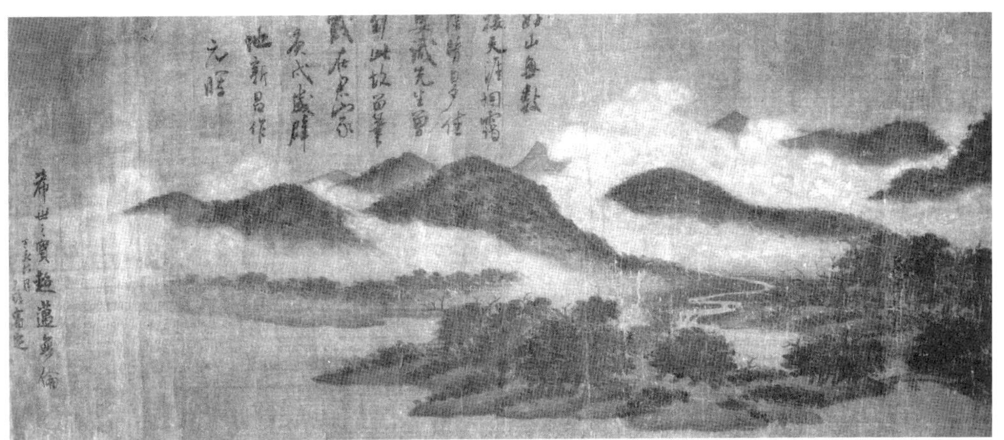

FIGURE 3
Mi Youren (1074–1151). *Cloudy Mountains*, dated 1130. Detail. Handscroll, ink, Chinese-white, and color on silk, 17$^{1}/_{8}$ × 76$^{1}/_{2}$ in. (43.4 × 194.3 cm). The Cleveland Museum of Art

low have the visual effect of jumping forward, a delimiting screen rather than true distance. This is continued in the full hill area where wooded mounds and carefully shaped clouds, while admitting an impression of substance in tight recession, more precisely take us up a richly painted surface until cut by the top edge. Forms are never truly liberated from surface (an effect somewhat neutralized by black-and-white reproductions). The small, warm passage of sharp undercut cliff just above the leftmost palace roofs hangs forward rather than back. While there is the convention of distant needlelike peaks, they jut colorfully upward (conveniently lower when the land is lower). They do not describe distance; they are simply repeated symbols of it.

Toward the close, the bridge with which we inevitably identify passage ends only at the briefest of plateaus blocked by a steep hill. Nor is there distance above. Pines are consciously open, but there is little depth to branch and needle clusters as they fan right and left of central writhing trunks. Nor is there marked depth between or behind these trees that lead us across rich patterns of water, cloud, hill, and peak to the very top of the scroll.

Marked, too, are jumps in scale which disrupt the physically logical relation of form to form and form to space. Arbitrary scaling is most succinctly summed up in the treatment of pines. Taken by itself, the opening promontory with its six pines and low crackling plums, its cranes, and an upper thin bright path leading to the thick grove of evergreens is believably scaled to a near and receding mid-distance. But moving leftward from it we are too quickly thrust into a screenlike tapestry of deliberate painting. Abruptly the pine-clad hills, even in the foreground, are conventionalized into daubs of green and black. When recognizable pines do return at scroll's end, their scale is two or three times the height of the original six trees. Yet they are spatially only slightly closer to us, for the eroded bank where earth meets water—restlessly active in its depiction—locates the land on the same forward plane from scroll's beginning until blocked by its steep ending, and the final hill is only marginally, a bridge-length at most, closer to us. Again, suddenly, almost magically, we have been brought back to a world of descriptive forms.

However, it is the patterning of those descriptive forms that dominates: brittle mesh of angled plum twigs, flat cloud, lines of water, silhouetted arrows of long-necked bird-flight, boneless bridge coloring, and pines—pines rising to the scroll's full height, spread like cutouts on its surface. The pines dominate and their branches, especially the curving cushions of needles, are carefully isolated to right and left of writhing trunks, creating a deliberately repetitive play with similar curves of cloud, hill, wave, and hollows of undercut land-banks. At this key ending, despite the increase of physical detail, the painting is unmistakably drawn into formal painterly expression.[16]

While thus transforming easy nature, the rejection is hardly complete. Forms in this final passage—tree, cloud, hillocks, bird-flight—echoing the late Song single-corner composition, are arranged to aim the view back toward the scroll's beginnings: pine to cloud, cloud to rooftop, to hidden valley, to bright path, to high tree grove, sky, moon; or, alternatively, from hidden valley to a line of plums back to landspit, water, night and moon. But while scale-jumps and other painterly arrangements still remind of nature, and despite the recognition of a specific place, an artist's insistence on formal structure, shape, color, and placement sets up a deliberate tension between expectations of a "normal" view and a personal inward vision of such a view. Nature enters into the realm of idea and imagination.

Seen in historical context, it is remarkable that such expression should be evident so early. If Zhao Bosu was the painter, the scroll must, of course, have been painted before his death in 1182. Perhaps we might assume a general date of the decade of the seventies. This is not to say that the ideals as such were not present, for they were well at hand by the beginning of the twelfth century, anchored in Su Shi, Li Gonglin (ca. 1041–1106), and Mi Fu. But the evidence of surviving painting does not support such painterly execution until well into the thirteenth century. In mentioning artists who appear to have influenced the style of *Palace in the Pines*—Zhao Danian, Mi Youren, Ma Hezhi—paintings have been suggested that differ markedly from the more precise style of artists working closely within the traditions of the Song academy. At the same time, however differing in the handling of the brush, they reflect an acceptance of the fact that those personal brushstrokes, colors, or wash must fit within a consistent spatial arrangement, a generally direct viewpoint which preserved a logical progression from foreground into, if desired, the furthest of distances.

Thus, Mi Youren's *Cloudy Mountains* of 1130 (fig. 3) offers an impeccably concrete view of an island of form where landspit, tree grove, stream, mountain, and cloud are so arranged as to create the illusion of forms progressing in orderly fashion toward believable physical distances. Because of its first colophon, the well-known scroll *Dream Journey Through the Xiao and Xiang Rivers* (*Xiao Xiang woyou tu*), in the Tokyo National Museum,[17] is datable to 1170 or shortly before, bringing us to a time in the late maturity of Zhao Bosu. It, too, defines the landscape with a unique personal touch based on ephemeral moist passages of melting ink. Still, spatial arrangements, while consistent with the dreamlike mood of the scroll, are convincingly unambiguous. This is especially true of a deep river-valley recession, a major focus of the scroll and one analogous to the river valley in Mi Youren's painting.

At the other end of the spectrum of twelfth-century painting is the art of Li Tang (ca. 1070s–1150s) and its strong influence on academic painting in the Southern Song. This is unmistakable in key surviving works of unquestioned authenticity: Jia Shigu (active ca. 1130–60), *Temple by the Cliff Pass* (*Yanguan gusi*), National Palace Museum, Taipei; Yan Ciping (active ca. 1162–89), *Villa by the Pine Path* (*Songdeng qinglu*), National Palace Museum, Taipei; Yan Ciyu (active ca. 1162–89), *Hostelry in the Mountains* (*Shancun guiqi*)—more accurately, *Mountain Market, Clear with Rising Mist*, one of the *Eight Views of the Xiao and Xiang*—Freer Gallery of Art. These are all signed works, but the manner can be extended to an additional anonymous group in the National Palace Museum, Taipei: *Strange Peaks* (*Qifeng wan mu*), a painting sometimes attributed to Li Tang;[18] *Pure Summer in the Water Village* (*Shuicun qingxia*), with a signature that has been interpreted, with some uncertainty, as that of Ma Kui (active late 12th–early 13th century), Ma Yuan's (active ca. 1190–1225) brother; and *The Fisherman Awakes* (*Pengchuang shuiqi*). None of these paintings are dated, but Yan Ciping and Yan Ciyu painted during the reign of Xiaozong, appar-

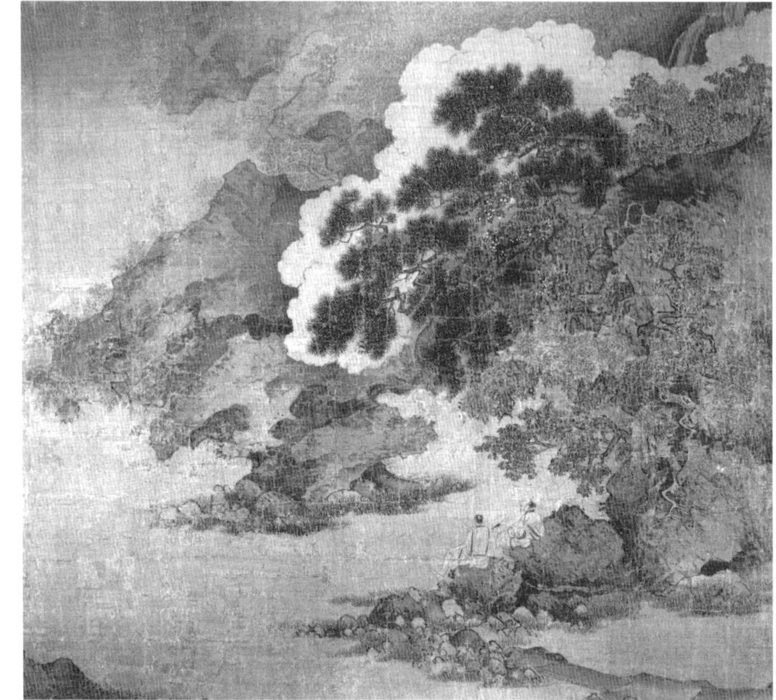

FIGURE 4
Unidentified artist. *Watching the Clouds*, in the tradition of Li Tang. Album leaf, ink on silk, 10⅞ × 11⅞ in. (27.7 × 30 cm). National Palace Museum, Taipei

ently active through the decade of the eighties.[19] *The Fisherman Awakes* has long been given to Gaozong. However, with careful reevaluation, both the imperial seal and the calligraphy are now accepted as belonging to Xiaozong during his period of retirement from 1189 to 1194.[20] The painting appears to be of the academy close to that time. Thus the style continued well to and beyond the end of Zhao Bosu's life in 1182.

It was a balanced style linking carefully ordered forms, often precisely rendered, with justly arranged spaces. When the stability of those forms and spaces began to change, when they became looser in themselves, distorted or less consistent in placement, there was a consequential change in meaning. Since the meaning, however, was still dependent on the original inception of those forms, it can only follow them, and we have moved to a later style. This clearly happened to paintings within the Li Tang tradition. An outstanding example of such change is an album leaf (fig. 4) attributed to that artist, *Watching the Clouds* (*Zuoshi kanyun*; lit. "seated on boulders, watching the clouds"), now in the National Palace Museum, Taipei.

The relation to Li Tang is unmistakable: outlined angled rocks, jabs of ax-strokes, tree roots dancing out of a rocky perch, thick clusters of pine needles, outlined clouds echoing the shapes of tree foliage, precisely arced falling water. But the whole receives a special animation. There is a zigzag entrance leftward from the lower right corner over a thin slab of bridge, back to the sharp boulderly perch of the two seated scholars. We continue to a wall of rock and tree from which, at an upward angle, we turn back again to cloud, more rock-wall, and fading mist-rock distance. The view, with minor variants, is an angled one from lower right to upper left. Within, detail reflects that angularity: corners of rocks, elbows of root and branch, jabs of a brush held at an angle, a sharp pine needle. But to these are added further complexities imposed by curving shapes: clusters of rounded foreground boulders, cavelike rock erosions, concentrations of needle and leaf, swelling clouds.

Based on a single-corner composition, with ambiguous leftward recession, this small painting offers a complex play of surface with the effect of denying expected physicality in the objects presented. The major definition of the painting hangs over space—water turning to cloud. Cliffs, themselves eroded, hidden or penetrated by cloud, rest imaginatively on, or hover over, a deeply honeycombed column of rock. The openness of the upper left might be read as tipped-up water or sky, except that close looking reveals shadowy foliage. It is a film of cloud-mist. The prominent placing and precise drawing of the two back-turned foreground figures present a rather over-intrusive "narrative" element. Yes, they, like us, are watching the clouds.

Watching the Clouds is of special interest in evaluating *Palace in the Pines* since it presents an academy-style version, in mirror reverse, of the ending of the latter scroll: sharp rise of land, prominent leaning pines, lesser deciduous trees, watery foreground, rocks honeycombed with cavelike erosions, deliberate bright patterns of clouds, the shutting off of distance so that there is a surface play of the varied forms presented. Neither could be considered a restrained objective view of nature. In both, the conscious intrusion of artistic device is present. Both are expressionist paintings. Since, however, both paintings rest on clearly established traditions, both must be considered as coming late within those traditions. The question is how late?

It is generally accepted that the famous styles of Ma Yuan and Xia Gui (active ca. 1195–1230) were aesthetically a continuation of Li Tang. Thus they carried the tradition well into the thirteenth century. Because of its conservative nature, the signed fan painting *Watching the Waterfall*

(*Guanpu tu*), in the National Palace Museum, Taipei, can be considered an early Xia Gui and thus painted in the latter part of the twelfth century, his more mature and "characteristic" works carrying us well into the thirteenth century. Yet even in these latter works, when characteristic Xia Gui brushwork is apparent, there is a continued sense of classic restraint—firm forms and unquestioned distances. Thus, when Xia Gui inserted the suggestion of cavelike water erosion at the base of a towering cliff in his *Pure and Remote View of Streams and Mountains* (*Xishan qingyuan*), the long handscroll in the National Palace Museum, Taipei, he did not play upon it, and the power of the cliff itself along with the firmness of succeeding mountain peaks belies any possible sense of instability (fig. 5). For Ma Yuan, firm dated paintings are similarly lacking. Yet from the evidence of seal legends, possible dates may be given to two high-quality works: *Twelve Views of Water* (*Shuitu*), datable to 1222, in the Palace Museum, Beijing, and *Solitary Fisherman* (*Hanjiang dudiao tu*), of about 1211, in the Tokyo National Museum.[21] Although the subject matter is limited and of different nature, neither of these paintings shows the complex expressiveness that characterizes *Watching the Clouds*. However, the presentation of water by Ma Yuan as a linear pattern fading into a far distance parallels the similar but more limited distance over water at the beginning of *Palace in the Pines*. Generally speaking, the style of Ma Yuan did

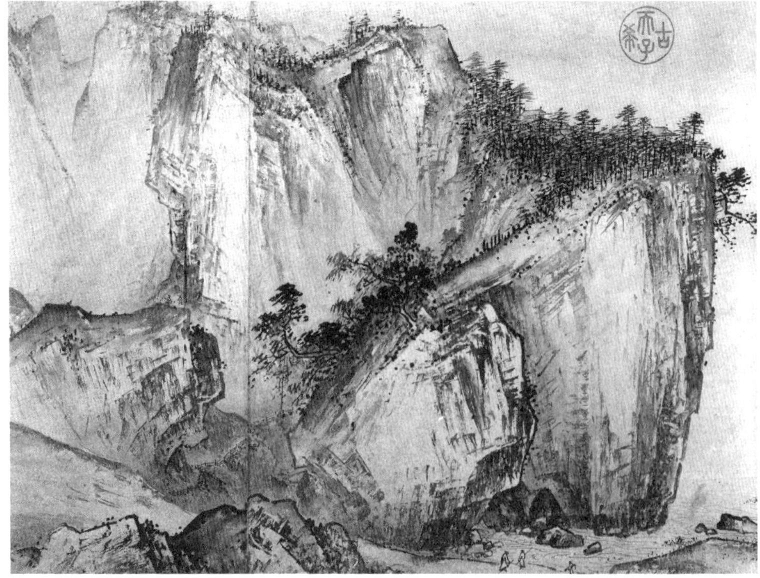

FIGURE 5
Xia Gui (active ca. 1195–1230). *Pure and Remote View of Streams and Mountains*. Detail. Handscroll, ink on paper, 18¼ × 350 in. (46.5 × 889.1 cm). National Palace Museum, Taipei

not turn to extensive expressionism until it reached the hand of his son, Ma Lin (ca. 1180–after 1256), whose datable works extend as late as 1256.[22] All the more, one thinks of these tendencies as indicating a thirteenth-century phenomenon. *Palace in the Pines* rests most convincingly in this later environment.

However, the comparison between one tradition—Zhao Danian—and another—Li Tang—need not necessarily lead us to conclude that they evolved at exactly the same rate. Here one must explore the ideological content of Zhao Bosu's approach to painting. Cao Xun (1098–1174), military official, calligrapher and connoisseur, supporter of Gaozong's legitimacy, instrumental in negotiating the return of Gaozong's mother from captivity under the Jin, and a close friend of both Zhao Boju and Zhao Bosu,[23] in a statement rare for this period tells directly, after praising both brothers, of having heard Zhao Bosu speak of his painting:

> In the brushing of human figures, fauna, and flora, the general run of painters have the skills to craft a likeness. But at the heart of those such as I is the need for a measure of expression [*yi zhong fenggui*], a spirit that is spontaneous, harmonies that are pure and far reaching, not insisting on the appearances of things even though they have aspects of beauty. Moreover, what I would have endure is not a pleasing of the world, and yet an ability to relate to common feelings. This is what needs to be understood.[24]

To a degree this is the universal complaint of the creative artist, who wants it understood that he is not caged by the expected. Li Tang, possibly in the uncertain times between the fall of Kaifeng and the reestablishment of the capital at Hangzhou, had voiced similar sentiments in a brief poem touched with irony:

> In snow the mist-wrapped village
> In rain the rapids.
> Easy it seems
> But the doing is hard.
> Had I known it would not please man's eyes,
> Far better buy rouge and paint peonies.[25]

While both asserted that their art went beyond superficial notions of beauty, Zhao Bosu consciously moved to a more intangible level that is easy to associate with the scholarly ideals that became so prominent in the Yuan. Yet Zhao Bosu was no rebellious recluse. After all, he was of the royal family. He held important government positions. He was honored by his contemporaries. However, his insistence that he wished to retain an ability to reach "common feelings" (*zhongqinq*) suggests a special aspect of Song taste. The ordinary world was still important. While rejecting the "beauty" of that world, Li Tang's "peonies," and apparently the accepted academic approach, he still wished to identify with general experience, but on a spontaneous, penetrating, and ideal level. All of this gives strong support to what we see in *Palace in the Pines*—the painting of a familiar place (the imperial palace at Hangzhou) at a time of universal experience (moonlight in spring) through the eyes of a unique personal vision.

Xu Bangda (b. 1911) has added further textual evidence in concluding that this scroll is the single surviving work not only of Zhao Bosu, but of Zhao Boju and the famous Tang predecessors in the mode, Li Sixun (653–718) and Li Zhaodao.[26] Noting its early acceptance by Zhao Mengfu, Ni Zan, and Zhang Shen, he picks up its importance in the seventeenth and eighteenth centuries. There are seals of the great collectors Liang Qingbiao (1620–1691) and An Qi (1683–ca. 1744), and of the Qing imperial collection—Qianlong (r. 1736–95), Jiaqing (r. 1796–1820), Xuantong (r. 1909–11). But it was not recorded in the imperial catalogue *Shiqu baoji*. The painting was fully published in *Daguan lu* of 1712. The compiler, Wu Sheng, made particular note of its unusual brushwork: "Dots vertical and horizontal, large and small, like trees, yet not trees, like texture-strokes, yet not texture-strokes."[27] An Qi also published an unusually complete description in his *Moyuan huiguan* of 1742. He indicated its stylistic dependence on Li Zhaodao (color), Dong Yuan (active 930s–60s; spirit-rhythm of brush), and Mi Youren (mountains and dotting). He stressed the boneless (*mogu*) quality of the color, including the use of gold, and that even the architectural elements—palace and bridge— made no use of ink.[28]

Xu cites a colophon ("copied by a friend") that Liang Qingbiao wrote on a hanging scroll, *Orchid Pavilion Gathering* (*Lanting xiuxi tu*), attributed to Zhao Boju:

> In collecting over seven hundred paintings from different periods only the paintings of Boju and his younger brother are as rare as the horn of the *qilin* or a feather of the phoenix. Fortunately I was able to purchase Bosu's handscroll *Palace in the Pines* [*Wansong jinque*].

> It has colophons by Zhao Mengfu, Ni Zan, Zhang Shen etc. (I suspect only half there). I heard that Dai Mingshuo [*jinshi* 1634] had in his collection a small silk fan, *Cranes Roosting in a Pine Grove* [*Songlin xihe*] with Gaozong's poem-colophon. By borrowing to compare, I then knew that *Palace* was genuine beyond doubt.[29]

Unfortunately today we lack the physical evidence to affirm that *Palace in the Pines* is "genuine beyond doubt." Careful examination, however, maintains that possibility, perhaps probability. The nature of the painting—its style, quality, and meaning—are "beyond doubt": "a spirit that is spontaneous, harmonies that are far reaching," these, too, are evident. Still there is the gnawing question: were these ideals expressed in this manner so early in history? It is a painting that has moved a measurable distance from clear roots in the art of Zhao Danian. Yet Zhao Danian was praised in a similar fashion. Mi Fu, in connecting him to the style of Wang Wei, wrote that Zhao captured "the idea of river and lake" (*you jianghu yi*).[30] This clearly was not the standard realism of the academy. His contemporary Li Chi (late 11th–early 12th century), while attributing excellence to his aristocratic heritage, was firm in "the beauty of his talents and the nobility of his life." He praised his "well modulated" color and his closeness to the Tang. This was continued by Deng Chun in his writing of 1167. He noted the "pure beauty" (*qingli*) of his many small hanging scrolls, and not only his closeness to Wang Wei in snow landscapes, but that he studied Su Shi in the theme of "small mountains and bamboo thickets."[31]

Moreover, for Zhao Danian we have selected preserved paintings that affirm the importance of his style shortly after 1100. In particular, two important paintings clearly fit the mold: Liang Shimin's (active early 12th century) *Heavy Snow on the Lu-Grass Landspits* (*Luting mixue tu*), in the Palace Museum, Beijing,[32] and the small, impeccable *Cottages in a Misty Grove in Autumn* by Li Anzhong (active second half of the 12th century), in the Cleveland Museum. Both are inscribed, the latter dated to 1117. Liang Shimin was active in the court of Huizong. Both join subtle touches of individuality to a secure stability in the relation of form to form and form to space, an enhancement rather than a violation of the accepted world of space and time.

While Zhao Bosu's statement about his art appears to point directly to the style exhibited in *Palace in the Pines*, words can be deceptive. Theory throws a broad net. Only specific works can define what is caught in that net. Lacking others, the surviving painting of Ma Hezhi may bring us closest to acceptance. Scraps of theory in the earliest texts aim in that direction. Zhuang Su (active late 13th century), discussing Ma Hezhi directly after Zhao Boju and Zhao Bosu, declared of Ma's revival of the Wu (Daozi, ca. 650s–after 758) manner, that his brush was "floating and untrammeled" (*piaoyi*), that he strove to eliminate "[mere] decorative beauty" (*huazao*). Tang Hou (active late 13th–early 14th century) reaffirmed Ma's reliance on Wu Daozi's manner, repeated the same phrase to describe his brush, and added that he was "able to cast off vulgar habits and lodge his mind in the lofty and ancient." We thus have the picture of an artist paralleling the aims of Zhao Bosu: reviving antiquity, consciously creating a personal style, and striving for an effect beyond the superficialities of common taste.[33]

As to the time of Ma Hezhi's activity—his dates have never been recorded—Zhuang Su claimed that Ma's famous series of illustrations to the *Shijing* (Classic of Poetry) were the result of collaboration with emperor Xiaozong. This, then, could extend his work from the early 1160s through the 1180s, much of it contemporary with the last two decades of Zhao Bosu's life. Nor would this exclude closeness to Gaozong, since the latter remained in retirement until 1187, outliving Zhao Bosu by five years. The earliest authority to claim Gaozong as the initiator of the *Classic of Poetry* was Xia Wenyan, in 1365, but he comprehensively included service to both courts.[34]

Stylistically, however, Ma Hezhi was a special case. He painted few landscapes. His major surviving work, illustrations to the *Classic of Poetry*, whether by him, by collaborators, or by early copyists, forced the artist into a world of ideas. By the very nature of the subject, he was pressed out of the present into the ancient past. He was not concerned with direct observation. Reflecting more orthodox expectation as late as the end of the thirteenth century, Zhuang Su hinted at difficulties in concluding that while he created a unique style there were also spots that were deficient, careless (or coarse)—*shuque chu*. When pure landscapes do occur, however, his "floating and untrammeled" brush appears disciplined to the coherence of a late Song view. The Boston Museum's *The Southern Mountains Have Tai Plants* neatly frames a mist-filled receding ravine with hills to right and left. *Lofty Are the Mountain Peaks*, in the Fujii Yurinkan, displays a Northern Song-type mountainscape directly observed behind a deep foreground recession of water and lowland. Level-ground evergreens are small, naturalistically scaled to the great mountains.

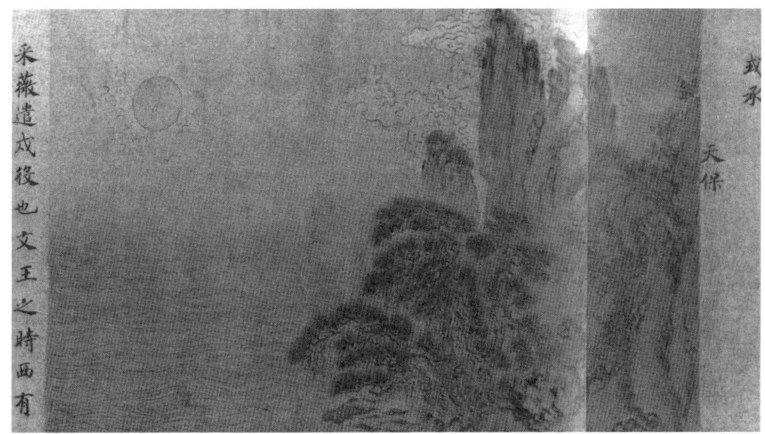

FIGURE 6
Ma Hezhi (active ca. 1130–ca. 1170). *Heaven Protects*. Detail. Handscroll, ink and color on silk, 71.1 × 340 in. (28 × 864 cm). (From the *Book of Odes*, *Luming zhi shi*: "Ten of 'The Deer Call'"). Palace Museum, Beijing

To return to Zhao Bosu, Ma Hezhi's *Heaven Protects* (*Tianbao*; fig. 6), in the Palace Museum, Beijing, perhaps offers the closest parallel to *Palace in the Pines*. Like the moonlit opening attributed to Zhao Bosu, Ma Hezhi has placed land—to the right and in the form of a sharp cliff—to offset wave-defined water receding into a misty distance. The bright orb of a red sun, rather than the moon, hangs insistently over the scene. But, once again, Ma Hezhi did not markedly distort his view. The tall cliff with its growth of trees frames and stabilizes our view into space. However personal the touch, he does not do violence to our expectation of nature's physical stability. Yet this is exactly what has occurred in *Palace in the Pines*.

The question still lingers. How far would Zhao Bosu have moved from nature's appearance as most generally perceived in the twelfth century and still have remained true to his goal of relating to "common feelings"? A definite answer is not precisely at hand. What remains certain, however, is the unique quality and personal creativity of the scroll itself—the representation in a short handscroll of a specific place, but a place that is imbued by the artist both with tradition and with penetrating personal insight. It is an artistic accomplishment that is most securely found in the early Yuan. One thinks of Qian Xuan's (ca. 1235–before 1307) *Floating Jade Mountain Retreat* (*Fouyu shanju tu*) in the Shanghai Museum, and Zhao Mengfu's *Autumn Colors on the Que and Hua Mountains* (*Que Hua qiuse*) of 1296 in the National Palace Museum, Taipei. It was Chu-tsing Li's pioneering study of the latter scroll that brought us to understand both its significance and the importance of its creator. [35] Are we now to extend the genre back into the second half of the twelfth century?

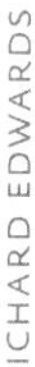

NOTES

I would like to acknowledge the importance of a fellowship administered by the Committee on Scholarly Communication with the People's Republic of China, which some years ago, in 1980, allowed me to gain my first acquaintance—albeit under glass in exhibition—with the scroll that is the main topic of this paper. Thanks also are to be given to Dr. Marshall Wu for assistance in some difficult points of translation. The errors, however, remain mine.

1. For a biography of Zhou Bida, see T. Kinugawa 1976, 275–77.
2. Laing 1976, 8–9.
3. The "Zhao Bosu Divine Way Stele" is to be found in Zhou Bida 1971, ch. 70, pp. 9–15.
4. For Gaozong's commitment to the calligraphy of Mi Fu, see Murray 1985a, 48.
5. For mention of Fan Chengda's mission, see *Songshi* 1977, ch. 34, pp. 648, 649. The mission as well as Fan's account of the trip are fully discussed in Hargett 1984, 119–77. Zhou Bida wrote the "divine way stele" for Fan Chengda (see ibid., 133 ff.) as well as that for Zhao Bosu. In the latter (Zhou Bida 1971, 10a-b) both missions are mentioned, the second one being headed by Zhao Xiong (1129–1190). To further emphasize connections between important Song personalities, it was in 1170, on the 26th day of the sixth month, that the poet Lu Yu, on his way to Sichuan, met Fan Chengda, with whom he had been connected eight years previously in the Bureau of Records. The meeting was at Zhenjiang near the Yangzi River crossing for travel to the north. Fan was there on his way north. Lu Yu comments on the temporarily received titles that made him suitable to be Petition Envoy to the Jin. See Chang and Smythe 1981, 52.
6. For reproductions of this scroll as well as others cited, but not illustrated in this text, consult Cahill 1980. An important, generally clear reproduction of *Palace in the Pines* is in *Zhongguo wenwu* 4 (1980): 1–8. This includes the three colophons and an important assessment by Xu Bangda that will be discussed below. For additional reproductions see *Zhongguo lidai huihua* 1982, pls. 56–63 and pp. 9–10; *Yiyuan duoying* 30 (1985): 27–28; and Suzuki Kei 1988, illustration vol., no. 3.
7. Wen Fong, seeing the painting as "a Daoist paradise, an immortal's heavenly abode on earth," has suggested that Ni Zan's colophon, especially the line "Immortals seem to beckon to me from the edge of heaven," reflected Ni's personal desire to escape from the mundane world. See Fong 1984, 2. The fact that Zhao Bosu himself designed Daoist temples gives general support to this idea. For Zhang Shen, see Yu Jianhua 1981, 850. The calligraphy is followed by a single seal: "*Shixing fu*." Shixing was his *zi*, or style name, traditionally given on attaining maturity. For the official title and its date, see Hucker 1985, 127, no. 487.
8. *Qingqiu shiji zhu* (*Sibubeiyao* ed.), Shanghai, n.d., ch. 9, pp. 17b–18a. The poem's beginning is an imaginative extension of what we see: "Tall pines lifting beards like a company of dragons; / Below, palace gates encircled—a thousand layers of cloud. / The head of Phoenix Mountain facing forward halls, / Sun out of a sea gate, a tide begins to rise. / White cranes come fly-

ing, approach immortal's hands." The "immortal's hands" is an architectural reference, Han Wudi having raised a cypress beam supported by a bronze pillar, like an immortal raising a dish to receive sweet dew. Phoenix Mountain locates us in Hangzhou's palace area. Gao Qi interprets the scene as rising dawn rather than full moonlight. Is this poetic license or a different version?

9. Maeda 1970, 246.

10. Li 1981, 350. Li is quoting Zhao Xigu, *Dongtian qinglu ji* (*Meishu congshu* ed.), 28b. Zhao Xigu also points out that while the color style is different from painting in ink, it is subject to the same weaknesses, thus bringing the handling of blue-green color and the handling of ink into close association, an aspect that historically seems often to have linked the two modes and why both were so acceptable within the range of later scholar-painting.

11. Soper 1949, 23.

12. Maeda 1970, 245; Vandier-Nicolas 1967, 80; Deng Chun 1963, ch. 2, p. 8.

13. Maeda 1970, 244, 245. The source is *Huaji*, ch. 2, p. 9.

14. Gernet 1962, 32 (reference is to the *Bulletin of Chinese Studies* 4, Chengdu, 1944).

15. Maeda 1970, 253. He is referring to *The Southern Mountains Have Tai Plants*, now in the Museum of Fine Arts, Boston. Maeda stresses not only the Mi-style and Ma Hezhi relationship, but ties them both to Zhao Danian.

16. Suzuki Kei has called attention to Japanese scholarship in mentioning the apparent availability of the scroll in south China and possible influence on Yuan painting, particularly the pine trees of Qian Xuan. See Suzuki Kei 1988, vol. 2, p. 7, n. 9. The scholarship in question is Shimada Hidemasa 1983, 267–98. Shimada gives a detailed discussion of the scroll relating it to such artists as Mi Youren and Ma Hezhi. Without affirming certain authenticity, he connects it with a creative twelfth-century period allied to the reestablishment of the dynasty in the south.

17. For reproductions of the painting see Cahill 1980, 202. It is also reproduced and briefly discussed in Li 1965, 49.

18. Cahill 1960, 42. The paintings listed here have previously been brought together in a consistent context in Edwards 1981, 37–72. For other reproductions of paintings cited, consult Cahill 1980.

19. Edwards 1975, 81.

20. See Chu Hui-liang 1991, 300–301; Wu 1997, 178–79.

21. Edwards 1976, 111. The date of the *Water* painting depends on the title in the empress' seal. The reading is now to be shifted from "*guifei*" to "*guijie*" (noble consort) and related to the later time when she was an established empress. See Lee 1994, 272.

22. Loehr 1961, 278. An album leaf in the Cleveland Museum extends Loehr's dates to 1256. See Lee 1974, 26, 27.

23. See Murray 1985b, 1–29.

24. The passage is to be found in Cao Xun 1977, ch. 30, pp. 12a–b. It is cited in Xu Bangda 1980, 8. It is contained in the second of two essays: *Jingshan luohan ji* and *Jingshan xu luohan ji* (Record of Jingshan luohan and its supplement). These essays reveal Cao Xun's friendship with and admiration for the two gifted brothers. In fact, they become paragons of brotherly love. Toward each other they show affection as in the blossom of the wild cherry, respect as the wagtail on the high plain (metaphors for brotherly relations from *Book of Odes*). "The elder comforts the younger; the younger

serves the elder. The elder says, 'sit,' and [the younger] sits; says 'eat,' and [the younger] grasps ladle and chopsticks to eat" (p. 12a). Cao Xun tells of Zhao Boju painting 100 scrolls with the subject of 500 luohan. The two compositions are both dated, the first to 1160 and the second to 1173. In the latter we are told that Zhao Boju had been dead a number of years (p. 12b). It seems clear that he did not outlive the decade of the sixties.

25. The poem is quoted by Song Qi of the fourteenth century following a Li Tang painting, *Bo Yi and Shu Qi in the Wilderness*, now in the Palace Museum, Beijing. See *Zhongguo lidai huihua* 1982, 4.

26. Xu Bangda 1980, 8.

27. Wu Sheng, *Daguan lu*, preface 1712, ch. 14, 1.

28. An Qi, *Moyuan huiguan*, preface 1742 (1908 ed.), painting, *shang*, 27–28a. He speaks also of having seen a Li Tang painting of the same subject, of high quality, but not the equal of this.

29. Xu Bangda 1980, 8.

30. Vandier-Nicolas 1967, 80 and n. 2. As the translator indicates, the mention of river and lake suggested the recluse absorbed in nature as opposed to the formalities of court and academy. Tang Hou in the 1320s appears to indicate the same in telling us his painting "went beyond brush and ink." The passage is somewhat suspect, as if to include Zhao Danian the commentator had to turn to another edition. The passage starts out with the mention of only Zhao Boju and Zhao Bosu. See Tang Hou 1959, 50 and n. 1. Xia Wenyan does not mention Zhao Danian in his seemingly comprehensive *Tuhui baojian* of 1365. However, Robert Maeda's doubts about including Zhao Danian as a "full-fledged *wenren* painter" should be modified (Maeda 1970, 244, n. 11). He was not a leading figure, but his values—archaisms, lofty personal expression, and a search for inner truth rather than mere outward likeness—fit the *wenren* mold. Certainly later literati painters often drew upon his manner.

31. For Li Chi and Deng Chun, see notes 11 and 12 above.

32. For a reproduction, in addition to Cahill 1980, see *Zhongguo lidai huihua* 1981, pls. 52–59 and p. 8.

33. Murray 1993, 32–33; Zhuang Su 1963, ch. 1, p. 4; Tang Hou 1959, 53. Murray isolates seven significant "primary" scrolls with text and illustrations of the *Classic of Poetry* but concludes that the calligraphy reflects a general dependence on Gaozong rather than being authentically by his hand.

34. Zhuang Su 1963, ch. 1, p. 4. Xia Wenyan 1936, ch. 4, p. 72.

35. Li 1965.

REFERENCES

Cahill, James. 1960. *Chinese Painting*. Geneva: Skira.

———. 1980. *An Index of Early Chinese Painters and Paintings: T'ang, Sung, and Yüan*. Berkeley: University of California Press.

Cao Xun. 1977. *Songyin wenji* (*Siku quanshu* edition, 1776). Reprint. Taipei.

Chang, Chun-shu and Joan Smythe, trans. 1981. *South China in the Twelfth Century*. Hong Kong.

Chu Hui-liang. 1991. Imperial Calligraphy of the Southern Sung. In *Words and Images: Chinese Poetry, Calligraphy, and Painting*, ed. Alfreda Murck and Wen C. Fong. New York: The Metropolitan Museum of Art.

Deng Chun. 1963. *Huaji* (1167). In *Huaji, Huaji buyi*. Beijing.

Edwards, Richard. 1975. The Yen Family and the Influence of Li T'ang. *Ars Orientalis* 10.

———. 1976. Ma Yüan. In *Sung Biographies: Painters*, ed. Herbert Franke. Wiesbaden.

———. 1981. The Real World: Style and Object (*Wu*) in Late Sung Painting. In *Proceedings of the International Conference on Sinology* (Section of History of Arts). Taiwan.

Fong, Wen C. 1984. Words and Images in Song and Yüan Paintings. In International Symposium of Art Historical Studies, *Landscape Painting of Far East II*. Osaka: The Society for International Exchange of Art Historical Studies.

Fontein, Jan and Tung Wu. 1973. *Unearthing China's Past*. Boston: Museum of Fine Arts, Boston.

Gernet, Jacques. 1962. *Daily Life in China on the Eve of the Mongol Invasion 1250–1276*. Trans. H.M. Wright. Stanford: Stanford University Press.

Hargett, James. 1984. Fan Ch'eng-ta's *Lan-p'ei lu: A Southern Sung Diplomatic Travelogue*. *Tsing Hua Journal of Chinese Studies* 16, nos. 1, 2 (December).

Hucker, Charles O. 1985. *A Dictionary of Official Titles in Imperial China*. Stanford: Stanford University Press.

Kinugawa, T. 1976. Chou Pi-ta. In *Sung Biographies*, ed. Herbert Franke. Vol. 1. Wiesbaden.

Laing, Ellen. 1976. Chao Po-chü, Chao Po-su. In *Sung Biographies: Painters*, ed. Herbert Franke. Wiesbaden.

Lee, Hui-shu. 1994. The Domain of Empress Yang (1163–1233). PhD diss., Yale University.

Lee, Sherman E. 1974. *The Colors of Ink*. New York.

Li, Chu-tsing. 1965. *The Autumn Colors on the Ch'iao and Hua Mountains: A Landscape by Chao Meng-fu*. Ascona, Switzerland: Artibus Asaie.

———. 1981. The Role of Wu-hsing in Early Yüan Artistic Development Under Mongol Rule. In *China Under Mongol Rule*, ed. John D. Langlois Jr. Princeton: Princeton University Press.

Loehr, Max. 1961. Chinese Paintings with Sung Dated Inscriptions. *Ars Orientalis* 4.

Maeda, Robert J. 1970. The Chao Ta-nien Tradition. *Ars Orientalis* 8.

Murray, Julia K. 1985a. The Role of Art in Southern Sung Dynastic Revival. *Bulletin of Sung-Yüan Studies* 19.

————. 1985b. Ts'ao Hsün and Two Southern Sung History Scrolls. *Ars Orientalis* 15.

————. 1993. *Ma Hezhi and the Illustration of the Book of Odes*. Cambridge: Cambridge University Press.

Shimada Hidemasa. 1983. Den Chō Hakushuku hitsu 'Banshō kinketsu zukan' ni tsuite. *Sōdai no shakai to bunka*. Tokyo.

Songshi. 1977. Zhonghua shuju. Beijing.

Soper, Alexander C. 1949. A Northern Sung Descriptive Catalogue of Paintings (the *Hua-p'in* of Li Ch'ih). *Journal of the American Oriental Society* 69 (March).

Suzuki Kei. 1988. *Chūgoku kaigashi*. Vol. 2b (Yuan). Tokyo.

Tang Hou. 1959. *Huajian* (ca. 1320). Beijing: Renming meishu chubanshe.

Vandier-Nicolas, Nicole. 1967. *Le Hua-che de Mi Fou*. Paris.

Wu, Tung. 1997. *Tales from the Land of Dragons*. Boston: Museum of Fine Arts, Boston.

Xia Wenyan. 1936. *Tuhui baojian* (1365). Shanghai.

Xu Bangda .1980. Cong Qinglu shanshui chuantong tan Zhao Bosu *Wansong jinque tu*. *Zhongguo wenwu* 4.

Yu Jianhua. 1981. *Zhongguo meishu jia renming zidian*. Shanghai.

Zhongguo lidai huihua. 1981. Beijing.

Zhongguo lidai huihua 3 (Song vol. 2). 1982. Beijing.

Zhou Bida. 1971. *Pingyuan xugao. Wenzhong ji*. Taipei: Commercial Press.

Zhuang Su. 1963. *Huaji puyi* (1298). Beijing.

STUDIES IN HONOR OF CHU-TSING LI

Song Mimesis and Beyond

WEN C. FONG

In Chinese painting history there occurred an irrevocable shift in painting style after the Southern Song period (1127–1279). What distinguishes Southern Song painting from the painting of later periods is the artist's fascination with mimetic representation and descriptive specificity.[1] In examining "realism" in Southern Song painting (fig. 1), it is difficult to explain how such veracity—"form-likeness" (*xingsi*), or conformity to what the eye sees—was achieved without the benefit of Western scientific techniques of perspective and illusionism, and why it was never again achieved in Chinese art.

SONG MIMESIS

Indeed, it is difficult to know what realism meant in a cultural context that is so different from that of the modern world. In my book *Beyond Representation*, I used the term "magic realism" to describe Southern Song art.[2] By "magic," or "supernatural realism," I was referring to the fourth-century painter Gu Kaizhi's (ca. 345–406) definition of painting as that which "captures the spirit [*shen*] through the form [*xing*]" (*yixing xieshen*),[3] meaning that through form-likeness an image becomes "supernaturally real" (*shensi*). A well-known legend tells how Gu Kaizhi, in order to attract the attention of a young lady he admired, painted her in such a lifelike manner that he was able to awaken her feelings for him by pricking the heart of the painted image with a needle.[4] This story illustrates how mimetic realism in early Chinese painting was considered functionally "real."

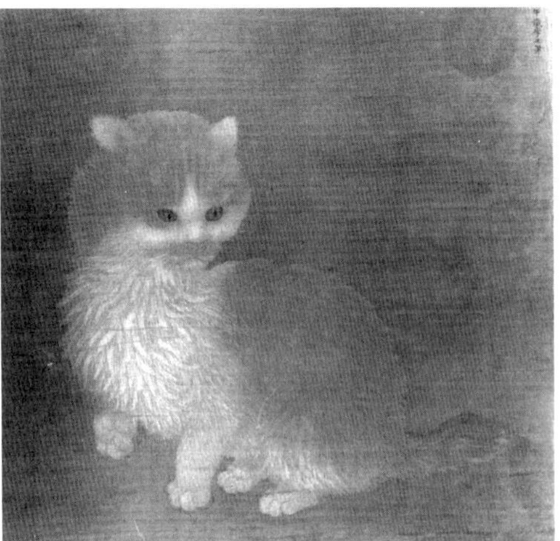

FIGURE 1
Li Di (active ca. 1163–after 1197). *Kitten*, dated 1174. Album leaf, ink and color on silk, 9¼ × 9½ in. (23.6 × 24.1 cm). National Palace Museum, Taipei

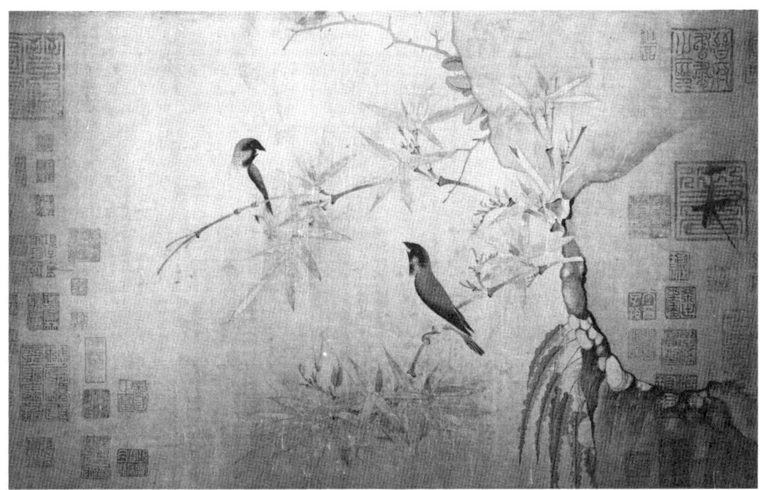

FIGURE 2
Emperor Huizong (1082–1135; r. 1101–25). *Finches and Bamboo.* Handscroll, ink and color on silk, 11 × 18 in. (27.9 × 45.7 cm). The Metropolitan Museum of Art. John M. Crawford, Jr. Collection, Purchase, Douglas Dillon Gift, 1981

Gu Kaizhi's view of achieving realism in painting reflects the prehistoric principle of sympathetic magic, by which the represented image, through the Law of Similarity, was perceived as the prototype in reality.[5] According to the Law of Similarity, image reproduces prototype. In his article "Concepts of *Lei* and *Kan-lei* in Early Chinese Art Theory," Kiyohiko Munakata established a theoretical basis for understanding ancient Chinese concepts of representation, including early landscape painting, whereby "sympathetic responsiveness" (*gan*) to the essential nature of various "kinds" (*lei*) of objects and things in nature generates through sympathetic magic an image that reproduces not only the appearance but also the energized embodiment of the prototype.[6] According to Munakata, the principle of *ganlei*, which was based on ancient magical practice as reflected by the hexagrams of the *Yijing* (The Book of Changes), worked as the "symbolic correlation system" in the fundamental Chinese cosmic order of harmonious interaction, in what Joseph Needham describes as an "ordered harmony of wills without an ordainer."[7]

From the Han through the Song dynasty (3rd century B.C.–13th century A.D.), a period that Max Loehr called China's Age of Representational Art,[8] when the function of mimetic representation or form-likeness (Gu Kaizhi's "capturing the spirit through the form") dominated the field of knowledge, supernatural realism was a reflection of a higher reality—that of the interdependent and correlative nature of the universe. Although Chinese painters developed neither an anatomical approach to figural representation nor an approach to space based on linear perspective, they

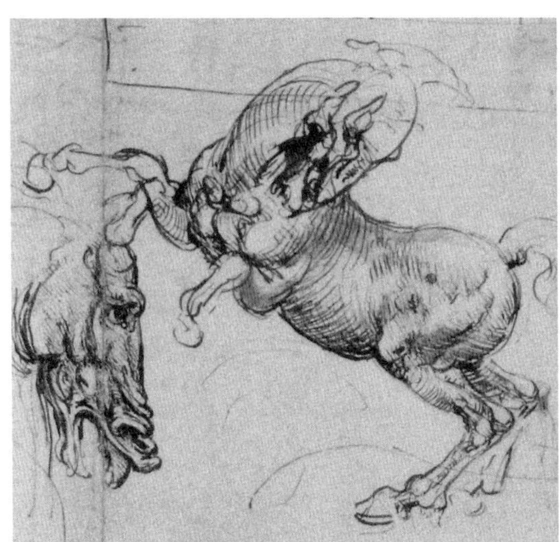

FIGURE 3
Leonardo da Vinci (1452–1519). *Horses and other Studies for the Battle of Anghiari.* Detail. Pen and brown ink and wash (with traces of black and red chalk), 7¾ × 12⅛ in. (19.6 × 30.8 cm). Royal Library, Windsor Castle, no. 12326r. From Rosand 1988, fig. 48, p. 39

nevertheless incorporated in their work representational skills that had accumulated from the Western Han through the end of the Song period. In a process E.H. Gombrich called "schema and correction," early Chinese art of representation developed by "making before matching [reality]."[9]

In his *Finches and Bamboo* (fig. 2), done in about 1120, the late Northern Song emperor Huizong (r. 1101–25), who was an occult Daoist adept, saw his painting as the "perceptive viewing" (*ruilan*) of a new, narrowly focused intensive realism.[10] In Huizong's *Xuanhe huapu* (Catalogue of the Imperial Painting Collection During the Xuanhe Era; preface dated 1120), we read:

> Where the essences of the Five Elements, pure and unadulterated, are concentrated in certain places between Heaven and Earth, a single inhalation of the *yin* and *yang* will cause [life] to spread out in its full glory.[11]

In the painting, the male finch, poised delicately on the swaying lower bamboo branch, sings to the female perched on the spray of bamboo above, as she coquettishly looks away. The lush painting surface sparkles with the intense jade-green patterns of the bamboo leaves, while the birds' eyes are accentuated by three-dimensional dots of shiny raw black lacquer, which serve to heighten the magical effect of vivaciousness.

Because Chinese painting is an art of the brush—more precisely, drawing with a brush—it has, as Norman Bryson has pointed out, "always selected forms that permit a maximum of integrity and visibility to the constitutive strokes of the brush: foliage, bamboo ... the patterns of fur, feather, reeds, branches."[12] The magic of Huizong's realism, however, depended on the artist's ability to match "seeing and making." In his study of Leonardo da Vinci's art of drawing (fig. 3), David Rosand writes: "Seeing and making are simultaneous acts for Leonardo ... The object being rendered, the form coming into being on the paper, comes to exist as a body confronting that of the draftsman, existing in a space that is implicitly a continuum with his or hers. The act of drawing, then, is an act of projection, of self-projection."[13] For the Chinese painter, who drew with the brush without pictorial involvement with aerial perspective, sfumato, and chiaroscuro, the challenge of mimetic representation lay precisely in the discovery of what Rosand calls "a [total] correspondence between the form of motion in nature and the motion of his own hand in drawing."[14] In Huizong's painting, while the drawing of the finches and bamboo shows a wonderful correspondence with their forms of motion in nature, the motion of the calligraphic brushwork nevertheless falls short of effectively matching the ridges and folds of the large mountain boulder on the right side of the painting.

THE BRUSH IDIOM AND SURFACE PATTERN

The comparison of Huizong's art with Leonardo's reveals a fundamental dichotomy between Chinese and European traditions of painting. While in the Western painting tradition drawings and preliminary oil sketches are often treated, in Norman Bryson's words, "primarily as an erasive medium," Chinese interest in the "constitutive strokes of the brush" lent paramount importance to the brush idiom as the basic "method" (*bifa*) by which the painter captured the image by "writing" it calligraphically.

In landscape painting, which became a major art form during the early Northern Song period (960–1127), mountain and rock forms were represented by brush patterns known as *cun*, or "texture methods." In Fan Kuan's (active ca. 990–1030) monumental landscape hanging scroll, *Travelers Amid Streams and Mountains* (fig. 4), dating to around 1000, for example, the pointillistic technique, described as the "raindrop" (*yutian*) texture pattern, vividly captures the rocky landscape of the artist's native Shaanxi region in northwestern China, where trees and brush grow in rich alluviun soil wind-deposited on steep mountaintops. In 1121, four

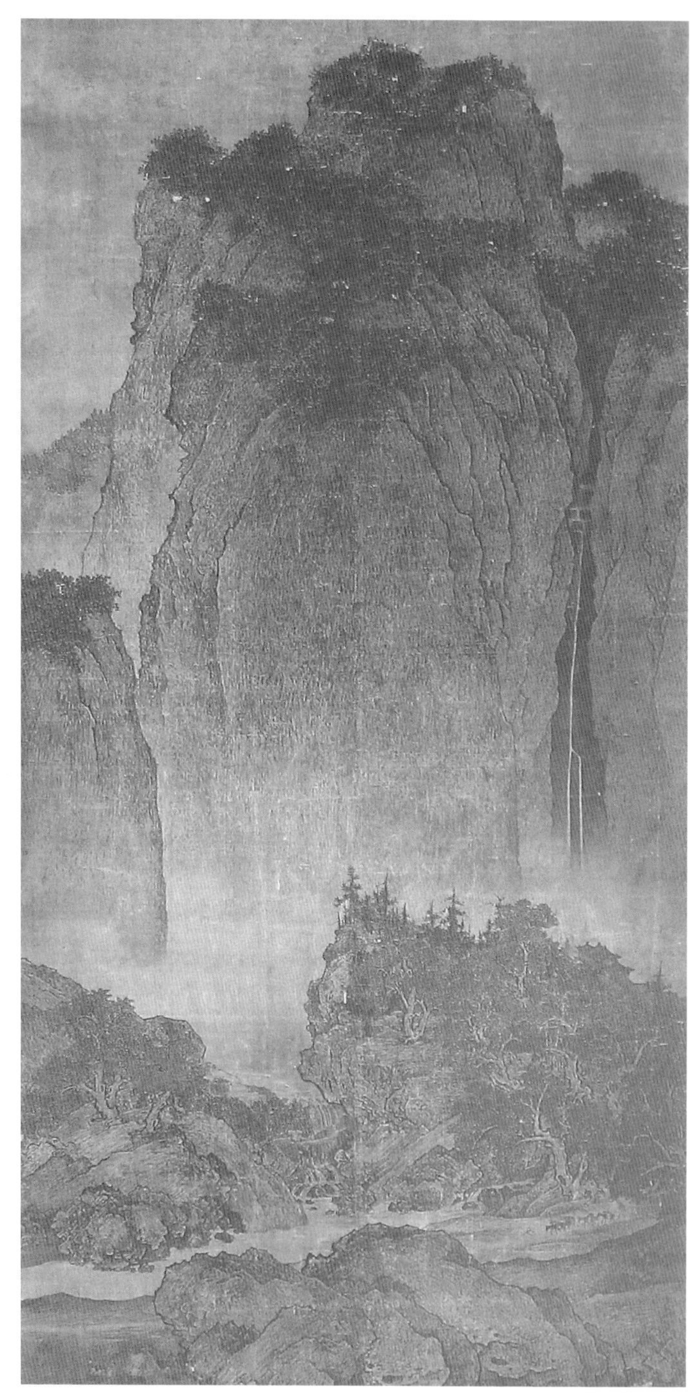

FIGURE 4
Fan Kuan (active ca. 990–1030). *Travelers Amid Streams and Mountains*, ca. 1000. Hanging scroll, ink and color on silk, 81¼ × 40¾ in. (206.3 × 103.3 cm). National Palace Museum, Taipei

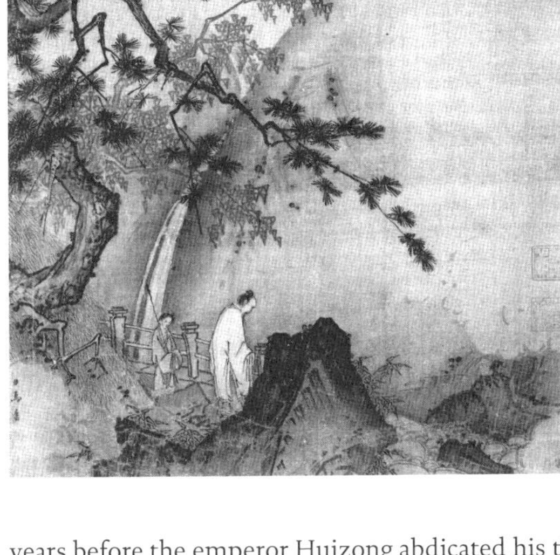

FIGURE 5
Ma Yuan (active ca. 1190–1225). *Scholar Viewing a Waterfall.* Album leaf, ink and color on silk, 9⅞ × 10¼ in. (24.9 × 26 cm). The Metropolitan Museum of Art. Gift of the Dillon Fund, 1973

years before the emperor Huizong abdicated his throne at the end of the Northern Song, Han Zhuo (active ca. 1119–26), a member of Huizong's Imperial Painting Academy, described various kinds of texture patterns for modeling rocks as follows:

> There is the *pima* [draping hemp-fiber] *cun*, the *diancuo* [dotting and crossing] *cun*..., the *zhuota* [cutting] *cun*, the *heng* [horizontal] *cun*, and the *yuner lianshui* [uniform and connected, water-like] *cun*. For every dot and every stroke there exist both ancient and modern styles and methods.[15]

Han Zhuo's catalogue of earlier representational techniques as texture patterns, or brush idioms, corresponded to the Southern Song academic interest in methods and rules, which led to the emphasis on surface patterns and abstraction—the very opposite of mimetic representation—in painting.

By the middle of the twelfth century, the shift from the monumental landscape painting of the Northern Song to the narrowly focused and intimate vision of Southern Song painting was complete.[16] In the early thirteenth century, a new generation of academy painters, under the leadership of Ma Yuan (active ca. 1190–1225; fig. 5) and Xia Gui (active ca. 1195–1230), developed through meditative introspection a lyric style that became the hallmark of Southern Song art. By using the "ax-cut" (*fupi*) stroke, which enlarged Fan Kuan's pointillistic technique to a broad,

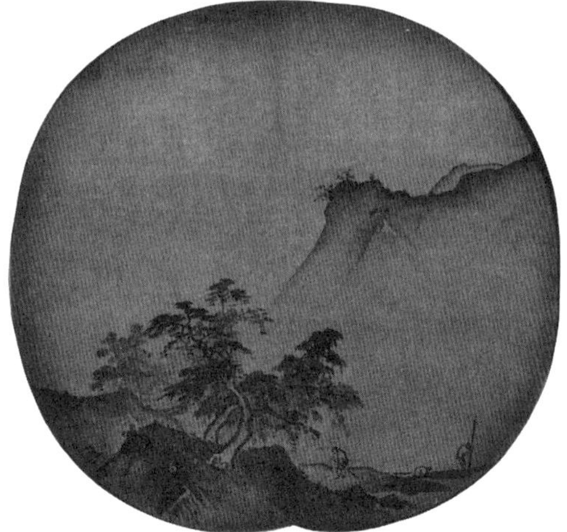

FIGURE 6
Style of Xia Gui (active ca. 1195–1230). *Windswept Lakeshore*. Fan mounted as an album leaf, ink on silk, 10¼ × 10⅝ in. (26 × 27 cm). The Metropolitan Museum of Art. Purchase, Theodore M. Davis Collection, Bequest of Theodore M. Davis, by exchange, 1973

angular stroke that effectively described the rugged chipped-off facets of the rock surface, these painters practiced the distinct Ma Yuan and Xia Gui (fig. 6) brush idioms in an increasingly stylized and facile manner. In a paper entitled "How Real is Real: The Thirteenth-Century Painter's Eye," Richard Edwards compares stylization in late Southern Song painting to that of late Italian Renaissance Mannerist art.[17] He quotes John Shearman, the well-known scholar on Mannerism, who adds in his interpretation of the Italian word *maniera* the connotation of "effortless accomplishment." Describing it as "[speaking] a silver-tongued language of… stylish style," Shearman claims for the term *maniera* a connection with an artistic environment "[where] the swing has gone beyond the mean."[18]

In thirteenth-century Southern Song art, as in Italian Mannerist art, the new stylization, having emerged after mimetic representation had reached its peak, manifested a highly emotional, expressionist content. Lu Xinzhong's *Sixteen Luohans* (fig. 7), dating to the late thirteenth century,[19] for example, shows a stylized treatment in both the figures and the modeling of the rocks that is in stark contrast to the naturalistic portrayal of Zhou Jichang's *Five Hundred Luohans* (fig. 8) dated to 1178–88, about one hundred years earlier. Lu's highly charged flat surface patterns, decorated in brilliant colors, dramatize the image of the luohan as a miracle worker, who perches high on a tree branch peering down at a pair of fierce dragons chasing a pearl. In another work from the second half of the thirteenth century, *A Bridge Over a Stream Among Steep Mountain Peaks* (fig. 9), the artist uses a schematic archaistic technique to depict frontally

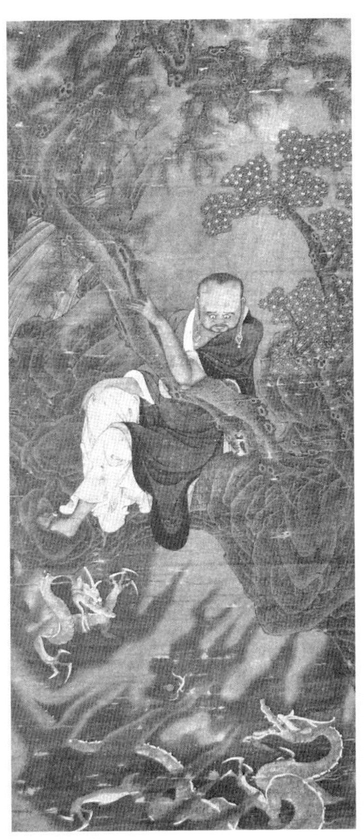

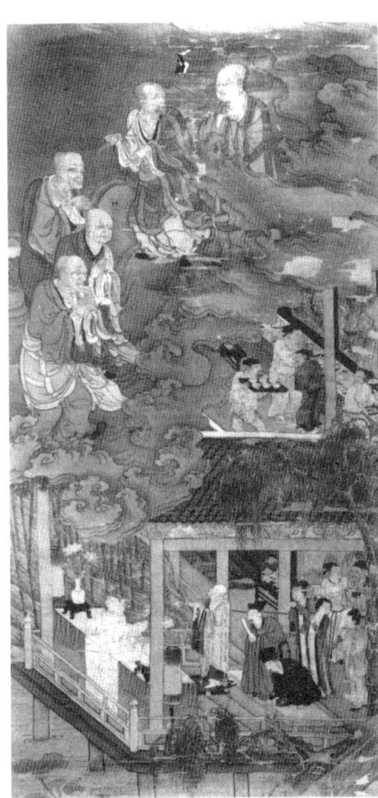

FIGURE 7
Lu Xinzhong (active 13th century). *Sixteen Luohans*, late 13th century. One of 16 hanging scrolls, ink and color on silk. Shōkokuji, Kyoto

FIGURE 8
Zhou Jichang (active late 12th century). *Feast of the Luohans*, from *Five Hundred Luohans*, ca. 1178–88. Hanging scroll, ink and color on silk, 44³⁄₈ × 21 in. (112.8 × 53.4 cm). Daitoku-ji, Kyoto

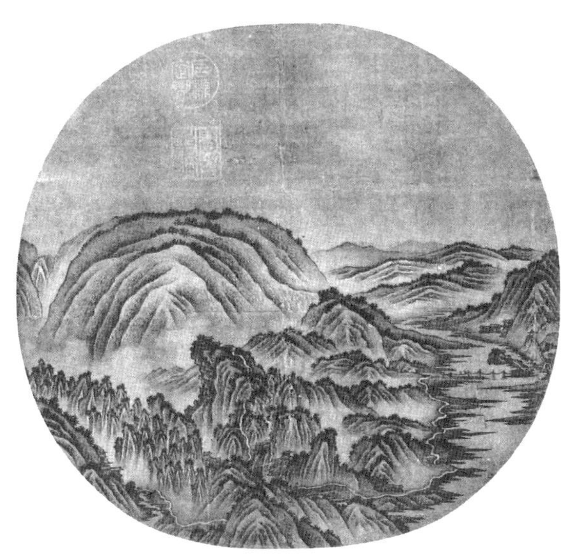

FIGURE 9
Unidentified artist. *A Bridge Over a Stream Among Steep Mountain Peaks*, second half of the 13th century. Fan mounted as an album leaf, ink and light color on silk, 9⁷⁄₈ × 10⁵⁄₈ in. (25 × 27 cm). Liaoning Provincial Museum

viewed triangular mountain motifs with parallel folds receding diagonally across the vertical picture plane; the texture pattern displays a dotting technique that refers back not only to Fan Kuan, but also to Fan's antecedents, Jing Hao (active ca. 870–ca. 930) and Guan Tong (active ca. 907–23).[20] There is a great stillness in this miniature portrait of the vast universe, where the earth abides and stasis rules. Through the schematic surface pattern, with its evenly textured folds and dots, the late Southern Song artist gives expression to the malaise of his time.

THE ART OF MA LIN

It was during the late Southern Song period that mimetic representation in Chinese painting finally reached its zenith before coming to an abrupt end following the Mongol conquest of 1279. Thereafter, literati painters, turning back to art history, used a calligraphic idiom of art historical styles to "write ideas" (*xieyi*) or to express their inner feelings.[21] The redirection from mimetic to art historical representation, which changed forever the function and meaning of later Chinese painting, is traditionally attributed to the leading early Yuan scholar-artist Zhao Mengfu (1254–1322). I would like to suggest that this shift from realistic to calligraphic representation began earlier, with Ma Lin (ca. 1180–after 1256), the last great realist of the Southern Song painting academy.

A fifth-generation member of the preeminent Ma family of Southern Song court painters, Ma Lin began his career working in the family style made famous by his father, Ma Yuan. Ma Lin's painting of two branches of blossoming plum entitled *Layers of Icy Silk* (fig. 10), which is accompanied by a poem written by the empress Yang Meizi (1162–1232), dated 1216, compares closely with Ma Yuan's *Apricot Blossoms* (fig. 11), dating to about 1210, also inscribed by the empress. In both paintings, the frail, delicate flowers are minutely observed and realistically depicted. The poem on the "palace plum," symbol of a court beauty, inscribed by Empress Yang on Ma Lin's painting is replete with allusions to the impermanence of erotic love and life itself:

> Like a cold butterfly passing the night in the corolla,
> Embracing the rouge center while recalling a past encounter.
> How lovely are the buds at the tip of the chilled branch:
> Such is the beauty that adorned the Han palace.

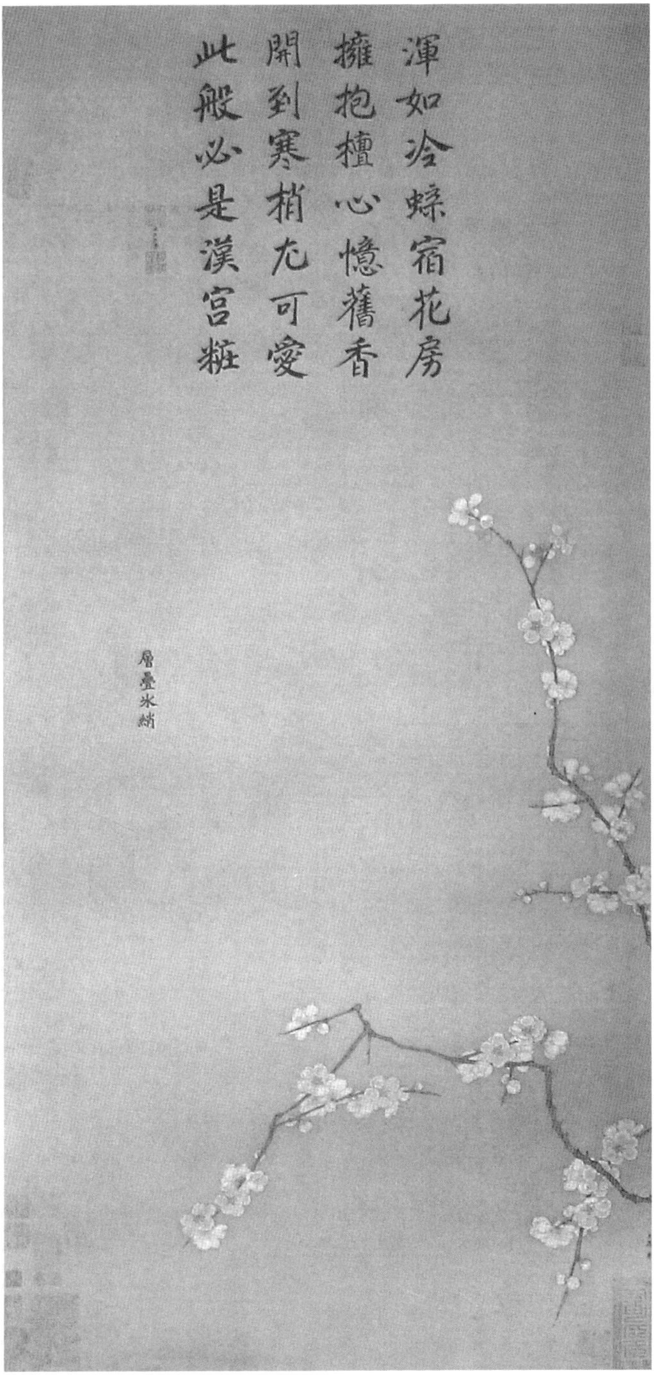

FIGURE 10
Ma Lin (ca. 1180–after 1256). *Layers of Icy Silk*, dated 1216. Hanging scroll, ink, color, and gold on silk, 40 × 19½ in. (101.7 × 49.6 cm). Palace Museum, Beijing

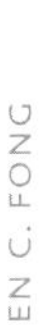

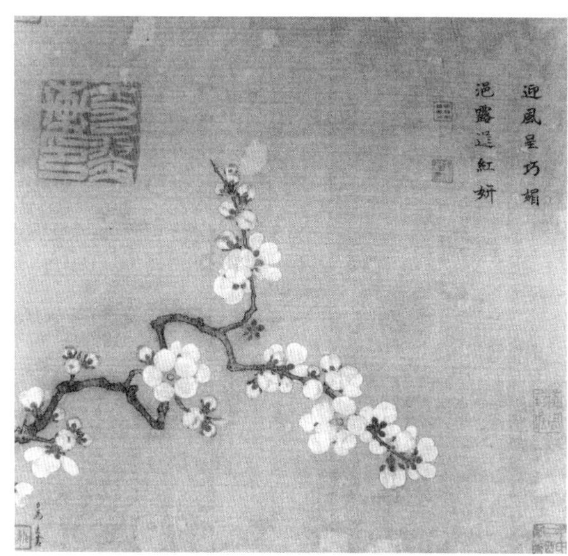

FIGURE 11
Ma Yuan (active ca. 1190–1225). *Apricot Blossoms*, ca. 1210. Album leaf, ink and color on silk, 9⅞ × 10 in. (25.1 × 25.4 cm). National Palace Museum, Taipei

In his study of Southern Song lyric poetry, Shuen-fu Lin describes what he sees as "an increasing narrowness of vision, a sensual plenitude of images," culminating in "the retreat toward the object." According to Lin, this development paralleled the Southern Song Neo-Confucian philosopher Zhu Xi's (1130–1220) epistemological process "in which the mind reaches outward toward the object."[22] Lin's phrase "the retreat toward the object" aptly describes Song mimetic realism, in which the artist, in Lin's words, "maintain[s] an attitude of detachment with regard to the object."[23] While his subtle rendering of the delicate plum blossoms vividly captures the empress's rich poetic imagery, Ma Lin, as a silent partner in a collaborative effort, painted a work that complements the words that were written by his imperial patroness rather than one that expresses his own feelings.

Two early landscape paintings by Ma Lin, *Fragrant Spring, Clearing after Rain*, dated to around 1224,[24] and *Night Vigil by Candlelight* (fig. 12), dating to the late 1220s, show how the artist, under imperial patronage, continued to use his father's brush idioms (see fig. 5) to depict the landscape of the Southern Song capital Lin'an (modern Hangzhou) and its imperial precincts. Ma Lin's paintings show the same—though somewhat hard and simpler—knotty, angular tree branches and the same ax-cut strokes in the modeling of rocks found in Ma Yuan's work. Both paintings illustrate poetic inscriptions written by Ma Lin's imperial

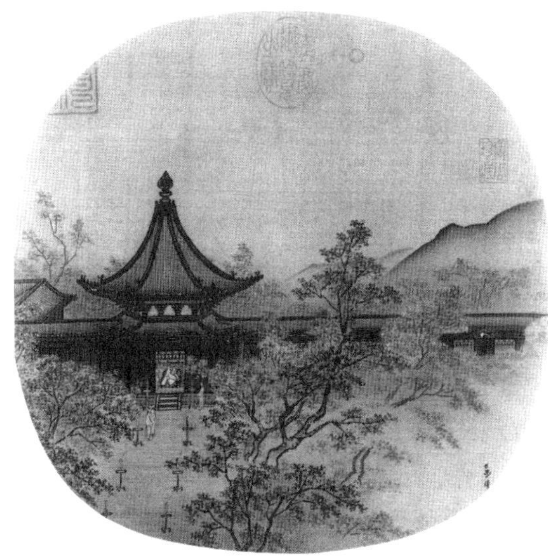

FIGURE 12
Ma Lin (ca. 1180–after 1256). *Night Vigil by Candelight.* Fan mounted as an album leaf, ink and color on silk, 9¾ × 10 in. (24.8 × 25.4 cm). National Palace Museum, Taipei

patrons. According to Li Lincan, the fan painting *Night Vigil by Candlelight* was once accompanied by Emperor Lizong's (r. 1224–64) transcription of a couplet from a poem by Su Shi (1037–1101) lamenting the ephemeral nature of crab-apple blossoms:

> Only fearful that when the night is deep, the flowers will fall asleep,
> Tall candles are lit brightly to shine on the red blossoms.[25]

The change in Ma Lin's work from the aesthetic of mimetic representation to that of calligraphic presentation, or performance, appears to date to around 1230, when Ma was commissioned by Emperor Lizong to execute *Confucian Sages and Worthies* (fig. 13), a set of thirteen idealized images of ancient sovereigns and worthies (five of which are extant). During the Southern Song, a group of ultraconservative Neo-Confucian philosophers under the leadership of Zhu Xi, known as the Dao Learning school (Daoxue), created an Orthodox Lineage of the Dao (*Daotong*) that positioned them as direct heirs of the legendary sage-kings Fuxi, Yao, and Shun, the Zhou kings Wen and Wu, and the sage Confucius and his disciples.[26] Although it was at first banned as heterodoxy, in 1241 Emperor Lizong, in an attempt to bolster his own legitimacy and demonstrate that the Song rulers, not the invading Mongols, were the rightful heirs of the Confucian tradition, proclaimed the Dao Learning— now designated the school of Moral Principles (*Lixue*)—as the official state orthodoxy.[27]

The *Confucian Sages and Worthies* marked the first time that a ruling dynasty used the Confucian orthodox lineage of Dao to lend support to its political legitimacy. For this historical project of portraying thirteen near-lifesize images of ancient sages, to be displayed at the National Academy (*Guozi jian*), Ma Lin chose a style markedly different from that of traditional imperial portraiture. This traditional style is represented by a portrait of the emperor Lizong (fig. 14), in which the face is meant to be magically "real" and the courtly robe and furnishings are drawn with craftsmanlike precision.[28] Ma Lin's idealized images of ancient sages, in contrast, show generalized facial features and a bold, calligraphic idiom better suited for public didactic purposes.

Compared to his *Layers of Icy Silk* (see fig. 10) of 1216, Ma Lin's *Orchids* (fig. 15), a work done perhaps twenty years later, in the late 1230s, manifests a new conceptual discipline. The delicate flowers, outlined in ink, are colored in a soft malachite green and salmon pink and touched with white highlights, while the leaves, colored in a deep malachite blue-green, are etched out calligraphically against the blank space. Rather than being sub-

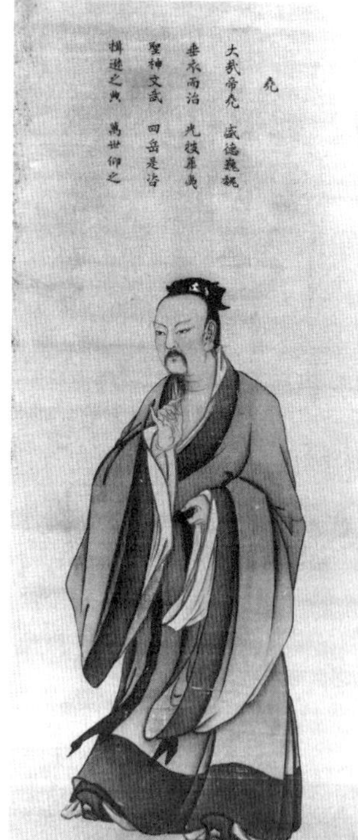

FIGURE 13
Ma Lin (ca. 1180–after 1256). *Portrait of King Yao*, from *Confucian Sages and Worthies*. Group of 5 hanging scrolls from an original set of 13, ink and color on silk, 97½ × 43¾ in. (248 × 111.1 cm.). National Palace Museum, Taipei

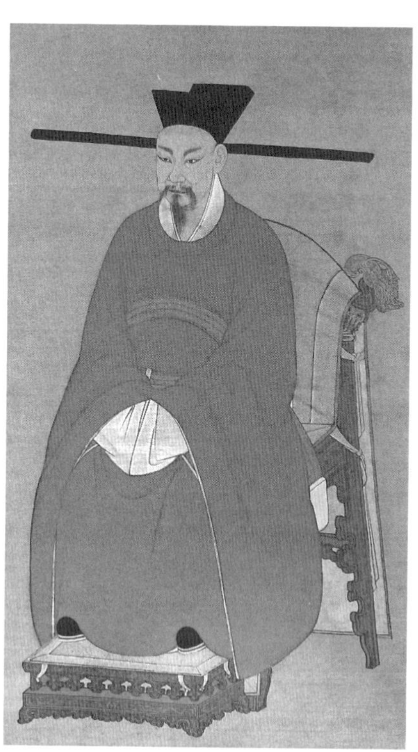

FIGURE 14
Portrait of Emperor Lizong (r. 1224–64). Hanging scroll, ink and color on silk, 74½ × 42¾ in. (189 × 108.5 cm). National Palace Museum, Taipei

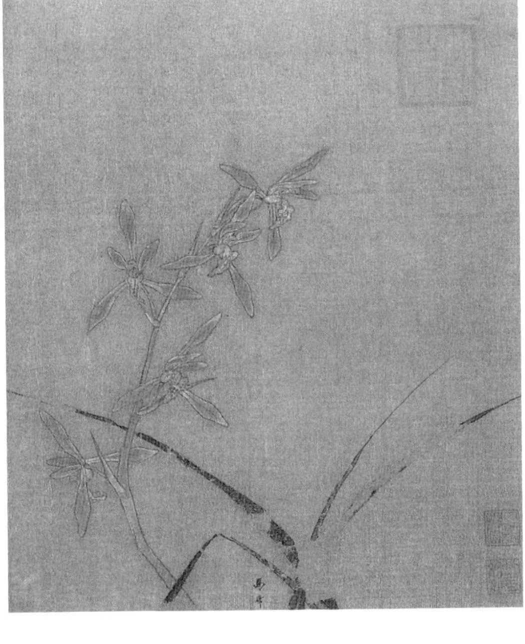

FIGURE 15
Ma Lin (ca. 1180–after 1256). *Orchids*. Album leaf, ink and color on silk, 10⅜ × 8⅞ in. (26.2 × 22.4 cm). The Metropolitan Museum of Art. Gift of the Dillon Fund, 1973

ordinated to representation, the brushwork is independently assertive and gestural. Norman Bryson has characterized calligraphic painting as "the work of the brush in 'real time' and as extension of the painter's own body."[29] Ma Lin's carefully planned composition is informed by a subtle balancing of the painter's body movements and counter-movements.

Perhaps the most astonishing work by Ma Lin is the large hanging scroll *Listening to the Wind in the Pines* (fig. 16), the title of which, dated 1246, is inscribed by Emperor Lizong. The two figures portrayed in the painting—a scholar accompanied by a boy servant—are surrounded by abstract brushstrokes that calligraphically transform the gnarled tree trunks, windblown pine needles, and draping vines into a cacophony of squiggly lines and dots. In turning to calligraphic abstraction, Ma Lin, the court painter, has reified calligraphy as the preeminent art form of expressive intent. In the painting the seated figure casts a sideway glance over the shoulder of his attendant, as if to draw the viewer's attention to the signature in the lower left corner, which reads: "Painted by the Servitor Ma Lin." But it is through his calligraphic performance rather than his signature that Ma Lin, now no longer a mere silent partner of the imperial patron who writes the title of the painting, has directly inscribed his own physical presence onto his painting.

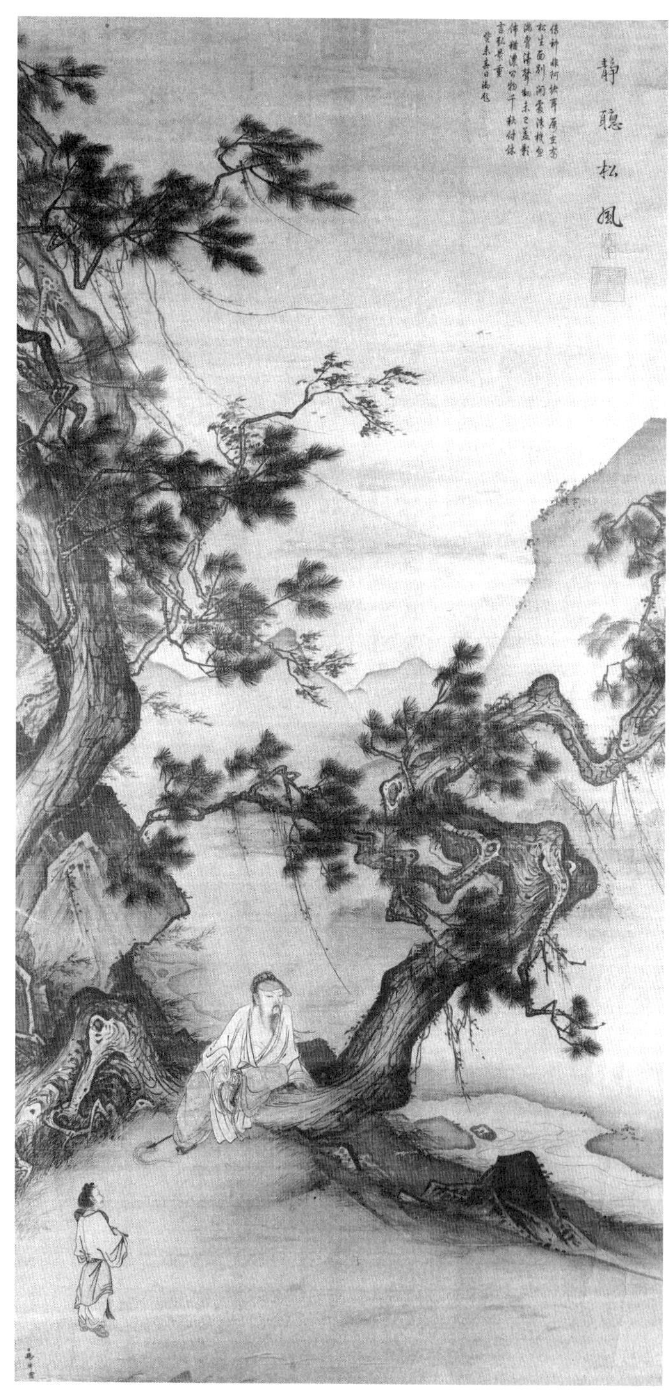

FIGURE 16
Ma Lin (ca. 1180–after 1256). *Listening to the Wind in the Pines*, datable to 1246. Hanging scroll, ink and color on silk, 89 1/8 × 43 1/2 in. (226.6 × 110.3 cm). National Palace Museum, Taipei

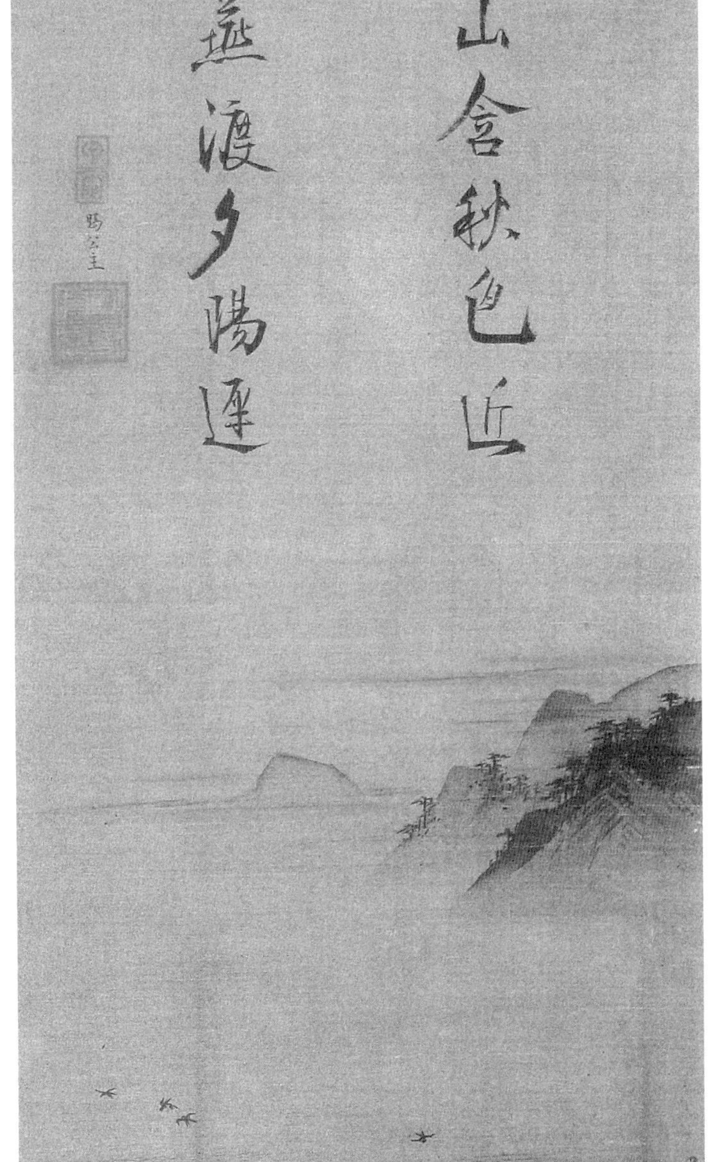

FIGURE 17
Ma Lin (ca. 1180–after 1256). *Evening Sun*, dated 1254. Hanging scroll, ink and color on silk, 20¼ × 10⅝ in. (51.5 × 27 cm). Nezu Institute of Fine Arts, Tokyo

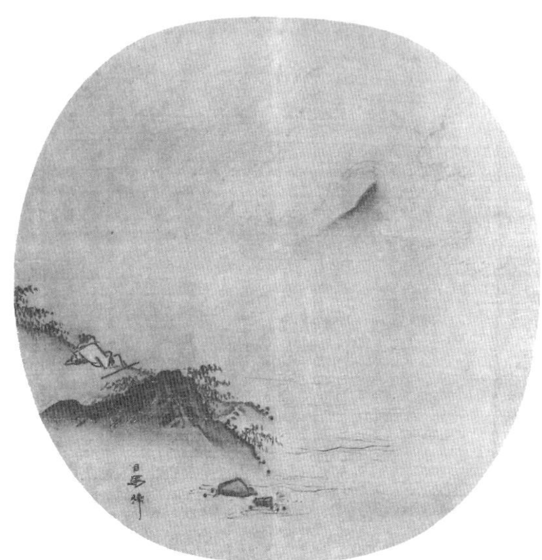

FIGURE 18A
Ma Lin (ca. 1180–after 1256). *Scholar Reclining and Watching Rising Clouds.* Album leaf, ink and color on silk, 9⅞ in. (25.1 cm). The Cleveland Museum of Art. John L. Severance Fund 61.421

In *Evening Sun* (fig. 17), Ma Lin meditates on the idea of the Southern Song capital Lin'an, or "Temporary Peace." A five-word couplet by the emperor Lizong, dated 1254 (originally written on a separate leaf), accompanies the painting:

> The mountains hold the autumn colors nearby,
> Where the swallows traverse the late evening sun.

The evening is calm; there is no wind on the lake. Three overlapping mountain peaks, with simple ax-cut strokes visible only on the nearest peak, recede and disappear beyond the horizon. The four tiny swallows scattered in the light of the setting sun—faint streaks of pink brush in the gray ink wash—complete an indelible image of the Southern Song empire in twilight.

Finally, in *Scholar Reclining and Watching Rising Clouds* (fig. 18a), Ma Lin's portrayal of a scholar reclining on the riverbank mediating on rising clouds is accompanied by Lizong's transcription (fig. 18b), dated 1256, of a famous couplet by the Tang poet Wang Wei (700–761):

> I walk to where the water ends,
> I sit and view the clouds as they rise.[30]

Instead of organizing his feelings around an object, as he did earlier in *Layers of Icy Silk* (see fig. 10), Ma Lin now evokes the poetic vision with an

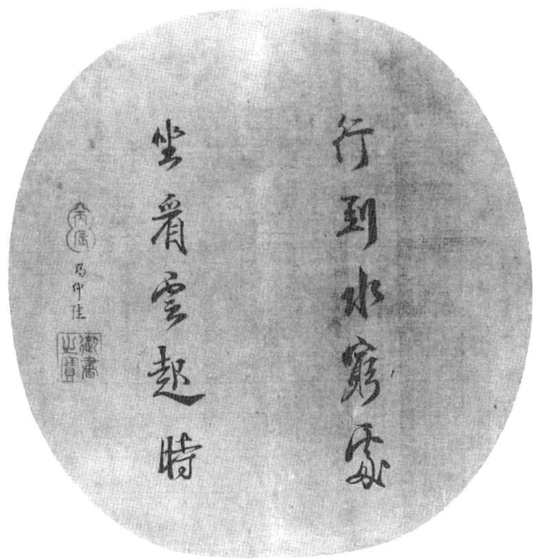

FIGURE 18B
Emperor Lizong (1205–1264; r. 1224–64). *Poem by Wang Wei*, dated 1256. Album leaf, ink on silk, 9⅞ in. (25.1 cm). The Cleveland Museum of Art. John L. Severance Fund 61.422

abstract language of angular rock forms and ax-cut strokes, drawing us kinesthetically into the pictorial space.

BEYOND REPRESENTATION

It was after the fall of the Southern Song to the Mongol Yuan dynasty in 1279, which marked the end of mimetic representation, that the scholar-artist Zhao Mengfu turned to the "writing of ideas and feelings" (*xieyi*) to express other kinds of realities. This shift from mimetic representation to calligraphic self-expression in fourteenth-century Yuan China bears a striking resemblance to the displacement of the representative by the expressive in Western modernism.

According to the meta-historian and philosopher Michel Foucault, a fundamental epistemological change from the representation of resemblance to that of the language of "signification" occurred in European culture on the eve of the modern age. From the nineteenth century onward, Foucault writes, "the theory of representation disappears as the universal foundation [of knowledge] ... a profound historicity penetrates into the heart of things ... To enable this history to emerge clearly ... the new grammar is immediately diachronic. How could it have been otherwise, since its positivity could be established only by a break between language and representation?"[31] Applying Foucault's insights to Zhao Mengfu's art, we find Zhao making a systematic study of art historical styles, translating them into the abstract language of calligraphy and creating a new language of "signification" for "writing ideas" in landscape painting.

In his book *A Cultural History of Civil Examinations in Late Imperial China*, Benjamin Elman relates the Southern Song concept of the Confucian Orthodox Lineage of the Dao and the Dao Learning to the struggle between Han Chinese and non-Han conquerors for political control and cultural legitimacy as the rightful rulers of China. In 1313 the Mongol Yuan court adopted the Dao Learning as the official examination curriculum, even though, as Elman points out, "the creation of a single-minded and monocular [Dao Learning] orthodoxy, which built on Song and Yuan precedents, was principally a Ming dynasty construction."[32] From this perspective, Zhao Mengfu's systematic study of art historical styles, in which he updated the classical canon both in calligraphy and in figure and landscape painting, not only paralleled the Confucian Orthodox Lineage of the Dao, but also served the all-important purpose of establishing Han Chinese cultural autonomy under alien Mongol rule.

A polymath trained as a calligrapher, poet, and connoisseur-collector as well as a painter, Zhao Mengfu revolutionized calligraphy and painting by reexamining ancient models. From 1286 to 1294, Zhao served at the court of Kubilai Khan (Yuan Shizu; r. 1260–94) in Beijing, where he dedicated himself to rediscovering lost ancient models from North China. In order to break away from the Southern Song calligraphic style, he studied Jin and Tang (4th–8th century) calligraphy as well as ancient (2nd–6th century) stone stele inscriptions from North China.[33] He also made a systematic study of Northern Song landscape painting styles which had been neglected during the Southern Song, defining them calligraphically in terms of brush patterns and techniques. Beginning with an archaic linear idiom inspired by the iron-wire technique of seal-style

FIGURE 19
Zhao Mengfu (1254–1322). *Twin Pines, Level Distance*, ca. 1310. Handscroll, ink on paper, 10½ × 42¼ in. (26.9 × 107.4 cm). The Metropolitan Museum of Art. Gift of the Dillon Fund, 1973

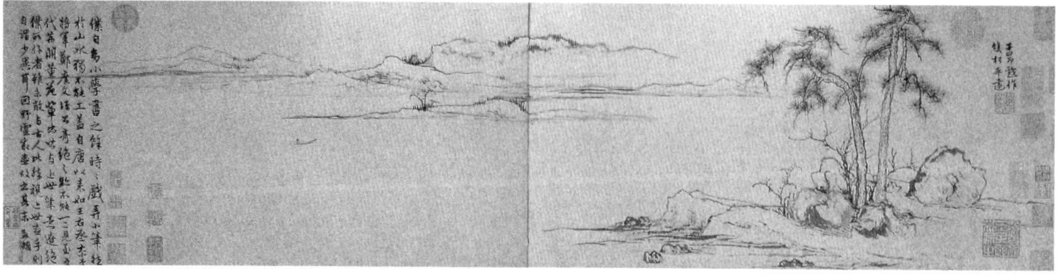

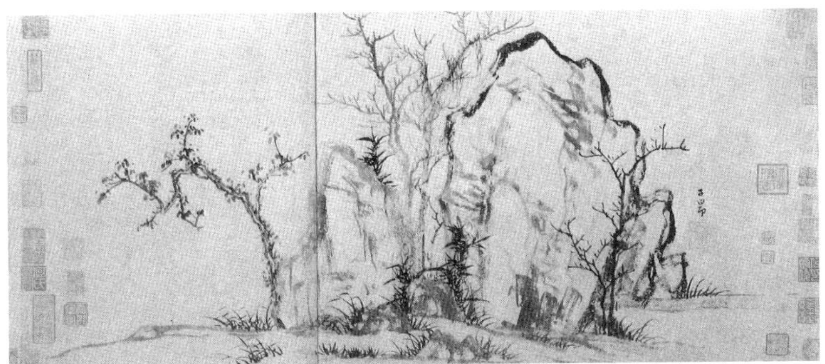

FIGURE 20
Zhao Mengfu (1254–1322). *Elegant Rocks and Sparse Trees*, ca. 1310. Handscroll, ink on paper, 10¾ × 24¾ in. (27.3 × 62.9 cm). Palace Museum, Beijing

calligraphy, he went on to experiment with the hemp-fiber brush idiom of Dong Yuan (active 930s–60s) as well as the devil-face and crab-claw brush patterns of Guo Xi (ca. 1000–ca. 1090).[34] In a famous colophon Zhao wrote:

> In painting one must capture the spirit of antiquity [*guyi*]; without it all technical skill is in vain. Modern painters know only how to draw with a fine line and to use brilliant colors ... My own paintings may appear simple and casually rendered, but connoisseurs will know that they are based on ancient models and so will judge them to be of high merit.[35]

By "capturing the spirit of antiquity," Zhao meant "writing" the different ancient brush patterns or methods calligraphically. In *Twin Pines, Level Distance* (fig. 19), dated to around 1310, he draws two pine trees in the style of the Northern Song master Guo Xi, turning Guo's representational brushwork into a calligraphic formula.[36] In his colophon at the end of the scroll, Zhao writes:

> As for the Five Dynasties [907–960] masters Jing [Hao], Guan [Tong], Dong [Yuan], and Fan [Kuan], all of whom succeeded one another, their brush ideas [*biyi*] are totally different from those of the more recent painters. What I paint may not equal the work of the ancient masters, but compared with more recent paintings I daresay mine are quite different.

According to Sun Guoting (648?–703?), a calligrapher "must study both large and small seal styles, the split style, draft cursive, and flying-white," and learn to juxtapose and harmonize different script styles.[37] In a colophon to *Elegant Rocks and Sparse Trees* (fig. 20), a work dating to around 1310, Zhao explains how he structures his brushwork in painting by combining different calligraphic scripts:

> Rocks as in flying-white [running-clerical script], trees
> as in seal script;
> When painting bamboo, I use the spreading-eight [late
> clerical] method.
> Only when one masters this secret,
> Will he understand that calligraphy and painting have
> always been the same.[38]

Freed from mimetic representation and placed against a plain white ground, Zhao's individual brushstrokes have, as isolated gestures, an independent energy of their own. Compared to Huizong's *Finches and Bamboo* (see fig. 2), Zhao's calligraphic image shows a new way of matching "seeing and making." By integrating different brush techniques of round and square, centered and oblique, internal and external movements to create a porous and illusionistic pictorial surface, he achieves in his calligraphic brushwork a new correspondence with forms of motion in nature. Because calligraphy is never divorced from the physical body of the artist who produced it, Zhao Mengfu thus accomplished a fundamental redirection in painting, turning pictorial representation into calligraphic self-representation.

NOTES

1. See Lee 2001.
2. See Fong 1992, 30, 182–87, 363–69.
3. Zhang Yanyuan 1963, *juan* 5, p. 67.
4. Ibid., 68.
5. It was Sir James G. Frazer (Frazer 1911, 52) who first articulated the principle of sympathetic magic: "First, like produces like ... Second, things which have once been in contact with each other continue to act on each other at a distance after the physical contact has been severed. The former principle may be called the Law of Similarity, the latter the Law of Contact or Contagion. From the first of these principles, namely the Law of Similarity, the magician infers that he can produce any effect he desires merely by imitating it." See also Freedberg 1989, 272–74.
6. Munakata Kiyohiko 1983, 105–31.
7. For Joseph Needham's discussion of the Han philosopher Dong Zhongshu's (ca. 179–ca. 104 B.C.) "symbolic correlative system," see Needham 1956, 281–83. Needham describes a symbolic correlative system of magical efficacy structuring the cosmos that "ordered harmony of wills without an ordainer"; see ibid., p. 28.
8. See Loehr 1964, 186; 1972, 286.
9. See Gombrich 1960, 116ff.
10. See Deng Chun 1963, *juan* 1, p. 1.
11. *Xuanhe huapu*, in Yu Anlan 1963, vol. 2, *juan* 15, p. 163.
12. Bryson 1983, 89.
13. Rosand 1988, 39.
14. Ibid., 30.
15. Maeda 1970, 25.
16. See Fong 1984, 55–60.
17. Edwards 2001, 9.
18. Shearman 1967, 17ff.
19. The inscription "Qingyuanfu" dates the paintings to before 1279, when the name of the city was changed to Qingyuanlu.
20. For a study and re-dating of Anonymous painting in the style of Yen Wenkuei (Yan Wengui) *A Buddhist Monastery in Autumn Mountains*, The Metropolitan Museum of Art, see Fong, 1984, 66.
21. See Fong 1992, 431ff.
22. Lin 1978, 8, 47.
23. Lin 1982, 313–14.
24. The poetic title of this painting, "Fangchun Yuji" (Fragrant Spring, Clearing after Rain), has been attributed to Emperor Ningzong (r. 1194–1224); see Wang Yaoting 1996, 271; 286, fig. 14.1.
25. Li Lincan 1973, vol. 1, pp. 187–91.
26. See Fong 1996, 257–59.
27. See Liu 1973.
28. For ancestor portraits, see Stuart and Rawski 2001.
29. Bryson 1983, 89.
30. Harrist 1991, 301–23.
31. Foucault 1973, xxiii, 293.
32. Elman 2000, xxv.
33. See Fong 1984, 97–102.
34. See Fong 1992, 438–39.
35. Ibid., 436.
36. See ibid., 439–40.
37. Fong 1999, 36.
38. Fong 1992, 439.

REFERENCES

Bryson, Norman. 1983. *Vision and Painting: The Logic of the Gaze*. New Haven: Yale University Press.

Deng, Chun. 1963. Biography of the Emperor Huizong, in *Huaji*. In *Huashi congshu*, ed. Yu Anlan. Shanghai: Shanghai renmin chubanshe.

Edwards, Richard. 2001. How Real is Real: The Thirteenth-Century Painter's Eye. Paper presented at a symposium on Southern Song art and culture, The China Institute, New York.

Elman, Benjamin A. 2000. *A Cultural History of Civil Examinations in Late Imperial China*. Berkeley: University of California Press.

Fong, Wen C. et al. 1984. *Images of the Mind: Selections from the Edward L. Elliott Family and John B. Elliott Collections of Chinese Calligraphy and Painting at The Art Museum, Princeton University*. Princeton: The Art Museum, Princeton University.

———. 1992. *Beyond Representation: Chinese Painting and Calligraphy 8th–14th Century*. New York: The Metropolitan Museum of Art.

———. 1996. The Orthodox Lineage of Tao. In *Possessing the Past: Treasures from the National Palace Museum, Taipei*, by Wen C. Fong and James C.Y. Watt, et al. New York: The Metropolitan Museum of Art.

———. 1999. Chinese Calligraphy: Theory and History. In *The Embodied Image: Chinese Calligraphy from the John B. Elliott Collection*, ed. Robert E. Harrist, Jr. and Wen C. Fong. Princeton: The Art Museum, Princeton University.

Foucault, Michel. 1973. *The Order of Things: An Archaeology of the Human Sciences*. New York: Vintage Books.

Frazer, James G. 1911. *The Golden Bough*. Part 1 of *The Magic Art and the Evolution of Kings*. London: Macmillan.

Freedberg, David. 1989. *The Power of Images: Studies in the History and Theory of Response*. Chicago: University of Chicago Press.

Gombrich, E.H. 1960. *Art and Illusion: A Study in the Psychology of Pictorial Representation*. New York: Pantheon Books.

Harrist, Robert E. Jr. 1991. Watching Clouds Rise: A Tang Dynasty Couplet and Its Illustration in Song Painting. *The Bulletin of The Cleveland Museum of Art* 78, no. 7 (November), 301–23.

Lee, Hui-shu. 2001. *Exquisite Moments: West Lake and Southern Song Art*. New York: China Institute of America.

Li Lincan. 1973. Ma Lin *Bingzhu yeyou tu* (Ma Lin's *Night Vigil by Candlelight*). In *Zhongguo minghua yanjiu* (*Studies of famous Chinese paintings*). Taipei: Yiwen yinshuguan.

Lin, Shuen-fu. 1978. *The Transformation of the Chinese Lyrical Tradition: Chiang K'uei and Southern Sung Tz'u Poetry*. Princeton: Princeton University Press.

———. 1982. The Importance of Context. *Chinese Literature: Essays, Articles, Reviews* 4, no. 2 (July), 303–14.

Liu, James T.C. 1973. How Did a Neo-Confucian School Became the State Orthodoxy? *Philosophy East and West* 23, no. 4 (October), 483–505.

Loehr, Max. 1964. Some Fundamental Issues in the History of Chinese Painting. *The Journal of Asian Studies* 23, no. 2 (February), 186–92.

———. 1972. Phases and Content in Chinese Painting. In *Proceedings of the International Symposium on Chinese Painting, National Palace Museum, Taipei, June 18–24, 1970*. Taipei: National Palace Museum, Taipei.

Maeda, Robert J. 1970. Two Twelfth-Century Texts on Chinese Painting: Translations of the *Shan-shui ch'un-ch'üan chi* by Han Cho and Chapters nine and ten of *Hua-chi* by Teng Ch'un. Michigan Papers in Chinese Studies, no. 8. Ann Arbor: University of Michigan, Center for Chinese Studies.

Munakata, Kiyohiko. 1983.Concepts of *Lei* and *Kan-lei* in Early Chinese Art Theory. In *Theories of the Arts in China*, ed. Susan Bush and Christian Murck. Princeton: Princeton University Press.

Needham, Joseph, with Wang Ling. 1956. *History of Scientific Thought.* Vol. 2 of *Science and Civilization in China.* Cambridge: Cambridge University Press.

Rosand, David. 1988. *The Meaning of the Mark: Leonardo and Titian.* The Franklin D. Murphy Lectures, 8. Lawrence: Spencer Museum of Art, University of Kansas.

Shearman, John K.G. 1967. *Mannerism.* Harmondsworth, England and New York: Penguin.

Stuart, Jan and Evelyn S. Rawski. 2001. *Worshipping the Ancestors: Chinese Commemorative Portraits.* Washington, D.C.: Freer Gallery of Art and Arthur M. Sackler Gallery, Smithsonian Institution.

Wang Yaoting. 1996. From *Spring Fragrance, Clearing after Rain* to *Listening to the Wind in the Pines*: Some Proposals for the Courtly Context of Paintings by Ma Lin in the Collection of the National Palace Museum, Taipei. In *Arts of the Sung and Yüan*, ed. Maxwell K. Hearn and Judith G. Smith. New York: The Metropolitan Museum of Art.

Yu Anlan, ed. 1963. *Huashi congshu.* Shanghai: Shanghai renmin chubanshe.

Zhang Yanyuan. 1963. Biography of Gu Kaizhi, in *Lidai minghua ji.* In *Huashi congshu*, ed. Yu Anlan. Shanghai: Shanghai renmin chubanshe.

STUDIES IN HONOR OF CHU-TSING LI

The Emergence and Ideology of the *Three Laughers* and Its Derivative, the *Two Laughers*

AN-YI PAN

Between the middle and late Tang dynasty (618–907), an intriguing story emerged about Huiyuan (334–416), the eminent Buddhist monk of the Eastern Jin dynasty, and his supposed friendship with the Daoist Lu Xiujing (406–477) and the Confucian scholar-recluse Tao Yuanming (Tao Qian; 365–427). By the Five Dynasties (907–960) this story was already well known in literati circles and had been adopted as a subject by such artists as the famous monk-painter Shi Ke (10th century).[1] Into the Northern Song (960–1127) period, the title *Three Laughers* (*Sanxiao tu*) was applied to this specific painting subject.[2]

Huiyuan was said to have determined to remain within the precincts of Donglin Monastery on Mount Lu, in present-day Jiangxi Province, where he led an austere life. When Lu Xiujing and Tao Yuanming came to visit, the three engaged in philosophical discussion; at their parting, Huiyuan would occasionally forget his own resolution and see his two friends off at Tiger Stream Bridge, so named because whenever Huiyuan crossed it, a tiger would roar to remind him that the bridge marked the boundary of the monastery. When the group realized that Huiyuan had once again gone too far, all three would burst into laughter.[3] Pictorial representations of this story usually focused on the climax—the Three Laughers. For example, in an anonymous Southern Song (1127–1279) handscroll in the National Palace Museum, Taipei, the three figures are shown laughing uproariously by Tiger Stream Bridge (fig. 1); to their left wait two attendants holding a donkey by a rope, indicating the prolonged farewell.

The Three Laughers story was derived from a devotional religious organization, later named Lotus Society (*Lianshe*) or White Lotus Society (*Bailianshe*), founded by Huiyuan and consisting of one hundred twenty-three members who together vowed in front of an image of Amitabha Buddha to be reborn in his Western Paradise.[4] By the late Tang, however, this original group was condensed into the so-called Eighteen Noble Worthies of the Lotus Society and "three non-members"—Tao Yuanming, Lu Xiujing, and the Confucian scholar Xie Lingyun (385–433).[5] In this new configuration, the Three Laughers theme was altered: it retained Huiyuan seeing off Lu Xiujing, but Tao Yuanming became an independent wanderer who refused an invitation from Huiyuan to join the Lotus Society, and thus it became the Two Laughers. In pictorial representations, Huiyuan and Lu are part of a larger composition, the *Lotus Society*, originally painted by the great Northern Song literatus painter Li Gonglin (ca. 1041–1106). They are depicted engaged in conversation by Tiger Stream Bridge,

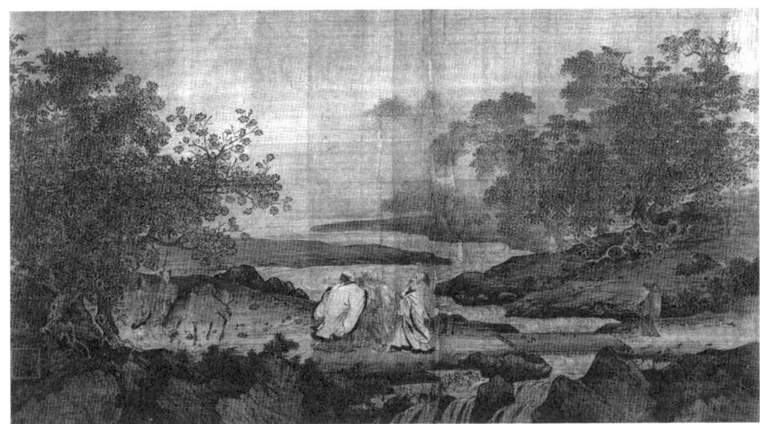

FIGURE 1
Unidentified artist. *Lotus Society*, Southern Song dynasty (1127–1279). Handscroll, ink and color on silk, 10⅜ × 18¾ in. (26.4 × 47.6 cm). National Palace Museum, Taipei

as seen in a handscroll copied by the painter's nephew Zhang Ji (active second half of the 11th century–first half of the 12th century), in the Liaoning Provincial Museum (fig. 2).[6] They are reserved in demeanor compared to the figures in the Taipei *Three Laughers*. In an anonymous Southern Song handscroll version of the *Lotus Society* in the Shanghai Museum (fig. 3), Tao Yuanming, however, is shown drunk, slumped in a square, flat-bottomed basket suspended on a pole carried by two young male attendants.

These three figures had all been active on Mount Lu during the Eastern Jin (317–420) and Six Dynasties (220–589) periods. Huiyuan, however, was thirty years older than Tao Yuanming, and in Tao's writings he is never mentioned. Furthermore, there is no reliable evidence indicating that the two men ever met.[7] Lu Xiujing was only ten years old and living in Wuxing (in present-day Jiangsu Province) at the time of Huiyian's death, in 416, so the chance of an encounter between the two would have been extremely slim; even if they had met, their encounter could not have resembled its depictions in Song dynasty *Three Laughers* or *Two Laughers* paintings.[8] Clearly both versions of this story are without historical validity. This raises two questions: under what circumstances were these stories created, and how did the genres of Three Laughers and Two Laughers serve their historical and ideological purposes?

Huiyuan and Lu Xiujing were not viewed as important figures in the first few centuries after their death, but this assessment changed in the middle Tang. An investigation into Huiyuan's and Lu's attitudes toward and roles in debates between the "Three Religions"—Buddhism, Confucianism, and Daoism—and the ups-and-downs of their historical reputations, provides a background for the development of the Three Laughers and Two Laughers genres. In particular, the contrast between Tao Yuanming's refusal to join the Lotus Society and Xie Lingyun's eagerness to join sheds light on the pervasive influence of Hongzhou Chan in the Mount Lu area during the late Tang that brought about the change in the trio's configuration. Finally, the literary and visual evidence shows that the formation of the Three Laughers story mirrored the Buddhist community's perspective on the issue of the Three Religions.

HUIYUAN, ARBITER OF THE THREE RELIGIONS AND PATRIARCH OF CHINESE PURE LAND BUDDHISM

According to the *Gaoseng zhuan* (Biographies of Eminent Monks) by the Liang dynasty monk Huijiao (497–554), Huiyuan was a child prodigy from Shanxi Province, who in his youth was already well versed in the *Six Confucian Classics*, *Zhuangzi*, and *Laozi*.[9] After he turned twenty-one, Huiyuan planned to study with the Confucian scholar Fan Xuan (active second half of 4th century) in another region of the country, but his plan was shattered by social unrest that prevented him from traveling far;[10] he ended up on Mount Taihang as a disciple of the monk Daoan (312 or 314–385).[11] In 381 he traveled to Mount Lu, built Donglin Monastery, and lived there until his death in 416.[12] At the monastery he was well acquainted with, and highly respected by, Confucian scholar-officials and recluses;[13] their communication and friendship formed the basis for the Eighteen Noble Worthies of the Lotus Society in later times.

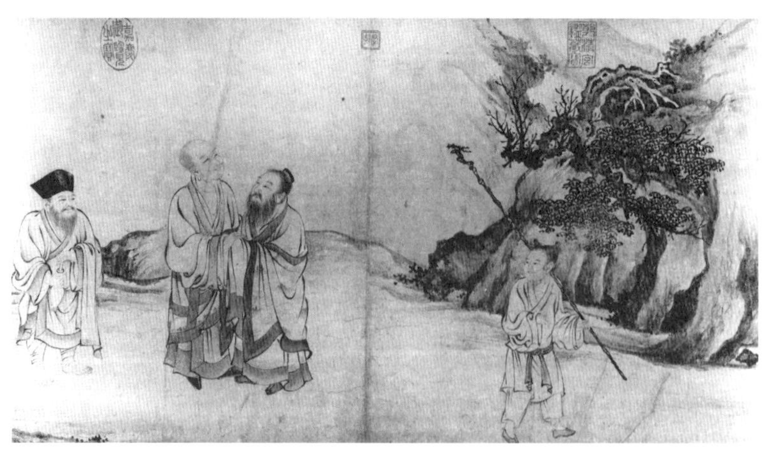

FIGURE 2
Zhang Ji (active second half of the 11th century–first half of the 12th century). *Lotus Society*. Detail. Handscroll, ink on paper, 13¾ × 334¼ in. (34.9 × 849 cm). Liaoning Provincial Museum

Among Huiyuan's contributions, his actions as an arbiter of the Three Religions and his *Banzhou samadhi* Pure Land practice (discussed below) secured his pivotal position in Chinese Buddhist history. His well-rounded Confucian and Lao–Zhuang philosophical education enabled him to utilize the philosophies of both schools of thought. Once, when his audience could not understand a Buddhist scripture he was preaching, he explained it using Daoist concepts.[14] His syncretic approach was highly regarded by his master, Daoan.[15] In his later years Huiyuan was often drawn into disputes between Confucians and Buddhists.[16] Despite disagreeing with Confucian scholars on certain issues, he emphasized that:

> As for the laws of Buddhism and the teachings of Confucianism, and as for Shakyamuni, [the ancient sage king] Yao, and Kong [Confucius], their inceptions may be different, but they influence each other. Their origins are indeed different, but their goals are the same.[17]

Huiyuan even played the dual role of Confucian and Daoist instructor. He discussed the meaning of the *Yijing* (The Book of Changes) with Yin Zhongkan (late 4th–early 5th century) and preached the Confucian *Sangfujing* (Classic of Mourning Garb) to Confucian scholars.[18] His efforts to bridge gaps between the Three Religions, however, went unnoticed for centuries, until the middle to late Tang, when the Three Laughers story was emerging. Before discussing the belated recognition of Huiyuan's syncretic contribution, I will first summarize his *Banzhou samadhi* Pure Land practice and the common perceptions of this practice prior to the middle Tang.[19]

Banzhou means "appearance of the Buddha," and *samadhi* is a meditation (*ding*) technique in which the meditator seeks union with the object of meditation. There are two kinds of *ding*: *shengding*, an innate ability, and *xiuding*, an intense meditative technique through which one obtains Buddhist wisdom and *karma*. Huiyuan's meditation (*dhyana*) practice utilized the *xiuding* technique.[20] To this end, he built a meditation hall at Donglin Monastery, where he led his disciples in earnest meditation day and night with the goal of visualizing Buddha.[21]

This self-reliant (*zili*) practice depended entirely on one's will, determination, and persistence. Only scholars of leisure could adopt the austere lifestyle it demanded; it was impractical for the masses, who could not spend long hours in meditation. For this reason, Huiyuan's influence was not widely felt in the years immediately following his death. Meanwhile, the Northern Wei (386–534) Pure Land evangelist Tanluan (475–after 554) had been promoting the *tali* method, through which, with the Buddha's intercession, one could be reborn in the Western Paradise.[22] Tanluan's disciple Daochuo (562–645) made this method even more accessible to the masses by altering the abstract concept of *nianfo* (to contemplate or be mindful of the Buddha) to the more tangible *nianfo* (to invoke the name of the Buddha).[23] Although both methods continued to be practiced, the latter became more popular. There was a tendency among Sui (581–618) and Tang Pure Land monks to ignore or even criticize Huiyuan's practice. In Daochuo's *Anle ji* (Collections of Essays on the Western Paradise), Huiyuan was not listed among the "six virtuous Pure Land evangelists."[24] Later, the renowned eighth-century Pure Land master Jiacai wrote in his *Jingtu lunji* (Exposition on Pure Land):

> Although the ancient masters Huiyuan, Xie Lingyun, and the like, all hoped to be born in the Western Paradise, they only cultivated themselves, and later followers were unable to continue the tradition.[25]

This statement summed up the distinction between Huiyuan's method and the criteria of later Pure Land evangelists. The influence of Huiyuan's practice and his contribution in bridging philosophies of the Three Religions were not realized until the middle Tang. Before examining this issue, I shall consider Lu Xiujing and Tao Yuanming, the other characters in the trio.

LU XIUJING, RESTORER AND DEFENDER OF DAOISM

Early records of Lu Xiujing are scant. Most extant materials were written by Buddhist monks who often gave unfair and distorted accounts of him. The earliest record of Lu written from a Daoist perspective was the early-Tang author Wu Yun's "Stele of Lu Xiujing" of 675, which recounts Lu's activities and contributions but rarely mentions corresponding dates.[26] Nonetheless, considering sources from both religious and official histories, we know that Lu Xiujing was an important Daoist master in the Liu Song (420–479) court of the Southern Dynasties.

Born in 406 in Wuxing, Lu lived for a few years on Mount Lu before he was summoned to court by the Liu Song emperor Mingdi (r. 465–72).[27] While there, he lived in the Hall of Relevance to the Void (*Chongxu guan*),

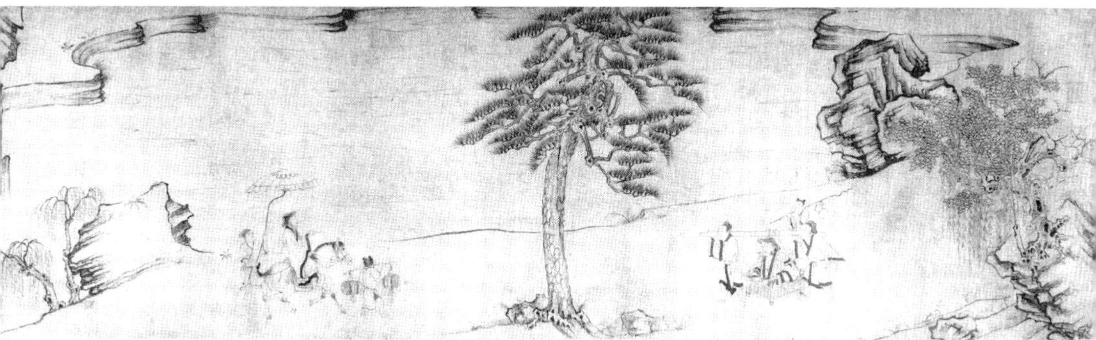

FIGURE 3
Unidentified artist. *Lotus Society*, Southern Song dynasty (1127–1279). Detail. Handscroll, ink on paper, 11 1/8 × 180 3/4 in. (28.1 × 459 cm). Shanghai Museum

where he contributed greatly to the Daoist canon. He reorganized and systematically canonized earlier Daoist scriptures and submitted them to the throne in 471.[28] He also standardized various Daoist rituals, which were followed by Tang Daoists.[29] Lu imitated formal aspects of Buddhism by worshipping triads of images installed in Daoist halls.[30] This form of worship embellished Daoist rituals, and made Daoism a more tangible and therefore more competitive religion.

Buddhist and Daoist sources conflict as to Lu Xiujing's later activities. His hagiographer Wu Yun recorded that he passed away in 477 in the capital, Jiankang (present-day Nanjing).[31] Buddhist sources claim that Lu fled to the north upon the issuing of the *Shedao wen* (Article on Abandoning Daoism) by Emperor Wu (r. 502–50) of the Liang,[32] but Lu, in fact, had died several decades earlier. In the north, as the Buddhist story goes, Lu, hoping to revive Daoism, bribed important officials; in 555 he reputedly received an order from Emperor Wenxuan (r. 550–60) of the Northern Qi to attend a debate with Buddhist monks.[33] This second event, however, could only have taken place had Lu reached the improbable age of 149.[34]

Because of his importance in Daoist history, Lu Xiujing and his accomplishments were brought up in debates between the Three Religions. As early as the Liang dynasty, the Buddhist monk Sengyou (445–518) accused him of practicing *jiaolu zhai*, a Daoist ritual that Sengyou described as extremely immoral and an assault on Chinese tradition because it allowed sexual intimacy between men and women regardless of their age.[35] Lu's setting up of triads in Daoist worship halls was also described as stealing Buddhist ideas.[36] Of all the attacks, the most severe concerned the Daoist canonical texts that Lu had submitted to the Liu Song emperor.[37] The monk Daoxuan (596–667) wrote derisively that:

> The canonical catalogues submitted [by Lu Xiujing to the emperor] indicated [there were still some scriptures] preserved in palaces in Heaven. But in the past one hundred and some years, we have not heard of [Daoist] heavenly beings descending from Heaven, nor witnessed Daoists ascending to Heaven. I wonder how those Daoist scriptures got here.[38]

The monk Falin (572–640) further railed:

> It is absurd that Lu Xiujing's canonical catalogue did not have the original copies. Lu Xiujing's catalogue is already a big forgery. Today's *Xuandu* catalogue [which comprised 2,040 scrolls] is the forgery of forgeries.[39]

That Lu Xiujing was so reviled by Buddhists was inevitable, given the religious environment of the early Tang, when Buddhism was under severe attack by other religions. First, the newly ruling Li clan, who were supported by Daoists during their rise to power, claimed to be the descendants of Laozi.[40] Second, in the power struggle between Prince Li Shimin and his brother Prince Li Jiancheng, the Buddhist community had backed the loser, Li Jiancheng.[41] Because of these circumstances, the court of Li Shimin (Emperor Taizong, r. 626–49) favored Daoism. Confucians and Daoists united in attacking what they called the "barbaric" (*hu*) religion of Buddhism. At court, the Grand Astrologer Fu Yi (active 618–49) was the most vocal opponent, and Daoists rose in support. Among them was Li Zhongqing, who used the spurious *Laozi huahu jing* (Scripture of Laozi Converting the Barbarians) to claim Daoism's legitimacy and superiority over Buddhism.[42] Li Zhongqing's tactic in turn spurred three severe Buddhist counterattacks wherein monks urged the court to destroy this Daoist apocrypha, and ultimately succeeded.[43] But Daoists quickly fought back, insisting on the negative influences and ill intentions of the "barbaric" faith. Wu Yun wrote:

> Noble scholars are hurt and they commiserate in silence ... The insidious, barbaric books [Buddhist sutras] rely on Chinese brushes to propagate [them]. Their traces cannot be found or proven in Ban [Gu] and Sima [Qian's writings]; their principles are only stolen from Lao[zi] and Zhuang[zi]. They praise the barbaric corners as the central land, and relegate the entire Xia [Chinese territory] to the backward regions. They aim to slander Confucianism and

> swallow Daoism, curb the emperors and pressure the kings so as to take over the emperor's power by force and seize the principle of the beginning of creation.[44]

Here we see Wu Yun's rationale in his reactionary urge to protect and preserve Confucian and Daoist principles. The distinctions between the Chinese (*xia*) and the barbarians (*hu*) can be traced back to the central point of the *Scripture of Laozi Converting the Barbarians*, which juxtaposes Chinese chauvinism with the "inferior" cultures of neighboring nations. These attacks and counterattacks explain why Lu Xiujing, who was the first to re-catalogue and canonize Daoist scriptures, was an easy target. The significance of Wu Yun's drafting of Lu Xiujing's hagiography amid these heated debates may thus be understood as a deliberate effort to rehabilitate Lu and use his contributions to bolster Daoism.

Hostilities between the Three Religions would last until the mid-Tang, when the poisonous atmosphere was replaced by a friendlier one. Though some still voiced anti-Buddhist sentiment, most elite members of the Three Religions advocated tolerance. Buddhists and Daoists no longer attacked each other at court but instead concluded their debates amicably. Many schools of Buddhism adopted Daoist thought and methods in their rituals and doctrines, and Daoist schools reciprocated.[45]

While some Confucian scholars continued to attack Buddhism, leading Buddhist monks and laymen offered reconciliation. In a rebuttal to the Confucian scholar Han Yu's (768–824) memorial against Buddhism, presented in 819, the renowned Huayan master Zongmi (780–841), for example, echoed a view expressed by Huiyuan a few centuries earlier:

> Confucius, Laozi, and Shakyamuni are all sages ... they together benefit the masses.[46]

Also in reaction to Han Yu's criticism, the ninth-century monk Shenqing wrote *Beishan lu* (Record of North Mountain), a work admired by scholars and distinguished clergymen as having "embodied the philosophies of the Three Religions."[47] Among Confucian-Buddhist scholars, Bai Juyi (772–846) equated the *Six Confucian Classics* with the twelve categories of Buddhist sutras, and the ten disciples of Confucius with the ten disciples of Shakyamuni.[48] Liu Zongyuan (773–819), a Confucian and Pure Land Buddhist practitioner, turned to Six Dynasties Buddhist history for precedents of harmonious relations between the Three Religions:

> In the past, leading clerics were all fond of befriending learned Confucian scholars. Since the Jin and Song, there were Daolin, Daoan, the master [Hui]yuan and Xiushangren. The people whom they befriended were Xie Anshi, Wang Yishao, Xi Zhaochi, Xie Lingyun, Bao Zhao, and the like.[49]

Liu Zongyuan viewed Buddhist clergy as initiators who not only tolerated but also befriended Confucians. The fabricated story of Huiyuan's "inviting" Tao Yuanming to join the Lotus Society, discussed below, epitomized this trend during the late Tang.

TAO YUANMING, PARAGON OF LIBERATED BEINGS

Like the dubious encounter between the Buddhist master and Lu Xiujing, Huiyuan and Tao Yuanming probably never met. The *Fozu tongji* (Record of the Lineage of the Buddha and Patriarchs), by the Southern Song monk Zhipan (active 1258–69), however, states that:

> [Tao] often went back and forth to Mount Lu, [and] he had one of his disciples and two sons carry [him in] the basket. At that time, Master Yuan formed the Lotus Society with many worthies, and he invited Yuanming by letter. Yuanming replied, "Only if I am allowed to drink will I go." [Huiyuan] approved it. Thereafter, Yuanming came to visit, but suddenly he was discontented. He turned around and left.[50]

This passage describes the awkward relationship between Tao Yuanming and the Donglin circle resulting from Tao's indifference to Buddhism. Nonetheless, Tao's high-mindedness, combined with his love for liquor, is integral to this legend.[51]

In the Shanghai Museum version of the *Lotus Society* (see fig. 3), Tao rides in a basket carried by two porters, his son, in front, and his student, in back.[52] The fourth figure, carrying liquor in a gourd suspended from a staff, is probably another son, mentioned in the *Jinshu* (Jin History).[53] The significance of Tao Yuanming in this new configuration must be compared with that of Xie Lingyun, who in the same handscroll is depicted on horseback.

XIE LINGYUN ON HORSEBACK

In the legendary account of the Lotus Society, Xie Lingyun was rejected for membership by Huiyuan:

> Xie Lingyun was talented but arrogant. Since his youth he respected few people. But once he met Master [Hui]yuan, he respected him wholeheartedly. Therefore he dug [two] ponds and [used the soil from them to] build a platform to translate the *Nirvana Sutra*. He asked to join the "Pure Society," [but] Master [Huiyuan] refused him on grounds that his mind was too distracted.[54]

In reality Xie had been not only a devout Buddhist famous for participating in translating and promoting new sutras, but also a devoted follower of Huiyuan. Moreover, in the Six Dynasties or early Tang period, he was not perceived as having been rejected by Huiyuan. In fact, Pure Land masters such as Jiacai and Feixi (active mid-8th century) noted that Xie Lingyun was among those who vowed with Huiyuan in front of an image of the Amitabha Buddha, the focal image in Pure Land Buddhism, to practice *nianfo* (mindfulness of the Buddha).[55]

The term *xinza* (distracted mind), noted in Zhipan's text cited above, was key to the later perception that Xie Lingyun was rejected by Huiyan, and aptly summarizes Xie's personality and life. Born into one of the two most prominent families of the Eastern Jin dynasty, and a grandson of the nobleman Xie An (320–385), Xie Lingyun inherited the title Marquis of Kangle (*Kanglehou*).[56] Though talented, he was spoiled, unruly, and rebellious.[57] His haughty and overbearing manner interfered with his personal relationships, so he was never given a favorable official assignment.[58] He finally rebelled against the emperor, an act that cost him his life.[59]

In the Shanghai Museum scroll (see fig. 3), Xie Lingyun is mounted on a horse, symbolizing his unique social status. His interest in Buddhism is indicated by the Sanskrit sutra he holds respectfully and the two bundles of sutra fascicles carried by a servant boy. The most intriguing element in the picture, one that reveals Xie's personality and role in the Lotus Society tradition, is the curved-stem parasol (*quli*)[60] carried by another servant, who is walking behind Xie. According to the *Shishuo xinyu* (New Tales of the World), by Liu Yiqing (402–444):

> Xie Lingyun preferred to use a curved-stem parasol (*quli*). The hermit Kong [Chunzhi] asked him: "Sir, if you wish to be aloof, why can't you leave behind the affectation of a curved-[stem] parasol?" Xie replied: "He who is not afraid of [his own] shadow cannot be completely unfettered."[61]

The meaning of this passage becomes clear when we return to its original source, the *Yufupian* ("Fisherman Chapter") of the *Zhuangzi*:

> Confucius ... bowed again and stood up, saying: "I was exiled twice from the state of Lu, escaped from the state of Wei, was defeated in the state of Song, and surrounded in the state of Chencai. I did not know what misconduct I had committed to have brought about these four insults. Why?" The [fisherman] guest was saddened and spoke with worry: "Alas! You are really obstinately adhering to misconceptions. There are those afraid of shadows and traces, so they run away from them. But the more they run, the more traces they leave behind, [and] the faster they walk, the faster their shadows follow. They think they are walking too slowly, so they speed up relentlessly until they exhaust themselves to death. They do not know [the method of] staying in shade to elude shadows, remaining still to evade traces. They are really stupid. Sir, you comprehend benevolence and righteousness, distinguish differences, observe the transformations resulting from actions, adapt the etiquette of giving and receiving, manage the motions of liking and despising, harmonize joy and anger. But still you cannot evade troubles. You should scrupulously cultivate your character and preserve your true nature. Be sure things and people are treated accordingly. Then you will have no worries. Now you do not cultivate yourself, but only request others [to do so]. Aren't you asking too much from externality?"[62]

Here, Confucius is portrayed as a man struggling in worldly affairs; the wise fisherman advises him to seek truth by cultivating his mind inwardly. This dichotomy between worries caused by external phenomena and self-cultivation to bring about lasting internal peace parallels the Buddhist concept of the illusion and defilement that conceal innate purity and *tathagatagarbha* (Buddha-nature) within each sentient being. Only after one is able to see through the illusory world will one realize one's true potential from within.

Thus the depiction of Xie Lingyun shaded by a curved-stem parasol refers to Xie and Kong's dialogue, and Xie's effort to steep himself in and utilize the classics in philosophical debates. In reality, Xie only understood the classics on a theoretical level; he probably never believed in self-restraint or introspection, nor sought answers from within. There was a conflict between his intellectual arrogance and the precepts of Buddhism. The pictorial representation of Xie Lingyun, while acknowledging his Buddhist faith and contribution in Buddhist history, points out this dilemma and the psychological flaws that led to both his outsider status in the Lotus Society tradition and his subsequent demise.

Tao Yuanming, unlike Xie Lingyun, struggled throughout his life to free himself from officialdom. This fundamental difference in their philosophy of life affected Tao's and Xie's relative historical positions in several ways. Tao's naïve spontaneity (*tianzhen ziran*), for example, won him higher respect in literary history than did Xie Lingyun's linguistic exquisiteness (*jinggong*).[63] Tao's quality of an unfettered mind was earnestly sought by both literati and Chan monks in the Tang and Song dynasties.[64] Tao Yuanming riding in his basket epitomizes the aloof gentleman and true hermit, while Xie Lingyun, on horseback and sheltered by a curved-stem parasol, is the image of arrogance, hindered by his "distracted mind." Together Tao and Xie would remind viewers of the importance of detachment from worldly desires and truthfulness to one's own nature on the path to enlightenment, a key point of Hongzhou Chan ideology.

HONGZHOU CHAN IDEOLOGY AS REVEALED IN THE JUXTAPOSITION OF TAO YUANMING AND XIE LINGYUN

Hongzhou Chan refers to the Chan tradition founded by the Tang Buddhist monk Mazu Daoyi (709–788) in Hongzhou (modern Nanchang, Jiangsu Province), near Mount Lu, where the legends of the Three Laughers, Two Laughers, and the Eighteen Noble Worthies of the Lotus Society were formulated. Daoyi's Chan thought can be summarized in the term *pingchangxin* (ordinary mind). Based on this principle, Daoyi fostered a new approach to the Mahayana practice of the bodhisattva path:

> One need not practice the Way, but just do not allow contamination. What is contamination? If the thought of birth and death occurs, or pretentiousness, [or] ingratiation, it is contamination.

> If one wishes to comprehend the Way directly, then Ordinary Mind is the Way. What is Ordinary Mind? [In it] there is no pretentiousness, no attachment nor rejection, no annihilation nor permanence, no commoners nor saints. A sutra said: "It is not the path of commoners, nor the path of saints; it is the path of bodhisattvas." Everyday walking, living, sitting, sleeping, and responses to things are the Way. The Way is *dharmadhatu*.[65]

Daoyi's concept of Ordinary Mind disregarded all methods based on scriptures, and argued that simply living one's life as usual was tantamount to practicing the bodhisattva path. This assertion corresponded to the Chan claim that practices such as studying sutras, meditation, and worshipping Buddhas were no longer viable means for reaching enlightenment. The Huayan master Zongmi characterized Daoyi's Ordinary Mind as *tianzhen ziran* (naïve and unpretentious revelation of one's nature) and *renyun zizai* (naturally living out one's own destiny); he even called those who possessed such qualities *jietuo ren* (liberated beings), signifying a synthesis of Chan and Daoist concepts.[66]

Parallel to Daoyi's concept of Ordinary Mind is his view that both good and evil conduct are merely the manifestation of one's *tathagatagarbha*.[67] Zongmi characterized this aspect of Hongzhou Chan in this way:

> The meaning of Hongzhou [Chan] is that any arising of mind and thought, the flicking of [one's] fingers, the moving of [one's] eyes, any conduct and behavior is [the manifestation of] *tathagatagarbha* ... Greed, anger, ignorance, committing good or vicious deeds, receiving happiness and suffering are all [manifestations of one's] *tathagatagarbha*.[68]

Since Daoyi identified evil deeds as the manifestation of one's *tathagatagarbha*, he disregarded the rules of conduct founded on Buddhist precepts and other social norms. He began to formulate unconventional teaching methods of kicking, hitting, and shouting at his disciples to jolt them into a sudden awakening to the truth.[69] Daoyi's new methods foresaw the later use of even more bizarre behavior and language by Chan masters. Linji Yixuan (d. 867), the founder of the Linji school of Chan, for example, boldly exhorted:

> Practitioners ... when you encounter a Buddha, kill him; when you

> encounter your [*dharma*] master, kill him; when you encounter an arhat, kill him; when you encounter your parents, kill them; and when you encounter your relatives, kill them. Then you can be liberated.[70]

Yixuan was not actually encouraging his disciples to commit murder, but his astonishing use of language took Daoyi's methods to an extreme. In another famous example of bizarre behavior, the Chan master Danxia's (738–823) burning of a wooden statue of the Buddha to keep warm in winter was certainly, in conventional views, profane. Yet among Chan circles this story became a favored painting subject to address the insubstantiality of reality.[71]

Given the Hongzhou Chan ideological context, one can understand why Tao Yuanming was removed from the Three Laughers story to be paired with Xie Lingyun. The image of Xie Lingyun on horseback reverently holding a sutra, with his attendant carrying bundles of sutras (see fig. 3), was a clear indication of Xie's fondness for studying Buddhist scriptures. I have already shown the paradox in Xie's attempt to use words in debates rather than to cultivate his mind. Moreover, his habit of drawing attention to himself is a perfect example of the "pretentiousness" reproved by Hongzhou Chan, and a form of contamination (*wuran*) in Daoyi's philosophy. This contamination parallels the "diagnosis" of *xinza* (distracted mind) given to Xie Lingyun in the Lotus Society legends. Thus, it is not surprising that even after Xie had shown his sincerity by digging ponds to plant lotus flowers and using the excavated earth to build a platform for translating the *Nirvana Sutra*, he was still rejected by Huiyuan for membership in the society.

Tao Yuanming, Xie's counterpart in this depiction, was by contrast a paragon of Hongzhou Chan. Under the guidance of the concepts of the Ordinary Mind and *Dao buyongxiu* (no need to practice the Way), and the notion that the daily routines of walking, sitting, and sleeping were in fact means of practicing the Way, one no longer had consciously to live and act according to conventional religious precepts and principles. In this context, Tao's spontaneous lifestyle was a perfect manifestation of Hongzhou Chan. Since irrational behavior could be considered the true revelation of one's *tathagatagarbha*, Tao's alcoholism could easily be interpreted as the unpretentious manifestation of his true nature, that is *tianzhen ziran*, the goal epitomized by Zongmi's *jietuo ren*.

These characteristics of Hongzhou Chan were instrumental in the formation of the legend of Huiyuan's invitation to Tao Yuanming to join the Lotus Society. His supposed willingness to allow Tao to drink, violating the Buddhist precepts that Huiyuan himself obeyed to the last moment of his life, implies the acceptance of irrational behavior as an expression of a liberated being. Tao's rejection of Huiyuan's invitation carried further the notion of total disregard for laws regulating the *sangha* (Buddhist community) by liberated beings. The juxtaposition of Xie Lingyun ("distracted mind") on horseback and holding a Sanskrit sutra, with Tao Yuanming ("liberated mind") riding in his basket and refusing to enter the Lotus Society, suggests that the Hongzhou Chan concept of Ordinary Mind was the underlying philosophy for separating Tao Yuanming from the trio of the Three Laughers.

To summarize the formation of the Three Laughers stories, I shall begin with the earliest hagiography of Huiyuan, by the sixth-century monk Huijiao:

> Huiyuan's shadow did not leave Mount [Lu] and his path did not enter the mundane world. When he sent his guests off, he would not leave the boundary [of Donglin Monastery].[72]

Huijiao mentions neither the two remaining characters in the Three Laughers story nor Tiger Stream Bridge. Nonetheless, the notion that Huiyuan did not easily step beyond the limits of Donglin Monastery is established. The Liang dynasty monk Sengyou once condemned Lu Xiujing for his practice of *jiaolu zhai* and scolded him for immorality. Considering the negative perception of Lu Xiujing during that period, it is highly unlikely that Huijiao's record had anything to do with the Three Laughers story. The Sui dynasty author Fei Changfang's *Lidai sanbao ji* (Record of Three Treasures of Successive Dynasties) followed Huijiao's writing without further embellishments, another indication that the trio had not yet been formulated.[73] In the early Tang, while Huiyuan's teachings were deemed unsuitable for propagation and ignored, Lu Xiujing's reputation came under the most severe scrutiny by Buddhist monks. It is inconceivable that the Three Laughers story was created in that hostile environment.

The next stage of development of the story is evident in the Tang poet Li Bai's (701–763) poem "Saying Farewell to the Monk of Donglin":

At the parting place of Donglin Monastery,
The moon rose and white gibbons howled;
Laughingly saying farewell to [Hui]yuan of Mount Lu,
Why bother crossing Tiger Stream Bridge?[74]

Although it does not explicitly refer to Lu Xiujing and Tao Yuanming, Li Bai's poem does mention laughter (*xiao*) and Tiger Stream Bridge. By the tenth century, as the Chan monk, poet, and painter Guanxiu's (832–912) poem indicates, Tao Yuanming had been extracted from the trio to form the new Two Laughers story:

[Huiyuan] loved the official Tao, who was hopelessly drunk.
He saw off the Daoist Lu, a prolonged [farewell].
Buying liquor and crossing over the bridge broke both rules.
Who were they who made the master behave like this?

[*Poet's Comments:*] He never crossed Tiger Stream Bridge when seeing off guests, regardless of their status. But when seeing off the Daoist Lu Xiujing, he passed Tiger Stream, [walking] several hundred steps. Nowadays, the Daoist Hill is in front of the gate [of the monastery]. This was where [Huiyuan] stopped when seeing off the Daoist.[75]

Thus the compilation of the Three Laughers and Two Laughers stories must have occurred between the time of Li Bai and Guanxiu (8th–10th century). Because Li and Guanxiu were closely affiliated with the Mount Lu circle, their views toward the Three Laughers and the Two Laughers most likely reflected the attitude of the larger Mount Lu Buddhist community around Donglin Monastery.

The Three Laughers were a perfect representation of the spirit of closing philosophical gaps and building consensus. All three figures were active on Mount Lu during the Eastern Jin and Southern Dynasties periods, even though they never actually met. Their prominence in their respective schools made them suitable candidates for inclusion in the Three Laughers story. Ironically, neither Huiyuan nor Lu Xiujing consistently won high regard for their achievements. They only became prominent when social and historic conditions were favorable, and their life stories and accomplishments were only useful through a filtered historical lens. Once the Three Laughers story became known, it was used as a paragon and applied by monks and Confucian scholars to promote syncretism. Like Zongmi, Shenqing, Bai Juyi, and Liu Zongyuan, the Northern Song monk Zanning revered Huiyuan and his teacher Daoan:

> Being a monk, one cannot be better than Daoan. [Dao]an's befriending Xi Zhaochi was respectful of Confucianism. Being a monk, one cannot be better than Huiyuan; [Hui]yuan's seeing off Lu Xiujing beyond Tiger Stream [Bridge] was respectful of Daoism. I admire both for their veneration of Confucianism and Daoism.[76]

While Daoan's friendship with Xi Zhaochi (second half of the 4th century) was a historical fact, Huiyuan's seeing off Lu Xiujing was a fabrication. Both stories came into existence in the late Tang and Northern Song because they reflected Buddhist perspectives on the Three Religions. A poem by the late Northern Song literatus Wang Shipeng (1112–1171) evokes the rapprochement of the Three Religions represented by the Three Laughers:

> Yuanming and Xiujing did not practice meditation;
> They were worthies within the gates of Confucius and Laozi.
> After the three laughingly said farewell at Tiger Stream,
> White clouds and flowing waters were both sorrowful.[77]

In this context, the trio becomes the representative of the Three Religions, standing together like Shakyamuni, Laozi, and Confucius in a Three Religions picture.[78]

Just as Tao Yuanming was easily included as one of the Three Laughers, he was singled out to be paired with Xie Lingyun as a paragon of Hongzhou Chan's *pingchangxin* (ordinary mind). Historicity was irrelevant, and inclusion or exclusion of these figures served to propagate specific social and religious agendas. Furthermore, Liu Zongyuan's and Zanning's statements show that it was Buddhist monks who initiated contact with and befriended Confucians and Daoists, conveying a solely Buddhist perspective that automatically put Buddhism foremost among the three. The Northern Song monk-historian Mingjiao Qisong (1011–1072) reinforced this hierarchical attitude:

> Though [Lu] Xiujing was a scholar of a heretical religion, [Huiyuan's] seeing him off beyond Tiger Stream Bridge did not [mean] he abandoned him merely because of his [Lu's] statements.[79]

Qisong's statement naturally put Lu Xiujing in an inferior position. This hierarchy is evident in visual representations of the Three Laughers and Two Laughers, again echoing compositions of Three Religions pictures. In the National Palace Museum's *Three Laughers* (see fig. 1), Huiyuan wears a red robe and is flanked by the other two nobles, making him the focal point of the composition.[80] The same configuration is found in the majority of Three Religions pictures, in which Shakyamuni is the central figure, flanked by Laozi and Confucius. In the *Two Laughers*, a small portion of the *Lotus Society* picture as represented by the Liaoning scroll (see fig. 2), Huiyuan is larger and stands higher than Lu Xiujing. Gazing into space, he pats Lu's hands paternalistically, while Lu looks up at him reverently. The hierarchy is unmistakable.

The Three Laughers story and its derivative, the Two Laughers, were created in the middle to late Tang. They appeared only when social and religious conditions encouraged the creation of new images to signify the harmonious relationships between the Three Religions and the promotion of the concepts of Hongzhou Chan. They reflect a Buddhist perspective in that a hierarchical relationship is expressed through the writings of Buddhist clergy and literati, and in paintings represented by the National Palace Museum, Shanghai Museum, and Liaoning Provincial Museum scrolls.

NOTES

1. Su Shi 1975, vol. 49, p. 46b.
2. Su Shi 1964, vol. 13, p. 3. See also Chen Shunyu 1932–34, vol. 2, p. 5a.
3. Chen Shunyu 1932–34, vol. 2, p. 5a.
4. Huijiao 1932–34, 358c.
5. The earliest records of the Eighteen Noble Worthies of the Lotus Society can be found in late Tang writings. The earliest surviving complete *Biographies of the Eighteen Noble Worthies of the Lotus Society* is in Chen Shunyu's *Lu-shan ji.* Chen noted in his preface that the Eighteen Noble Worthies was a popular story on Mount Lu, but his writings never mentioned the "three non-members"; see Chen Shunyu 1932–34. That phrase first appeared in the Southern Song monk Zhipan's version of *Biographies of the Eighteen Noble Worthies of the Lotus Society*; see Zhipan 1932–34. Zhipan wrote in his preface that in the early Daguan reign (1107–10), the monk Huaiwu noted that Chen Shunyu's records of the Eighteen Noble Worthies were not complete and he added them to Chen's writing. Based on *Lushan ji* (Chen Shunyu 1932–34), *Gaoseng zhuan* (Hujiao 1932–34), *Jinshu*, and *Songshu*, Zhipan further augmented Huaiwu's writing. Also see Tang Yongtong 1991, 366.
6. The man behind Huiyuan, holding a *kundika*, is the snake-catcher. For a detailed study of this figure, see Pan 1997, 113–19.
7. Tang Yongtang 1991, 370.
8. Ibid. See also Wu Yun 1983a, vol. 926, pp. 21b–23b. According to Wu Yun, Lu died in 477 at the age of seventy-two. If we calculate from that year, Lu would have been just ten years old when Huiyuan died, and Lu did not move to Mount Lu until much later. See Wu Yun 1983a, vol. 926, p. 22a.
9. Hujiao 1932–34, 357c.
10. Ibid.
11. Ibid., 358a.
12. Ibid., 358a–61b.
13. Ibid., 358c. See also Daoxuan 1932–34a, 267a.
14. This was a daring approach in a period when non-Buddhist thought and books were considered vulgar by some Buddhists. See Hujiao 1932–34, 358a, and Kimura Eiichi 1962, 513.
15. Hujiao 1932–34, 358.
16. Most typical of the issues addressed by Confucian scholars in this period were why monks did not bow to rulers and how monks' robes contradicted Confucian decorum. The contents of these disputes are preserved in Sengyou 1932–34, 31a.
17. Ibid.
18. Kimura Eiichi 1962, 513.
19. The Sui dynasty Tiantai patriarch Zhiyi promoted the four forms of *samadhi*, which included Huiyuan's *Banzhou samadhi* practice. Tiantai Pure Land practices did not develop fully until the Northern Song, owing to the efforts of such eminent monks as Zhili and Zunshi. In this article I consider only the common practices of the Tang dynasty.
20. Fang Lifu 1984, 123.
21. Ibid., 361b.
22. Nogami Shunjō 1962, 227.
23. Daoxuan 1932–34c, 593–94.
24. Nogami Shunjō 1962, 227.
25. Jiacai 1932–34, 83.
26. Wu Yun 1983a, 22a.
27. Ibid.
28. Ibid. For contradictory information, see Daoxuan 1932–34b, 737, and Xuanni 1932–34, 561a and 563c.
29. Wu Yun 1983a, 22b.
30. Falin 1932–34a, 535b.

31. According to Wu Yun, three days after Lu Xiujing's death his students on Mount Lu saw his soul flying back to his old residence. See Wu Yun 1983a, 23a.
32. Daoxuan 1932–34b, 737a–b; 1932–34c, 525a–b; 1932–34a, 112c; and Xuanni 1931–34, 569. Emperor Wu issued a *Shedao wen* in 504 (see *Quan shanggu Sandai Qin Han Sanguo Liuchao wen, Quan Liangwen* 1965, vol. 4, p. 9a-b), but the *Shedao wen* seems irrelevant to the life of Lu Xiujing, who had died a few decades earlier.
33. Daoxuan 1932–34b, 737a–b.
34. Though it is unclear if Lu fled to the north, he did attend debates between Buddhists and Daoists. The details of these debates are not known, except from the Tang monk Falin's *Poxie lun* (*On Destroying Evils*), written in response to Confucian and Daoist attacks, in which he mentioned that Lu wrote *Dui shamen ji* (*Record of Rebutting Monks*). See Falin 1932–34b, 485.
35. Sengyou 1932–34, 48b.
36. Falin 1932–34a, 535b.
37. All records except one (Yancong 1932–34, 209c) claim that this event happened in 471. Yancong's account of Lu's submission of the Daoist canon to the Liu Song emperor in 465 is questionable because, according to Daoist writings, Lu Xiujing was at Mount Lu at the time.
38. Yancong 1932–34, 209c; Daoxuan 1932–34a, 174c.
39. Falin 1932–34a, 547.
40. Ren Jiyu 1981, 267–69.
41. Qing Xitai 1988, 774. Falin led Buddhists in supporting Li Jiancheng, and Wang Zhiyuan led Daoists in supporting Li Shimin.
42. Written in 305 by Wang Fu of the Western Jin, this text emphasizes the superiority of Daoism over the imported religion, Buddhism. See Qing Xitai 1988, 770.
43. Ibid., 783.
44. Wu Yun 1983b, vol. 925, pp. 2a–b.
45. Qing Xitai 1988, 789.
46. Zongmi 1932–34, 505a–12c. While purporting to promote filial piety, this work is full of syncretic promulgations; also see Wu Yun 1983a, vol. 920, p. 2a.
47. Zanning 1932–34b, 741; Shenqing 1932–34, 573–636.
48. Bai Juyi 1983, vol. 677, p. 17b. This records a debate between the Three Religions held at the Tang court. Bai Juyi was close to Pure Land circles on Mount Lu, and built a retreat near Donglin Monastery, which he named Yi'ai Thatched Studio (*Yi'ai Caotang*). According to Chen Shunyu, it was located northeast of Donglin Monastery; see Chen Shunyu 1932–34, 7.
49. Liu Zongyuan 1964, vol. 25, pp. 422–32.
50. Zhipan 1932–34, vol. 26, pp. 269c–270a.
51. Liquor was probably not the pretext for Tao's refusal to join the Lotus Society, because one of his drinking partners, Zhang Ye, was among Huiyuan's closest lay followers and was included in the Eighteen Noble Worthies of the Lotus Society. This fabrication was created using Tao Yuanming's and Huiyuan's most prominent characteristics. Huiyuan was esteemed for his scrupulous adherence to Buddhist precepts. A quintessential example of this occurred in the final days of Huiyuan's life, when his disciples encouraged him to take rice wine, perhaps to ease his pain or for medicinal purposes. Huiyuan instead instructed them to consult the sutras to see whether drinking would be in accord with the precepts (see Hujiao 1932–34, vol. 16, p. 361b). In contrast, Tao

Yuanming's passion for liquor surpassed his love of life. In his late years he imagined he had died, and drafted three eulogies for himself. Sentences such as: "I regret when I was alive, I did not get to drink enough," and "In the past I had no wine to drink. Now I only brood on an empty cup," most aptly describe his alcoholism. (Translations follow Davis 1982, vol. 1, p. 173.)

52. See Li Chongyuan n.d., vol. 3, pp. 29b–30a.

53. *Jinshu* 1974, vol. 94, p. 2462.

54. Chen Shunyu 1932–34, p. 1039b. A similar passage in the same work reads: "In the past, Xie Lingyun was insolent because of his talent. Since his youth he respected few people. Once he met Master [Hui]yuan, he totally submitted to him. Thereupon he translated the *Nirvana Sutra* at the monastery. Thus he dug lotus ponds [and used the excavated earth] to build a platform, and planted white lotus flowers in them. He named this platform the 'Sutra-translation Platform.'" (Ibid., 1028a.)

55. Tang Yongtong 1991, 371. Tang notes that Xie went to Mount Lu eleven years after the vow. For Jiacai's record, see Jiacai 1932–34, 83b; for Feixi's, see Feixi 1932–34, 140b.

56. See his biography in *Nanshi* 1979, vol. 19, pp. 538–46.

57. Ibid.

58. Ibid.

59. Ibid.

60. This term was identified by Li Chongyuan of the Song dynasty in his *Lianshe tu ji*; see Li Chongyuan n.d.

61. Xu Zhen'e 1984, 89.

62. Huang Jinhong 1985, 355–56.

63. The Southern Song critic Yan Yu compared the two men's works: "The reason Xie is inferior to Tao is that [Xie] Kangle's poems are exquisite, whereas [Tao] Yuanming's are plain and natural." See Yan Yu 1983, 13a.

64. Su Shi, for example, was an ardent promoter of Tao Yuanming during the Northern Song.

65. The original text is in *Mazu Daoyi Chanshi yulu* 1995, 406c. Also see Wang Zhiyuan 1992, 230.

66. While there is no way to confirm whether Daoyi actually incorporated these concepts into his philosophy and preaching, they nevertheless corresponded to his fundamental approach to bodhisattvahood. Given the importance of Zongmi's view in Chan history, these terms and the concepts derived from them were regarded as Hongzhou Chan norms during the Northern Song.

67. Though other sutras, such as *Adushiwang jing* and *Yangjue moluo jing*, advocated similar views, Daoyi's definition of *tathagatagarbha* was inspired by the concept of *shan bushan yin* (good and evil causes) from the *Lengqie jing*, which accepts both good and evil deeds as equal components of *tathagatagarbha*. See Wang Zhiyuan 1992, 304.

68. The original text is in Zongmi's *Chanmen shizi chengxi tu*, quoted in Kamata Shigeo 1975, 350–51.

69. Wang Zhiyuan 1992, 223–40.

70. Ibid., 304. Daoyi's ideology was followed by the Linji school of Chan. Through Linji Chan, the influence of Hongzhou Chan extended into the Northern Song.

71. Puji 1984, vol. 5, p. 262. While some Chan monks disliked this tradition, which they disparagingly termed "wild fox Chan" (*yehu Chan*), it was still widespread in the Song.

72. Hujiao 1932–34, 361a.

73. Fei Changfang 1932–34, 6b–7b.

74. Li Bai 1977, vol. 15, p. 729.

75. See Li Tiaoyuan 1992, vol. 9, p. 1132.

76. Zanning 1932–34a, 255b.
77. This poem, titled "Donglin si," is preserved in Su Shi 1975, vol. 49, p. 39a, b.
78. For a Song dynasty rubbing of a Three Religions picture, dated to 1209, see Fong 1992, fig. 138. For a less formal example of a Three Religions picture by the late Ming painter Ding Yunpeng, see Barnhart et al. 1997, pl. 221.
79. Qisong 1932–34, 719.
80. For a color reproduction of this painting, see *Yuanming zhiqu tezhan tulu* 1988, pl. 9.

REFERENCES

Bai Juyi. 1983. *Sanjiao lunheng*. In *Quan Tangwen*. Beijing: Zhonghua shuju.

Barnhart, Richard M. et al. 1997. *Three Thousand Years of Chinese Painting*. New Haven and Beijing: Yale University and Foreign Languages Press.

Chen Shunyu. 1932–34. *Lushan ji*. In *Taishō shinshū daizōkyō*. Vol. 51. Tokyo: Daizō shuppan.

Daoxuan. 1932–34a. *Guang Hongming ji*. In *Taishō shinshū daizōkyō*. Vol. 52. Tokyo: Daizō shuppan.

———. 1932–34b. *Ji gujin fodao lunheng*. In *Taishō shinshū daizōkyō*. Vol. 52. Tokyo: Daizō shuppan.

———. 1932–34c. *Xu gaoseng zhuan*. In *Taishō shinshū daizōkyō*. Vol. 50. Tokyo: Daizō shuppan.

Davis, A.R. 1982. *T'ao Yuan-ming* (A.D. 365–427)*: His Works and Their Meaning*. Cambridge: Cambridge University Press.

Falin. 1932–34a. *Bianzheng lun*. In *Taishō shinshū daizōkyō*. Vol. 52. Tokyo: Daizō shuppan.

———. 1932–34b. *Poxie lun*. In *Taishō shinshū daizōkyō*. Vol. 52. Tokyo: Daizō shuppan.

Fang Lifu. 1984. *Huiyuan ji qi Foxue*. Beijing: Zhongguo Renmin Daxue chubanshe.

Fei Changfang. 1932–34. *Lidai sanbao ji*. In *Taishō shinshū daizōkyō*. Vol. 49. Tokyo: Daizō shuppan.

Feixi. 1932–34. *Nianfo sanmei baowang lun*. In *Taishō shinshū daizōkyō*. Vol. 47. Tokyo: Daizō shuppan.

Fong, Wen C. 1992. *Beyond Representation: Chinese Calligraphy and Painting 8th–14th Century*. New York: The Metropolitan Museum of Art.

Hedong ji. n.d. Beijing: Zhonghua shuju.

Huang Jinhong. 1985. *Xinyi Zhuangzi duben*. Taipei: Sanmin shuju.

Huijiao. 1932–34. *Gaoseng zhuan*. In *Taishō shinshū daizōkyō*. Vol. 50. Tokyo: Daizō shuppan.

Jiacai. 1932–34. *Jingtu lunji*. In *Taishō shinshū daizōkyō*. Vol. 47. Tokyo: Daizō shuppan.

Jinshu. 1974. Beijing: Zhonghua shuju.

Kamata Shigeo. 1975. *Shūmitsu kyōgaku no shisō shi teki kenkyū*. Tokyo: Tokyo Daigaku shuppansha.

Kimura Eiichi. 1962. Lu-shan in the History of Medieval Chinese Thought. In *Eon Kenkyū*. Kyoto: Kyoto University, Research Institute for Humanistic Studies.

Li Bai. 1977. *Bie Donglin si seng*. In *Li Taibai quanji*. Beijing: Xinhua shudian.

Li Chongyuan. n.d. *Lianshe tu ji*. In *Jiangcun shuhua xiaoxia lu*, Gao Shiqi (preface 1693). Baoyitang repr.

Li Tiaoyuan. 1992. *Quan Wudai shi*. Repr. Sichuan: Xinhua chubanshe.

Liu Zongyuan. 1964. Song Wenchang shangren deng Wutai zhu you Hesuo xu. In *Liu Hedong ji*. Beijing: Zhonghua shuju.

Mazu Daoyi Chanshi yulu. 1995. Xuzangjing, vol. 119. Taipei: Xinwenfeng chubanshe.

Nanshi. 1979. Taipei: Dingwen shuju.

Nogami Shunjō. 1962. Hui-yuan and Later Chinese Buddhist Salvationism. In *Eon Kenkyū*. Kyoto: Kyoto University, Research Institute for Humanistic Studies.

Pan, An-yi. 1997. Li Gonglin's Buddhist Faith and His *Lotus Society Picture*: An Iconographic Diagram of the Bodhisattva Path. PhD diss., University of Kansas.

Puji. 1984. *Wudeng Huiyuan* (1252, Su Yuanlei collated edition). Repr. Beijing: Zhonghua shuju.

Qing Xitai. 1988. *Zhongguo Daojiao shi*. Chengdu: Renmin chubanshe, 1988.

Qisong. 1932–34. Ti Yuangong yingtang bei. In *Tanjin wenji*. *Taishō shinshū daizōkyō*. Vol. 52. Tokyo: Daizō shuppan.

Quan shanggu Sandai Qin Han Sanguo Liuchao wen, Quan Liangwen 1965. Beijing: Zhonghua shuju.

Ren Jiyu, ed. 1981. *Zhongguo fojiao shi*. Beijing: Xinhua shuju.

Sengyou. 1932–34. *Hongming ji*. In *Taishō shinshū daizōkyō*. Vol. 50. Tokyo: Daizō shuppan.

Shenqing. 1932–34. *Beishan lu*. In *Taishō shinshū daizōkyō*. Vol. 52. Tokyo: Daizō shuppan.

Su Shi. 1964. *Sanxiao tu* zan. In *Su Dongpo quanji, xuji*. Taipei: Shijie shuju.

————. 1975. Ti *Sanxiao tu* zan. In *Jiujiang fuzhi*. Taipei: Chengwen chubanshe.

Su Wenzhou. n.d. Liu Zongyuan yu fojiao zhi guanxi. In *Dalu zazhi* 5, no. 55.

Tang Yongtong. 1991. *Han Wei Liang Jin Nanbeichao Fojiao shi*. Repr. Taipei: Commercial Press.

Wang Zhiyuan. 1992. *Zhongguo Chanzong sixiang licheng*. Beijing: Jinri Zhongguo chubanshe.

Wu Yun. 1983a. *Jianji xiansheng Lujun bei*. In *Quan Tangwen*. Beijing: Zhonghua shuju.

————. 1983b. *Si huaiquan fu*. In *Quan Tangwen*. Beijing: Zhonghua shuju.

Xu Zhen'e. 1984. *Shishuo xinyu jiaojian*. Beijing: Zhonghua chubanshe.

Xuanni. 1932–34. *Zhenzheng lun*. In *Taishō shinshū daizōkyō*. Vol. 52. Tokyo: Daizō shuppan.

Yan Yu. 1983. *Canglang shihua*. *Siku quanshu* edition, vol. 419. Beijing: Beijing Tushuguan chubanshe.

Yancong. 1932–34. *Tang hufa shamen Falin biezhuan*. In *Taishō shinshū daizōkyō*. Vol. 50. Tokyo: Daizō shuppan.

Yuanming zhiqu tezhan tulu. 1988. Taipei: National Palace Museum.

Zanning. 1932–34a. *Da Song gaoseng shilue*. In *Taishō shinshū daizōkyō*. Vol. 50. Tokyo: Daizō shuppan.

———. 1932–34b. *Song gaoseng zhuan*. In *Taishō shinshū daizōkyō*. Vol. 50. Tokyo: Daizō shuppan.

Zhipan. 1932–34. *Fozu tongji*. In *Taishō shinshū daizōkyō*. Vol. 2035. Tokyo: Daizō shuppan.

Zongmi. 1932–34. *Foshuo Yulanpen jingshu*. In *Taishō shinshū daizōkyō*. Vol. 39. Tokyo: Daizō shuppan.

A Landscape Painting and Its Literary Sources: Taigu Yimin's *Traveling Among Streams and Mountains*

JANET LOUISE CARPENTER

The handscroll *Traveling Among Streams and Mountains* (*Jiangshan xinglü tu*; fig. 1, fig. 1a–e) signed Taigu Yimin and bearing the seal "Donggao," in the Nelson-Atkins Museum of Art, is generally acknowledged to have been painted in northern China in the first half of the thirteenth century, during the Jin dynasty (1115–1234) or the transition period between the Jin and the Yuan (1272–1368) dynasty.[1] The artist's sobriquet Taigu Yimin (which may be translated as "a leftover subject from antiquity") is linked with literati values of the Northern Song dynasty (960–1127) and with the early fifth-century poet Tao Qian (365–427), who became the model practitioner of reclusion for scholar-officials of the Northern Song and later periods. Moreover, the text of the artist's seal, "Donggao" (Eastern Bank or East Hill), appears in a significant passage in Tao Qian's poem *Guiqulai ci* ("Returning Home").[2]

The investigation of the subject of a painting is essential to an understanding of the work and its context. Recent studies have focused on various aspects of content, aside from religious iconography.[3] These include studies on court painting as propaganda, the political iconography of literati painting, and the illustration of traditional literary themes. These inquiries, which have elucidated the meaning and significance of specific subjects of individual works and groups of paintings, underlie the present investigation of Taigu Yimin's *Traveling Among Streams and Mountains*. In the following sections we will examine the subject of the painting in light of the artist's sobriquet and identify issues of subject and content as defined by the evidence of the painting itself as well as sources in the visual and literary arts. The discussion will focus on what the artist is describing in the painting and how the ideas discerned in the painting are related to those in other pictorial and literary works of the time.

The *Xuanhe huapu* (Catalogue of the Imperial Painting Collection During the Xuanhe Era; preface dated 1120), the official catalogue of the collection of the Northern Song emperor Huizong (r. 1102–25), lists nine categories of painting according to general subject matter.[4] This text is useful in understanding the importance of subject in Chinese painting, especially

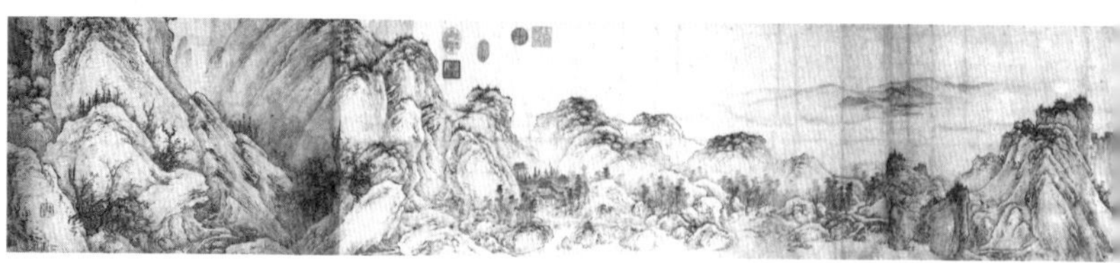

FIGURE 1
Taigu Yimin, *Traveling Among Streams and Mountains*, first half of the 13th century. Handscroll, ink on paper, 15⅛ × 164½ in. (38.4 × 418 cm). The Nelson-Atkins Museum of Art, Kansas City, Missouri (Purchase: the Kenneth A. and Helen F. Spencer Foundation Acquisition Fund)

during the Song period. Beyond that general categorization, however, the particular images depicted within each genre have a specific meaning, and reflect the artist's motives, concerns, and philosophy. In some instances, these concerns are indicated in an artist's inscription and can be correlated with the accompanying visual image.[5] In the case of the Nelson-Atkins scroll *Traveling Among Streams and Mountains*, which bears no inscription by the artist, we must instead rely solely on the visual image to decipher the meaning and significance of the work.

THE ARRANGEMENT OF PICTORIAL ELEMENTS

The essential structure of *Traveling Among Streams and Mountains* is defined by the arrangement of architecture, human figures, and animals—the built environment. The kinds of elements the artist chose to portray are, in turn, critical to the meaning of the painting. An analysis of the arrangement of pictorial elements in the scroll reveals an underlying theme, which, as we shall see, signifies a more complex meaning. In the opening section of the painting (fig. 1a), we are introduced quite abruptly into a landscape that contains many signs of human habitation. At the lower right stand three buildings, one of which, probably a mill, houses a water wheel. Walking away from these buildings, toward the right, is a lone figure with a pack. A grove of tall trees growing from a foreground hill draws the viewer's eye leftward to a small village comprising several groups of buildings with plastered walls and thatch roofs.[6] Above one building flies a flag, perhaps the sign of a wine shop or hostelry. The detailed depiction of figures and beasts of burden reveals the artist's interest in evoking everyday life. In the foreground building, three figures are engaged in conversation, while one figure seems to be pointing out directions to another. Others converse around a table in the adjacent building. A mule driver is shown leaving the village, while another figure, astride a donkey and accompanied by two servants, approaches from the left.

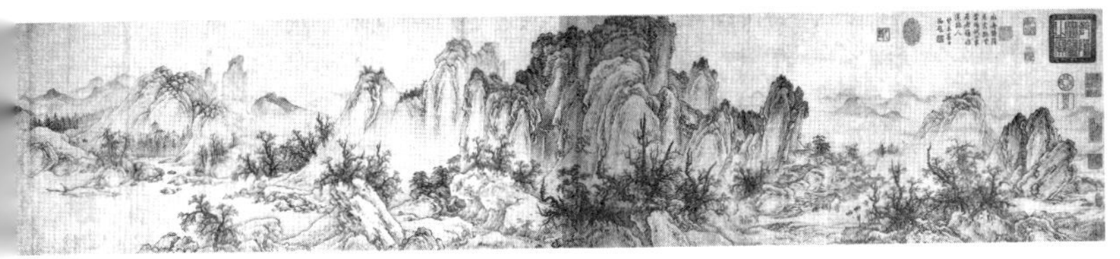

The structures the viewer next encounters, located on the far side of the mountain at the foot of a rocky crag (fig. 1b), are different from the thatched cottages and places of business in the preceding village. Perhaps part of a shrine or villa, this cluster of buildings, which includes a tall structure with a roofed porch, is perched over a misty void and appears inaccessible. Below these buildings, in the foreground, a lone traveler, hunched over and walking with a staff, emerges from behind rocks. Further to the left, enshrouded in mist and sheltered by a grove, is another group of even larger buildings.[7] Two boats, one with a lone fisherman, ply the waters below.

The next segment of the scroll is dominated by a large structure spanning a wide body of water (fig. 1c). This unusual structure is known as a *shuiguan*, a strategic construction designed to control navigation in times of war.[8] Boats could pass beneath its central arch, but the passageway could be closed by lowering a gate. Under ordinary circumstances, this type of structure served to prevent flooding of low-lying areas or to provide a sheltered harbor by creating a protected bay. The architectural style of the structure depicted here, which is probably an accurate ren-

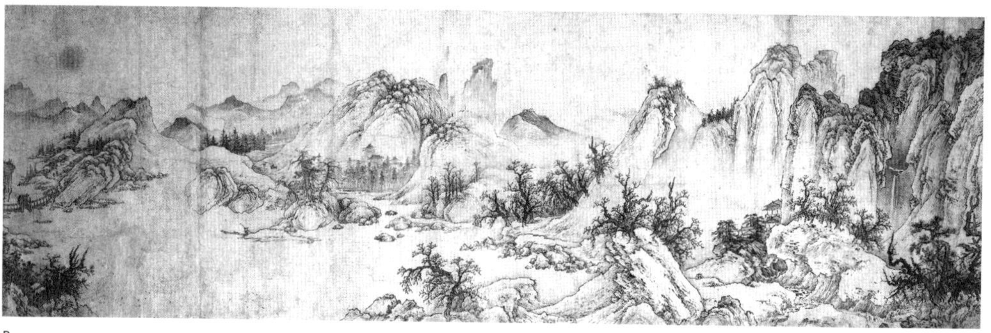

B

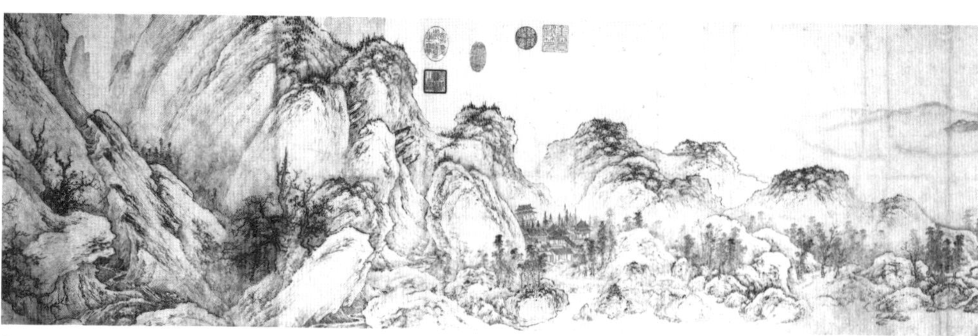

D

dering of an actual *shuiguan*,[9] may date to the Song dynasty or possibly the early or mid-Yuan period. The roofed pavilion above the central arch resembles structures sometimes found atop walls on mountain passes or on city gates. Beyond the *shuiguan* is a fishing village with several boats tied up at the shore. In the foreground, on the near shore, two roofs emerge through foliage; further to the left, two figures travel along a hilly path.

In the final section of the scroll is a clearly rendered image of a villa (fig. 1d). The villa's gate faces the viewer, so that one lateral precinct is hidden and only one of what would normally be a pair of two-storied towers is visible. The main hall contains what appears to be an altar. Behind the hall is the tallest structure in the complex; to the right of that building, and mostly hidden from view, is a thatched hut. At the very end of the scroll, nestled deep in the mountains, is a small thatched pavilion (fig. 1e). Below and to the right of that modest retreat lies another structure, as yet unidentified.

While this final scene might at first seem rather undramatic, the artist has, in fact, been building up to this image of a rustic retreat from the beginning of the scroll. He takes the viewer on a spiritual journey, from

FIGURE 1A–D
Taigu Yimin, *Traveling Among Streams and Mountains*, first half of the 13th century. Details

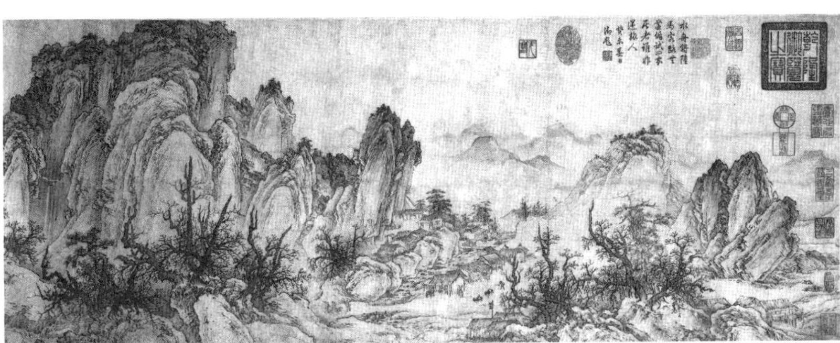

A

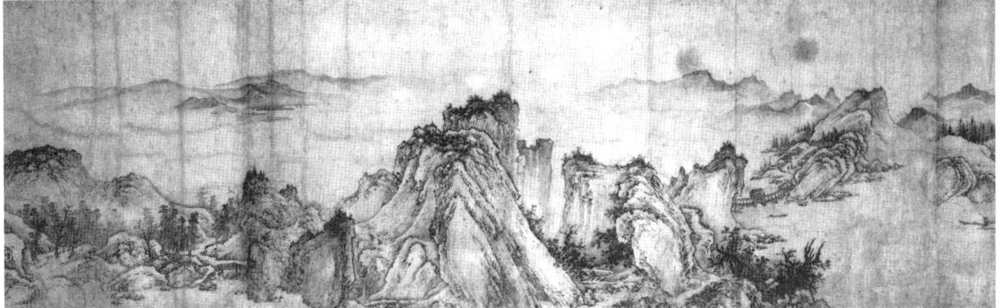

C

idyllic views of the labor and leisure of rural life (depicted in the villages), to the tranquil life of study and contemplation (represented by the country villas), and finally to the ultimate place of repose, a symbol of the ideal of reclusion (the thatched pavilion). The arrangement of the picture elements, in which scenes of human habitation alternate with depictions of natural scenery, reveals the concerns of the artist. The painting represents a continuation of the Northern Song scholarly tradition articulated by the preeminent scholar-official artist Su Shi (1037–1101) and his circle, in which nature was informed by humanistic concerns and ideas. These ideas are presented in the painting on a superficial level in the architecture and figures, which are a subtle but prominent feature of the work. The artist's personal interests are expressed on a deeper level in the painting's narrative themes. The viewer moves through village scenes into a landscape punctuated by travelers, villas, and waterways to a modest dwelling in the mountains. This peaceful retreat is the focal point of the painting, and, by implication, the goal of the traveler.

INNOVATIONS IN COMPOSITION

The specific arrangement of pictorial elements in Taigu Yimin's *Traveling Among Streams and Mountains* is unusual in the history of Chinese painting prior to the Yuan dynasty. This becomes clear when we compare the work with other twelfth- and thirteenth-century landscape handscrolls: *Pavilions by Rivers and Mountains* (*Jiangshan louguan tu*), in the Osaka Municipal Art Museum;[10] *Streams and Mountains Without End* (*Xishan wujin tu*), in The Cleveland Museum of Art;[11] *Dream Journey Through the Xiao and Xiang Rivers* (*Xiao Xiang woyou tu*), in the Tokyo National Museum;[12] *Ten Thousand Li of Rivers and Mountains* (*Jiangshan wanli tu*),

FIGURE 1E
Taigu Yimin, *Traveling Among Streams and Mountains*, first half of the 13th century. Detail

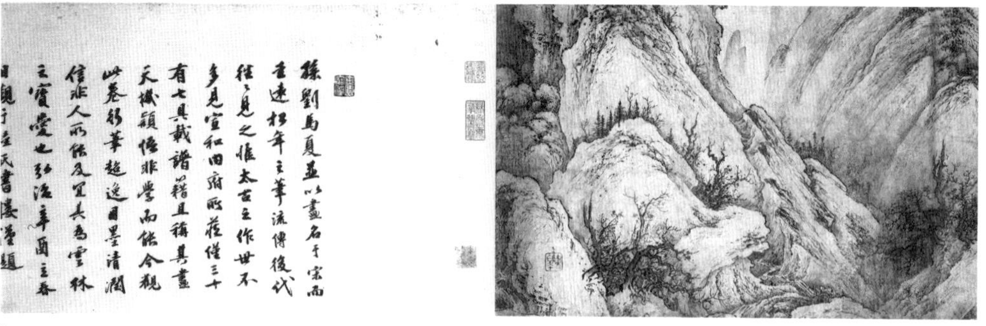

E

by Zhao Fu (active 1131–62), in the Palace Museum, Beijing;[13] and *Streams and Mountains, Pure and Remote* (*Xishan qingyuan tu*), by Xia Gui (active ca. 1195–1230), in the National Palace Museum, Taipei.[14]

The Osaka landscape, *Pavilions by Rivers and Mountains*, is undoubtedly the earliest of several handscrolls that are comparable in organization to Taigu Yimin's *Traveling Among Streams and Mountains*. Arrayed along its length from right to left are villas, boats at anchor, large and small pavilions, a temple, mountain dwellings, and travelers. In contrast to those depicted in the Nelson-Atkins scroll, all the buildings seem to be carefully arranged as part of a single community or vignette, with little sense of the passage of time or movement. Even allowing for its relative brevity, the work is the product of an entirely different compositional concept from that of the Taigu Yimin painting.

Streams and Mountains Without End, in the Cleveland Museum, is a similarly focused composition. At the center of the painting a group of gentlemen stand by a thatched pavilion on the shore, awaiting the arrival of another group shown approaching in a skiff. Directly across the inlet is another pavilion, the mirror image of that on the opposite shore. While there are other scenes of human habitation—dwellings that stand in clearings or beside a path, and a temple that rises above a misty valley—the painting focuses on the architecture and figures at the center.

In the Tokyo National Museum's *Dream Journey Through the Xiao and Xiang Rivers*, originally ascribed to Li Gonglin (ca. 1041–1106), architecture and figures are subordinated to nature. The scroll presents a vast watery landscape occupied by single houses, villages, travelers, and a few boats. The figures, though clearly depicted, are minute, emphasizing the vastness of the surrounding landscape.

In his *Ten Thousand Li of Rivers and Mountains*, Zhao Fu organized the composition by interspersing mountains and water. The same kinds of man-made elements found in the Taigu Yimin scroll are encountered here. Narrative details also interest the artist: travelers, visitors, and fishermen all take their place in the composition and the fabric of rural life. These elements, however, are not presented in the same sequence as Taigu Yimin's painting, nor is there a sense of continuity among them. Rather, they are conceived as individual vignettes, isolated by landscape elements. The composition culminates in a passage depicting a temple perched on a rocky cliff above crashing waves. This ending is as visually dramatic as that of the Taigu Yimin scroll, but in the Taigu Yimin painting the element of drama is expressed as much by the brushwork as by the change in scale of the landscape forms.

Xia Gui's *Streams and Mountains, Pure and Remote* also lacks the sequential treatment of pictorial elements that characterizes the Taigu Yimin scroll. Temples, fishing villages, a walled city, villas, and pavilions are interspersed randomly throughout the painting. Toward the end of the extant portion of the painting[15] is a thatch-roof hut tucked away in the mountains. This small structure resembles that depicted in *Traveling Among Streams and Mountains*, but its position and significance are not similar enough to warrant comparison beyond its isolation within the overall landscape. While the landscape forms and the brushwork in the Xia Gui scroll show many similarities with those of the Taigu Yimin, the order of the pictorial elements signifies no more than a simple rural landscape setting.

The five paintings discussed above fall into one of two groups based on the artists' treatment of the built environment. The specific issues that concern us here are: the focus of the composition, either on a single aspect of the subject or on multiple aspects; the amount of detail and the artist's attention to detail; the separation or integration of motifs; and the artist's concern with universality (the dissociation from references to a specific place and time). The Osaka, Cleveland, and Tokyo paintings, three of the earliest of these works, belong to the first group. The subject centers on one major cluster of buildings and/or figures in the middle of the composition; the built environment is not treated in great detail; and the figures are subordinate to the surrounding landscape. The second group is represented by the Zhao Fu and Xia Gui paintings. The Taigu Yimin scroll also fits within this group. In each of these works, the artist focuses on multiple aspects of the subject. Architectural and figural elements are arrayed along the entire length of the scroll, and no one group takes precedence over the others. The figures are described in detail and treated with empathy; they are not subordinate to nature, as in the first type, but instead take their place in the spaces created by the landscape.

THE NARRATIVE LANDSCAPE

The multiple-focus composition seen in the Zhao Fu and Xia Gui handscrolls is taken one step further in Taigu Yimin's *Traveling Among Streams and Mountains*. The artist organizes the architectural and figural elements in a sequence that culminates at the end of the scroll in close-up mountains that fill the picture plane.[16] These architectural and genre elements seem to be more than mere formal innovations, particularly when examined in light of the references to Tao Qian in Taigu Yimin's signature and seal.[17] The sequence in which these elements are presented resembles that in roughly contemporaneous illustrations of Tao's poem "Returning Home" (*Guiqulai ci*), such as the long handscroll *Tao Yuanming's Homecoming Ode* (*Guizhuang tu*) by the Yuan court painter He Cheng (1224–after 1315), in the Jilin Provincial Museum.[18] Like the Taigu Yimin scroll, He Cheng's painting is characterized by a succession of intimate vignettes and village scenes ending in a passage that serves as the focus of the entire painting: the depiction of a place of retreat from worldly affairs. In their sympathetic and detailed portrayal of human activities, both artists convey an interest in extolling the virtues and pleasures of rural life.

The Taigu Yimin painting, which at first glance seems unrelated to Tao Qian's poem, differs from the He Cheng scroll in its lack of a continuous narrative and recurring central figure and in the depiction of the lone thatched hut, which is less literal. Rather, the viewer is led progressively through a physical environment that echoes a spiritual path. The lack of a specific reference to an individual or a circumstance renders the ideas in the Taigu Yimin scroll universal. These non-literal references to Tao Qian's poem are consistent with the ideals of the artist as represented by his sobriquets.[19]

This interpretation of the Taigu Yimin composition is consistent with the importance that was attached to the eremitic ideal, and its association with Tao Qian, during the Jin dynasty. References to Tao Qian appear throughout the poetry of Yuan Haowen (1190–1257), the most illustrious admirer and proponent of Tao Qian's poetry and his way of life in the Jin period.[20] The connection of *Traveling Among Streams and Mountains* with the Tao Qian tradition is further reinforced by the dozen or so poems on paintings inspired by Tao's poetry that are included in Yuan Haowen's collection of Jin dynasty poetry, the *Zhongzhou ji* (Anthology of the Central Land).[21]

As mentioned above, the significance of Taigu Yimin's composition lies in the function of the landscape as narrative. Shifts among near, middle, and far distance alternate dramatically in a zigzag pattern through space. The landscape forms stretch the limits of the space allotted them, particularly at the end where the middle and background are completely obscured in the final upward sweep of the mountains. The organization of the landscape elements serves to emphasize the singularity of the architecture and figures occupying the space. Each cluster of buildings and each traveler (whether alone or in a group) occupy a distinct place in the composition. Each group is separated from the others by a landscape of great solitude, which serves to isolate and emphasize the human and architectural elements in the painting. Through variations on motifs, such as the spiky dry trees and the flinty foreground rocks, the landscape leads us along the route the artist has planned. The direction of movement is emphasized by the rocks that jut out at angles to the right or left. Many of these jutting rocks oppose each other, momentarily arresting the viewer's attention. While it may be said that all handscrolls, at least from the standpoint of the viewer when unrolling the scroll, are to a certain extent narrative in form, this work possesses greater narrative force than many landscape handscrolls of the period.[22]

THE DEVELOPMENT OF SUBJECT MATTER IN THE SCHOLARLY TRADITION

In his *Hualun* (Discussions on Painting), the Yuan dynasty critic Tang Hou listed the subjects that were considered most appropriate for scholars' painting in Yuan times:

> Landscapes, ink bamboos, blossoming plums and orchids, leafless trees and strange rocks, ink flowers and birds, etc., the playing with brush and ink in which men of high character and superior scholars have given form to inspiration and sketched ideas.[23]

The development of a scholarly style for landscape painting began during the Northern Song period, in the writings of Su Shi, Mi Fu (1052–1107), and other critics.[24] Landscape became invested with certain concepts, which were often associated with the styles of particular artists. Certain landscape styles, such as those of Wang Wei (700–761), Li Cheng (919–967), Dong Yuan (active 930s–60s), and Mi Fu,[25] were preferred by the literati. The qualities of naturalness, blandness, and lofty antiquity, for example, were associated with the landscape style of Dong Yuan.[26] In the Jin period, these ideas were fused with an appreciation of the style of Li Cheng, all in the pursuit of a new type of landscape painting. It was in the Jin period that the thought of the Northern Song literati, most notably the political and cultural views of Su Shi, was put into practice in the painting of certain genres and subjects, especially landscape.[27]

The influence of the Northern Song literati in painting is reflected in the writings of later theorists such as Tang Hou. In his *Discussions on Painting*, Tang praised the scholar-artists Wang Tingyun (1151–1202) and Zhao Mengfu (1254–1322) as the best painters since the Northern Song period:

> Zhao Mengfu of this [Yuan] dynasty and Wang Tingyun of the Jin are unmatched by anyone during the two hundred years after the Song crossed the river to the south.[28]

Tang Hou recognized this north-south dichotomy as significant. Although a scholarly landscape style was developed during the Southern Song period, that style was based on models different from those followed in the north under the Jin. Literati art of the Southern Song consisted mainly of such subjects as bamboo, orchid, and plum, which were developed in and associated with court painting.[29] This interest in subjects other than landscape can be found in the art of three major Southern Song *yimin* (leftover subject) painters: Zheng Sixiao (1239–1316), Gong Kai (1222–1307), and, to a lesser extent, Qian Xuan (ca. 1235–before 1307). Landscape as a literati subject, which was developed almost exclusively in the north under the Jin, fully matured during the Yuan period under the influence of the Jin painting tradition.

The development of landscape as a genre embodying literati concepts differed from that of bamboo, orchid, and plum. Unlike those subjects, landscape did not have an intrinsic symbolic content. The literati element in landscape painting was instead expressed through references to the styles of earlier masters or literary subjects and through the use of iconographic elements—for example, the recluse-fisherman or the scholar's retreat—that embodied certain ideas, such as eremitism, which had matured in literature.

Traveling Among Streams and Mountains is an early example, perhaps the prototype, of this kind of landscape painting. While it does not ostensibly represent a specific literary subject, the painting nonetheless has a scholarly theme—the ideal of a humble retreat in the mountains where one can find physical and emotional release from the cares of the everyday world.[30] For this reason, the scroll has an intimacy lacking in earlier landscape handscrolls, in which, even when there are figures, the focus is on nature's grandeur rather than the humans occupying it. While it may be argued that it is also preoccupied with the intimate view, Southern Song painting relies more on atmospheric effects and genre details to achieve this effect. *Traveling Among Streams and Mountains* is a more personal work. The references to eremitism, both in the painting and in the artist's signature and seal, identify the theme as more than a simple depiction of a pastoral scene. The artist uses the handscroll format to develop a theme leading up to its climactic conclusion in the final section, not simply to portray natural and man-made elements in an additive manner. Formal elements, such as the twisted, sharp-branched trees and the telescoping mountains that obscure the horizon, propel us toward the end of the painting through their repetition and shear force.

QUOTATIONS FROM THE VISUAL PAST

In *Traveling Among Streams and Mountains*, Taigu Yimin has consciously quoted the styles of past masters. He derives his own style from a variety of sources, and this borrowing of styles is integral to the subject and content of the painting. Past styles are referred to selectively rather than used wholesale as in earlier paintings. For example, mountains in the brush manner of Juran (active ca. 960–95) surround a group of upright rocks near a spit of land that recalls the Guo Xi (ca. 1000–ca. 1090) manner (fig. 1b). In such passages, the different styles are combined, but not integrated, as seen, for instance, in the work of the later artist Zhao Mengfu. By combining and integrating ancient styles, painters used the art of the past as a source of inspiration for their own creativity.

The so-called archaism practiced by later Northern Song masters, such as Li Gonglin, Wang Shen (ca. 1048–after 1104), Mi Fu, Zhao Lingrang (active ca. 1080–1100), Li Tang (ca. 1070s–1150s), Wang Ximeng (1096–1119), Zhao Boju (ca. 1120–1162), and Qiao Zhongchang (active first half of the 12th century), is not "archaism" in the strict sense of the term as it came to be applied to Yuan painting. Rather, it is simply a reference to and use of a past style in a particular work. The beginning of true archaism — the integration of various styles of the past with reference to their specific meaning —took place in the Jin period as a development of the ideas of Su Shi. Jin artists were aware of past traditions in landscape painting, as can be gathered from their writings and paintings, such as Li Shan's (active early 13th century) *Wind and Snow in the Fir-Pines* and Wu Yuanzhi's (active late 12th–early 13th century) *Red Cliff*, which reveal a continuation and evolution of the late Northern Song monumental landscape style.[31] In quoting from previous styles and combining those styles in a new way, Taigu Yimin goes beyond simple remembrance to create a painting that is a purposeful homage to the past. The history of Chinese art plays a prominent role in the painting, which in its brushwork, composition, and individual pictorial elements is replete with quotations from the work of past masters, including Fan Kuan (active ca. 960–1030), Juran, Yan Wengui (active ca. 970–1030), Xu Daoning (ca. 1000–after 1066), and Guo Xi.[32]

THEMATIC PRECEDENTS IN PAINTING

There are two specific precedents for the subject and thematic elements in *Traveling Among Streams and Mountains*: Wang Wei's (700–761) *Wangchuan Villa* (*Wangchuan tu*), which had long captured the imagination of scholars in the north,[33] and Li Gonglin's *Dwelling in the Longmian Mountains* (*Shanzhuang tu*), a work inspired by Wang Wei's composition. There is evidence that the paintings of Li Gonglin were known in the north in the Jin period[34] and that the study of his works led to the development of a literati landscape style that was different from that of the Mi-family style in the south.[35] The subject and idea of Wang Wei's famous depiction of his garden retreat, *Wangchuan Villa*, were known through literature and tradition.[36] A good example of a work that refers specifically to ideas associated with Wang Wei is *Dream Journey to Mount Xizhou* (*Jiashan guimeng tu juan*), a now-lost painting done by Li Yu for Yuan Haowen, with colophons by various friends of Yuan, including Yang Yunyi (1170–1228), Zhao Yuan, and Zhao Bingwen.[37] While we can only deduce the painting's general composition from the recorded colophons, the relationship of the painting to the Wang Wei tradition is clear. In the painting, which can be dated to 1221 based on Yuan Haowen's series of poems,[38] Li Yu evokes Yuan Haowen's native home of Xinxian, Shansi Province, which he had been forced to flee six years earlier, in 1215, following the surrender of Xinxian to the Mongols.[39]

The topographical and narrative elements traditionally associated with Wang Wei's *Wangchuan Villa*, which represents in handscroll format a country estate and the surrounding landscape, are present in Taigu Yimin's *Traveling Among Streams and Mountains*. A comparison of the painting with one of the many rubbings of the 1617 stone engraving based on a copy of *Wangchuan Villa* attributed to the tenth-century artist Guo

Zhongshu reveals several similarities in composition, spatial organization, and thematic elements. Although the space is more integrated in the Taigu Yimin painting, the arrangement of architectural elements, such as buildings and bridges, in space cells carved out of the area between foreground rocks and background mountains reflects that of the earlier composition.

THEMATIC PRECEDENTS IN POETRY AND PROSE

Another important precedent for the subject of *Traveling Among Streams and Mountains* is derived from poetry. In Jin dynasty poetry, certain themes, particularly those drawn from the poet's own everyday experiences and surroundings, took precedence over poetic expression. Although they emphasized subjects that were previously considered mundane, Jin poets drew heavily on past Chinese poetic traditions as models for their own work.[40]

The same emphasis on theme occurred in Jin painting, as evidenced by the predominance of literary subjects in recorded colophons. Some ten percent of Yuan Haowen's own collected poems consist of colophons on paintings of the Tang, Five Dynasties, Northern Song, and Jin.[41] Moreover, in his collection of Jin dynasty poetry, *Zhongzhou ji*, he included more than ninety poems on painting.[42] In Zhao Bingwen's collected works, *Fushui wenji*, we find a similar number of such poems. These poems include information on painting themes; they also provide us with much information about the artistic milieu of the time and the importance of painting to the litterateurs of the period.

Evidence points to a lively exchange about the arts among the cultural elite during the Jin period.[43] There existed a large network of literati for whom the appreciation of paintings played an important role.[44] Literature, particularly poetry, both inspired and was inspired by paintings, continuing a trend that began in the Northern Song period. In our examination of the Taigu Yimin scroll, it is important to consider this connection between literature and painting and the literary sources that painters drew upon for their subjects.

According to the titles of paintings recorded in literary sources, the three most popular subjects of paintings during the twelfth and early thirteenth centuries were Su Shi's *Chibi fu* ("The Red Cliff") and Tao Qian's *Taoyuan ji* ("Peach Blossom Spring") and *Guiqulai ci* ("Returning Home"). The popularity of such literary subjects is seen, for example, in Wu Yuanzhi's painting of the Red Cliff and the painting of the Peach Blossom Spring recorded in a colophon by Yuan Haowen.[45] The favor accorded these literary subjects seems to have reached its peak during the twelfth and thirteenth centuries, concurrent with the growing interest in "Su studies," which, following the academic tradition of Su Shi, emphasized training in literature,[46] and with the concomitant ascent in the popularity of Tao Qian.

The poetry of Tao Qian acquired new significance in the Jin dynasty through the efforts of Yuan Haowen and his predecessors, as part of the general trend in Su studies.[47] There was little parallel interest in Su Shi in the south during the corresponding Southern Song period, and the models for Southern Song eremites were those other than Tao Qian. The ideas and the styles of Su Shi and Huang Tingjian (1045–1105) were rejected in favor of the styles of the Tang period, at least in literature.[48] Unlike the south, where scholarly influence was on the wane, in the north the ideas of scholar-officials held sway.[49] The power invested in the world of ideas afforded a great deal of freedom from strictly political concerns. During the Jin, the literati participated in a wide range of cultural activities, rich in both literary and artistic expression. However, in contrast to the Southern Song, Confucian philosophical studies were rather unsophisticated, and Jin learning was independent of the flowering of Neo-Confucian thought in the south.[50]

The importance attached to Tao Qian in the north under the Jin may also have had political overtones, considering the popularity of certain overtly eremitic subjects in Tao's oeuvre, such as "Peach Blossom Spring" and "Returning Home." Evidence of this can be found in Jin period literature, in which references to and even suggestions of an obsession with Tao Qian and Su studies are abundant. Perhaps the poetry of Tao Qian attracted the attention and admiration of Jin scholar-officials because of their own concern with eremitism and nature. Another factor contributing to the popularity of the literary works by Su Shi and Tao Qian discussed here is that the ideas expressed in these works lent themselves to translation into pictorial language. It may also reflect a growing concern with the expression of ideas in painting, rather than simply the depiction of grand landscape. The Jin interest in Northern Song culture, especially the ideas of Su Shi and the culture of the recluse as embodied in the person of Tao Qian, which also came to be associated with the concept of antiquity in art, provided an ideal background for the creation of Taigu Yimin's *Traveling Among Streams and Mountains.*

TRAVELING AMONG STREAMS AND MOUNTAINS AND EARLY VERSIONS OF "RETURNING HOME"

The signature, Taigu Yimin, and the seal, reading "Donggao" (Eastern Bank or East Hill), on *Traveling Among Streams and Mountains* both refer directly to Tao Qian. The seal (probably the artist's *zi*, or courtesy name) is derived from the last stanza of Tao's poem "Returning Home."[51] It is logical, therefore, to look for other references to Tao Qian in the painting. These allusions, while subtle, become clear when we turn to various early versions of "Returning Home."

Perhaps the earliest extant pictorial rendition of the poem is the handscroll *Tao Yuanming Returning to Seclusion*, in the Freer Gallery of Art, a work formerly attributed to Li Gonglin.[52] It is a fairly literal rendering of the poem, and probably unrelated to Li Gonglin.[53] A handscroll in the National Palace Museum, Taipei, has nearly the same composition; it may be related to the Li Gonglin tradition, though it is probably later than the Freer painting.[54] Two other early renditions of the subject are the handscrolls *Returning Home* (*Guiqulai tu*), by Qian Xuan, in The Metropolitan Museum of Art,[55] and *Tao Yuanming's Return to His Village* (*Guiqulai ci tu*), in The Cleveland Museum of Art.[56] In the formation of the rocks and in the brushwork—for example, the hatching and modulated outline of the rocks—the Cleveland painting bears some similarity to the Taigu Yimin scroll. However, in the Cleveland painting the modulated outline is more loosely drawn and the rocks are rendered in alternating tones of light and dark ink, whereas in the Taigu Yimin scroll there is a subtle use of wash and no emphasis on the contrast between light and dark. The Cleveland scroll has been catalogued as a fourteenth-century painting, but it is more likely a late-thirteenth-century relative of Taigu Yimin's *Traveling Among Streams and Mountains*—perhaps the artist's interpretation of common stylistic antecedents.

The most important of the early renditions of "Returning Home" is the previously mentioned work by He Cheng, *Tao Yuanming's Homecoming Ode*, which represents a version of the Li Gonglin legacy in the early Yuan period and is stylistically the most closely related to the Taigu Yimin scroll.[57] He Cheng, a northern artist, was, according to contemporary writers, indebted to Jin painters.[58] He was also considered a follower of Li Gonglin through the Southern Song monk Fanlong, the best known Li follower. Of the extant paintings of "Returning Home" dating from the pre-

Ming period, He Cheng's handscroll may be the closest reflection of the Li Gonglin tradition. It is in the context of that tradition as interpreted in the early Yuan that He Cheng's painting bears the most intriguing stylistic similarities, both in brushwork and motifs, to the Nelson-Atkins scroll.

Although no credible painting of "Returning Home" by him survives, Li Gonglin is intimately associated with the subject. A description of a depiction of the poem by Li is found in the *Xuanhe huapu*:

> In Li Gonglin's illustration of Tao Qian's *Guiqulai* [Returning Home] he did not insist on the fields, gardens, the pine trees and the chrysanthemums, but rather on the enjoyment of the clear flowing water.[59]

In his colophon to the Freer Gallery's *Tao Yuanming Returning to Seclusion*, written in 1110, Li Peng stated:

> Once, in the home of Shan-gu [Huang Tingjian, 1050–1110] I saw a small screen by Li Boshi [Li Gonglin] illustrating the *Guiqulai*. Its touch was light but its flavor subtle, and it is quite similar to this painting.[60]

Li Peng's comments on Li Gonglin's painting agree more with the description in the *Xuanhe huapu* than with the Freer scroll, which seems not to represent the style of Li Gonglin either as a whole or in its individual elements. The description in the *Xuanhe huapu* would seem to have little relationship to extant paintings attributed to Li Gonglin, which are full of genre details. The most reliable evidence of Li's rendering of "Returning Home" as transmitted in the Yuan period is that provided by He Cheng, but the relationship of He's painting to Li Gonglin's style is not direct. A good example of the legacy of Li Gonglin in landscape painting, which seems to accord with the *Xuanhe huapu* passage, is *Illustration to the Second Prose Poem on the Red Cliff* (*Houchibi tu*), by Li's follower Qiao Zhongchang, now in the Nelson-Atkins Museum. In this painting, Qiao interprets Li Gonglin's dry brushwork and simplified composition.[61]

TRAVELING AMONG STREAMS AND MOUNTAINS AND "RETURNING HOME"

In its rendering of motifs that appear in the original literary work, *Traveling Among Streams and Mountains* is related to the aforementioned group of early illustrations of "Returning Home." These motifs are drawn particularly from the last stanza of the poem, from which the artist also derived his style name "Donggao." The painting, a depiction of a literal and spiritual journey to a retreat that evokes Tao Qian's poem, portrays nature in early spring. Some of the trees, particularly those near the water, have newly sprouted leaves; others are still without foliage. The twisted trees with numerous tiny branches in the foreground, found also in He Cheng's painting and in the Cleveland Museum scroll, are probably plum trees or peach trees, both of which recall Tao Qian. The plum, in particular, is associated with Tao's retreat and with hermits' retreats in general. The pines, which are also mentioned in the poem, occur in most pictorial illustrations of the work. The trees in Taigu Yimin's painting, then, serve mainly as iconographical elements, and have meaning with reference to the subject of the painting.

The overhanging rock formations, which also appear in the Freer and Cleveland scrolls as well as the paintings by Qian Xuan and He Cheng, may also serve as iconographical elements. While they probably have a generalized archaic reference, the specific significance of these landscape elements lies in their association with the figure of Tao Qian.

A second group of motifs in *Traveling Among Streams and Mountains* that relate to the poem refer to genre details. For example, at the beginning of the scroll the artist alludes to the commerce of town life. A solitary traveler is seen headed toward the mountains, where there is a retreat and, further on, a modest hut. (These elements also appear in more literal depictions of the subject.) There are other such genre references in the boats that dot the waterway, the solitary fisherman, and the traveler carrying a zither. Indeed, the entire composition is a spiritual narrative, in which the viewer is carried from a bustling town scene across waterways and finally to a thatched hut in the mountains, the pictorial culmination of the composition. There are no extraneous genre details, such as chrysanthemums, farming scenes, and family gatherings, as seen in other paintings of the subject. Instead, the artist focuses solely on the enjoyment of nature. In this way, the painting mirrors the description of Li Gonglin's illustration of "Returning Home" in the *Xuanhe huapu*. Although not a literal depiction of Tao Qian's poem, the work renders in a more poetic and meaningful way the essence of the poem's eremitic theme. The poetic and indirect ways of treating classical themes, observed, for example, in Qian Xuan's rendition of "Returning Home," may have originated in such paintings as *Traveling Among Streams and Mountains*, which reflect ideas derived from

Northern Song depictions of the poem, such as those by Li Gonglin.[62]

Traveling Among Streams and Mountains is organized as a narrative in which present and past are interwoven. Thus, it is in keeping with the rich and varied culture of the Jin dynasty, which sought to preserve and build upon Northern Song culture and thereby forge a connection to it. In the work of more conservative artists, this effort resulted simply in a continuation of Northern Song and Five Dynasties (907–960) styles. Innovative artists like Taigu Yimin, the painter of the Nelson-Atkins *Traveling Among Streams and Mountains*, were able to draw on earlier painting traditions to create new styles and new ideas. Taigu Yimin's notable innovation lies in his transformation of these past styles into a motif that itself becomes a subject of the painting.

NOTES

1. For a partial review of the literature on Jin dynasty painting, see Carpenter 1994.
2. The signature, Taigu Yimin, and the seal, "Donggao," are generally accepted as those of the artist. See Carpenter 1994, 29–31. In Tao Qian's "Returning Home" (*Guiqulai ci*), the fourth line from the end, "Deng Donggao yi shu xiao," refers to Donggao, the literal meaning of which is "marshy field." The word is often translated as Eastern Slope or Eastern Bank. "East" refers to the spring planting season and the hopes for a successful year. Several poems refer to the Eastern Slope, among them "Zati shi," by the Liang dynasty (502–527) poet Jiang Yan, and "Yewang shi," by the early Tang poet Wang Ji, but Tao Qian's poem is unquestionably the best known. The artist's sobriquet Taigu Yimin reflects an eremitic sentiment expressed in Tao's poem.

   A discussion of Tao Qian's dates can be found in Hightower 1970, 3–4, n. 6.
3. For an overview of these studies, see Silbergeld 1987, 867–74.
4. See *Xuanhe huapu* 1120.
5. An example is Huang Gongwang's (1269–1354) inscription on his *Dwelling in the Fuchun Mountains*, dated 1350, in the National Palace Museum, Taipei. See Chang Kuang-pin 1975, pl. 102.
6. It is difficult to ascertain from the style of the vernacular architecture when these types of buildings were constructed; dating the painting from such evidence is, therefore, unreliable. See Fu Xinian 1993, 93–94, for a discussion of the structures in the scroll. For a discussion of architecture in Chinese painting, see Liu Dunzhen 1980.
7. The multistoried construction of these buildings indicates a type of monumental architecture common to palaces and temples. A good diagram of such structures is found in Sickman and Soper 1971, pl. 261(A).
8. See Bian Yongyu 1682, 11:71. Bian mentions this structure in his description of the painting. I have not seen this type of structure in any other Chinese painting.

9. See Liu Dunzhen 1980. A somewhat similar structure is seen in Xiao Yuncong's (1596–1673) woodblock print *Landscape of Taiping*, originally published in Zheng Zhenduo 1648, pl. 1. For a reproduction of the print, see Lee and Ho 1968, 94, fig. 19a.

10. Reproduced in *Osaka shiritsu bijutsukan-zō Chūgoku kaiga* 1975, pl. 19. This scroll, attributed to Yan Wengui (active ca. 970–1030), is dated variously from the early eleventh to the early twelfth century. The layered mountains and the contrasting light mist and dark land masses are similar to the Cleveland Museum's *Streams and Mountains Without End* (see n. 11 below).

11. The painting, dated variously from the late eleventh to the mid-twelfth century, is illustrated in Lee and Fong 1967. See also Fong 1975, pl. 36 and n. 14.

12. Published in *Sō Gen no kaiga* 1962, 92–93. The painting is probably a mid-twelfth-century work. See Loehr 1961, 219–84.

13. For information on Zhao Fu, see Xia Wenyan 1365, *juan* 4.

14. Published in *Gugong minghua sanbaizhong* 1959, pl. 115. The earliest colophon to the painting, by Chen Chuan, is dated 1378. The painting probably dates to the early thirteenth century. See *Gugong shuhua lu* 1964. See also Suzuki Kei 1972.

15. At least one section (that with the signature) of the Xia Gui painting is missing. Compared with two copies, in the Freer Gallery of Art (11.169) and The Metropolitan Museum of Art (14.220.18), some of the beginning sections of the scroll have also been lost. See Suzuki Kei 1972, 417–35.

16. These characteristics of the Taigu Yimin scroll find their fullest expression in later paintings, such as Huang Gongwang's *Dwelling in the Fuchun Mountains* (see n. 5 above). Huang's scroll, like that of Taigu Yimin, ends in a passage that is executed in somewhat looser brushwork. The rendering of a real place and an actual experience poses a veristic idea, which the artist presents in opposition to his individualistic brushwork in the painting. This dichotomy between verism and expression also appears in Taigu Yimin's *Traveling Among Streams and Mountains*, where, for example, the brushwork in the mountains in the last section begins to emerge as an independent force in the work.

17. See n. 2 above.

18. He Cheng's scroll is published in *Yiyuan duoying* 6. There is some controversy about He Cheng's dates. He was possibly active until the early fourteenth century. See Weidner 1982, 112–14. For a discussion of the painting, see ibid., 114–26.

19. See n. 2 above.

20. For a study of Yuan Haowen's literary criticism, see Wixted 1982. For one example that makes clear his regard for Tao Qian, see Mai Chaoshu 1958, 525. For a biography of Yuan Haowen and a discussion of his poetry, see Yoshikawa Kōjirō 1989, 28–42.

21. See Yuan Haowen 2002.

22. Awaiting further study is the similarity of certain compositional elements in *Traveling Among Streams and Mountains* to those of Fanlong's (active first half of the 12th century) *Sixteen Luohan*, in the Freer Gallery. The latter scroll culminates in a close-up view of grottoes beside a stream, which also serve as a retreat for a meditating figure. It is possible that, in addition to the eremitic ideal, the artist of *Traveling Among Streams and Mountains* may have had in mind the Buddhist concept of retreat embodied

in *Sixteen Luohan* and other such works. Fanlong is mentioned in Xia Wenyan 1365, *juan* 4. The Fanlong scroll is illustrated in Lawton 1973, pl. 20.

23. See Tang Hou 1986b, 4a, and translation in Bush 1971, 97.

24. See, for example, Mi Fu 1986.

25. See Tang Hou 1986b. See also Tang Hou 1986a.

26. For comments on the relationship of these ideas to the archaizing tendencies of Song literati, see Bush 1971, 72–73.

27. For a discussion of Su studies in the Jin period, see Yoshikawa Kōjirō 1989, 46–47.

28. Tang Hou 1986b, 4a.

29. See Malenfer 1990.

30. This ideal follows the tradition of Li Gonglin's *Mountain Villa* (*Shanzhuang tu*). See Harrist 1989 and 1998.

31. The collected poems in Yuan Haowen's *Zhongzhou ji* shed some light on which paintings from the past were extant during the Jin and early Yuan periods, and which were popular and therefore available as models for painters. For an illustration of the Li Shan painting, now in the Freer Gallery of Art, see Fong 1992, p. 189, fig. 80. The Wu Yuanzhi painting is in the National Palace Museum, Taipei.

32. The structure and brushwork of *Traveling Among Streams and Mountains* indicate that the artist was familiar with the works of Five Dynasties and Northern Song landscapists. For example, the hatching along the rock edges can be seen in the art of Yan Wengui, particularly in *Pavilions by Rivers and Mountains*, a work attributed to him (see n. 10, above). The double- and triple-pronged mountains may also derive from Yan's style, as seen in the Metropolitan Museum's *Summer Mountains*, attributed to Yan's follower, Qu Ding (Fong 1975, pl. 13). The tilting foreground rock topped by a gnarled tree is also seen in *Summer Mountains*. The jagged rock fragments that jut out from the main rock masses are found in the work of the Northern Song master Xu Daoning. An example is *Fishing Boats on an Autumn River*, in the Nelson-Atkins Museum, attributed to Xu (Ho and Lee 1980, pl. 12). These forms probably ultimately derive from Li Cheng; they are seen, for example, in a painting attributed to Li Cheng, *Buddhist Temple in the Hills after Rain*, also in the Nelson-Atkins Museum (Ho and Lee 1980, pl. 10). The treatment of the dry trees with forked tops and spiky branches recalls the painting of Fan Kuan, a follower of Li Cheng, as seen in the copy after Fan Kuan entitled *Winter Landscape* (*Gugong minghua sanbaizhong* 1959, pl. 66) and the seventeenth-century copy after Li Cheng's *Snow Scene* (Fong 1975, pl. 8), both in the National Palace Museum, Taipei.

33. See Harrist 1989 and 1998. The paintings that Zhao Mengfu collected in north China, which included works by Wang Wei, Li Sixun (651–716), Dong Yuan, Sun Zhiwei, Li Cheng, and Wang Shen, provides evidence of the admiration that artists and scholars in the north felt for Wang Wei's work. See Li 1965, 20–21. (Li mentions a landscape by Sun Zhiwei, but there are only two figure paintings by him recorded in Zhao Mengfu's collection.) Zhao's collection is recorded in Zhou Mi 1986, 2:13a–16a. See ibid., 18b–19b, for Zhao's father's collection; see ibid., 19b, for the Southern Song imperial collection, which also contained Tang and Northern Song works.

Upon his return to the south in 1295, Zhao Mengfu brought Wang Wei to prominence. See Li 1965, 36–44. A version of Wang Wei's *Wangchuan Villa*, perhaps authentic, was likely to have been in a collection in North China during the Jin period. See Li 1965, especially p. 40. Wang's *Wangchuan Villa* was associated with northern influence in Zhao's *Autumn Colors on the Que and Hua Mountains* of 1296. See Li 1965, 38; Li states that there was a deep appreciation of Wang Wei in the north.

It is not possible to determine whether Zhao Mengfu saw Taigu Yimin's *Traveling Among Streams and Mountains*, but it is probable, judging from the ideas he brought back from the north, that he saw works similar to it. See Li 1965, 20–21. The paintings that Zhao collected in the north are listed in *Yunyan guoyan lu*, ISTP ed., 87–93.

34. See Mai Chaoshu 1958, 3:17b–18a.

35. For literati developments in the Southern Song, see Bush 1971, 87–111.

36. Paintings by Wang Wei are praised by Yuan Haowen in his poems. See Mai Chaoshu 1958, 4:14b–15a.

37. See Bush 1971, 89–90, and Mai Chaoshu 1958, *fu lu*, 7a–b, 9b, 13a. See also the discussion of the colophons to the Li Yu painting in Suzuki Shūji 1965, 118–122. Li Yu is represented by six poems in the *Zhongzhou ji*; see Yuan Haowen 2002, 5:13b (repr., 253–54). For Zhao Yuan's colophon, see ibid., 271; for Zhao Bingwen's colophon, see ibid., 165; for Yang Yunyi's colophon, see ibid., 219. For Yuan Haowen's poems on the subject of "homecoming," see Mai Chaoshu 1958, 11:23b–24a. See also the discussion in Wu Mei-yü 1976, 52–53. Yuan Haowen's poems on homecoming are translated in Cram 1970, 101–102.

38. See Mai Chaoshu 1958, 4:14b–15a.

39. Yoshikawa Kōjirō 1989, 30–31.

40. The most prominent example is Yuan Haowen. See ibid., 28–42.

41. Mai Chaoshu 1958. See also Wu Mei-yü 1976, 48.

42. Yuan Haowen 2002.

43. See the biography of Ren Xun (*jinshi* 1157), which mentions Ren's collection of paintings and calligraphy, in Yuan Haowen 2002, 2:17b (repr., 87).

44. On this subject, see Bush 1971, 88–91.

45. See Mai Chaoshu 1958, 14:6a–b. Artists such as Wu Yuanzhi were associated with two or three of these subjects. Colophons to paintings on the subject of "The Red Cliff," "Peach Blossom Spring," and "Returning Home" are also recorded in Fang Qi, *He Fen zhulao shi ji*, *juan* 3, and Yuan Haowen 2002, *juan* 2.

46. Yoshikawa Kōjirō 1989, 19.

47. Northern scholars' adoration for Tao Qian was carried over to the Yuan period. For example, see Tu Wei-ming 1982, 248–49, for a discussion of Liu Yin's (1249–1293) eighty poems rhyming with some of Tao's well-known verses. The significance of the subject of Tao Qian's retirement for Yuan Confucian scholars is discussed in Mote 1960, 286–87; Mote translates and comments on Zhao Mengfu's poem on a painting of the "Homecoming." See also Weidner 1982, 225, n. 61.

48. Bush 1971, 91–92.

49. Ibid., 94–97.

50. See Tu Wei-ming 1982, 248–50.

51. See n. 17 above.

52. According to Lawton 1973, 38–40, the painting likely dates from the twelfth century based on the similarity in the style of the calligraphy in the text of the *Guiqulai* and the colophon by Li Peng, dated 1110, although, as Lawton notes, some scholars have suggested that the colophon may not have been originally part of the scroll.

53. See discussions in Lawton 1973 and Weidner 1986, 11.

54. See Weidner 1986, 21, n. 30.

55. Illustrated in Fong 1992, pp. 314–15, pl. 70.

56. The Cleveland scroll was formerly ascribed to Li Tang (interpolated signature). It bears Northern Song imperial seals (spurious) and Yuan seals of Ke Jiusu (genuine?). The painting is published in Barnhart et al. 1977, pl. 53–54, as a possible Jin painting. It is catalogued at the Cleveland Museum (82.152) as a fourteenth-century work, but has also been ascribed to the early Ming period. See Weidner 1986, 22, n. 40. The painting bears a closer relationship to the works of Jin and early Yuan dynasty followers of Li Cheng and Guo Xi.

57. See n. 18 above.

58. See Weidner 1982, 125–27. See also Xue Yongnian 1973, 26–29.

59. Sirén 1956–58, vol. 2, p. 40. Cited in Weidner 1982, 116 and 226, n. 67. See also *Xuanhe huapu* 1120, 7:9.

60. Lawton 1973, 38. Cited in Weidner 1982, 115 and 226, n. 65.

61. See Loehr 1961, 244–45; Cahill 1976, pl. 93, and 1980, 75–76. While doubts have been expressed about the authenticity of this painting, it represents the late Northern Song literati style.

62. See Nelson 1986, 32, for an analysis of Qian Xuan's contribution to the treatment of themes from the poetry of Tao Qian during the Yuan period.

REFERENCES

Barnhart, Richard M., Iriya Yoshitaka, and Nakata Yūjirō, eds. 1977. *Tō Gen, Kyonen* (Dong Yuan, Zhuran). Vol. 2, *Bunjinga suihen*. Tokyo.

Bian Yongyu. 1682. *Shigutang shuhua huikao* (Notes and records on calligraphy and painting). 60 *juan*. Facsimile repr. Taipei: Zhengzhong shuju, 1958.

Bush, Susan. 1971. *The Chinese Literati on Painting: Su Shih (1037–1101) to Tung Ch'i-ch'ang (1555–1636)*. Harvard-Yenching Institute Studies 27. Cambridge: Harvard University Press.

Cahill, James. 1976. *Hills Beyond a River: Chinese Painting of the Yüan Dynasty, 1279–1368*. New York: Weatherhill.

———. 1980. *An Index of Early Chinese Painters and Paintings: T'ang, Sung, and Yüan*. Berkeley: University of California Press.

Carpenter, Janet Louise. 1994. Traveling Among Streams and Mountains and Chin Period Landscape Painting. PhD diss., University of Kansas.

Chang Kuang-pin. 1975. *Yuan sidajia: Huang Gongwang, Wu Zhen, Ni Zan, Wang Meng* (The four great masters of the Yuan: Huang Gongwang, Wu Zhen, Ni Zan, Wang Meng). Taipei: National Palace Museum.

Cram, Richard Anthony. 1970. A Chinese Poet at War: A Study of Yuan Hao-wen up to the Fall of the Chin Dynasty in 1234. Master's thesis, University of Washington.

Fang Qi. n.d. *He Fen zhulao shi ji* (Poetry anthology of elders from the He and Fen Rivers). 8 *juan*. Repr. *Sibu congkan chubian*, vol. 107. Shanghai: Shangwu yinshuguan.

Fong, Wen C. 1975. *Summer Mountains: The Timeless Landcape.* New York: The Metropolitan Museum of Art.

———. 1992. *Beyond Representation: Chinese Painting and Calligraphy 8th–14th Century.* New York: The Metropolitan Museum of Art.

Fu Xinian. 1993. Fan Mei suo jian Zhongguo gudai minghua zhaji, shang (Notes on pre-modern Chinese paintings seen in the United States, Part 1). *Wenwu.*

Gugong minghua sanbaizhong (Three hundred masterpieces of Chinese painting in the National Palace Museum). 1959. Taichung: National Palace Museum.

Gugong shuhua lu (Catalogue of calligraphy and paintings in the National Palace Museum and National Central Museum). 1964. 4 vols. Taipei: National Palace Museum.

Harrist, Robert E. Jr. 1989. A Scholar's Landscape: Shan-chuang t'u by Li Kung-lin. PhD diss., Princeton University.

———. 1998. *Painting and Private Life in Eleventh-Century China: Mountain Villa by Li Gonglin.* Princeton: Princeton University Press.

Hightower, J.R. 1970. *The Poetry of T'ao Ch'ien.* Oxford: Clarendon.

Ho, Wai-kam, Sherman E. Lee, Laurence Sickman, and Marc F. Wilson. 1980. *Eight Dynasties of Chinese Painting: The Collections of the Nelson Gallery-Atkins Museum, Kansas City, and The Cleveland Museum of Art.* Cleveland: The Cleveland Museum of Art.

Lawton, Thomas. 1973. *Freer Gallery of Art Fiftieth Anniversary Exhibition II: Chinese Figure Painting.* Washington: Smithsonian Institution.

Lee, Sherman E. and Wen C. Fong. 1967. *Streams and Mountains Without End: A Northern Sung Handscroll and Its Significance in the History of Early Chinese Painting.* Ascona, Switzerland: Artibus Asiae.

Lee, Sherman E. and Wai-kam Ho. 1968. *Chinese Art Under the Mongols: The Yüan Dynasty (1279–1368).* Cleveland: The Cleveland Museum of Art.

Li, Chu-tsing. 1965. *The Autumn Colors on the Ch'iao and Hua Mountains: A Landscape by Chao Meng-fu.* Ascona, Switzerland: Artibus Asiae.

Liu Dunzhen. 1980. *Zhongguo gudai jianzhu shi* (History of ancient Chinese architecture). Beijing: Zhongguo jianzhu gongye chubanshe.

Loehr, Max. 1961. Chinese Paintings with Sung-dated Inscriptions. *Ars Orientalis* 4.

Mai Chaoshu, ed. 1958. *Yuan Yishan shiji jianzhu* (Anthology of the poetry of Yuan Yishan with notes and commentaries). Beijing.

Malenfer, Valerie Marie. 1990. Dream Journey over Xiao and Xiang: Scholar-Amateur Landscape Painting in Southern Song China (1127–1179). PhD diss., Harvard University.

Mi Fu. 1986. *Huashi* (History of painting). 1 *juan.* Repr. *Meishu congshu*, 3 vols. Ed. Huang Binhong and Deng Shi. Rev. ed. Yangzhou: Jiangsu guji chubanshe.

Mote, F.W. 1960. Confucian Eremitism in the Yuan Period. In *The Confucian Persuasion*, ed. Arthur Wright. Stanford: Stanford University Press.

Nelson, Susan E. 1986. On Through to the Beyond: The Peach Blossom Spring as Paradise. *Archives of Asian Art* 39.

Osaka shiritsu bijutsukan-zō Chūgoku kaiga (Chinese paintings in the collection of the Osaka Municipal Museum of Art). 1975. Tokyo: Asahi Shimbunsha.

Sickman, Laurence and Alexander Soper. 1971. *The Art and Architecture of China.* Rev. ed. New York: Penguin Books.

Silbergeld, Jerome. 1987. Chinese Painting Studies in the West: A State-of-the-Field Article. *Journal of Asian Studies* 46 (November).

Sirén, Osvald. 1956–58. *Chinese Painting: Leading Masters and Principles.* London: Lund, Humphries.

Sō Gen no kaiga (Song and Yuan Paintings). 1962. Kyoto: Benrido.

Suzuki Kei. 1972. Hsia Kuei and the Academic Style of the Southern Sung Court. In *Proceedings of the International Symposium on Chinese Painting.* Taipei: National Palace Museum.

Suzuki Shūji. 1965. Gen Kōmon. Vol. 20 of *Kanshi taikei.* Tokyo: Shūeisha.

Tang Hou. 1986a. *Huajian (Gujin huajian).* 1 *juan.* Repr. *Meishu congshu.* 3 vols. Ed. Huang Binhong and Deng Shi. Rev. ed. Yangzhou: Jiangsu guji chubanshe.

———. 1986b. *Hualun* (Discussions on painting). Repr. *Meishu congshu.* 3 vols. Ed. Huang Binhong and Deng Shi. Rev. ed. Yangzhou: Jiangsu guji chubanshe.

Tu Wei-ming. 1982. Liu Yin's Confucian Eremitism. In *Yüan Thought: Chinese Thought and Religion under the Mongols*, ed. Hok-lam Chan and Wm. Theodore DeBary. New York: Columbia University Press.

Weidner, Marsha S. 1982. Painting and Patronage at the Mongol Court of China, 1260–1368. PhD diss., University of California, Berkeley.

———. 1986. Ho Ch'eng and Early Yüan Dynasty Painting in Northern China. *Archives of Asian Art* 39.

Wixted, John Timothy. 1982. *Poems on Poetry: Literary Criticism by Yuan Hao-wen (1190–1257).* Münchener Ostasiatische Studien, 33. Wiesbaden: Franz Steiner Verlag.

Wu Mei-yü. 1976. *Yuan Yishan shi yanjiu* (A study of Yuan Yishan's poems). Taipei: Chia Hsin Foundation.

Xia Wenyan. 1365. *Tu hui baojian* (Precious mirror of painting). 5 *juan.* In *Huashi congshu.* Taipei: Wenshizhe chubanshe, 1983.

Xuanhe huapu (Catalogue of the imperial painting collection during the Xuanhe era; preface dated 1120). Facsimile ed. Taipei: National Palace Museum, Taipei.

Xue Yongnian. 1973. He Cheng he tade "Guizhuang tu" (He Cheng and his handscroll "The Homecoming"). *Wenwu*, no. 8.

Yoshikawa Kōjirō. 1989. *Five Hundred Years of Chinese Poetry (1150–1650).* Trans. John Timothy Wixted. Princeton: Princeton University Press.

Yuan Haowen. 2002. *Zhongzhou ji* (Anthology of the Central Land). Repr. *Sibu congkan.* Beijing: Beijing shu tong wenxian shuzihua jishu youxian gongsi.

Zheng Zhenduo. 1648. *Zhongguo banhuashi tulu* (History of Chinese woodblock prints). Repr. Shanghai, 1940.

Zhou Mi. 1986. *Yunyan guoyan lu* (A record [of painting and calligraphy] that drifted before my eyes). In *Meishu congshu*, ed. Huang Binhong and Deng Shi. Rev.ed. Yangzhou: Jiangsu guji chubanshe.

STUDIES IN HONOR OF CHU-TSING LI

Allegories, Metaphors, and Satires: Writing About Painting in the Early Yuan Dynasty

ANKENEY WEITZ

During the transition from the Song (960–1279) to the Yuan (1272–1368) dynasty, in the last quarter of the thirteenth century, the art market in China expanded dramatically.[1] Suddenly, a far greater number of art objects were in circulation than in the previous decades, during which most paintings had been hidden behind palace walls or locked up in storehouses of wealthy aristocrats or highly placed officials.[2] The vibrant early-Yuan art market encouraged many newly prosperous men to begin studying and appreciating art. No longer was collecting art the prerogative of the aristocratic gentleman of leisure; now, bureaucrats and military officials found that the activity provided important benefits, not the least of which was social prestige.

Although owning paintings and other objets d'art functioned on one level as a straightforward expression of status, some early Yuan art collectors played a much more sophisticated game with their collected objects, a game whose roots lie in the social power of what Pierre Bourdieu calls the "symbolic production of the work."[3] This essay studies the process through which these collectors symbolically produced (or perhaps we could say "re-produced") paintings by affixing interpretive texts to the scrolls. These texts not only ascribed value to the paintings through the agency of interpretation, but they also linked them to the conditions of the collector's own life. During this period of political transition and social flux, the "singularizing" process of inscribing paintings allowed the collector to both demonstrate his aesthetic discernment and position himself in the broad spectrum of social and political possibilities—from staunch Song loyalist to dignified Confucian statesman.[4]

When we talk about the reception of paintings in China, we must recognize that the collection and appreciation of paintings was not a private affair; collectors held parties to show off their recent acquisitions, and often brought out scrolls to show the spontaneous visitor.[5] Given the important social dimension of art appreciation and art collecting, we should not be surprised to discover a preoccupation among some collectors with the propriety of certain types of knowledge, as well as the modes of expressing their knowledge at painting-viewing parties. For example, Tang Hou, a collector and art historian active from the late thirteenth to the early fourteenth century,[6] advised:

> One who is beginning to learn about viewing paintings must be able to analyze essentials and subtleties and should look over notes

> and documents. Otherwise, even though he is versed in connoisseurship and is able on seeing a painting to distinguish quality, he will be confused and unable to reply when asked about the reasons for these aesthetic opinions.[7]

He went on to ridicule those who had not studied painting texts:

> Upon unrolling a scroll they just begin to admire it; but if someone asks them where its wonderful qualities lie, they do not know how to answer. The [paintings] are all "average" or "old," and the viewer is suddenly tired of looking. Some men will, on the spur of the moment, try to force an interpretation without knowing its origin. This is profoundly ludicrous.[8]

Tang Hou's comments suggest several important things: First, that in the early decades of the Yuan, the practice of art collecting and appreciation had expanded beyond the bounds of a few high-minded and knowledgeable men to include a new breed of philistines, at least from Tang Hou's perspective. Second, Tang contended that the correct manner of knowing and speaking about paintings could be learned by studying art-historical texts and theoretical treatises, as well as following a system that he called the "Six Methods," which conveniently parroted the fifth-century painter Xie He's (active ca. 479–502) "Six Principles."[9] Tang asserted that sons of good families should pay attention to these matters because "they will benefit in many other areas. All the famous men and venerable personages of the past, without exception, paid attention to these subjects."[10] Thus, Tang clearly considered mastering correct "art speak" an indispensable form of cultural capital for politically ambitious young men.

In presenting his Six Methods—configured as a set of conditions for understanding a painting rather than for producing one—Tang Hou derided his contemporaries for, among other things, their interest in the narrative content of paintings and urged them to pay attention to more abstruse formal qualities like "spirit resonance" (*qiyun*) and "brush conception" (*biyi*).[11] Tang seems to have proposed this method as an antidote for the more common, hermeneutic practice of early Yuan collectors: reading antique paintings as allegories, metaphors, or even satires of contemporary events or persons. Yuan literary sources in fact show that many collectors, not just the parvenus, found much to be admired and interpreted in the subject matter of paintings. Even scholarly collectors in Tang's father's generation, several of whom are mentioned in Tang Hou's text *Huajian*, inscribed clever metaphorical readings on paintings without referring to critical concepts like *qiyun* or *biyi*. Thus Tang's Six Methods should not necessarily be taken as a reflection of common connoisseurial practices during his time.

The custom of reading paintings as metaphors or allegories certainly was not new to the Yuan period. In the late eleventh century the Northern Song scholar-official artist Mi Fu (1052–1107) had stated that the best paintings provided the viewer with "exhortations and warnings."[12] Mi placed Buddhist and narrative paintings at the top of his hierarchy of subjects because they could be interpreted as object lessons in ethical behavior. Paintings of landscapes, bamboo, trees, water, and rocks followed in sequence; those of court ladies and birds were relegated to the bottom category. This hierarchy of subjects was still in force among the collectors of the late thirteenth century, as indicated by the *Yunyan guoyan lu*, a collectors' catalogue compiled by Zhou Mi (1232–1296) in the 1280s and 1290s.[13] Included in the approximately forty early Yuan collections recorded in that text were a total of two hundred sixty-eight paintings. Of these, over forty percent portrayed figural subjects, a third of which were Buddhist figures. Another third of the figural paintings depicted historical narratives or illustrations of the classics, such as *Duke Wen of Jin Recovering His State* or *The Classic of Filial Piety*.[14] The popularity of these types of subjects among early Yuan collectors probably resided in their conduciveness to allegorical readings. In particular, the subjects of the two aforementioned scrolls—the recovery of occupied territory and the virtues of loyalty—resonated powerfully with former Song and Jin (1115–1234) dynasty officials.

Although narrative paintings, portraits of religious and historical personages, and illustrations of the classics were collected in great numbers and provided readily accessible allegories, other subjects also provided compelling material for interpretation. Paintings of cows and horses were perennial favorites, given the richness of the literary metaphors associated with these animals. In literati painting, the horse often signified a loyal official, while the cow was a frequent symbol for a high-minded recluse.[15] For example, Zhao Mengfu's (1254–1322) reading of Han Huang's (723–787) *Five Oxen*, familiar to us from Chu-tsing Li's penetrating study of Zhao's animal paintings, draws on the cow's association with loyalty in reclusion. As translated by Dr. Li, Zhao's second inscription on Huang's painting reads in part:

> In the past the Emperor Wu of the Liang dynasty [502–557] wanted to make Tao Hong-ching [Dao Hongjing, 452–536] an official. Hung-jing painted two buffalos, one with a golden halter on his head and the other freely grazing in the water and among grasses. [After seeing it], Emperor Wu of Liang sighed with respect for his high ideals and did not force him. This painting may have depicted the meaning of that story.[16]

We might read this inscription as an expression of the ambivalence that Zhao Mengfu, a scion of the Song imperial family, felt about serving in the Yuan government. However, we should also realize that he expressed this sentiment not in private correspondence or in his personal diary but on a painting frequently shown to guests and soon sold to another collector. Because paintings were objects of public display and circulation, inscriptions and colophons were also public acts; thus, a seemingly personal sentiment became a statement of position. In this case Zhao was perhaps expressing less his own discomfort in office than his appreciation for those who chose not to assume "the golden halter."[17]

The political and personal issue of one's relationship with the Yuan government was, of course, a major concern of many southerners, who used their inscriptions on antique paintings to publicly express their position on the subject. Consider, for instance, the Song loyalist Qiu Yuan's (1247–after 1327) complete colophon on a painting of one hundred oxen attributed to the early Southern Song artist Jiang Shen (ca. 1090–1138), which reads:

> Shanzhongren showed me this painting of one hundred oxen and said, "King Xuan's royal herds [grazing] by riverbanks and by ponds [numbered] more than ninety head. This is really bragging about how many oxen he had—and, how much more so the two hundred flapping ears [seen here]! Old farm dwellers always take lots of oxen to be a sign of prosperity. But how about retiring with one golden calf to plow at the base of a southern mountain? What I love is the single cow!" And, he closed the scroll with a laugh.[18]

In her partial translation and study of this colophon, Scarlett Jang dwells on Qiu Yuan's reference to King Xuan of Zhou (r. 827–782 B.C.) and draws out the metaphorical meaning of this general subject (herding oxen or one hundred oxen) through a literary allusion to the *Book of Odes*. Quoting several other colophons from a later period, she builds a case for reading herds of oxen as metaphors for the emperor's "concern for his people's livelihood" or, alternately, "a time of peace" due to benevolent leadership. She also notes that gifts of ox-herding paintings functioned "as reminders to officials of how to govern well."[19]

Nevertheless, reading Qiu Yuan's entire inscription shows that he actually had subversive intentions in making the passing reference to King Xuan. Far from praising the government, Qiu scoffed at the idea of serving as an official and declared that he would rather stay home and plow his field with one beloved calf than be known for his great skill as a herdsman. Qiu Yuan thus expressed his disdain for those men of the scholarly class who sought official appointment, while also positioning himself as morally superior to those who fell prey to the temptations of fame and fortune.

Along the same lines, we find another southerner, Jie Xisi (1274–1344), using an antique painting to complain about the northern Chinese and Central Asian officials who had been sent to oversee the Yuan consolidation of power in the former Southern Song (1127–1279) territories. Jie's inscription, which appeared on a now-lost painting of wild geese, reads:

> Freezing, they come to Jiangnan to warm up;
> Hungry, they come to Jiangnan to eat their fill.
> All their things are from Jiangnan;
> But they do not say Jiangnan is good.[20]

Although at first glance this might appear to be a rather curious poem, Jie's younger contemporary Kong Keqi (active 14th century) provides us with the following gloss:

> Now this is a satire of Central Asian and northern [officials] who came to Jiangnan and went from poverty to great wealth, from having nothing to having everything. [Yet] they unceasingly complained about and demeaned Jiangnan. They saw themselves as being from honorable families of noble status, while regarding southerners as akin to slaves. For this reason, southerners also lowered their opinion of northerners a notch, and often ridiculed them like this.[21]

I suspect that Jie Xisi wrote his inscription before his fortieth year (1314), when he first traveled to the Yuan capital Dadu (modern Beijing) in search of work and began his slow rise through the government bureaucracy.[22] Although we cannot know the precise conditions under which the inscription was written, we can read it as Jie's appropriation of an existing painting to express his own bitterness at the social conditions of his time, without regard for the original intent of the artist or even the symbolic meanings in common use during the Song and Yuan.[23]

To suggest the lengths to which Yuan collectors went to singularize their possessions and transform them into objects of self-expression, we can turn to one final example of a politicized reading of an otherwise unassuming subject. On a painting of a purple turnip attributed to the Song emperor Huizong (r. 1101–25), Mou Yan (1227–1311) wrote the following poem:

> The old turnip lay in an abandoned garden;
> The leaves and roots large in the emptiness.
> Bitter and tough, it would have burned a human mouth;
> So, unfit for human needs, it was thrown out.
> Ants descended upon it by the millions;
> They saw that there was something left to suck on.[24]

How are we to understand this strange poem? As a disenfranchised former Song official, Mou Yan witnessed the disappointing surrender of the Southern Song capital Hangzhou to the Yuan armies. Could his reading of this still-life painting be a lament on the failure of the Song to tend its own garden? In this interpretation, the old turnip lying forlornly in an unprotected garden is a metaphor for the abandoned authority of the Song; it falls easy prey to an army of ants, that is, Jurchen and Mongol soldiers.[25] This meaning could not have been intended by Emperor Huizong, one of the agents of the Northern Song's demise in 1127; thus if this reading is correct, Mou clearly appropriated the painting to convey his own message with no regard for the intentions of the artist.

Although Tang Hou decried such readings as ludicrous, for many early Yuan collectors the artistic past was ripe for creative manipulation. Individual collectors acquired paintings and objects not only for their aesthetic merit, but also for their symbolic content, which they used to express their opinion on social or political values in which they had a stake. Thus, the building of an art collection was a process of creating a public image through which the collector self-consciously positioned himself in a social field. Collectors (and their invited friends) wrote interpretive texts on their paintings in order to manufacture a calculated image of their social, moral, and political status. Through the social activity of displaying paintings, either in his own home or at connoisseurs' parties, a collector not only presented himself as a man of aesthetic discernment, but also disseminated his views on a variety of contemporary issues. Thus, the collecting of antique paintings was a conscious act of self-creation and social distinction, in which aesthetic taste was subsumed into an embracing concept of self-interest.

NOTES

1. The early Yuan art market was the subject of my dissertation, done under Dr. Chu-tsing Li's direction. The present article, first presented in 1997 at the Association for Asian Studies Annual Conference, is a rethinking of some of the ideas presented in the dissertation. See Weitz 1994.

2. The early Yuan connoisseur Tang Hou wrote: "At the end of the Song dynasty many scholars did not know about painting. Although they had the reputation of being connoisseurs, they were very careless. Since the finest objects were all in the imperial collection, not many remained among the people, and [even those] were often seized by the powerful. When Jia Sidao [1213–1275] arrogated power over the country, he became interested in collecting. At that time, many courtiers and followers were consumed with searching out paintings to present to [him]." See Tang Hou 1963, 7. This translation is adapted, with significant changes, from that in Bush and Shih 1985, 257.

3. Bourdieu 1993, 37.

4. I borrow the idea of "singularization" from Kopytoff 1986, 64–91.

5. Guo Bi's (1280–1335) diary of a trip to Hangzhou in 1308 (*Ke Hang riji*) described many occasions at which he was shown paintings by his hosts. Most of these painting-viewing sessions were *ad hoc* affairs. Guest lists for more formal parties still survive. See, for example, Bian Yongyu 1991, *shu* 6: 15b-16b; Lu You 1962, *shang*: 15; and Ren Daobin 1984, 50. For an extended discussion of early Yuan parties, see Weitz 1994, 40–50.

6. See Chou 1999.

7. See Tang Hou 1962, 65. Translation from Bush and Shih 1985, 259.

8. Tang Hou 1963, 9.

9. "As to the methods of looking at painting, first look at the spirit resonance (*qiyun*), next at the brush conception (*biyi*), formal structure (*gufa*), placement and coloring, and lastly at formal likeness. These are the Six Methods." See Tang Hou 1963, 9, and Bush and Shih 1985, 261.

10. Tang Hou 1962, 66. Translation from Bush and Shih 1985, 260.

11. The translations of these terms are from Bush and Shih 1985, 261.

12. See Mi Fu 1982, 214. Translation from Bush and Shih 1985, 235.

13. See Weitz 1994, Appendix D, 571–73.

14. Paintings illustrating these two classics are in The Metropolitan Museum of Art. See Fong 1992, pls. 8a-g (*The Classic of Filial Piety*) and pls. 26a-h (*Duke Wen of Jin Recovering His State*).

15. On this subject see Li 1968, 279–326; Jang 1992, 54–93; Silbergeld 1985, 159–202; and Harrist 1997.

16. Li 1968, 292.

17. Chu-tsing Li writes about this inscription: "This is Chao Meng-fu's way of reading meaning into the painting of Han Huang. How correct he was in his interpretation is something quite difficult to surmise, for there was no direct indication of its meaning from the artist ... In his approach to literati painting, with its symbolic overtones, Chao began to see something more than the formal and aesthetic aspects. The fact that paintings of buffalos evoked in his mind such symbolic meaning is important, for it can shed some light on his own depiction of animals." See Li 1968, 313–14.

18. Qiu Yuan 1983–89, 38b.

19. Jang 1992, 67–70.

20. Quoted in Kong Keqi 1987, 3:31a. Another, slightly different version of the inscription appears in Jie's collected writings; see *Jie Xisi quanji* 1985, *shi xuji*: 145. My provisional translation reads:

> Freezing, they come to Jiangnan
> to warm up;
> Hungry, they come to Jiangnan
> to eat their fill.
> No one says that Jiangnan hates
> [them],
> We must speak of Jiangnan's
> love.

Jiangnan refers to the region south of the Yangzi River.

21. Kong Keqi 1987, 3:31a.

22. For Jie Xisi's biography, see *Yuanren juanji ziliao suoyin* 1985, 3:1385–7, and Jiang Yihan 1981, 124–29.

23. Like ox-herding, the theme of wild geese could refer to a poem from the *Shijing* (Classic of Poetry). Wen Fong describes the Song emperor Gaozong's (r. 1127–62) fondness for this theme, and comments on a painting by Ma Hezhi (ca. 1130–ca. 1170): "The settling of the wild geese symbolizes, in the courtly panegyric, the reestablishment of peace under Gaozong." See Fong 1992, 220–22.

24. Mou Yan 1983–89, 2:6a.

25. A more blatant criticism of Huizong's failure appears in a colophon by Hu Zhiyu (1227–1295), a northerner who served in influential positions at Khubilai's court. See his "Colophon for Huizong's Painting" in Chen Gaohua 1984, 617.

REFERENCES

Bian Yongyu. 1991. *Shigutang shuhua huikao*. Shanghai: Shanghai guji chubanshe.

Bourdieu, Pierre. 1993. The Field of Cultural Production, or: The Economic World Reversed. In *The Field of Cultural Production: Essays on Art and Literature*, ed. Randal Johnson. New York: Columbia University Press.

Bush, Susan and Hsio-yen Shih. 1985. *Chinese Texts on Painting*. Cambridge: Harvard University Press.

Chen Gaohua, ed. 1984. *Song Liao Jin huajia shiliao*. Beijing: Wenwu chubanshe.

Chou, Yeongchau. 1999. Re-dating Tang Hou's Biography (1260s–mid-1310s) and his *Huajian* (Critical Notes on Paintings and Painters). Paper presented at the annual conference of the Association for Asian Studies.

Fong, Wen C. 1992. *Beyond Representation: Chinese Painting and Calligraphy, 8th–14th Century*. New York: The Metropolitan Museum of Art.

Harrist, Robert E. Jr. 1997. *Power and Virtue: The Horse in Chinese Art*. New York: China Institute.

Jang, Scarlett. 1992. Ox-herding Painting in the Sung Dynasty. *Artibus Asiae* 52, nos. 1, 2.

Jiang Yihan. 1981. *Yuandai Kuizhangge ji Kuizhangge renwu*. Taipei: Lianjing chuban shiye gongsi.

Jie Xisi quanji. 1985. Shanghai: Guji chubanshe.

Kong Keqi. 1987. *Zhizheng zhiji. Song Yuan biji congshu* edition. Shanghai: Guji chubanshe.

Kopytoff, Igor. 1986. The Cultural Biography of Things: Commoditization as Process. In *The Social Lives of Things: Commodities in Cultural Perspective*, ed. Arjun Appadurai. Cambridge: Cambridge University Press.

Li, Chu-tsing. 1968. The Freer "Sheep and Goat" and Chao Meng-fu's Horse Paintings. *Artibus Asiae* 30, no. 4.

Lu You. 1962. *Yanbei zashi*. In *Biji xiaoshuo daguan*, vol. 1:5. Taipei: Xinxing shudian.

Mi Fu. 1982. *Huashi*. In *Huapin congshu*, ed. Yu Anlan. Shanghai: renmin meishu chubanshe.

Mou Yan. 1983–89. *Lingyang ji. Wenyuange siku chuanshu* edition. Taipei: Shangwu.

Qiu Yuan. 1983–89. *Shancun yiji. Wenyuange siku chuanshu* edition. Taipei: Shangwu.

Ren Daobin. 1984. *Zhao Mengfu xinian*. Henan: Henan renmin chubanshe.

Silbergeld, Jerome. 1985. In Praise of Government: Chao Yung's Painting "Noble Steeds" and Late Yüan Politics. *Artibus Asiae* 46, no. 3.

Tang Hou. 1962. *Hualun*. Edition in *Huajian*, comp. Ma Cui. Beijing.

———. 1963. *Hualun. Meishu congshu* edition. Taipei: Yiwen yinshuguan.

Weitz, Ankeney. 1994. Collecting and Connoisseurship in Early Yuan China: Zhou Mi's *Yunyan guoyan lu*. PhD diss., University of Kansas.

Yuanren juanji ziliao suoyin. 1985. Taipei: Xinwen feng chuban gongsi.

STUDIES IN HONOR OF CHU-TSING LI

Chen Hongshou's *Children Paying Homage to the Buddha*: An Illustration to the *Lotus Sutra*

HSING-LI TSAI

The late Ming period (1368–1644) witnessed the revival of Buddhism and its predominant influence on art in China.[1] Many of the foremost figure painters of the time concentrated on the depiction of Buddhist subjects and themes.[2] Among them, Chen Hongshou (1598–1652), a bohemian artist but a pious Buddhist,[3] is perhaps the most original in terms of the selection and treatment of Buddhist themes. Unique to his Buddhist painting is his endeavor to embrace Buddhist concepts in art. Chen's painting *Children Paying Homage to the Buddha* (fig. 1) is a good example of the intimate relationship Chen sought to establish between art and the prevailing Buddhist thought of the time. The aim of this paper is to investigate the meaning of the painting[4] and its link with other paintings by Chen Hongshou that convey similar Buddhist concepts prevalent in the first half of the seventeenth century.

Children Paying Homage to the Buddha portrays in a large hanging-scroll format four boys with a sculpture of a Buddha in front of a Taihu rock. The Buddha, seated on a stone stand supported by the rock, commands the attention of three of the children, all of whom appear to be wholeheartedly worshipping him. The child standing in the foreground and wearing a brown robe takes the lead and offers to the Buddha a vase containing chrysanthemums and bamboo. Behind him and partly obscured, the second child pays his utmost respect to the Buddha by kneeling with his forehead and forearms on the ground (apparently unaware that his bare buttocks are boldly turned up), while the third raises his hands together in a gesture of worship. The fourth child, his eyes fixed on his three companions and holding a chisel in his right hand, appears to be making a pagoda.

The portrayal of children with a Buddhist figure has at least two precedents in Chinese painting. Children are most commonly associated with Maitreya, the Buddha of the Future, and Guanyin, the Bodhisattva of Compassion. Maitreya often manifests himself as the benevolent, big-bellied Budai, who is recorded as having been accompanied by sixteen children, but is usually depicted with a group of six children playing around him.[5] Unlike the joyful children associated with a laughing Budai, Chen Hongshou's little boys wear solemn facial expressions, showing full respect to the sculpture of the Buddha. In this they are more reminiscent of the boy pilgrim Sudhana, who often accompanies Guanyin and is shown raising his hands, palms together, in a gesture of reverence to his spiritual mentor.[6]

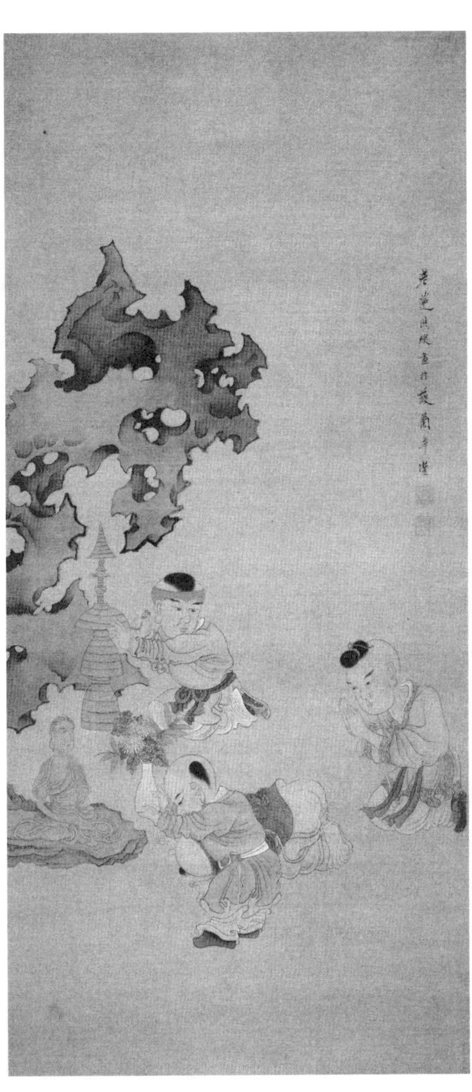

FIGURE 1
Chen Hongshou (1598–1652). *Children Paying Homage to the Buddha.* Hanging scroll, ink and color on silk, 58⅞ × 26⅝ in. (149.5 × 67.5 cm). Palace Museum, Beijing

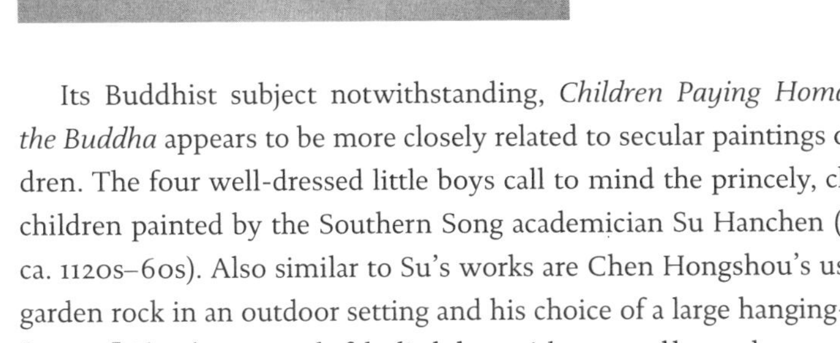

Its Buddhist subject notwithstanding, *Children Paying Homage to the Buddha* appears to be more closely related to secular paintings of children. The four well-dressed little boys call to mind the princely, chubby children painted by the Southern Song academician Su Hanchen (active ca. 1120s–60s). Also similar to Su's works are Chen Hongshou's use of a garden rock in an outdoor setting and his choice of a large hanging-scroll format.[7] Chen's portrayal of the little boy with exposed buttocks may derive from the well-known knick-knack peddler paintings by Li Song (active ca.

1190–1230), another Southern Song painter of children.[8] Another example of this type of figure is found in an anonymous Ming painting, which was possibly influenced by Li Song's realistic depictions of the lower classes.[9] Paintings showing children amusing themselves with toys, including those by Lü Wenying (active late 15th century), were popular in the Ming.[10] Such paintings may have inspired Chen Hongshou to combine secular scenes from genre painting with a serious Buddhist theme.

Having noted the stylistic similarities of Chen Hongshou's children to their religious and secular predecessors, we now turn to an examination of the four activities performed by the children in Chen's painting. Is Chen simply portraying ordinary boys mischievously playing with two toys, a Buddhist sculpture and a pagoda, in a garden setting? The first three activities—offering flowers to the Buddhist image, prostrating before the Buddha, and worshipping the Buddha with raised hands—are forms of respect commonly shown by Buddhist believers. But why does Chen depict children instead of adults engaged in these forms of worship? Why does he include the making of a pagoda, which seems irrelevant to the other three activities? Also, do the chrysanthemums and the pagoda serve only as props, or do they have special meaning? Finally, what does the Buddhist image symbolize, and why did the artist portray an image of a Buddha rather than that of a bodhisattva?

The inscription on the upper right corner of the painting, which bears only the names of the artist and his studio, offers no clues to the questions raised here.[11] To find the answers, we have to turn to the sutras that were familiar to Chen Hongshou. The most likely source is the *Lotus Sutra*, one of the most important of the sacred scriptures of Mahayana Buddhism,[12] which Chen may have read in his early twenties.[13] The three activities of worship mentioned above are described in the second chapter of the sutra:

> If anyone, even with distracted thought,
> And with so much as a single flower,
> Makes offering to a painted image,
> He shall at length see numberless Buddhas.
> There will be some who prostrate themselves ceremoniously;
> Others, again, who merely join palms;
> Others yet who do no more than raise one hand,
> Others yet again who incline their heads but slightly—
> All, in these several ways, honoring the images.
> They shall at length see incalculable Buddhas,

Themselves achieve the Unexcelled Path,
Broadly rescue numberless multitudes,
And enter into nirvana without residue,
As, when the kindling wood is exhausted, the fire goes out.
If any, even with distracted thought,
Shall enter a stupa or mausoleum,
And recite Namo Buddhaya [Homage to the Buddha] but once,
They have all achieved the Buddha Path.[14]

According to the sutra, the act of offering flowers, prostrating oneself, raising one's hands, or lowering one's head as a gesture of respect to a Buddhist image lead to the Buddha Path. But, again, why in Chen's painting are children shown performing these activities, and why is another child shown making a pagoda? The answers to these questions can be found in the same chapter of the *Lotus Sutra*, which states that even children are able to achieve the Buddha Path:[15]

There are even children who in play
Gather sand and make it into Buddha-stupas.
Persons like these
Have all achieved the Buddha Path.[16]

It is now clear why Chen Hongshou included in his painting the figure of a child making a pagoda; this is not a randomly portrayed activity, but a crucial image that offers a clue to the meaning of the painting and confirms its link with the *Lotus Sutra*. Like the first three activities, the making of a pagoda is recognized in the scripture as one of the numerous ways that lead to the attainment of Buddhahood. All of these activities are included in the ten passages addressing the ways of achieving the Buddha Path.[17] Some ways are abstract, such as keeping the precepts, showing forbearance, cultivating wisdom, or accumulating merits; others are concrete, such as making pagodas, sculptures, and paintings, and paying respect to Buddhist images.

The four activities depicted by Chen are, as stated in the *Lotus Sutra*, among those that lead to the Buddha Path. But how do they represent the ultimate teaching, and what is the ultimate teaching revealed in the *Lotus Sutra*? Why did Chen Hongshou consider it important to embrace this concept in his painting? The sutra refers to these activities as "expedient devices," the convenient and practical ways that lead to the goal of Buddhahood promised in the sutra. The purpose of adopting the expedient devices is to achieve the ultimate truth of Buddhist teaching, the Buddha Vehicle or the so-called One Vehicle:

Within the Buddha-lands of the ten directions
There is the Dharma of only One Vehicle.
There are not two, nor are there yet three.[18]

The sutra confirms that all the Buddhas teach this single vehicle or truth:

All the World-Honored Ones,
All of them, preach the Way of the One Vehicle.
Now these great multitudes
Are all to purge their doubts and uncertainties.
The Buddhas say without differing
That there is only One Vehicle, not two.[19]

The sutra then promises that all the expedient devices lead to the attainment of Buddhahood:

All the Thus Come Ones,
By resort to incalculable expedient devices,
Save the living beings,
That they may enter into the Buddha's wisdom free of outflows.
Of any who hear the Dharma,
None shall fail to achieve Buddhahood.[20]

Not only did those who had already become Buddhas—namely, the Buddhas of the past and the present—preach the One Vehicle, but the future Buddhas, though teaching myriad ways, still direct their teachings to the One Vehicle. The sutra reads:

The Buddhas of ages to come,
Though they shall preach hundreds of thousands of millions
Of numberless gateways to the Dharma,
Shall, in fact, be doing it for the sake of the One Vehicle.

The teaching of the One Vehicle is further illuminated in this passage from the sutra:

All dharmas without exception are empty and quiescent,
Having no birth and no extinction,
Neither great nor small,
Having no outflows and no ado.
With this in mind,
We experienced no pleasure.

Throughout the long night of time,
For Buddha-wisdom, we had no craving and no attachment,
Nor yet any hope.
On the contrary, where Dharma is concerned, to ourselves
We said: "This is the ultimate!"[21]

The breaking of the contradiction between two conflicting forces, such as birth and extinction, greatness and smallness, leads to the ultimate attainment of Buddhahood, the One Vehicle, which can only be taught by the Buddha:

They know the prime Quiet Extinction;
By resort to expedient devices
They may demonstrate various paths, but
They do so, in fact, for the sake of the Buddha Vehicle.[22]

It is evident that Chen Hongshou understood the One Vehicle as equivalent to the ultimate Buddhahood since what he portrayed in his painting is clearly an image of a Buddha rather than that of a bodhisattva. Dressed in an Indian robe, the Buddha sits in a meditative pose, his hands placed in his lap, one on top of the other with palms up, in the mudra of concentration. The image of the Buddha, the object of the children's reverence, symbolizes the One Vehicle, or the attainment of Buddhahood, taught in the *Lotus Sutra*.

If *Children Paying Homage to the Buddha* illustrates the teaching of the One Vehicle, how does Chen Hongshou embrace this teaching, and how is the concept of breaking the boundary between two conflicting forces presented in the painting? Chen demonstrates the breaking of the contradiction between greatness and smallness with the whimsical contrast between the small size of the Buddha sculpture and the larger figures of the four children. The Buddha is usually portrayed as the largest and most prominent figure in a group, as in the assemblies in sutra frontispieces,[23] but in Chen's painting he is portrayed as the smallest image. In this departure from the orthodox canon, Chen not only challenges long-established iconographic conventions but brilliantly embraces the concept of nondualism, a central aspect of Mahayana Buddhism set forth in the *Lotus Sutra*.

Chen Hongshou's attempt to break the boundary between contradictory forces is also shown in the human expression of the Buddha. Although bearing his traditional attributes, the *ushnisha*, *urna*, and elongated earlobes, the Buddha is portrayed with a humanized face. (The humanization of Buddhist figures is characteristic of much late Ming Buddhist painting,[24] but seems to be even more pronounced and deliberate in Chen's Buddhist paintings.[25]) The nature of the Buddha is also made ambiguous. Chen seems to depict a game played by the children, making the sculpture of the Buddha look like one of the children's toys. The children, however, are shown with serious expressions on their faces, and appear instead to conduct a ritual focused on the Buddha. The ambiguity of the Buddha image, which can be seen as either a toy or an object of worship, underscores the artist's intention to detach the image from its traditional and practical functions and give it new meaning.

The specific identity of the Buddha image is also not clear. It might be Shakyamuni, the historical Buddha, or Bhaishajyaguru, the Buddha of Medicine (*Yaoshi*), as chrysanthemums symbolize the ninth month, when the birthday of the Medicine Buddha is celebrated. This ambiguity may signify that the identity of the Buddha is of little importance since all Buddhas share a universal language and teach the same ultimate goal of the One Vehicle.

Chen Hongshou's depiction of children rather than adults performing activities of worship would seem to be in marked contrast to the complexities of Buddhist teaching. However, the apparent contradiction between the naïveté of children and the abstruseness of Buddhist teaching is hardly noticeable in the painting, as the artist has ingeniously transformed a solemn subject into a delightful picture by adding beautiful colors and an element of humor in the image of the little boy with upturned buttocks. The result coincides with the ultimate teaching of the *Lotus Sutra*: the One Vehicle, the attainment of Buddhahood with no limitation and no contradiction between any conflicting forces or elements.

The embrace of Buddhist concepts is found not only in *Children Paying Homage to the Buddha*, but in at least five other paintings by Chen Hongshou. Two of these paintings are also directly associated with Buddhist scriptures. In *Self-Image in the Guise of Vimalakirti*, Chen juxtaposes the image of himself as Vimalakirti with the text of the *Heart Sutra*, which teaches the relief from attachments through comprehension of the nonexistence of dualism.[26] The link with Vimalakirti, whose ultimate teaching is said to eliminate dualities in both the physical and the spiritual worlds, confirms that the theme of the painting is the concept of nondualism,[27] a term synonymous with the One Vehicle and widely adopted by late Ming literati.[28] *Shakyamuni and Subhuti*, an album leaf by Chen inscribed with the phrase "No law can be taught," is the epitome of the *Diamond Sutra*, a scripture that also advocates the elimination of contradictory elements.[29]

Three of Chen Hongshou's paintings exemplify his deep interest as a late Ming literatus in the concept of nondualism. One of the poems inscribed on the handscroll *The Four Pleasures of Nan Shenglu* conveys Chen's understanding of nonabiding, the method leading to the attainment of nonduality.[30] In another painting, *Seeking the Truth*, Chen portrays the Buddhist master Zhude, his hand raised in a gesture of nonduality, accompanied by a lay Buddhist, signifying the spiritual communion between monks and lay Buddhists and the wide interest in the concept of nondualism in the late Ming.[31] Chen's interest in the concept of nondualism is also expressed in his painting *Elegant Gathering*, which portrays the famous Ming essayist Yuan Hongdao (1568–1610), who in his book *Xifang helun* discussed the Buddhist teaching of nonduality, and one of his brothers at a gathering with six lay Buddhists and a monk.[32]

Appealing and humorous as it is, *Children Paying Homage to the Buddha* evidences Chen Hongshou's endeavor to embrace in painting the Buddhist concepts in the *Lotus Sutra*. The four activities of the children refer to the expedient devices that lead to the attainment of Buddhahood, the Buddha Vehicle or the so-called One Vehicle. The image of the Buddha symbolizes the teaching of the One Vehicle, as the Buddhas of the past, present, and future all teach the same ultimate goal of the One Vehicle. The One Vehicle can be achieved by eliminating the contradiction between opposing forces, the concept of nonduality taught in many sutras. This concept is substantiated in art by breaking the boundary of the established canon or formula, such as the portrayal of the small Buddha and the large children in Chen Hongshou's painting. *Children Paying Homage to the Buddha* demonstrates Chen's unprecedented enthusiasm in advocating Buddhist beliefs and concepts through art, and his commitment to create new Buddhist subjects and attach philosophical meaning to them. It also serves as an embodiment of the *Lotus Sutra* in art and exemplifies a parallel development between art and the prevailing Buddhist thought in the late Ming period. At the same time, the painting can be regarded as an important pictorial document that attests to the late Ming literati's profound interest in Buddhist scriptures and their attempt to apply Buddhist concepts in their life and art.

NOTES

1. For a discussion of the revival of Buddhism in the late Ming, see Yü 1981 and 1975, 93–140; Hsü 1979; Shih Sheng-yen 1987. For a discussion of Ming Buddhism in general, see Weidner 1994a, 51–83 and 2001, 1–9.

2. Chen Hongshou, Wu Bin (active ca. 1591–1626), Ding Yunpeng (1547–ca. 1621), and Cui Zizhong (ca. 1595–1644) are the best known. For the discussion of Chen Hongshou's Buddhist painting, see Tsai 1997, 36–107, 127–65. For Ding Yunpeng, see Oertling 1980. For Cui Zizhong, see Andrews 1984, 180–227. Many of the paintings by these artists are reproduced in *Wan Ming bianxing zhuyi huajia zuopin zhan* 1977.

3. For Chen Hongshou's Buddhist life, see Tsai 1997, 8–35; Burkus 1987, 202–31.

4. This paper is adapted in part from my dissertation; see Tsai 1997, 137–44. At least three versions of the painting discussed here survive, suggesting its popularity during the artist's lifetime. Five different Chinese titles have been given to the painting (the artist did not entitle the work in his inscription). *Xiying tu* (*Zhongguo lidai huihua, Gugong bowuyuan canghua ji*, vol. 6, p. 143) and *Yingxi tu* (*Chen Hongshou zuopin ji*, pl. 27; *Zhongguo huihuashi tulu*, pl. 435; Weng 1997, vol. 2, p. 120), both used by the Palace Museum, Beijing, can be translated as *Children at Play*. The third title, *Tungzi bai Guanyin* (Children Paying Homage to Guanyin), was given to the painting in the Ho Yü-hua Collection, Taipei (*Zhongguo shuhua, I, renwu hua*, 98), discussed below. The last two titles, *Qunying bai fo tu* (Weng 1997, vol. 1, p. 153) and *Tungzi bai fo tu*, both translated as *Children Paying Homage to the Buddha*, in my view describe more clearly the meaning of the painting and the activities portrayed.

The two versions of Chen's painting in the Palace Museum, Beijing, bear different inscriptions, brushwork, and slightly different motifs. The one with highly refined brushwork (*Zhongguo lidai huihua, Gugong bowuyuan canghua ji*, vol. 6, p. 143), which is discussed in this paper, may have been created in the late 1640s or early 1650s, a period when Chen Hongshou's mastery of lines attained perfection. This painting, though skillfully executed, may have been a collaborative work with Chen's student, which is true of many of his works. While the Buddha and the four children display Chen's peculiar free-flowing but intense brushwork, the Taihu rock displays little solidity and reveals a weaker hand. Also, the Taihu rock, on which the pagoda is placed in other paintings, no longer serves as a stand and may have been added later by Chen's student. The other Beijing version (*Chen Hongshou zuopin ji*, pl. 27) may have been done in the mid-1640s, a period characteristic of Chen's angular, agitated lines. It is most likely a copy of the third version, in the Mu-fei Collection, Cambridge, England (*The Journal of the Institute of Chinese Studies of The Chinese University of Hong Kong*, vol. 8, no. 12 [1976], pl. 8). Although the two versions bear the same inscription, reading "Lianlao Hongshou hua yu Qingyuan tang" (Old Lotus Hongshou painted in the Hall of Purity and Seclusion), the Beijing mid-1640s painting betrays traces of a copy in the writing of the calligraphy. The brushwork and the motifs further support the Mu-fei painting as the original. For instance, the contour lines of the rock in the Beijing painting do not display the spontaneity and vitality of those in the Mu-fei painting. A section of rock at the lower left corner in the Mu-fei version has been removed, which also suggests that the Beijing painting is a copy. In addition, the painting listed in the Ho Yü-hua Collection, Taipei, appears from the reproduction to be a copy of the Beijing mid-1640s version. Wango Weng also discussed the authenticity of a similar painting published in *Christie's Catalogue* (New York, June 1988, pl. 43), and suspected it to be a copy of the Beijing mid-1640s painting. See Weng 1997, vol. 2, pp. 153–54. I shall reserve my judgment until I have seen the actual paintings.

5. The record is found in Zhipan, *Fozu tongji*, in *Dazong jing*, vol. 49, p. 390; cited in Lessing 1942, 25, and discussed in Weidner 1994b, 392. An example of Budai surrounded by six children is an anonymous painting titled *Maitreya as Budai with Children*, dated 1503, in the Museum of Fine Arts, Boston. For an illustration, see Hyland 1987, 19; Barnhart 1993, 118; and Weidner 1994b, pl. 28.

6. Many examples portraying Guanyin and Sudhana can be found in Ming paintings. See Weidner 1994b, pls. 22–24.

7. Examples of paintings attributed to Su Hanchen are *Fifteen Children Playing Around a Garden Rock*, in the Palace Museum, Beijing, and *Children at Play*, in the National Palace Museum, Taipei.

8. Two paintings of Li Song's *Knick-knack Peddler* survive. A fan painting, in the National Palace Museum, Taipei, is reproduced in *National Palace Museum Masterpieces*, vol. 2, pp. 19, 28. A handscroll, in the Palace Museum, Beijing, is reproduced in *Zhongguo meishu chuanji, huihua bian*, vol. 4, pp. 86–87.

9. *Beverage Peddler and Fan Painter*, in the Saint Louis Art Museum. See Barnhart 1993, cat. 35.

10. Lü Wenying's *The Toy Peddlers*, a pair of hanging scrolls in the Tokyo University of the Arts, is reproduced in Barnhart 1993, cat. 36a–b.

11. The inscription reads, "Lianlao Hongshou hua yu Hulan caotang" (Old Lotus Hongshou painted in the Thatched Hall of Protecting Orchid).

Wei Dong has suggested that the activities depicted in Chen's painting refer to a children's game of the late Ming period that was popular in the artist's hometown Shaoxing, Zhejiang Province. In celebration of the Buddhist Festival *yulan penhui*, on the fifteenth day of the seventh lunar month, children would make a pagoda, place a lighted lamp inside it, and then walk around the pagoda. However, aside from the making of a pagoda, this game does not accord with the other activities depicted in Chen's painting. Wei Dong 1991, 89. See also Burkus 2002, 327.

12. I am indebted to Prof. Marsha Weidner for this reference.

13. Chen Hongshou possibly read the *Lotus Sutra* in 1619; he also mentioned having discussed this sutra with a friend (Chen Hongshou, *Baolun tangji*, 9/67a). See Tsai 1997, 10–11.

14. Hurvitz 1976, 40.

15. The children are mentioned in two activities: making the pagoda and painting Buddhist images with grass, sticks, brushes, or even their fingernails. For the translation, see Hurvitz 1976, 38–39.

16. Ibid., 1976, 38–39.

17. For the translation of the ten passages, see ibid., 38–40.

18. Ibid., 34.

19. Ibid., 37.

20. Ibid., 40–41. I have translated the

character *zhi* as "wisdom," which is more accurate than Hurviz's rendering, "knowledge."

21. The translation is mainly taken from Hurvitz 1976, 96. I have replaced the term "Buddha-knowledge" with "Buddha-wisdom," which is a more accurate rendering of the original text.

22. Ibid., 1976, 41.

23. Examples of the frontispieces illustrating sutras can be found in Weidner 1994b, cats. 39–42 and pl. 20.

24. For examples, see Tsai 1997, 48.

25. Another example is the bodhisattva in Chen Hongshou's *Elegant Gathering*, in the Shanghai Museum of Art (see note 32 below). The head of this Buddhist image looks like that of the other figures in the painting except for the crown, *urna*, and elongated earlobes. For a discussion of the image, see Tsai 1997, 46–49, 102–107.

26. The painting, in the Jilin Museum, is reproduced in *Zhongguo meishu chuanji, huihua bian*, vol. 8, p. 181; Weng 1997, vol. 2, p. 135. For a discussion of the painting, see Tsai 1997, 131–34.

27. Tsai 1997, 131–34.

28. For example, Chen Hongshou expressed his seeking of the meaning of nonduality in a poem datable to 1650 (Chen Hongshou, *Baolun tang ji*, 9/50a), and the celebrated essayist Zhang Dai named his studio the Studio of Nonduality (Zhang Dai, *Taoan mengyi*, 16–17). Cited in Tsai 1997, 147.

29. The painting, one of eight leaves in an album in the Palace Museum, Beijing, is reproduced in *Zhongguo meishu chuanji, huihua bian*, vol. 8, p. 192; and Weng 1997, vol. 2, p. 159. For a discussion of the painting, see Tsai 1997, 134–37.

30. The painting, in the Charles A. Drenowatz Collection, Zurich, is illustrated in Li 1974, vol. 2, fig. 5; and Weng 1997, vol. 2, p. 184. Chen's poem reads:

> People speak of the smell of
> lotus flower;
> I say fragrance of sandalwood.
> Whenever encountering no
> solution,
> [I] then understand the way of
> not abiding in [anything].

For a discussion of the painting, see Tsai 1997, 150–51.

31. The painting, in the Palace Museum, Beijing, is reproduced in Weng 1997, vol. 2, pp. 268–70. For a discussion of the painting, see Tsai 1997, 145–50.

32. The painting, in the Shanghai Museum, is reproduced in *Zhongguo meishu chuanji, huihua bian*, vol. 8, 186–87; *Chen Hongshou zuopin ji*, pl. 69; and Weng 1997, vol. 2, pp. 142–44. For a discussion of the painting, see Tsai 1997, 36–107. A different interpretation is found in Burkus 2002, 315–30.

REFERENCES

Andrews, Julia. 1984. The Significance of Style and Subject Matter in the Painting of Cui Zizhong. PhD diss., University of California, Berkeley.

Barnhart, Richard M. 1993. *Painters of the Great Ming: The Imperial Court and the Zhe School.* Dallas: Dallas Museum of Art.

Burkus, Anne. 1987. The Artefacts of Biography in Ch'en Hung-shou's "Pao-lun-t'ang chi." PhD diss., University of California, Berkeley.

———. 2002. Between Representations: The Historical and the Visionary in Chen Hongshou's *Yaji*. *The Art Bulletin* 2, 315–30.

Hsü, Sung-p'eng. 1979. *A Buddhist Leader in Ming China: The Life and Thought of Han-shan Te-ch'ing*. University Park: Pennsylvania State University Press.

Hurvitz, Leon, trans. 1976. *Scripture of the Lotus Blossom of the Fine Dharma (The Lotus Sutra)*. New York: Columbia University Press.

Hyland, Alice R. M. 1987. *Deities, Emperors, Ladies and Literati: Figure Painting of the Ming and Qing Dynasties*. Birmingham: Birmingham Museum of Art.

Lessing, F. D. 1942. *Yung-ho kung, An Iconography of the Lamaist Cathedral in Peking*. Stockholm: Reports from the Scientific Expedition to the North-western Provinces of China under the Leadership of Dr. Sven Hedin, publication 18.

Li, Chu-tsing. 1974. *A Thousand Peaks and Myriad Ravines: Chinese Paintings in the Charles A. Drenowatz Collection*. 2 vols. Ascona, Switzerland: Artibus Asiae.

Oterling, Sewall Jerome. 1980. Ting Yün-p'eng: A Chinese Artist of the Late Ming Dynasty. PhD diss., University of Michigan.

Shih Sheng-yen. 1987. *Mingmo Zhongguo Fojiao zhi yanjiu*. Taipei: Tung-ch'u.

Tsai, Hsing-li. 1997. Ch'en Hung-shou's *Elegant Gathering*: A Late-Ming Pictorial Manifesto of Pure Land Buddhism. PhD diss., University of Kansas.

Yü, Chün-fang. 1975. Chu-hung and Lay Buddhism in the Late Ming. In *The Unfolding of Neo-Confucianism*, ed. Wm. Theodore de Bary. New York and London: Columbia University Press.

———. 1981. *The Renewal of Buddhism in China: Chu-hung and the Late Ming Synthesis*. New York: Columbia University Press.

Wan Ming bianxing zhuyi huajia zuopin zhan. 1977. Taipei: National Palace Museum.

Wei Dong. 1991. Chen Hongshou *Xiying tu* xintan. *Wenwu* 11: 88–90.

Weidner, Marsha. 1994a. Buddhist Pictorial Art in the Ming Dynasty (1368–1644): Patronage, Regionalism, and Internationalism. In *Latter Days of the Law: Images of Chinese Buddhism, 850–1850*, ed. Marsha Weidner. Lawrence: Spencer Museum of Art, University of Kansas.

———, ed. 1994b. *Latter Days of the Law: Images of Chinese Buddhism, 850–1850*. Lawrence: Spencer Museum of Art, University of Kansas.

———, ed. 2001. *Cultural Intersections in Later Chinese Buddhism*. Honolulu: University of Hawaii Press.

Weng, Wan-go. 1997. *Chen Hongshou*. 3 vols. Shanghai: Shanghai renmin meishu chubanshe.

STUDIES IN HONOR OF CHU-TSING LI

Ming Paintings of Xiang Furen from the *Nine Songs*

XUE YONGNIAN

明人九歌圖中的湘夫人

薛永年

帝子降兮北渚,
目眇眇兮愁予,
嫋嫋兮秋風,
洞庭波兮木葉下。

這段情景交融的歌詞，是屈原《九歌》湘夫人一章中的名句。詩人以細膩抒情的藝術語言創造的動人意境，一直吸引著歷代以《九歌》為題材的畫家，促使他們在描繪這一畫面時刻意經營，在前代畫家奠立的基礎上，進行新的探索。南京大學歷史系文物館所藏明人《九歌圖》的"湘夫人"，在明代描寫"湘君"、"湘夫人"的作品中，十分突出。又與美國波士頓美術館藏張敦禮《九歌圖》中的"二湘"大同小異，恰是這同中之異，使之更富於表現力與感染力。有趣的是，上述同中之異又正是南大《九歌圖》湘夫人與黑龍江省博物館傳李公麟《九歌圖》湘夫人的異中之同，因此很值得探討論列。

三個本子及其時代

上述二個本子的"湘夫人"與一個本子的"二湘"，都是不同《九歌圖》的組成部分。因此在進入藝術上的比較討論之前，有必要對三本《九歌圖》的概貌和時代作一說明。

傳張敦禮《九歌圖》卷(以下簡稱"傳張本")今藏美國波士頓美術館。其中"湘君、湘夫人"一節曾刊入日本國原田謹次郎所編《支那名畫寶鑒》，全圖為鄭振鐸收入《域外所藏中國古畫集》。二書編者均以為作者是元代張渥。該圖為絹本，設色。依屈原《九歌》分九段繪成，依次是"東皇太一、雲中君"，"湘君、湘夫人"，"大司命"，"少司命"，"東君"，"河伯"，"山鬼"，"國殤"，"禮魂"，長短不等。每段後篆書《九歌》有關章節，各段均有背景，畫法為勾勒著色。人物衣紋及樹石畫法仍具宋人規模，但已見元人溫雅情調，其底本或早於元人。經求教於徐邦達先生，他以為從圖片看，作者非張敦禮，亦非張渥，應是元人手筆。

孫承澤舊藏傳李公麟《九歌圖》卷(以下簡稱"傳李本")，今存黑龍江省博物館，此圖為牙黃紙本，無款。圖卷中依次畫《九歌》中神祇，唯缺"國殤"及"禮魂"二段。每段後隸書《九歌》有關篇章。引首為景暘所書，圖後有元代趙忠和虞集的長跋並書《九歌》原文。又有林溫、王沂、周伯琦、林希之、劉鶚、賀方、錢惟善、易恒等九人題跋。清孫承澤亦跋二處，均真：圖中押賈似道氏長腳"封"字印，偽。此圖畫法，諸神祇皆為白描，但衣領袖口處則墨染，用筆柔韌富於彈力，輕重變化較大，似有南宋馬和之影響。一些段落有簡略的襯景，景物亦用水墨渲染，雖在充分發揮水暈墨章上近於南宋人，但筆墨已較含蓄，區別於南宋馬遠、夏圭派的陽剛之美。至於狀物傳神，則倍極生動。如"河伯"一段，畫河神迎面而來，頃身坐黿上，順流而下，頗饒動勢。為表現逆風前進，畫家還精細地描繪了冠帶的飛揚，鬍鬚的飄拂。其側又點綴荷葉三、四，俯仰有致，深得物情。荷葉間撇以蘆葦多莖，亦因風勢而向一方搖曳。天空圓日一輪，則用水墨烘染其四周。畫荷葉所用水墨點染的方法而生動，亦有近於南宋牧谿之處。七十年代初葉，我曾親見此圖，以為是宋末元初人之作，已故著名鑒定家張珩定為元初人所作，徐邦達以為作者是南宋人。總之，在本文討論的三本中，此圖時代最早。

南京大學歷史系文物館所藏《九歌圖》卷(下文簡稱"南大本")在三本中，為時最晚。筆者在七十年代末葉，蒙考古學家蔣纘初教授慨然出示，得以獲觀。此圖紙本，墨筆白描，無款。依次畫《九歌》，無"禮魂"一段。每段後均篆書本詞文本。書前方鈐九疊文"之印"半印，白文"徐榮印"，圖中押"會稽太守之印"，前隔水有清同治癸亥年僧人果差一題。拖尾有清人伊念曾、費丹旭、姚燮、許榮、吳鐘駿、杜聲、蓮衣等諸人題跋。從題跋印記看，明以前無考。而清人伊氏、費氏、姚氏都斷為明人或明初人之作。各段或有景，或無景，畫法風格在人物用筆及佈景筆墨上取法南宋，但亦可看到元人影響。六十年代，書畫鑒賞家張珩、韓慎先雖定南宋作品，今天看來，徐邦達以為不早于明初是有根據的。

南大本與傳張本的同中之異

南大本中的"湘夫人"一段，是幅很有情調的佳作：雲鬢漆黑身著縞素的兩個少女，一正一側地坐在秋林中，沉靜地默望前方，袖手而待。在她們周圍是秋風吹動著的樹木，攀附在樹身上的藤絡隨風揚起，吹落的秋葉，尚在空中無主地飄搖。身邊的叢叢嫩竹也戰顫在秋風中，倒向一側。少女膝下和竹樹根部都隱沒在光影中，無際的光影一直籠罩了遠方泛起微波的江水。一種期待之情，如光如影地充溢於畫內。圖中的一切都是在狀物，同時又都是在抒情。畫家不是以形象圖解文本，而是以繪畫語言重現詩歌的情境。清代一些觀者有感於此，紛紛在跋文中發出讚歎。伊念曾稱其"氣韻生動"，費丹旭稱其"筆筆著意遠出仇唐之上"，姚燮說它"寓恣肆於嚴密"，費氏還專門借臨一過。

這幅畫在藝術上所達到的水平，無疑是高超的，比仇英、唐寅一般的仕女畫，也更具感染力。但是，如果用以對照傳張本的"二湘"一段，就並不令人感到過於驚歎了。就會看出，作者原來是在前人成就的基礎上取得了新的發展。二本在人物神情動態的描繪上，在人物環境的經營位置上，均十分相近。傳張本的"二湘"，也是兩位少女一正一側袖手坐於秋林中，若暇思，亦若期待。但正坐者著白衣，側坐者著淡色衣。所有衣領袖邊皆以較重色墨渲染。從局部考察，被衣領袖邊強調的動勢線，特別是袖口那下垂而拖曳的勢態加強了人物靜坐以待的情態。然而，從全局看，傳張本的"二湘"色調的柔和就遠不如南大本白衣烏髮不染領袖且以灰調子為背景那麼鮮明動人了。在背景的描繪上，二者都是一片秋林，江波泛起，秋葉飄蕭，藤絡舞動，但亦有不同處：傳張本秋林以馬尾松為主。松葉的倒垂，藤條的舞動，枯枝的臨風搖曳，固然在以松樹象徵人物的情操方面或有命意，也造成了秋風颯颯的感覺，可是未能突出湘水之畔的景色特點，把江水畫得像馬遠《水圖》中的"疊浪層層"或者旨在襯托人物內心的不平靜，但已不是文本中"嫋嫋兮秋風"的抒情意味了。南大本的"湘夫人"則與此不同，背景也有松樹，但不以松為主，還描寫了另些雜樹與枯樹，纏上樹上的藤絡得到了突出，飛落飄泊的樹葉被有意識地描繪於空曠的光影中，異常醒目。少女身邊添加的秋風中的嫩竹，既能與感取喻，令人聯想少女的命運，又恰切地交待了湘江之畔自然環境的特點。文本中"嫋嫋兮秋風，洞庭波兮木葉下"的情感氣氛在此得到了妥貼地表現。江水畫在遠方，只是微波泛起，象馬遠《水圖》中的"秋波杳杳"，又隱現於光影明滅中，景的渺遠，恰恰表達了文本中"目眇眇兮愁予"的哀愁與眷念之情的悠長。圖中不畫地面，用閃動的光影略去不必交待的無關宏旨的細節，遂使人物、秋林、江水聯成一體，在虛實的結合滲透中令愁思彌漫於廣闊的空間，意深情遠，耐人尋味。

南大本與傳李本的異中之同

傳李本《九歌圖》中的"湘夫人"在藝術上也是相當高妙的。構圖雖簡，而表現力很強。圖中只畫一女子、一老樹，但在渲染氣氛處理虛實濃淡上頗為精到。女子用筆殊簡，衣縞素，髮濃黑，袖手立雲中。其軟髮向上飄舉，身旁為土坡上老樹一株，仿佛自天而下"降兮北渚"。老樹軀幹巨大，枝葉已枯，俯身立秋風中。樹身以淡墨染，形成灰色塊，正好反襯白描畫成的女子。女子烏鬢與白衣的對比，使之在畫中非常突出。觀者會開卷便注意到她那微微俯首若有所思的情態。樹上之纏藤以濃墨點葉，與女人濃黑的雲鬢相呼應，在單純中饒有豐富的韻律感。作者遠從畫面的左上向右下以淡墨染出數道，有若風勢，造成了"秋風秋雨愁煞人"的氣氛。以此圖與南大本"湘夫人"對照，也可以發現藝術表現上的某些相同之處。其一，正面而坐的少女顏面較豐腴，並且幾乎一模一樣；其二，少女雲鬢漆黑，衣裳雪白，對比強烈，又處在灰色背景的烘托之下，十分鮮明突出；其三，少女下半身以"虛"的手法加以省略，突出其上半身的情態動作；其四，自畫面左上向右下用淡墨染出風的感覺。雖然如此，南大本與傳李本的相同或相似之處，已巧妙地融入本身完整統一的藝術境象中了，因此相同中有變異。變異合理的依據，除去更符合文本交待的細節外，主要是按畫家對文本的理解強化藝術表現。比如，傳李本著重描寫"湘夫人"隨風勢自天而降，故強調風勢中樹影的遠離與人物的若有若無，對洞庭木落未予直接表現。而南大本則著重描寫"湘夫人"在靜中有動的環境中期待沉思，所以描寫環境較具體，又為了不致影響人物的突出，遂以環境統一於灰色調中而突出了黑髮白衣的人物。對洞庭秋風落葉的細節，亦以竹樹纏藤的飄動，落葉的片片刻意顯示。二者與傳張本比較，傳張本畫法實而不虛，傳李本虛中有實，而南大本實中有虛，傳李本虛之以風勢，南大本則主要虛之以光影。

同一母題在繼承中的發展

以上三本《九歌圖》的作者已無法獲知。明初南大本《九歌圖》作者是否一定見到過完成時間更早的另兩本亦無可考。但是，由於相傳為李公麟創作的《九歌圖》在宋元以來流傳甚多。傳張本與傳李本應均有底本以致摹本。從前文三圖有關部分的比較可以使人相信，即使南大本作者從沒有見到過另二本，至少也會見到過另二本的底本、別本或摹本。另二本的構圖或藝術家理顯然影響了南大本的出現，而南大本作者在因革取捨間是注入了自身對原詩文本的理解及一定的生活體驗的，故而別具新意。

在傳李本《九歌圖》中，"湘君"和"湘夫人"是分做兩段描繪的，有每段旁邊所錄的原詩為證。"湘君"一段，畫一男子戴冠有鬚，回首立雲端。"湘夫人"一段緊接其後。不難從這種編排中看出，作者是把"湘夫人"當作《九歌》中的神祇之一來描寫的。這種處理意味著作者並沒有把"湘夫人"視為古史傳說中的唐堯的女兒。持這種理解者也不乏其人，顧炎武便說“《九歌》‘湘君’‘湘夫人’自是二神。此之為神，與天地並，不得謂堯女也。”按照這種理解來構思命筆，自然會很重視文本中的“帝子降兮北渚”，從而選取了湘夫人自天而降軟髮逆風揚起的瞬間，其足下流動著雲氣，正是以別於人的構想的產物。選取自天而降的瞬間，表現在一段時間內持續的“目眇眇兮愁予”是有困難的。為此，作者便以景襯人，寓意于景，靠充滿風勢的簡潔明瞭的秋樹，烘托出湘夫人內心無法平靜的愁思。

傳張本與此不同。“湘君”“湘夫人”被處理成一段，旁邊書寫了“湘君”“湘夫人”兩章詩歌。二湘都畫成了女子。顯然，作者沒有把“湘君”和“湘夫人”視為配偶神，甚至於也不打算把她們畫成神祇。韓愈在《黃陵廟碑》中說“堯之長女‘娥皇’，為舜之正妃，故為君。其二女‘女英’自宜降為夫人也。”看來，傳張本正是按照這種古老傳說中的理解來描繪的。二湘在作者心目中已成為人間失戀的少女，她們的丈夫舜死了，故充滿了悲哀愁苦與沒有結果的期待。因此，作者沒有畫雲氣，也沒有選取“帝子降兮北渚”的刹那，而是讓二湘腳踏實地生活於人間的洞庭湖畔，在“目眇眇兮愁予，嫋嫋兮秋風，洞庭波兮木葉下”三句上下功夫。通過人物坐等的靜止的場景描寫，強調了久候不至望眼欲穿的寂寞憂傷。這種把二湘理解為娥皇，女英的認識，與文徵明畫《二湘圖》的立意是一致的。文氏在該圖中題道：“余少時閱趙魏公畫湘君湘夫人，行筆設色皆極高古。石田先生命余臨之，余輒不敢。今二十年矣。偶見畫娥皇、女英者，作唐妝，雖極精工，而古意略盡，固仿趙公為此設色……。”據此可知，從趙孟頫的二湘圖，就已不作配偶神可視為“堯之二女”—“有舜二妃”了，本此立意畫二湘者在明代也仍有人在。

南大本《九歌圖》“湘夫人”一段，雖構圖與人物安排雖頗似傳張本“二湘”一段，但此本另有“湘君”一段，此段題為“湘夫人”，這又何以索解？查王逸注《楚辭》時，即以“湘君”為水神，以“湘夫人”為娥皇女英了。看來，南大本《九歌圖》作者正是本此理解的。圖中別的段落仍作神祇處理，唯湘夫人一段按傳說中的娥皇女英處理，也正因為如此，傳張本的二湘因具體內容契合，因而被當作重要構圖依據而有所變異了。湘竹的著意描寫，似乎即是為引起“湘妃竹”的聯想而增益的，充溢畫面的光影除了傳情之外，也可以給人以追懷往古流光的啟示。此圖湘夫人所受傳李本或其別本摹本的影響，顯然主要只在藝術表現方面。

通過以上分析，不難看出，南大本《九歌圖》“湘夫人”較高的藝術水平是建立在前人多種探索和已有成效的基礎之上的。它啟示我們想到這樣一個帶有普遍意義的問題：在中國繪畫史上，有些傳統母題在不同時代不同畫家筆下一畫再畫，似乎是重復，然而如果不屬於臨摹復製的話，就一定會有所變異。實際上，重復的只是題材，也許在構圖和形象上有所取法，但不僅在對題材的理解上會有所不同，而且在藝術表現上總會有因有革，有承繼，也有發展。研究同一母題乃至同一構圖在歷史發展中的演進變化，對於瞭解中國畫家怎樣在自己的文化背景下進行藝術探索，對於瞭解不同時代不同素養的畫家怎樣在處理傳統題材上發揮創造才能，對於不脫離歷史地估價一些作品的成就，都會是有益的。

The Mirror in the Garden: Courtesans' Painting of the Late Ming Dynasty

JEAN WETZEL

One of the more provocative titles for a major art exhibition in recent years was "Bad Girls."[1] Viewers of this display of works by twentieth-century feminist artists might have been astonished to learn that another group of women artists who might qualify as "bad girls" was active in China at least as early as the seventeenth century. These were the painters of the courtesan class. Like their contemporaries in seventeenth-century Europe, Chinese courtesans were not outcasts, but played a significant role in the aesthetic culture of their time. While the role of European courtesans in the visual arts remained that of muse and object for the idealized portrayals created by male painters,[2] however, some Chinese courtesans of this period were themselves highly acclaimed painters.

This paper is an initial exploration of the phenomenon of the success of courtesan-painters in the late Ming dynasty (1368–1644). As such, it addresses the following three questions: Why do courtesans constitute such a large percentage of women artists recorded as active in the Ming dynasty? How did these courtesan-artists serve as a mirror of the social, intellectual, and aesthetic desires and priorities of their male patrons? Finally, how did their talent as painters provide opportunities for Ming courtesans to subvert and transcend, even to a small extent, limitations traditionally imposed upon those of their class and gender?

It would be wrong to foster the impression that a large number of Chinese women artists of any class are represented in either records or actual paintings before the twentieth century; this is not the case in Chinese art history any more than it is in that of Europe. The role of women in painting in China, however, is established in ancient mythological accounts. Tradition has it that painting was invented by Lei, the younger sister of the legendary emperor Shun (ca. 2200 B.C.). Still, the paucity of records of women artists prior to the tenth century suggests that, like their male contemporaries, most were anonymous artisans who produced didactic works for temples and palaces. The largest number of known women painters appears in records dating from between 1300 and 1912. This may be because most of these women were of, or attached to, the scholar-gentry (literati) class, which formed the dominant school of painting in China after 1300.[3] Although we know more about women artists during this period, the material available in historical records, and even in contemporary research on Chinese painting, is still sparse in comparison to the wealth of information about male painters. The available sources suggest, however, that courtesans formed a major subclass among Chinese women painters, particularly in the Ming dynasty.

The *Yutai huashi* (Painting History of the Jade Terrace), an important nineteenth-century work compiled from earlier sources by Tang Souyu, the wife of a Hangzhou scholar and book collector, is a history of women painters from the Tang (618–907) to the Qing (1644–1911) dynasty. Tang Souyu categorizes the painters according to social class: court and noblewomen, gentry women, concubines and second wives, and "acclaimed prostitutes" (*mingji*). Of the approximately 230 women artists recorded in the volume, palace women and concubines account for only 31 and 17, respectively. While women of the gentry class constitute the largest group at 127, courtesan-artists form the second largest group, with 41 artists of this class recorded as having been active between the Tang and Qing dynasties.[4] What is perhaps most striking is the dramatic increase in women painters of these last two classes during the Ming dynasty. Between the Yuan (1279–1368) and Ming, the number of gentry women painters recorded by Tang Sonyu jumps from 9 to 56, a sixfold increase. For courtesan painters, the number surges from 4 in the Song dynasty (960–1279) to 32 in the Ming, an eightfold increase.[5] It is also noteworthy that, although there is a significant disparity in the total number of gentry women and courtesan-artists included in the *Yutai huashi*, the difference in number in the Ming period is not that great. A confluence of several factors in the late Ming seems to have created an atmosphere conducive to the activities of courtesans schooled in the art of painting.

HISTORY OF AND ATTITUDES TOWARD COURTESANS

One of the major factors that enabled courtesans of the Ming dynasty to achieve public prominence and success in the visual arts may have been the power of history and tradition that underlay much of Chinese culture. While her ancient ancestor was a sexual slave, by the Ming dynasty the courtesan had evolved into what Eloise Hibbert has romanticized as "the emancipated woman of ancient China. Men of intellect sought her company because she was at home in their society. And what was more she carried on the musical and artistic traditions of her country."[6]

Historically, there were three classifications of prostitutes in China. State or official prostitutes (*guanji*) were the ancient predecessors of the Ming dynasty courtesans who became artists.[7] Around the seventh century B.C., the practice had evolved of taking into bondage the women of the families of convicted criminals to serve in the state bordellos as reparation for the family member's crimes. (Male members of the family often would be required to serve as slaves to government officials.) The *guanji* class later also came to include women from poor families who either could not afford dowries or who were forced to sell their daughters to the brothels to pay off family debts.[8] Since their lives as prostitutes often involved sacrifice for the family or other circumstances that could easily be interpreted as "fate," these women were often viewed sympathetically rather than reviled as immoral.

The function of *guanji* seemed to change dramatically in the early Tang period when this class of prostitutes, who had evolved over the centuries into entertainers trained in singing and dancing, also began to be educated in the classics and poetry. By the Song dynasty, *guanji* were invited by members of the Imperial Academy to take part in dinners with poetry contests, and many famous poets of the period had affairs with and took as concubines courtesans with whom they carried on poetic correspondence.[9] As in many areas of art and culture, the Ming dynasty may have looked back to this Song precedent. By the Ming period, not all courtesans were unfortunate women sold to brothels by poor families; some were lower-class women who were either too beautiful or too intellectually and artistically gifted to be satisfied with men of their own class. These women may have chosen the profession for its social mobility—the possibility of becoming a wife or concubine of a distinguished scholar or official—and the freedom to pursue and express their talents.[10] The element of choice and the possibility of social mobility were unheard of for most Chinese women prior to the nineteenth and twentieth centuries. As is usually the case, however, this freedom was not total but relative; it came with costs. Ming courtesans lived on the razor's edge of paradox, aptly described by Lynn Lawner as "the continual dualism of courtesanry—at once free and bound, exhilarating and humiliating."[11] Yet, for the bright and talented Ming courtesan the possibilities for "freedom" and "exhilaration" were greater than those available to most women in the world in the seventeenth century.

The Ming dynasty seems to have been not only the apogee of courtesan culture in Chinese history, but also a period in which both men and women enjoyed a mobility in social, intellectual, and artistic circles unknown to earlier generations. As in Europe, this situation was created in China by a shift to a more urban culture and commercially based economy. The brothels of great cities were one of the primary sites where upwardly mobile poets, artists, and scholars of both genders were able to mingle. When Chinese rule was renewed under the Ming after almost a hundred years of Mongol occupation, brothels were revived and quickly became centers for men of culture to pursue "a dream vision of feminine enchantment."[12] Although active "pleasure districts" were prominent in most major Chinese cities, the arts were cultivated to the highest degree in those located in cities in the Jiangnan area, in southern China: Yangzhou, Suzhou, Jiaxing, Hangzhou, and, most particularly, Nanjing.

Upon his ascension to the throne, the first Ming emperor, Hongwu (r. 1368–98), established the Compound of Wealth and Pleasure near the Imperial Path Bridge in Nanjing. Prostitutes were brought from all over to work in the district's sixteen brothels, and wives of convicts, captives, executed rebels, and recalcitrant officials were forced to join them.[13] When the Ming capital was moved to Beijing, in 1421, Nanjing maintained its status as the southern capital, even including an Imperial Academy. It was also one of the major sites for the official examinations, which were the path to success in the Chinese bureaucratic system. Many scholars were assigned to Nanjing where they had leisure time to engage in calligraphy, painting, poetry, and book collecting, activities that by the early Ming had become the enthusiastic avocation (and sometimes vocation) of their class.[14] The Ming educational system was also among the most liberal, with examinations open to men of all classes and more examination candidates accepted from non-official families. The brothel quarter happened to be near the site at which the official examinations were held.[15]

Courtesans were both sought after and respected by the Nanjing scholars. According to Howard Levy, courtesans were praised and remembered not only for their physical beauty, but also for their skills and talents as entertainers and in the arts. A valued courtesan, like her scholar patron, dabbled in calligraphy and painting, collected books, played and sang music, recited poetry, acted out dramatic parts with distinction, and assisted at banquets with courtesy, refinement, and expertise. "It is evident that courtesans who enthralled members of high society did so primarily through artistic attainment rather than physical appeal."[16]

Although "learned courtesans" were extolled in Chinese literature at least as early as the ninth century when Sun Chi wrote a treatise on the lives of the courtesans, praising many for their "quick intelligence,"[17] the late Ming dynasty was the peak of visibility and respectability of courtesan culture. Dorothy Ko has pointed out three main characteristics of courtesan culture in the Ming: its indispensable role in the public lives of scholar-officials; the primacy of poetry and music (and, one might add, painting) as the language of social interaction and the recognition of women as creators; and the permeability of the boundary between the courtesan world and the domestic world.[18] Ko offers evidence of both the social fluidity of the courtesans' lives and their great value to the careers of the scholars who were their patrons. Through parties in the brothel district and, in the later Ming, at scholars' homes, courtesans provided an initiation for examination candidates "into the tastes and manners of the power elite. They also helped to introduce new dramas and poems [and painting styles?] created by their clients and themselves."[19]

That courtesans were highly valued is reflected in both legal and literary texts of the late Ming period. Rules governing relationships with courtesans were created, including how much of a patron's income was expected to be given to her. If an affair lasted more than three months, the man was expected to support the courtesan until he found someone equal in rank and assets to take his place.[20] And, as discussed below, attitudes toward courtesans came more often to reflect a male vision of the "ideal woman," rather than the harsher realities of courtesan life.

MANIFESTATIONS OF THE IDEAL

The courtesan lived a dual life—a life that was on the one hand reflected in her idealized image, and on the other hand rooted in the reality of being dependent upon a tenuous and often unpleasant system of support and self-support. "The literati blithely ignored the darker side of brothel life and indulged themselves in the brothels as a kind of cult of elegant living. And it was their idealization of these quarters that elevated this aspect of Ming cultural life away from the sordid and towards the sublime."[21]

One of the major historical objectives of the artist has been the creation of objects of beauty. Another has been the formation of an illusion of reality, or of a substitute reality in which the viewer can dwell for a time. Lynn Lawner has theorized that creating an art of dissimulation was one of the primary talents, and possibly functions, of the courtesan of Renaissance Europe. Moreover, the primary evidence for this function in both

Renaissance Europe and Ming China is that while this illusion was created and promoted by the courtesan herself, it was given added weight and credence by her powerful patrons' willingness to believe and actively support it. As Lawner has stated, men who tried to denigrate courtesans risked a "crime against dissimulation," since the courtesan was meant to be perceived as what she seemed rather than what she was. By exposing courtesans in an unflattering light, one risked "injuring society's own image of itself."[22]

Chinese of earlier periods were tolerant of and sympathetic toward prostitutes. In later dynasties courtesans were not only accorded high honor for their talent in the arts, but were praised for their virtue—a tantalizing trick of dissimulation if ever there was one. It is notable, however, that this transformation in the perception of courtesans often appears within or in connection with the arts, which, as stated above, are concerned with creating a convincing illusion of a more perfect reality. Consider, for example, drama. Several Chinese plays from the Yuan period onward feature courtesans in major roles. In these, the courtesan is usually represented as a woman of high moral and ethical qualities or at least an object of the viewer's sympathy. The cases in which she is portrayed as "bad" are rare.[23]

Another example of gilding the image of a former courtesan is found in the case of the painter Dong Bai (1625–1651). Dong was a Nanjing courtesan who became a concubine of the scholar Mao Xiang (1611–1693) in 1642, after a friend of his paid off her debts and bought her contract. After Dong's death, Mao wrote a reminiscence of their time together. He praised abundantly Dong's artistic tastes, intellectual talents, and empathy with his own highly evolved sense of aesthetics. Mao also lauded his new concubine for more traditional female "virtues": her industriousness around the house, ability to get along with his wife and his mother, dedicated tutoring of his sons, and keeping of his household accounts.[24]

The *Yutai huashi*'s section on famous courtesans of the Ming probably also reflects attempts to create an idealized image of this class of women artists. All the entries designate the women as courtesans and mention their talent in painting, calligraphy, and other arts; yet few make much ado of the women's erotic charms. Common are descriptions such as that of Fan Jue, said to be "pure and modest and of simple tastes," preferring to "retire and burn incense and soak tea."[25] A poem on a fan painting of a willow tree by the Nanjing courtesan Lin Nuer (active Chenghua era, 1465–

87) compares her to a gentle willow whose "tender twigs" were bruised by callous admirers.[26]

It is my contention that the courtesan-artists' rise to prominence in the Ming dynasty was due chiefly to their image in art and literature as "ideal women," an image created both by themselves and by their patrons. In addition, I believe that the patrons of courtesans actually came to identify with them, much as one identifies with one's own reflection in a mirror, for they embodied many of the qualities their patrons sought to cultivate in themselves. The remainder of this paper examines three major ways in which the devices of idealization of a certain type of woman and the commensurate mirroring of male desires and values in this ideal helped to elevate the status of women artists of the courtesan class in the Ming period.

EDUCATION AND WOMEN IN THE MING DYNASTY

Education played a primary role in the success of a Chinese courtesan of the seventeenth century, particularly in developing her skills in the visual arts. Attitudes about education for women, and the slow transformation in images of the "ideal women" in other classes of Chinese society, also opened doors for the acceptance and visibility of courtesans as artists and poets in Ming society.

The traditional Chinese attitude toward the role of women—particularly that of wives and mothers—in the artistic and intellectual realm is summed up in the popular saying: "A woman without talent has virtue."[27] Thus scholarly and aesthetically inclined men seeking "soul mates" typically looked outside the boundaries of their arranged marriages. The courtesan quarter provided the perfect opportunity to find talented (if not conventionally virtuous) women, as education was an essential vehicle for achieving success as a high-level courtesan.

Courtesans were the "Cosmo Girls" of earlier times, expected to dress beautifully and expensively. Since their primary role was to act as cultured companions for upper-class men, it was also essential that they be proficient in the arts of witty conversation, singing, dancing, and playing musical instruments.[28] It was not until the Ming dynasty, however, when painting and calligraphy were fully established as "gentlemen's accomplishments," that these visual arts were also cultivated by courtesans.[29] The means by which courtesans were educated remains sketchy, but much of their education probably took place after they were sold to brothels, usually around the age of twelve. Of the courtesan-artists featured in the Ming section of Tang Souyu's *Yutai huashi*, the majority are praised not only as painters, but also as poets, musicians, singers and dancers, and adept readers and collators of literary texts.[30] That they were most likely educated in these arts after entering the brothel, rather than before, is suggested by at least two considerations. One is the assumption that a twelve-year-old girl would have had to be an amazing prodigy in order to have learned so many skills before entering the courtesan ranks. The other is the frequency with which these courtesan-painters seem to have been attached to particular areas, especially the Jiuyuan (Old Compound) in the Chenghua section of Nanjing. The majority of the Ming courtesan-artists recorded by Tang Souyu were from Nanjing. At least four of these women lived in the Jiuyuan, which, according to Yu Huai's (1616–1696) *Banqiao zaji* (Diverse Records of the Wooden Bridge), was considered to be the most prestigious courtesan compound:

> Lowly and trifling prostitutes lived in the Southern City. Pearl City occasionally had an unusual beauty, but all the famous singing girls of the southern quarter and the foremost-ranking official prostitutes resided in the Old [Prostitution] Compound.[31]

This may suggest that brothels in the Jiuyuan chose only the best-educated and talented women, but is just as likely to signify that the women who ended up there received a superior education to those in the other compounds.

By the late Ming, however, courtesans and gentry women in China were not solely dependent on others for education, but had unprecedented opportunities for self-education. This is reflected in the dramatic upsurge in women painters of the courtesan and gentry classes noted in the *Yutai huashi* and in the increase in published women writers and poets at the end of the Ming. Dorothy Ko cites the booming publishing industry of the seventeenth century, which was a result of an increasingly urbanized and commercialized economy, as a major reason for this thriving subsociety of literary and artistic women.[32] Competition among publishers in major societies in the Jiangnan area kept production of books high and prices low, allowing much greater access to printed materials. Even if courtesans and gentry women were often confined to the "inner chambers," they had greater access to a wide range of literature, as both authors and audience,[33] than ever before in China's history.

Access to printed books also allowed women, both gentry and courtesans, to develop more sophisticated visual literacy. Books such as Gu Bing's *Gushi huapu* (Master Gu's Pictorial Album) of 1603 were designed to offer visual education in painting styles of the past for a would-be connoisseur. Craig Clunas states that this can "be seen on one level as part of the broader 'commodification of knowledge' observable for the first time in a number of areas of sixteenth–seventeenth-century culture; the purchaser acquires cultural capital by the acquisition of the volume."[34] This was particularly empowering to women. Not only did volumes like Gu Bing's allow women to become more authoritative when viewing and discussing art with their patrons, but such manuals allowed familiarity with models from the past, a knowledge of which had also become the aesthetic "cultural capital" among male scholar-artists even earlier than the Ming dynasty.

Thus, during the Ming period there arose a greater number of educated women among those with the money to purchase printed books and the leisure time and incentive to pour over them: the gentry and courtesan classes. As a result, the attitude toward talented women among the more enlightened men of the Ming also seemed to undergo a marked shift; the "ideal woman" (and, by association, the ideal candidate for a relationship with a man) was one with artistic and intellectual gifts. This located talented courtesan-painters less on the fringes of society and more in the mainstream of Ming social and aesthetic consciousness.

According to the Ming dynasty scholar and connoisseur Li Yu, talent in a woman consisted of four skills: an ability to write poetry and literature; to play musical instruments; to sing and dance; and to do needlework. These are clearly the skills traditionally taught to courtesans (who also, like many Chinese women of the upper classes, were expected to learn embroidery). Truly "cultivated ladies" (*guixiu*, or "ladies in the inner chamber"),[35] according to Li Yu, must also be proficient in the four arts of calligraphy, painting, zither, and chess, and "if they excel in any one of these arts they will gain fame as gifted women [*cainü*]."[36] This illustrates not only how well courtesan-painters fit into Li's loftiest category of women, but also the high status of the arts of painting and calligraphy in the Ming. Talent in painting or calligraphy alone would catapult a woman into the *cainü* stratosphere, as far as Li was concerned.

Even more significant as a reflection of the transformation of the womanly ideal was the celebration of the union of educated and talented men and women in the literature and thought of the late Ming and early Qing periods. Dorothy Ko sees the phenomenon as a confluence of two factors: the growing acceptance of educated women among the Ming literati and a greater value placed by male scholars on the concept of what she calls the Cult of *Qing* (feeling or emotion).[37] Traditional "female" and "male" diversions seemed to blur as "more men came to value women as emotional companions, either inside or outside the bounds of arranged marriage."[38] One crucial outcome of this was the growing emphasis, among educated males in the Jiangnan region, on the ideal of "companionate marriage" (although married women were still expected to maintain the traditional values of virtue and household industriousness, as well).[39] An ardent emotional and artistic relationship was what men traditionally sought in the courtesan quarter. Rather than reducing the importance of courtesans, however, the idealization of the companionate marriage in the late Ming dynasty only served to elevate the status of the courtesan through association.

This ideal became quite popular, as manifested in both "chaste" and "erotic" novels of the late Ming and early Qing. Keith McMahon has aptly illustrated the shift in attitudes toward women during this period as it appears in the frequency of the "beauty and the scholar" (*caizi jiaren*) theme in seventeenth-century novels: "One of the most prominent features of such works is their portrayal of smart, capable, chaste young women who are equal to and in some cases better than their male counterparts in terms of literary talent, moral fiber and wit."[40] One might notice that the late Ming courtesan-artist, like her educated sister of the gentry class, ably fulfilled all aspects of this description save for one: chastity. The alchemy for the transformation of the courtesan into a woman of purity befitting this ideal was deftly handled by the Ming courtesan-painter through the manipulation of visuality in at least two intriguing ways.

VISUALITY AND GENDER IN LATE MING CULTURE

Before examining the methods used by courtesans to purify their image, we must consider the intriguing relationship among gender, visuality, and the art of painting that became prominent in the late Ming period. Seventeenth-century Jiangnan, like seventeenth-century Rome, had a highly sophisticated visual culture. In both cases, paintings were considered prized commodities. In China, even more so than in Rome, paintings often embodied a potent combination of visual beauty and poetic resonance requiring sensitivity and intellectual acumen from the "gentlemen" who gazed at them both in public and in private. More often, however, this viewing was a type of social ritual, and was expected to be a shared act.[41]

It is rather startling to realize that many of these same values applied to the relationship between courtesans, their patrons, and painting. One of the most stunning manifestations of this, as Craig Clunas has pointed out, is the conflation of viewing a painting with viewing a beautiful woman:

> Perhaps the most startling analogy, and one which is repeated in a number of texts, is that between looking at a painting and looking at a woman. "Looking at a painting is like looking at a beautiful woman (*meiren*)," says the *Hui miao* ... Women were certainly considered as the objects of a connoisseurly gaze in the Ming, ranked and appraised like other forms of elite male consumption.[42]

This analogy is unfortunate in its accuracy when applied to the courtesan. She was prized for her beauty, associated with the arts and their appeal to the senses, and was available for purchase (although in the idealized view of the day, this involved a high degree of discrimination on the part of both the gifted courtesan and her cultivated patron). A conflation of women with beauty, the arts, intellectual pursuits, and, in some cases, sensuality, has many manifestations in the Ming dynasty; it will serve the present purpose to mention a few of those that may have benefited Chinese women, especially women artists.

If, as Craig Clunas has said, "in China ... every act of viewing was also an act of social interaction,"[43] then women seem to have been especially valued as partners in such interactions. Mao Xiang's choice of Dong Bai as his courtesan probably had a great deal to do with the fact that she was a highly accomplished calligrapher and an able painter. This is attested to by the fact that after Dong Bai's death Mao took two other women painters, Cai Han and Jin Yue, as concubines. Most of the paintings produced by Cai and Jin seem to have been joint works. Mao's inscriptions appear on many of these as dedications to the intended recipients, and some also clearly state that he "ordered" his concubines to execute the works.[44] This would suggest that Mao may have valued these women even more for their artistic talents than for their other assets. It also suggests that his concubines' works were a valued commodity for social exchange between Mao and his literati friends. Whether this was simply because the women were accomplished painters or because of some type of multifaceted evaluation of beauty, perhaps with erotic undertones, shared by the males involved is hard to say.

Women may have been indirectly empowered through the emphasis on visual culture in the Ming, as elucidated by Dorothy Ko. She equates the great popularity of illustrated printed books in the seventeenth century with "foregrounding" the needs of the stereotypical female reader. (Women were considered to be generally less intellectual than men and to prefer images, which had a more direct emotional impact, to complex text.)[45] Since women were not the primary audience for these or any books, this new emphasis on pictures (connected with text) may also have given greater prominence to values traditionally seen as "feminine."

An association—whether direct, metaphorical, or emotional—with the arts may have raised the status of both courtesans and gentry women who were painters in the late Ming dynasty; it certainly contributed to refining the image of the courtesan-artist and affording her more legitimacy within the mainstream of the contemporary urban art world. Whether the courtesan herself played the largest role in shaping this process is debatable. She did, however, employ certain visual tricks in order to create a more favorable image and legitimize herself in the eyes of her patrons and thus in the upper levels of seventeenth-century Jiangnan society.

CROSS-DRESSING AND CROSSING GENDER BOUNDARIES

In *The Second Sex*, Simone de Beauvoir uses the "image of the mirror as a key to the feminine condition" by saying that women are concerned with their own images, while men are concerned with "an enlarged self-image provided by their reflection in a woman."[46] Much of the discussion above has shown how seventeenth-century Chinese courtesans benefited from their role as a reflection of contemporary male desires and values. More fascinating, however, are some examples of courtesans manipulating visual expectations through mirroring actual male appearance and behavior.

One of the well-known examples of courtesan cross-dressing appears in the biographical records of the accomplished courtesan-painter Liu Yin (1618–1664). Even before meeting her primary patron and, later, husband, Qian Qianyi (1582–1664), Liu had been praised as both a poet and a painter. It is said that Liu, determined to meet Qian, dressed like a young male scholar and called on Qian to present her poetry.[47] Her bold move was successful, and after the death of his first wife Qian married Liu. Even after the marriage, she supposedly continued to dress like a man when she met with Qian and his friends to discuss literature and art.[48]

Another of the late Ming art world's most prominent courtesans, Xue Wu (Xue Susu, ca. 1573–1620), called herself the "Fifth Boy." When the literatus Hu Yinglin (1543–1581) met her for the first time, he addressed her as "Master Xue" (or "Student Xue").[49] Xue was known not only for her painting and calligraphy, but also for an athletic prowess rarely associated with courtesans (most of whom had bound feet). According to records, Xue Wu was acclaimed for her archery skill and particularly for a trick in which she would shoot two balls from her crossbow while galloping on horseback, making the second ball hit the first in mid-air.[50]

It has been suggested that late Ming courtesan-artists took on these male personae in order to become more accepted in the public, male world of the literati. That there may have been an erotically charged pretense in the acceptance of Liu Yin's disguises, by both the artist and her audience, is also suggested by Dorothy Ko:

> Liu did not, however present herself to her male friends and clients as an androgynous *person*; her identity was firmly based on her self-representations as an androgynous *woman*. In daring to be man-like in concerns and looks, Liu did not forget that her femininity was her ultimate attraction. Among women the courtesan was free to negotiate and even to violate gender norms and roles; yet at the same time she was committed to accentuating her feminine identity. This ambivalence was best expressed in Liu's pride in the small size of her bound feet. Even when dressed in men's robes, she made sure that her tiny feet protruded from the garments.[51]

It is fascinating to note that toying with an androgynous image through the device of cross-dressing was also a technique employed by courtesans in Renaissance Europe. Men's clothing, such as trousers (often concealed under long skirts), was popular courtesan couture in sixteenth-century Venice, as well as in other parts of Italy and in France. There may be several reasons for this, including a desire for greater freedom of movement or an erotic association with the boys and male lovers also favored by some upper-class Renaissance men.[52] The fact that this phenomenon appears among the highest levels of courtesanry in both China and Europe would suggest that it was a potent strategy that legitimized the courtesan through a mirroring of the male patron upon whom she was dependent. In any case, it is a distinctive manifestation of the social functions of style and visual culture worthy of further examination.

THE COURTESAN'S SELF-IMAGE IN PAINTING

For the art historian, of course, assumption of the role of painter was the most significant means utilized by the courtesan-artist in the transformation of her image. The contribution of painting, and the creation of self-image in painting, to the success of the courtesan in the late Ming cultural world of Jiangnan is presented here utilizing a few examples. These images constitute an attempt to present to the viewing public a self-portrait that would cast these courtesans in the most favorable light possible.

A courtesan's power rested upon her erotic and physical attraction. Yet if she was to be perceived as more than a sexual object, she also had to elicit either sympathy for her plight or, even more effective, respect for her virtue. As with most of the best literati painting in Chinese art history, the self-portraits by courtesans were not explicit, but metaphorical.[53] Many of the symbols chosen by courtesans for their paintings embody this constant shifting of identity from beautiful temptress to virtuous recluse.

One courtesan who employed this visual (and poetic) strategy of self-portraiture was Lin Nuer (Lin Jinlan), one of the famed courtesans of the Jiuyuan in Nanjing. She is said to have painted landscapes and figures in the style of the Southern Song painter Ma Yuan (active ca. 1190–1225), and her style was noted for its "feminine elegance."[54] Her paintings were appreciated by no less than Shen Zhou (1427–1509), one of the most important literati artists of the Ming period, who inscribed a poem on one of them. The painting of a willow on a fan mentioned above seems to be one of Lin's attempts to create a type of self-portrait. The willow was often employed to suggest ideal female attributes, such as a "willow waist" or "willow eyebrows." The first two lines of the inscription on Lin's painting allude to the willow as a symbol of female allure, as well as the dangers of such beauty to its possessor:

> In former times, [her] delicate waist swayed through the
> Changtai [brothel].

[Her] tender branches were plucked and injured by the
appointed officials.
If [her] sketching now enters into [the realm] of painting,
The East Wind [will not] be allowed to shake [her].[55]

The self-referential image was a subtle invocation to both the aesthetic imagination and the sympathy of the viewer-reader. It could evoke in the intended scholarly male audience a desire for the suggested female qualities. At the same time, the empathetic response would create a greater emotional bond between the viewer and the artist, thus helping to erase some of the distance inherent in the disparities between their classes and genders.

The most accomplished courtesan-painters, such as Xue Wu, Liu Yin, and Ma Shouzhen (1548–1604), probably painted many different subjects, much like their male contemporaries. In general, however, records of courtesans' paintings and the actual works seem to reflect a rather narrow range of subjects. The most popular among these seems to be the orchid, particularly monochrome renderings of orchids.[56] Of the thirty-two courtesan-painters of the Ming dynasty recorded in the *Yutai huashi*, at least half were praised for their paintings of orchids.[57] Of their three predecessors recorded in the Song dynasty, none was cited as an orchid specialist; all were acclaimed for their skill in rendering bamboo, usually in ink. This is not surprising, as ink bamboo was also a favored subject for the male literati painters who were probably the patrons of the courtesans during the Song and the succeeding Yuan dynasty.

In the Ming dynasty, however, the painting of orchids seems to be associated primarily with women painters of the courtesan class. Therefore, it is most likely that this subject was also one in which the courtesan-artist chose to lodge symbolically her self-identification. This practice may have become popularized by the illustrious Nanjing courtesan-painter Ma Shouzhen. A contemporary, Zhou Tianqiu (1514–1595), described Ma as "well enough refined in the 'female arts' to head the 'gay quarters.' In sketching orchids and bamboo she is without equal."[58] That Ma, who was also praised as a painter of other subjects, had a particular identification with the orchid is suggested not only by the large number of orchid paintings she executed,[59] but also by the fact that she called herself Xianglan, or orchid of the Xiang River.

In Chinese culture the orchid, like many other flowers, is associated with female beauty. Although the orchid has been interpreted elsewhere as an erotic symbol associated with the female body,[60] this was most likely not the intent of the courtesan painter of the Ming dynasty. The Chinese orchid is most noteworthy for its sweet fragrance, which one notices only if one takes the time to draw closer to it. Thus, the orchid became a symbol in earlier Chinese literati paintings of the "gentleman" whose modesty prevented his best qualities from being revealed, except to those who had the good taste and judgment to (be allowed to?) become more familiar with him. One can see how this association, cultivated in orchid paintings by courtesans, creates a mirroring of the male patron's own ideal image and aspirations as well as a more elevated image of the courtesan herself.

The rendering of orchids in ink was appreciated as a difficult art requiring considerable calligraphic skill, which reflected well on the talents of the courtesans, many of whom were accomplished calligraphers. Beyond its association with humility, the orchid was also a common symbol in Chinese art and literature for purity and seclusion because of its home in the "dark valleys of the rivers."[61] Chinese literati would eagerly have accepted the loaded analogy between finding a rare orchid hidden among the grasses of the riverbank and their alliances with the courtesans. Moreover, the image of the orchid had traditional symbolic resonance when applied to intimate human relationships. The Confucian classic of divination, the *Yijing* (The Book of Changes), employed this imagery to describe the serenity of being in spiritual and emotional rapport with someone, resulting in such phrases as "orchid relations" and "orchid friends."[62] Is it any wonder, then, in this period in which "companionate" relationships between men and women were being extolled by some literati, that the orchid became a subject that courtesans often painted for their patrons?

Not only did the courtesans utilize aesthetic association with the orchid as a catalyst for transforming their image into one of purity; their male patrons were also willing participants in this act of social alchemy. Poems composed by male patrons often compare courtesans to the purity, beauty, and delicacy of orchids (among other flowers). One such line was penned by the Nanjing scholar Yu Huai: "These [jasmine] ... were truly lewd buds of seductive night, bewitching weeds coquettishly attached to man. The Fukienese orchid [by way of contrast], was elegant and most uncommon."[63] Clearly the courtesans were cultivating an image of the "elegant and most uncommon."

One final example of a possibly more literal and bawdy self-portrait by a courtesan artist—a painting by the archer-athlete Xue Wu, now in the

Nanjing Museum—serves as a playful contrast to the "ideals" presented in the images described above. This work is especially notable, however, because it is rather unusual among courtesans' paintings and may represent a different aspect of self-imaging that was a more personal expression of the artist's own bold and mischievous personality. The painting portrays a beautiful woman in a garden setting seated near a rock and a grove of bamboo. The woman is playing a flute, and Xue's inscription reads: "When the jade flute can bear to be played on, the man is in the Phoenix Pavilion [a possible reference to paradise]." It is signed "Mistress Su of the Xue family with a playful brush."[64] This may be a very rare case of a courtesan deliberately portraying a subject with erotic implications obvious even to a twenty-first-century Western viewer. That it may also be a self-portrait is suggested by the fact that Xue was known to have played a real jade flute at parties.[65] Thus, self-expression is also one of the benefits that late Ming courtesans may have derived from their talent in painting.

COURTESANS, PAINTING, AND MOBILITY

This paper has been an examination of the way in which their talent provided the means for courtesans to transcend the limitations traditionally imposed upon those of their class and gender. This section briefly reviews how this mobility occurred on economic, personal, and social levels.

The ability to paint was an economic advantage to a woman, particularly in the late Ming when the art market had become so vital. Mao Xiang's "ordering" artwork by his two concubines may suggest that he was using their work for economic as well as social gain. Although the courtesans' freedom to come and go was relative and they operated under the handicap of having no legal status (unless they married or became concubines), their position afforded them the very unusual privilege of having little labor to perform and much leisure time to pursue activities such as painting. It also allowed them the possibility of an independent income, which was extremely rare among women in China.[66] Women could rely on painting to augment family finances or to earn a living when they lost the support of a husband or patron in their later years.[67]

As artists, women painters and poets in the late Ming dynasty often had an opportunity for self-expression that was denied the majority of Chinese women, who were usually of the slave or working classes.

Woman Playing a Bamboo Flute by Xue Wu is an example of a painting that seems to express the artist's own personality. Mao Xiang's description of the aesthetic activities of his concubine Dong Bai suggests that her motivation in painting and in looking at paintings was very personal. Mao wrote that Dong's love of painting and viewing ancient works was so great that when they were forced to flee their home at the end of the Ming, she chose to "abandon the articles of her dowry in order to bring along her writings and paintings."[68] Her efforts to save her treasures were unsuccessful: as Mao lamented, "Her writings and paintings were ill-fated, but she was body and soul with her hobby."[69] Ellen Laing has cited two later examples of women painters that also suggest the importance of art as an emotional outlet. The Qing painters Sun Baoshan and Ren Chunqi were both said to have died of grief after marrying men who forced them to give up painting.[70]

Being adept in the art of painting or poetry afforded women a great deal of social mobility in several contexts in the late Ming dynasty. The first was in the unusual opportunity to become famous for their personal talents rather than their Confucian sacrifice for family (the usual *lienu* model extolled in classical texts and special sections of provincial gazetteers). In this way, even if the courtesan did not wander far from home, her works and name might still become widely known. Ma Shouzhen represents just one example of this type of mobility. She was so well known as a painter that envoys supposedly came from as far away as Siam to buy her painted fans.[71] Several forgeries of her works also exist,[72] perhaps the highest compliment that can be paid a Chinese painter (imitation truly being one of the highest forms of flattery in Chinese art). As was the case with many women poets of the gentry class, whose families published their works in order to make them known to the cultured public, two volumes of Ma's poetry were published after her death by her admirer Wang Zhideng (1535–1612).[73]

Another important context in which painting allowed women of the courtesan class in the late Ming to gain greater freedom was in their relationships with other educated women. From its very origins, the male literati culture of China was characterized by its dependence on social intercourse and the sharing of aesthetic ideas and works of art. Poets and painters of the literati class not only exchanged their own works and collectively admired art by past masters, but also created joint works combining poetry, painting, and calligraphy; this precedent enabled educated women of the gentry and courtesan classes to follow suit. Poetry societies arose among women of the gentry class.[74] Women of the courtesan class executed joint works. As mentioned above, Mao Xiang's concubines Cai Han and Jin Yue (who may or may not have originally been courtesans) executed most of their paintings together. Xue Wu and Ma Shouzhen, two of the most accomplished painters among late Ming courtesans, knew each other and did at least one collaborative scroll, owned by the twentieth-century collector Pei Jingfu.[75] Art also provided a vehicle through which women of different classes could intermingle and form close relationships. The seventeenth-century gentry-class poet, scholar, and painter Huang Yuanjie painted at least one landscape as a gift for Liu Yin after Liu had become the wife of Qian Qianyi. The two women seem to have enjoyed a long friendship, with Liu having offered Huang a place to live in her Crimson Cloud Storied Pavilion on West Lake in Hangzhou.[76] Interestingly, during at least one of the periods Huang spent in Hangzhou, her next-door neighbor was none other than the (then retired) courtesan Xue Wu. It is said that the two women also spent time together and "entertained each other with calligraphy and paintings."[77] Xue also became friends with Yang Jiangzi, Liu Yin's sister, who enlarged Xue's sphere of activity in quite another way. Yang was dedicated to Chan Buddhism, and together the two women "discussed Chan Buddhism and composed poetry, vowing never to depend upon men again."[78] Near the end of Xue's life, they made pilgrimages to Mount Lu, in Jiangxi, and Mount Emei, in Sichuan; the vast distances and arduous climbs were significant undertakings for two solitary women of their day. Clearly the stereotype of the traditional Chinese upper-class woman as a *neiren* (indoor person) could be overcome in the Ming dynasty by women like Xue. Her courtesan-class standing put her somewhat outside the system of usual gender expectations, and her talent as a painter allowed her to expand her horizons through contact with many stimulating women and men.

A final means through which courtesans achieved a greater degree of freedom and mobility is the most obvious: their relationships with men. The courtesans' high degree of education coupled with their artistic prowess allowed them greater access to the most educated and accomplished, and often most liberal-minded, men of their generation. At the very least, they gained intellectually through the stimulation provided by the sharing of poetry, paintings, and conversation at the brothels and private parties at which they served as hostesses. At best, women like Liu Yin had the opportunity to marry well-known scholars who would support their artistic efforts, as well as give them the social status and stability that only alliance with a man could provide in traditional China. As stated earlier, this gave courtesans, especially those of the Ming dynasty, who often were born to poor families and sold into a type of slavery, a particularly dramatic and unusual opportunity to "jump class."

The late Ming period provided an atmosphere that was much more conducive to the flourishing of women in the arts than in previous dynasties, or even in contemporaneous cultures in other parts of the world. The women who were fortunate enough to have the freedom from domestic tasks and the access to education necessary for the development of artistic talent were still very few. While it may surprise us to realize that women of what is usually considered to be an underclass were among the privileged, the Chinese courtesans of the Ming period might have been the most well-positioned of all to utilize the potential of a burgeoning visual culture to "re-image" themselves and thus achieve higher status and greater potential for visibility and acclaim. Among many other factors, what made this possible was the courtesan's knack for "mirroring" the fantasies and values of the male clients who made her fame possible. The courtesan poet and painter Liu Yin manifests this aesthetic sleight of hand in a poem on one of eight album leaves, *Landscapes with Figures*, which reads in part:

> One layer of azure void, one layer of mist—
> A three-storied tower and pavilion: a bit of heaven.
> Most suitable for a man of talent is a beautiful woman;
> An immortal's fated partner must be the Goddess of the Moon.[79]

NOTES

1. Tanner and Tucker 1994.
2. A good source on the role of courtesans in the literary and visual culture of Renaissance Europe is Lawner 1987.
3. Weidner 1988, 13.
4. Tang Souyu 1963, vol. 5, pp. 3–8.
5. Tang Souyu does not record any women painters of the courtesan class in the Yuan dynasty. This does not mean that there were none.
6. Hibbert 1938, 30.
7. The other two classes of prostitutes were camp prostitutes (*yingji*), who were attached to army camps and sometimes were wives or daughters of captured non-Chinese minorities, and home prostitutes (*jiaji*), who lived in large households of upper-class men. The latter, who were ranked below concubines but above servants, served mainly as singers, dancers, and entertainers. See Wolfe 1980, 249–51.
8. See O'Hara 1971, 261.
9. Wolfe 1980, 255.
10. Hibbert 1938, 31.
11. Lawner 1987, 55.
12. Levy 1966, 21.
13. Ibid., 18–19.
14. Ibid., 16–17.
15. Ibid., 23–24.
16. Ibid., 9.
17. This praise appears in Sun Chi's *Beili zhi* of 858. See Tseng Yuho 1955, 201.
18. Ko 1994, 255.
19. Ibid., 255–56.
20. Hibbert 1938, 31.
21. Levy 1966, 4.
22. Lawner 1987, 80.
23. See Wolfe 1980, 241. Wolfe's conclusion is based on the examination of 683 plays contained in the three volumes compiled by Huang Wenchang in the eighteenth century.
24. Mao Xiang 1931, 43.
25. Tang Souyu 1963, 78.
26. Ibid., 70.
27. Laing 1990, 82.
28. Ibid., 81.
29. Ibid., 82.
30. Tang Souyu 1963, ch. 5.
31. Levy 1966, 33.
32. Ko 1994, 29.
33. Ibid., 34.
34. Clunas 1997, 138.
35. Ko 1994, 265.
36. From Li Yu's *Xianqing ouji* (published ca. 1671), as translated by Ko 1994, 265.
37. Ko does an excellent job of both defining *qing* and supporting her contention of its significance in late Ming culture; see Ko 1994, ch. 2.
38. Ibid., 111.
39. Ibid., 181.
40. McMahon 1994, 227.
41. Clunas 1997, 113.
42. Ibid., 116. This analogy seems to have originated in the writings of the literatus Tang Hou (active ca. 1320–30).
43. Ibid., 113.
44. Weidner 1988, 113.
45. Ko 1994, 50–51.
46. Chadwick 1996, 314.
47. Weidner 1988, 100; and Tseng Yuho 1955, 205.
48. Tseng Yuho 1955, 206.
49. Ibid., 204.
50. Weidner 1988, 86.
51. Ko 1994, 279 and n. 83.
52. Lawner 1987, 20.
53. In an essay on the use of the body in Chinese art, John Hay states that, with a few functional exceptions, nudes were not popular in Chinese art, even though it had a strong figural tradition. He goes on to explain that "the 'representation'

of the body is a process of construction, not mimesis." See Hay 1994, 43–44. This is distinctly different from European tradition and practice in the seventeenth century, in which courtesans were often portrayed figurally, either nude or seminude, by male painters.

54. Tang Souyu 1963, 70.

55. My translation of the inscription recorded in Tang Souyu 1963, 70–71.

56. Ellen Laing's investigation of the courtesan-artists recorded in Yu Jianhua's *Zhongguo meishu jia ren ming cidian* reveals that the next favorite subjects (in order) were: landscape, bamboo, stones and flowers, figures, bird-and-flower subjects, and plum blossoms. See Laing 1990, 91.

57. Tang Souyu 1963, ch. 5.

58. Weidner 1988, 72.

59. See ibid., 183, for a list of extant paintings by Ma Shouzhen.

60. For example, in the work of the twentieth-century American painter Georgia O'Keefe; see Slatkin 1993, 228–29. O'Keefe herself objected strongly to this interpretation.

61. Weidner 1988, 74.

62. Ibid.

63. Levy 1966, 41.

64. Cahill 1990, 107.

65. Ibid.

66. O'Hara 1971, 258.

67. Laing 1990, 88–89.

68. Mao Xiang 1931, 47.

69. Ibid.

70. Laing 1990, 88.

71. Weidner 1988, 72.

72. Cahill 1990, 108.

73. Tseng Yuho 1955, 199. An excellent discussion of the publication activities of gentry-class women poets can be found in Ko 1994, ch. 1.

74. See Ko 1994, ch. 3.

75. Tseng Yuho 1993, 254.

76. For information about Huang Yuanzhi and her relationship with Liu Yin, see Ko 1994, chs. 3 and 7.

77. Ibid., 285.

78. Tseng Yuho 1993, 254.

79. Weidner 1988, 100.

REFERENCES

Cahill, James. 1990. The Painting of Liu Yin. In *Flowering in the Shadows: Women in the History of Chinese and Japanese Painting*, ed. Marsha Weidner. Honolulu: University of Hawaii Press.

Chadwick, Whitney. 1996. *Women, Art and Society*. 2nd ed. London: Thames and Hudson, Inc.

Clunas, Craig. 1997. *Pictures and Visuality in Early Modern China*. Princeton: Princeton University Press.

Hay, John. 1994. The Body Invisible in Chinese Art. In *Body, Subject and Power in China*, ed. Tani Barlow and Angela Zito. Chicago: University of Chicago Press.

Hibbert, Eloise Talcott. 1938. *Embroidered Gauze: Portraits of Famous Chinese Ladies*. London: Union Brothers, Ltd.

Ko, Dorothy. 1994. *Teachers of the Inner Chambers: Women and Culture in Seventeenth-Century China*. Stanford: Stanford University Press.

Laing, Ellen Johnston. 1990. Women Painters in Traditional China. In *Flowering in the Shadows: Women in the History of Chinese and Japanese Painting*, ed. Marsha Weidner. Honolulu: University of Hawaii Press.

Lawner, Lynn. 1987. *Lives of the Courtesans: Portraits of the Renaissance*. New York: Rizzoli International Publications, Inc.

Levy, Howard. 1966. *A Feast of Mist and Flowers: The Gay Quarters of Nanking at the End of the Ming*. Yokohama.

Mao Xiang. 1931. *Yingmei an yiyu*. Trans. by Pan Tze-yen (Z.Q. Parker) as *The Reminiscences of Tung Hsiao-wan*. Shanghai: The Commercial Press, Ltd.

McMahon, Keith. 1994. The Classic "Beauty-Scholar" Romance and the Superiority of the Talented Woman. In *Body, Subject and Power in China*, ed. Tani Barlow and Angela Zito. Chicago: University of Chicago Press.

O'Hara, Albert Richard. 1971. *The Position of Women in Early China*. Taipei: Mei Ya Publications.

Slatkin, Wendy. 1993. *The Voices of Women Artists*. Englewood Cliffs, New Jersey: Prentice-Hall, Inc.

Tanner, Marcia and Marcia Tucker, eds. 1994. *Bad Girls*. New York: The New Museum of Contemporary Art.

Tang Souyu. 1963. *Yutai huashi*. In *Huashi congshu*, vol. 5., ed. Yu Anlan. Shanghai: Shanghai renmin chubanshe.

Tseng Yuho (Ecke). 1955. Hsueh Wu and Her Orchids in the Collection of the Honolulu Academy of the Arts. *Arts Asiatiques* 2, no. 3.

———. 1993. Women Painters of the Ming Dynasty. *Artibus Asiae* 53.

Weidner, Marsha. 1988. *Views from the Jade Terrace: Chinese Women Artists 1300–1912*. Indianapolis: Indianapolis Museum of Art.

Wolfe, Barnard. 1980. *The Daily Life of a Chinese Courtesan: Climbing Up a Tricky Ladder*. Hong Kong: Learner's Bookstore.

Ming Dynasty Aesthetic Theory

HSIO-YEN SHIH

The evaluation of Ming dynasty (1368–1644) art criticism and theory by art historians has been largely confined to texts dealing with painting. Commenting on such texts, Oswald Sirén noted, "The Ming critics were, on the whole, more interested in historical questions than were their predecessors, although their manner of representing the evolution of painting became constructive rather than analytical."[1] Susan Bush saw the constructive boundaries as determined by regional rivalries and the opposition of literati, or amateur, painters to professional painters, epitomized in the writings attributed to Dong Qichang (1555–1636), Mo Shilong (d. 1587), and Chen Jiru (1558–1639).[2] James Cahill was more explicit in stating that "This bipolar formulation of the history of Ming painting [that is, Zhe school vs. Wu school, Song vs. Yuan styles, professional vs. amateur status] was to culminate in the late Ming theory of the 'Northern and Southern schools' propounded by Tung Ch'i-ch'ang."[3] Both Bush and Cahill accepted such formulations as valid to a certain extent, particularly with respect to their widespread acceptance by later practitioners. However, both also acknowledged their inadequacies as demarcators of stylistic distinctions.

Even in the late Ming, literati painting was not identified with a Wu school as such. Dong Qichang merely named Shen Zhou (1427–1509) and Wen Zhengming (1470–1559) as the only members of his own dynasty who continued the literati tradition originating in Tang dynasty (618–906) painter-poet Wang Wei (700–761).[4] Dong's friend Fan Yunlin (*jinshi* 1595), a native of Wu county, Jiangsu Province, criticized his contemporaries for their ignorance of both literature and connoisseurship, "hastily creating out of their own minds," then selling their daubs in the marketplace. Even the few who followed Wen Zhengming's methods did not realize his sources in Song (960–1279) and Yuan (1272–1368) dynasty masters.[5] Possibly the association of literati painting with the Wu region derived from the numerical superiority of painters there. Tu Long (1542–1605), a poet and dramatist from Zhejiang Province, commented, "To understand painting one can follow the Song or the Yuan. There are even several hundreds of painters who embrace both, of whom the majority live in the Wu region. This is unmatched by the luminaries of all other regions."[6]

More significantly, and a fact generally disregarded by art historians, the Wu region was a center for writers on literary theory during the mid-Ming period. The importance of the late fifteenth and sixteenth centuries in the history of Chinese literary criticism and theory has been well recognized in recent years.[7] Moreover, it is in writings on poetry that we find elements of aesthetic theory that are elusive in the texts on painting. From the Yuan dynasty on, calligraphy, painting, and poetry were often created by the same practitioners, and their sharing of aesthetic principles should be recognized.

A long colophon inscribed by Shen Zhou on a hanging scroll of 1492, *Night Vigil*, in the National Palace Museum, Taipei, suggests the artist's concern with the relationship between sensual experience and the human consciousness. One passage reads:

> Sounds are cut off, colors obliterated; but, my will, absorbing these, alone endures. What is the so-called will? Is it inside me, after all, or outside? Does it exist in external things or does it come into being because of those things? In this [experience of absorbing sensation] there is a means of deciding these questions. Ah! I have, through this, decided them.[8]

Du Mu (1459–1525), a student of Shen Zhou, wrote about his teacher's poetry:

> [He] is famous for his poetry throughout the land, and his songs about things are especially marvelous. I used to study poetry with him and noted down many couplets by him ... [examples given include the seven-graph regulated verses on "Cash," "Sending off the Gate-God," "The Curtain," "Willow Blooms," and "Falling Flowers" included in Shen's collected writings.[9]] They are all clear and fresh, virile and hearty, uninhibited in their subject matter yet never departing from their content. It is in this that they are marvelous.[10]

Shen Zhou's words are not not directly descriptive of an artist's creative process, but they convey his awareness of internal repose to external stimuli. Du Mu, who was also known as an art critic, saw in his teacher's poetic works forthright expression of common experience. The spontaneity thus implied must have emerged from a transformative catalyst. What could such a catalyst be? Xu Zhenqing (1479–1511), the only southern member of the Seven Early Masters of Ming literature and one of the Four Talents of Wu—together with Tang Yin (1470–1524), Wen Zhengming, and Zhu Yunming (1461–1527)—offered as an answer "feeling" (*qing*):

> Feeling is the essence of the mind. It has no fixed place, but is startled into activity [*xing*] when stimulated emotionally. Then it is active within, and it must form itself into sound.
>
> Since feeling can move things, poetry must move people. From obscure vagueness spring the sprouts of feeling; vast and ever expanding is its burgeoning; endlessly unrolling like a coil of silk is one of its characteristics. Speeding forth, it dashes to one's life-force; with simple restraint and cautious estimation it can be thought's control.[11]

Though here applied to the creation of poetry, "feeling" must also have been perceived as the impetus for the act of painting. He Liangjun (1506–1573), who often discussed painting with Wen Zhengming, noted that Wen placed Shen Zhou above the Song painters "precisely because [his] resonances surpassed them. Moreover, superior men of the past would only take up the brush and paint when they were startled into activity [*xing*]."[12] It has also been suggested that painter-poets such as Shen Zhou continued a "tradition of expressionism," countering the archaist orthodoxy advocated by the northern members of the Seven Early Masters group.[13]

A generation later than the Seven Early Masters, Xie Zhen (1495–1575) was the founder of the literary group known as the Seven Later Masters. He further defined the role of "feeling" in creative enterprise, coupled with the inclusion of visual stimulus for the writing of poetry:

> Writing poetry originates with feeling.
> Feeling is isolated and cannot stand alone.
> If there is nothing [for it] to match with, then one rises
> to thought, and one's spirit meets those of antiquity.
>
> Inasmuch as there are a myriad of scenes and the seven emotions [*qing*] upon which one aspires to gaze, one's response must be true, one's joy or sorrow be distinguished, and one must concentrate upon one's direction. If leaning toward one side or the other, one will only perceive one half; if true in direction, one will see the whole. A mirror is like the mind, its light like the spirit. When thought penetrates, then darkness is reversed, and there is neither subject nor object. Thus are the secrets of creating poetry.

> Poetry is a vehicle for emulating feeling and scene. Feeling stimulates one within, deeply and at length; scene vivifies one without, widely and grandly.[14]

Xie saw the need for internal and external experience to be unified in poetry and for subject and object distinctions to be extinguished. This is precisely the synthesis that Shen Zhou sought in his *Night Vigil* meditation.

In the late Ming, a Wu-region scholar and minor painter, Gu Ningyuan, could begin his discussion of qualities and techniques in painting by again objectifying the phenomenal world. His attitude may suggest one of the reasons for the decline of literati painting in Wu. Gu wrote:

> When inspiration does not come and the wrist cannot be moved, direct feeling will continue in isolation, being stimulated by nothing. Then, one can seek with deep feeling and clear eyes the hidden meanings in dried logs, stone blocks, puddles of water, and thin groves, cast-offs from Creation and different from the fashionings of men. Painting these, lively meaning will emerge. This is a method just like picking out poetic phrases from a brocade bag.[15]

Feeling can, then, be transferred to the symbolic evocations of natural phenomena in isolation or in miniature. Subject matter, rather than the artist's transference of assimilated experience, became the content of painting for this artist at the time of Wu painters' decline.

The locus of discourse on poetics in the late Ming was no longer centered in the north, or even in the Wu region. Dong Qichang was an intimate of the Gongan school leaders from Hubei Province.

A major influence on these late Ming writers was Xu Wei (1521–1593), the only Ming painter to have made notable contributions to literary theory. Xu Wei came from Shaoxing, in Zhejiang. He was better known in his own time as a calligrapher, poet, and prose-writer, his dramatic works being especially popular.[16] Yuan Hongdao (1568–1610), the most prominent of the Gongan school writers, particularly admired Xu's poetry. He eulogized Xu as follows:

> From the things he saw—mountains running, seas standing, desert sands rising, thunder scudding, rain crashing, and trees falling—and, whether he found himself in secluded forests or great cities, any sight which could startle and surprise him, be it people,

> fish, or birds, all these did he manage to convey in his poetry ... As a result, the composition of his poetry is either like angry shouting or happy laughter, like water roaring through a canyon, like a seedling thrusting up through the earth, like a widow's night cries, like a homesick traveler getting up in the cold. Although his formal style is rather poor, his innate creativity always emerges naturally.[17]

For Yuan, Xu's poetry was natural because it was created in direct response to the strong stimulation of emotion. Not innate feeling but susceptibility to provoked passion was the catalyst for the creative act.

Xu Wei himself recognized the importance of catharsis in poetic effects. In a letter to a certain Xu Beikou on the latter's selection of poetry, he exclaimed:

> When I had a go at reading the selection of poetry you had sent to me, it succeeded in making me feel as if icy water had been poured down my back—a fantastic shock all at once! This really is the kind of poetry that inspires [*xing*] one, makes one observe, makes one fit for company, and is able to express grievances.[18]

Xing as used in the quotation cited above denotes a certain quality in poetry, but in another usage by Xu it connotes a poetic mode:

> The *xing* mode [*ti*] in poetry never has any meaning in its beginning line ... This [first line] is really the self-propulsion of natural creativity, sounding when stimulated to open [the way] to what follows and the feeling of wishing to describe. A silent understanding has its own wonders. One must not try to explain it.[19]

The unselfconscious utterance is the first result of the creative impulse, a revelation of catharsis. Spontaneity, originality, and expressivity are implicit in Xu's understanding of the creative process. His preference for extreme emotive effect is not only manifested in his poetic works but also in his painting. This, and his personal history, has led analysts of his pictorial works to view Xu as an irrational or "genuinely deranged" painter.[20] However, his own writings, as well as those of literary theorists influenced by him, demonstrate that his creative impulses and working methods were founded upon defined aesthetic principles.

The Gongan writers appreciated Xu Wei's freedom of expression, but were themselves more disciplined in their approaches to the creative process. Yuan Hongdao wrote about his younger brother Zhongdao (1570–1624), in a preface to the latter's collected works: "At times, his emotions and the scene would come together, and in an instant he would produce a thousand words, as naturally as the rivers flow east, enough to take one's breath away!"[21] Thus, a fusion of the internal and external worlds inspired the unforced creative act. Jonathan Chaves states that "for the Kung-an writers ... at least one of the functions of literature was to embody or communicate a perception of innate reality, through a process similar in some fashion to religious meditation."[22] A development of Shen Zhou's concerns, cited earlier in this paper, is echoed in this characterization.

A much-quoted account of Yuan Hongdao and his older brother Zongdao (1560–1600) visiting Dong Qichang has Dong answering a question as to whether such major recent painters as Wen Zhengming, Tang Yin, and Shen Zhou had something of the "brush conceptions" of the old masters: "The leading masters of recent times do not have a single brush stroke that does not resemble the old masters; but by not having any that do not resemble, in fact they do not have any that do resemble. One might call this 'no painting.'"[23] Yuan Hongdao's response to Dong was:

> These are the words of one who has perceived the Tao! For the good painter learns from things, not from other painters. The good philosopher learns from his mind, not from some doctrine. The good poet learns from the panoply of images, not from writers of the past. When one models oneself on the [poets of the] T'ang dynasty, it is not a question of modeling one's technique, lines and words on theirs. One models oneself on the spirit of their *not* being like the Han [poets], or the Wei [poets], or the Six Dynasties [poets]. This is the true "modeling."[24]

Yuan's statements offer two insights that may have influenced Dong. The first is that the visual artist's realm of experience lies in the material world, while the poet's lies in an imaginative one. The second is that understanding of past works requires an awareness of their individuality and originality rather than their formal patterns only. Implied in this is a conception of changing period styles as well.

Dong Qichang's main contribution to aesthetic theory derives from his notion of a "great synthesis," the practice of studying past masters to form the basis for invention, and of using the phenomenal world of nature as the model for creativity.[25] In focusing on these two aspects of artistic practice, he not only reiterated Yuan Hongdao's concerns, but was also able to reconcile the controversy between the archaist movement associated with the Seven Early and Seven Later Masters and the Gongan school of literary theorists. Dong wrote:

> The painter who studies ancient masters already belongs to the Upper Vehicle. Advancing one more step, he adopts nature as his teacher. Every morning, he observes the changing appearance of clouds and vapor, which resemble closely the mountains of his painting ... When he has made thorough observations, he is naturally able to transmit the spirit [of the landscape]. The transmission of the spirit depends upon the form. When there is a total accord between the form, the mind, and the hand, each forgets the others' separate existence.[26]

This quotation can be compared with one from Wang Shizhen (1526–1590), one of the Seven Later Masters identified with the archaist movement:

> I should make a discriminating selection of the very best of [ancient writings through the Han], and I should read all of these so thoroughly that I shall begin to swim in them and so let their infusive power flow vast and full in me. Then, when I have occasion to write, I shall be totally able to follow the inclinations of my inner creative powers, my spirit will surge forth in complete harmony with my intent, and my intuitive powers will form a unity with the objects of perception.[27]

Since he also compiled the *Wangshi huayuan* and *Wangshi shuyuan*, two major reference works of painting and calligraphy, Wang Shizhen must have been known to Dong Qichang. For Wang, study of early literature provided the power that allowed his own gifts full expression. For Dong, there seems to have been two steps for the painters to take: "scholar-artists should learn first to exhaust the limits of workmanship and technical refinement, making creation their teacher and friend."[28] Study of past masters and works was to ensure command of formal competencies, then to be discarded for a natural process of creativity. Dong's writings suggest that he considered creativity to be innate to the artist, as, for example, when he states, "Spirit-resonance [of Xie He's Six Laws of Painting] cannot be learnt. One is born knowing it, bestowed by the heavens from Nature," or "The Way of painting is to be found in the painter who controls the universe in his own hands. Wherever he looks he sees life, or the motivation for life."[29]

Dong Qichang's affiliation with certain tenets of Wang Yangming (1472–1529) and the Neo-Confucian School of the Mind has been noted by several scholars.[30] Wai-kam Ho saw in the emphasis on mind (*xin*), rather than principle (*li*), that: "One was to reconstruct or remodel the laws of nature or the old masters in accordance to one's own free will." Li Zhi (1527–1602), the most radical of the School of the Mind philosophers, admired Dong and was himself a primary influence on the Gongan school writers. Li and the Yuan brothers discerned in Dong an example of the extreme individualism and autonomous self that they considered to give rise to real creativity. On the other hand, Dong Qichang may also be considered a successful conciliator between those who sought legitimacy in a continuing tradition, albeit one that had to be redefined, and those who affirmed the primacy of self-realization. The seventeenth century's development of a "progressive" or "reformed" archaism "attempted to reconcile the individual with the tradition so that each could contribute to an increased and more profitable appreciation of the other."[31] Dong was at the forefront of this development.

Shen Hao (1586–ca. 1661), a Wu painter who was supposedly a member of Shen Zhou's clan, was familiar with Dong's division of the Northern and Southern schools through analogy with the schism in Chan Buddhism. He also saw that followers of Wen Zhengming and Dong Qichang had become frozen in "relying on inherited manners" so that independence could only be sought in new styles and a disengaged position. He therefore recommended that the painter "walk alone on [his] own way, preeminent in self-realization." Shen cites Ni Zan (1301–1374) as a painter who followed Five Dynasties (907–960) and Song masters, but "in his late years followed his own ideas in rubbing and brushing. He was like a lion walking alone, having discarded companions."[32]

Gong Xian (1619–1689), a Ming loyalist and generally viewed as an unorthodox painter, wrote in an inscription on a landscape of 1689, now in the Honolulu Academy of Arts:

> In painting one must first synthesize all Sung and Yuan methods, then, relaxing, one may create works in a simple untrammeled manner. [This way] a painting of a few sparse brushstrokes will embody all Six Principles. It will have a cultured breath and a good painting style.[33]

That two such different painters as Shen Hao and Gong Xian should both distinguish the study of past masters as a preliminary stage to self-expressive creation is confirmation of Dong Qichang's widespread influence.

The resolution of personal experience in artistic expression was of primary importance to Ming painter-poets. Shen Zhou and Xu Wei both articulated this concern, but arrived at different solutions. Shen sought to assimilate the world of the senses through innate sensitivity to its stimulus. Xu looked for sensual provocation and correspondent emotional reaction. Consciousness of the artist's individuality and expressive potential underlies their varying approaches and provides them with some common ground. In the late Ming, despite a more extreme emphasis on individualism and expressionism, Dong Qichang did not evoke feeling or emotion as the impetus for art. His was an intellectual schema founded on acquired knowledge and a more detached observation of material phenomena. Integration of an appropriated past with the artist's own perceptions could then satisfy the creative urge.

If literati painters are to be considered as visual artists who also engaged in literary activities, their significance becomes all the greater. Art historians usually seek primary evidence for their constructs in the physical features of pictorial works, but even these are inexplicable when the bases for their formulations are ignored. The importance of literature for the Chinese scholar lies in its revelation of subjective translation from the commonly experienced world. Throughout China's history, literary theory, and above all poetics, preceded other art theory in framing the aesthetic principles from which works of art were created.

NOTES

1. Sirén 1963, 124–25.
2. Bush 1971, 153–67.
3. Cahill 1978, 5.
4. Bush 1971, 169.
5. Ibid., 175. The *Shuliaoguan ji* passage is also quoted in Yu Jianhua 1973, vol. 1, p. 126. Another translation is given in Cahill 1982, 28–29.
6. *Huajian* 1923, series 1:6, p. 113.
7. Lynn 1975, 217–69; 1983, 317–40.
8. Cahill 1978, 90.
9. Shen Zhou 1968, vol. 2, pp. 632, 639, 640, 644, 646–648, 650.
10. Du Mu 1915, vol. 4, p. 14.
11. Xu Zhenqing 1770, vol. 16, pp. 492–93.
12. He Liangjun 1923, series 3:3, p. 37.
13. Lynn 1983, 332.
14. Xie Zhen n.d., 3:26b, 13a.
15. Gu Ningyuan 1923, series 1:4, p. 19.
16. Goodrich and Fang 1976, 609–12.
17. Lynn 1983, 333–34.
18. Ibid., 334.
19. In a letter to his friend Zhi Ben (1485–1563), cited by Guo Shaoyu n.d., 356.
20. Tseng Yu-ho 1963, 243; Cahill 1978, 159–63.
21. Chaves 1983, 358.
22. Ibid., 349.
23. Cahill 1982, 28.
24. Chaves 1983, 352.
25. See Cahill 1982, 118–23 for an exposition of these points.
26. Ibid., 121–22. Cahill's translation reads, "The painter who imitates ancient masters . . . ," but the text uses the verb *shi* rather than *fang*.
27. Lynn 1983, 328.
28. Cahill 1982, 96.
29. Ibid., 122.
30. Berger 1971, 29–30; Ho 1976, 13.
31. Lynn 1983, p. 337.
32. Shen Hao 1923, series 1:6, pp. 31, 38.
33. Fong 1984, 194, 196.

REFERENCES

Berger, Patricia. 1971. Real and Ideal: Intellectual Solutions in the Late Ming. In *The Restless Landscape: Chinese Painting of the Late Ming Period*, ed. James Cahill. Berkeley: University Art Museum.

Bush, Susan. 1971. *The Chinese Literati on Painting: Su Shih (1037–1101) to Tung Ch'i-ch'ang (1555–1636)*. Harvard-Yenching Institute Studies 27. Cambridge: Harvard University Press.

Cahill, James. 1978. *Parting at the Shore: Chinese Painting of the Early and Middle Ming Dynasty, 1368–1580*. New York and Tokyo: Weatherhill.

———. 1982. *The Distant Mountains: Chinese Painting of the Late Ming Dynasty, 1570–1644*. New York and Tokyo: Weatherhill.

Chaves, Jonathan. 1983. The Panoply of Images: A Reconsideration of the Literary Theory of the Kung-an School. In *Theories of the Arts in China*, ed. Susan Bush and Christian Murck. Princeton: Princeton University Press.

Du Mu. 1915 (preface). *Nanhao shihua*. In *Xu lidai shihua*. Repr. Taipei: Yiwen.

Fong, Wen C. et al. 1984. *Images of the Mind: Selections from the Edward L. Elliott Family and John B. Elliott Collections of Chinese Calligraphy and Painting at The Art Museum, Princeton University*. Princeton: The Art Museum, Princeton University.

Goodrich, L. Carrington and Chaoying Fang, eds. 1976. *Dictionary of Ming Biography*. New York: Columbia University Press.

Gu Ningyuan. 1923. *Huayin*. In *Meishu congshu*. Vol. 2. Shanghai: Shenzhou guoguangshe.

Guo Shaoyu. n.d. *Zhongquo wenxue piping shi*. Hong Kong: Hongzhi.

He Liangjun. 1923. *Siyouzhai hualun*. In *Meishu congshu*. Vol. 12. Shanghai: Shenzhou guoguangshe.

Ho,Wai-kam. 1976. Tung Ch'i-ch'ang's New Orthodoxy and the Southern School Theory. In *Artists and Traditions: Uses of the Past in Chinese Culture*, ed. Christian Murck. Princeton: Princeton University Press.

Huajian. 1923. In *Meishu congshu*. Vol. 3. Shanghai: Shenzhou guoguangshe.

Lynn, Richard John. 1975. Orthodoxy and Enlightenment: Wang Shih-chen's Theory of Poetry and Its Antecedents. In *The Unfolding of Neo Confucianism*, ed. Wm. T. de Bary. New York: Columbia University Press.

————. 1983. Alternate Routes to Self-Realization in Ming Theories of Poetry. In *Theories of the Arts in China*, ed. Susan Bush and Christian Murck. Princeton: Princeton University Press.

Shen Hao. 1923. *Huachen*. In *Meishu congshu*. Vol. 3. Shanghai: Shenzhou guoguangshe.

Shen Zhou. 1968. *Shitian xiansheng ji*. Taipei: Yiwen.

Sirén, Oswald. 1963. *The Chinese on the Art of Painting*. New York: Schocken Books.

Tseng Yuho (Ecke). 1963. A Study on Hsü Wei. *Ars Orientalis*.

Yu Jianhua. 1973. *Zhongguo hualun leibian*. Hong Kong: Zhonghua.

Xie Zhen. n.d. *Siming shihua*. In *Xu lidai shihua*. Vol. 4. Repr. Taipei: Yiwen.

Xu Zhenqing. 1770 (preface). *Tanyi lu*. In *Lidai shihua*. Repr. Taipei: Yiwen.

Wang Duo's Assessment of Ni Zan: A Reappraisal

ALAN G. ATKINSON

In 1645 the renowned calligrapher and former Grand Secretary Wang Duo (1593–1652) was among a small group of prominent literati of the Ming dynasty (1368–1644) who accepted service under the Manchus, founders of the succeeding Qing dynasty (1644–1911). At the time, Wang was well regarded by his peers as a poet and scholar of ancient texts. Examples of his dynamic calligraphy could be seen in palaces and homes of the aristocracy. Wang was also considered a knowledgeable connoisseur of painting, and his opinions were sought by both friends and professional acquaintances. His influence was such that his inscriptions on ancient paintings are second in prominence only to those of the eminent Ming art theorist and painter Dong Qichang (1555–1636).[1]

Despite the breadth of his interests and his accomplishments, it remains an unfortunate fact that in the view of Western scholars the defining moment of Wang Duo's artistic life is his well-known letter to his friend and student Dai Mingshuo (*jinshi* 1634):

> In regard to paintings that are bland and without strong feeling, such as the work of Ni Zan [1301–1374], although such compositions give the effect of quietude they cannot avoid being dry and weak, like a sick old man gasping for breath. They may be called airy and elegant, but how thin and insipid they really are! Great masters do not paint that way![2]

This statement, together with Zhang Geng's (1685–1760) declaration that Wang Duo followed the tenth-century masters Jing Hao (active ca. 870–ca. 930) and Guan Tong (active ca. 907–23), has been used to categorize Wang as "anti-Yuan" and an "opponent" of literati painting as practiced by followers of Dong Qichang's Southern School.[3] Wang Duo was, in fact, engaged in an effort, through his connoisseurship, to increase the number of orthodox models and, through his work as a painter of landscape, to enlarge the vocabulary of painting techniques by which creative engagement with those models took place. This paper will reexamine Wang's statement about Ni Zan in its original context, and, in the process, show that the statement has been fundamentally misunderstood.

Wang Duo was one of the few artists outside Dong Qichang's immediate circle who had acquired, through the study of works collected by friends and relatives, direct knowledge of some of the very paintings that Dong had endorsed as signs for various artists of his Southern School. Despite Wang's reputation as a follower of Jing Hao and Guan

Tong, the tenth-century master who received Wang's closest attention was Dong Yuan (active 930s–60s). The Dong–Ju style, as manifested in paintings attributed to Dong Yuan, Juran (active ca. 960–95), and Mi Fu (1052–1107), as well as works by Gao Kegong (1248–1310), exerted a strong influence on Wang's painting in the 1640s. His view of Dong Yuan encompassed that of Dong Qichang, but also went beyond it to include works newly attributed to Dong Yuan by Wang. As a result of his many opportunities to collect and study early paintings after his return to Beijing in 1645 as Minister of Rites under the Qing, Wang arguably had wider knowledge than Dong Qichang of Song landscape painting.

The mid-sixteenth century cataloguer He Liangjun (1506–1573) had recognized three main schools of Song landscape painting, all of which he considered orthodox: Jing–Guan, Dong–Ju, and Li (Cheng)–Fan (Kuan). Although he had emphasized the Dong–Ju school in his personal vision of the Southern School, Dong Qichang did not exclude the other two, declaring:

> [The painters] I [most] want to study are [the tenth-century masters] Ching [Hao], Kuan [T'ung], [Tung] Yüan, Chü [-jan], and Li Ch'eng. But it is precisely these five whose genuine works are particularly scarce. The Sung paintings [preserved] in the south are not even worth examining.[4]

Because their painting styles had never exerted any notable influence on the Yuan dynasty (1272–1368) artists who, with the possible exception of Ni Zan, were important to Dong's explication of his Southern School, Jing Hao and Guan Tong never became important subjects of Dong's attention as either connoisseur or painter. With respect to their study of early landscape painting, the most significant distinction between Wang Duo and Dong Qichang is the former's attention to these two early masters. Wang's attempt to revive the Jing–Guan style as part of the orthodox canon is clearly evidenced in his connoisseurship and painting, and as noted by his contemporaries, such as Zhang Geng, was the distinguishing characteristic of his late career.

Although the monumental landscape painting of the Five Dynasties (907–960) and Northern Song (960–1127) played a prominent role in the formation of his mature style, Yuan painters were also important to Wang Duo's development as an artist. Wang was by no means opposed to Yuan

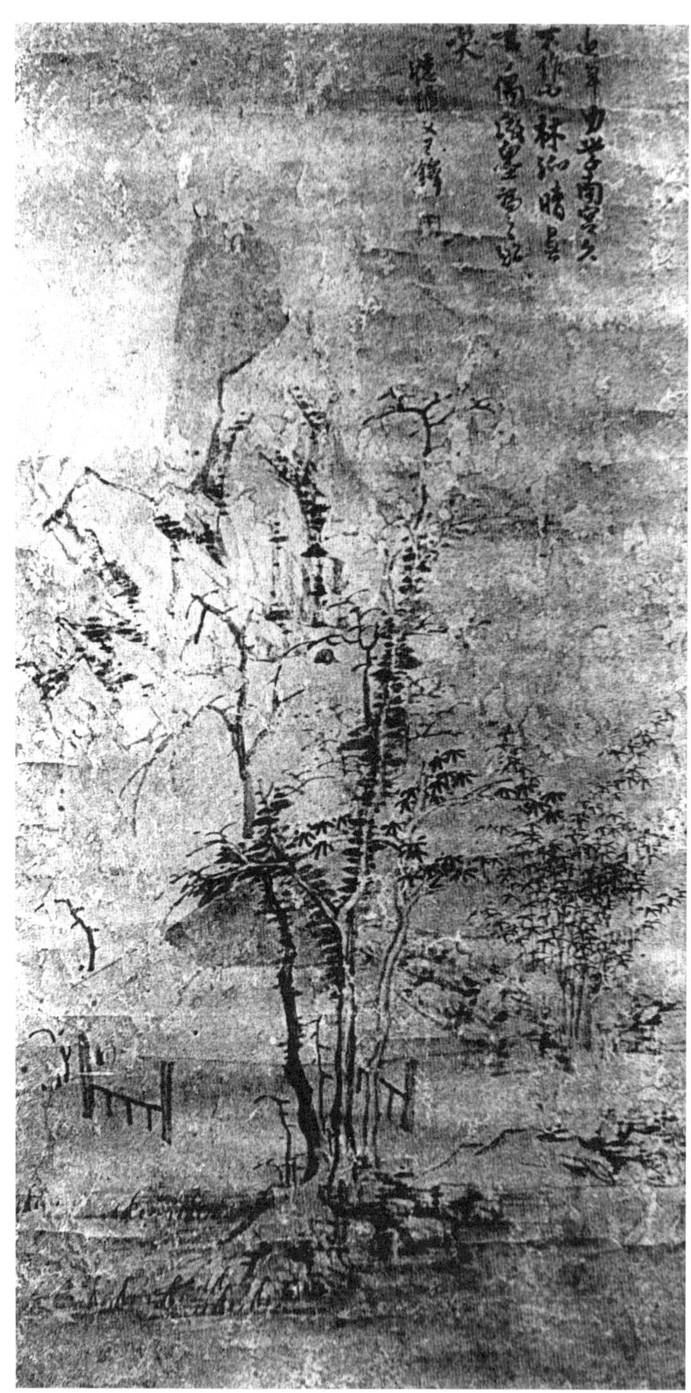

FIGURE 1
Wang Duo (1593–1652). *Landscape.* Hanging scroll, ink on paper, $51^{1}/_{8} \times 28^{3}/_{4}$ in. (130 × 73 cm). Collection unknown. From *Shenzhou guoguangshe* 4, 1909

painting. He praised the painting of Zhao Mengfu (1254–1322), Gao Kegong, Wu Zhen (1280–1354), and Huang Gongwang (1269–1354).[5] Gao Kegong and Wu Zhen, in particular, were important to his interpretation of the Dong–Ju tradition. In addition, Wang wrote a poem on a painting by Yao Tingmei (14th century) and owned what he believed to be a painting by Wang Meng (ca. 1308–1385).[6]

The notable exception was Ni Zan, who alone among Yuan artists was singled out by Wang Duo for special criticism. The great irony of this is that Ni Zan was also the only Yuan artist Wang ever named specifically as the model for one of his own landscape paintings, an undated hanging scroll in ink on paper (fig. 1).[7] Wang's inscription reads in part:

> Last year I rigorously studied Mi Fu. It has been a long time since I painted a Ni Zan.

The painting features a stand of three trees, each different from the others, in front of an empty thatched pavilion. A small clump of bamboo grows beside the pavilion. The trees and the pavilion stand on a low spit of land; a tall craggy mountain rises in the distance. In his drawing of the rocks, Wang emphasizes the horizontal lines, which are thinner and dryer than usual for Wang. Moss dots are scattered along the vertical elements. Here, Wang is consciously imitating Ni Zan on several levels: subject, composition, and brush technique. As a representation of Ni Zan's style, the painting includes all the necessary pictorial elements, but lacks the astringency of Ni Zan-style paintings by other seventeenth-century painters, such as Li Liufang (1575–1629), Wang Jian (1598–1677), Dan Zhongguang (1623–1692), or even Dong Qichang.

In order to demonstrate its relevance to our understanding of Wang Duo's pronouncements about Ni Zan, we must first determine where this painting fits chronologically in Wang's oeuvre. Clues to the date of the painting can be found in the inscription, the calligraphy, and the brushwork. In his inscription, Wang states that "last year I rigorously studied Mi Fu." The specific year in which Wang's work shows a pronounced dependence on Mi Fu is 1649–50, culminating in the long handscroll *Calligraphy with Mountain Landscape*, in the Osaka Municipal Museum of Art.[8] The only extant painting by Wang that explicitly acknowledges the Mi-family style as a model is a large undated album leaf in the collection of Rongbaozhai, Beijing.[9] The painting's softly modeled mountains are constructed from large wet Mi-dots laid on horizontally, combined with ropy vertical texture strokes. The inscription reads in part:

> For the last ten years I have been feeling the corners of Dong Yuan.
> It has been a long time since I did a Mi Fu-style painting.

The work of Dong Yuan was one of Wang's predominant concerns throughout the 1640s. A Mi Fu-style painting done after ten years of "feeling the corners of Dong Yuan" would most probably have been painted after 1649.

The calligraphy of Wang's inscription on his landscape after Ni Zan (see fig. 1) also supports a date for the painting from the late 1640s to 1650. Although the inscription is relatively short, and the best available reproduction rather poor, the calligraphy is characteristic of Wang's work during his fifties. These years also coincide with the period of his most intense experimentation with Mi Fu's calligraphy, in the mid- to late 1640s. It is possible that Wang's "rigorous study" of Mi Fu included the study of Mi's calligraphy as well as his painting. The signature on the painting is distinctive, and appears only on a few other works by Wang, including an album of landscapes dated to 1650, in the Liaoning Provincial Museum.

The poor quality of the reproduction of the painting and the unusual nature of the composition in comparison with other Wang Duo paintings make any definitive statements about style difficult. However, nothing that can be determined about the brushwork or types of tree forms contradicts a date of 1649 or 1650 for the painting. In other words, Wang painted his own Ni Zan-style landscape within months of the inscription that he wrote in the latter part of 1649 on the side mounting of a painting he attributed to Guan Tong:

> The works of great masters are substantial like this. Followers of Ni Zan, on the other hand, quarrel over who can be the thinnest and most mannered. When they have produced two trees, one stone, and a sandy bank they proclaim it a landscape! A landscape![10]

Wang Duo's statement contradicts Dong Qichang's opinion, subsequently parroted by many other literati painters, that Ni Zan's style represented the Yuan continuation, and therefore the orthodox version, of the Jing–Guan manner. Wang was not alone in his opposition to Dong Qichang's declaration that Ni's style was derived from Guan Tong. His denigration of Ni Zan's style in relation to his praise for Jing Hao and Guan Tong was well understood by at least some of his contemporaries. The early

Qing cataloguer Gu Fu, for example, states in his section on Guan Tong: "In his painting Ni Zan is widely said to have been excellent in the study of Jing and Guan ... [but] what I have seen of Jing and Guan has nothing to do with Ni's conception!"[11] This begs the question, what had Gu Fu seen that he considered representative of the Jing–Guan manner? Even if he was relying solely on Wang Duo's attributions as evidence, Gu's statement is an indication that Wang's attempt to separate the Ni Zan style from the Jing–Guan tradition had supporters outside his immediate circle.

It seems clear that Wang's criticism of Ni Zan should be understood within the context of his reappraisal of the painting tradition of Jing Hao and Guan Tong after his arrival in Beijing in 1645. Viewed in this context, Wang's critique of Ni Zan belies the supposition that his appreciation of Five Dynasties and Northern Song landscape painting as models implies a corresponding denigration of Yuan painting. Wang's declarations about Ni Zan were in effect rhetorical devices designed to call attention to his own attempts to revive the Jing–Guan manner. By attacking Ni Zan, the only recognized transmitter of the Jing–Guan style in Dong Qichang's Southern School, Wang prepared the way for consideration of his more authoritative version of the Jing–Guan style as an aspect of the Southern School orthodoxy. In addition, Wang's own version of a Ni Zan, which he describes as "scattering ink for a laugh," can be seen as a satiric demonstration of the inability of the Ni Zan style, as practiced in Wang's day, to invoke the Jing–Guan manner as Wang understood it. Seen in this light, it becomes apparent that Wang Duo's opposition to Ni Zan was not a direct critique of Dong Qichang and his theories, but instead part of Wang's strategy to expand the scope of the Southern School orthodoxy by re-establishing the Jing–Guan manner on a more historical basis.

Wang Duo's increasing involvement in artistic pursuits during his last years was the primary way he dealt with his decision to serve the Manchu conquerors. An intriguing insight into Wang's attitude toward his accommodation with the Manchus is found in an inscription written by him on the handscroll *Night Revels of Han Xizai*, attributed to Gu Hongzhong (active ca. 943–60), in the Palace Museum, Beijing.[12] By the end of the Song dynasty, this painting had become an important document in support of the literati's revisionist legend of Han Xizai (907–970), who had fled North China and offered his services to the Southern Tang dynasty.[13] It was seen as visual evidence that Han, a worthy official distrusted by his emperor, had in self-defense disguised his true nature behind the mask of a playboy devoted to sensual pleasures. This was clearly the reading of the painting implied by the Yuan scholar Ban Weizhi in a poem he appended to the scroll in 1326. Commenting on the meaning of the painting, Wang Duo's friend Sun Chengze (1592–1676), a former Ming official who, like Wang, had chosen to accept service under the Manchu rulers, wrote:

> [Han] realized that the government he served was rapidly degenerating, and he was ashamed to assume the position of Prime Minister. He thus hid himself in sensual pleasures. He often told his friend Monk Deming: "I act this way to avoid assignment."[14]

In his inscription on the painting, which immediately follows Ban's poem, Wang Duo praised Han Xizai for his "profoundly silent and remote mind," invoking the image of the noble Confucian scholar who adopts the persona of a dissolute official. Though the inscription is undated and bears no seal, the style of the calligraphy suggests a date after the mid-1640s. Sun Chengze's interpretation of the painting reflects the historical understanding of the scroll's imagery, but Sun was no doubt also aware of the similarity between Han Xizai's situation and that of his friend Wang Duo.[15] Sun's observation brings to mind Qian Qianyi's (1582–1664) comments in his memorial essay for Wang about Wang's dalliance with dancing girls and indulgence in drink during his last years in Beijing, as well as the remark by Zhang Yi that Wang was "muddleheaded and decrepit" after joining the Manchus.[16] Though the evidence is circumstantial, the biographical details of this period of his life, together with his sympathetic colophon on Gu Hongzhong's painting, suggest that Wang consciously adopted Han Xizai's pose during his years as a Qing official.

During the last five years of his life, Wang served as little more than a ceremonial functionary, charged with putting the best face on the Manchu Confucian façade. This left him with little real responsibility, except to perpetuate through his artistic activities the ideals of the literati class. For Wang, that task included preserving the shape of Dong Qichang's orthodoxy, broadening its base, where possible, through connoisseurship, and reinforcing it with his own painting.

In reinforcing the status of Jing Hao and Guan Tong as orthodox models, Wang Duo realized his best opportunity to employ art to cover the blemish on his political career. In this respect, Wang Duo might be seen as the seventeenth-century embodiment of a historical type: the upright Chinese official, who, for reasons known only to himself, chooses a position that appears to undermine his moral standing and then attempts through artistic activity to demonstrate his steadfast loyalty to the cultural ideals that represent the true China. In this endeavor, Wang Duo would be following none other than Zhao Mengfu, who turned a precarious political position into an enduring artistic achievement by determined effort and artistic brilliance. In his memorial essay, Qian Qianyi supports this view of Wang's last years, comparing him to Wang Ruoxu (*jinshi* 1197), another official who served two dynasties without losing his moral standing.[17]

Wang's focus on the paintings of Jing Hao and Guan Tong was an opportunistic response to a new historical situation. He realized that his access to a little-known group of early and as yet unattributed landscape paintings was his chance to make a contribution to the study of the history of Chinese landscape painting that could rival Dong Qichang's inquiries into the styles of Wang Wei (700–761) and Dong Yuan. Wang Duo's revival of the long-dormant image of Jing and Guan would allow him to strengthen the foundation of the Southern School on which later literati painters could build and thus secure for himself an important place in Chinese art history.

As we have seen, this attempt to revive the Jing–Guan manner is the source of Wang Duo's presumed difficulty with Dong's Qichang's Southern School orthodoxy. Wang ran afoul of the conventional belief, especially prevalent among southern literati artists of the so-called Songjiang school, that Ni Zan was the Southern School representative of the Jing–Guan style. This belief became widespread because Dong Qichang had been less thorough in his elucidation of the Jing–Guan style than that of the styles of other early landscape masters in his Southern School pantheon. Wang's ambition to restore and elevate the Jing–Guan model necessitated his apparent rejection of the orthodox canon proposed by Dong Qichang. This does not mean that Wang opposed Dong's theories or his specific choice of models, but that he believed his own understanding of the Jing-Guan style was superior to Dong's. By Wang Duo's time, the Songjiang school had come to represent a style of painting that was incompatible with the Jing–Guan manner as Wang understood it. In his view, those who believed that Ni Zan's style best represented that tradition were departing from the orthodox canon.

Wang Duo was ultimately successful in establishing his own version of the Jing–Guan manner as the orthodox norm, and his attributions form a large part of the core monuments upon which modern investigations into that style have been based. On the other hand, while he may have been satisfied with this authoritative contribution to the shape of orthodoxy, Wang's attempts to rehabilitate himself through painting proved unsuccessful. The Qing dynasty, unlike the short-lived Yuan, endured for several hundred years after Wang's death. This meant that there was never an opportunity for the sort of historical reconsideration of Wang Duo by artists of the next generation that had been granted Zhao Mengfu and his art.

NOTES

1. Fu Shen 1981, 30
2. Wang Duo 1986, 395–96. Translation from Zhang Geng 1739, 21, based on Judith Whitbeck in Cahill 1971, 118. Slightly different translations are found in Sirén 1978, 3, and Yonezawa Yoshio 1956, 30. The letter was most likely written sometime between 1645 and 1650.
3. Cahill 1982, 166–67. Wang's presumed opposition to Yuan painting models, and his advocacy of direct reference to Song models, has been supported by this statement by Dai Mingshuo: "The styles of the Northern Song masters have not been carried on for a long time. Now I have had a try at it, in opposition to the Songjiang manner" (Cahill 1982, 166).
4. From a letter to Chen Jiru, ca. 1590s, in *Huachan shi suibi*, 1720, *juan* 2, p. 13, quoted in Reily 1992, 398.
5. Wang's knowledge of Yuan painting is addressed in Atkinson 1997, chap. 3 (Wang Duo as a Collector and Connoisseur of Painting), 173–233.
6. Wang Duo, *Nishanyuan xuanji*, vol. 3, p. 1156.
7. Illustrated in *Shenzhou guoguangji* 4, 1909. The current location of this work is unknown.
8. Illustrated in *Chinese Painting in the Osaka Municipal Museum of Art* 1975.
9. Viewed by the author in October 1989.
10. Quoted in Cahill 1971, 118. The painting is reproduced in *Gugong shuhua tulu* 1989, vol. 1, p. 57.
11. *Pingsheng zhuangguan* 1962, 6/70. Quoted in Nelson 1980, 86, n. 5.
12. *Zhongguo lidai huihua* 1978, vol. 1, p. 15. For a discussion of Want's accommodation with the Manchus, see Atkinson 1997, 68–74.
13. For a discussion of the painting and the "textual shells" that enclose it, see Wu Hung 1996, 29–47.
14. Ibid., 46–47.
15. Sun Chengze's knowledge of the scroll and his comments suggest that he saw it in the north, probably in the collection of Wang Changhuan, who owned the painting at the time that Wang Duo inscribed it. He may also have seen the painting after it passed to Liang Qingbiao, sometime after the 1650s.
16. Qian Qianyi 1910, 30/6. The remark by Zhang Yi, author of *Xiaowen xubi*

(17th century), is quoted in Murakami Sando 1983, vol. 2, p. 202.

17. Wang Ruoxu served as an official of both the Song and the Jin dynasties. Wang considered the Jin dynasty to be the continuation of the Song mandate in the north because it was protecting China from the nomads of the steppe. See Murakami Sando 1983, vol. 1, p. 240

REFERENCES

Atkinson, Alan G. 1997. New Songs for Old Tunes: The Life and Art of Wang Duo. PhD diss., The University of Kansas.

Cahill, James, ed. 1971. *The Restless Landscape: Chinese Painting of the Late Ming Period.* Berkeley: University Art Museum.

———. 1982. *The Distant Mountains: Chinese Painting of the Late Ming Dynasty, 1570–1644.* New York and Tokyo: Weatherhill.

Chinese Painting in the Osaka Municipal Museum of Art. 1975. Tokyo.

Fu Shen. 1981. Wang To and His Circle: The Rise of Northern Connoisseur-Collectors. Unpublished paper presented at the Symposium on Chinese Painting, The Cleveland Museum of Art, March.

Gugong shuhua tulu. 1989. Taipei: National Palace Museum, Taipei.

Murakami Sando, ed. 1983. *Otaku no Shoga* (Wang Duo's calligraphy). 5 vols. Tokyo: Nigensha.

Nelson, Susan E. 1980. Rocks Beside a River: Ni Tsan and the Ching-Kuan Style in the Eyes of Seventeenth-Century Critics. *Archives of Asian Art* 33.

Pingsheng zhuangguan. 1962. Shanghai.

Qian Qianyi. 1910. *Muzhai chuxue ji.* Beijing: Suihan zhai.

Reily, Celia Carrington. 1992. Tung Ch'i-ch'ang's Life. In *The Century of Tung Ch'i-ch'ang 1555–1636*, vol. 2, ed. Wai-Kam Ho and Judith G. Smith. Kansas City: The Nelson-Atkins Museum of Art.

Sirén, Osvald. 1978. *A History of Later Chinese Painting.* 2 vols. New York: Hacker.

Wang Duo. 1986. *Nishanyuan tie.* Repr. Jiangsu: Jiangsu guji chubanshe.

Wu Hung. 1996. *The Double Screen: Medium and Representation in Chinese Painting.* Chicago: The University of Chicago Press.

Yonezawa Yoshio. 1956. *Painting in the Ming Dynasty.* Tokyo: Mayuyama and Co.

Zhang Geng. 1963. *Guochao huacheng lu* (Painters of the Qing dynasty; 1739). In *Huashi congshu*, ed. Yu Anlan. Shanghai: Renmin meishu chubanshe.

Zhongguo lidai huihua: Gugong bowuyuan canghuaji. 1978. Beijing: Renmin meishu chubanshe.

Real-Scenery Landscape Painting in China, Korea, and Japan in the Seventeenth and Eighteenth Century

JUNGHEE HAN

It remains debatable whether the prevalence of real-scenery landscape painting (frequently called *chin'gyŏng sansu*, or true-view landscape) in eighteenth-century Korea originated independently or instead derived from the new trend in painting generally witnessed throughout East Asia at the time. In an essay entitled "The Influence of China on Late Chosŏn Painting," I attributed the origin of this type of painting in Korea to the latter.[1] In this essay, I will examine the actual modes and specific content of the new trend in landscape painting of the seventeenth to eighteenth century. I will also compare and contrast the similarities and differences among China, Korea, and Japan in the portrayal of real scenery and specific sites.

Although the representation of real scenery in China, Korea, and Japan has a long history, it was not until the seventeenth and eighteenth centuries that it flourished widely. While painters depicted celebrated locales in their own countries in their own way, there appear to have been several common social and cultural factors that contributed to the contemporaneous development of similar styles of painting in the three countries: a shared philosophical background, the popularization of travel made possible by economic prosperity, the development of travel literature, and the introduction and circulation of woodblock print albums. This essay investigates these common factors.

Shitao (1642–1707), one of the most prolific real-scenery landscape painters in seventeenth-century China, remarked, "Ancient masters' beards and eyebrows will not grow on my face." He also noted, "There are Southern and Northern Schools in painting, and the two Wangs' laws in calligraphy. But I follow my own principles." The distinction between Southern and Northern Schools was formulated by Dong Qichang (1555–1636), who established the practice of *fangzuo*, or painting in the manner of ancient masters, as a form of art creation. According to Shitao's remarks, it appears that the emergence of real-scenery landscape painting was counter to *fangzuo* and was drastically different from it in many aspects. Yet, the development of real-scenery landscape painting reveals that creative imitation and real-scenery landscape painting coexisted without clear distinction in the seventeenth and eighteenth centuries and only slowly became increasingly independent. This non-differentiation constitutes another characteristic of real-scenery landscape painting in this period.

As real-scenery landscape painting acquired great popularity, painters in China, Korea, and Japan tended to concentrate on portraying specific sites in their own countries, such as Mount Huang in China, Mount Kŭmgang in Korea, and Mount Fuji in Japan. They also tended to paint in the manner of specific artists; Hongren (1610–1664) was emulated in China, Chŏng Sŏn (1676–1759) in Korea, and Ike Taiga (1723–1776) in Japan.

CAUSATIVE FACTORS FOR THE PREVALENCE OF REAL-SCENERY LANDSCAPE PAINTING

As noted above, in China, Korea, and Japan several common factors served to elevate real scenery as a prevalent subject of landscape painting in the seventeenth and eighteenth centuries. Among these were similar philosophical ideas, the development of travel literature in conjunction with the growing interest in travel, and the wide circulation of albums of woodblock landscape prints.

PHILOSOPHICAL IDEAS. The School of Practical Learning (Kr. *Sirhak*) was the most influential among many philosophical schools. In the essay mentioned earlier, I dealt specifically with the influence of the School of Practical Learning on Chinese and Korean real-scenery landscape painting, but this applies to Japan as well. The term "practical learning" originally was coined to distinguish Confucian philosophy from Buddhist and Daoist thinking that emphasized nothingness. The meaning of the term changed by the time of the Ming (1368–1644) and Qing (1644–1911) dynasties, when, in contrast to earlier philosophical ideas, the School of Practical Learning was founded upon scientific attitudes stimulated by the influence of Western civilization. Although the terms and concepts of Practical Learning had appeared much earlier in Chinese history, it is the School of Practical Learning of the Ming and Qing periods that is most relevant to seventeenth- and eighteenth-century real-scenery landscape painting.[2]

Practical Learning of Ming–Qing China was introduced into Korea and Japan and promoted the trend that emphasized empiricism under the influence of Western scholarship and science. Western books translated into Chinese were imported along with the new philosophy; also introduced were Western natural sciences and the Catholic religion. In Japan, where Western civilization and culture had been introduced much earlier via Dutch Learning, or Rangaku, the impact of Western science and philosophy spread even more quickly and in all areas of society. The School of Practical Learning established a number of principles as fundamental:

Practical Reason, Practical Emotion, Practical Achievements, Practical Conduct, and so on. The aspiration for the empirical embodied in these principles seems to have resulted in real-scenery landscape painting.

In China, the theory of Practical Learning was systematized by Luo Qinshun (1465–1544) and Wang Tingxiang (1474–1544) in the mid-Ming and further developed by the Donglin school in the late Ming.[3] These scholars advocated empirical philosophy and practical attitudes in opposition to the ideational and conceptual Neo-Confucianism and the School of the Mind, which had pursued vain reasoning and empty argument far from empirical reality. Although Gu Yanwu (1613–1682), Huang Zongxi (1610–1695), Fang Yizhi (1611–1671), and Wang Fuzhi (1619–1692) developed the theory of Practical Learning even further in the Qing dynasty, the government, under the rule of the Manchus, suppressed it. The newly emerging School of Han Learning eventually replaced Practical Learning in the Qing period.[4] Ming–Qing Practical Learning nonetheless widely affected literature and the arts, especially writers such as Li Zhi (1527–1602), Tang Xianzu (1550–1616), and the Gongan school, and artists such as Shitao and the Huangshan school.[5]

Chinese Practical Learning was first introduced into Korea in the seventeenth century. Yi Su-gwang's (1563–1628) *Chibong yusŏl* and Yi Ik's (1681–1763) *Sŏngho sasŏl* are usually said to be the first publications by Korean scholars influenced by the newly introduced empirical philosophy, but in the cultural sphere Hŭh Kyun (d. 1618) and Yun Tu-sŏ (1668–1715) were also influenced by the new ideas. The artist Yun Tu-sŏ, in particular, is a prime example of the wide influence of empirical thinking on arts and culture; he was interested in practical skills and various applied sciences, and produced not only real-scenery landscape paintings but also genre paintings.[6] Renowned scholars such as Hong Tae-yong (1731–1783) and Pak Chi-wŏn (1737–1805), both of whom wrote accounts of their travels to China, further developed empirical philosophy and ventured into the subjects of astronomy, geology, history, mathematics, medicine, and military science.

The promotion and practice of Practical Learning in Korea are characterized by an emphasis on the improvement of social and economic life. It was supported by kings Yŏngjo (r. 1724–76) and Chŏngjo (r. 1776–1800) of the Chosŏn dynasty (1392–1910), who, unlike the Manchu rulers in China, actively encouraged philosophical exploration and its application. Contemporary Chosŏn society, however, was so saturated with Neo-

Confucianism that the growth of liberal philosophy was undermined. Thus, explored within the limits of Neo-Confucianism or at least acknowledging its basic terms, Korean Practical Learning did not bring about fundamental social change.

Japan differed from both China and Korea in the application of Practical Learning. Although scientific achievement in the field of Practical Learning did not match that of the other two countries, modern theorists, including Fukuzawa Yukichi (1835–1901), actively applied the theories to practical social issues and thus accelerated the modernization of Japan. To put it simply, Japan succeeded in the realization and actual application of the philosophy of Practical Learning. Numerous scholars of the Edo period (1615–1868), among them Nakae Tōju (1608–1648), Kumazawa Banzan (1619–1691), Kaibara Ekken (1630–1714), and Miura Baien (1723–1789), embraced Chinese Practical Learning, while founding its theoretical basis upon Zhang Zai's (1020–1077) Qi Philosophy of the Song period (960–1279).[7] The integration of Dutch Learning and Practical Learning was one of the strengths of Japanese Practical Learning. Dutch Learning was pivotal in introducing Western science and arts, which in turn helped Japanese intellectuals and artists incorporate without much difficulty Western science and Practical Learning.

Practical Learning negated Neo-Confucianism and the School of the Mind, attempting to overcome their unrealistically conceptualized teachings. The active exploration of Practical Learning provided the foundation for new philosophical ideas and the creative impulse shared by China, Korea, and Japan—namely, the emphasis on the practical and empirical in philosophy, the respect for individual ideas and instincts in literature, and the representation of real scenery in art.

THE VOGUE OF TRAVEL. The second factor that helped to promote real-scenery landscape painting was the popularity of travel and the consequential growth in travel literature. In all three countries, traveling and travel literature became popular as the newly emergent civil class gained economic power.[8]

There are several reasons why travel became so popular in Ming period China: the desire to enjoy the nature of the homeland regained from the Mongols (excursion journey); the need to go into the mountains to protect oneself from harsh politics (seclusion in nature); and the anti-dogmatic and anti-traditional tendency to return to nature under the influence of the School of the Mind, which encouraged the literati class to become absorbed in *xingling* (mind and personality) amidst the mountains and waters.[9] The Left School of the School of the Mind, in particular, acknowledged human desire and allowed the pursuit of pleasure in eating, drinking, and the enjoyment of entertainment. Excursions (*langyou* or *tuoyou*) were considered to be the ultimate phase of such entertainment. Anthologies of travel literature, such as *Tianxia mingshan lansheng ji* and *Mingshan zhusheng yilan ji*, were published, and the literati built their own gardens to enjoy nature and entertainment. Contemporary leisure and entertainment are recorded in Wang Shizhen's (1526–1590) *You jinling zhuyuan ji* and Wen Zhengming's (1470–1559) *Zhuozheng yuan ji*. Most outstanding of the Ming period travel writers is Xu Xiake (1586–1641), who traveled all over China. His *Xu Xiake youji* reveals a new scientific and empirical attitude distinct from the sentimentalism of the previous period; his scientific interest even extended to geographical and geological explorations of soil, the formation of mountains, cave structures, flora and fauna, and meteorology. Accounts of journeys to Mount Huang by Xu Xiake and many others played a pivotal role in the emergence of the Huangshan school in the early Qing.[10] Xu's admiration for Mount Huang attests that it was venerated as the best among Chinese mountains:

> I did not see mountains after I had seen the Five Peaks, but I do not visit the Five Peaks now that I have seen Mount Huang. Nothing compares to Mount Huang in Anhui Province, and I can no longer see another mountain as there is no better mountain on earth when I am on the top of Mount Huang.[11]

In Korea, real-scenery landscape painting likewise increased with the proliferation of travel literature in the seventeenth and eighteenth centuries. Among the various types of travels recorded, those undertaken for the enjoyment of nature were most popular, but there were also official travels for executing government orders, journeys for emulating Chinese literary models or searching for a truly fine site and paradise, and therapeutic travels for healing the mind and spirit. In addition, there are records of travels to China and Japan written by diplomats or their escorts, records of exile in the countryside, and writings of maritime explorations.[12] In terms of content, it is noticeable that the emphasis in Korean travel literature shifted from Buddhist concerns to Neo-Confucian thinking, from an ascetic or transcendental vision to a more human or earthly realm exemplified by historically or culturally specific sites and the individual's experience of those places.[13] Numerous mountains were admired, but Mount Kŭmgang was considered the best. Along with the Eight Views of Kwandong, Mount Kŭmgang was the most widely celebrated by painters and poets.[14]

In Japan, travel literature had similarly become abundant by the modern period due to the improved economic situation, which allowed frequent and easy travel. In the Edo period are found numerous writings, among them Matsuo Bashō's (1644–1694) *Oku no hosomichi*, Koga Koshōken's *Tōyū zakki* and *Seiyū zakki*, Hayashi Razan's (1583–1657) *Heishin kikō*, Yoshida Shigefusa's *Chikushi kikō*, and Shiba Kōkan's (1738–1818) *Seiyū nikki*. Bashō's beautiful lines of *haikai* in his travel accounts were re-created in *haiga* paintings by Yosa Buson (1716–1783). Shiba Kōkan included in his books his own real-scenery landscape sketches, exemplifying the incorporation of landscape painting and travel literature.[15]

WOODBLOCK PRINT ALBUMS. The third factor that resulted in the simultaneous proliferation of real-scenery landscape painting in the three countries was the wide circulation of landscape print albums. Albums of woodblock prints were the only available form of reproduction at the time, and Chinese albums introduced into Korea and Japan contributed greatly to the development and dissemination of real-scenery landscape painting in those countries. The albums provided painters with specific techniques and skills, while giving common people an opportunity to appreciate a variety of forms of landscape painting.[16]

Landscape print albums were published along with many other albums of woodblock prints in Ming China. *Gushi huapu* (Master Gu's Pictorial Album) of 1603 was an album of landscape prints, but it cannot be considered a proper album of real-scenery landscape painting since it was intended to introduce old masterpieces for the practice of painting in the *fangzuo* style. The albums that actually contributed to the production of real-scenery landscape paintings are the *Sancai tuhui* of 1607, *Hainei qiguan* of 1609, *Mingshan tu* of 1633, and *Taiping shanshui tu* of 1648.[17] It is known that these albums had been introduced to Korea by the seventeenth century, and later to Japan.[18] Deploying a rather conventional style of expression, *Sancai tuhui* and *Hainei qiguan* do not show a systematic use of linear perspective. In contrast, *Mingshan tu* and *Taiping shanshui tu*, which were highly appreciated and often emulated by Korean and Japanese landscape painters, are more sophisticated in terms of composition, the use of perspective, and the rendering of distance.

According to a record in Japan, Gion Nankai (1677–1751) had the *Taiping shanshui tu* and let Ike Taiga copy the album. Okada Beisanjin (1744–1820) had copied the *Lingxu shan*, indicating that the album had been introduced to Japan by the eighteenth century.[19]

These three factors—the shared philosophical background, the vogue of travel and travel literature, and the circulation of albums of woodblock prints—resulted in the contemporaneous development of real-scenery landscape painting in China, Korea, and Japan in the seventeenth and eighteenth centuries. Despite their distinctive characteristics owing to the specific social conditions of each country, these common factors served to produce more or less similar aspects and tendencies in art. Thus, although portraying specific indigenous sites and locales, the real-scenery landscape paintings of all three countries reflect certain shared perceptions and ideas.

SPECIFIC SITES AND PARTICULAR STYLES

Based on shared philosophical and cultural values, artists in the three countries developed their own modes of expression by depicting particular sites in various artistic styles. Mount Huang was most celebrated in China, Mount Kŭmgang in Korea, and Mount Fuji in Japan. Mount Kŭmgang and Mount Fuji, in particular, had long been admired, but it was only in the seventeenth and eighteenth centuries that they began to be widely portrayed.[20]

The Chinese admiration for Mount Huang is clearly revealed in Xu Xiake's remarks quoted earlier. The veneration for Mount Kŭmgang and Mount Fuji is quite similar. On the subject of Mount Kŭmgang, the writers Kim Ch'ang-hyŭp (1651–1708) and Ŏ Yu-bong (1671–1744) noted, respectively:

> After all, there is no mountain like Mount Kŭmgang in terms of grandeur. It truly deserves the fame it now enjoys.[21]

> Mount Kŭmgang is the best mountain in this country, and the Biro Peak is the best in Mount Kŭmgang. It is a shame for a Korean not to have seen Mount Kŭmgang, and unless you climb up to the top of Biro Peak, you have not seen Mount Kŭmgang at all.[22]

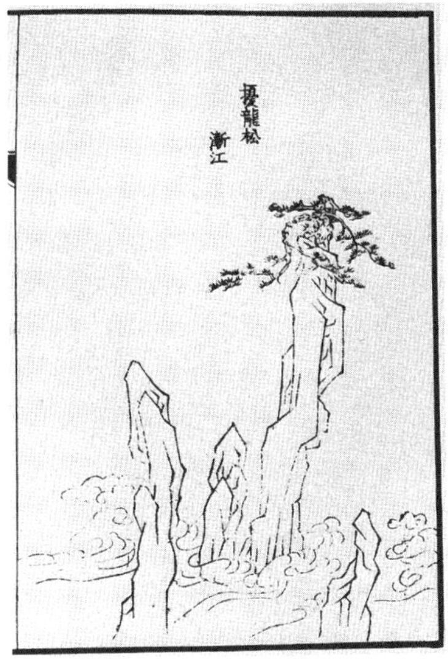

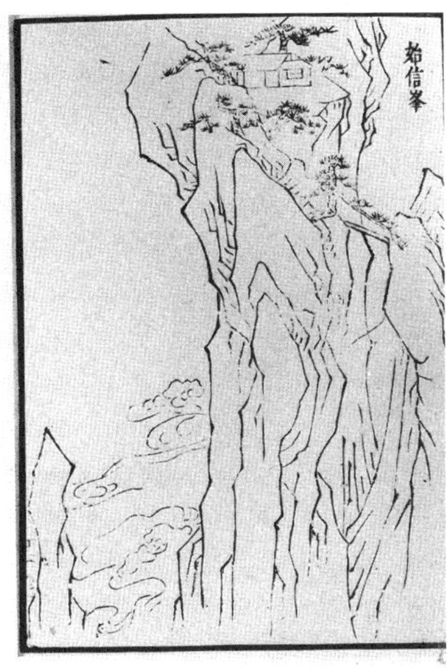

FIGURE 1
Hongren (1610–1664), *Shixin Peak* and *Tamed Dragon Pine*, from *Huangshan ji*, 1667. Woodblock print. Anhui Municipal Library

Numerous Edo period landscape paintings of Mount Fuji reveal a similar interest in traveling to the mountain and appreciating the experience of nature. Ike Taiga, a representative artist of real-scenery landscape painting of the eighteenth century who was renowned for his paintings of Mount Fuji, wrote:

> When I visited Edo last year, I climbed Mount Fuji, made obeisance at Nikko, and looked around the scenic sites of Matsu. The view of the sea seen from Shiogama and Matsushima was spectacular. The islands wrapped in fog were simple and modest, but conveyed a sense of the long history of time. I was astonished to find such a beautiful place on earth. This year, I came to Kanazawa in the Kaga area and talked about Mount Fuji and Matsushima with many people. The scenery of Mount Fuji is widely known because many people have climbed the mountain and seen its beauty, but Matsu is so remote that there are very few people who have seen it.[23]

Taiga's account testifies to the appreciation by the Japanese people of Mount Fuji, the most celebrated site in the literature and art of Japan.[24]

In depicting specific sites in their own country, landscape artists developed distinct styles in terms of the expressive mode. When painting Mount Huang, Chinese artists portrayed the peaks as the main subject; renowned peaks including Tiandu, Shixin, and Lianhua were especially preferred. Particular attractions in Mount Huang, such as Tangchi and Mingxianquan, and pine trees on cliffs, were also popular subjects (fig. 1).[25] Korean landscape artists, in contrast, placed the peaks of Mount Kŭmgang in the background, focusing on a temple rather than the peaks themselves as the central motif. It may be that there were many temples at almost all scenic sites in Mount Kŭmgang; among the most popular were Chang'an-sa (fig. 2), P'yohun-sa, and Chŏng'yang-sa. Other frequently painted scenic attractions at Mount Kŭmgang were Manp'ok-tong, Paekch'ŏn-tong, Kŭmgang-dae, and Guryong-pok.[26]

Japanese landscape painting is different from that of the other two countries. In their depictions of Mount Fuji, artists characteristically emphasize the mountain's peak and juxtapose it with various views of the mountain seen from the far distance. It may be that because Mount Fuji is not composed of many peaks but is itself one huge peak, the only variation in the view was that offered by the different landscapes surrounding the mountain. This kind of juxtaposition is especially distinct in *Thirty-six Scenes of Fuji*, an album of paintings by Katsushika Hokusai (1760–1849) and in landscape paintings by Shiba Kōkan (fig. 3).[27]

Along with the three famous mountains—Mount Huang, Mount Kŭmgang, and Mount Fuji—other sites were also portrayed in real-scenery landscape painting: in China, Mount Hua, Mount Jing, Mount Qingbian, Huqiu (Suzhou), Mount Zhijing, Mount Wuyi, and Mount Taibai;

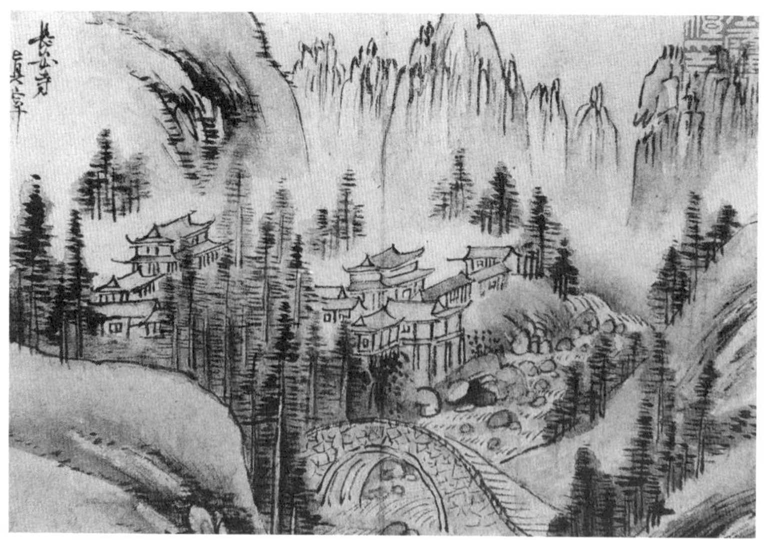

FIGURE 2
Kim Yun-gyŏm (1711–1775), *Chang'an-sa Temple*, 1768. Ink and color on paper. The National Museum of Korea, Seoul

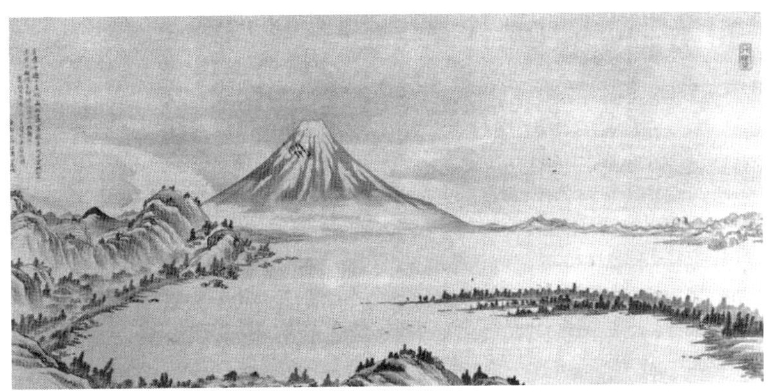

FIGURE 3
Shiba Kōkan (1738–1818), *Mount Fuji Seen from Miho Matsubara.* Private collection

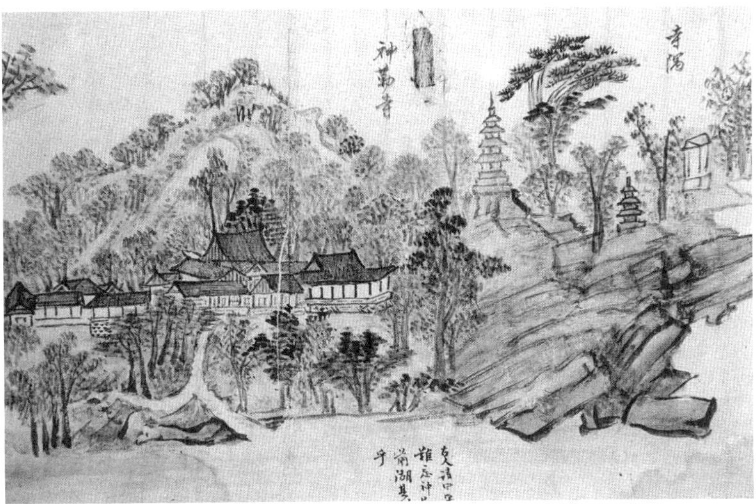

FIGURE 4
Chŏng Su-yŏng (1743–1831), *Shilluk-sa Temple,* from *View Along the Han and Imjin Rivers,* 18th century. Detail. Ink and color on paper. The National Museum of Korea, Seoul

in Korea, Eight Views of Kwandong, Ten Views of Kwansŏ, many historical sites in Seoul and Kyŏnggi province, Songdo (present-day Kaesong), and P'yŏng'yang. The Korean landscape painter Chŏng Su-yŏng (1743–1831), for instance, painted not only Mount Kŭmgang, but also Kwangju, where he began his journey, and other places he visited along the way to the mountain, such as Yongp'yong, Sakryong, and T'osan. Chŏng's 52-foot-long scroll, in which he depicted consecutive scenes of his journey in various dynamic compositions, is monumental in terms of both size and scale (fig. 4).[28] In some cases, such as the *Nanxun tu,* the series of twelve scrolls depicting the Kangxi emperor's (r. 1662–1722) second southern inspection tour, several artists participated in the production of a landscape painting.

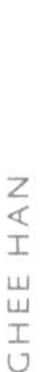

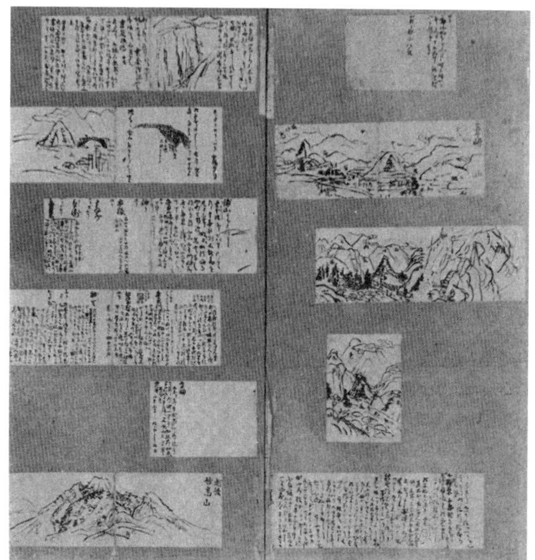

FIGURE 5
Ike Taiga (1723–1776), *Diary of the Journey to the Three Peaks*. Kyoto National Museum

In Japan, other frequently portrayed sites were Mount Asama (almost second to Mount Fuji in popularity), Kojima Bay, Miho Matsubara, and Nachi Waterfall.[29] In 1780, Ike Taiga made sketches and travel notes on his journey to Hakusan, Tateyama, and Mount Fuji. Originally assembled by the artist in a small folding book, they were later made into an eight-panel screen, now in the collection of the Kyoto National Museum (fig. 5).[30] Some nineteenth-century Japanese artists made numerous landscape prints of one place, such as Hokusai's *Thirty-six Scenes of Fuji* or Utagawa Hiroshige's (1797–1858) *Fifty-three Stations of Tōkaidō Road* and *One Hundred Scenes of Edo*.

Interestingly, some Korean and Japanese landscape paintings portray Chinese sites. Chŏng Sŏn's *Waterfall at Mount Lu* and Ike Taiga's *West Lake* and *Red Cliff* are such examples. These artists painted Chinese scenery from their imagination, but portrayed it as if they had actually visited the site. It seems that they recreated the scenes based on Chinese landscape paintings or print albums. Particular types of Chinese real-scenery landscape painting albums, such as Zhang Huanzhen's *Album for Celebrating Longevity*, had a great influence in Japan. This album contained paintings of the Yueyanglou and Zuiwengting at Lake Dongting, several of which Taiga seems to have copied or referred to in his work. In order to recreate Lake Dongting more vividly, Taiga visited Lake Biwa, which was similar to the renowned Chinese site in its scenery and mood.[31]

In all three countries, real-scenery landscape painters chose not only to portray particular sites and famous scenic attractions, but various other places as well. There are, for example, landscape paintings portraying the houses in which the artists lived. Such examples include Chŏng Sŏn's *Recluse in Inwang Valley*, *Clearing after Rain on Mount Inwang*, and *Residence in Inwang Valley*, and Ike Taiga's *The Taigado*. Taiga's painting, in which the house and its surroundings are depicted in bird's-eye view, is highly realistic, more vivid and naturalistic than Chŏng Sŏn's *Residence in Inwang Valley*, which seems comparatively static. In China, gardens were preferred to houses as subject matter, as in Sun Kehong's (1533–1611) *Scenes of a Garden*, Mi Wanzhong's (active 1595–1628) *Scene of Diaoyuan Garden*, and Shen Shichong's (active ca. 1607–40) *Twelve Scenes of Jiaoyuan*.[32] These paintings, mainly depicting a study or pavilion in the mountains, are exquisite in their fresh colors and simple compositions.

Landscape painters in each of the three countries preferred particular styles as well as particular sites and scenes. Chinese artists painted uniquely geometric images in the manner of Hongren; Korean artists favored Chŏng Sŏn's direct and powerful style; and Japanese painters were drawn to Ike Taiga's nuanced and lyrical expressions. Thus, contrary to the general assumption that they painted scenes in their own styles and modes of expression, seventeenth- and eighteenth-century real-scenery landscape artists portrayed specific sites in specific manners following a particular artist's mode of expression. Hongren's geometric style was succeeded by that of Cheng Sui (1602–after 1690), Wang Zhirui (active mid-17th century), Jiang Zhu (b. 1625), and Zhu Chang, and further transformed by Xiao Yuncong (1596–1673), Mei Qing (1623–1697), and Shitao, but Hongren's innovative mode of representation was maintained throughout.[33] Zhang Geng (1685–1760) praised Hongren's style as follows:

> Hongren was prominent in poetry and prose, and learned landscape painting from Ni Zan [1301–1374]. Artists of Xin'an, who painted in the manner of Ni Zan, did that following Hongren's model. I have seen his painting in which the valleys were deep and the peaks lofty and wide. It was entirely different from the work of painters who self-indulgently call themselves Kaoshi after having painting just a few pine trees and dried bushes.[34]

The new mode of expression employed by Hongren, Xiao Yuncong, and Mei Qing was introduced to Korea by the eighteenth century and made a huge impact on Korean landscape painting. Works by Yi In-sang (1710–1760), Kang Se-hwang (1713–1791), Yi Yun-yŏng (1714–1759), and Chŏng Su-yŏng, for example, show a geometric quality influenced by the new current in Chinese landscapes.[35] Nevertheless, in Korea, Chŏng Sŏn's energetic, dynamic, and spontaneous style was equally loved by numerous painters. Kang Hŭi-ŏn (1710–1764), Ch'oe Puk (1712–ca. 1786), Kim Yungyŏm (1711–1775), and Chŏng Su-yŏng are such examples. Through their real-scenery landscape paintings, Chŏng Sŏn also influenced the artists Sim Sa-jŏng (1707–1769), Kang Se-hwang, and Kim Hong-do (1745–1806).

Again, we see a similar phenomenon in Japan, where Ike Taiga's simple, lyrical style was followed by Kō Fuyō (1722–1784), Kuwayama Gyokushū (1746–1799), Noro Kaiseki (1747–1828), Kimura Kōkyō (Kenkadō; 1736–1802), Aoki Shukuya (d. ca. 1802), and Aoki Mokubei (1767–1833).[36] While *nanga* (Southern painting) artists favored Taiga's lyrical style, such painters as Niwa Kagen (1742–1786), Maruyama Ōkyo (1733–1795), Hokusai, Tani Bunchō (1763–1840), and Watanabe Kazan (1793–1841) adopted a more realistic style of real-scenery landscape painting.

In China, there were two stylistic tendencies in real-scenery landscape painting, the Wu school and the Huangshan school. They were introduced to Korea, where they coexisted with the style of Chŏng Sŏn. In Japan, instead of adopting the Chinese geometric style, real-scenery landscape painters favored Taiga's abbreviated, allusive style, which was later to coexist with Western realism.

DIFFERENCES IN MODES OF EXPRESSION IN CHINA, KOREA, AND JAPAN

We have seen in the preceding discussion why artists in China, Korea, and Japan came to be interested in representing specific sites and how they developed their own artistic styles in real-scenery landscape painting. In this section, my aim is to show how different the specific modes of expression were in the three countries. In the case of Korea and Japan, Chinese-influenced styles coexisted with indigenous ones. Thus, we will first see what kind of artistic styles were prevalent in China, then examine which expressive modes of these various artistic styles were transmitted to Korea and Japan to exert influence on new landscape painting and coexist with indigenous landscape traditions.

In China, the paintings of Mount Huang, produced in great number in the seventeenth century, can be divided into three categories. The

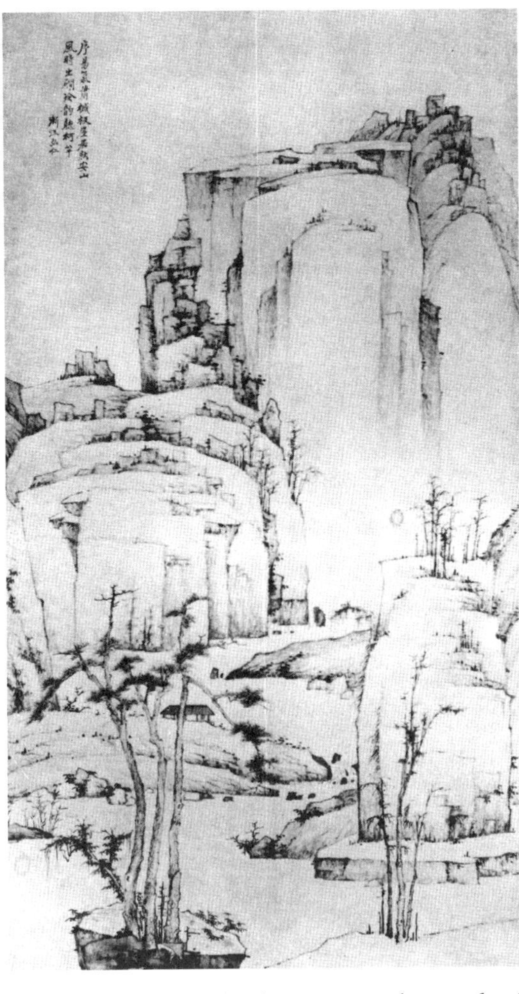

FIGURE 6
Hongren (1610–1664), *The Coming of Autumn.* Ink on paper. Honolulu Academy of Arts

first is the geometric, almost semi-abstract landscape style developed by Hongren, which later became the most typical mode of representing Mount Huang.[37] Although Ni Zan's style formed the basic foundation of the style, Hongren's transformation of it deserves special notice. The geometric style (see fig. 1), though highly schematized, can be easily found in other landscape paintings (fig. 6). Many artists such as Zha Shibiao (1615–1698), Zou Zhilin (active early 17th century), and Xiao Yuncong followed this trend. Xiao Yuncong, in particular, used this geometric style even in his painting in the manner of old masters. In his *Landscape in the Manner of Jing Hao* (fig. 7), for example, Xiao employed the new style but described it as a *fangzuo*, or imitation copy, in the manner of the tenth-

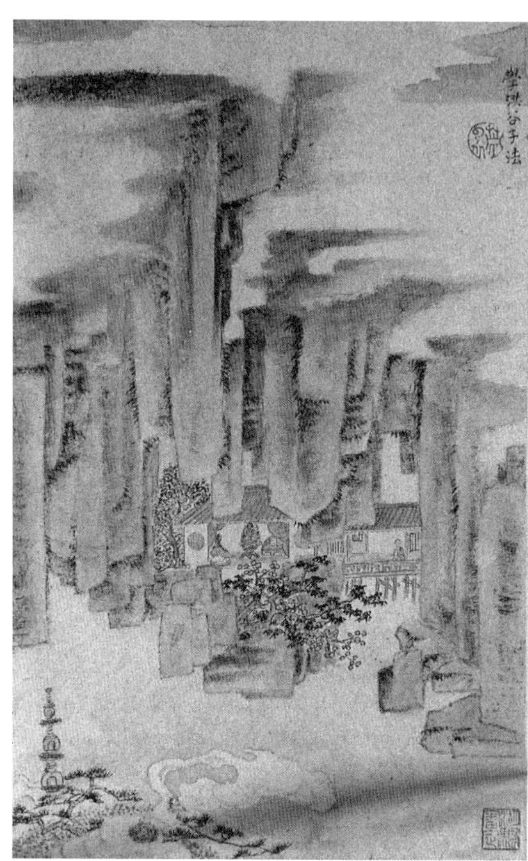

FIGURE 7
Xiao Yuncong (1596–1673), *Landscape in the Manner of Jing Hao*, from *Album of Landscapes*, 1654. Shanghai Museum

century master Jing Hao. This is also true of his *Landscape in the Manner of Guan Tong*, where the characteristically massive, solid quality of Guan Tong's (active ca. 907–23) style is hardly visible.[38] These works bear witness to the fact that Xiao did not hesitate to use in his so-called *fangzuo* the newly developed and innovative style of real-scenery landscape painting.

The second category of landscape painting is characterized by curving forms full of rhythmic movement. Again, Xiao Yuncong's work is representative of this style, as exemplified in a leaf from a landscape album (fig. 8). The undulating lines of rocks, resembling lava flowing from a volcano, are drastically different from the geometric language of the first type. This organic, curved form was adopted by many other painters. Among the examples are Shitao's *Mountain Retreat* from an album of landscapes (fig.

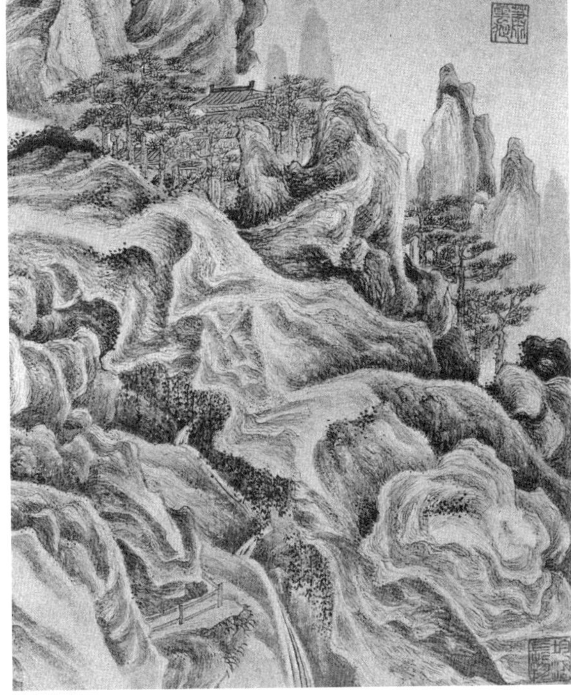

FIGURE 8
Xiao Yuncong (1596–1673), *Landscape*, from *Album of Landscapes*, 1654. Shanghai Museum

9) and Mei Qing's *One Leaf in a Landscape Album*, in which lines of rocks are flowing as if dancing. It is noteworthy that Xiao Yuncong made a rare case for adopting at the same time the two opposed styles of geometric and curving forms.

The last category is a combination of the first two, employing more complicated compositions and more natural expressions. Shitao is representative of this type of eclectic landscape painting. Instead of radically distorting or transforming shapes, Shitao tried new variations in terms of perspective, spatial arrangement, and coloring, and thus enjoyed more popularity.[39]

Of the three categories, the first type, or geometric style, was introduced into Korea. This geometric style is often found in paintings by Kang Se-hwang, Yi In-sang, and Yi Yun-yŏng, clearly affirming the influence of

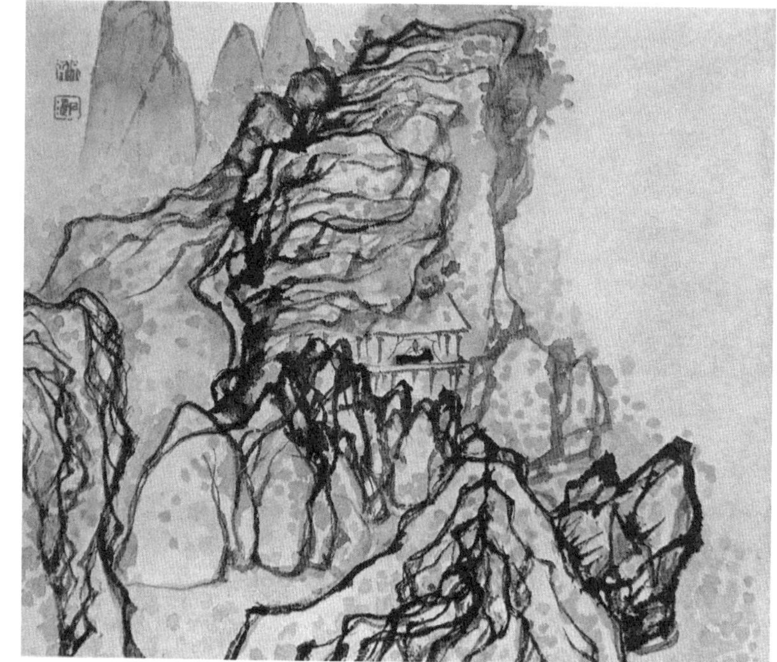

FIGURE 9
Shitao (1642–1707), *Mountain Retreat*, from *Landscape Album for Elder Yu*. Ink and color on paper. Private collection

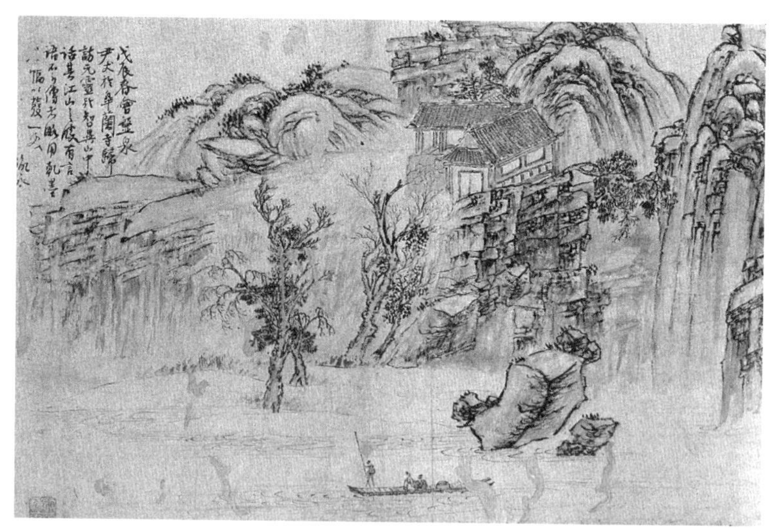

FIGURE 10
Yi Yun-yŏng (1714–1759), *Goran-sa Temple*, 1748. Ink and color on paper. Private collection

China. Yi Yun-yŏng's *Goran-sa Temple* (fig. 10) renders a cliff by means of many small cubic forms, which are prevalent in works of Chinese artists such as Hongren, Xiao Yuncong, and Mei Qing. This style is also found in Yi In-sang's treatment of rocks and Chŏng Su-yŏng's paintings of Mount

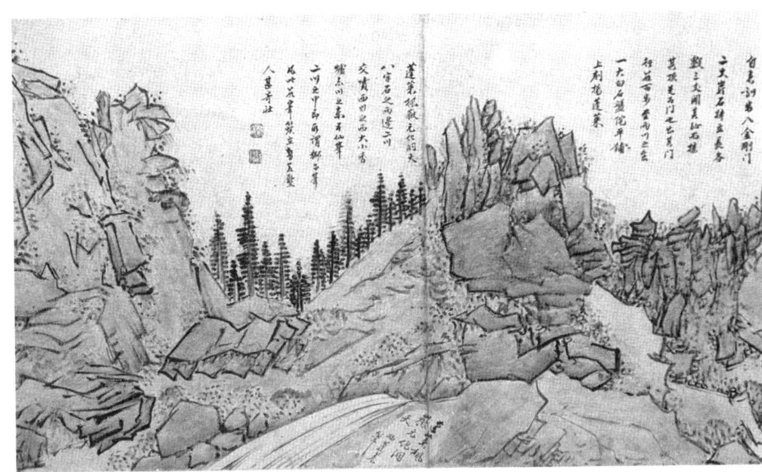

FIGURE 11
Chŏng Su-yŏng (1743–1831), *View Along the Han and Imjin Rivers*, 18th century. Detail. Ink and color on paper. The National Museum of Korea, Seoul

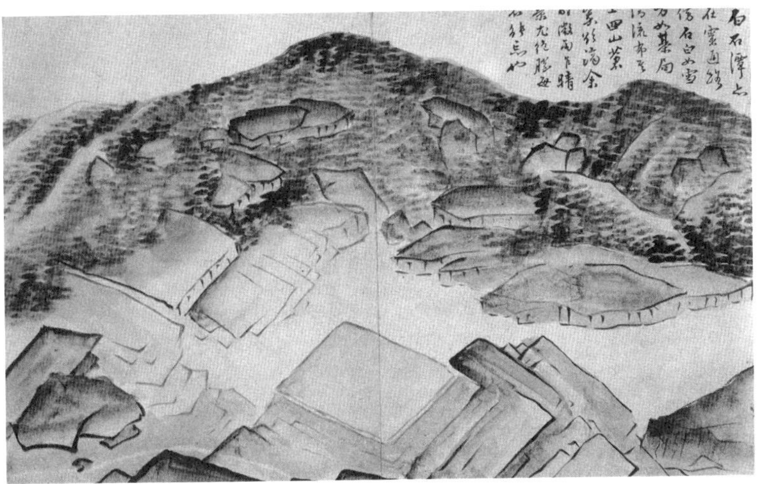

FIGURE 12
Kang Se-hwang (1713–1791), *Peaksok-dam*, from *Album of a Journey to Songdo*. Ink and color on paper. The National Museum of Korea, Seoul

Kŭmgang.[40] Chŏng Su-yŏng's *View Along the Han and Imjin Rivers* (fig. 11) renders rocks in the style of the Huangshan school. He further develops the Chinese style by using pointillist techniques for the autumn leaves. Also creative and witty is the way in which Chŏng Su-yŏng inscribed characters on the rocks in the foreground.

Another Korean transformation of Chinese style is found in a leaf from Kang Se-hwang's *Album of a Journey to Songdo* (fig. 12). Here, the background mountains are painted in short, Mi ink-dots, whereas the foreground rocks are defined in more abstract, geometrical shapes. This innovative combination of the traditional Mi-style with the new geometric forms can be seen as a revolutionary transformation of Chinese styles based on the specific situation and sensibility of Chosŏn period Korea. Kang Se-hwang's transformative impulse is also revealed in his other albums, in which he incorporated the traditional Chinese Mi-style with a Western mode of representation. This combination of two distinct traditions testifies to Kang's exquisite sensibility of form. He achieved a new sense of beauty in his ingenious integration of the geometric style of the Huangshan school and Western techniques of rendering shadows.[41]

The greatest achievement in Korean real-scenery landscape painting is Chŏng Sŏn's use of using vertical strokes and Mi ink-dots together with wild brushstrokes. The needlelike sharp peaks in his painting are the real view of specific mountains, but it is also possible that he might have adopted some expressive motif from Chinese woodblock prints. Along with the bold and expressive brushstrokes used in mountain peaks, his treatment of pine trees is also innovative. He transformed the new way in which Chinese literati artists like Shen Zhou (1427–1509) rendered pine trees, achieving a more powerful, dynamic, and natural expression. This new expression, which is almost completely "Koreanized," is found in Chŏng's *Manp'ok-dong* (fig. 13) and *Hyŏlmang-bong*.[42]

Chŏng Sŏn's new style attracted many followers, among them Kim Tŭk-sin (1754–1822), Ch'oe Puk (1712–ca. 1786), Kang Hŭi-ŏn (1710–1764), Chŏng Hwang (b. 1735), Chŏng Ch'ung-yup (active 18th century), Kim Yun-gyŏm (1711–1775), and Kim Ŭng-hwan (1742–1789), who created paintings based on the new expressive mode. Kŏyon-dang's (active late 18th century) landscape painting, though not of excellent quality, summarizes Chŏng Sŏn's stylistic characteristics.[43] In the treatment of tree branches, in particular, his brushstrokes appear almost exactly the same as his predecessor's, which bears witness to the fact that Chŏng Sŏn's style had come to be easily used as a reference point. Along with the geometric mode of the Huangshan school, Chŏng Sŏn's style constituted one of the two main currents in Korean real-scenery landscape painting in this period.

In the development of artistic styles in real-scenery landscape painting, Japan differed from China and Korea, which were more closely related stylistically. As mentioned earlier, many *nanga* painters engaged in real-scenery landscape painting in Japan. *Nanga* (Southern painting), known also as *bunjinga*, "painting of the literati," had been developed under the influence of paintings of the Ming–Qing period in China and the late Chosŏn period in Korea. However similar in style and appearance to those

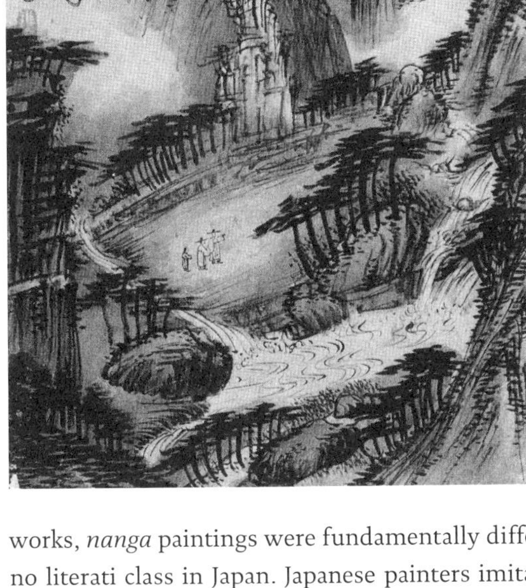

FIGURE 13
Chŏng Sŏn (1676–1759), *Manp'ok-dong*. Ink and color on silk. Museum of Seoul National University

works, *nanga* paintings were fundamentally different because there was no literati class in Japan. Japanese painters imitated Chinese models of pure literati painting or conceptual painting. For real-scenery landscape painting, however, they could neither imitate Chinese landscapes nor adopt the literati style due to the particular subject matter of real scenery. In this rather peculiar situation, Japanese painters eventually developed their own style based on literati landscape painting.

The *nanga* painter Ike Taiga is one of the most prolific landscapists of the eighteenth century. His paintings, called true-view landscape painting (*shingei-zu*) instead of real-scenery landscape painting, include several dozen images, among them *Diary of the Journey to the Three Peaks* (see fig. 5).[44] He portrayed numerous sites, including Mount Fuji, Mount Asama, and the Bay of Kojima, but his paintings are hardly identifiable either as real-scenery landscapes or as literati painting. In his *Mount Fuji* (fig. 14), for instance, the peak is easily recognizable as that of Mount Fuji, but the

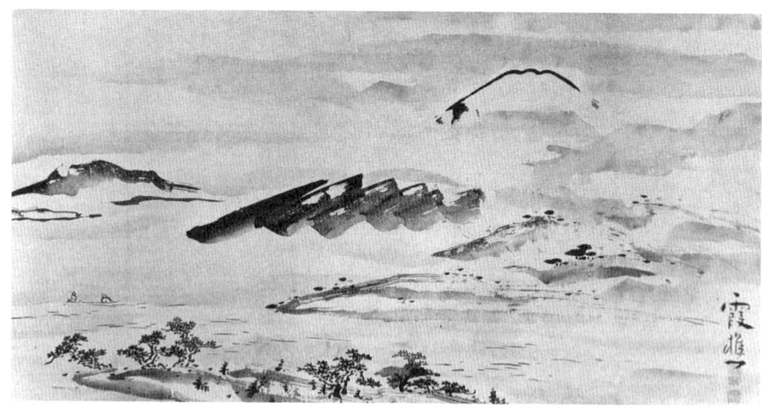

FIGURE 14
Ike Taiga (1723–1776), *Mount Fuji*. Ink on paper

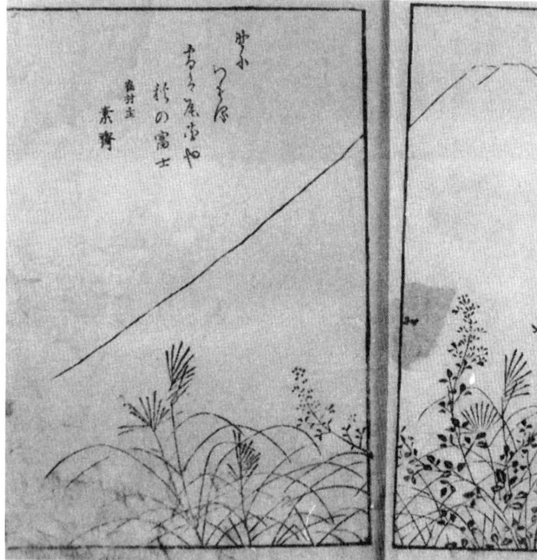

FIGURE 15
Kawamura Minsetsu (active 18th century), *White Mount Fuji*, 1771. Private collection

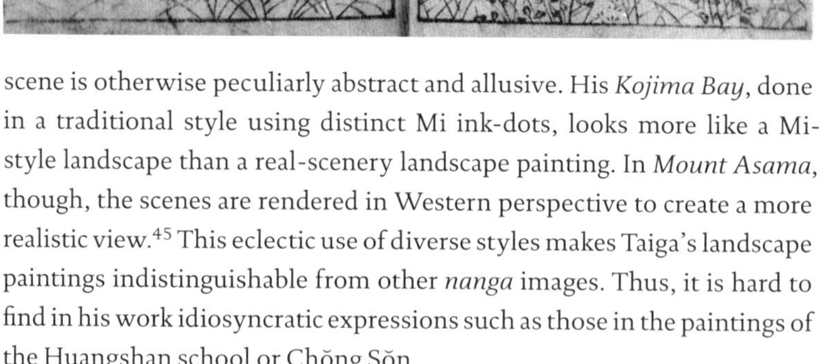

scene is otherwise peculiarly abstract and allusive. His *Kojima Bay*, done in a traditional style using distinct Mi ink-dots, looks more like a Mi-style landscape than a real-scenery landscape painting. In *Mount Asama*, though, the scenes are rendered in Western perspective to create a more realistic view.[45] This eclectic use of diverse styles makes Taiga's landscape paintings indistinguishable from other *nanga* images. Thus, it is hard to find in his work idiosyncratic expressions such as those in the paintings of the Huangshan school or Chŏng Sŏn.

Like Taiga, other Japanese artists painted Mount Fuji more often than any other site. But their expressions were extremely conventional or arbi-

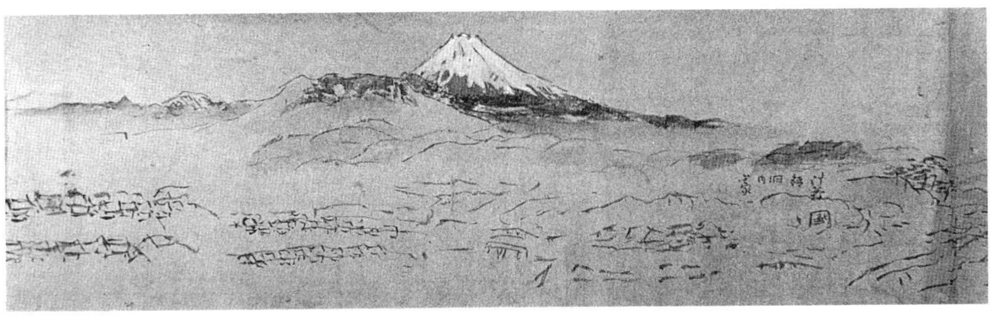

FIGURE 16
Kano Tan'yū (1602–1674), *Mount Fuji Seen from Tōkaidō*, from a handscroll of sketches. Ink and color on paper

trary, as they were merely interested in conspicuously portraying the three small peaks on the top of Mount Fuji. Kawamura Minsetsu's *White Mount Fuji* (fig. 15) of the eighteenth century showcases this Japanese taste; the three peaks are set in the background almost like a standard pattern, and the conventional motifs of traditional Japanese painting, such as flowering trees, an expanse of reeds, or a small stream, are placed in the foreground. This mode of expression following established tradition betrays the conservatism of the Japanese, while the simplified, patternlike form testifies to their distinguished sense of design.

Taiga assumes a similar place in the history of Japanese landscape painting as that of Chŏng Sŏn in Korea. He had a great number of followers who imitated his style and failed to develop their own artistic expression. Nakayama Kōyō's landscape paintings or Noro Kaiseki's *Mount Fuji* are such examples.[46] The plain, lifeless peaks, as well as the trees or hills done in the literati style, reveal limits similar to those of Taiga's literati-style landscape paintings.[47] However, these paintings depart from the tradition of Taiga in that they do not use any of his characteristic techniques, such as ambiguous smoky clouds or Mi ink-dots.

Another characteristic of Mount Fuji landscapes of Japan is that the site was favored as a subject by artists regardless of their schools or artistic styles, ranging from *nanga* painters to artists of the Kano school, Western-style painters, Ukiyo-e artists, and even printmakers. In his *Mount Fuji Seen from Tōkaidō* (fig. 16), for example, Kano Tan'yū (1602–1674) placed Mount Fuji in the center of the background with the village spread out below. A preliminary sketch, it nevertheless reveals not only patternlike expressions characteristic of the Kano school but also some new aspects of Kano Tan'yū's painting.

The Western-style painter Shiba Kōkan also painted numerous landscapes of Mount Fuji, most of which were done in oil. While employing the Western method of linear perspective to portray the scene realistically, he still shows vestiges of traditional Japanese painting in the treatment of the trees in the foreground and the depiction of waves (fig. 17).[48] Though in their paintings most artists placed Mount Fuji in the far distance, Nakazawa Rosetsu (1754–1799), of the Maruyama and Shijō schools, put the peaks of the mountain in the center of his landscapes. He adopted Western techniques in rendering the mountain as if seen from above and in adding gradations of light and dark to the valleys. Yet he also included the traditional Japanese motif of flying cranes, incorporating the two distinct traditions into his work.

Thus, Japanese painters portrayed Mount Fuji in a variety of ways according to the stylistic traditions to which they belonged. What they have in common is their placement of the three peaks of Mount Fuji in the background and the use of their own styles for rendering the middle and the foreground. This clearly differentiates Japanese landscapes from those of China and Korea that deal with actual scenery of real sites as a major motif. Hokusai's prints, especially those depicting views of the mountain on a bright, sunny day (fig. 18), can be regarded as the culmination of Japanese real-scenery landscape painting. The simplified composition, with its absence of extraneous details, attests to a unique sense of plastic beauty. The delicately rendered clouds and beautiful colors suggest that Mount Fuji was as fully explored as an object of beauty as Mount Huang in the paintings of the Huangshan school in China. In another view of Mount Fuji, Hokusai portrays a lively and energetic scene of the mountain. The huge, soaring waves can be said to be a magnified version of the tra-

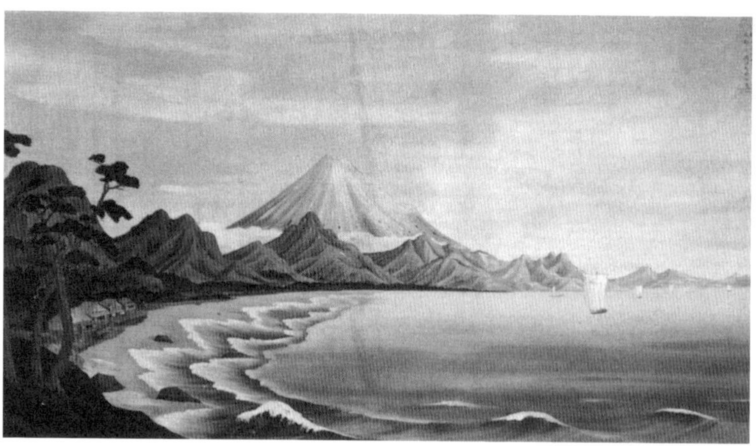

FIGURE 17
Shiba Kōkan (1738–1818), *Mount Fuji Seen from Far Distance.* Shizuoka Prefecture Museum

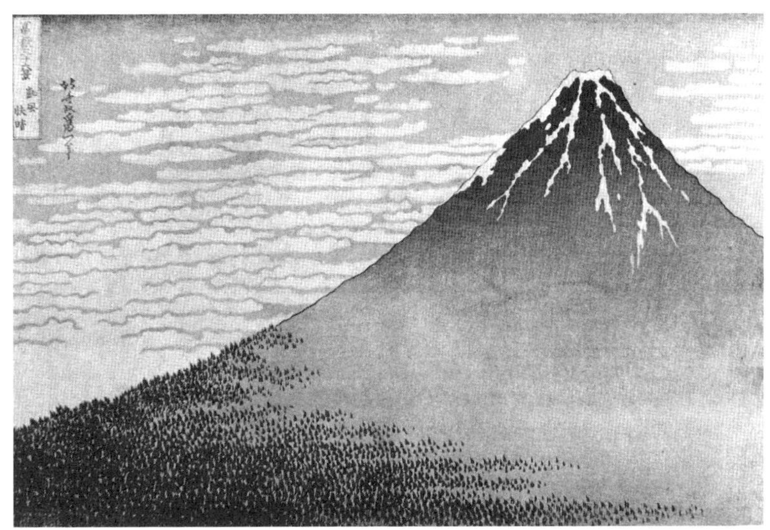

FIGURE 18
Katsushika Hokusai (1760–1849), *Mount Fuji*, from *Thirty-six Scenes of Mount Fuji*, 1825. Woodblock print

ditional expression of ripples. Seen through the huge waves, Mount Fuji seems to tell viewers its own history of existence and endurance. The fact that Mount Fuji had been a central subject of Japanese landscape painting from the Kamakura period (1185–1333) up to the nineteenth century testifies to the almost religious status of the mountain for Japanese painters. This admiration for a certain mountain is, as we have seen, also found in China and Korea, where Mount Huang and Mount Kŭmgang were portrayed as a main subject up to the twentieth century. These three mountains were not mere objects of nature, but rather a field of visual exploration where artists experimented with new modes of expression.

Real-scenery landscape painting flourished in China, Korea, and Japan almost simultaneously due to the rapid introduction of landscape paintings of the Chinese Huangshan school into Korea and Japan. Although there were earlier examples of real-scenery landscape paintings in each of the three countries, the paintings produced in the seventeenth and eighteenth centuries were fundamentally different from those works in both their process of development and their content. First, the mode of expression established by the Huangshan school influenced the landscape traditions of Korea and Japan. Second, the artists did not limit themselves to the realistic depiction of real scenery, but rather experimented with various artistic styles by incorporating the literati painting tradition or by executing radical transformations of that tradition.

In China, there were several types of real-scenery landscape painting. Among them, the geometric style of Hongren, introduced to Korea in the eighteenth century, made a great impact on Korean real-scenery landscape painting. In Korea, however, the style of Chŏng Sŏn constituted the mainstream of landscape painting. Though revealing certain influences of the woodblock print style of China, Chŏng Sŏn's style was not imitative of it; rather, it was founded upon the indigenous tradition of the mid-Chosŏn period. His influence on the following generations was so great that his style became representative of a unique Korean mode of expression. Both in China and in Korea, literati painters actively engaged in real-scenery landscape painting and painted actual scenes in the literati style.

Japan's relationship to China was not as close as that of Korea. Yet, because *nanga* painters,who aspired to the literati style, developed real-scenery landscape painting, Chinese real-scenery landscape was eventually imported to Japan. Ike Taiga and his followers combined the indigenous Japanese expression and the Chinese literati style in their paintings of Mount Fuji. Though highly eclectic, these paintings rarely contain particularly geometric or curvilinear elements. Thus, further investigation is needed to determine whether the geometric expressions in the works of Nakabayashi Chikutō (1776–1853) or Kameda Bōsai (1752–1826) resulted from the influence of the Huangshan school of China. Although Japanese artists of various schools painted Mount Fuji in their own styles, their landscape paintings have in common decorative patterns and traditional or conservative tendencies.

China, Korea, and Japan were clearly different in terms of specific expressions in real-scenery landscape painting. In general, while China and Korea were rather closely related, Japan took an independent path. Further exploration of new resources and materials, as well as an in-depth study of woodblock prints of landscape painting, such as the *Jiezi Yuan huazhuan* (Mustard Seed Garden Painting Manual) and *Taiping shanshui tu*, is necessary to expand our understanding of seventeenth- and eighteenth-century real-scenery landscape painting in the three countries.

NOTES

1. Han 1996; 1999, 216–55.
2. For the formation of the concepts of Practical Learning, see Ju Chil-sŏng 1998, 321–30; Korean Practical Learning Research Association 1998, 529–66.
3. For the history of Practical Learning during the Ming–Qing period, see Ju Chil-sŏng 1998, 328–45; Korean Practical Learning Research Association 1998, 245–581; Korean Practical Learning Research Association 1996; Ge Rongjin 1992.
4. By the late Ming period, the School of the Mind had been divided into three sects: the Right School, the Left School, and the Orthodox School. Sometimes called *Xiancheng pai* or School of Taizhou, the Left School went to an extreme degree of abandoning social mores, propagating that one can do whatever one wishes if one makes up one's mind. Practical Learning attempted to overcome the conceptual or idealist element of the School of the Mind and Neo-Confucianism by emphasizing practical aspects of social, political, and economic life, thus differentiating itself from its predecessors.
5. For the relation of Chinese real-scenery landscape painting to contemporary philosophy, see Ganza 1990. Ganza positions real-scenery landscape paintings of Ming–Qing China within the context of contemporary philosophical currents. He suggests that real-scenery landscape painting of the late Ming and the early Qing was closely related to the Left School and the Right School of the School of the Mind, respectively. In his dissertation, Ganza does not use the term "practical learning," which came to be widely used only in the 1990s.
6. For Practical Learning of Korea, see History Association 1973; Yi Ulho 1983; Kum Changtae 1987; Kang Mankil 1998; Bu Jinzhi 1998, 567–81. Chŏng Sŏn, who came after Yun Tu-sŏ, is believed to have been influenced by this new current in philosophy. Some scholars have suggested that the literary theory of the Gongan school of Ming China, such as the theory of Tianji or Xingling, gave an impetus to Chŏng Sŏn's real-scenery landscape painting. However, since it is now widely agreed that the philosophical background of the Gongan school was the School of Practical Learning rather than the School of the Mind, we can rightly argue that it was the Practical Learning of the Ming–Qing period that provided the philosophical foundation for real-scenery landscape painting. In their opposition to reactionary revivalism, both the theory of Tianji and the theory of Xingling were influenced by the School of the Mind and Practical Learning. For the theory of Tianji, see Pak Eun-sun 1997; 2002, 258.
7. For Japanese Practical Learning, see Minamoto Ryoen 1980. Minamoto characterizes Japanese Practical Learning as follows: a tendency toward the School of the Mind; an emphasis on self-enlightenment; an interest in practical social benefits; a broad range of intellectual engagement including among Confucian scholars, soldiers, merchants, and the peasant class; the strong power of empirical rationalist lineage following the School of Qi. He suggests that all of these elements contributed to the rapid modernization of Japan.
8. The first travel literature in China appeared during the Han dynasty and Six Dynasties. *Yu sabulsan-ki*, written by Chinjŏng Kuksa in the Koryŏ dynasty, and *Tosa Ikki*, written in 935 in the Heian

era, are believed to be the first travel literature in Korea and Japan, respectively. For more information, see (for China) Lin Pangqun 1992; and (for Korea) Yi Hye-sun 1997 and Choe Kang-hyŭn 1982. For Korean literature on travels to China and Japan, see Sŏ Chae-yong and Kim Tae-jun 1985, especially the parts on China and Japan.

9. Zhang Bigong 1992, 332–38.

10. Among those who wrote about the journey to Mount Huang are Yuan Zhongtao, Yao Zhisu, Huang Ruxiang, Xu Xiake, Yang Bu, Huang Jimo, and Qian Qianyi.

11. Xu Xiake, recorded in Zhang Bigong 1992, 381.

12. Choe Kang-hyŭn 1982.

13. Yi Hye-sun 1997, 30–42.

14. For Korean literature about Mount Kŭmgang, see Choe Kang-hyŭn 1992, 1773–1827; Kim Dong-joo 1999.

15. For Japanese travel literature, see Suzuki Dōjō 1984; Matsuo Bashō 1998.

16. For Chinese woodblock prints in general, see Kobayashi Hiromitsu 2002. For the influence of Chinese prints on Japanese painting, see Machida Municipal International Print Museum 1990, vols. 1, 2.

17. The scenes depicted in *Hainei qiguan*, *Mingshan tu*, and *Taiping shanshui tu* can be found in *Ancient Chinese Prints* 1994, vol. 2, no. 11.

18. Ko Yŭn-hee 2001, 74–90.

19. Chen Chuanxi 1990, 86–92; Okada Beisanjin's *Lingxu shan* can be found in Machida Municipal International Print Museum 1990, vol. 2, p. 154.

20. For the history of paintings of Mount Kŭmgang, see Pak Eun-soon 1997. For the history of paintings of Mount Fuji, see Naruse Fujio 1998.

21. Kim Chang-hyŭp, *Nongam-jip*, vol. 11.

22. Ŏ Yu-bong, *Kiwon-jip*, vol. 21.

23. Kobayashi Yūko 1996, 252–53.

24. Takayaki Mitsuhisa 1973.

25. The mode of depicting pine trees on a cliff originated in Hongren's album on Mount Huang. Before Hongren, the prevalent method was to portray the entire view of mountains, as in the *Sancai tuhui* or *Hainei qiguan*. The *Mingshan tu* and *Taiping shanshui tu* also followed the artistic tradition of portraying the entire view.

26. Paintings of Mount Kŭmgang with multiple scenes had started with Cho Sok in the mid-Chosŏn dynasty. He made one album of eight paintings, depicting such subjects as *Jangan-sa Temple*, *Jangan-sa Temple Viewed from the North*, and *Pyohun-sa Temple*. The album was executed in the early seventeenth century, when Hongren produced his Mount Huang album.

27. It is recorded that paintings of Mount Fuji had appeared as early as the tenth century. Among the oldest is *Prince Shōtoku Taishi eden*, of the eleventh century, which portrays the story of Prince Shōtoku ascending Mount Fuji on a black horse. The famous three peaks of Mount Fuji seen from Fujishan City in Shizuoka Prefecture had been painted since the Kamakura period.

28. Yi Su-mi 1995, 217–43; Park Jŭng-ae 1999.

29. For the paintings of Miho Matsubara, see Yamashita Zenya 1995, 244–49.

30. For Taiga's *Diary of the Journey to Three Peaks*, see Suzuki Susumu 1975, 87–88; Kobayashi Yūko 1996, 255–56.

31. Kobayashi Yūko 1996, 253.

32. For a reproduction of the paintings, see Cahill 1982b, color pl. 7, and pls. 25, 83; *Yuanlin minghua tezhan tulu* 2001, pls. 18/1–18/4.

33. For the stylistic characteristics of painters of the Huangshan school, see

Cahill 1981; Kuo Chi-sheng 1980; Chen Chuanxi 1996; Ko Yŭn-hee 1996.

34. Zhang Geng, 1963, chapter on Hongren.

35. For detailed information, see Han 1996.

36. For the works of these artists, see Naruse Fujio 1998, 204–10.

37. Hongren's paintings can be found in *Zhongguo meishu quanji* 1988, vol. 9; Cahill 1981; and *Selected Paintings of Ming and Qing Anhui Painters* 1988.

38. In *Taiping shanshui tu*, Xiao Yuncong wrote on each leaf "After a certain ancient master," which reveals an undifferentiated phase of real-scenery landscape painting and *fangzuo*. This phenomenon is also found in some of Taiga's paintings and several Korean real-scenery landscape paintings, such as Kim Ung-hwan's *Entire View of Mount Kŭmgang* and Yun Je-hong's *Oksun-bong* in the manner of Yi In-sang.

39. For Shitao's painting, see Edwards 1967; Cahill 1982.

40. For further information, see Han 1996, 78–79.

41. On Kang Se-hwang, see Byŭn Yŏng-sup 1988.

42. For Chŏng Sŏn's paintings, see *Beauty of Korea* 1977, series no. 1, and *Exhibition of Chŏng Sŏn* 1998.

43. For Kŏyon-dang's paintings, see Ahn Hwi-joon 1982, pls. 99, 100.

44. For Ike Taiga, see Takeuchi 1992.

45. Ibid. *Mount Asama* is reproduced in pl. 29, *Kojima Bay* in pl. 47.

46. For the images, see Naruse Fujio 1988, pls. 155–57.

47. Kobayashi Tadashi 1983, 32–33.

48. Tsukahara Akira 1996, 281–98; Iwasaki Yoshikazu and Harada Minoru 1998, 51–60.

REFERENCES

Ahn Hwi-joon, ed. 1982. *Landscape Painting* II. Seoul: Jung'ang Daily Co.

Ancient Chinese Prints. 1994. Shanghai: Guji chubanshe.

Beauty of Korea. 1977. Seoul: Jung'ang Daily Co.

Bu Jinzhi. 1998. Differences and Similarities of Philosophical Ideas of Practical Learning of China and Korea. In *A Study on the History of Practical Learning in China and Korea*, Korean Practical Learning Research Association. Seoul: Min'umsa.

Byŭn Yŏng-sup. 1988. *Study on Paintings of Kang Se-hwang*. Seoul: Iljisa.

Cahill, James, ed. 1981. *Shadows of Mt. Huang: Chinese Painting and Printing of the Anhui School*. Berkeley: University Art Museum.

———. 1982. *The Compelling Image: Nature and Style in Seventeenth-Century Chinese Painting*. Cambridge: Harvard University Press.

———. 1982b. *The Distant Mountains: Chinese Painting of the Late Ming Dynasty, 1570–1644*. New York and Tokyo: Weatherhill.

Chen Chuanxi. 1990. Youguan Xiao Yuncong Taiping shanshui shihua wenti. *Duoyun* 25. Shanghai: Shuhua chubanshe.

————. 1996. *Hongren.* Jilin: Meishu chubanshe.

Choe Kang-hyŭn. 1982. *A Study of Korean Travel Literature.* Seoul: Iljisa.

————. 1992. A study of Mt. Kŭmgang Literature. *Songgoknonchong* 23.

Edwards, Richard. 1967. *The Paintings of Tao-chi.* Ann Arbor: University of Michigan.

Exhibition of Chŏng Sŏn. 1998. Daelim Gallery.

Ganza, Kenneth S. 1990. The Artist as Traveler: The Origin and Development of Travel as a Theme in Chinese Landscape Painting of the Fourteenth to Seventeenth Century. PhD diss., Indiana University.

Ge Rongjin, ed. 1992. *The History of Practical Learning of China and Japan* (Chinese Social Science Publication).

Han, Junghee. 1996. The Influence of China on Late Chosŏn Painting. *Art Historical Investigation* 206 (Korean Art History Association).

————. 1999. *Painting of China and Korea.* Hakgojae.

History Association, ed. 1973. *Introduction to the Study of Practical Learning.* Ilchogak.

Iwasaki Yoshikazu and Harada Minoru. 1998. *History of Modern Japanese Painting.* Trans. by Kang Dŏk-hui. Seoul: Yekyong.

Ju Chil-sŏng et al. 1998. *Traditional Philosophy of East Asia.* Yaemoon Seowon.

Kang Mankil et al. 1998. *Ideas of Korean Practial Learning.* Seoul: Samsung Publishing Co.

Kim Dong-joo, trans. and ed. 1999. *Mt. Kŭmgang Travel Literature.* Jontong munhua yonguhui.

Ko Yŭn-hee. 1996. Paintings of Mt. Huang by Anhui School. Master's thesis, Hongik University.

————. 2001. *Travel Arts of the Late Chosŏn Dynasty.* Seoul: Iljisa.

Kobayashi Hiromitsu. 2002. *Traditional Prints of China.* Trans. by Kim Myŭng-sŏn. Sikongsa.

Kobayashi Tadashi. 1983. *Edo Kaiga,* II, *Nihon no Bijutsu.* Shibundō.

Kobayashi Yūko. 1996. Ike no Taiga. *Art History Forum* 4. Shikongsa.

Korean Practical Learning Research Association. 1996. *Issues and Future Prospect of East Asian Practical Learning* (summary publication of the Fourth International Conference of East Asian Practical Learning).

————. 1998. *A Study on the History of Practical Learning in China and Korea.* Seoul: Min'umsa.

Kum Changtae. 1987. *The Study of Ideas of Korean Practical Learning.* Chibmundang.

Kuo Chi-sheng. 1980. *The Paintings of Hung-jen.* PhD diss., University of Michigan.

Lin Pangqun, ed. 1992. *Litai Youjixian.* Zhongguo qingnian chubanshe.

Machida Municipal International Print Museum. 1990. *Modern Japanese Painting and Prints.*

Matsuo Bashō. 1998. *Bashō's Haiku.* Trans. by Kim Jŏngrae. Badachulpansa.

Minamoto Ryōen. 1980. *A Study on Practical Learning in the Early Modern Period.* Seibunsha.

Naruse Fujio. 1998. *Japanese Painting and Its Expression of Landscape.* Chūō kōron bijutsu shuppan.

Pak Eun-sun. 1997. *A Study of Landscape Painting of Mt. Kŭmgang.* Seoul: Iljisa.

————. 2002. Viewpoint and Subject of Real-Scenery Landscape Painting. In *Our Land, Our Real Scenes.* Ch'uncheon National Museum.

Park Jŭng-ae. 1999. Landscape Painting of Chŏng Su-yŏng. Master's thesis, Hongik University.

Selected Paintings of Ming and Qing Anhui Painters. 1988. Anhui: Meishu chubanshe.

Sŏ Chae-yong and Kim Tae-jun, eds. 1985. *Literature of Journey and Experience.* Minjok munhua mungo kanhaeng hui.

Suzuki Dōjō. 1984. Note on Travel. In *Dictionary of Japanese Classic Literature,* vol. 2. Iwanami Shoten.

Suzuki Susumu. 1975. Ike no Taiga. *Nihon no Bijutsu* 114. Tokyo: Shibundō.

Takayaki Mitsuhisa. 1973. Mt. Fuji and Literature. In *Study on Mt. Fuji.* Meicho shuppansha.

Takeuchi, Melinda. 1992. *Taiga's True View: The Language of Landscape Painting in Eighteenth Century Japan.* Stanford: Stanford University Press.

Tsukahara Akira. 1996. Shiba Kōkan: His Landscape Expression and Consciousness of Enlightenment. *Art History Forum* 3.

Yamashita Zenya. 1995. The Formation and Development of Painting of Mt. Fuji. *Art History Forum* 2. Shikongsa.

Yi Hye-sun et al. 1997. *Mountain Travel Literature of the Mid-Chosŏn Dynasty.* Jipmundang.

Yi Su-mi. 1995. A Study of Chosŏn period Paintings of Famous Sites around the Han River: Chŏng Su-yŏng's Painting of Famous Sites along the Han River. *Seoulhak Yongu* 6.

Yi Ulho, ed. 1983. *Anthology of Scholarly Essays on Practical Learning.* Chŏn-nam University Press.

Yuanlin minghua tezhan tulu. 2001. Taipei: National Palace Museum, Taipei.

Zhang Bigong. 1992. *History of Travel in China.* Yunnan: Renmin chubanshe.

Zhang Geng. 1963. *Guochao huacheng lu* (Painters of the Qing dynasty; 1739). In *Huashi congshu,* ed. Yu Anlan. Shanghai: Renmin meishu chubanshe.

Zhongguo meishu quanji. 1988. Shanghai: Renmin meishu chubanshe.

STUDIES IN HONOR OF CHU-TSING LI

Chain of Causation: Fang Shishu's *The Autumn Colors on the Que and Hua Mountains after Zhao Mengfu and Dong Qichang*

JU-HSI CHOU

In *Scent of Ink: The Roy and Marilyn Papp Collection of Chinese Painting*, I argued for the restoration of the orthodox painter Fang Shishu's (1692–1752) place in the art of Yangzhou,[1] demonstrating how central Fang was to the culture of that city. Fang, himself a failed salt merchant, was at home with the wealthy merchants of the salt trade, some of whom were undisputed leaders in the patronage of art and artists. Not surprisingly, he frequently associated with them and also participated in their "elegant gatherings" (fig. 1).[2] It is a modern myth that in the eighteenth century Yangzhou painting was given over to the so-called eccentric modes of painting.[3] Another myth is that the orthodox school, of which Fang Shishu was a prominent member, was little more than a backdrop for the emergence of the eccentric artists. In the end, we may have to recognize that Yangzhou's eminence as a thriving artistic center was not due to the eccentrics alone, but rather to the vital competition among diverse trends in the arts, including that represented by Fang Shishu.

Fang Shishu's hanging scroll *The Autumn Colors on the Que and Hua Mountains after Zhao Mengfu and Dong Qichang* (fig. 2), in the Roy and Marilyn Papp Collection, demonstrates that Fang was in the inner circle of Yangzhou's community of salt merchants and art patrons.[4] The painting was executed in the fourth month of 1734. The occasion, as Fang Shishu recorded elsewhere, was a gathering at Xiao Linglang Shanguan (Small and Exquisite Mountain Lodge),[5] the well-known estate of the poets and bibliophiles Ma Yueguan (1688–1755) and his younger brother Ma Yuelu (1697–after 1766),[6] whose family was engaged in the Yangzhou salt business. At that gathering, Ma Yueguan showed his guests a painting by the Ming mas-

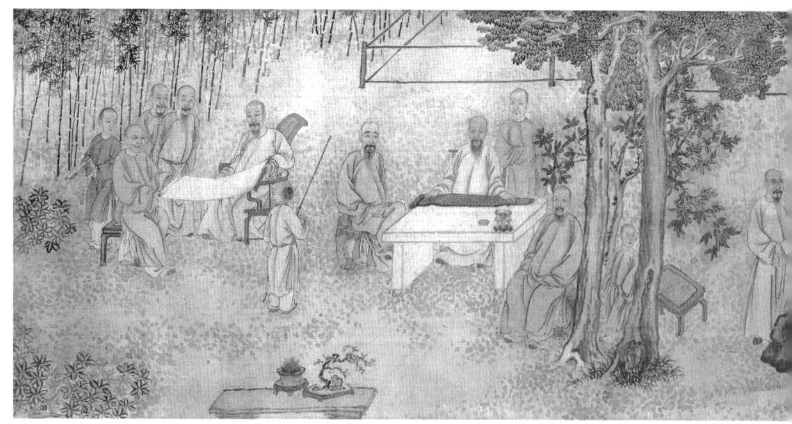

FIGURE 1
Fang Shishu (1692–1752) and Ye Fanglin (active late 17th–early 18th century). *The Ninth Day Literary Gathering at Xing'an*, 1743. Detail. Handscroll, ink and color on silk, 12½ × 79⅛ in. (31.7 × 201 cm). The Cleveland Museum of Art, The Severance and Greta Millikin Purchase Fund. 1979.72

ter Dong Qichang (1555–1636) done in "homage" to Zhao Mengfu's (1254–1322) famous handscroll *Autumn Colors on the Que and Hua Mountains*, of 1296, now in the National Palace Museum, Taipei, which Dong had once owned.[7] Afterward, Fang Shishu, having secured permission from his hosts to borrow it, took the painting home and made a copy of it. At a subsequent gathering, which took place during the *duanwu* (fifth day of the fifth month) festival, he showed his finished copy to the Ma brothers. In response, they wrote verses in appreciation, lauding the artist as a worthy successor to Zhao Mengfu and Dong Qichang.[8] These poems were inscribed on the silk border of the painting as a gesture of humility, allowing other guests, namely the elderly scholar Fang Zhenguan (1679–1747)[9] and the artist's half-brother, Fang Shijie (b. 1697), to add their inscriptions in the premium space, at the upper part of the painting.

As recorded in his *Tianyong an biji*, Fang Shishu responded to the Ma brothers' poems with a verse of his own:

> Where indeed are the Que and Hua mountains?
> I saw them at your upper floor.
> Shrouded by mist and vines, your studio was quieted.
> Autumn's clearing sky tinted the mountains with an emerald hue.
> I am so pleased we had this gathering,
> For we seemed to have made the journey to Jinan.
> I have recited your poems and contemplated your painting.
> How envious was I of your impeccable life style.[10]

Why was Fang's poem not inscribed on the painting? One reason is that

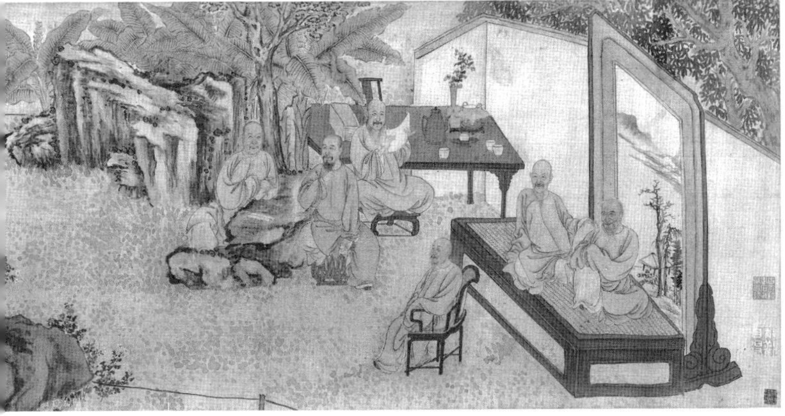

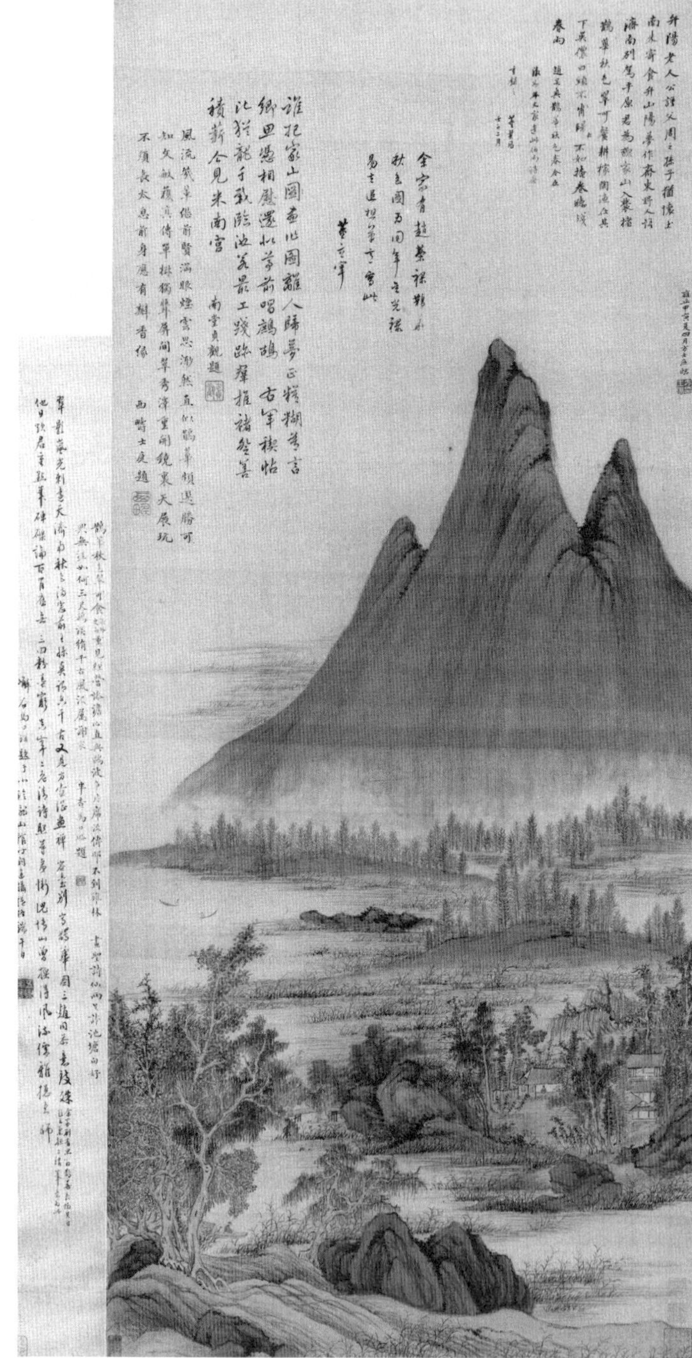

FIGURE 2
Fang Shishu (1692–1752). *The Autumn Colors on the Que and Hua Mountains after Zhao Mengfu and Dong Qichang*, 1734. Hanging scroll, ink and color on silk, 60⅞ × 26⅛ in. (154.6 × 66.5 cm). Collection of Roy and Marilyn Papp, Courtesy of Phoenix Art Museum (photography by Craig Smith)

it was most likely written after the *duanwu* gathering. Fang Shishu was not quick witted; when given a poetic assignment, he "wrinkled his eyebrows, cringed his shoulders and, invariably, produced his poems with the utmost difficulty and pain."[11] However, when they were completed, his poems appeared "so well integrated as if being issued from Heaven, for [his artistry was such] that it was like a spring breeze sweeping over a lake surface, leaving no [human] trace whatsoever."[12]

In the events recounted here, one may observe a chain of cause and effect. The first link in the chain is Zhao Mengfu's short handscroll *Autumn Colors*. The second link is Dong Qichang's rendering of *Autumn Colors*, the location of which is currently unknown. What we know about Dong's painting comes mainly from Fang Shishu's copy, the last link in the chain. The following discussion examines the nature of this chain: how it was formed, and how each link is related to, and distinguished from, the others.

ZHAO MENGFU'S AUTUMN COLORS

Let us start with Zhao Mengfu and his *Autumn Colors on the Que and Hua Mountains*,[13] ostensibly a depiction of the countryside near Jinan, Shandong Province, dominated by the two hills Que and Huabuzhu. Zhao Mengfu served as a vice governor in this ancient region of Qizhou from 1292 to 1294, when he was recalled to the Yuan capital, Dadu (modern Beijing). Zhao returned to his home in Wuxing, Jiangsu Province, in late 1295, after nearly a decade in the north, and several months later, in January 1296, painted the scroll for Zhou Mi (1232–1298), a close friend whose ancestral roots lay in the Shandong region. Because of centuries of political strife, Zhou Mi had never had the opportunity to visit his ancestral land; it was up to Zhao Mengfu to depict for him the scenery of the region. Thus, Zhao's painting was a personal memento, signaling a bond between friends and carrying with it an emotional overtone.

While the scenery of Shandong provided the initial impetus for the painting, its transformation under Zhao Mengfu's hand is apparent. His approach is utopian, a celebration of a simple, rustic life set in a remote antiquity. Here, fishermen and peasants toil beneath the hills, where all is peaceful and tranquil. To reinforce this utopian theme, Zhao employs an "archaic" style, a throwback to a presumed stage of art before skill and artistry were apparent. Despite the allusions to Dong Yuan (active 930s–60s) and Juran (active ca. 960–95), exemplified in the texture patterns (*cun*) and the depiction of the rolling hills, or even to Li Cheng (919–967), in the twisting tree trunks and branches, there is nothing grand about the scroll. With its low hills, quiet surroundings, and intimate scale, the painting represents a critical departure from the monumental landscape tradition of the tenth and eleventh centuries. Nonetheless, one cannot ignore its urgent call for the revival of ancient heritages, which prefigured the orthodox movement in the late Ming (1368–1644) and Qing (1644–1911) periods. In that movement, Dong Qichang was the undisputed leader, and Fang Shishu an important eighteenth-century follower.[14]

Since its creation, Zhao Mengfu's handscroll has attracted much critical acclaim and admiration. One indication of this is the eminence of those who left inscriptions and seal impressions on the scroll.[15] Another is the number of known imitations and variations on the painting's theme, among which Yao Shou's (1423–1495) free improvisation led the way.[16] Wen Zhengming's (1470–1559) rendering of the theme has not survived, but we know that he added distant hills and a trailing city wall at the end.[17] In the Qing period, Wang Hui (1632–1717) produced a stretched-out version, which retains the lyricism, though at the expense of the mythic vision.[18] Following suit, a Qing court painter, Sun Hu (active Qianlong era, 1736–95), made a less-than-inspired attempt, perhaps after having seen the original scroll, which was then in the imperial collection.[19] The last known work created along the same lines is an album leaf by Wu Hufan (1894–1968), which extended this tradition of producing works after Zhao Mengfu's masterpiece into the twentieth century.[20] Surveying these works, we observe few exact copies; all contain some degree of modification. None of them, however, can equal the extent of changes made by Dong Qichang.

Or was it Dong Qichang at all?

DONG QICHANG'S AUTUMN COLORS

In one of his five inscriptions on Zhao Mengfu's *Autumn Colors*, Dong Qichang relates that in 1602 he received the scroll as a gift from Xiang Deming (Xiang Huifu; probably active 1573–1630),[21] who presumably had inherited it from his father, the great collector Xiang Yuanbian (1525–1590), whose seals are prominently displayed on the scroll. According to other existing documents, sometime afterward, between 1605 and 1616, Dong traded the painting for another work in the collection of Wu Zhengzhi (d. ca. 1619), of Yixing, Jiangsu Province, a close friend and a major collector in his own right.[22] The two inscriptions that Fang Shishu copied from his prototype in his *Autumn Colors* painting shed some light on this trade. The first (Inscription A), at the upper center of the painting, reads:

> Once I had Zhao Ronglu's [Mengfu] *Autumn Colors on the Que and Hua* in my collection. It was exchanged [for another work] with my *tongnian*,[23] Master Wu, the assistant minister of the Court of Imperial Entertainment [*Guanglu*]. I searched in my memory of [Zhao Mengfu's] brush idea and wrote [painted] this.

Master Wu is none other than Wu Zhengzhi. Dong Qichang dedicated a number of his own works to him, including two handscrolls, *Invitation to Reclusion at Jingxi*, of 1611, now in The Metropolitan Museum of Art,[24] and *After Mi Youren's "Wonderful Scenery of the Xiao and Xiang Rivers,"* of about 1616, in the Museum für Ostasiatische Kunst, Berlin,[25] and a hanging scroll, *Strange Peak and White Cloud*, in the National Palace Museum, Taipei (fig. 3). In all of these paintings, Dong addresses Wu by his *hao*, Cheru.

The second inscription (Inscription B), at the upper right, testifies that Dong Qichang sought to insert—or reinsert—into the context of *Autumn Colors* a poem by Zhang Yu (1277–1348), a Daoist poet and painter who was friendly with both Zhao Mengfu and Zhou Mi.[26] The inscription consists of a transcription of Zhang's poem, followed by an explanatory note, in which Dong contends that the poem was missing from the sequence of inscriptions on Zhao Mengfu's handscroll and that he was making partial amends by recording it in his own work.[27] Dong wrote the inscription in 1612,[28] by which time, according to Dong, the Zhao Mengfu scroll had passed into the hands of a collector whose *zi* or *hao* reads "Aoru." (Dong Qichang addresses him as *nianzhang*, suggesting that he is of an older generation.)[29]

Based on the two inscriptions, the sequence of events would be as follows: First, there was an exchange of paintings between Dong Qichang and Wu Zhengzhi, who obtained Zhao Mengfu's scroll *Autumn Colors*; second, Wu Zhengzhi allowed the scroll to pass on to a new owner, Aoru, by 1612. The question is: Was that really the case? The answer is: Hardly.

We learn from Zhang Chou (1577–1643), author of the important compilation *Qinghe shuhua fang*, that Zhao Mengfu's scroll was in the hands of the Wu family of Yixing sometime before 1616, that being the date of

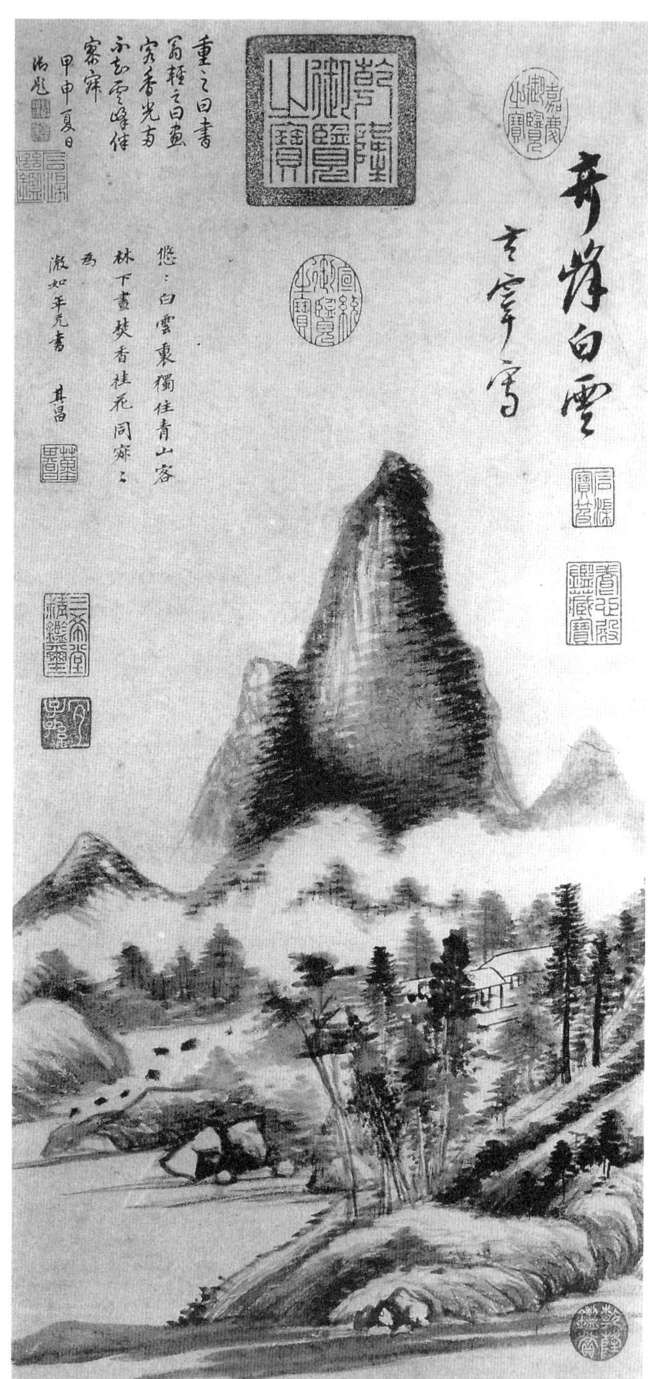

FIGURE 3
Dong Qichang (1555–1636), *Strange Peak and White Cloud.* Hanging scroll, ink on paper, 25¾ × 12 in. (65.5 × 30.4 cm). National Palace Museum, Taipei

the preface to Zhang's publication.[30] In addition, there is the testimonial of Dong Qichang himself, who, in an inscription on Zhao's *Water Village*, asserted that Master Wu, the assistant minister of the Court of Imperial Entertainment, still had *Autumn Colors* as late as 1619, around the time of his death.[31] In other words, the scroll did not change hands before 1619, but remained in Wu Zhengzhi's collection from the time the exchange took place.

If, in fact, the ownership of the scroll had not changed, it would seem that the name Aoru in Inscription B on Fang Shishu's painting might be a mistranscription. Indeed, in appearance it is not dissimilar from Cheru, the name written by Dong Qichang in the above-mentioned works dedicated to Wu Zhengzhi, such as *Strange Peak and White Cloud* (fig. 3a). It would only take someone who was not familiar with the character *che*, which is not at all commonplace, to produce a character that might at first glimpse be related to it but could also be read as something else. As innocuous as it may appear, this misreading of the character compels us to ask: Who made the error? Were Fang Shishu the culprit, it would not raise further questions. On the other hand, if the mistake was made in Fang's prototype, the so-called Dong Qichang, it may have other ramifications. Since its authorship has not yet been ascertained (see below), it may be useful to designate the prototype as Version X.

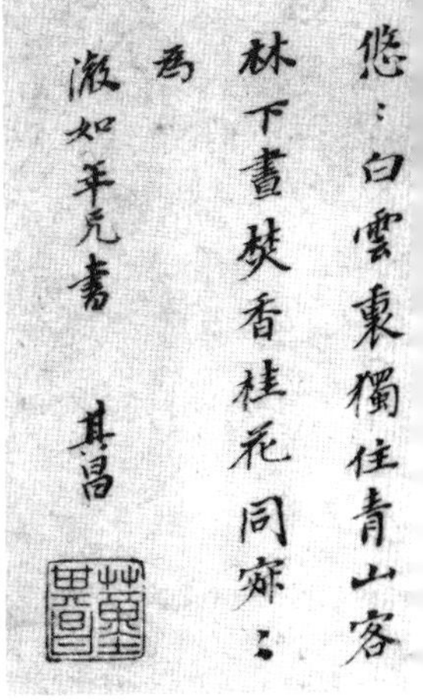

FIGURE 3A
Detail of Fig. 3

A preliminary investigation reveals that there was a known version of Dong Qichang's *Autumn Colors* in circulation in the Jiangnan region during the late Kangxi period (1662–1722). In that version, which was recorded by Wu Sheng (active ca. 1670–1713) in his *Daguan lu*, the inscriptions are identical to those copied by Fang Shishu.[32] More significantly, there appears the same error in the rendering of Wu Zhengzhi's *hao*, Cheru, as Aoru. This suggests that the *Autumn Colors* painting recorded by Wu Sheng may very well be the same painting that eventually made its way into Ma Yueguan's collection (that is, Version X). Although less likely, it might also be a derivative of that work (Version XX).

It should be pointed out here that Wu Sheng was a disciple of Wang Shimin (1592–1680), who studied under Dong Qichang and was well acquainted with Dong's style. Upon examining the aforementioned *Autumn Colors* scroll, he expressed dismay that "it was lacking in ink and brush methods, and was imbued rather by the manner of a professional."[33] He concluded that it was probably a *daibi* (ghost painting), as the silk was of a fine quality and the calligraphy of the two inscriptions excellent. Apparently, these were positive attributes pointing to Dong Qichang as the writer of the inscriptions, if not the author of the painting.

The error made in the transcription of Wu Zhengzhi's *hao* was in itself, however, a critical faux pas. Its commission eliminates any possibility that Dong Qichang could be the author of the inscriptions, as he did not make the same mistake elsewhere. In short, the painting (Version X or Version XX) was far from being a genuine work by Dong Qichang. Nor can it qualify as a *daibi*: In a *daibi*, the painting might be done by a ghost painter, but the purported author of the work would write the inscription in his own hand. We must conclude, therefore, that only a copyist—or more likely a forger—could make such a mistake. At the time that he was engaged in replicating perhaps an existing prototype (Version Y), the forger was neither familiar with Dong Qichang's circle of friends nor able to decipher the key character. The question, then, is: If the version seen by Wu Sheng was spurious, what might Version Y be?

I believe that Version Y could well be a *daibi*, one in which Dong Qichang not only wrote the set of inscriptions that have been preserved in Fang Shishu's copy, but also wielded considerable influence in the execution of the pictorial image.[34] I arrive at this conclusion first through an examination of style and then from a conceptual appraisal. As seen in Fang Shishu's copy, both Versions X and Y would have departed markedly in style from Dong Qichang's known range. Dong's style is often described as "intellectual" and "abstract," thriving on the potential of brush and ink. By contrast, Fang Shishu presents to us a painting whose model clearly favors pictorial and atmospheric effects. Granted, with neither Version X nor Version Y available for comparison, we are not able to ascertain the extent of Fang Shishu's transformation of his model. However, judging from the angular profile of Mount Huabuzhu, the smooth and silky appearance of the mountain's surface, and the free flow of ink, the author of the work that Fang sought to emulate could hardly be Dong Qichang. These features instead remind one of Zhao Zuo (ca. 1570–after 1633), a well-known ghost painter in Dong's service as well as, it may be postulated, a number of other Susong school painters.[35] We may compare Fang's *Autumn Colors* to Zhao Zuo's *Mist and Rain in Lakes and Hills*, in the collection of the Arthur M. Sackler Museum, Harvard University Museums, which, although thematically different, is similar in its rendition of the central peak.[36] Another Zhao Zuo painting, *Fishing by the Distant Mountains*, dated 1619, in the Palace Museum, Beijing, displays the characteristic shape of the peak and the "lotus vein" texture pattern inspired by Mount Huabuzhu.[37] A third work, attributed to Dong Qichang but again linkable to the broader context of the Susong school, is also typically misty and atmospheric.[38] One can note in that painting, as well as in the Fang Shishu version of *Autumn Colors*, the presence of taller trees at the lower left corner, a feature that was enlarged from the original scroll when the handscroll format was changed into a hanging scroll.

This leads to the next point. Conceptually, even though Version Y was likely a *daibi*, it could also have been instigated, or based on a work, by Dong Qichang. (Here, I am raising the possibility of a Version Z.) This conclusion is based on several factors. First, Dong Qichang knew Zhao Mengfu's *Autumn Colors* intimately, far better than any of the ghost painters in his service, to whom he usually allowed considerable liberty. At least eight versions of *Autumn Colors* are attributed to Dong, one, if not more, of which could have been from his own hand.[39] Second, unlike any previous attempt, either by Yao Shou or even Wen Zhengming, this series involved a radical change in format, from handscroll to hanging scroll. This change in turn necessitated a major adjustment in composition, which resulted in an emphasis on Mount Huabuzhu as the predominant pictorial element and the elimination of Mount Que. (Also, as a result of this change in format, the marshland appears to recede, rather than, as in Zhao Mengfu's original composition, to stretch out laterally in a series of sandbars and land outcroppings.) Such boldness is more typical of Dong Qichang than, say, Zhao Zuo, whose painting style observed a steady progression and gradual denouement in motifs and in movement and had none of the unexpected burst or unimpeded willfulness of Dong's. It was Dong Qichang who sought to achieve resemblance through non-resemblance.[40] Dong's attitude toward Zhao Mengfu ranged from grudging admiration of the artist to an irrepressible urge to challenge him.[41] In his approach to *Autumn Colors*, Dong took the Shandong geography and emasculated it. In so doing, he undermined the source of the warm sentiment shared between two friends, Zhao Mengfu and Zhou Mi. It is not far-fetched to suggest that Dong's painting signals a contest of will between the past and the present. As Ruan Yuan (1764–1849), who also had a version of Dong's *Autumn Colors*, put it, Dong Qichang's approach verges upon the "combative."[42] Few artists in the late Ming displayed such an obsessive desire to stand proud in the face of ancient masters. Only Dong Qichang succeeded.

Thus, beginning with Dong Qichang and then extending to his ghost painters and followers, Zhao Mengfu's *Autumn Colors* underwent a dramatic transformation—something close to a mutation. Judging by the work of those painters who willingly took up the replicating process, this new approach was surprisingly influential. Among those who took this mutated image seriously were Chen Guan (1563–ca. 1647),[43] Lan Ying (1585–ca. 1644),[44] and Yun Shouping (1633–1690).[45] Their collective efforts produced a pictorial series that spans the Ming and Qing dynasties. Individual variations notwithstanding, one persistent feature unites this group of paintings: Mount Huabuzhu rarely exceeds in height a third of the whole composition.[46] Knowing this prepares us to examine more closely Fang Shishu's painting (see fig. 2).

FANG SHISHU'S AUTUMN COLORS

In Yangzhou, where Fang Shishu lived, Zhao Mengfu's original scroll was not available, but its legend was well known.[47] In that city there were copies of the scroll by local and migrant artists. Yu Zhiding (1647–after 1709), a famous portraitist and landscape painter associated with the city, produced a well-known version which entered the collection of the connoisseur Gao Shiqi (1645–1703).[48] Zhu Wenzhen (active ca. 1740–70), originally from Shandong and a disciple of Zheng Xie (1693–1765), is also known to have made a large handscroll in ink monochrome, which was said to rival Wang Hui's.[49] A painting by Luo Pin (1733–1799) shows the artist and his friend, a native of Jinan to whom he dedicated the painting, against the backdrop of Mount Huabuzhu.[50] Luo executed the work with full awareness of the genesis of the *Autumn Colors* theme and the friendship between Zhao Mengfu and Zhou Mi.

There were two versions of Dong Qichang's *Autumn Colors* in Yangzhou, one in the collection of Ma Yueguan (our Version X) and the other in the collection of the scholar-official Ruan Yuan.[51] The latter version was probably not known to Fang Shishu in 1734, when he produced his version of *Autumn Colors*, and even today remains unknown. It was Version X that caught Fang Shishu's eye. Fang was not the only artist who was captivated by the work; Wang Nanmin, a contemporary and friend of Fang Shishu, is also known to have copied it.[52] It matters little whether Version X was a genuine work by Dong Qichang. Unlike us, Fang Shishu did not question the authorship of the painting. He cherished the unexpected encounter with the scroll at the Ma brothers' gathering, and then undertook to emulate it with respect for his artistic forebear. Unlike Dong Qichang, who rose to challenge his predecessor, Fang Shishu sought to merge with him.[53] As Fang makes clear in his inscription, it was not so much a matter of "*fang*," as simply a desire to emulate, that is, *lin* (to copy). Lending weight to this contention is Fang's faithful replication, in content as well as style, of the inscriptions in an attempt to approximate the appearance of the original.[54]

Emulation is an act of homage, not a battle of wits. That being the case, we must agree that the major portion of Fang's painting is derivative. By Fang's time the transformation of Zhao's *Autumn Colors* into hanging-scroll format was a fait accompli. Also, the silky surface of Mount Huabuzhu was characteristic neither of Dong Qichang's style nor of Fang Shishu's, which favored dry, textured passages, at times tremulous and changing.[55] Light washes of the blue-green can still be seen, echoing not so much Zhao Mengfu as the pseudo-Dong Qichang's preference. In terms of what was once present in Zhao Mengfu's scroll, and also keeping in mind an unknown intermediary, we may point to such features as the two crescent-shaped fishing boats in the lake, the rows of evergreens, and the shorelines with reeds. Some of the tree groupings are vaguely reminiscent of those in Zhao Mengfu's original work; other elements are repositioned (the crescent-shaped boats with fishermen transposed from the right to the left side of the painting), reduced (the diminished role of the willows, for instance), or modified (the change in the scale of the motifs).

Fang Shishu, however, was not totally faithful to his prototype. Like many painters with sufficient artistic maturity, he held his own views and convictions. The act of copying, as Fang states in his treatise *Tianyong an biji*, does not mean to repeat, stroke by stroke, an existing image.[56] On the contrary, it is similar to creating an original work. Consequently, as he puts it, "the idea must precede the brush," a familiar saying placed in a new context.[57] The process of creating a painting calls for constant adjustment and readjustment, in response to a given model or to the newly emerging image itself. The end result need not be identical to the model, but can encompass a wide range—from close approximation to something startlingly fresh.

One major alteration in the composition of the painting, which Fang Shishu must have conceived at the outset, is the increased prominence of Mount Huabuzhu. In Fang's version, Mount Huabuzhu represents approximately one-half the total pictorial surface, compared to one-third in most of the seventeenth-century versions discussed here. As a result, Mount Huabuzhu, which in reality is nothing more than a small rocky promontory, has been transformed into a lofty mountain, rising thousands of feet above the flat plain. By contrast, the marshland below, with its diminished scale, is made more complex. The number of trees increases dramatically, and large boulders, not present in Zhao Mengfu's *Autumn Colors* or virtually any versions of the painting attributed to Dong Qichang or his followers, make their appearance in the foreground. Darkened for dramatic effect, the boulders contribute to the ebb and flow of the land formation and also serve to define the space cells that accommodate the dwellings. These changes produce an unexpected effect: We become much more aware of the presence of the small figures in the thatched hut and on the boats, which are highlighted by touches of bright color. Fang's figures create a greater empathetic response than those depicted in the remote time and space of the original Zhao Mengfu painting or even in the "generic" landscapes of Dong Qichang and his followers. The result is a keen sense of immediacy, a world of tangibles. This was undoubtedly what Fang Shishu had in mind when he said that the ideal artist was one who, like the masters of the Five Dynasties (907–960) and Song (960–1279) periods, could turn the realm of imagination (*xu* or "vacuous") into one of substance and reality (*shi* or "the solid").[58]

What does all of this mean in the chain of causation? Fang Shishu, it is clear, began with the intent of emulation, but ended by stressing the physical nature of the landscape and its interactive dimension with the hermetic ideal. He may not have visited Shandong, but this did not prevent him from trying to make Mount Huabuzhu as tangible and substantial as he could—even monumental.[59] The urge was to return, in a roundabout way, to the site that had initially inspired Zhao Mengfu. While it could still accommodate the hermits and scholars, Fang's landscape was intended to be a real place.

In conclusion, there are three or more paintings at stake here, linked images that span roughly six or seven hundred years. The first, Zhao Mengfu's *Autumn Colors*—inspired by friendship, founded on real topography, and transformed by a utopian ideal—is still with us. In its avowed interest in reviving the past, it provided impetus for the later orthodox movement in Chinese painting. The second, which began as a challenge, produced a mutation potent enough to become a sub-genre of, if not a major

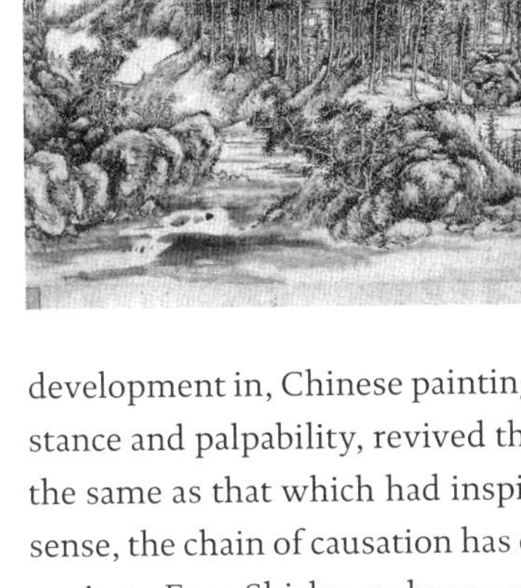

FIGURE 4
Fang Shishu (1692–1752), *Mists on the Summer Mountains after Dong Yuan*, 1737. Hanging scroll, ink and light color on paper, 89 7/8 × 34 1/2 in. (228.3 × 87.5 cm). National Palace Museum, Taipei

development in, Chinese painting. The last link, distinguished by its substance and palpability, revived the reality of the landscape, although not the same as that which had inspired the original *Autumn Colors*. In this sense, the chain of causation has come full circle.

As to Fang Shishu, only one question remains: Was his experience in emulating *Autumn Colors*, especially with his insight into Dong Qichang's bold attempt, a beneficial one? Apparently so. It has been suggested that both Fang Shishu and his teacher, Huang Ding (1660–1730), were skilled in emulating the ancients.[60] It is not known if Huang Ding, the master, ever attempted to turn a horizontal image into a vertical one, in the manner of Dong Qichang's transformation of Zhao Mengfu's *Autumn Colors*. However, Fang Shishu, the disciple, not only attempted this in his re-creation of what he perceived to be the late Ming master's effort, but was inspired to try his hand at it again. Three years later, in 1737, when another ancient masterpiece—*Mists in Summer Mountains*, a handscroll attributed to the tenth-century master Dong Yuan, now in the collection of the Shanghai Museum[61]—came to his attention, he re-enacted a similar transformation. Like Zhao Mengfu's *Autumn Colors*, the scroll was formerly in Dong Qichang's collection. During the early Qianlong reign (1736–95), no later than 1737, it fell into the possession of Wang Tingzhang,[62] a wealthy salt merchant in Yangzhou and Fang Shishu's major patron. It was Wang who willingly paid a thousand taels of silver for Huang Ding to come to Yangzhou to teach Fang Shishu the secret of painting.[63] It is not surprising, then, that Fang Shishu was allowed the privilege of examining the Dong Yuan scroll immediately after Wang acquired it. Sometime later, he must have borrowed the painting for closer scrutiny and eventually decided to rework Dong Yuan's composition into a large, imposing vertical scroll (fig. 4).

This artistic impulse came, once again, from a painting formerly in Dong Qichang's collection, an ancient masterpiece that, in Fang Shishu's eyes, had received Dong's sanction. This time, however, Fang Shishu no longer required an intermediary to lead the way, but approached the task on his own. Armed with his previous experience, he proceeded to merge his own being with that of the ancient master. Fang's observations of the art of Dong Yuan, noted in the inscription accompanying his painting, found expression in his own version of Dong's work:

> The hills and rock forms are done primarily by dotting. By this means he makes clear the veins and arteries. Everywhere it is even and rounded. There is not a single instance of angular protrusions. This is vastly different from the usual variety of imitations.

Mists on the Summer Mountains after Dong Yuan, which stands at the apex of Fang Shishu's own artistic career, evinces a grandeur and monumentality that can co-exist with the Dong Yuan.

NOTES

Professor Chu-tsing Li's study of the thirteenth-century master Zhao Mengfu's handscroll *Autumn Colors on the Que and Hua Mountains*, published in 1965, remains a classic in the field of Chinese art history. Chinese painting scholars have all recognized the pivotal role this study has played in advancing scholarship in the field. After forty years, it remains an exemplary account of a single work of art. The present paper is related to that painting. In the way that the eighteenth-century painter Fang Shishu celebrated Zhao Mengfu's *Autumn Colors*, I present it in homage to a senior scholar in the field.

1. Chou 1994b, cat. no. 26, pp. 88–91.
2. For a brief introduction to the painting illustrated in fig. 1, *The Ninth-Day Literary Gathering at Xing'an*, see Chou and Brown 1985, cat. no. 45. In this famous painting, jointly executed by Fang Shishu (landscape) and Ye Fanglin (figures), Fang (the sixth figure from the right) and his half-brother, Fang Shijie, appear among major salt merchants and other prominent personages of Yangzhou. The estate of Xing'an belonged to the brothers Ma Yueguan and Ma Yuelu, who are also featured in the painting.
3. See Chou 1991, 329–50.
4. See Chou 1994b, cat. no. 26, pp. 88–92.
5. See Fang Shishu, *Tianyong an biji*, *juan* 2, p. 15.
6. For a brief biographical account of the Ma brothers, see Hummel 1943, 559–60.
7. For an illustration of the Zhao Mengfu painting, see Li 1965, fig. 1; Fong and Watt 1996, 274–75, pl. 140.
8. See Ma Yueguan, *Shaheyilao xiaogao*, *juan* 1, pp. 3b–4a, in which Ma Yueguan records the three verses he wrote on the silk border of the painting. Ma Yuelu's verses appear only on the painting and are not recorded in his published works.
9. Fang Zhenguan was a native of Tongcheng, Anhui Province. Although not related to him, he considered Fang Shishu a nephew. See Feng Jinbo, *Guochao huashi*, vol. 71, p. 705.
10. Fang Shishu, *Tianyong an biji*, *juan* 2, p. 15.
11. Ruan Yuan 1971, *juan* 3, pp. 19b–20a.
12. Ibid.
13. Most of the data on and interpretation of Zhao's painting provided below are culled from Li 1965. Ding Xiyuan has presented a different view, contending that Zhao Mengfu's painting may not be a genuine work; see Ding Xiyuan 1991. At the time of his writing, Ding may not have seen the original painting, and he also failed to unearth any new documentary sources beyond those supplied in Professor Chu-tsing Li's study. For Ding's more recent research on the painting, see Ding Xiyuan 1994, 748–66, and 1998; also see Zhao Zhicheng's rebuttal in Zhao Zhicheng 1998.
14. It may be noted that Fang Shishu was a student of Huang Ding (1660–1730), who studied under Wang Yuanqi (1642–1715), the grandson of Wang Shimin (1592–1680), a favorite disciple of Dong Qichang.
15. For a discussion of the authors of these inscriptions, see Li 1965, 20–35.
16. For a convenient reference, see *Zhongguo gudai shuhua tumu* 1987, Hu 1-0328, leaf A, in an album dated 1494.
17. See *Wen Zhengming huigao* 1929, vol. 2, pp. 9a–b.
18. See *Zhongguo gudai shuhua tumu*

1990, Hu 1–2947, sections 3–4. The painting is one of four extant paintings from Wang Hui's *Six Realms*, painted for Song Lao (1634–1713), who once owned Zhao Mengfu's *Autumn Colors*.

19. See Christie's, New York 1983, lot no. 713.

20. See Sotheby's, Hong Kong 1994, lot no. 991a.

21. Dong's inscriptions were written before, during, and after the period in which he owned the painting. For the inscription referred to here, see Wang Shiqing 1992, 471.

22. That Wu Zhengzhi was a major collector is beyond question. He is remembered as the owner of Huang Gongwang's (1269–1354) *Dwelling in the Fuchun Mountains*. For Wu Zhengzhi's life and his collecting activities, see Huang Guan 1975, 42–45, and Riely 1992, 411–15. For Dong Qichang's interaction with the Wu family, see Dong Qichang 1968, vol. 3, pp. 1277–79 ("Eulogy for Wu Zhengzhi"), and vol. 1, pp. 491–94 ("On the Lanshu or Orchid Villa, built by Wu's son according to his specifications"). Regarding the whereabouts of the Zhao Mengfu scroll, we learn from Dong Qichang that he still had the scroll in 1605 (see his inscription). In that year, he took it to his official quarters in Wuchang and aired it in the sun. In his *Qinghe shuhua fang*, published in 1616, Zhang Chou mentions that *Autumn Colors* was in the collection of the Wu family of Yixing. That is to say, Wu Zhengzhi took possession of the scroll sometime before 1616. If the inscription (Inscription B) copied in Fang Shishu's painting is reliable, the trade could have taken place prior to 1612 (see discussion below). Most intriguing, however, is Dong Qichang's willingness to part with Zhao Mengfu's *Autumn Colors*. He was aware that the original scroll should have had Zhang Yu's inscription on it, a deficiency that caused him to consider transcribing it on the scroll years later, in 1630. Also, in a colophon appended to Zhao Mengfu's *Water Village*, Dong made it clear that he regarded *Autumn Colors* in a lesser light. See *Shiqu baoji* 1971, vol. 1, pp. 577–85.

23. The term *tongnian* refers to those who passed the same civil service examination in a given year. Wu and Dong both received their *jinshi* (presented scholar) degree in 1589.

24. See Ho and Smith 1992, vol. 1, pl. 18.

25. Ibid., vol. 1, fig. 40.

26. The poem is also found in Zhang Yu, *Juqu waishi zhenju xiansheng shiji*, *juan* 3, p. 26.

27. Chou 1994b, 91.

28. Eighteen years later, in 1630, Dong reinserted the poem by Zhang Yu in the original Zhao Mengfu scroll, at the request of a certain Huisheng, the owner of the painting at that time. See Li 1965, fig. 1a.

29. *Nianzhang* is an ambiguous term. It usually designates those who are elderly. Dong Qichang also addresses Wu Zhengzhi by this term in his eulogy for Wu; see Dong Qichang 1968, vol. 3, p. 1277.

30. See Zhang Chou 1888, *juan* 10, pp. 47a–48a. I find it puzzling that Zhang Chou recorded a version of Zhao Mengfu's *Autumn Colors* that is different from that in the National Palace Museum, Taipei. First, the peak(s) were said to be in the blue-green style; and second, the poem by Zhang Yu, still intact, was the only remaining inscription. Relative to the first issue, the blue-green style, it may be illusory at best, since there are also those who regarded the National Palace Museum version as such an exam-

ple, even though indigo blue was used, not malachite and azurite powder. In fact, Wang Shimao described the painting as such; see Wang Shimao 1969, vol. 4, p. 2408. Regarding the second issue, Wang's comment also supports Zhang Chou's eyewitness account that there survived a version of Zhao's *Autumn Colors* bearing Zhang Yu's poem as the lone inscription. See Wu Sheng 1920, *juan* 16, pp. 10a–b.

31. In *Midian zhulin, Shiqi baoji* 1971, 584, Dong Qichang writes: "This [Zhao Mengfu's *Water Village*] is Zi'ang's own prized painting. It is superior to the *Que and Hua* scroll . . . Both were [at one time] in my possession. The *Que and Hua* went to my *tongnian*, Wu, the assistant minister of the Court of Imperial Entertainment. This scroll entered into [the collection of] Cheng Jibai." Dong's inscription is dated 1619. At the time he wrote it, he appeared to be pleased that both paintings had found their rightful homes. Also, according to Celia Riely's calculation, Wu Zhengzi died before 1620; see Riely 1992, n. 276.

32. See Wu Sheng 1920, *juan* 19, p. 35b, which records a painting with a set of inscriptions identical to Fang Shishu's. This allows us to conclude that this painting was known during the late Kangxi period and could have been done in either the late Ming or the early Qing period. If the connection with the Susong school is to be sustained, then a late Ming date is more probable.

33. Ibid.

34. I am aware that there may be another possibility: The author of Version X could have interjected a stylistic mode not present in Version Y. Version Y, therefore, could have been a full-fledged Dong Qichang or something close to it.

35. The best evidence of Zhao Zuo's activities as a *daibi* for Dong Qichang is *Visit to Lake Dongting;* see Chou 1994b, cat. no. 5, pp. 26–28. The painting bears a colophon by Dong, which mentions that Zhao Zuo accompanied him to Lake Dongting and that, on the way back, they cooperated on the painting. As far as I can ascertain, the scroll bears the stylistic imprint of Zhao Zuo, not Dong Qichang.

36. See *Haiwai yizhen* 1988, no. 80.

37. For an illustration of the painting, see *Paintings from the Ming Dynasty from the Palace Museum* 1988, no. 65.

38. See Li 1965, fig. 2.

39. The eight paintings are: (1) the version recorded by Wu Jingyun in his 1662 inscription on Zhao Mengfu's *Autumn Colors* scroll; (2) the version copied by Fang Shishu, which was in the collection of Ma Yueguan; (3) the version recorded by Wu Sheng in his *Daguan lu, juan* 19, p. 35b; (4) the version mentioned by Ma Yueguan in his inscription on the silk border of Fang Shishu's copy, described as "a long hanging scroll after *Que and Hua.*" Dong Qichang's own inscription suggested that he had done the scroll by incorporating the idea of "Three Zhaos," that is, Zhao Boju, Zhao Danian, and Zhao Mengfu. See also Dong Qichang 1968, vol. 4, p. 2121; (5) the version owned by Ruan Yuan, a hanging scroll dated 1603; see Mao Chenglin 1926, vol. 1, pp. 354–55; (6) *Landscape in Color after Zhao Mengfu*, reproduced in Li 1965, fig. 2; (7) one leaf from an album featuring motifs derived from *Autumn Colors*. It is dated 1602, after Dong's acquisition of Zhao Mengfu's *Autumn Colors* handscroll from Xiang Deming. See Qingfu Shanren, *Dong Huating shuhua lu*, p. 29; and (8) a version by Dong Qichang; see Mao Chenglin 1926, vol. 1, p. 365.

40. See Chou 1989, 243–47, describing the act of *fang* as conceived by Dong Qichang and emulated by later artists.

41. See, for instance, Dong Qichang 1968, vol. 4, pp. 1951–52, 2006–7 (on calligraphy), 2098–99, 2103, 2104–05, and 2121 (on painting). In Dong Qichang's own words, the act of *fang* is a combat of wills, between the self and the past, and, figuratively speaking, a "bloody battle." See Chou 1989, 243–76, especially 246–47.

42. I refer to Ruan Yuan's line in his poem on another version of the painting by Dong Qichang. His contention was that Dong often sought to compete against Zhao Mengfu. See Mao Chenglin 1926, vol. 1, p. 355.

43. See Christie's, New York 1988, lot no. 76. Chen Guan's painting combines both the Que and Hua mountains in a hanging-scroll composition. It was dedicated to Chen Jiru (1558–1639); Dong Qichang wrote an inscription on the painting, in which he mentioned that Zhao Mengfu's original was the chief inspiration for the work.

44. See Christie's, New York 1992, lot no. 64. Lan Ying made it clear that his painting was painted after the style of Zhao Mengfu. See also a leaf from the album *Landscapes after the Song and Yuan Masters*, in Sotheby's, New York 1991, lot no. 33. It was painted in 1630 with Dong Qichang's version in mind.

45. See National Palace Museum, Taipei 1987, pl. 67. The painting is dated 1664.

46. This obviously is not applicable to the album format, where the proportion of height to width is such that it tends to undermine such pictorial possibilities inherent in hanging scrolls.

47. See Mao Chenglin 1926, vol. 1, pp. 352–53. It is conceivable that Gao Fenghan, a Shandong native who was stationed near Yangzhou in the mid-1730s and paid visits to the city, could have spread his knowledge about Zhao Mengfu's painting and the vicissitudes it endured in the late Ming and early Qing periods. It should also be noted that Fang Shishu saw a number of paintings attributed to Zhao Mengfu during his lifetime; see Fang Shishu, *Tianyong an biji*, passim. Fang also made a copy of Zhao's *Water Village;* see ibid., *juan* 2, p. 21.

48. See Gao Shiqi 1968. The painting eventually went to a Jiaxing collector; see Mao Chenglin 1926, vol. 1, pp. 352–53.

49. See Li Yufen 1981, 143.

50. See Mao Chenglin 1926, vol. 1, pp. 328–29.

51. See ibid., 354–56.

52. See Ma Yueguan, *Shahe yilao xiaogao, juan* 1, p. 6a. Fang Shishu wrote a laudatory verse about Wang's painting; see Fang Shishu, *Tianyong an biji, juan* 2, p. 17.

53. In his *Tianyong an biji, juan* 1, p. 12, Fang wrote to the effect that: "To attain transformation in painting, one must be mindful of the resplendence of the ancients, merging form and technique; in the end, one can then trust one's hand to move in whichever way to produce form and structure. In this way, the emotion will be engendered from the brush tip and, as the inner being does not dwell on a fixed image, the artistic manifestation will not be bound by fixed forms. The key is to read voluminously and to cultivate one's spirit [or *qi*], thus bringing fullness to one's own being. Afterward the heart will attain a state of harmony and the brush will be tinged with a state of peace and tranquility; the emerging painting will be 'antique' and the spirit will be liberated."

54. As I have argued in Chou 1994b, 90, Inscription A is oddly placed; it dangles

at the central axis of the silk surface, just above a lesser ridge of Mount Huabuzhu. Inscription B, however, rests comfortably in the upper right corner of the painting. Based on the content of the two inscriptions, Inscription A appears to come before Inscription B. Its priority makes the placement even more precarious, that is, if it should be the first to appear in the sequence in Version X. My explanation is this: when Fang Shishu completed the painting, he wrote his own inscription discretely at the far right side. Then, when his work was presented at the *duanwu* gathering, Fang Zhenguan and Fang Shijie were invited to write their comments first. After that, Fang Shishu attempted to emulate Dong Qichang's inscriptions. While Inscription B remains where it is, Inscription A could have been pushed to its present, central location from a previous, still unknown, setting. It could have been to the left side of the silk surface above the landscape.

55. Compare this with another work by Fang Shishu, *Maples on the Hill*, in Chou and Brown 1985, no. 43, in which the hand of Fang Shishu is present everywhere. Characteristic of his personal manner, he moves his brush at a deliberate pace, dealing with a continual struggle of contending elements and overcoming the obstacles every step of the way. This is part of Fang Shishu's legacy and also his special charm. His was an orthodoxy that promised no easy solutions.

56. See Fang Shishu, *Tianyong an biji*, *juan* 1, p. 2: "[In copying], the idea must precede the brush. In areas full of details, one must strive not to cause disorder. In areas that are sparse, one should try to avoid being scattered. As soon as the flavor appears, that's it. Do not only aim at the effect of *zhuo* [awkward or unskilled] but leave *qiao* [skilled or ingenious] unattended. This is truly what is meant by purifying one's heart and clearing one's sight. If one can savor the bittersweetness in the ancients' experience, and discriminate between the incorrect and correct ways, this is truly the orthodox way."

57. See n. 55 above.

58. See Fang Shishu, *Tianyong an biji*, *juan* 1, pp. 1–2: "Mountain and stream, plants and woods pertain to Nature and its mysterious ways. This is reality [as we know it]. Generating images in one's heart and then carrying them by means of one's hand: this is the realm of imagination. From imagination to achieve reality, this depends on the effect of brush and ink, whether they are able to measure right from wrong and to settle the skilled or the unskilled." Fang Shishu further writes that the ability to bridge the binary realms of *xu* and *shi* is contingent upon a dynamic process of sweeping movements of contrary forces, which he terms as *zhong* (vertical movement) and *heng* (horizontal movement). This is a typical formulation of eighteenth-century theorists and is also reminiscent of Wang Yuanqi's original ideas of *kaihe* (open and closed) and *qifu* (rise and fall). See Chou 1994a, 321–43.

59. See Fang Shishu, *Tianyong an biji*, *juan* 2, p. 15.

60. See Qin Zuyong's appraisal of Huang Ding's and Fang Shishu's skill in imitating ancient masterworks, in *Tongyin lunhua*, *Yishu congbian* edition, 29, 35–36.

61. For an illustration, see *Zhongguo meishu quanji: huihua bian* 1988, vol. 2, pl. 68, 144–47; see also explanatory text, 38–39. For a full account of the painting's inscriptions and seals, see Pang Yuanji 1971, vol. 1, pp. 53–61.

62. See Pang Yuanji 1971, particularly p. 57. The painting bears Wang's collector's seal. Also see Fang Shishu's inscription, as well as that of Fang Zhenguan. For Wang Tingzhang's biography, see Li Dou 1969, 745–46.

63. See Li Dou 1969, 748–51. For the chronology of this event, see Fang Shishu, *Tianyong an biji*, *juan* 2, p. 18, autobiographical verse inscribed on a painting *Return to the Mountain*, by Master Fengyi. The arrival of Huang Ding is said to have taken place in the decade after 1721, when Fang Shishu was 30 *sui*.

REFERENCES

Chou, Ju-hsi. 1989. Tung Ch'i-Ch'ang's Mimetic Cult and Its Legacy. In *Wen-lin: Studies in the Chinese Humanities*, ed. Tse-tsung Chow. Vol. 2. Madison and Hong Kong.

————. 1991. Rubric and Art History: The Case of the Eight Eccentrics of Yangzhou. In *Chinese Painting Under the Qianlong Emperor*, ed. Ju-hsi Chou and Claudia Brown. *Phoebus* 6, no. 2. Tempe, Arizona.

————. 1994a. Painting Theory in Eighteenth-Century China. In *The Power of Culture: Studies in Chinese Cultural History*, ed. Willard Peterson, Andrew Plaks, and Ying-shih Yu. Hong Kong.

————. 1994b. *Scent of Ink: The Roy and Marilyn Papp Collection of Chinese Painting*. Phoenix: Phoenix Art Museum.

Chou, Ju-hsi and Claudia Brown. 1985. *The Elegant Brush: Chinese Painting Under the Qianlong Emperor, 1735–1795*. Phoenix: Phoenix Art Museum.

Christie's, New York. 1983. *Fine Chinese Ceramics, Paintings and Works of Art*, June 23–24.

————. 1988. *Fine Chinese Paintings and Calligraphy*, November 30.

————. 1992. *Fine Chinese Paintings and Calligraphy*, June 2.

Ding Xiyuan. 1991. Zhao Mengfu "Quehua qiuse tujuan" xinkao. *Mingjia Hanmo* no. 3 (February): 94–112.

————. 1994. "Quehua qiuse tujuan" zaikao. In *Zhao Mengfu yanjiu lunwen ji*. Shanghai.

————. 1998. "Quehua qiuse tujuan" zai zaikao. *Wenwu* no. 6: 77–85.

Dong Qichang. 1968. *Rongtai ji*. Repr. Taipei.

Fang Shishu. *Tianyong an biji. Yishu congbian* edition.

Feng Jinbo. *Guochao huashi*. In *Qingdai zhuanji congkan*.

Fong, Wen C., James C.Y. Watt, et al. 1996. *Possessing The Past: Treasures from the National Palace Museum, Taipei*. New York: The Metropolitan Museum of Art.

Gao Shiqi. 1968. *Jiangcun shuhua mu*. Hong Kong.

Haiwai yizhen. 1988. Vol. 2. Taipei.

Ho, Wai-kam and Judith G. Smith, eds. 1992. *The Century of Tung Ch'i-chang, 1555–1636*. 2 vols. Kansas City: The Nelson-Atkins Museum of Art.

Huang Guan. 1975. Wu Zhiju yu Yunqi Lou. *Mingbao Yuekan*, vol. 10, no. 5 (May).

Hummel, Arthur, ed. 1943. *Eminent Chinese of the Ch'ing Period.* Washington D.C.

Li, Chu-tsing. 1965. *The Autumn Colors on the Ch'iao and Hua Mountains: A Landscape by Chao Meng-fu.* Ascona, Switzerland: Artibus Asiae.

Li Dou. 1969. *Yangzhou huafang lu.* Repr. Taipei.

Li Yufen. 1981. *Ouboluo shi shuhua guomu Kao.* Repr. Taipei.

Ma Yueguan. *Shahe yilao xiaogao. Yueya tang congshu* edition.

Mao Chenglin. 1926. *Xuxiu licheng xianzhi.* Repr. Taipei.

Midian zhulin, Shiqu baoji. 1971. Taipei.

National Palace Museum, Taipei. 1987. *Lanqian shanguan Minghua mulu.*

Paintings from the Ming Dynasty from the Palace Museum. 1988. Hong Kong.

Pang Yuanji. 1971. *Xuzhai Minghua lu.* Repr. Taipei.

Qingfu Shanren. *Dong Huating shuhua lu. Meishu congshu* edition.

Riely, Celia Carrington. 1992. Tung Ch'i-Ch'ang's Life, 1555–1636. In *The Century of Tung Ch'i-Ch'ang, 1555–1636*, ed. Wai-kam Ho and Judith G. Smith. Vol. 2. Kansas City: The Nelson-Atkins Museum of Art.

Ruan Yuan. 1971. *Guanglin shishi.* Taipei.

Shiqu baoji. 1971. Taipei.

Sotheby's, Hong Kong. 1994. *Fine Modern and Contemporary Chinese Paintings*, May.

Sotheby's, New York. 1991. *Fine Chinese Paintings*, November 25.

Wang Shimao. 1969. *Danpo huapin.* In *Peiwen zhai shuhua pu.* Taipei.

Wang Shiqing. 1992. Dong Qichang di jiaoyou. In *The Century of Tung Ch'i-Ch'ang, 1555–1636*, ed. Wai-kam Ho and Judith G. Smith. Vol. 2. Kansas City: The Nelson-Atkins Museum of Art.

Wen Zhengming huigao. 1929. Shanghai.

Wu Sheng. 1920. *Daguan lu.*

Zhang Chou. 1888. *Qinghe shuhua fang.*

Zhang Yu. *Juqu waishi zhenju xiansheng shiji. Sibu congkan* edition.

Zhao Zhicheng. 1998. Zhao Mengfu "Quehua qiuse tujuan" xinkao bianzhen. *Wenwu* no. 6: 396–409.

Zhongguo gudai shuhua tumu. 1987. Shanghai.

———. 1990. Shanghai.

Zhongguo meishu quanji: huihua bian. 1988. Beijing.

STUDIES IN HONOR OF CHU-TSING LI

Painting and the Qing Court: Scholar-Artists, 1736–1850

CLAUDIA BROWN

Historians have often described the literary and artistic endeavors of the emperors of the Manchu Qing dynasty (1644–1911) as grand pretense, calculated solely for political gain.[1] Harold L. Kahn, for example, has written of the monumental projects of the Qianlong emperor (r. 1736–95) as "public but not popular art, meant to reaffirm hegemonic sovereignty, omnicompetence, imperial legitimacy and the natural, harmonious order of things."[2] Recent art historical studies have helped to clarify the politics of art at the court, identifying a complex mixture of motives for the Qing rulers' patronage of art.[3] Other studies point out the importance of another aspect of painting at the Qing court, namely, the adoption by the Manchus of the literati ideal of the Han Chinese tradition.[4] These studies show that the Qing monarchs and their inner circle of officials regarded the traditional practice of painting and calligraphy as part of their life, duty, and culture.

An impression of the enthusiasm for painting at the Qing court, especially beginning with the patronage of the Kangxi emperor (r. 1662–1722), can be obtained from the Qing imperial catalogues of paintings and calligraphy, including the three editions of the *Shiqu baoji* and the *Bidian zhulin*. Today these catalogues are most often consulted for records of pre-Qing works. However, more than two-thirds of the paintings and calligraphies listed there were produced after 1644, the year in which the Qing dynasty was founded.[5] About one percent of the recorded works are by artists assigned to the Academy of Painting,[6] while nearly fifty percent are by government officials, princes, and emperors. This extraordinary participation in art by scholar-bureaucrats and imperial relatives has not received sufficient attention in the exploration of art at the court in Beijing during the eighteenth and early nineteenth centuries.[7]

The Qing court early on embraced the ideal of the Chinese scholar and the style of literati painting. Portraits of the Kangxi emperor show him surrounded by books or writing at a desk.[8] Patronage of scholar-artists was already underway with the Kangxi emperor's recruitment of Wang Hui (1632–1717) to supervise the production of the series of twelve scrolls (*Nanxun tu*) depicting the emperor's second southern inspection tour in 1689[9] and Wang Yuanqi (1642–1715) to oversee the production of paintings documenting the emperor's sixtieth birthday celebration (*Wanshou tu*) in 1713. The urge to commemorate an important occasion was paramount in these two collaborative projects. Also important to the practice of painting at court, however, was the expressive personal style of these artists, especially Wang Yuanqi, whose orthodox manner was a direct inheritance through his grandfather Wang Shimin (1592–1680) and ultimately Dong Qichang (1555–1636). Ju-hsi Chou has described the Kangxi emperor's personal observation of Wang Yuanqi painting in the imperial Southern Study.[10] This set the precedent for one of the most intriguing—and least appreciated—aspects of court painting under the Manchus, that is, the direct participation of the emperors and imperial relatives in China's highest cultural expression, painting and calligraphy. It was Tangdai (d. 1754), a Manchu disciple of Wang Yuanqi at the Qing court, who stimulated the Qianlong emperor's early interest in painting. Qianlong's admiration for Tangdai's paintings paralleled his grandfather Kangxi's fascination with the works of Wang Yuanqi.[11]

In the late 1720s, some six years before he became the Qianlong emperor, Hongli, then a prince in his late teens, took up painting. By that time he had been well trained in calligraphy and had a substantial interest in collecting both old and new paintings. During the first eight years of his reign, the young emperor either painted rarely or preserved little of his work. However, by the mid-1740s he seems to have become a prolific painter, an avocation he would pursue continuously until at least the age of eighty-seven. The year 1744 seems to have been a benchmark. In that year, he produced at least twenty-five paintings, which were preserved in the imperial collection, and commissioned the first catalogues of the ancient and modern paintings and calligraphies in the collection: the *Bidian zhulin*, a record of Buddhist and Daoist texts and paintings, and the *Shiqu baoji*, a description of secular paintings and calligraphies. The emperor took a personal interest in the compilation of these catalogues, which was carried out under the supervision of Zhang Zhao (1691–1745), whose calligraphy was a force in molding Qianlong's own writing. Zhang was noted for his paintings of plum blossoms, a subject that Qianlong also adopted. The emperor's burst of creativity may have been partly inspired by his participation in the review of the palace collection. An even more compelling urge probably stemmed from his desire to be documented in the *Shiqu baoji* as emperor-artist and as the supreme practitioner and scholar of that tradition.

Another participant in the compilation of the *Shiqu baoji*, the scholar-artist Dong Bangda (1699–1769), may have been a major influence on Qianlong's painting at this time. More than one hundred twenty of Dong's own paintings are included in the catalogue.[12] He also interacted artistically with other court officials, both Manchu and Chinese. *A Pavilion under Pine Trees* (fig. 1), dated 1751, was painted by Dong for the Manchu official Jiefu (d. 1762) when both men were serving as examiners for the metropolitan civil service examination.[13] The painting has an informal quality about it, and it stands as a record of the quiet ideals of the men charged with the heavy responsibility of conducting the highest level of the national examination. The understated style and the subject—lofty gnarled pines, a symbolic reference to the wisdom and experience of the examiners themselves—together with Dong's reference to the Yuan dynasty (1272–1368) scholar-official and painter Zhao Mengfu (1254–1322) in his inscription place the painting fully within the literati tradition.

Zou Yigui (1686–1772), an official of the highest accomplishments who was responsible for improvements in the treatment of prison inmates and the broadening of ethnic eligibility for the civil service exam as well as other reforms,[14] also participated with the Qianlong emperor in the review of ancient paintings in the palace collection. A painting by Zou was appended along with another by Qianlong among the colophons on one of the emperor's most prized works, *Admonitions of the Instructress to the Palace Ladies*, attributed to Gu Kaizhi (ca. 345–406).[15] Zou Yigui's *Flower Studies* is a miniature album of sixteen leaves presented directly to the emperor, its last page (fig. 2) depicting the plant called *wannianqing* (ten-thousand years verdant), a wish for the emperor's long life.[16] Zou was connected through his wife to the legacy of Yun Shouping (1633–1690), who set the standard for flower painting among the painters of the orthodox school. The realistic depictions of flowers in this small album stem from Yun Shouping and other precedents within the Chinese tradition, but Zou knew Western painting as well. His comment on the spatial illusionism of European painting, sometimes interpreted as narrow-minded rejection of the value of European pictorial techniques,[17] may also be seen as evidence of his thoughtful reflection on the profound differences between the two painting traditions.

Qianlong's southern inspection tours, officially documented by the *Nanxun* scrolls, were also an occasion for more informal artistic interpretation on the part of the emperor and members of his court. An album by Prince Hongwu (d. 1811), *The Myriad Delights of Lake Shi* (fig. 3), now in the Roy and Marilyn Papp Collection, the Phoenix Art Museum, has been convincingly associated by Ju-hsi Chou with Qianlong's second southern inspection tour of 1757.[18] Hongwu may have accompanied the emperor

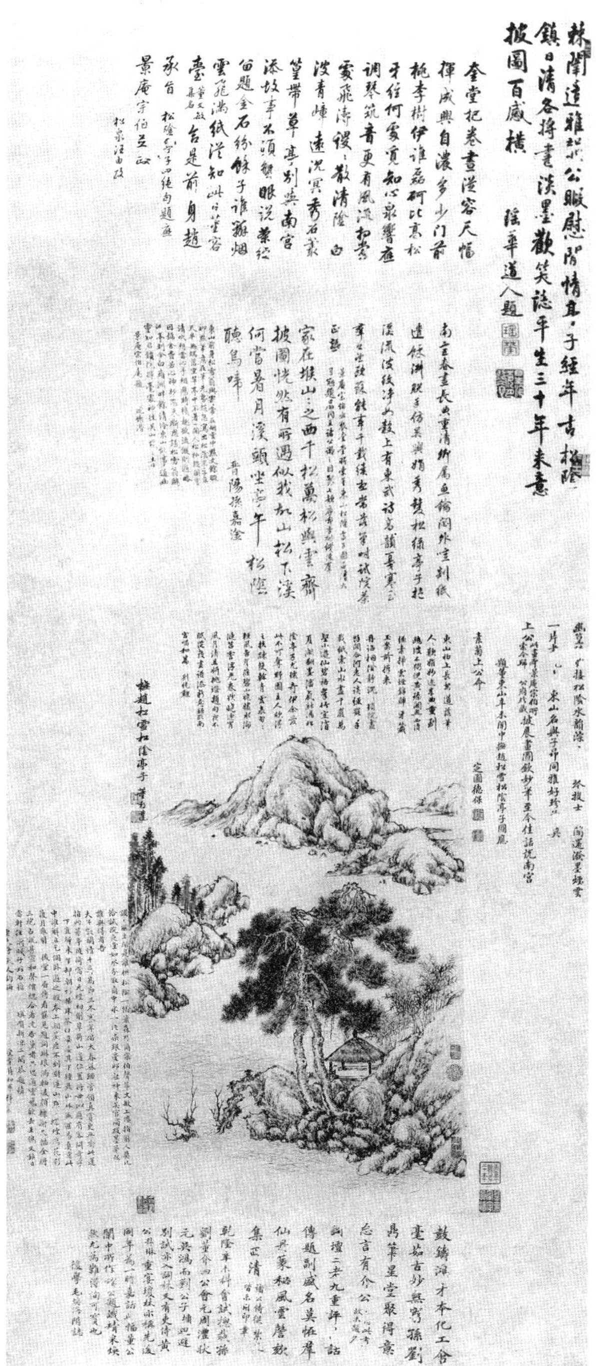

FIGURE 1
Dong Bangda (1699–1769), *A Pavilion under Pine Trees*, dated 1751. Hanging scroll, ink on paper, 21½ × 12 in. (54.6 × 30.5 cm). Roy and Marilyn Papp Collection. Photograph courtesy of the Phoenix Art Museum

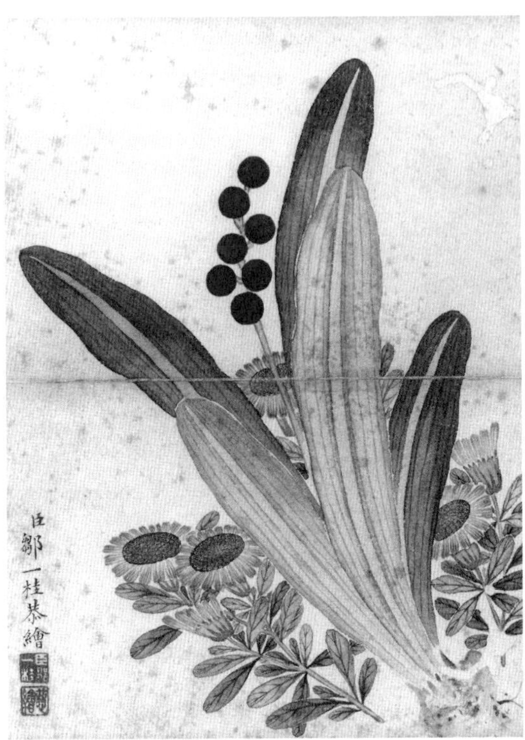

FIGURE 2
Zou Yigui (1686–1772), *Flower Studies*. One leaf from an album of 16 leaves, ink and color on paper, each leaf 7 × 5¼ in. (17.9 × 13.2 cm). Roy and Marilyn Papp Collection. Photograph courtesy of the Phoenix Art Museum

on that tour and personally viewed Lake Shi near Suzhou. In his album he responds to poems written by Qianlong on the tour. The album was prepared for but never received its inscriptions by the emperor and still has its temporary title slips.

Scholars have designated the decades of the 1760s and 1770s as a turning point that marked the beginning of reduced government sponsorship of the arts, establishing a trend that continued through the Jiaqing period (1796–1820). The imperial painting and craft workshops were reorganized,[19] with a resulting reduction in the size of the painting studio; many painters were reassigned to the enameling workshops, which produced a variety of palace decorations. The changes had notable effects in many of the decorative arts practiced at court as well. After this time, court painting, which had flourished during the early and middle years of Qianlong's reign, was now practiced more as decoration (on porcelain or in painted enamels on glass or metal).[20] Its use in monumental commemorative cycles such as the Southern Inspection Tour pictures became rare. However, painting related to the literati tradition continued to gain importance, encouraged by the arrival of more than one hundred sixty scholars at the court in the 1770s and 1780s to work on the *Siku quanshu* (Comprehensive Library of the Four Treasuries), a compendium of texts, reviews, and commentaries involving more than ten thousand titles.[21] One of the participants in the project was Weng Fanggang (1733–1818),[22] a brilliant scholar who had completed the *jinshi* degree while still a teenager. Weng's calligraphy was so highly admired that he was chosen to make one of the final manuscript copies of Qianlong's second compilation of poetry, as well as to take part in the production of a manuscript copy of the sixth-century model anthology of literature *Wenxuan*, compiled by Xiao Tong, Crown Prince Zhaoming of Liang (501–531), which was treasured by the emperor.

In the nineteenth century Beijing continued to attract scholars hopeful of success in government service, but a decentralizing trend was already under way. The reductions in palace staff and expenditures instituted by the Jiaqing emperor and his successor, Daoguang (r. 1821–50), made necessary by a serious depletion of the imperial treasury, sought to reduce court expenditures by enforcing frugality and discouraging ostentation. A resulting shift from public to private sponsorship and subsequent commercialization occurred in the decorative arts.[23]

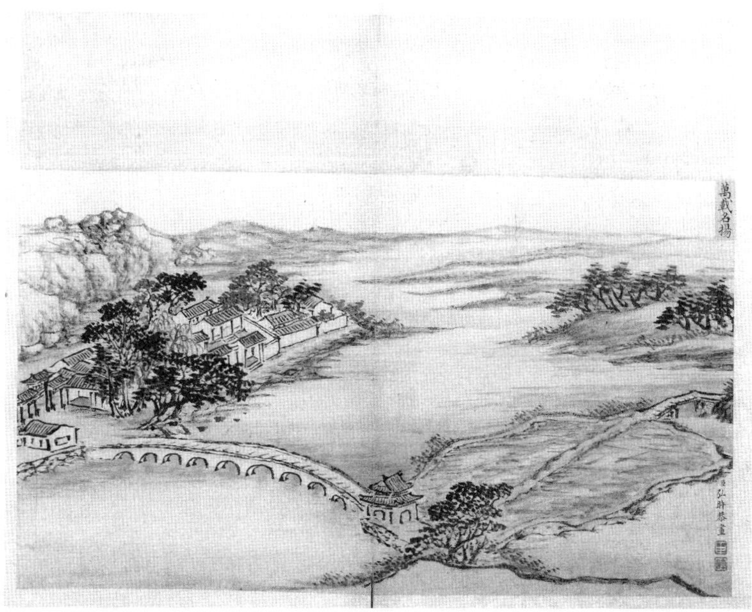

FIGURE 3
Hongwu (d. 1811), *The Myriad Delights of Lake Shi.* One leaf from an album of 10 leaves, ink and color on silk, each leaf 9 × 11½ in. (23 × 29.2 cm). Roy and Marilyn Papp Collection. Photograph courtesy of the Phoenix Art Museum

After Qianlong abdicated, in 1795, his son Jiaqing assumed only nominal rule, but following Qianlong's death, in 1799, he was at last able to formulate and carry out his own policies. Jiaqing's reforms, which began a few days after his father's death with a move against the corrupt clique of the Manchu official Heshen (1750–1799), included reductions in expenditures as well as the replacement of many administrators. Several important scholar-official artists, all of whom had stood fast against Heshen, continued as major advisors. Among them were Dong Gao (1740–1818), the son of Dong Bangda, whose version of the orthodox style had become a dominant trend at court, and the literary scholar and high official Liu Yong (1720–1805),[24] whose calligraphy was much admired by the Jiaqing emperor.

With few exceptions, Jiaqing continued to sponsor the arts, following the pattern maintained by his father for more than sixty years. (One of Jiaqing's most often used seals reads "rightful posterity.") Historians of Chinese ceramics and decorative arts have noted a continuation of court styles well into the Jiaqing reign, and the same appears to be true of painting. Although he did not paint, Jiaqing frequently composed poetry and inscribed many albums and scrolls, as recorded in the *Shiqu baoji sanbian* of 1816, the massive third and final sequel to the two painting catalogues commissioned by the Qianlong emperor. However, Hironobu Kohara has observed that the preparation of this final portion of the catalogue took less time than the previous editions because Jiaqing interfered less than had Qianlong.[25]

Jiaqing had relied on his brothers and half-brothers for a show of strength when he removed Heshen in 1799, and in the years thereafter these princes participated actively in the literary and artistic life of the court. The emperor had great respect for the calligraphic skills of his half-brother, the prince Yongxing (1752–1823);[26] in 1814 he ordered Yongxing to select examples of his calligraphy to be engraved on stone and reproduced as rubbings.[27] Prince Yongxuan (1746–1832), like Yongxing, was a frequent inscriber of court paintings and calligraphic works. In the 1780s, Yongxuan and Yongxing both served on the commission that compiled the *Siku quanshu*; Yongxuan later took charge of the imperial library and printing offices. The less-talented Prince Yonglin (1766–1820), younger brother of Jiaqing, also inscribed court works. A younger generation of princes also participated in artistic activities at the court. Miankai (1795–1839) and Minning (1782–1850), the future Daoguang emperor, added their

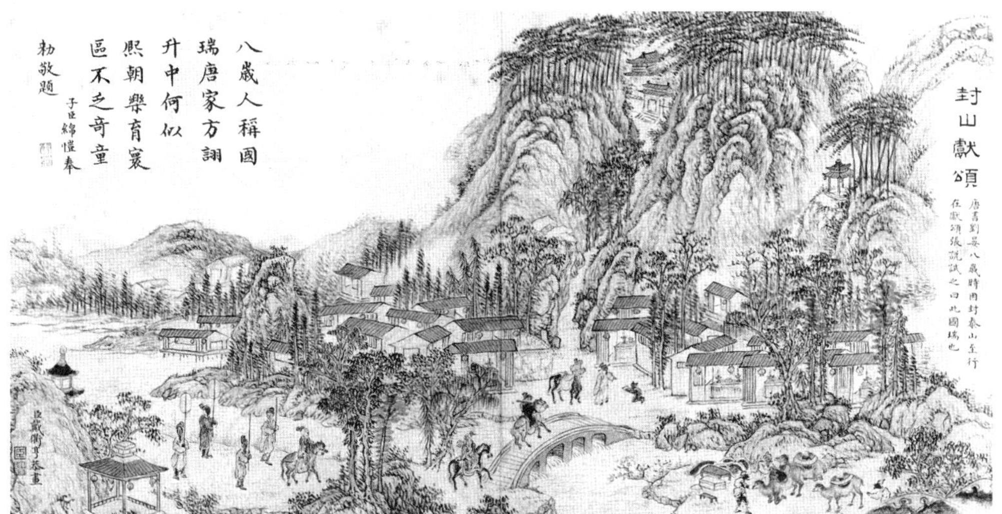

FIGURE 4
Dai Quheng (1755–1811), *In Celebration of Child Prodigies*. One leaf from an album of 8 leaves, ink and color on paper, each leaf 6¾ × 13 in. (17 × 33 cm). Roy and Marilyn Papp Collection. Photograph courtesy of the Phoenix Art Museum

inscriptions to works by Jiaqing as well as ones by Dong Gao and other scholar-official painters.[28] Mianyi (1764–1815) was a painter, and several of his works received the favor of Jiaqing's inscriptions. Aside from members of the imperial household, many high officials of the Jiaqing period participated in inscribing paintings and calligraphic works. Poetry, painting, and calligraphy played a central role in the education of princes in the palace school, as seen in a small album in the Papp Collection, *In Celebration of Child Prodigies* (fig. 4).[29] Each leaf of the album is painted by the high official Dai Quheng (1755–1811) and inscribed by Prince Miankai. A companion album is inscribed by Prince Minning.[30]

Although commissions for professional painters at court were seriously reduced as a result of the overall reductions in government expenditures, the artistic and literary conventions of inscribing poetic works by imperial family members and paintings by scholar-officials were maintained by the emperor Jiaqing. He also continued many of the scholarly projects begun under Qianlong's patronage, issuing, for example, in 1816 the third editions (*sanbian*) of the *Shiqu baoji* and *Bidian zhulin*. Dong Gao figured prominently in these pursuits of the Jiaqing court. He was one of the major compilers of the *Quan Tang wen* (Complete Prose of the Tang Dynasty), commissioned in 1808 and completed in 1814. His paintings, greatly favored by Qianlong,[31] enjoyed as well the favor of the Jiaqing emperor, who inscribed his albums of 1798 and 1803,[32] and Dong often participated directly with Jiaqing in calligraphic works.

As court sponsorship of such projects dwindled in the face of the economies of the Jiaqing and later periods, literary scholarship, now more likely to be based on the efforts of private individuals, assumed a more regional character. The epigrapher Ruan Yuan (1764–1849) was one of the compilers of the second catalogue of paintings and calligraphies in the imperial collection, the *Shiqu baoji xubian* and *Bidian zhulin xubian*, completed in 1793. Even though he served in a series of provincial posts, Ruan remained closely involved with painting and calligraphy at the court over the next two decades, participating with other high officials in inscribing works by the Qianlong and Jiaqing emperors. In 1801, as governor of Zhejiang Province, Ruan established in Hangzhou the Gujing Jingshe, an academy for the study of literature and the classics. In 1820, while serving as governor-general of Guangdong and Guangxi provinces, he founded in Canton Xuehai Tang (Sea of Learning Hall), which became a well-known center of scholarship. Among Ruan Yuan's circle in Beijing were the painters Zhu Henian (1760–1834)[33] and Yi Bingshou (1754–1815),[34] the latter best known for his distinctive style of calligraphy.

While imperial interest in painting declined after the Jiaqing period, it did not cease, despite political and military travails. The succeeding Daoguang period bore the first devastating blow of foreign incursion into China and witnessed growing domestic problems and new threats from corruption in the central government. The opium trade and the widespread addiction and corruption it fostered had by then reached a level of crisis. The Chinese government's attempt to halt the illicit trade at Canton was met by British resistance and ultimately led to the Opium War of 1839–42. The resulting Treaty of Nanjing (1842) had far-reaching effects: the forced opening of new ports, including Shanghai, and the surrender of the island of Hong Kong to British territory. The period ended with the outbreak of the Taiping Rebellion (1850–64).

The Daoguang emperor may be best known for having sent Commissioner Lin Zexu (1785–1850) to Canton to confront the British in the incident that sparked the Opium War. This profoundly important political event may be placed within a broader context of scholar-artists and their paintings. Lin Zexu, widely admired for his conduct as an official and his strong Confucian humanism, was associated with the New Statecraft School (*Xingjing shixue*), a precursor of the late Qing reform movement.[35] A handscroll in the Papp Collection by Wan Lan (active early 19th century; fig. 5) portrays Lin Zexu in a boat with other officials in the year 1837.[36]

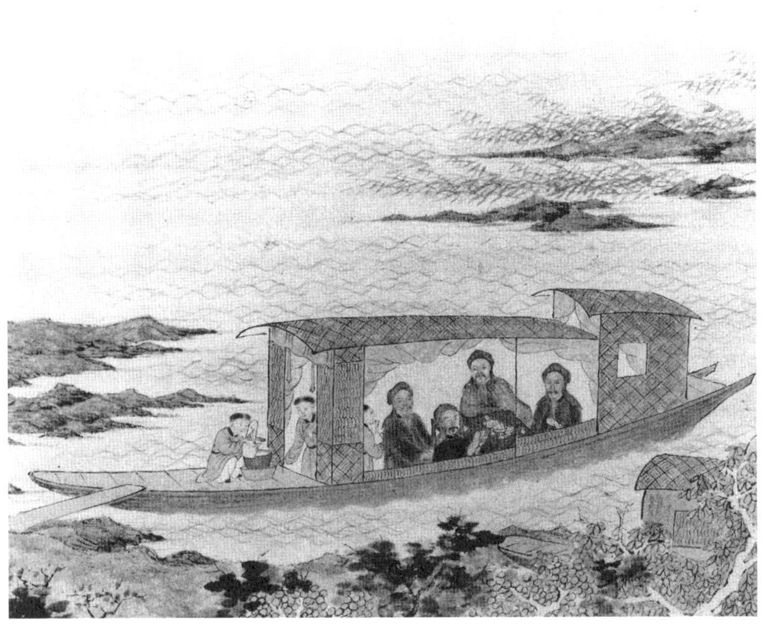

FIGURE 5
Wan Lan (active early 19th century), *Sharing a Cup of Wine in a Snowbound Boat*, dated 1837. Detail. Handscroll, ink and color on paper, 19½ × 72½ in. (49.5 × 184.1 cm). Roy and Marilyn Papp Collection. Photograph courtesy of the Phoenix Art Museum

Zhao Tingxi, head of Yangzhou Prefecture, had respectfully come out to meet Lin, then governor-general of Jiangsu, who was in transit on the Yangzi River.[37] Lin and his companions became stranded when a cold snap made the river impassable. Zhao later commissioned Wan Lan to commemorate their camaraderie with a group portrait, set in the snowbound boat with the scenery of the Jin and Jiao mountains in the distance.[38] The following year, in 1838, Lin Zexu arrived in Canton and made his stand against the British traffic in opium; and in 1839 he addressed his historic letter protesting the trade to Queen Victoria. Although the British surprised him by defending the opium trade and waging war to increase trade privileges, Lin eventually regained the emperor's favor and respect. He died on his way back to Guangdong and Guangxi, again on imperial assignment, to suppress the initial stages of the Taiping Rebellion. Attention to this new threat delayed the attempts begun by Lin and other Chinese intellectuals to study and disseminate Western texts on geography, history, law, and politics.

Although beset by domestic turmoil and foreign challenges, the Daoguang emperor nevertheless took an interest in painting. In 1838 the Hangzhou scholar-official and amateur painter Dai Xi (1801–1860) received an imperial appointment to serve as education commissioner of Guangdong.

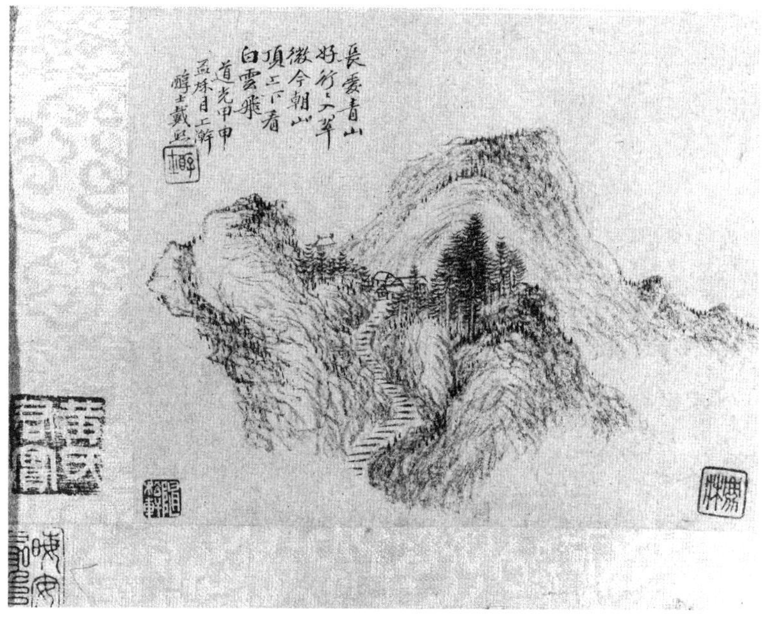

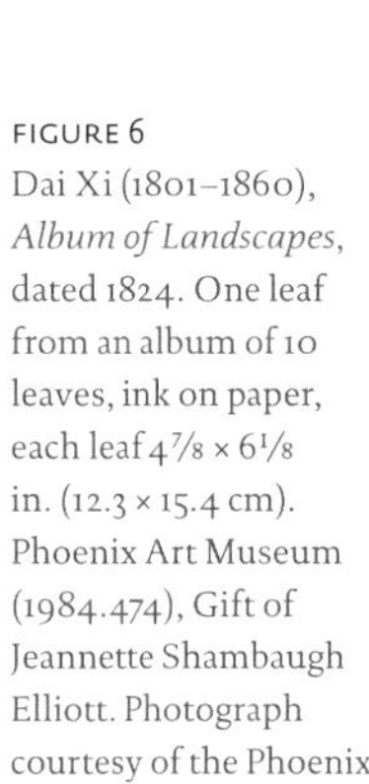

FIGURE 6
Dai Xi (1801–1860), *Album of Landscapes*, dated 1824. One leaf from an album of 10 leaves, ink on paper, each leaf 4⅞ × 6⅛ in. (12.3 × 15.4 cm). Phoenix Art Museum (1984.474), Gift of Jeannette Shambaugh Elliott. Photograph courtesy of the Phoenix Art Museum

Commending Dai Xi and commenting on his painting,[39] Daoguang suggested that the long trip to the south would allow Dai to see the famous scenery of Kuanglu (Mount Lu), Jiangxi Province, and Mount Luofu, Guangdong Province, and thus would broaden his view of landscape painting. Comparison of Dai Xi's early style of painting in a small-scale album, dated 1824, in the Jeannette Shambaugh Elliott Collection in the Phoenix Art Museum (fig. 6)[40] to his later large-scale works[41] may support Daoguang's prediction. Dai Xi outlived the Daoguang emperor by almost a decade; his life ended tragically in Hangzhou in 1860 when, upon the fall of the city to the Taiping rebels, he committed suicide.

The paintings discussed above reflect the varied ways in which the Qing court and its officials embraced the ideals of the Chinese scholar-artist. The emperor, the imperial princes, and their coterie of high officials, both Manchu and Chinese, took the role of scholar-artist seriously. The paintings and calligraphies produced at the court during this period went well beyond mere pretense, embodying intellectual and aesthetic as well as political content.

NOTES

1. This essay, which might well be subtitled "A View from Arizona Collections," is based in part on a paper presented at the annual meeting of the College Art Association held in Boston in February 1999.

2. See Kahn 1985, 291. Making a similar point about Qianlong's polylingualism, Pamela Kyle Crossley observes, "Whether on his monuments in Manchu, Mongolian, Tibetan, and Chinese (and, after the conquest of Turkestan, Uigur), or in the pages of the enormous multilingual dictionaries published repeatedly during his reign, the display of his cosmopolitanism was awesome in itself, but always pointed back to the emperor, as the center at which all cultures converged"; see Crossley 1997, 116.

3. Among these are Wu Hung 1995, 1996, and 1997.

4. Some of these studies, cited in the notes below, include works in Arizona collections. Pioneering work by Chu-tsing Li, particularly Li 1974 and 1979, paved the way in many respects for these collectors. Jeannette Shambaugh Elliott, whose collection is now preserved in The Art Museum, Princeton University, the Smart Museum of Art, University of Chicago, and the Phoenix Art Museum, received advice and support in collecting from Chu-tsing Li, his students, and many other art historians in Chinese painting. Another collection was formed recently by Roy and Marilyn Papp. The Papp collection has been shown in three exhibitions organized by the Phoenix Art Museum; see Chou and Brown 1989; Chou 1994b and 1998.

5. This and the following estimates are based on Rogers 1985, 303–304. Rogers took into account additional records of palace holdings; see ibid., 317, n. 1.

6. These paintings are a valuable source of historical information as well as a unique aspect of the history of art resulting from a vigorous mixing of, on the one hand, European artists with Chinese artists and, on the other, professional craftsmen with artists of literary background. Both aspects stem from the organization of palace workshops by the Kangxi emperor. His willingness to employ European craftsmen and foreign technology set the pace for later developments under the Yongzheng and Qianlong emperors. For example, the Kangxi emperor's new glasshouse was established in 1696 under the supervision of the German priest Kilian Stumpf; see Rabiner 1995, 17–18.

7. This body of material has been largely ignored by Qing historians in the West. For example, Rawski 1998, 51–55, discusses the Qing emperors' collecting of art, writing of colophons, and commissions to court academy painters, but makes no mention of the practice of painting and calligraphy by the emperors and their imperial relatives. If, as Howard Rogers has pointed out (see Rogers 1985, 305), the Qianlong emperor composed on average a poem a day, a calligraphy every two weeks, and a painting every month of his reign, then this should be taken as a serious element within the social history of the Qing court.

8. Often reproduced are a portrait of the young Kangxi at a desk with brush, paper, and ink, and another of him in his library; see, for example, *La Cité interdite* 1996, 100–101, figs. 86, 87. Later emperors, too, posed in the scholar's role; for example, the Daoguang emperor was

portrayed wearing a scholar's robe and holding a book (see ibid., 1996, 113, fig. 98).

9. For a full discussion of the series, see Hearn 1988. One scroll from the Kangxi series is now in the collection of Roy and Marilyn Papp; see Chou and Brown 1989, cat. no. 18. The Kangxi emperor made six tours, the first in 1684 and the last in 1707.

10. See Chou 1994b, 65–66. For a broader discussion of the importance of the orthodox movement, see Chou 1994a, 35–42.

11. See Chou 1988.

12. A fan with a landscape by Dong Bangda on one face and poetry inscribed by Wang Youdun (1692–1758) on the other, in the Roy and Marilyn Papp Collection, may be typical as a presentation work for the emperor. Wang Youdun was Grand Councilor from 1745 to 1758 and served as editor of Qianlong's collection of poetry. See Chou and Brown 1989, cat. no. 26.

13. The circumstances are fully described in Chou 1998, cat. no. 36.

14. These and other accomplishments are cited in Chou 1994b, p. 82.

15. Illustrated in Suzuki Kei 1982–83, E15–260, 261. See also Mason 2001, 33–34.

16. The album is fully illustrated in Chou 1994b, cat. no. 25, and in color in Chou 1999, cat. no. 27.

17. See Sirén 1956–58, vol. 5, p. 228.

18. The album is fully illustrated in Chou 1994b, cat. no. 36, and in color in Chou 1999, cat. no. 38. The Qianlong emperor made six tours, the first in 1751 and the last in 1784.

19. See Yang Boda 1991, 338–40.

20. Reassignment of artists from one studio to another may have occurred frequently. See, for example, Stuart 1995. Stuart points out that some artists were painters on porcelain under Yongzheng and painting academy members under Qianlong.

21. See Rawski 1998, 26, which suggests that the art and antiques district of Beijing, Liulichang, owed its rise at this time to this influx of scholars into the city.

22. A calligraphy couplet by Weng Fanggang, collected by Jeannette Shambaugh Elliott, is now in the Phoenix Art Museum (1984.588). For Weng's biography, see the entry by Fang Chao-ying in Hummel 1943, 856–58.

23. In glassmaking, for example, a significant decline in production occurred during the Jiaqing and Daoguang reigns. See Yang Boda 1987, 82.

24. An album by Liu Yong, *The Women's Classic of Filial Piety*, dated 1794, collected by Jeannette Shambaugh Elliott, is now in the Phoenix Art Museum (acc. no. 1986.25). Liu Yong and the scholar-official and painter Qian Feng (1740–1795) had been involved earlier in the courageous and successful prosecution of two of Heshen's henchmen. For Qian Feng, see Chou and Brown 1989, cat. no. 34.

25. According to Hironobu Kohara, the compilation of the *sanbian* took only sixteen months as opposed to the earlier two catalogues, each of which took more than two years. See Kohara 1988, 66–67.

26. A calligraphy fan by Yongxing collected by Jeannette Shambaugh Elliott is now in the Phoenix Art Museum (acc. no. 1996.93). In this work, dated 1821, Yongxing copied a poem written by the Qianlong emperor.

27. Lothar Ledderose has described a profound change in calligraphy beginning in this period. See Ledderose 1998, 189–207; 1970.

28. For a fuller discussion of painting at the Jiaqing court, see Brown and Chou 1992, 15–18.
29. The album is fully described and illustrated in Chou 1994b, cat. no. 35, and illustrated in color in Chou 1999, cat. no. 37.
30. See Chou 1994b, 114.
31. For a hanging scroll by Dong Gao in the Phoenix Art Museum, see Chou and Brown 1985, cat. no. 29.
32. These survive in the National Palace Museum, Taipei, and are recorded in Hu Jing 1816, 2964–66, 3610.
33. See Chou and Brown 1989, cat. no. 37.
34. Yi Bingshou's calligraphy *Fragrance of Antiquity*, dated 1811, was collected by Jeannette Shambaugh Elliott and is now in the collection of The Art Museum, Princeton University; see Ledderose 1998, fig. 2. For more on Yi Bingshou, see Brown and Chou 1992, 24–25.
35. On Lin and his role in this movement, see Fairbank and Liu 1980, 145–47.
36. See Chou 1998, cat. no. 48. Although he is not recorded, Wan Lan is assumed to be a professional artist, given the circumstances of the commission.
37. The identity of Zhao Tingxi and the details of the encounter have been clarified in Chou 1998, 155–57.
38. On related developments of the period and another painting of the same scenery, see Mei Yun-ch'iu 1999, 195–239, 244. Tao Shu (1779–1839), the patron of the scroll discussed in Mei's article, also inscribed the Wan Lan scroll described here.
39. Jane Wai-yee Leong has cited the emperor's comments and his bestowal of an imperial painting manual, an inkstone, and carved bamboo brushes on Dai Xi. See Brown and Chou 1992, 50. Dai Xi's long and successful career is the subject of a thesis by Leong; see Leong 1991.
40. The album (acc. no. 1984.474) is published in Siu 1985, 18–21.
41. Note, for instance, the masterful set of eight scrolls, dated 1849, in the Papp collection; see Chou 1994b, cat. no. 42.

REFERENCES

Brown, Claudia and Ju-hsi Chou. 1992. *Transcending Turmoil: Painting at the Close of China's Empire, 1796–1911*. Phoenix: Phoenix Art Museum.

Chou, Ju-hsi. 1988. Tangdai: A Biographical Sketch. *Phoebus* 6, no. 1, 132–40.

———. 1994a. In Defense of Qing Orthodoxy. In *The Jade Studio: Masterpieces of Ming and Qing Painting and Calligraphy from the Wong Nan-ping Collection*, by Richard M. Barnhart et al. New Haven: Yale University Press.

———. 1994b. *Scent of Ink: The Roy and Marilyn Papp Collection of Chinese Painting*. Phoenix: Phoenix Art Museum.

———. 1998. *Journeys on Paper and Silk: The Roy and Marilyn Papp Collection of Chinese Painting*. Phoenix: Phoenix Art Museum.

———. 1999. *Le Parfum de l'encre: Peintures chinoises de la collection Roy et Marilyn Papp*. Paris: Musée Cernuschi.

Chou, Ju-hsi and Claudia Brown. 1985. *The Elegant Brush: Chinese Painting Under the Qianlong Emperor, 1735–1795*. Phoenix: Phoenix Art Museum.

———. 1989. *Heritage of the Brush: The Roy and Marilyn Papp Collection of Chinese Paintings*. Phoenix: Phoenix Art Museum.

Crossley, Pamela Kyle. 1997. *The Manchus*. Oxford: Blackwell Publishers.

Fairbank, John K. and Kwang-ching Liu. 1980. *The Cambridge History of China, Volume 11: Late Ch'ing, 1800–1911*, part 2. Cambridge: Cambridge University Press.

Hearn, Maxwell K. 1988. Document and Portrait: The Southern Tour Paintings of Kangxi and Qianlong. *Phoebus* 6, no. 1, 91–131.

Hu Jing et al. 1816. *Shiqu baoji sanbian*. Reprint, Taipei: National Palace Museum, 1971.

Hummel, Arthur W., ed. 1943. *Eminent Chinese of the Ch'ing Period*. Washington D.C.

Kahn, Harold L. 1985. A Matter of Taste: The Monumental and Exotic in the Qianlong Reign. In *The Elegant Brush: Chinese Painting Under the Qianlong Emperor, 1735–1795*, by Ju-hsi Chou and Claudia Brown. Phoenix: Phoenix Art Museum.

Kohara, Hironobu. 1988. The Qianlong Emperor's Skill in the Connoisseurship of Painting. *Phoebus* 6, no. 1, 56–73.

La Cité interdite: Vie publique et privée des empereurs de Chine (1644–1911). 1996. Paris: Les Musées de la Ville de Paris.

Ledderose, Lothar. 1998. Calligraphy at the Close of the Chinese Empire. *Phoebus* 8, 189–207.

———. 1970. *Die Siegelschrift (Chuan-shu) in der Ch'ing-Zeit: Ein Beitrag zur Geschichte der chinesischen Schriftkunst*. Wiesbaden.

Leong, Jane Wai-yee. 1991. *The Art of Dai Xi (1801–1860)*. Master's thesis, Arizona State University.

Li, Chu-tsing. 1974. *A Thousand Peaks and Myriad Ravines: Chinese Paintings in the Charles A. Drenowatz Collection*. Ascona, Switzerland: Artibus Asiae.

———. 1979. *Trends in Modern Chinese Painting: The C. A. Drenowatz Collection*. Ascona, Switzerland: Artibus Asiae.

Mason, Charles. 2001. The British Museum *Admonitions* Scroll: A Cultural Biography. *Orientations* 32, no. 6 (June), 30–34.

Mei Yun-ch'iu. 1999. Chang Yin's Handscroll *Chin-k'ou san-shan t'u*: Landscape Imagery and the New Statecraft School of the Tao-kuang Period (1821–1850). *Meishu shi yanjiu jikan (Taida Journal of Art History)*, no. 6 (March), 195–239.

Rabiner, Donald. 1995. Chinese Glass and the West. In *A Chorus of Colors: Chinese Glass from Three American Collections*. San Francisco: Asian Art Museum of San Francisco.

Rawski, Evelyn. 1998. *The Last Emperors: A Social History of Qing Imperial Institutions*. Berkeley and Los Angeles: University of California Press.

Rogers, Howard. 1985. Court Painting Under the Qianlong Emperor. In *The Elegant Brush: Chinese Painting Under the Qianlong Emperor, 1735–1795*, by Ju-hsi Chou and Claudia Brown. Phoenix: Phoenix Art Museum.

Sirén, Osvald. 1956–58. *Chinese Painting: Leading Masters and Principles.* New York: Ronald Press.

Siu, Wai-fong. 1985. *The Modern Spirit in Chinese Painting: Selections from the Jeannette Shambaugh Elliott Collection.* Phoenix: Phoenix Art Museum.

Stuart, Jan. 1995. Unified Style in Chinese Painting and Porcelain in the 18th Century. *Oriental Art*, vol. 41, no. 2 (Summer), 32–46.

Suzuki Kei et al. 1982–83. *Comprehensive Illustrated Catalogue of Chinese Paintings.* Tokyo: University of Tokyo Press.

Wu Hung. 1995. Emperor's Masquerade: "Costume Portraits" of Yongzheng and Qianlong. *Orientations* 26, no. 7, 25–41.

———. 1996. *The Double Screen: Medium and Representation in Chinese Painting.* Chicago: University of Chicago Press.

———. 1997. Beyond Stereotypes: The Twelve Beauties in Qing Court Art and the "Dream of the Red Chamber." In *Writing Women in Late Imperial China*, ed. Ellen Widmer and Kang-i Sun Chang. Stanford: Stanford University Press.

Yang Boda. 1987. A Brief Account of Qing Dynasty Glass. In *Chinese Glass of the Qing Dynasty, 1644–1911: The Robert H. Clague Collection*, by Claudia Brown and Donald Rabiner. Phoenix: Phoenix Art Museum.

———. 1991. The Development of the Ch'ien-lung Painting Academy. In *Words and Images: Chinese Poetry, Calligraphy, and Painting*, ed. Alfreda Murck and Wen C. Fong, New York: The Metropolitan Museum of Art and Princeton University Press.

STUDIES IN HONOR OF CHU-TSING LI

Returning to the Subject of Poetry as the Expression of Heartfelt Sentiments

RAO ZONGYI

詩言志再辨——以郭店楚簡資料為中心

饒宗頤

"詩言志"語，初見于今文《尚書·堯典》，《詩大序》："詩者，志之所之也。在心為志，發言為詩"。作為中國學術史、文學史上一大課題，多年來已有學人仔細討論過。郭店楚簡裏面，提供一些"詩"和"志"有關嶄新的文學語言，使我們對這一問題可以重新考慮。

《語叢一》說：

> 《易》所以會天道、人道也。
>
> 《詩》所以會古含(今)之𢘑(志)也者。
>
> 《春秋》所以會古今之事也。

"𢘑"字從心從寺，此處"𢘑"應是"志"字的繁寫。從心從寺與從㞢相同，讀為"恃"或直釋為"詩"，都不甚妥當。[1]《詩》(經)是一部會集古今人之"志"的詩篇。《春秋》是一部會集古今之事的著作。"志"與"事"對言，這和所謂記事、記言同例，《詩》是另一類記"志"的書，以表示之：

> 書 ——記"言"
>
> 詩 ——記"志"
>
> 春秋 ——記"事"

言、事、志三者，古代似是分開的，他們對"志"非常重視。

《語叢一》又說：

> 𧫷(察)天道以𢡺(化)民𣲖(氣)。
>
> 凡又(有)血𣲖(氣)者，皆又喜，又有怒，……
>
> 其豊(體)又容、又頟、又聖(聲)、又臭(嗅)、又未(味)、又𣲖、又志。……
>
> 容𦀚(色)，目𤔲(司)也。聖，耳𤔲也。臭，鼻𤔲也。未(味)口𤔲也。𣲖(氣)，容𤔲也。志，心𤔲。

能觀察天道，便可變化民"氣"，有點像後來所謂變化氣質。楚人習慣"氣"字寫作𣲖，見於楚帛書皆相同。氣與志駢列，氣與志凡是血氣之倫之所同有，與五蘊眾覺的眼、耳、口、鼻並生。氣為容之所司，而志為心之所司。故凡民皆有氣有志。志與氣的相互關係於茲可見其重要性。孟子因之有“志，氣之帥也”的說法。古人極重視“志”。“志”為“心”所主宰，故云“志，心𢼄”。“志”可說是一種“中心思維”，思想上具有核心作用。《尚書．般庚》三篇有兩處言及“志”云：

若射之有志(上篇)

各設中於乃心(中篇)

“中”是旗幟，設旗旃於心，作行為之指導。旗幟淵源甚古，《世本》云：“黃帝作旃。”殷卜辭屢見“立中亡風”之占，“立中”可讀為“位中”。“設中於心”便是“志”。立志是儒家思想起點的要義，故曰“志於道”，語見《論語》，郭店簡亦見之(3:1)。簡又云：

㤀由敬作。(21:1)

敬生於㢿(儼)。

仁生於人，義生於道，或生於內，或生於外。(11:1)

孟子因之有集義養氣之論。“㤀”字可讀為“持”。故曰“持其志，無暴其氣”。持志必小心翼翼，故云“持由敬作”。持即持志之志。舉動詞作為名詞。於心中樹立旗幟以指揮行動。《春秋》有“象物而動”一語，為能用兵的象徵。(《左傳》記蔿敖為宰事)。物是雜色旗。劉熙《釋名》：“將帥之所建也。”志所以為氣之帥，正如“旗”、“物”之為兵之帥，軍隊之立旗，與心之設“中”，道理沒有二致的。

㮡 —— 容之所司

志 —— 心之所司

孟子(《公孫丑章》)所以“志至焉，氣次焉”，又曰“持其志，無暴其氣”。“配義與道，無是餒也”。楚簡云“其體有容有色有聲有嗅有味有氣有志”，證以孟子說“氣，體之充也”，可作這段話的注解。持志必主敬，“敬生於㢿”，㢿即嚴，讀為儼。《曲禮》云“儼若思”，是其義。

* * *

“志”在心理上地位的重要性有如上述。《詩》之為書，為篇章的總集，正薈萃著古今人的“志”之所托。“詩以道志”即所以見古今之志。通過這些詩，可以使民變化氣質。儒家對詩的功用，從斷章零簡的語言，略可捉摸到古人立言的大體。

楚簡中所見的“詩”字有許多不同寫法，郭店簡《緇衣》篇引“詩云”，均作“寺身”，或“大頣(雅)員”、“少(小)頣員”，直以“寺”字代“詩”。上海博物館的楚簡《緇衣》引詩則作“峕員”；其《孔子閒居》篇作“詣曰”。“寺”字改從口，不從ㄋ。

金文《熊章鐘》：“永時用亯”，曾侯乙樂器銘：“詐時用冬”，即“作持用終”。《詩緯 · 含神霧》：“詩者，持也。”[2] “詩”與“持”同訓，互相借用。楚簡《唐虞之道》末引《吳陟》曰：

> 大明不出，完(萬)勿(物)膚(皆)訠(揞)。聖者不在上，天下必壞。幻(治)之，至敚(養)不喿(肖)，亂之至滅臤(賢)。

大明指日月，讀為揞，《方言》：“揞，藏也。荊楚曰揞。不喿借為不肖，與賢人對文。此即“天地閉、賢人隱”之意。萬物與萬事遣詞略同。《書 · 益稷》有股肱之歌：“股肱惰哉，萬事墮哉”。此吳陟，裘錫圭謂即虞詩。陟讀為詩，按楚文字，從言亦可從陟。包山簡諓(誹)亦作[illegible]、[illegible]、[illegible](阩、陞、隥)，可証。

楚簡《性自命出》篇云：

> 凡人雖有性，心無定志，待物而後作，待悅而後行，待習而後定。喜、怒、哀、悲之奨，性也。及其見於外，則物取之也。……凡心有志也，無與不[可]……好、惡，性也。所好、所惡，物也。……

指出喜怒、好惡、哀悲之氣都是性。以証《左傳》昭二十五年傳，(鄭)吉對趙簡子的說話，引用他父親子產有名的議論云：

> 民有好惡喜怒哀樂，生於六氣，是故審則宜類，以制六志。哀有哭泣，樂有歌舞，喜有施捨，怒有戰鬥，喜生於好，怒生於惡。是故審行信令，禍福賞罰，以判死生。生，好物也，死，惡物也。好物，樂也，惡物，哀也。哀樂不失，乃能協於天地之性，是以長久。

喜怒、哀樂於好惡，是謂六志，出於心之情感。後代稱為六情(參朱自清書引孔穎達《毛詩正義》)。詩經裏面詩人對於生死慨歎的文句屢有所見，例如：

> 鮮瓦之聲，不如死之久矣(《穀風之什蓼莪》)

> 知我如此，不如無生(《小雅 · 苕之華》)

死傷無日，無幾相見(《小雅 · 頍弁》)

死傷之感，兄弟孔懷(《小雅 · 棠棣》)

生是人之所好，死是人之所惡。哀樂及喜怒隨之而生。六志因氣而來。六氣者，杜預注說指陰陽、風雨晦明，氣候的變化，是人的情緒亦跟著而變化。子產認為民人的行動，隨六志而變遷，必以禮約束其性，使不失於正。他說：

> 禮，天之經也，地之義也，民之行也。天地之經而民則之。則天之明，因地之性，生其六氣，則其五行。……淫則昏亂，民失其性。時故微禮以奉志。

他的意思是說凡滋味、聲色過則傷性，五色令人目迷，五音令人耳聾，一過其分則損害於性，故必以禮約束之，此之謂"禮以奉志。"以圖表示如下：

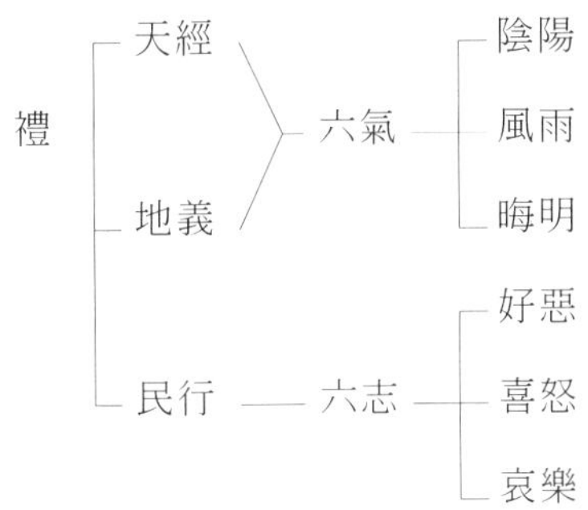

他以六氣配六志，使六志有節度，能夠曲折以赴禮，然後的稱為"成人"。他是孔孟以前一位通天地人三方來倡行以禮奉志的重要學術人物。郭店楚簡本章對於定志和六志都有精闢的見解。如說："道始於情，情生於性。"心無定志，則六情(六志)的哀樂喜怒好惡遂有不能節制，不能協於天地之性。故必心有定志，這個意見與子產之說有許多相關之處，值得再進一步的研究。

楚簡本章又說：

> 詩、書、禮、樂皆源於人。其始出皆生於人。是，又為為之也；書，有言為之也；禮樂有為舉之也。聖人比其類而會也；觀其先後而逆(迎)訓之；體其義而次第之；理其情而出入之。然後復以教，所以生德於中也。

這段話從人本主義的立場來說詩書禮樂的產生，始於人性，很可令人作深長思的。詩與志之不可分。必認識"定志"的重要。揚雄《法言．寡見》："說志者莫辨乎詩"。班固稱："省其詩而志正"(《禮樂志》)。"詩以正言，義之用也"。(《藝文志》)具見詩以道志已成為漢人司空見慣的恒言。

* * *

中心必須有定志，所以春秋以來，許多重要人物都有教詩明志之說，如申叔時之輩(《國語．楚語》)；孔子亦命諸弟子"各言爾志"(《論語．公冶長》)。關於獻詩陳志、賦詩言志的事，朱書已討論過，不用多贅。孔子稱"詩三百，一言以蔽之曰思無邪"(《論語．為政》)，這是隨便摘取《魯頌．駉之什》第四章中一句，其實尚有思無疆、思無期、思無斁三句。今見於郭店簡中有"思無疆，思無期，思无怠，思無不由義者"語，其章號作墨釘，似有意給以標誌。這些"思無疆"等語，顯然摘自《魯頌》，可以尋味。《論語》原本是否只單用"思無邪"一句，亦很難說。但可見斷章取義以說詩，從楚簡引詩句的情形看來，孔門和儒家無不如此!

"定志"要持敬。在較早的文獻像《尚書．皋陶謨》引禹曰：

> 安汝止，惟幾惟康。其弼直，惟動丕應。徯志以昭受上帝，天其申命用休。

徯訓待。這句《史記》譯作"清意以昭待上帝令"。他認為行動可以得到好的反應，要清明志意以等待上帝的耿命。古代人人心中有一個上帝，《詩經》裏面"上帝"共十九見，"上帝臨汝"二見，"上帝不臨"一見，可以為證。"惟幾惟康"是思危纔能致安，這是政治上"徯志"的教訓。"徯志"不能不先從"定志"做起。志與氣可以結成複合詞曰"志氣"。所謂"清明在躬，志氣如神"，史公言"清意"，便是這樣的境界。

詩以言志，賦亦同樣要顯志(馮衍有《顯志賦》)。《昭明文選》特立"志"一類。班固作《幽通賦》，亦"以致命遂志"。其言曰："蓋惴惴之臨深兮，乃二雅之所祗"。"神先心以定命兮，命隨行以消息。"曹大家注："祗，敬也。""言人之行各隨其命。命者，神先定之。"楚簡《性自命出》章："性自命出，命自天降"。"始者近情，終者近義"。臨深履薄的警惕，賦家對於心中定志，亦惓惓於懷呢!

* * *

根據《尚書》記載，"志"之觀念，由來已久。其實，占卜亦要言"志"。我在《貞的哲學》[3] 一文中，已作過具體的研究。占卜有"繇"詞，亦是"詩"的性質。殷代《歸藏》的繇辭，已在湖北王家台的秦簡發現。"繇"亦是"詩"的一種，是占卜的副產品。古代枚卜，要先"蔽志"，再"昆命於元龜"。其志先定，然後通過占卜的手續，詢謀僉同，天人共同認可(見《大禹謨》)。"蔽"訓決斷。事先作好決定，然後問卜，打定主意，亦是"定志"的事。

《左傳》有幾個故事，足以驗證"志"與卜筮的關係。左哀十八年傳：

> 子國之卜也，觀瞻曰：如"志"。故命之。及巴師至，收卜帥。王曰："寧如志，何卜焉？"使帥師而行。……君子曰：惠王知志。《夏書》曰："官占，唯能卜志"其是之。謂乎。志曰："聖人不煩卜筮。"惠王有焉。

此志稱讚惠王能夠"知志"。所引《夏書》，即上述《大禹謨》兩句，足見其語非出虛構。

又襄二十七年傳：

> 趙孟七子賦詩。伯有賦《鶉之賁賁》，卒享。文子告叔向曰：伯有將為戮矣!詩以言志，志誣其上而公怨之以為賓榮，其能久乎？

同傳：

> 子木論晉楚無信，事利而已。苟得志焉，焉用有信。

> 令尹將死矣，不及三年，求逞志而棄信，志將逞乎？志以發言，言以出信，信以立志，參以定之。何以及之？

暢論信以立志、志以發言、信——志——言三者的連環關係，志必以信為基，民無信不立，沒有信，則志將無所依存。志須依信以立言，信即貞(正)也。

又昭十二年傳：

> 南蒯筮，遇坤☷之比☵，為黃裳元吉，大吉之象。惠伯告以忠信則可，不然必敗。外強內溫，忠也。和以率貞，信也。故曰黃裳元吉。

必和順而行貞正之事，始能取信於人，而得到大吉。上述諸項，可為舊作《貞的哲學》補充說明，皆與志有關，故附帶及之，以見

《易》之有"繇"，與"詩"同一本源，都與"志"有一定的關係。

附表

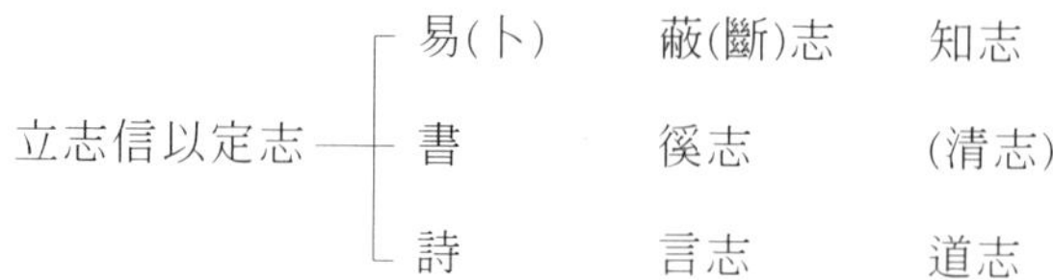

詩字異文表

寺	(省言)
峙	(志)在心為志，從之與從寺同(信陽楚簡亦有　字[4])
𡴭	從口之，口與言同意
詩	從言
哇	從口與從言同意，借為'持'
陭	改從阝
埒	從阝、從土同意，借作'持'

注

(本論文曾在武漢大學接受名譽教授時宣讀，略有增訂，作者附識)

1. 近見廖名春《郭店楚簡引〈書〉論〈書〉考》引此第38、39簡亦讀"㤅"字即"志"，引信陽楚簡"戔人剛㤅"亦應讀作志，甚說是。

2. 參拙著《固庵文錄》:《詩——言三訓辯》。

3. 文見《華學》第3期，北京清華大學出版。

4. 信陽楚簡"戔人剛㤅"(1–02簡)劉雨釋作恃。

Zhao Zhiqian and the Emergence of Self-Expression in Seal Carving

PHILIP C.J. WU

As in the West in the eighteenth century, in China the rise of archaeology not only energized the field of antiquarian study, but also generated new approaches in art. Trained in the methods of evidential scholarship (*kaozheng*),[1] including philology and etymology, artists inspired by the newly discovered ancient bronzes, stelae, coins, and engravings integrated them into their painting, calligraphy, and seal carving. Epigraphic artists, such as Huang Yi (1744–1802), Wu Xizai (1799–1870), and Zhao Zhiqian (1829–1884), represented a distinctive development in the revival of interest in *jinshixue*, or the study of ancient bronze and stone objects, in the Qing period (1644–1911).[2] Although Jin Nong (1687–1763), one of the so-called Eight Eccentrics of Yangzhou, is often credited as the pioneer of epigraphical calligraphy (which became known as the Stele school), the noted scholar and bibliophile Zhao Zhiqian was the first to truly master the Three Accomplishments: painting, calligraphy, and seal carving.[3] With the increasing circulation in the art market of archaeologically recovered materials, Zhao and those who followed him were able to use their evidential research skills to verify the ancient materials, thereby bridging gaps in the historical record. Zhao's approach to evidential research also inspired the painting as well as the seal carving and calligraphy of the later masters Wu Changshuo (1844–1927) and Qi Baishi (1864–1957). The *jinshi* flavor in painting and calligraphy became a criterion for judging modern Chinese painting, as can be seen in the assessment of works by Huang Binhong (1865–1955), Pan Tianshou (1897–1971), and Li Keran (1907–1989).[4]

THE SEARCH FOR SELF-EXPRESSION

Nearly without exception, the subject matter of the seals of late Ming (1368–1644) and early Qing artists can be grouped in three categories: personal names, studio names, and phrases from poetry. Beginning in the mid-eighteenth century, with the seal carvers known as the Eight Masters of Xiling, [5] a new trend can be found in seal carving. Alongside seals that bore only names and formal titles, some seal carvers began to add personal comments and other jottings. Ding Jing (1695–1765), Huang Yi, and Xi Gang (1746–1803), for example, recognized that it was no longer necessary simply to imitate ancient seals. Seals could function as a form of self-expression, which can be seen in the seals they carved for themselves. In his seal *Wo shi rulai zuixiao zhi di* of 1759, Ding Jing presents an interesting view of himself as the "youngest brother of the Buddha."[6] Huang Yi's *Maihua maishan* (Selling a painting [to] purchase a mountain [for retirement]), carved in 1763 for his friend Lu Fei, mocks his foolishness.[7] Xi Gang's seal *Jinshi pi*, dated 1788, humorously embodies his "Obsession with metal and stone."[8]

Zhao Zhiqian, with his rich epigraphic background, was alert to the self-expressive possibilities of seals. Besides the seals he made that bear names and poetic phrases, there are others that disclose his personal circumstances or that record a specific occasion. Zhao also often engraved his thoughts and comments on the sides of the seal, in the process creating an even richer form of expression. These types of seals, which are discussed below, constitute Zhao's distinctive contribution to the art of seal carving.

Zhao was born into a merchant family in Kuaiji, present-day Shaoxing, Zhejiang Province. Determined to pass the national *jinshi* (presented scholar) examinations and become a government official, he attained the degree of government student (*shengyuan*) in 1848 and passed the provincial examinations (*juren*) in 1859 in Hangzhou. In 1860, when the city was taken by Taiping rebels, Zhao was forced to flee Hangzhou and subsequently returned to his hometown.

In 1862 Zhao produced several seals that expressed his reaction to troubling events. Two of these concerned his profound sorrow at the deaths of his wife and daughter, who had died in Shaoxing while he was traveling in Fujian Province. The seal *Beian* (Cloister of Sorrow; fig. 1) bears an inscription reading: "My family is broken and members deceased, [I therefore] changed my *hao* to make [this seal]." The seal *Sanshisi sui jiapo renwang nai hao Beian* ([When] thirty-four years old, with my family broken and family members deceased, I therefore changed my *hao* to the Cloister of Sorrow) explains why he took the new style name Beian.

FIGURE 1
Zhao Zhiqian (1829–1884). *Beian*. Seal, dated 1862. Collection unknown

In the same year, he carved another seal, *Sheng feng Yao Shun jun buren bian yongjue* (Having been born in the time similar to [that of] the emperors Yao and Shun, I could not endure to depart [from them]), which compared the Qing emperor Tongzhi (r. 1862–74) to the legendary emperors Yao and Shun of the Xia dynasty (ca. 2100–ca. 1600 B.C.), who were considered the paradigm of Chinese emperors.[9] The side inscription of this seal reads: "The Beian jushi [secular devotee of Cloister of Sorrow] had become extremely depressed after *xinyou* [1861]. The reason why I did not commit suicide was because I still had the hope to go to the capital and rely on the beams of the sun and moon [of the emperors] to repay myself like a horse and a dog. Unfortunately, I am not only poor and old, but I also disgraced myself during the rebellion. This indeed brings shame on my parents and country. I engraved these words to demonstrate my moral fortitude." During the Taiping Rebellion (1850–64), many loyal Qing literati were killed or committed suicide.[10] Though Zhao's statement might be seen as self-justification, his words reveal not only his personal dilemma, but also the turmoil felt by many men of his class during this period.

Another seal from 1862, *Naner sheng bu chengming shen yilao* (Having not become accomplished, one feels aged already), expresses his regret at having failed the *jinshi* examination and his determination to succeed on the next try,[11] while the *Canjing yangnian* (Consuming [Buddhist] sutra to cultivate one's life; fig. 2), produced two years later, in 1864, concerns his conversion to Buddhism.[12] Such dated inscriptions provide us with concrete details of the different stages of Zhao's personal life. In this regard, Zhao added a documentary function to the art of seal carving.

In addition to seals that refer to personal circumstances, Zhao Zhiqian produced an unusually large number of seals that record or commemorate a specific occasion. The majority of the seals carved for special occasions were done for his friends.[13] Zhao's *Jixi Hu Shu Chuansha Shen Shuyong Renhe Wei Xizeng Jiasun Kuaiji Zhao Zhiqian tongshi shending yin* (fig. 3) of 1863 is unique because it contains the names of four epigraphic scholars on one seal.[14] In the side inscription, Zhao noted that "on the ninth day of the ninth month of the second year of Tongzhi, [this seal was made

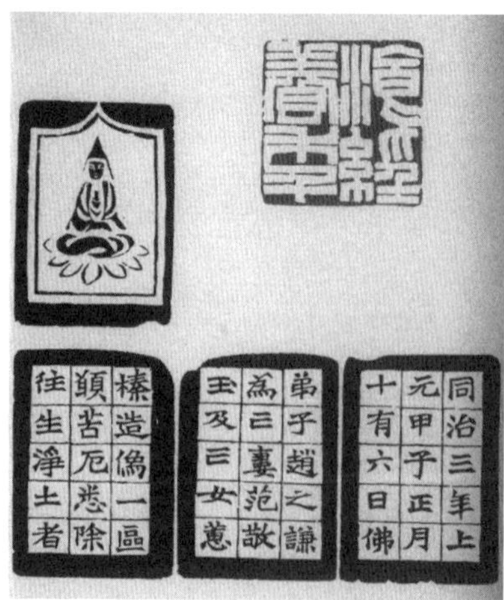

FIGURE 2
Zhao Zhiqian (1829–1884). *Canjing yangnian.* Seal, dated 1864. Juntao yishu yuan collection

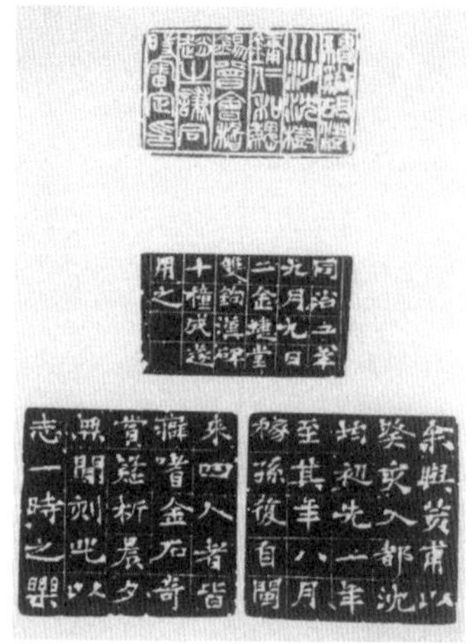

FIGURE 3
Zhao Zhiqian (1829–1884). *Jixi Hu Shu Chuansha Shen Shuyong Renhe Wei Xizeng Jiasun Kuaiji Zhao Zhiqian tongshi shending yin.* Seal, dated 1863. Juntao yishu yuan collection

for] the completion of the tracing copies of ten Han stelae by *Er jindie tang*."[15] The seal not only recorded a memorable event, but also expressed the friendship of the four men and their mutual interest in *jinshi* studies. Zhao wrote in the side inscription:

> Gaifu [Hu Shu] and I arrived in the capital [Beijing] in the year of *guihai* [1863]. Shen Yunchu [Shuyong] arrived one year earlier. On the eighth month of that year, [Wei] Jiasun also came from Min [to Beijing]. The four of us are all enthusiasts of metal-and-stone. [Together we] appreciate the wonder and analyze the problems, almost from morning until evening. [I] engraved this to jot down the joy. Ninth day of the ninth month of the second year of Tongzhi [1863].

Zhao also carved seals for close friends on certain other occasions. For Shen Shuyong (1832–1873), he carved over thirty seals, two of which are worth noting. The *Han shijing shi* was carved in 1863, during Zhao's sojourn in Beijing. In the side inscription, he states:

> I heard that a broken fragment of the Han Stone Classics of the Xiao Penglai ge [Huang Yi's studio name] is still available.[16] Yunchu planned to look for them. I carved the studio name [for him] in advance to wait [for the rubbings to enter his collection]. In the autumn of *guihai* [1863].

A second inscription follows:

> On the eve of the new year of this year, Yunchu came to tell me that he had obtained the Stone Classics. The next morning, I got up early and went to congratulate him. [He] displayed what he had collected, and [we] had a great time. [I] therefore carved these words on stone.

Besides explaining why the seal was carved, Zhao's inscriptions celebrate Shen Shuyong's success in locating the rubbings of the Stone Classics. The *Han shijing shi* thus combines artistic expression, epigraphic knowledge, and training in evidential research.

Another seal that Zhao carved for Shen Shuyong displays similar interests. *Zhengzhai jinshi* (Metal and stone [collected by] Zhengzhai) was done in 1863 when Zhao and his *jinshi* friends were in Beijing. Zhao inscribed on the side of the seal:

> Among the calligraphers of the Northern Wei dynasty [386–534], Zhengxibo of Yingyang surpassed others. Yunchu had acquired the complete ink rubbings of the *Yunfeng* and *Taiji* stelae.[17] He therefore requested me to inscribe [on the rubbings] and carve this seal. In the tenth month of the second year of Tongzhi [1863], noted by Beian.

The seal *Shenshi jinshi* (Metal and stone [collected by] Shen) was also carved in 1863, with the following long inscription:

> Yunchu obtained this stone, on which was an inscription by Xiaosong [Huang Yi]. Nevertheless, it was a shame that the characters had been ground away by others. I remember that Xiaosong engraved the *Zhaoshi jinshi yin* for my relative [Zhao] Zhuan. Therefore, I imitated [Xiaosong's] style to engrave this for Yunchu. [By doing this] I would somehow compensate for the loss [of the missing characters]. Eighty-seven years later [after Huang Yi's seal].[18] In the *guihai* year of Tongzhi [1863], Zhao Zhiqian of Guiji inscribed. Attended by Wei Xizeng [Jiasun] of Renhe.

This work is especially significant because the inscription was carved on an old seal that had once been owned by Zhao's deceased relative and originally bore an inscription by one of the Xiling Masters, Huang Yi. It represents not only a commemorative work, executed for Zhao's friend Shen Shuyong in the presence of another close friend, Wei Xizeng, but also a cumulative gesture, signaling the continuity of the great tradition initiated by the Xiling Masters.

ZHAO ZHIQIAN'S SIDE INSCRIPTIONS

Although seal carvers of the Ming occasionally added side inscriptions (*biankuan*) to their seals, these generally consisted of the carver's name, the date of the seal, and sometimes a brief dedication. Beginning in the mid-Qing, around the time of Ding Jing, who was known as the founder of the Zhe school of seal carving, seal carvers added more and more words to their side inscriptions. The new trend suggests that, in the nearly two hundred years since the development of the literati movement of seal carving, Chinese seal carvers had overcome technical barriers and were able to handle the medium in a more versatile way. Jiang Ren (1743–1795), one of the Eight Masters of Xiling, seems in particular to have favored inscribing on the sides of a seal. The four sides of his *Jiang Shantang yin*, dated 1780, are packed with hundreds of words from two of his poems. In another work, *Zhenshui wuxiang*, dated 1784 and dedicated to Hu Zuoqu (active mid- to late 18th century), Jiang inscribed the sides of the seal with a short essay, including details concerning the reason for the inscription.[19] Visually, Jiang's side inscriptions call to mind the energetic brushwork and dense composition of the paintings of the Yuan artist Wang Meng (ca. 1308–1385). Jiang's lengthy inscription signals that he was consciously exploring the sides of a seal as a way to add literary elements. Seal carving had by now matured as form of literati art.

It was Zhao Zhiqian who most fully explored the potential of side inscriptions, in the process inspiring many others to emulate his efforts. In comparison to other seal carvers of his time, Zhao was much more sensitive to and knowledgeable about epigraphic sources from the Warring States period (475–221 B.C.) to the Six Dynasties (220–589). He developed many intriguing innovations in his side inscriptions, borrowing, for instance, the epitaph format from the Six Dynasties and pictorial images from engravings of the Han period. Sometimes he would combine various formats to create a new one. For example, in the seal of 1863 mentioned above (see fig. 3), the side inscription imitates the chessboard-like epitaphs of the Six Dynasties. Although Zhao was not the first to apply the grid to a seal, his use of the single-knife method, in which the characters are carved directly on the stone, created a stronger epigraphic flavor than the work of Deng Shiru (1743–1805), whose seal carvings strongly influenced Zhao.[20]

The rich fund of epigraphic materials in Beijing must have inspired Zhao Zhiqian. His completion of the draft of *Liuchao biezi ji* (Varied Characters of the Six Dynasties; preface dated 1864), is evidence that Zhao took advantage of these resources. His *jinshi* friends, Wei Xizeng, Hu Shu, and Shen Shuyong, moreover, played an important role in Zhao's studies, both in helping him to sharpen his skills in textual analysis and in sharing collected materials. Judging from dated works by Zhao, the years from 1863 to 1865 were not only productive for the quantity of the seals he produced but also for the versatility of styles. For instance, the side inscription of *Canjing yangnian* (Consuming [Buddhist] sutra to cultivate one's life), a seal made in 1864 to commemorate the deaths of his wife and daughter two years earlier, consists, on one side, of the image of Guanyin (Avalo-

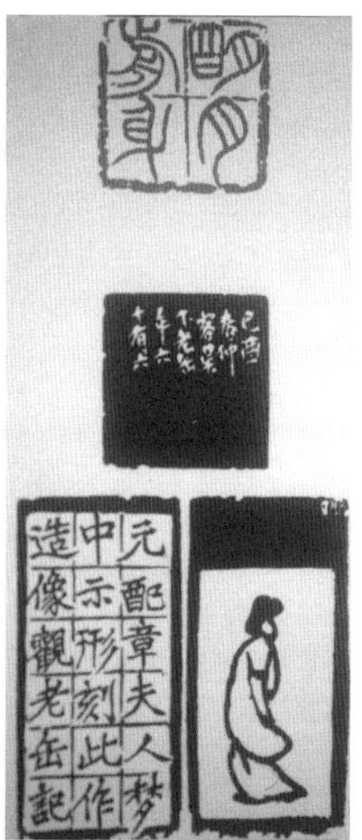

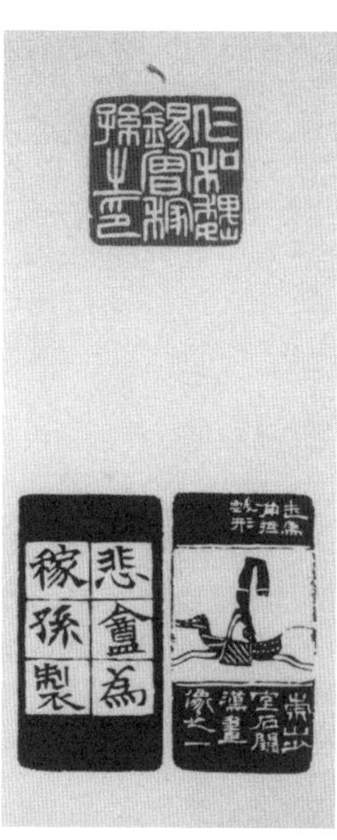

FIGURE 4
Wu Changshuo (1844–1927). Side inscription of *Mingyue qianshen*. Seal, dated 1906. Collection unknown

FIGURE 5
Zhao Zhiqian (1829–1884). *Renhe Wei Xizeng Jiasun zhi yin*. Seal, undated. Collection unknown

kiteshvara) and of engraved characters on the other three sides.[21] The characters are arranged within a grid, which resemble the *Shiping gong zaoxiang ji* (Title Inscription of Buddhist Image Constructed by Duke Shiping; dated 498). It is important to note that Zhao carved the characters in relief, which had never been attempted in side inscriptions by any other artist. Echoing the commemorative nature of the seal is the skillful combination of Northern Wei-style block script and the Guanyin image. In this regard, the style, content, and use of the epitaphic form of the seal are coherently unified. It is not surprising to see that one of Zhao's admirers, Wu Changshuo, made a similar seal, with a side inscription in the same block script of the *Shiping gong zaoxiang ji*, to commemorate his deceased wife (fig. 4).

Something more daring can be found on the sides of two large seals made by Zhao Zhiqian in 1862.[22] The grid patterns on the side inscriptions are similar to those of *Canjing yangnian*, but here Zhao adopted the epitaph format from the Six Dynasties. Judging from the smooth silhouettes of the carved characters, these inscriptions were executed in the double-knife method, in which the characters are first written on the stone and then engraved. The overall effect is that the side inscriptions look as if they are miniature epitaphs from the Six Dynasties.[23]

Besides the ancient epitaph format, Zhao also pioneered in applying pictorial figures from the Han dynasty. On the sides of the undated seal *Renhe Wei Xizeng Jiasun zhi yin* (fig. 5), Zhao carved a circus figure astride a horse and six characters, which read *Beian wei Jiasun zhi* (Beian made this for [Wei] Jiasun). Zhao's pictorial model is from the Han dynasty *Songshan Shaoshi shique* (Stone pillar of Shaoshi), dated 123 (fig.6), while the block script is identical to that of the *Shiping gong zaoxiang ji* of the Northern Wei dynasty.

For his friend Hu Shu, Zhao carved a double (top and bottom) seal with two side inscriptions and a dragon (fig. 7). The dragon was obviously modeled after the *Songshan Shaoshi shique* (see fig. 6). Using the single-knife method, Zhao carved the words *Songshan Shaoshi shique Han huaxiang long* (Pictorial figure of a dragon from the *Songshan Shaoshi shique* of the Han dynasty). The fluency of the writing demonstrates Zhao's knowledge of seal script as well as his confidence in handling the carving knife.

On the sides of another double-sided seal, dated 1867, Zhao carved the image of a house in a landscape. The seal was made for Cao Gemin (1800–ca. 1875), a book dealer from Renhe, Zhejiang, and an important patron of

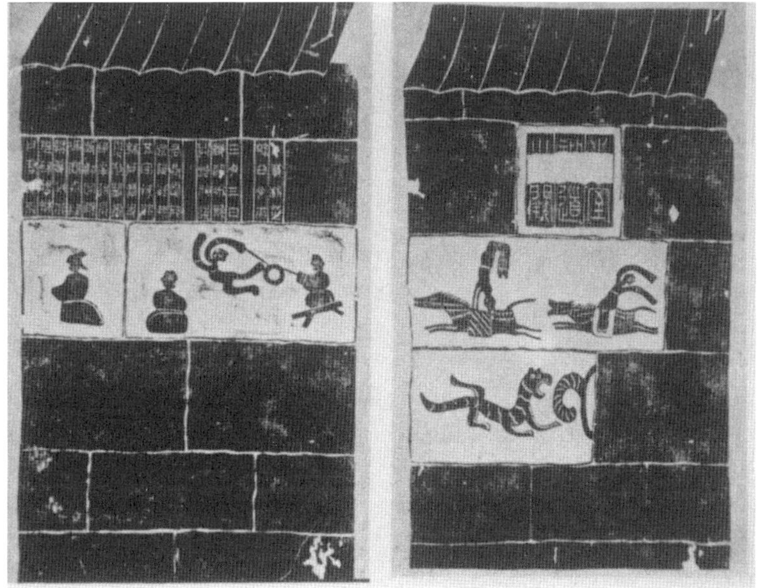

FIGURE 6
Songshan Shaoshi shique. Han dynasty, dated 123

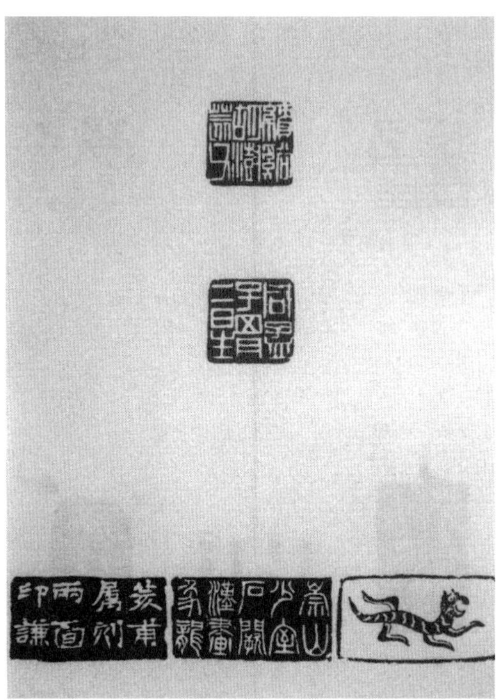

FIGURE 7
Zhao Zhiqian(1829–1884). Side inscription from a double-sided seal for Hu Shu, undated

Zhao Zhiqian.[24] In the side inscription, Zhao wrote, "Gemin requested [me to] carve. There are some broken scraps on the seal. [I] therefore altered [the scrapped patterns] to the *Writing a Book in Stone House*. This is only for expressing a general idea instead of demanding accuracy. In the seventh month of the *dingmao* year [1867] of Tongzhi." On the other side of the stone, Zhao engraved the two characters *shiwu* (stone house) in clerical script, similar to the style of Deng Shiru.[25]

Zhao Zhiqian was not the first to carve pictorial images on seals. There is an abundance of pictorial seals from the Warring States, Qin, and Han periods. Zhao had a few precursors in the Qing era: Zhou Hao (1685–1773) carved a floral subject on the side of one of his seals, and Zhang Yanchang (1738–1814) carved the image of a gentleman on the side of a seal, accompanied by the text of Tao Qian's (Tao Yuanming; 365–427) essay "Biography of Master Five Willows" (Wuliu xiansheng zhuan). Zhao Zhiqian, however, was the first Qing seal carver who explored the potential of pictorial elements on his seals. The strong correlation of his pictorial images with the contents of the seal legend and the side inscriptions inspired many of the seal carvers who followed him.

NOTES

1. For the emergence and development of *kaozheng* scholarship in the late Ming and Qing periods, see Elman 1990.

2. Huang Yi, one of the Eight Masters of Xiling and an amateur archaeologist, located the Wu Family shrines in Shandong Province in 1786. He meticulously documented his travels to seek out ancient stelae in his *Xiao penglai ge jinshi wenzi* (Epigraphical studies of the Xiao penglai ge; preface dated 1800) and *Songluo fangbei riji* (Diary of seeking stelae in the Mount Song and Luo area; 1853). For a biographical account of Wu Xizai and his contribution to epigraphical studies, see *Guang yinren zhuan* 1997, 369.

3. In Chinese art history, the term "Three Accomplishments" traditionally refers to poetry, calligraphy, and painting. Along with the rise of the Epigraphic school in the eighteenth century, seal carving became a new category for the evaluation of the works of artists. Yang Yi noted that Zhao Zhiqian "excelled in painting, calligraphy, and seal carving." See Yang Yi 1988, *juan* 3, p. 10.

4. For the signifigance of the *jinshi* school, see Wan Qingli 2005, 16.

5. The Eight Masters of Xiling refers to a group of seal carvers who worked in Hangzhou, Zhejiang Province, from the early eighteenth to the mid-nineteenth century.

6. This seal was requested by Ding's friend Liang Tongshu (1723–1815). The side inscription reads: "Shanzhou [Liang Tongshu] requested me to carve this seal. However, he was afraid of offending [the Buddha]. I told him that if one could understand the Buddha through one's heart, the Buddha would treat one like a friend or even like his younger brother."

7. The phrase "selling a painting to purchase a mountain" is taken from a poem by the Ming painter Tang Yin (1470–1524): "People dislike the rice field on the lake [because of flooding problems]; [Likewise,] who will purchase the mountains in my painting?" In the side inscription to his seal, Huang Yi wrote: "Xiaoyin [Lu Fei] planned to purchase a place for hermitage. He began to paint ink plum blossom for sale. How silly he was!"

8. Huang Yi engraved a seal with the same words. Wang Qishu (1728–1800), a noted epigraphic scholar from Shexian, Anhui Province, called himself *Yinpi xiansheng* (a gentleman obsessed with seals), and Wei Xizeng (Jiasun), a close friend of Zhao Zhiqian and fellow *jinshi* scholar, referred to himself as *yinnu* (seal slave).

9. Zhao's statement seems, on the one hand, to flatter Emperor Tongzhi, and, on the other, to excuse him from being absent from the battle against the Taiping rebels in Hangzhou.

10. Among the Qing literati artists who either committed suicide or died during the Taiping Rebellion were Dai Xi (1801–1860), Qian Song (d. 1860), Mao Geng (d. 1861), Tang Yifen (1778–1853), and Zhao Zhichen (1780–1860).

11. Zhao tried three times without success to pass the national *jinshi* examination in Beijing.

12. Although Chinese Confucian scholars had a long history of engaging with Buddhism, Zhao Zhiqian's conversion to Buddhism exemplifies the intellectual crisis of Confucian scholars of his time. For a discussion of late Qing intellectuals, such as Kang Youwei (1858–1927), Zhang Taiyan (1868–1936), Tan

Sitong (1865–1898), and Liu Shipei (1884–1919), see Chang Hao 1987.

13. Qian Juntao has noted that fewer than sixty people were recipients of Zhao's seals, the majority of which were dedicated to or requested by Wei Xizeng (Jiasun), Hu Shu, and Shen Shuyong. See Qian Juntao 1960, no. 9., pp. 366–68.

14. In the inscription to a seal dated 1919, Wu Changshuo, following Zhao Zhiqian's lead, mentioned himself and two others, Chu Teyi and Zhang Zengxi.

15. *Erjindie tang* is a studio name of Zhao Zhiqian.

16. In 175 A.D., the Eastern Han emperor Lingdi (r. 168–89), in response to a proposal by Cai Yong (ca. 133–92), initiated a project of standardizing the Six Confucian Classics. In 183, forty-six stone tablets were erected in front of the Imperial Academy in Luoyang, the capital of the Eastern Han. Because they represented the official version of the Confucian texts and the highest standard of calligraphy in that period, the Stone Classics were considered important by later scholars and calligraphers. See Chang and Miller 1990, 360–61.

17. The title of the *Yunfeng* stele, also called *Zheng Wengong bei* or *Zheng Xi xiabei*, dated 511, was written by Zheng Daozhao, Regional Inspector of Guangzhou, in present-day Shandong Province, in the Northern Wei dynasty. Zheng had the text carved on Mount Yunfeng to memorize his father, Zheng Xi. The *Taiji* stele (not dated) is located in Laicheng, Shandong. For a discussion of these two stelae, see Yu Huansu et al. 1989, vol.6., pp. 166–68.

18. Huang Yi's original inscription was dated 1777.

19. For the complete text of Jiang's inscription, see Yu Huansu et al. 1989, vol. 16, p. 168. For a discussion of Jiang's inscription, see Huang Dun 1994, 232–33.

20. There are two methods for carving inscriptions on the side of seals. In the first method, called *shuangdao fa* (double-knife method), the characters are written on the stone and then carved. In the second method, *dandao fa* (single-knife method), the characters are carved directly in the stone without a preliminary draft. Though it requires more skill, this method conveys more closely the appearance of characters on ancient stelae.

21. Zhao's inscription reads: "On the sixteenth day of the first month of the third year of Tongzhi [1864], the Buddhist disciple Zhao Zhiqian made an image for my deceased wife Fang Jingyu and daughter Huizhen. [I] wish all the suffering can be discharged from them and [that they can] be reborn in the Pure Land."

22. According to Elizabeth Bennett, these two seals are in a private collection in Tokyo. For the English translation of the inscriptions, see Bennett 1983, vol. 1, p. 4.

23. Qian Juntao stated that these two seals were either carved by Zhao Zhiqian's disciple Qian Shi or completed by Qian Shi because Zhao had not finished the carving. See Qian Juntao 1987, under the year 1861. Nevertheless, the original idea and design of the seals and inscriptions would have been Zhao's.

24. Zhao also painted the *Shiwu wenzi wujin deng tu* for Cao Gemin in 1869. The painting is illustrated in *Beian shengmo* 1992, vol. 2, p. 2. It is very likely that Zhao had access to Cao's book collection and repaid Cao for this favor with seals and paintings.

25. For Deng's influence on Zhao's calligraphy, see Wu 2002, chap. 3.

REFERENCES

Beian shengmo. 1992. Taipei: Zhonghua shuhua chubanshe.

Bennett, Elizabeth. 1983. *Chao Chi-ch'ien (1829–1884), A Late Nineteenth-Century Artist: His Life, Calligraphy, and Painting*. PhD diss., Yale University.

Chang Hao. 1987. *Chinese Intellectuals in Crisis: Search for Order and Meaning (1890–1911)*. Berkeley: University of California Press.

Chang, Léon Long-yien and Peter Miller. 1990. *Four Thousand Years of Chinese Calligraphy*. Chicago and London: The University of Chicago Press.

Elman, Benjamin A. 1990. *From Philosophy to Philology: Intellectual and Social Aspects of Change in Late Imperial China*. Council on East Asian Studies, Harvard University. 2nd ed. Cambridge, MA and London: Harvard University Press.

Guang yinren zhuan (Expanded biography of seal carvers; preface dated 1916). 1997. In *Ming-Qing yinren zhuan jicheng*, ed. Zhou Lianggong. Taipei: Wenshizhe chubanshe.

Huang Dun. 1994. *Zhongguo gudai yinlun shi* (History of ancient Chinese seal carving). Shanghai: Shanghai shuhua chubanshe.

Qian Juntao. 1960. Zhao Zhiqian keyin ersan shi (Remarks on Zhao Zhiqian's seal carving). In *Yilin conglu*, ed. Da Tang. Hong Kong: Shangwu.

———. 1987. Zhao Zhiqian dashi ji (Chronological account of Zhao Zhiqian). In *Zhao Zhiqian*, ed. Qian Juntao. Hangzhou: Zhejiang renmin meishu chubanshe.

Wan Qingli. 2005. *Bingfei shuai luo de bainian*. Taipei: Xiongshi tushu.

Wu, Philip. 2002. Between Tradition and Modernity: Strange Fish of Different Species, Products of Wenzhou by Zhao Zhiqian (1829–1884) and their Relationship to the Epigraphic Studies of Late Qing. PhD diss., University of Kansas.

Yang Yi. 1988. *Haishang Molin* (The Ink Forest of Shanghai). Repr. Taipei: Wenshizhe.

Yu Huansu et al. 1989. *Shudao quanji* (Compendium of Chinese calligraphy). Taipei: Dalu chubanshe.

STUDIES IN HONOR OF CHU-TSING LI

The Transformation in Jiangnan: A Glimpse of Chinese Art History in the Nineteenth and Early Twentieth Century

WAN QINGLI

> Paintings in recent times have indeed declined.[1]
> There is no painting in the Qing dynasty.[2]
> From about the year 1800 on, painting in China
> became rather repetitive; the creative force was spent.[3]

In the past, presumptuous statements such as those quoted above greatly hindered the study of Chinese painting of the modern era. Consequently, the history of this period has become as difficult to discern as distant mountains shrouded in mist. Although the study of twentieth-century Chinese painting during the last thirty years has aroused some interest in the development of painting in the nineteenth century, the period studied has been mostly limited to that after 1840,[4] and the area confined to that of Shanghai.

It is my belief that the study of twentieth-century Chinese painting is very much limited by what we do not know, or fail to understand, about painting history in the nineteenth and even the eighteenth century. The changes and reforms that took place in painting in the twentieth century did not happen suddenly; their causes were rooted in the previous two centuries and were part of a continuous process of change in the social, economic, ideological, and cultural history of China. I will focus here on the Jiangnan region of southern China as an example and point out the different aspects of this process of change that should be investigated.

Confucianism, the main ideological entity of the eighteenth and nineteenth centuries, had been subjected to profound changes. During the early Qing dynasty (1644–1911), Confucian scholars, who disapproved of the esoteric discourse that was prevalent in the Ming dynasty (1368–1644), devoted themselves to the study of the classics. They were strict in upholding the practice of moral principles and advocated the application of the classics to the conduct of current affairs. During the reigns of Yongzheng (r. 1723–35) and Qianlong (r. 1736–95), many scholars, fearing persecution, turned to the study of philology. In the Qianlong and Jiaqing (1796–1820) eras, Han Learning (*kaojuxue*, or the School of Evidential Research) became popular.[5] Toward the end of the Qing period, the Gongyang School of Confucianism (*Chunqiu gongyang xue*) was revived and provided the intellectual base for the Reform Movement.[6] It would seem that in the development of Confucianism in the Qing period, the efforts of Confucian scholars to understand the principles of the classics and to utilize them to save the country were in contradiction to the trend toward textual research in the Qianlong and Jiaqing eras. Actually, the two complemented each other, combining the desire for change and the readiness to accept Western learning that was widespread at the end of the Qing dynasty.

Against such an intellectual background, certain aspects related to the development of the arts and culture should be examined. Here, I shall point out only two. First was the change in the Confucian concept of "agriculture as the basic occupation, commerce as the last" to that of "emphasizing commercialism."[7] Second, *kaojuxue* caused the growth of *beixue* (stele school) principles and the popularity of *jinshixue* (the study of ancient metal and stone artifacts). The first aspect represented the rise of the urban economy and the corresponding merchant class; the second reflected the change in the aesthetic standards of the time.

Although China was known as an agricultural country, less than one-tenth of the country's total territory was arable.[8] By the Jiaqing and Daoguang (r. 1821–50) eras, the population exceeded 400 million, three-quarters of which was concentrated in the fertile southeastern region, particularly in the Jiangnan area. As a result of war and famine, many people moved from the countryside to the cities, where some joined the industrial workforce and others became merchants. The economy in the cities was often dictated by groups of rich businessmen, such as the salt merchants, who held the monopolies, the securities merchants, who controlled the movement of capital, and the trade merchants, who were in charge of specific trades. Among the different strata of society, these wealthy merchants wielded the most power. Their participation in cultural affairs directed, to a certain extent, the social and cultural transformation of China. I believe that the role of these rich merchants was not confined to patronage (such as that of the Yangzhou painters by the salt merchants or the Xin'an painters by the Anhui merchants), but extended to direct participation in artistic creation. Some even became the founders of new art schools and leading figures in art circles. Ding Jing (1695–1765), a wine merchant, was a *jinshi* scholar and the leader of the Eight Masters of Xiling.[9] As the founder of the Zhe school of seal carving, which influenced the development of the art of seal carving for the next two centuries, Ding is said to have rectified the impure qualities of being "refined and charming," which were associated with some Ming artists. He started the new trend of carving "integrated, thick, pure, and archaic" seals. Ding and his close friend and neighbor Jin Nong (1687–1763) were both engaged in the antiques trade.[10] Zhang Zikun (1734–1791), a wealthy cloth merchant of Zhenjiang, was proficient in painting and encouraged his son, Zhang Yin (1761–1829), to develop a new painting style. Subsequently, Zhang Yin became the leader of the Jingjiang school of painting.[11] Zhao Zhiqian (1829–1884), who came from a bankrupt merchant family in Shaoxing, was esteemed as the foremost master of the *jinshi* school of painting. He applied the principles of the northern stele (*beibei*) calligraphy to painting and blended them with poetry, painting, and seal carving. If the example of the literati painter Qian Dong (1752–1817), who "gave up the life of a literatus to become a merchant," was considered an exception in late-eighteenth-century Yangzhou, by the early twentieth century the phenomenon had become commonplace. Even Cai Yuanpei (1868–1940), the father of modern education in China, once operated a *doufu* shop in Paris.[12] Wang Zhen (1867–1938), the leading painter in Shanghai after Wu Changshuo (1844–1927), was a well-known comprador in a trading house.[13] Another significant figure in Shanghai was Zheng Chang (1894–1952), a painter, art historian, and publisher.[14] Jin Cheng (1877–1926), the so-called godfather of Beijing painting circles in the early years of the Republic (1912–1949), was a government official and a comprador of a British bank, and owned an antiquity shop. All of the above cannot be aptly described as "literati painters or artists." Their work shared the common characteristics of being "archaic and clumsy," "embedded and thick," "robust and strong." Their intention was to depart from the orthodox literati tradition of Loudong and Yushan and to establish a new and different style. These artists represented the aesthetic pursuit of part of the intelligentsia. [15] It is important to realize that the "taste of the common people" is rich in content and does not always mean "vulgar" or "wild." To make such a generalized allegation would be unfair.[16]

During the Qing dynasty, Chinese calligraphy underwent a major transformation. This revolution in calligraphy not only set a new style for the period, but altered the basic aesthetic standards by which calligraphy was to be judged. This in turn affected, directly and indirectly, painting and other visual arts. The theories concerning the study of ancient monuments associated with calligraphy, the *jinshi* flavor found in painting, and the various schools of seal carving that emerged during the period were the products of *kaojuxue*, or the School of Evidential Research. These were important accomplishments of Chinese modern art. They were not caused by the impact of Western culture, a common misconception that continues to hinder a better understanding of these accomplishments. A fair evaluation of them is still wanting.

Although calligraphy had attained substantial heights in the Ming dynasty, it was nevertheless a continuation of the Jin and Tang traditions.[17] In the early Qing period, with the growing popularity of the School of Evidential Research and the trend toward works modeled after the calligraphy of ancient monuments, many calligraphers turned to the study of bronze (*jin*) and stone (*shi*) inscriptions and began to practice the ancient forms of characters, such as the old seal script and the Qin new seal script, the Han clerical script, and the Wei regular script. With the growing interest in these ancient styles came a change in aesthetic values. The scholar-artist Fu Shan (1607–1684/85) was one of the forerunners who led the change in aesthetic standards in the late Ming and early Qing periods. Possessing a wide knowledge of early script forms, Fu was able to extract feelings of antiquity from the seal and clerical scripts and inject them into his own calligraphy. His running script was unadorned and clumsy, while his seal and clerical scripts contained elements of the running script, causing orthodox calligraphers to label him as "strange." Fu reiterated the importance of learning the seal and clerical scripts,[18] stressing that in writing one should strive to be clumsy rather than artful, ugly rather than charming, disorderly rather than polished, and straightforward rather than arranged.[19] Such aesthetic qualities as clumsy, awkward, disorderly, and straightforward were present in some eighteenth-century works and became more evident later. The painting and calligraphy of Jin Nong, Zheng Xie (1693–1765), Gao Fenghan (1683–1748), and others signified the beginning of a new "artistic trend."[20] If one were to say that the *qishu*[21] of Jin Nong and the *liufenbanshu*[22] of Zheng Xie were arranged and affected, lacking in the qualities of being straightforward and natural, then the painting of Jin Nong, with its characteristic clumsiness, demonstrated the combination of natural flavor and *jinshi* learning. By the beginning of the nineteenth century, *beixue*, the study of inscriptions on stone stelae, became more dominant. The well-known epigraphers and calligraphers Ruan Yuan (1764–1849), Bao Shichen (1775–1855), and Kang Youwei (1858–1927) propagated the theories of *beixue*, praising the study of *bei* and deprecating the use of *tie* (model-books of ink rubbings taken from engraved stone or wood), and advocating the style of the Wei over that of the Tang. By doing so, they instigated the reforms in the calligraphic style of the era.

The revolution in calligraphy also stimulated reform in painting through the introduction of elements of seal, clerical, and Wei *bei* calligraphy. Painters generally sought to convey in their works the antique flavor of metal and stone inscriptions and paid attention to issues of placement and balance on the picture plane. The *jinshi* school of painting, which began to develop in the mid-nineteenth century and continued well into the twentieth century, was represented by Zhao Zhiqian, Wu Changshuo, and Qi Baishi (1864–1957). They not only excelled in poetry, calligraphy, and painting, but were excellent seal carvers whose respective styles had lasting influence. They broadened the traditional Chinese painting concept of "Excellence in Three" to that of "Perfection in Four," namely, poetry, calligraphy, painting, and seal carving. Other painters who, though not famous as seal carvers, were similarly influenced by *bei* calligraphy include Chen Shizeng (1876–1923), Lu Fengzi (1885–1959), Pan Tianshou (1897–1971), and Zhang Daqian (1899–1983). Even the Westernized painters and art educators Xu Beihong (1895–1953) and Liu Haisu (1896–1994) were at one time students of Kang Youwei. Calligraphers devoted to *bei* were numerous. The most respected was He Shaoji (1799–1873), whose work was regarded as characteristic of the time. It has been said that as a result of his work, "calligraphy in the last few hundred years was given an energizing jolt."[23] Some even equate him with the revered fourth-century calligrapher Wang Xizhi (303–361). He Shaoji's running and cursive scripts fully realized the calligraphic standards advocated by Fu Shan. From the decorous, graceful, feminine, and refined calligraphic tradition of more than a thousand years came the change to the irregular, masculine, unadorned and vigorous, artless and clumsy, embedded and coarse. This change also reflected a psychological reaction: Many artists wanted to pursue a bold and strong style in the midst of the unremitting corruption of the Qing court and the dying fortunes of the country.

The dissemination of Western art in China hastened the transformation of Chinese art. Historical records concerning the activities of Christian foreign missionaries at the Qing court are well known, but what is perhaps not fully comprehended is that the influence of Western painting was not confined to the court.[24] As early as the beginning of the seventeenth century, religious sculpture and woodblock prints used by the missionaries for preaching were being circulated among the common people.[25] The number of Christian converts increased quickly, from the modest figure of just over a hundred in 1596 to more than ten thousand at the end of the Ming dynasty, in 1644.[26] During that period, religious pictures and figurines were produced in China to meet the growing demand for such objects. Among the missionaries who painted these religious pictures were You Wenhui (Pereira Yeou, 1575–1633), a native of Macau, and the Chinese-Japanese Eurasian Ni Yagu (Jacques Niva, 1579–1633).[27] One can easily discern the influence of Western chiaroscuro and perspective[28] in eighteenth-century Suzhou woodblock prints,[29] "western mirror" (*xinyangjing*) painting,[30] and the popular painting[31] of the Jiangnan region. Historical documents record Chinese painters adept in Western painting methods, including Zhang Shu,[32] Ding Yuntai, and Ding Yu.[33] By the eighteenth century, there were a number of workshops of Western painting in Guangdong that sold their goods to clients in Europe and America.[34] In the mid-nineteenth century, the Catholic bishop of Shanghai established an arts and crafts factory in the city to manufacture articles for use in preaching; the factory, which remained active until the early twentieth century, trained at least a hundred oil and woodblock painters as well as sculptors.[35] Among them were the precursors of Chinese advertising and private art school professionals, such as Zhou Xiang (1871–1933), Zhang Yuguang (1885–1966), Xu Yongqing (1880–1953), Hang Zhiying (1900–1947), and Zhang Chongren (1907–1998). (At the beginning of the twentieth century, Western realistic painting methods were being widely used in commercial advertising, calendar painting, and *bapo* paintings.[36] At the time when Kang Youwei, Cai Yuanpei, Chen Duxiu (1879–1942), and others were advocating reform and the "blending of China and the West," Western realistic painting methods were already being practiced in Chinese society.

The main achievement of the Self-Strengthening Movement and the Reform Movement of the nineteenth century was the instigation of change in China's education system. In 1901 schools were divided into primary, secondary, and tertiary levels, modeled on the Western system. The teaching of practical scientific knowledge was emphasized; Chinese classics accounted for only one-seventh of the curriculum, signifying the end of the old learning. These drastic reforms threatened the existence of the traditional civil examination system, which was based on Confucianism and the classics and had been in place for more than a thousand years. In 1905 the examinations were finally abolished.[37] With the new education system firmly in place, the structure of learning was changed and a new system of selecting government officials was established. The old system of scholar-bureaucrats and the literati class came to an end. At the beginning of the twentieth century, the group of Chinese artists who went to Japan, Europe, and America to study constituted the principal founders of China's art education. The role they were to play in the transformation of Chinese modern art is well known.

The contribution to and the influence on Chinese modern art by artists in the Jiangnan region are subjects particularly worthy of investigation. From the nineteenth to the early twentieth century, hundreds of art societies sprang up in Shanghai, Hangzhou, Suzhou, and other Jiangnan cities. The first art society in Beijing, Songyuan Huashe, was formed during the period 1861–69 by Qin Bingwen (1803–1873), a native of Wuxi who was a member of the Pinghua Shuhuhui,[38] a painting society set up in Shanghai in 1851. Many influential people who lived in Beijing at the beginning of the twentieth century were from the Jiangnan area, including Cai Yuanpei, Jin Cheng, Tang Dingzhi (1878–1946), Lu Xun (1881–1936), Shou Shigong (1885–1950), Chen Banding (1876–1969), Zhou Zhaoxiang (1880–1953), Yu Shaosong (1882–1955), and Xu Beihong. Tang Dingzhi and Yu Shaosong organized the Xuannan Huashe, which included many famous painters from Jiangnan.[39]

It is popular among scholars nowadays to use Western art theories in interpreting the development of Chinese art history. In the face of many unfilled gaps and unanswered questions, I believe that we must embark on a search for primary research materials and thereby discover the main principles of the history of modern Chinese art.

NOTES

This paper is adapted from an article by the author in *Journal of Oriental Studies* (Centre of Asian Studies, University of Hong Kong) 35, no. 1 (1997): 14–21.

1. Kang Youwei 1977, 1.

2. Chen Xiaodie 1934, no. 2, 18–19; no. 3, 37.

3. Lee 1973, 456.

4. Case studies of the first half of the nineteenth century are few in number. See, for example, Zhao Li 1992. For general historical accounts, see Wan Qingli 1992–94.

5. See Liu Yizheng 1988, vol. 2, sect. 2, chap. 25; sect. 3, chap. 7.

6. See Wei Zhengtong 1991, vol. 1, chap. 3, 75–130.

7. In the late Ming, Huang Zongxi pointed out that "industry and commerce are all the basis." The inclinations of Anhui mechants "to trade and to take pleasure in the Confucian classics" and "to trade as well as to study" reflected the change in the thinking of the time. In the late Qing, Zheng Guanying (1842–1921), a famous merchant in Jiangnan who turned to politics and became an important and influential thinker, advocated using "commerce as the basis" and wrote *Jingshi weiyan*.

8. Weng Zhiyong 1965, 36.

9. *Hangzhou fuzhi*, vol. 145; *Wenyuan*, Guangxu version, 29.

10. Hang Shijun 1792, vol. 33, 10–11. Deng Zhicheng 1992, 4.

11. See note 4 above.

12. Feng Zhi and Liu Yongbiao 1992, 9.

13. *Zhongguo jindai huajia mingjian* 1992, 11.

14. Ibid., 25.

15. For example, in his colophon on *Xifa Loudong shanshui zhou*, Zhang Yin wrote: "Our Run [the other name for Zhenjiang] painters use their own methods, and do not follow Loudong." He also stated in an inscription on another painting, *Shanshui zhou*, "Yuan painters abandoned completely the impure qualities of Song painters ... the qualities of vigor and luxuriance are present. Baishiweng [Shen Zhou, 1407–1529] learned from Meihua Daoren [Wu Zhen, 1280–1354], but added his own flavor of vigor and luxuriance. That is why he was the best in the Ming dynasty. Robust and strong like Tang Ziwei, refined and graceful like Qiu Shizhou, yet they cannot surpass him. This shows that in calligraphy and painting, archaic and unadorned were the best, and competence is secondary." Both paintings mentioned here are in the Zhenjiang City Museum.

16. Wang Yuanqi, in *Lutai huaba*, wrote: "Guangling and Baixia, their foul habits are not dissimilar to those of the Zhe school." (Guangling and Baixia refer, respectively, to the Yangzhou and Zhenjiang area.) Here, Wang, besides criticizing the dry, stiff, blatant style of the Zhe school and its bad influence on posterity, also showed that he considered the Yangzhou and Zhenjiang painters similar to those of the Zhe school. This, however, inadvertently demonstrates that some people liked the masculine, robust, and forthright visual effects of this kind of painting.

17. Wan Qingli 1992–94, vol. 264, pp. 113–20.

18. Fu Shan 1911, vol. 25, p. 2.

19. Wan Qingli 1992–94, vol. 264, pp. 113–15.

20. Kang Youwei 1936, 8.

21. Jin Nong jokingly referred to his clerical-style calligraphy as *qishu*, or

"painted calligraphy," because it appeared to be executed with a painting brush rather than a writing brush.

22. Zheng Xie used the term *liufenbanshu* (six and a half parts) to describe his clerical script (*lishu*). By this, he meant that his calligraphy was not as perfect as the ancient clerical script known as *bafen* (eight parts).

23. Yang Kan 1988, 26.

24. Wang Bomin 1988, 149; see also *Gugong bowuyuan cang Qingdai gongtinghuihua* 1995.

25. Luo Guang 1996, no. 4, p. 405.

26. Xiong Yuezhi 1994, 32.

27. Fang Hao 1988, 166; see also Rong Zhenhua 1995, 495.

28. See Sullivan 1973, 41–88.

29. *Zhongguo yangfeng huazhan* 1995, 376.

30. "People in Jiangning made a square or round wooden box, and painted on the inside flowers, trees, fish or birds, creating a strange and mysterious kind of game. A hole was made on the outside, using the five colors of the transparent tortoise shell. When one looked through the hole, the obstruction became smaller and the vision broadened. This was the Western mirror." See Li Dou 1968, vol. 17, p. 23.

31. See note 29 above.

32. See Li Dou 1968, vol. 2, *caohelu*, p. 15, which states: "Zhang Shu, *zi* Jinren, skilled in Western painting methods, from close up to far away, from big to small, even in minute details he abided by the rules. Even Westerners were not better than he."

33. See *Guochao huazheng xulu* 1963, 116–17, which states: "Ding Yuntai, from Qiantang, skilled in realistic painting, specialized in the Western method of using wash to throw the objects into sharp relief. His daughter, Ding Yu, who acquired her family's skills, specialized in portraits."

34. Wan Qingli 1997, 158–72.

35. *Dongnan wenhua* 1992, no. 5, pp. 124–30. See also Wan Qingli 1994, 98–104.

36. Berliner 1992, 61–70.

37. See *Guangxu zhengyao* 1958, vol. 4, pp. 4619–816; vol. 5, pp. 5285–466.

38. Wan Qingli 1992–94, vol. 274, p. 103.

39. Huang Pingsun 1987, 155–56.

REFERENCES

Berliner, Nancy. 1992. The "Eight Brokens" Chinese Trompe-l'oeil Painting. *Orientations* vol. 23, no. 2.

Chen Xiaodie. 1934. Qingdai wu hualun. *Guohua yuekan* (Shanghai), nos. 2 and 3.

Deng Zhicheng. 1992. *Gudong suoji*, "Jin Dongxin." Vol. 6. Beijing: Zhongguo shudian.

Fang Hao. 1988. *Zhongguo tianzhujiaoshi renwuzhuan*. Beijing: Zhonghua shuju.

Feng Zhi and Liu Yongbiao. 1992. *Minguo mingren yiwenlu*. Nanjing: Jiangsu guji chubanshe.

Fu Shan. 1911. *Shuanghongkan quanji*, Dingbaoquan kanben, vol. 25.

Guangxu zhengyao, Guangxuchao donghualu. 1958. Beijing, Zhonghua shuju.

Gugong bowuyuan cang Qingdai gongtinghuihua. 1995. Beijing: Wenwu chubanshe.
Guochao huazheng xulu. 1963. Vol. 2, *Huashi congshu* (3). Shanghai: Shanghai renmin meishu chubanshe.
Hang Shijun. 1792. *Daogu tangji*. Qianlong version, vol. 33.
Huang Pingsun. 1987. Yu Shaosong qiren qishi. *Duoyun*. Shanghai.
Kang Youwei. 1936. *Guangyizhou shuangji, zunbei* 2. Beijing: Zhonghua shuju.
———. 1977. *Wanmu caotang cang Zhongguo huamu xu*. Taipei: Wenshizhe chubanshe.
Lee, Sherman E. 1973. *A History of Far Eastern Art*. New York: Prentice-Hall, Inc.
Li Dou. 1968. *Yangzhou huafanglu*. Taipei: Xuehai chubanshe.
Liu Yizheng. 1988. *Zhongguo wenhuashi*. Shanghai: Dabaike quanshu chubanshe.
Luo Guang, trans. 1996. *Limadou quanji*. Shanghai: Guangqi chubanshe.
Rong Zhenhua. 1995. *Zaihua Yesuhuishi liezhuan ji shumububian*. Trans. Geng Sheng. Hong Kong: Zhonghua shuju.
Sullivan, Michael. 1973. *The Meeting of Eastern and Western Art: From the Sixteenth Century to the Present Day*. New York: Graphic Society.
Wan Qingli. 1992–94. Bingfei shuailuode bainian: shijiushiji Zhongguo huihuashi. *Xiongshi meishu* (Taipei), vols. 254–78.
———. 1994. Zhongguo xiyanghua zhi yaolan. *Xiongshi meishu* (Taipei), vol. 276, no. 2.
———. 1997. Guangdong waixiaohua jianshi. *Huajia yuhuashi*. Hangzhou: China National Art Academy Press.
Wang Bomin, ed. 1988. *Zhongguo meishu tongshi*. Jinan: Shandong jiaoyu chubanshe.
Wei Zhengtong. 1991. *Zhongguo shijiushiji sixiangshi*. Taipei: Dongda tushu gongsi.
Weng Zhiyong. 1965. *Zhongguo jingji wenti tanyuan*. Taipei: Zhengzhong shuju.
Xiong Yuezhi. 1994. *Wanqing shehui yu xixue dongjian*. Shanghai: Shanghai renmin chubanshe.
Yang Kan. 1988. *Xike zazhu*. Suzhou: Suzhou guji chubanshe.
Zhao Li. 1992. *Jingjiang huapai yanjiu*. Changsha: Hunan meishu chubanshe.
Zhongguo jindai huajia mingjian. 1992. Hong Kong: Hanmoxuan Publishing Co. Ltd.
Zhongguo yangfeng huazhan–Mingmo zhi Qingdaide huihua, banhua, chatuben. 1995. Majita City, Japan: International Art Museum of Prints.

STUDIES IN HONOR OF CHU-TSING LI

The Commodification of Chinese Painting and Calligraphy and Its Relationship to the Production of Forgeries

YANG XIN

商品經濟、世風與書畫作偽

楊新

偽造他人書畫作品，究竟起於何時，已無從查考。《世說新語》載："鍾會是荀濟北(勖)從舅，二人情好不協，荀有寶劍，可值百萬，常在母鍾夫人許。會善書，學荀手跡作書與母取劍，乃竊去不還。"鍾會狡獪，和荀勖開了個小小玩笑，可說是文人們賣弄風流，但故事卻說明三國時期已有偽造他人手跡的行為。至於摹仿複製前人作品，和將無名氏作品題為前代名家之筆，至少在初唐時期是很普通的事。成書於貞觀十三年(369 年)的裴孝源《貞觀公私畫史》曾明確指出"今人所蓄，多是陳(善見)王(知慎)寫榻，都非楊(契丹)鄭(法士)之真筆"。又說在他所記載的畫卷中，"其間有二十三卷恐非晉宋人真跡，多當時工人所作，後人強題名氏"。這些都只能說，從行為、技術和手段上，為書畫作偽準備好了條件。

真正的書畫作偽，是在書畫作品進入市場成為商品之後，使它在觀賞價值之外，同時還具有金錢財產的價值。唐・張彥遠《歷代名畫記》載："董伯仁、鄭法士、楊子華、孫尚子、閻立本、吳道玄，屏風一片，值金二萬，次者售一萬五千。其楊契丹、田僧亮、鄭法輪、(尉遲)乙僧、閻立德，一扇值金一萬。"由此可見書畫作品作為商品在市場上流通，在唐末已很盛行，而且價值昂貴，這就誘使了一些商人和其他人在其中弄虛作假，製造偽品以魚目混珠。因為這不需要多的投資，便可謀取極大的收益，是一本萬利的生意。在中國歷史上，曾經出現過三次書畫作偽的高潮，都是與商品經濟的發展緊密相聯繫的。

第一次高潮約出現在十一世紀後半葉至十二世紀初，正當北宋王朝的後期。北宋結束了五代紛爭的局面，在統一全國之後經過一段社會安定，使城市商業經濟有了突出的發展。當時的都城汴京(今開封)是全國最繁華的商業城市，居民二十余萬戶，八方輻輳，商店林立，大街小巷，無論是白天黑夜，都可以進行貿易活動。據孟元老《東京夢華錄》點滴記載，在汴京頻繁的商業活動中，書畫的交易也相當引人注目。如著名大相國寺殿后的集市，潘樓東街巷的攤販店鋪中，都有書畫珍玩的買賣。年節時，宣和樓前及其它街上，有"賣時行紙畫"及"小像兒並紙畫"，以及"門神、鍾馗、桃板、桃符及財門"之類。在這樣大的市場中，書畫偽品混跡其中，是可以想像得到的。

這一時期假書畫的製造，已達到令人吃驚的程度。《宣和畫譜》李成傳記中記載："自成歿後，名益著，其畫益難得，故學成者，皆摹仿成所畫峰巒泉石，至於刻畫圖記名字等，庶幾亂真，可以欺世。”偽作李成繪畫流布之廣，據鑒賞家米芾說，在他所見到的三百餘本中，真跡“只見二本”，對此他很憤慨，“欲為無李論”(《畫史》)。其實，米芾自己就是一個造偽者，不過他不隱瞞，有點玩世不恭，請聽他的自白：“王詵每餘到都下，邀過其第，即大出書帖索余臨學，因櫃中翻索書畫，見余所臨王子敬(獻之)《鵝群帖》，染古色麻紙，滿目皺紋，錦囊玉軸，裝剪他書上跋連於其後。又以臨虞(世南)貼裝染，使公卿跋。余適見大笑，王就手奪去，諒其他尚多，未出示。又余少時，使一蘇州背匠之子呂彥直，今在三館為胥，王詵嘗留門下，使雙鉤書貼。又嘗見摹《黃庭經》一卷，上用所刻勾德無圖書記，乃余驗破者”。(《書史》)這裏米芾揭破，呂彥直就是一個作偽者，而在王詵的家裏，就有著一個小小的造假書畫“作坊”。

除了偽造前人古人的作品外，也偽造時人作品。當時有一上畫家叫劉宗道，京師人，畫“照盆孩兒”最為精到而知名，為了防止假冒和仿製，“每作一扇，必畫數百本，然後出貨，即日流布”(《畫繼》)。可見當時假畫製造的猖獗。至於對前流傳下來的古舊作品，進行改頭換面或亂定名號以提高身價者，更比比皆是。蘇軾曾指出“世所收吳(道子)畫，多朱繇筆也”(《東坡全集》卷九)。朱繇為唐末人，“工畫佛道，酷類吳生”(《圖畫見聞志》)，但他的名氣，遠不能與吳道子相匹，所以其作品就被改造或有意定為吳道子筆跡了。亂定古畫名目，米芾有過尖銳批評，他說：“世俗見馬即命為曹(霸)韓(幹)韋(偃)，見牛即命為韓滉，戴嵩，甚可笑”。並引民諺云：“牛即戴嵩，馬即韓幹，鶴即杜荀，象即章得”(《畫史》)。韓幹、戴嵩為唐畫馬、牛專家，而杜荀鶴、章得象即唐、宋間兩名人姓字，非畫鶴畫象專家，針對社會現象，民諺嘲諷，可謂辛辣。

終北宋之世，偽造古書畫之風，有增無減。鄧椿《畫繼》(成書於 1167 年)中記錄“銘心絕品”二百餘件，附記中特別申明：“右前所載圖軸，皆千之百，百之十，十之一中之所擇也，若盡載平日所見，必成兩牛腰矣！然不載者，皆米元章(芾)所謂慚惶殺人之物(指偽劣作品一筆者)，何足以銘心哉。”可見偽品書畫在社會上存在的情況。

第二次高潮約出現在西元十六至十七世紀前期，即明代的中晚期。明代自朱元璋 1368 年建國以後，經過一個半世紀的休養生息，社會相對安定，所謂“承平日久”，“海內宴安”，生產和經濟都較之前代有更大發展。特別突出的是，江南地區城鎮手工業、商業發展尤速，商品一貨幣經濟空前高漲。在店鋪林立、百貨雲集中，逐漸形成了骨董行業，專門經營古今字畫和珍玩，買賣相當活躍。沈德符《萬曆野獲編》記北京"廟市日期"中說："城隍廟開市在貫城以西，每月亦三日，陳設甚夥，人生日用所需，精粗畢備，羈旅之客，但持阿堵入市，頃刻富有完美。以至書畫骨董，真偽錯陳，北人不能鑒別，往往為吳儂以賤值收之。"北京的集市貿易，除城隍廟外，還有大明門左右的朝前市，東華門外的燈市，正陽橋的日昃市等，每次集市百貨中，都少不了書畫骨董。集市貿易僅只是書畫商品交換的一種形式，經常性的交換是那些固定的店鋪，以及收藏者、作者、掮客之間的直接交易，這在南方城鎮尤盛。南京、蘇州、杭州、松江、新安等地，都是當時較大的書畫市場。

書畫市場的繁榮，再一次地掀起了書畫作偽的高潮。當時的蘇州，可說是全國製造假骨董假書畫的中心。《萬曆野獲編》載："骨董自來多贋，而吳中尤甚，文士藉以糊口。近日前輩，修潔莫如張伯起(鳳翼)，然亦不免向此中生活。至王伯穀(穉登)則全以此作品計然策矣。"張、王為有地位名望的文人，尚且如此，那些衣食無著的寒儒和工匠們就更不待說了。沈周和文徵明是蘇州畫壇鉅子，他們的作品，在市場上很暢銷，而且價格看好。王世貞《觚不觚錄》記載道："畫當重宋，而三十年來，忽重元人，乃至倪元鎮(瓚)以逮明沈周，價驟增十倍"。正因如此，所以沈周的作品"片縑朝出，午已見副本，有不十日，到處有之"(祝允明：《記石田先生畫》)。沈周、文徵明為人寬厚，有時竟然為偽造自己的作品題款字。馮時可在《文待詔小傳》中說："有偽公書畫以博利者，或告之公，公曰：'彼其才藝，本出吾上，惜乎世不能知，而老夫徒以先飯占虛名也。'其後偽者不復憚公，後操以求公題款，公即隨手與之，略無難色。"王世貞補充道："以故先生書畫遍海內，往往真不能當贋十二，而環吳之裏居者，潤澤于先生手幾四十年。"(《弇州山人四部稿》"文先生傳")蘇州畫家，知名海內，而書畫作偽，也出了名。顧炎武考察全國歷史地理、風土民情，寫成《肇域志》一書，於蘇州特別寫道："蘇州人聰慧好古，亦善仿古法為之，收畫之臨摹，鼎彝之冶淬，能令真贋不辨之。"從現存的實物來看，書畫偽品中有名的"蘇州片"，作品既多，流布亦廣，就是在這一時期內興盛起來的。"蘇州片"的作品內容，形式，規格有著統一性，時間的延續也較長，由此來分析，不是少數人的單幹，而是集體的製作，看來有著專門的生間作坊，可惜這方面，尚缺乏充足的文獻記載。

其它地區的書畫作偽，雖遠遜于蘇州，但也不乏其人，最典型的例子莫過於張泰階。張字愛平，上海人，萬曆四十七年(1619年)進士，于崇禎六年(1633年)著成《寶繪錄》一書，載有晉、唐至明名家作品甚夥，《四庫全書總目提要》及吳修《論畫絕句》均指出，作者記錄的作品全系偽品。吳修譏諷他道："不為傳名定愛錢，笑他張姓謊連天。可知泥古成何用，已被人欺二百年。"附注云："崇禎時有張泰階者，集所造晉、唐以來偽畫二百件，刻為《寶繪錄》二十卷，自六朝至元朝，無朝不備。宋以前諸圖，皆趙松雪(孟頫)、俞紫芝(和)、鄧善之(文原)、柯丹丘(九思)、黃大癡(公望)、吳仲圭(鎮)、王叔明(蒙)、袁海叟(凱)十數題識，終文衡山(徵明)，不雜他人。數十年間，全見數十種，其詩跋乃一人所寫，用松江黃粉箋紙居多。"看來張泰階這二百來件偽品，都還確有實物作底，也決非他一人所能完成，其家中亦可能存在一個作偽作坊。既製造偽品，還著書宣傳，可謂有"創造"性。其製造偽品手段，也是登峰造極了。

第三次高潮約出現在西元十九世紀後半葉至二十世紀初，即清代的後期。清代是中國最末一個封建王朝，自 1644 年建立以來，經過康熙、雍正、乾隆之治，社會生產和經濟得到很大的發展。乾隆、嘉慶時期，手工業與農業越來越趨勢分離，農業的專門化、手工業內部行業分工與地域分工，比以前變化更加明顯。社會分工的不斷擴大，使產品交換也隨之擴大，貨幣流通加速，需求增加，都直接促進了商品經濟的日益繁榮，也刺激了中國本土資本主義萌芽的滋長。1840 年的鴉片戰爭，西方帝國主義用槍炮撞開了閉關自守的中國大門，使中國逐步淪為半封建半殖民地社會。西方帝國主義的自由出入，使一些重要通商口岸，成為帶有國際性的貿易城市。

在整個社會商業的發展當中，書畫古玩業也隨之變化，專業分工的傾向越來越明顯，店鋪也相對地有所集中，形成專業經營區域。例如在北京，自乾隆後期開始，琉璃廠一帶逐漸形成為文化街市，書籍、文具、古玩字畫的店鋪都集中於此，馳名全國。據近人孫殿起所輯《琉璃廠小志》一書搜集的資料，從咸豐，同治時期起至民國時期，在琉璃廠一帶專門經營古玩字畫的店鋪字型大小，先後有一百三十餘家。其中博古齋從咸豐時開業，至光緒年間，凡三易其主，而經營項目不變。而有些字號的牌匾，至今猶存。可以想見當時書畫買賣之盛。除北京外，上海是一個新興商業大埠，書畫古玩的買賣有後來居上之勢，店鋪大概集中於城隍廟一帶。此外天津、青島、武漢、長沙、廣州等城市，都不乏類似的情形，可惜這方面的資料，尚缺乏收集整理。

在於此聲勢浩大的書畫買賣中，尤其是有洋人參與其事，頗有根基的古書畫偽造，便再度地掀起高潮。在北京，有著名的"後門造"，專一偽造清宮廷畫家如郎世寧輩的作品，因出現於後門橋一帶而得名。據聞上海城隍廟一帶的畫師，專門偽造海上名家的作品。長沙犁頭街一帶書畫鋪，則專門偽造明末清初名人字畫，偽造品傾銷武漢轉手至上海，稱為"長沙貨"。被壓抑多年的石濤、揚州八怪的作品，逐漸為人們所欣賞，揚州、廣州就有他們的偽品出現，分別被鑒賞家命名為"揚州造"和"廣東貨"。作偽的方法、手段、技巧等，也日益精能，臨、摹、仿、造、挖、改、拆、配，無所不用其極，如染色作舊，其潮黴、腐敗、蟲蝕等，巧若天成，至於用照相複製圖章印記，凡令真贋難辨。在偽造之中，亦不乏高手，張大千先生晚出，此中奇士者也，早年偽造石濤等人作品，使當時頗有聲望的鑒賞家，也不免墮其彀中，先生亦由此著名。

書畫作偽是隨著商品經濟的興盛繁榮而高潮疊起的，但是，書畫作品畢竟與其它的商業產品有所差別，那就是它的文化藝術本質內含，因此，書畫買賣的興衰發展，除了經濟的因素之外，還與一定的社會文化思想緊密相聯繫，直接與之有關的是社會上的好古之風與收藏家隊伍的變化。

北宋時代的好古之風是從文學上的復古主義開始的。北宋初期，詩壇上有所謂"西昆派"，他們繼承了唐末五代以來的唯美浮靡風氣，追求聲律，提倡駢體，綺詞麗句，窮妍極態。針對此種風氣，最早有柳開、穆修等人，積極提倡韓愈、柳宗元的古文，與之頡頏。繼之者有歐陽修、蘇舜欽、梅堯臣、王安石、王令、蘇洵、蘇軾、蘇轍、曾鞏等，提倡"文以載道"，復興儒學，逐漸成一股強大的"復古"運動。

由思想文化的復古，而產生了生活情趣上的好古之風，許多文壇上的復古健將，也同時是古書畫的收藏愛好者，如蘇舜欽、蘇軾、黃庭堅、秦觀、晁補之等。此外王詵、米芾、趙希鵠等則是私人收藏最富有者，可謂好古之士。米芾甚連衣服帽子都仿古人裝束，人稱"衣冠唐制度，人物晉風流"。

由於社會財富的積累，商品經濟的活躍，在復古、好古之風的倡導之下，使收藏者隊伍迅速變化和擴大。北宋以前，書畫收藏主要是宮廷、少數顯貴和特殊愛好者，而此一時期則擴大到一般的官僚、地主和商人家庭，特別是那些新貴和商業暴發戶。米芾曾將書畫收藏分為"鑒賞家"和"好事者"兩類，說："鑒賞家，謂其篤好，遍閱記錄，又複心得，或能自畫，故所收皆精品。近世人或有貲力，元無酷好，意作標韻，至假耳目於人，此謂之好事者。置錦囊玉軸，以為珍秘，開之或笑倒，餘輒撫案大叫曰：慚惶殺人！"(《畫史》)米芾挖苦和抨擊"好事者"，從另一側面反映了此一時期內，書畫收藏者隊伍的重大變化和不斷擴大。據米氏《書史》、《畫史》、《寶章待訪錄》三書略加統計，僅他一人所接觸到的收藏者就在百名以上。鄧椿《畫記》"銘心絕品"一章，則記有三十七位收藏家。

收藏家增多，特別是好事者增多，直接影響了書畫市場的繁榮，同時也就使僞品有了廣闊的銷路，使作僞形成高潮。米芾曾看邵必家的收藏品，說："略似江南畫，即題曰徐熙，蜀畫星神，便題曰閻立本、王維、韓滉，皆可絕倒"。還說楊囊家的收藏，也與此差不多。鄧椿《畫繼》記了一則故事："政和間，有外宅宗室不記名，多蓄珍圖，往往王公貴人令其別識，於是遂與常賣交通，凡有奇跡，必用詭計勾致其家，即時臨摹，易其真者，其主莫能別也。復以真本厚價易之，至有循環三、四者，故當時號曰'便宜三'。"此種技倆，米芾亦有之，前述王詵家中，也約略相似。

與北宋後期有某些雷同之處，明代在中後期的文學上，也出現了一股復古主義思潮，反對的是前期華而不實的"台閣體"，主張"文必秦漢，詩必盛唐"，代表人物是前後七子，他們是李夢陽、何景明、徐禎卿、邊貢、康海、王九思、王廷相(前七子)，李攀龍、王世貞、謝榛、宗臣、梁有譽、徐中行、吳國倫(後七子)。在此影響下的好古之風，比北宋有過之而無不及。而收藏家之盛，互相之間的勾心鬥角，更有甚於前。《萬曆野獲編》載："嘉靖末年，海內宴安，士大夫富厚者，以治園亭，教歌舞之隙，間及古玩，如吳中吳文恪公之孫(吳寬？)，溧陽史尚寶之子(史際)，皆世藏珍秘，不假外索。延陵則稽太史應科，雲間則朱太史大韶，吾郡(浙江嘉興)項太學錫山(項元淇)、安太學(安國？)、華戶部(華鑰)輩，不吝重貲收購，名播江南。南都則姚太守汝循，胡太史汝嘉，亦稱好事。若輦下則此風稍遜，惟分宜相國父子(嚴嵩、嚴世蕃)、朱成公兄弟，並以將相當途，富貴盈溢，旁及雅道。於是嚴以勢劫，朱以貨取，所蓄幾及天府，未幾冰山既泮，金穴亦空，或沒內帑，或售豪家，轉眼已不守矣。今上初年，張江陵(張居正)當國，亦有此嗜，但所入之途稍狹，而所收精好，蓋人畏其焰，無敢欺之，亦不旋踵歸大內散人間，時韓太史世能在京，頗以廉直收之。"吾郡項氏，以高價鉤之，間及王弇州兄弟(王世貞、王世懋)，而吳越間浮慕者，皆起稱大賞鑒矣。近年董太史其昌最後起，名亦最重，人以法眼歸之，篋笥之藏，為時所豔。山陰朱太常敬循，同時以好古知名，互購相軋，市賈又交構其間，至以考功法中董外遷，而東壁西園，遂成戰壘。比來則徽人為政，以臨邛程卓之貲，高談宣和博古圖書畫譜。鍾家兄弟(應為鍾繇鍾會父子——引者)之偽書，米海岳(米芾)之假帖，澠水燕談之唐琴，往往珍為異寶。吳門(蘇州)新都(安徽新安)諸市古董者，如幻人之化黃龍，如板橋三娘子之變驢，又如宜君縣夷民改換人肢體面目，其稱貴公子大富人者，日飲蒙汗茶，而甘之若飴矣！"此段概括敍述了當時的收藏家情況，也簡略勾畫了在好古風尚下，人們的種種變態。萬曆以後及沈德符所未記的好古收藏之著名者尚有陳繼儒、孫克弘、李日華、張丑、都穆、詹景鳳、郁逢慶、朱存理、朱之赤等。

明末的好古收藏在官僚中很普遍，吳江沈孟描寫北京城隍廟骨董市肆的情況道：“……未到廟市一里余，雜陳寶玉古圖書。公卿卻與台省步，摩肩接踵皆華裙。阿監飛龍內廄馬，高出人頭俯屋瓦。錦衣袠帽出西華，二十四衙齊放假。亦有波斯僧喇嘛，西先生老鼻如瓜。擠擠挨挨稠人裏，華與鄰交市一家。……”(轉引自《帝京景物略》)這裏值得注意的是，骨董買賣中有太監和外國商人。明代太監受皇帝寵信，權勢極大，他們搶奪骨董書畫，完全是為了攫取財富。著名的《清明上河圖》真跡，自嚴嵩家裏抄沒入內府之後，很快就落到了太監馮保手中，尾紙上有他題跋云：“餘侍御之暇，賞閱圖籍，見宋時張擇端《清明上河圖》，觀其人物界畫之精，樹木舟車之妙，市橋村廓，迥出神品，儼真景之在目也，不覺心思爽然，雖有隋珠和璧，不足云貴，誠希世之珍歟？宜珍藏之。時萬曆六年歲在戊寅(1578年)仲秋之吉，欽差總督東廠官校辦事兼賞御用監司禮太監鎮陽雙林馮保跋。”此跋自供出馮保的偷盜行徑。在宮中尚且如此，市肆之中可想而知。《清明上河圖》偽作在明末大量出現，說明好事者之多，互相間的劫奪欺詐。

一般商人也參與好事者行列，但他們沒有社會地位和勢力，只能憑藉貲財。1987年考古工作者在江蘇淮安發掘出王鎮夫婦墓，即其一例。據墓誌所載，王鎮，字伯安，祖籍揚州儀真，曾祖父在洪武年間移家淮安。“父叔好貨殖，家資頗足用”，本人則“聿承先業，治家勤儉，生財有道，由是家益豐盛”。全家十七餘口，但沒有讀書做官的，可見社會地位低下。然而王鎮卻對“古今圖畫墨蹟，最為心所鍾愛，終日披覽玩賞不替，不啻好色之娛目，美味之悅口。尤善識其真偽，收藏之頃，不計價值”。隨墓葬出土有二十五件書畫作品，應是他生前精心收藏。(淮安縣博物館：《淮安縣明代王鎮夫婦合葬墓清理簡報》，載《文物》1987年第三期)這二十五件作品中，除同時代不甚知名的畫家作品系真跡外(其中李在作品亦真)，兩幅有款的元代作品，任仁發的《人馬圖》和王淵的《秋塘圖》，均為偽品，像王鎮這樣中小商人而喜好收藏者，徽州，淮揚一帶居多。“好事者”，是書畫作偽“家”們主要獵取對象。

與前兩次有不盡相同之處，清代後期出現的書畫買賣熱潮，不完全是出自復古、好古之風的推波助瀾。乾隆、嘉慶時期，思想學術界由於對理學的不滿，提倡有樸實學風的漢儒考據訓詁之學，興起一股考據學又稱漢學的思潮。乾、嘉時期的學者們，在搜集、整理、考據古代經籍文獻的時候，也注意到對包括碑帖書畫在內的地面和傳世文物的搜集整理。如金石歷史學家畢沅，同時也是一個書畫的收藏鑒賞學者，思學哲學家龔自珍則特別注重收集古代碑帖拓本。“乾嘉學派”的學風一直延續到晚清和民國初年，它對書法創作的影響，便是碑學的興起，對繪畫創作的影響，便追求金石味筆法。它所造成的一股“厚古薄今”的思想風氣，也影響到對古代書畫作品的鑒藏，形成了這一時期對古代書畫收集、著錄之盛。其最顯者有陳焯、孫星衍、金瑗、張大鏞、阮元、陶樑、胡積堂、吳榮光、梁章鉅、迮朗、吳辟疆、潘正煒、謝堃、蔣光煦、韓泰華、史夢蘭、徐康、孔廣鏞、孔廣陶、李佐賢、方濬頤、杜瑞聯、顧文彬、顧麟士、楊思壽、沈樹鏞、陸心源、邵松年、龐元濟、周嵩堯、葛金烺、潘世璜、羅振玉、廉泉、崇彝、汪士元、秦潛、郭葆昌、關冕鈞等等。以上諸人均有著錄著作行於世，或者記錄自己收藏或祖傳的書畫作品，或者記錄他人一家所藏或零散觀閱過的作品。這其中還有許許多多的收藏者，是沒有留下文字記錄的。

自從西方帝國主義撞開了中國大門以後，一些外國學者也進入中國國境，特別是敦煌石窟的被發現，其文物為斯坦因等大批盜往歐洲，引起了西方學者對中國古老的文化藝術極大興趣。因此一些不法分子和商人不惜採取各種手段，在中國大量搜集文物。開始由對宗教石窟寺廟和墓葬出土文物的興趣，漸而對傳世的古代繪畫和書法的注意。在此中，日本由於和中國有古老的文化藝術淵源，對中國的繪畫書法的收集較早，繼之才是歐美國家。如美國的福開森氏於1886年來中國，在北京大量收買中國古畫，在1912年至1916年時分三批運往美國。這些作品曾由馮思崐編成目錄，名曰《名畫彙錄》，而未及運走的至今留在南京大學。由於大量的中國藝術品流往歐美和日本，促使在西方國家形成和建立起了中國藝術史專門學科。

再由於在這近百年間，在中國本土上，書畫收藏者隊伍空前壯大，再加上西方國家對中國書畫收藏興趣，直接造成了中國書畫市場的空前繁榮，再次地掀起了偽造假書畫的高潮。偽造者除了針對中國的好事者，也針對國外的商人和好事者。尤其是後者，由於他們對中國文化的陌生，更不懂得中國書畫藝術和中國傳統的鑒定方法，僅只憑藉那麼一點藝術的靈感，也最容易上當。1984年我曾經有機會到美國研究和考察中國藝術史一年，在各大小博物館中參觀瞭解中國古書畫的收藏，其中的許多偽品，就是在這一時期搗騰和製造出來的。

書畫作偽既然與市場經濟緊密相聯繫，同時也以商業營利為主要目的，那麼我們今天在清理鑒定古代書畫偽品時，就不能不對古代的書畫市場也要有所瞭解和清理；在識破一切作偽的手段和技倆時，不能不緊緊抓住有利或無利可圖這一中心要害環節，從中摸索和探討規律。例如，在對古舊書畫進行改造中，挖款，改款、添款時，總是把近改古，把小名家改成大名家，使無款變有款等。對於臨仿臆造，也是大名家多於小名家。古代多於近代和當代。只有這樣，作偽者才能花少力而獲大利。

時代的遠近是相對的，世風的變化也是與時推移的。北宋人臨摹仿造唐及其以前的名人作品，到了明代被誤認為真跡，根據偽品再作偽，這也並不奇怪。因此，宋人、明人即使是大鑒賞家所確認的名跡，我們也不能全信，如董其昌所確認的王維，乃至於荊浩、關仝、董源、巨然的作品，我們也必需要重新加以認識和研究。

時世風氣的變化與美術史的發展關係極為密切，造偽者大多數雖然不懂得美術史，但卻會根據市場窺測方向。有一個極好的例子，據史籍記載，在元代盛懋和吳鎮同時，並曾經一度比鄰而居，都以賣畫而生。但是盛家門口，求畫人多，門庭若市，而吳家則冷冷清清。這種情況使吳夫人有些眼熱，就對丈夫叨叨說：你看人家多興旺。吳鎮正在追求一種新的文人畫風格，作品還不被社會所承認，只好苦笑著說：二十年以後再看罷。仍然我行我素，一直窮老終生。很顯然，在元代盛懋的名氣大過吳鎮，同時代的作偽者，只有可能作盛懋的假，而不可能去作吳鎮的假，因為吳鎮的親筆都少人問津，惶論偽作？孫作(字大雅，江陰人)在吳鎮去世後不久，曾到吳鎮生活過的地方去找尋他的作品，說道：“餘留秀州(今浙江嘉興，吳鎮故鄉)三年，遍訪士大夫家，征其筆跡，蔑有存者，然更復百年，知好者畫，復當幾人耶。”(孫作《滄螺集》卷三)連吳鎮故鄉的士大夫家中，都少有他的作品，那就更不要說外地他鄉和好事者家中了。孫作躭心吳鎮的名字，將要為時間所泯滅，然而歷史的運轉，卻大出孫作的預料之外。吳鎮死後一百五十年前後，吳門畫派興起，如日中天，再過一百年，董其昌崛起於畫壇，叱吒風雲。文人畫由山澗小溪，匯而成滾滾洪流。吳鎮和另外三名元代畫家，黃公望、倪瓚和王蒙，被人們重新喚起，稱為“元四大家”，他們的作品，崇為畫學的楷模，聲名不但未被歷史湮沒，反而越來越高漲，形成一股“四家熱”，鑒賞家、畫家和好事者們，都在競相搜集收藏他們的作品。吳鎮身價既高，作品又求之不易，於是偽作便應時而出。鑒定家徐邦達先生曾發現，明代有一個叫詹僖的人，專門僞造吳鎮的墨竹。詹僖，字仲和，浙江寧波人，活躍於明代正德、嘉靖時候，“寫墨竹，風枝露葉，可追仲圭(吳鎮)”(《無聲詩史》)。因為他有本款作品存世，所以我們能從吳鎮偽品中認識到他，至於那些專一作偽者，就不知凡幾了。

與吳鎮的命運相反，明代前期、中期的宮廷畫家，在當時名氣很大，但由於他們服務的對象主要是宮廷和少數達官貴人，作品主要不在市場上流通，同時代作偽者很少。到了明代晚期，宮廷畫派畫風，受到文人畫家的打擊和排斥，在復古之風中，他們的作品流落到市場中，很多就被改頭換面成宋代的作品出售了。顧復《平生壯觀》記載云："先君云：文進(邊景昭)、延振(呂紀)、以善(林良)翎毛花卉，宋人餘教未衰。髫年時見紀《蘆雁》、良《松鶴》，極佳。中歲惟究心山水於元人，三人之跡屏棄而不視矣。邇來三人之筆寥寥，說者謂洗去名款，竟作宋人易之，好事家所見之翎毛花卉宋人款者，強半三人筆也。予不能不為三人危之。"顧復的話一點也不誇張，在實物中，現已恢復名譽的石銳《嵩祝圖》(藏美國克利夫蘭博物館)和《漁村圖》，就曾被加題跋題簽分別說成是唐李昭道和宋許道寧的作品。在一些出版物中，也曾見將朱端的作品改添款為宋郭熙、呂紀風格的作品添款為遼肖瀜等，例證舉不勝舉，較為普遍。此風一直延續到清初，到清中期明代宮廷名家作品，亦稱名貴，晚期的書畫作偽高手中，也就很少人再幹這種事。

市場隨風倒，掌握世風及市場的演變和發展，對於我們摸清偽品的製作年代，作偽規律和恢復歷史本來面貌非常必要。

總結中國歷史上三次書畫作偽高潮的出現，除了是在商品經濟繁榮的時代之外，同時也都是處在一個王朝的沒落之中，這是一個更為廣闊的社會問題，非本文所承擔的任務。

The Art of Pu Xinyu

JANE C. JU

Immediately after his death in 1963, Pu Xinyu (1896–1963) was praised as "the last brush of literati painting."[1] Although "last" may be too final and a bit exaggerated, Pu was indeed one of the very few artists in modern China who truly fit the definition of a literatus. He was a scholar, credited with several publications of commentaries on the classical texts and known for his poetry in the classical style, published in several volumes. Pu was an adept calligrapher, who excelled in different styles and scripts and left a large body of calligraphic works written in different formats and stylistic traditions. In fact, a standard feature in Pu's paintings is the inclusion of his own poems inscribed in his own hand. Finally, Pu was a master of painting. He was proficient in executing a wide variety of subjects, including horses, monkeys, birds and flowers, figures, and landscapes. HisΩ brush skills reflect a wide range of stylistic traditions, from refined and detailed outline paintings to expressive and spontaneous monochrome ink renditions.

Much has been written about Pu Xinyu in Chinese, primarily subjective and impressionistic accounts of his art and life, in magazines and newspapers. As for Pu's paintings, there have been several exhibitions organized and painting catalogues published in Taiwan and Hong Kong. These publications, however, merely reproduce Pu's works and do not offer any detailed, analytical study of his artistic expression, nor do they discuss the significance of his work in the context of modern Chinese art.[2]

In the West, there has been a dearth of writings on Pu Xinyu, likely perhaps because of his traditionalism. In studies on modern Chinese painting, the emphasis and interest have been more often directed toward the new and radical elements in its development. One reason for this is no doubt the Western critical emphasis on originality and the individual creative talent. Moreover, for many art historians, traditionalism is at best a passive attempt to preserve the past and at worst a stubborn effort to stifle progress and creativity. Paintings that do not demonstrate innovation in either form or content are often dismissed as retrogressive.

To have a fuller understanding of the development of modern Chinese art it is important to examine all its various aspects. Traditionalism, to be sure, plays a significant role in the formation of modern Chinese painting. Thus, as an influential artist working in the traditional mode, Pu Xinyu deserves critical attention. What follows is a brief study of Pu's art and its significance in modern Chinese art history.[3] Since changes in politics and culture affected Pu's career, this discussion will also touch upon those developments that led to the emergence of Pu as a prominent artist both in Beijing during the 1930s and 1940s and in Taiwan after 1949.

Pu Xinyu was born in 1896 as Prince Pu Ju of the Manchu imperial family, Aixin jueluo (Aisin gioro), which founded the Qing dynasty (1644–1911). In accordance with tradition, Pu, the name given to the princes of his generation, became their family name. Xinyu was Prince Pu Ju's alternative given name, and later became commonly used. He was the great-grandson of Emperor Daoguang (r. 1821–50) and the grandson of Prince Gong, the younger brother of Emperor Xianfeng (r. 1851–61).

According to his autobiography, Pu Xinyu did not start painting until he was nearly thirty years old, that is, in the early 1920s. Despite this late start, he was regarded as one of the foremost traditional artists in Beijing during the 1930s and 1940s. It should be noted that Pu emerged during a time of active movement to revivify traditional culture. During the 1920s and 1930s, in response to the political weakness of the country and also as a reaction to the iconoclasm of the May Fourth Movement of 1919, a group of intellectuals called for a revitalization of traditional culture as a means of raising national awareness of China's rich heritage, an effort termed *zhengli guogu* (restoration of the national heritage). As defined by the reform leader Hu Shih (1891–1962) in 1919, *zhengli guogu* denoted efforts by scholars to reevaluate Chinese history, the classics, and religion according to modern methods of historiography and criticism.[4] These efforts stimulated the founding of art associations to promote traditional art by organizing exhibitions and publishing art periodicals. Such activities were facilitated by the unprecedented availability of ancient masterpieces for viewing by the general public and artists, as the treasures of the imperial collection were nationalized and opened for public viewing by 1925. Museums and galleries promoting traditional art mushroomed. All of these activities gravitated toward Beijing, the imperial capital, with the exception of a few brief intervals, since the time of the Mongol Yuan dynasty (1272–1368) and thus the unquestioned center of traditional culture. At this time, Pu Xinyu, a resident of Beijing, gained prominence as one of the leading younger artists working in the traditional mode.

The most influential group of traditional artists in Beijing during the Republican years was the Research Association of Chinese Painting (Zhongguo huaxue yanjiuhui).[5] The founding members of the group, including such important artists as Jin Cheng (1877–1926), Chen Banding

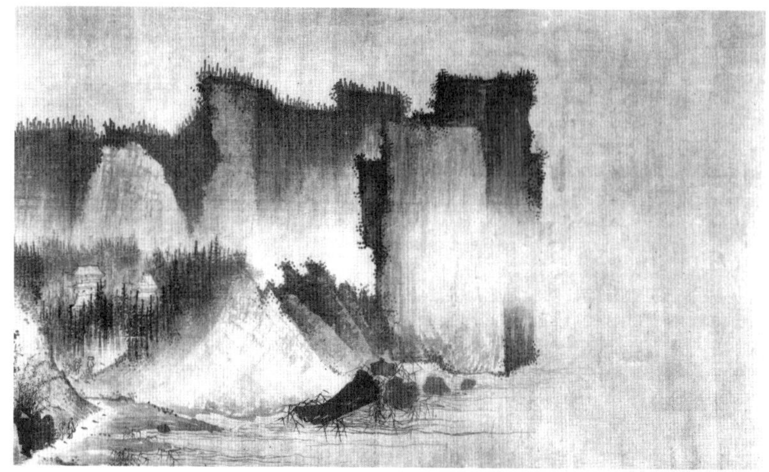

(1876–1969), Yu Feian (1881–1959), and Hu Peiheng (1891–1962), sought to promote traditional painting through the careful study of ancient styles and to teach the proper techniques through publications and exhibitions. Motivated by their desire to perpetuate literati painting, association members studied the works of the Song (960–1279) and Yuan dynasty masters as well as their own more immediate predecessors, the Four Wangs of the early Qing. As a result, the paintings of these modern Beijing painters share common characteristics with works of the Four Wangs, although they were, in fact, breaking away from the orthodoxy of those masters.

Beijing attracted talented artists from other parts of the country, who brought with them concerns and interests that were to reinvigorate traditional painting. For example, Xiao Sun (1883–1944) introduced artistic traditions from his native Anhui Province,[6] most importantly the art of the Qing individualist Shitao (1642–1707). Shitao's artistic choice not to imitate Song and Yuan models but to render nature in his own distinctive style offered an alternative for early twentieth-century Chinese artists who wanted to move away from the orthodox school. Inspired by Shitao and other Anhui painters, Xiao Sun created dramatic and spectacular scenes of Mount Huang in southern Anhui. The artistic concerns of Shitao and the Anhui school were also adopted by other artists of the Republican period, notably Huang Binhong (1865–1955), whose influence can still be seen in the works of many contemporary artists in China. Another artist, Chen Hengke (1876–1923), from Jiangxi Province, focused on other individualist painters of the Ming (1368–1644) and Qing periods, such as Xu

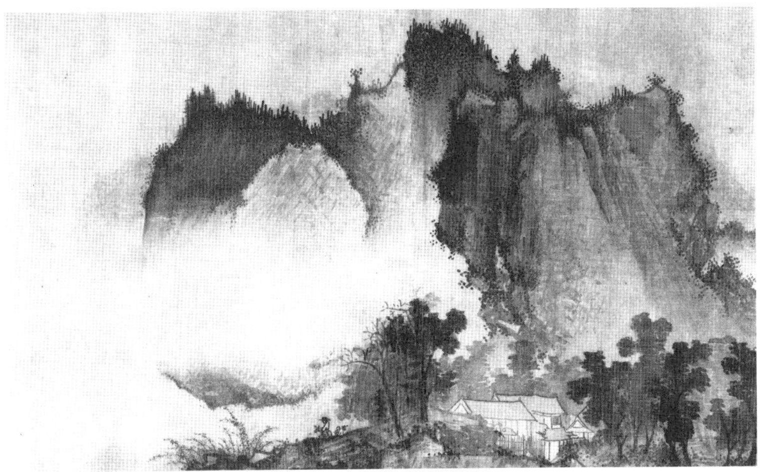

FIGURE 1
Unidentified artist. *Landscape*, late 14th–early 15th century. Detail. Handscroll, ink and light color on silk, 9 3/8 × 190 1/2 in. (28.3 × 475.5 cm). The Nelson-Atkins Museum of Art. Nelson Fund

Wei (1521–1593), Zhu Da (1626–1705), and Gong Xian (1619–1689).[7] For Chen and many early twentieth-century Chinese artists looking for fresh and new approaches, the artistic expression of these individualists offered inspiring alternatives.

Pu Xinyu was no doubt influenced by and benefited from this collective effort to preserve and promote traditional Chinese painting. As a younger artist, Pu experimented with the various traditional painting styles prevalent at the time. He also worked in the academic style of painting, a term sometimes used interchangeably with the so-called Northern school to denote the refined, elegant, and courtly painting style associated with the Southern Song Academy. Because he was a member of the deposed Qing imperial family and worked in the Southern Song style, Pu is often categorized as an academic painter. However, his paintings went beyond copying Southern Song painting. As a member of the imperial family, Pu had access to works of ancient masters in the palace collection; because of this exposure as well as his own temperament, Pu chose to work in various genres and styles, disregarding the arbitrary categories established by Chinese art historians since the seventeenth century. Like most scholar-artists of the twentieth century, Pu perpetuated the literati tradition by emulating the masters of the Song, Yuan, and Ming dynasties. On the other hand, he also painted many subjects not typically in the oeuvre of later literati, such as horses and grooms in the Tang dynasty (618–907) tradition and paintings of Buddhist deities and of historical and mythological figures.

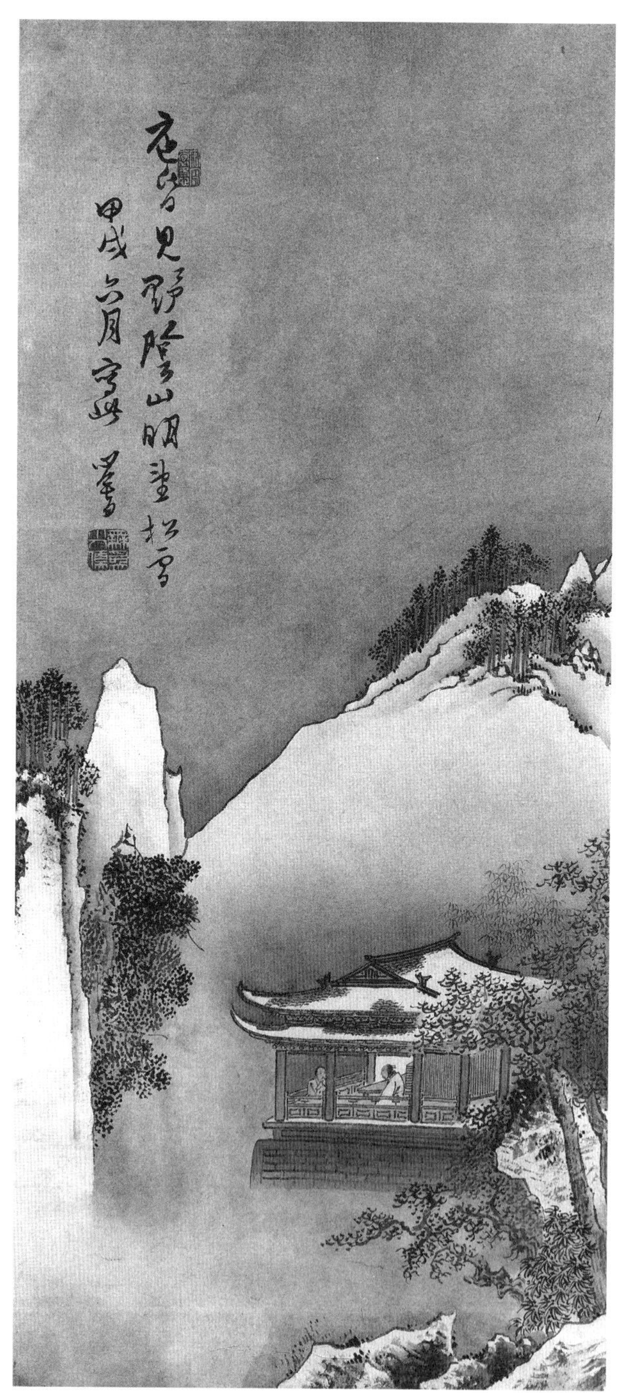

FIGURE 2
Pu Xinyu (1896–1963). *Pavilion in Snow*, 1934. Hanging scroll, ink and color on paper, 24¾ × 11⅛ in. (62.9 × 28.2 cm). The Nelson-Atkins Museum of Art

Pu Xinyu was most successful in expressing his literati ideals through his landscapes. In his search for form and content that best suited his artistic interests, Pu looked to the Song period for inspiration. In his personal collection was an anonymous Song landscape handscroll (fig. 1), now in the Nelson-Atkins Museum of Art, that was to have a tremendous impact on his painting development. Although attributed to the Song period,[8] the handscroll presents a curious amalgamation of Song stylistic features, suggesting that it may be of later date, possibly the early Ming period when there was a conscious effort by artists to emulate Song traditions. However, the date of the Nelson-Atkins handscroll is not essential to the discussion here; it is clearly an example of a Song style that influenced Pu's choices from the past for study and emulation. In addition to being a model for many of Pu's landscapes, the Nelson-Atkins scroll led Pu to masterpieces attributed to the tradition of the Southern Song academy masters Ma Yuan (active ca. 1190–1225) and Xia Gui (active ca. 1195–1230). Of the many works Pu executed in the Ma–Xia tradition, the hanging scroll *Pavilion in Snow* (fig. 2) is of special interest since it seems to have been one of Pu's favorite subjects. Signed and dated 1934, this painting, formerly in the possession of Laurence Sickman and now in the Nelson-Atkins, is the earliest extant work by Pu depicting two scholars in conversation sitting in a snow-covered pavilion. The pavilion is elevated above an empty space that can be presumed to be a layer of mist. Craggy rocks and trees flank the pavilion to the right, while two steep rocks rise to the left. In the background towers a large rounded mountain. As is typical of a work in the Ma–Xia tradition, *Pavilion in Snow* is composed in geometric divisions of land masses, with the shapes of the mountains effectively highlighted by heavy outlines. The trees on the mountaintops, like those in the Nelson-Atkins handscroll (see fig. 1), are delineated by vertical brushstrokes. Although the painting features many attributes of the Ma–Xia tradition, it lacks the atmospheric sense of depth. The simple composition and lack of attention to detail may suggest that Pu was simply interested in experimenting with the basic techniques of the tradition. Through this painting and many others, Pu Xinyu reintroduced a Southern Song painting mode that had been ignored by later literati, and thus opened up a new avenue for modern Chinese literati landscape painters.

Pu's interest in Song landscape painting eventually led him to his mid-Ming predecessors and their interpretations of works by earlier masters of the twelfth through the fourteenth century. Some of the styles favored by

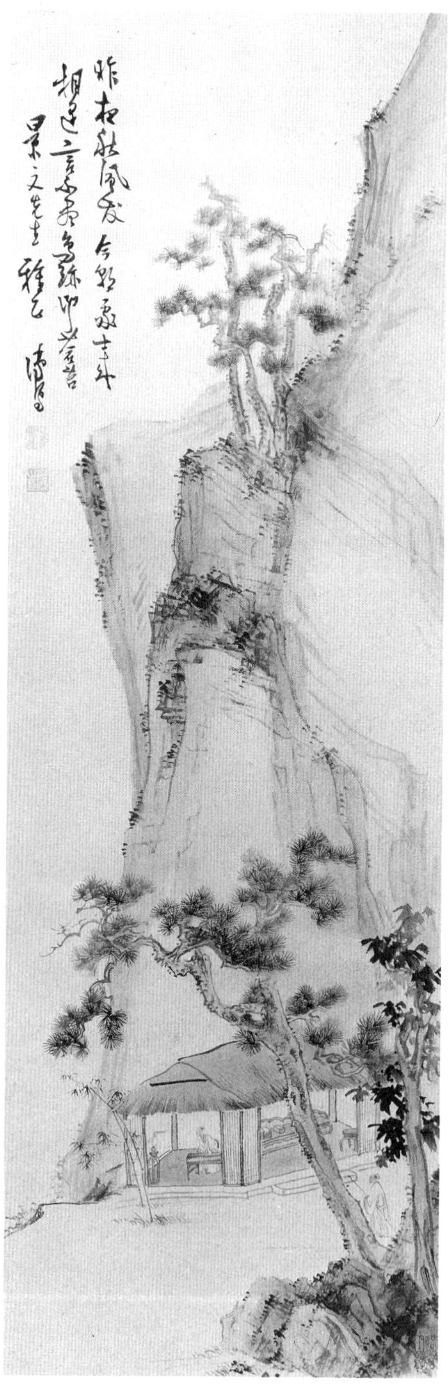

FIGURE 3
Pu Xinyu (1896–1963). *Visiting a Friend in Autumn.* Hanging scroll, ink and light color on paper. The Harvard University Art Museums, F.Y. Chang Collection; Collection of Stuart and Julia Chang Bloch

these mid-Ming literati are also those preferred by the early Ming painters of the academy. As such, Pu shared with the mid-Ming artists an interest in both the literati and the academic styles. Moreover, Pu's ties with the Ming masters are suggested by the works of artists in his own collection, notably the landscapes of Du Qiong (1396–1474), Yao Shou (1423–1495), and Chen Chun (1483–1544).[9] In several of his paintings Pu specifically acknowledges the Ming artists Xu Wei, Wen Zhengming (1470–1559), and Song Xu (1525–ca. 1607) as his inspiration. He also made close copies of landscapes by Tang Yin (1470–1524) and Qiu Ying (ca. 1495–1552).

An example of Pu Xinyu's indebtedness to the mid-Ming artists is his landscape *Visiting a Friend in Autumn* (fig. 3), in The Harvard University Art Museums.[10] Although no specific references to the past are indicated in the inscription, the painting contains several elements characteristic of many sixteenth-century literati landscapes. Its depiction of a scholar in his studio was a popular subject with Tang Yin and Wen Zhengming and their circle, and the close relationship between Pu's landscape and those of the Ming masters is evident in the composition. The focal point of the scholar's studio, for example, recalls Wen Zhengming's *Qin and Crane* or Tang Yin's *Sipping Tea*, both now in the National Palace Museum, Taipei. Furthermore, all three scholars' retreats are flanked by trees and mountains. Pu, like Wen Zhengming, uses very dry ink to create the forms of the rocks and trees and washes these forms with subdued colors. The broad and angular pattern strokes are not unlike Tang Yin's use of the Southern Song ax-cut strokes.

Unlike his contemporary literati, Pu worked comfortably in both the Northern and the Southern school style. In fact, he distinguished himself by incorporating the stylistic features of these two schools into his own personal expression. Viewed in this light, he was no mere slavish imitator but an innovative interpreter of past traditions.

As with all Chinese of his time, Pu Xinyu's life changed dramatically after World War II. Politics was to play an important role in his life and art. The period following the civil war, from 1949 to the mid-1970s, saw the de facto establishment of "two Chinas": the People's Republic of China founded by the Communists on the mainland and the Republic of China founded by the retreating Nationalists and their supporters, among them Pu Xinyu, on Taiwan. The direction of art in China under the Communists came to be dictated by Mao Zedong's theories, which were to some extent an adaptation of the Socialist Realism advocated by the Soviet Union.

Artistic ideas from the West were rejected because they were considered products of a decadent capitalist culture. Under direct official control, romantic revolutionary art became dominant. At the same time, traditional Chinese painting was deemed ideologically unacceptable in the new proletarian society, unless its practitioners adopted a socialist perspective. In some cases, traditional styles and methods of ink and brush were used to depict the new socialist themes in landscapes and figure paintings.

On the other side of the strait, Taiwan was rebuilding after liberation from Japanese occupation. Due to the long period of Japanese control, from 1895 to 1945, the art and culture of Taiwan reflected a mixture of Chinese and Japanese characteristics;[11] from the 1950s onward, however, both gradually moved in a decidedly Chinese direction. The dominance of the culture of the ruling mainlanders resulted from government efforts to become more directly engaged in cultural matters. After settling in Taiwan, the Nationalist government engaged in intense soul searching in an effort to determine the reasons for its loss of mainland China to the Communists.[12] Among the many reasons proposed was its underestimation of the effectiveness of literature and art as a political tool. Moreover, it had failed to recognize the impact of political and psychological warfare by countering the Communists' "unlimited war with limited war."[13] As a result, the government determined to become more involved in the arts as a means to win the support of the people. Writers were encouraged to produce works with anti-Communist sentiments and themes. Several awards in art and literature were established by the government, and art and literary associations were set up. In the two supplementary chapters to Sun Yat-sen's (1866–1925) *Principles of People's Livelihood Concerning Education and Recreation*, Chiang Kai-shek (1887–1975) called for "artistic work of truth and beauty which expresses the essential spirit of the Chinese nation."[14] Although this exhortation lacked specifics, especially in comparison to Mao Zedong's highly detailed directives, Chiang mandated Taiwan to continue the cultural development of pre-1949 China as a reaction against the new and radical direction taken by the Communists after that year.

It was natural, then, that artists and writers who had roots in the mainland gained immediate prominence and dominated the artistic and literary worlds. Pu Xinyu and Huang Junbi (1898–1991) were the dominant figures in traditional painting during the 1950s and 1960s. The reasons for Pu's rise to prominence are several. As a member of the Qing imperial family and a renowned literatus in Beijing, he provided a link to China's cultural past; moreover, as a skilled literati painter, Pu was able to introduce many artistic theories and techniques from the past to a younger generation of artists in Taiwan.

Today, traditional painting continues to play an important role in the development of art in Taiwan, persisting even while younger artists of the 1960s, inspired by ideas from the West—especially American abstract expressionism, pop art, and the like—have emerged to challenge the old order. One reason for this has been the success of the Nationalist government's educational policies, a top priority of which has been to preserve and nourish traditional Chinese culture, supposedly being destroyed on the mainland. It must be emphasized, however, that the development of traditional painting in Taiwan took on some special characteristics. The art practiced by those who came over from the mainland was limited in scope, representing only a small segment of the artistic development that had been taking place since the turn of the century. Along with continued isolation from artistic developments and trends in China, the result has been a distinctive Taiwan style of traditional painting. Most significantly, Taiwan's ties with the United States have made it easier for younger artists to turn to modern Western models, leading to interesting artistic developments as they have attempted to reconcile the traditional with the modern.

Pu Xinyu lived in Taiwan for thirteen years, until his death in 1963. This last stage of Pu's life was also a period during which the government was going through intensive political and socio-economic reconstruction in an effort to rebuild and stabilize its authority and its power. It was a time for survival, both for the government and population, and life in exile on the island was hard. The situation for artists was even more difficult. For Pu, life became very simple. In addition to a small income as the Manchu representative to the National Assembly and other honorary appointments on boards of government-owned industries, he supported himself with his art. Pu was a faculty member in the Art Department of Taiwan Normal University where he was given the responsibility of teaching figure painting in the Chinese section of the department.

Although Pu spent more than a decade in Taiwan, his later paintings were not dramatically different from his early ones; most works from his Taiwan period reflect styles and compositions already evident in his Beijing period. For example, he continued to create narrative landscapes in

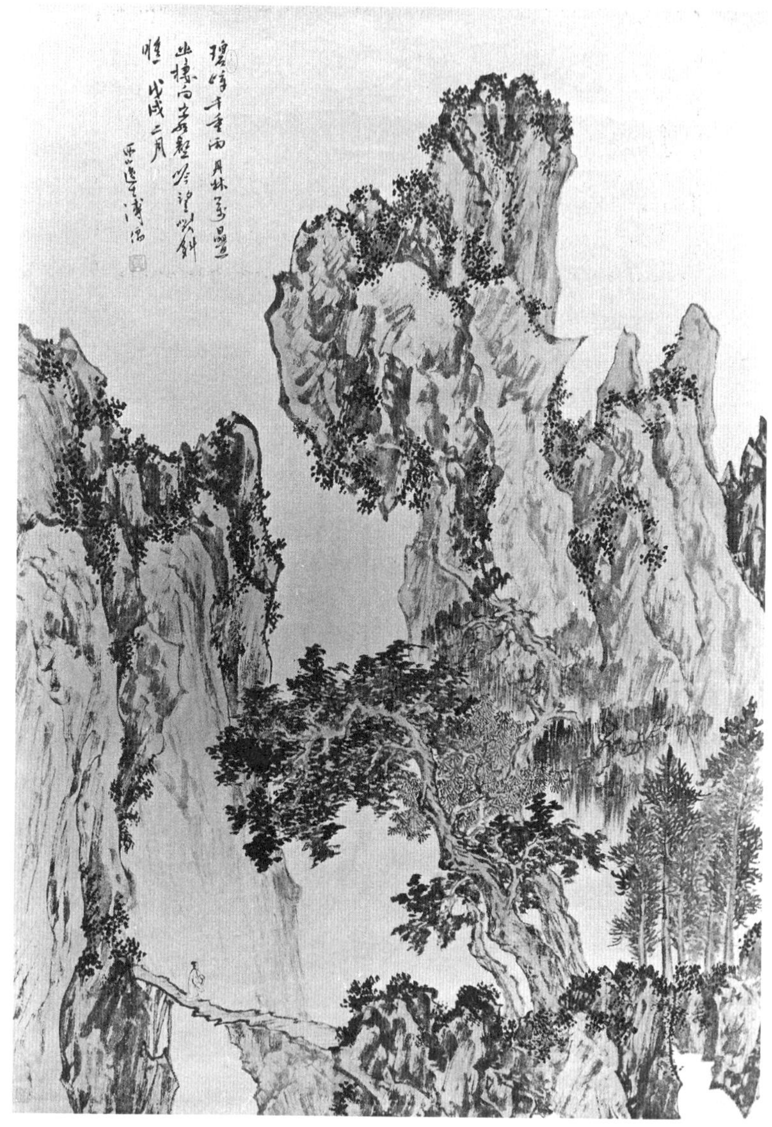

FIGURE 4
Pu Xinyu (1896–1963). *Autumn Colors and Verdant Peaks*, 1958. Hanging scroll, ink and color on paper, 53½ × 37¼ in. (136 × 94.5 cm)

the handscroll format of the Nelson-Atkins painting (see fig. 1). He also repeated certain subjects, such as the pavilion in snow, and continued to work in the Ma–Xia style as well as in the Yuan and Ming literati traditions.

If one were to choose a single work from this later period that best exemplifies Pu Xinyu's distinctive landscape style, it would be the 1958 landscape *Autumn Colors and Verdant Peaks* (fig. 4), formerly in the Cathay Art Museum, Taipei.[15] Unlike typical mountainscapes that give equal attention to the lower, the middle, and the upper sections of the composition, *Autumn Colors* places major emphasis on the mountains in the upper section. To the lower right of the painting is the mouth of a stream that meanders down the mountains through the rocks. To the left of the stream is the rocky peak of a lower mountain, topped by trees that lean toward the next mountain. The elevation of the two mountains is suggested by the deep space between them, over which a bridge tenuously connects them. The height of the mountains is emphasized by a small figure walking alone on the bridge beneath the towering trees. The tallest peak consists of a long, narrow rock jutting out of a large group of rocks and looming over the rest of the landscape.

The composition of *Autumn Colors and Verdant Peaks* is based on Northern Song monumental landscapes, but Pu's painting focuses on one area, the towering mountain. Instead of presenting a balanced three-level composition, starting from the riverbank at the bottom and moving upward to the mountaintop, he takes us directly to the top, eliminating any signs of the lower part of the mountain. The painting seems like a close-up view, and, like many of Tang Yin's best surviving works, is endowed with a sense of immediacy as a result of the swift and powerful brushstrokes. Pu uses long, agitated brushstrokes to create earth and rocks, which are animated by the dramatic light and dark texturing of the pattern strokes. In addition, the painting shows Pu's creative adaptation of the angular ax-cut strokes of the Ma–Xia tradition. Pu's brushwork is done in a free and spontaneous manner, resulting in a bold and dynamic composition rather than the quiet and refined landscapes of the Southern Song.

Pu Xinyu's position as a traditional artist in Taiwan became especially important after his death. From the mid-1960s to the 1970s, the Nationalist government promoted its Cultural Renaissance Movement as part of a reaction to the Cultural Revolution taking place on the mainland. This movement was intended to preserve traditional values on an island that, with urbanization and industrialization, was rapidly becoming Westernized. Pu's art thus accorded well with the government's cultural agenda, although it must be emphasized that Pu was not merely a token artist for the Nationalist program. He was a great master of Chinese painting in his own right, and the impact of his art on later artists is far-reaching and significant. As a teacher, Pu influenced and inspired a number of younger artists. Through the works of two of his students, Liu Guosong (b. 1932) and Jiang Zhaoshen (1925–1996), we can see the legacy of Pu's art and the role of traditionalism in modern Chinese art.

In 1949, at the age of seventeen, Liu Guosong arrived in Taiwan with the Nationalist government.[16] After graduating from high school, he was accepted into the Art Department of Taiwan Normal University and graduated at the top of his class in 1956. Though his major area was oil painting, Liu was required to study both Western and Chinese painting as part of the art program. In Chinese painting classes, students learned by copying and imitating examples of the professor's works. The most prominent faculty member in the department was Pu Xinyu, and examples of Liu Guosong's early works in the traditional style show how closely he followed Pu's technique and style.

In 1957, Liu Guosong and several of his friends founded the Fifth Moon Group, one of the many art associations that sprang up in Taipei in the 1950s and that eventually became the best known internationally. Like many of his contemporaries, Liu was strongly critical of traditional art and looked to the West for new ideas. After several years of experimentation in Western styles and techniques, especially the new and influential abstract expressionism, Liu, like other members of the Fifth Moon Group, became dissatisfied with his progress and decided that total Westernization was not the answer to the problems of modern Chinese art. As an alternative, Liu sought to combine Western artistic ideas with Chinese tradition. In many of his later works, on which he built an international reputation, Liu applied traditional techniques of ink and brush while incorporating the painterly techniques of the abstract expressionists. One example of his innovative style is *Yellow and Gray: A Landscape*, dated 1968 and now in the Spencer Museum of Art, Lawrence, Kansas (fig. 5). It is painted on rice paper with broad sweeping angular brushstrokes in ink, reminiscent of those in the Ma–Xia tradition. Pieces of painted paper are pasted on to the large sheet of rice paper to create textures and space. Strands of fiber have been removed from the inked paper to create lines of patterns. Although

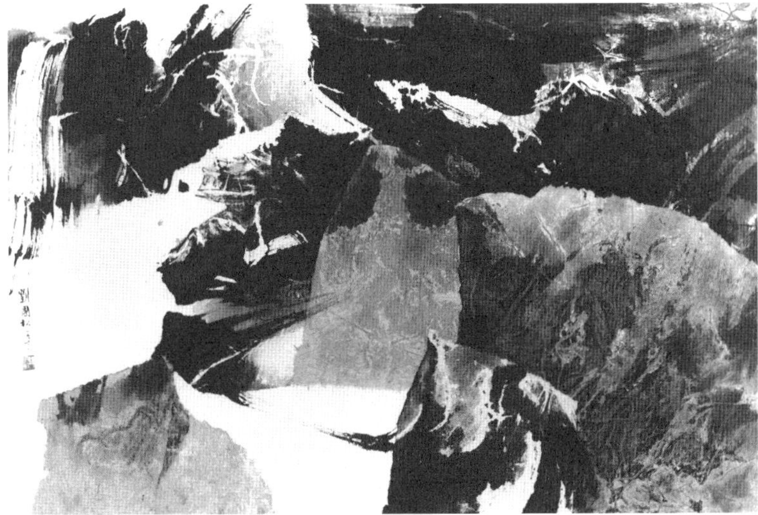

FIGURE 5
Liu Guosong (b. 1932). *Yellow and Gray: A Landscape*, 1968. Ink and color on paper, 23¾ × 36 in. (60.2 × 91.5 cm). Spencer Museum of Art, University of Kansas. Gift of the Ssu-ch'uan-k'o Collection

abstract in form, the painting evokes in its juxtaposition of shapes, colors, and textures the dynamic forces of the monumental landscape in traditional Chinese painting.

At the peak of Liu Guosong's success in the 1960s, the Nationalists in Taiwan were especially sensitive to the activities of the Cultural Revolution in China. Novel artistic expression was often wrongly accused of being inspired by the Communists, who were thought determined to undermine the traditional foundations of Chinese culture. Liu Guosong took part in a series of heated debates between the traditional thinkers and the more progressive critics regarding the direction of modern art. As a result of indirect political pressure, Liu finally left Taiwan in 1971 for a position at the Chinese University of Hong Kong. His works are exhibited internationally and, beginning in 1983, have been shown in several cities in China.

Although he had only an indirect influence on Liu Guosong, who uses traditional Chinese art as his point of departure in creating a style strongly suggesting Western influences, Pu Xinyu may have had a more direct influence on Jiang Zhaoshen, who sought to make innovations to landscape painting within the literati tradition. Born in Anhui in 1925, several years before Liu Guosong, Jiang Zhaoshen began his artistic development early in his childhood.[17] Trained in the traditional manner, he learned painting, calligraphy, and seal carving from several prominent literati friends of his family. After his formal education ended, when he dropped out of fourth grade in 1934, Jiang studied on his own. His writing skills and command of literature were already recognized early in his life. After moving to Taiwan with the Nationalists, he wrote a letter to Pu Xinyu in 1951, in which he asked Pu to accept him as a painting student. Pu responded:

> I have been traveling for some time and just now received your flattering request. To find calligraphy and essays of your quality in today's world is like seeing a phoenix in the heavens! [I do not want to accept you as a painting student because] I paint only for a living in the little time left over from my teaching duties. In reading your poems, however, I was impressed by the high path you had pursued and the refinement you had shown in both thoughts and diction. Should you come to Taipei, I would enjoy discussing with you poetry among other things.[18]

Thus, began a series of exchanges between Jiang Zhaoshen and Pu Xinyu.

Jiang Zhaoshen often referred to this initial correspondence with Pu Xinyu to point out that he did not actually study painting with him. Although his artistic debt to Pu cannot be clearly documented, his paintings and scholarly writings clearly suggest Pu's influence. Jiang became prominent in the art world following his appointment as associate research fellow at the National Palace Museum, Taipei, in 1965, after building a reputation for his research in art history. Interestingly, his earliest research was on the identity of Empress Yang Meizi (1162–1232), consort to the Southern Song emperor Ningzong (r. 1194–1224), and on the paintings of Ma Yuan. He then devoted several years to studying Tang Yin and Wen Zhengming, producing the most important studies on the two artists to date. In 1972 Jiang became the curator of painting and calligraphy at the National Palace Museum, and in the following years, organized the exhibition *Ninety Years of Wu School Painting*, which contributed greatly to the scholarship on Ming painting. Jiang served as vice-director of the National Palace Museum and continued painting until his death in 1996.

Jiang Zhaoshen never explicitly stated that it was Pu Xinyu who inspired his interest in the Ming artists Tang Yin and Wen Zhengming. But it seems too much of a coincidence that out of all the masters and masterpieces available for him to study at the National Palace Museum, he chose the two who were important for Pu's understanding of the past.

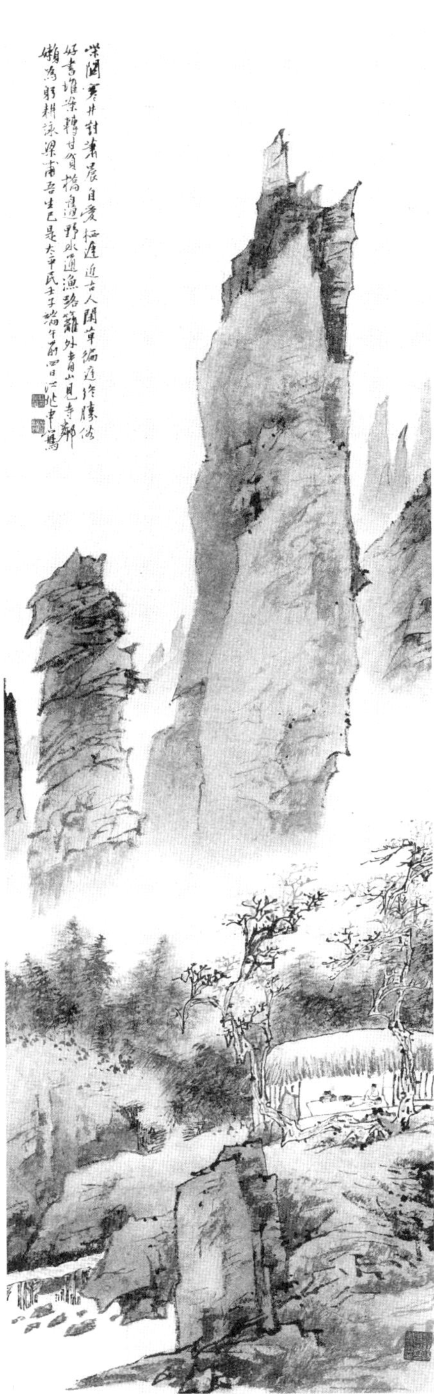

FIGURE 6
Jiang Zhaoshen (1925–1996). *Landscape*, 1972. Hanging scroll, ink and light color on paper, 37⅝ × 12½ in. (95.6 × 31.8 cm). Phoenix Art Museum. Gift of Jeannette Shambaugh Elliott

In addition to their shared interest in the Ming masters, the connection between Jiang Zhaoshen and Pu Xinyu can be discerned in the stylistic features of Jiang's landscape paintings. Recognized for both his creative and his scholarly works, Jiang was considered the foremost literati painter in Taiwan. Like most of his literati predecessors, however, he preferred to keep a low profile as a painter and be recognized instead for his scholarship in art history. Jiang has not had many one-man exhibitions in Taiwan, but his paintings are in great demand and command a high price. Many of his landscapes feature the subject of a scholar's studio-retreat, which was favored by the mid-Ming masters and by Pu Xinyu. His brush style reminds one of Pu's use of blunt and sharp edges in the Ma–Xia tradition.

Jiang's 1972 *Landscape* (fig. 6) illustrates his artistic kinship with Pu Xinyu. The painting, now in the Phoenix Art Museum, is closely related to several of Pu's landscapes discussed earlier in reference to the mid-Ming tradition. Like many of Pu's landscapes, Jiang's depiction of a scholar studying in his studio nestled in the mountains is reminiscent of works by mid-Ming artists, especially Wen Zhengming. The most notable element linking this painting to Pu's style is the tall and narrow mountains hovering over the rest of the composition, an arrangement that characterizes many of Pu's landscapes, such as *Autumn Colors and Verdant Peaks* (see fig. 4). In several of his other paintings as well, Jiang's blunt and angular brushwork is similar to Pu's.

The above discussion indicates to what extent Pu Xinyu influenced contemporary artists such as Liu Guosong and Jiang Zhaoshen. These are just two examples, however; the legacy of Pu's art can be seen in the paintings of many younger artists who worked, or still work, in the traditional mode. One of Pu's greatest contributions was the link he provided with the past; by reintroducing a style that had been ignored, Pu revitalized a tradition and put the past in proper perspective. Above all, Pu Xinyu provided a sense of history and continuity in the development of modern Chinese art. In the words of T.S. Eliot, an advocate of tradition as a context for modern criticism, there is an inseparable bond between the artist and the past:

> No poet, no artist of any art, has his complete meaning alone. His significance, his appreciation, is the appreciation of his relation to dead poets and artists. You cannot value him alone; you must set him, for contrast and comparison, among the dead.[19]

And, according to Eliot, the artist, no matter how "original" his works appear, is inevitably indebted to his predecessors:

> [W]e shall often find that not only the best, but the most individual parts of his work may be those in which the dead poets, his ancestors, assert their immortality most vigorously.[20]

Viewed from this perspective, the "most individual parts" in Pu's work are those elements in which his ancestors—such as Ma Yuan, Xia Gui, Tang Yin, and Wen Zhengming—"assert their immortality most vigorously." Finally, by transforming elements of the past into his own expression, Pu himself became a source of inspiration for later generations. Again, in Eliot's words:

> The existing monuments form an ideal order among themselves ... for order to persist after the supervention of novelty, the *whole* existing order must be, if ever so slightly, altered.[21]

As we see in the works of Liu Guosong and Jiang Zhaoshen, Pu made it possible for his followers and students to create innovative works out of the "existing order" within the traditional mode.

It has been over four decades since Pu Xinyu's death. The political situation in both "Chinas" has greatly altered since then, especially after 1978, when the People's Republic of China was recognized as the legitimate nation of China by the United States and consequently the rest of the world. Taiwan suddenly found itself a "non-nation" in world politics, and the development of art in Taiwan has since then either been slighted or neglected by many Western scholars. Yet, politics aside, the fact remains that art in Taiwan is an integral part of modern Chinese culture, and only by recognizing the significance of such artists as Pu Xinyu can we hope to gain a complete understanding of its development.

NOTES

1. Chou Ch'i-tzu n.d., 27–28.
2. Pu's art has also been the subject of scholarly studies. A recent example is the 1993 international conference on the art of Zhang Daqian and Pu Xinyu organized by the National Palace Museum, Taipei. See National Palace Museum, Taipei 1994.
3. This essay is excerpted from my dissertation. See Ju 1989.
4. Chow Tse-tsung 1960, 317.
5. Li 1979, 12.
6. Ibid.
7. Ibid.
8. Ho et al. 1980, 162.
9. Pu Xinyu listed the works that were in his collection in *Hualin yunye*, a two-volume collection of his writings, including anecdotes, stories, and commentaries on things he saw and read. See Pu Xinyu 1963.
10. Although it is not dated by inscription, the painting was probably done in the 1930s. F.Y. Chang acquired the work before 1949. Moreover, the style of inscription is similar to those written by Pu in the 1930s.
11. Lin Hsing-yu 1987, 15–72.
12. Lancashire 1982, 664.
13. Chiang Kai-shek 1957, 218, as quoted in Lancashire 1982, 663. By "unlimited war" Chiang meant the political and psychological warfare of the Communists; "limited war" referred to the military warfare of the Nationalists.
14. Lancashire 1982, 664.
15. Cathay Art Museum houses the collection of Tsai Chen-nan. As of October 1988, because of financial problems caused by the Tsai family corporate enterprises, Tsai's assets, including his art collection, were impounded by the Taiwan government. His art collection is now the property of a Taiwan bank.
16. The most extensive studies of Liu Guosong's work have been done by Chu-tsing Li. See, for example, Li 1969 and 1986.
17. *Jiang Zhaoshen zuopin ji* 1979, 90–93.
18. As quoted in ibid., 93.
19. Eliot 1971, 784.
20. Ibid.
21. Ibid., 784–85.

REFERENCES

Chiang Kai-shek. 1957. *Soviet Russia in China: A Summing-up at Seventy*. New York: Farrar, Straus and Cudahy.

Chou Ch'i-tzu. n.d. Zhongguo wenren hua de zui hou yi bi. *Wen Xing* 74: 27–28.

Chow Tse-tsung. 1960. *The May Fourth Movement: Intellectual Revolution in Modern China*. Cambridge: Harvard University Press.

Eliot, T. S. 1971. Tradition and the Individual Talent. In *Critical Theory Since Plato*, ed. Hazard Adams. New York: Harcourt Brace Jovanovich Publishers.

Ho, Wai-kam, Sherman E. Lee, Laurence Sickman, and Marc F. Wilson. 1980. *Eight Dynasties of Chinese Painting: The Collections of the Nelson Gallery-Atkins Museum, Kansas City and The Cleveland Museum of Art*. Cleveland: The Cleveland Museum of Art and Indiana University Press.

Jiang Zhaoshen zuopin ji. 1979. Taipei: Yunkang.

Ju, Jane C. 1989. The Art and Life of P'u Hsin-yü (1896–1963). PhD diss., University of Kansas.

Lancashire, Edel. 1982. Popeye and the Case of Guo Yidong, alias Bo Yang. *The China Quarterly* 92 (December).

Li, Chu-tsing. 1969. *Liu Guosong: The Growth of a Modern Chinese Artist*. Taipei: National Gallery of Art and Museum of History.

———. 1979. *Trends in Modern Chinese Painting*. Ascona, Switzerland: Artibus Asiae.

———. 1986. The Fifth Moon of Taiwan. *The Register of the Spencer Museum of Art*, vol. 6, no. 3.

Lin Hsing-yu. 1987. Taiwan meishu fengyun 40 nian. Taipei: Independent Evening Daily News.

National Palace Museum, Taipei. 1994. *Proceedings of the International Conference on the Poetry, Calligraphy, and Painting of Zhang Daqian and Pu Xinyu, June 21–23, 1993*.

Pu Xinyu. 1963. *Hualin yunye*. Taipei: Guangwen shu ji.

STUDIES IN HONOR OF CHU-TSING LI

The Inventor Wen-ying Tsai

SILIANG YANG

> Those who are inventors and interpreters between Nature and Man, compared with the reciters and trumpeters of the works of others, are to be considered simply as is an object in front of a mirror in comparison with its image when seen in the mirror, the one being something in itself, the other nothing.
>
> Leonardo da Vinci[1]

The ingeniously intricate works of the artist Wen-ying Tsai (b. 1928) are the result of a unique artistic vision as well as a sophisticated use of electronic instruments. In these works, which he describes as "cybernetic sculptures," Tsai has successfully combined art and science in the belief that these two disciplines are not opposites but that each is a component of the other.[2]

Tsai views this mutual interdependence of art and science as an "artistic attitude toward science and technology."[3] It can also be called a "scientific attitude toward art." While people today might find the notion peculiar, it was nothing new to Leonardo da Vinci and other Renaissance masters, for whom there was no demarcation between art and science. To them, art (*arte*) meant skill, and science (*scientia*) meant knowledge, both of which were needed for creation.[4] Leonardo emphasized that the creation of painting had to rely on knowledge. To him, it was the ignorance of this fact—that there was no art without science—which accounted for the low esteem in which his profession was often held. Leonardo did not want his work to be regarded as crafts, but rather to be classified among the Liberal Arts, which were based on knowledge. He loathed being thought of as merely an artist or craftsman; he regarded himself as an inventor, in the mold of the Creator, whose mission was to create something that did not exist before.[5]

The separation of art and science began with the rise of Romanticism in the late eighteenth century. The division of labor and the ever-increasing demand for specialization in the industrialized world made it easy to accept this separation. Science and art quickly came to be seen as two distinct, almost rival, disciplines. In the late nineteenth century, the tremendous achievements of science changed the world, while art, by contrast, appeared to be falling behind. Artists nevertheless wanted to take part in the task of changing society. Perhaps the most ambitious in this respect were the Cubists, who theorized that, to change the world, all one needed to do was to change the way one saw the world. This theory led Cubists to

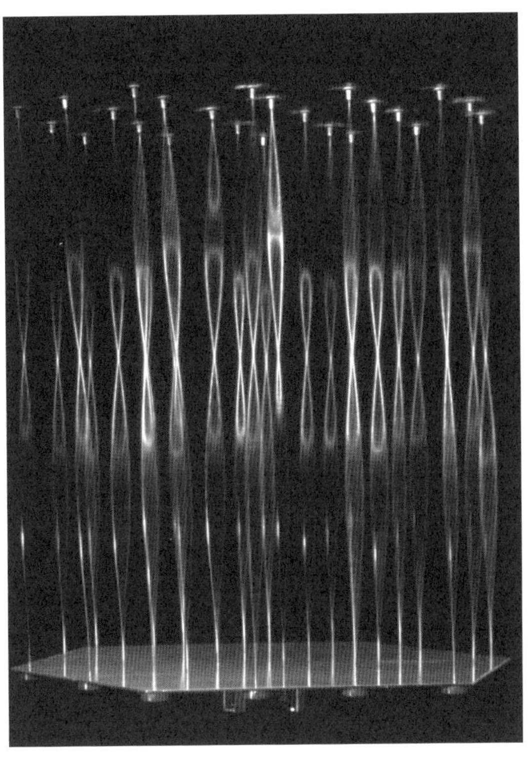

FIGURE 1
Wen-ying Tsai (b. 1928). *Harmonic Sculpture.* 1969. Stainless steel rods with square mirror tops, vibrator, 43 × 22½ × 19 in. (109.2 × 57.2 × 48.3 cm). Museo de Arte Contemporaneo, Caracas

create fragmented and abstracted paintings of three-dimensional reality. Although Cubist painting has been in existence for almost a century, we still do not see the world in a Cubist way, for the Cubist representation of three-dimensionality contradicts our natural way of seeing. The artists themselves were in fact aware of the limitations of their method, which is why they only painted ordinary and familiar objects, such as violins, guitars, and human figures. Cubism came into vogue not because it had helped to change the world or our way of seeing the world, but because of the false critical notion that art should progress as science had.[6]

Art does not progress in the same way as science, but an artist's skill can improve through the study of science. That they have taken for granted the separation of art and science may account for the fact that few modern artists have attained the level of achievement of the Renaissance masters, which no doubt has frustrated their aspirations. Wen-ying Tsai was one of those frustrated artists. After he won the John Hay Whitney Opportunity Fellowship for painting in 1963, Tsai gave up his career as an engineer to become a professional artist. Though he had more time to paint, he could not produce anything on canvas. "I was full of ideas, but I could not find a way to express myself in the old medium. I felt like building something by hand. I felt that if I were to be a whole person, I would have to combine art with science and technology. I would have to combine them, or I wouldn't be happy."[7]

Tsai's search for a new medium of expression is easy to understand: painting has had its glorious past, and anyone engaged in it has to compete, directly or indirectly, with his predecessors. Moreover, traditional painting has inherent limitations. Even though perspective allows the emulation of a three-dimensional world in a two-dimensional format, painting is limited in its capacity to represent movement. If the invention of the camera posed a serious challenge to realist art, the popularity of television posed an equally serious challenge to static images. People have become so used to seeing images in motion that static images may strike them as lacking something. This is perhaps why painting cannot satisfy the aesthetic demands of the contemporary world as it did in previous times. Artists must come up with new solutions in order to fulfill the expectations of a new society.

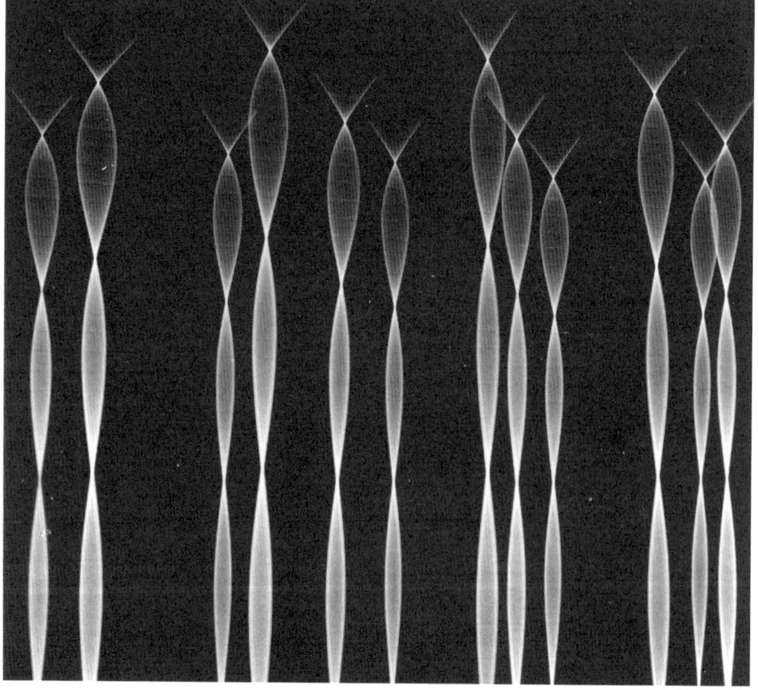

FIGURE 2
Wen-ying Tsai (b. 1928). *Cybernetic Sculpture Fiber Glass.* 1979/1989. Fiber glass, electronic audio feedback control system and stroboscopic light, vibrators, 7 units: 10 × 12 × 10 ft. (3.04 × 3.65 × 3.04 m); 5 units: 17 × 12 × 10 ft. (5.18 × 3.65 × 3.04 m). Taiwan Museum of Art, Taichung

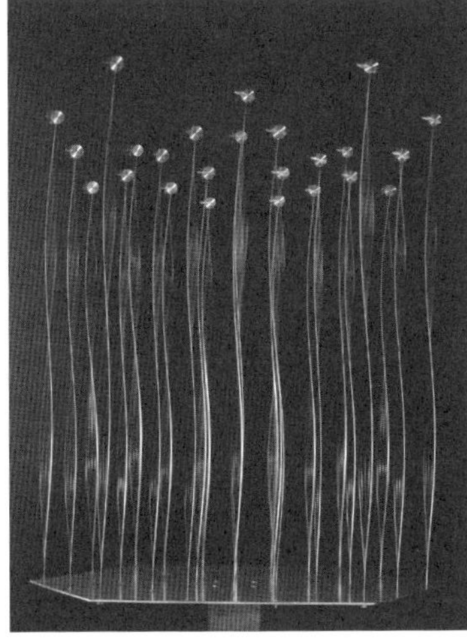

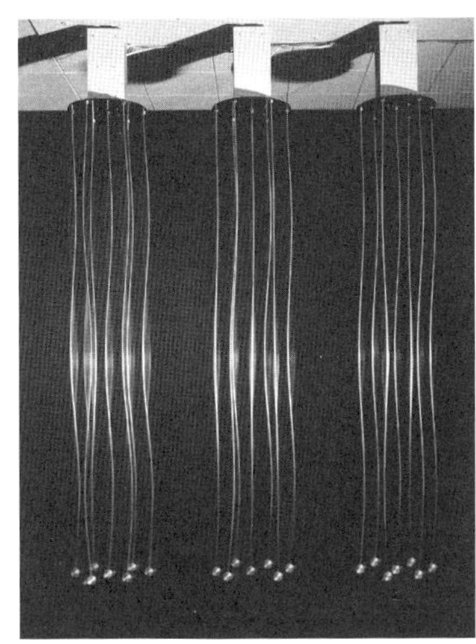

FIGURE 3
Wen-ying Tsai (b. 1928). *Double Level Diffraction*. 1971. Stainless steel rods with diffraction discs, electronic audio feedback control system and stroboscopic light, vibrator, 52 × 29 × 25 in. (132.1 × 73.7 × 63.5 cm). Centre Georges Pompidou, Paris

FIGURE 4
Wen-ying Tsai (b. 1928). *Suspended Cybernetic Sculpture*, 1979. Stainless steel rods with diffraction discs, vibrators, 96 × 60 × 12 in. (243.8 × 152.4 × 30.5 cm). Collection of the artist

In a sense, Leonardo was faced with the same problem. Many people believed that painting had reached its apex in the work of his contemporary Perugino. Leonardo knew that if he were to surpass Perugino, he had to create something new. He not only applied the advanced method of perspective in his painting, but continuously experimented with new methods and techniques. Indeed, he called himself a "disciple of experience."[8] Through his experiments, Leonardo achieved what most artists could only dream of achieving. For hundreds of years artists have imitated Leonardo, but none have come close to attaining his fame. A major reason they have not is that they are merely "artists."

Wen-ying Tsai differs from the majority of these followers. He is not merely an artist, but received thorough training in engineering as well as in painting. He also worked for ten years as a professional engineer. More importantly, he understands the true spirit of artistic creation. Like Leonardo, he uses the most advanced technology to express his vision, his imagination, and his feelings.[9] In modern terminology, Tsai uses science and technology to achieve artistic beauty.

Tsai is not an expressionist, least of all an abstract expressionist, although his works do possess abstract beauty. Unlike so many expressionists (and many modern artists), Tsai does not regard self-expression as the ultimate goal of art. Rather, he believes that inspiration is the first step toward artistic creation. In order to give shape to his artistic vision, he works more than sixteen hours every day. He prefers working during the night because, he says, it is easier to concentrate one's thought in the quiet of the night. Each of Tsai's "electrifying" works is the result of years of such disciplined work, of constant trial and error, and of tireless making and matching. As if this strict creation process were not enough to ensure perfection, Tsai puts each of his finished pieces through yet another test. When a work is technically completed, he sets it up in the studio for several months, and looks at it every day. If, and only if, he still judges it a satisfactory piece will he let it leave his hands.

Self-criticism is only one way to ensure success. Even more important is a refined taste, which comes from self-cultivation. Only when one has experienced beauty in the mind is it possible to recreate that beauty in one's work. Tsai's training as an engineer taught him the importance of self-criticism; his Chinese education taught him the importance of self-cultivation. In order to acquire a discriminating taste, Tsai visited many museums around the world. Because his works require knowledge and experience of movement, he took dance lessons from Erick Hawkins, the pioneering choreographer of modern dance, not with the intention of becoming a dancer but to experience "kinesthesia, the sensation of movement" and the "resonant vitality" of the human body.[10] The dancing lessons paid off. Many of his cybernetic works vividly express the beauty of human movement. *Harmonic Sculpture* (fig. 1) and *Cybernetic Sculpture Fiber Glass* (fig. 2), for example, reveal the kind of resonant vitality and gracefulness often seen in choreography, especially in Chinese folk dance.[11] The lifeless rods suddenly become elegant dancers; moments

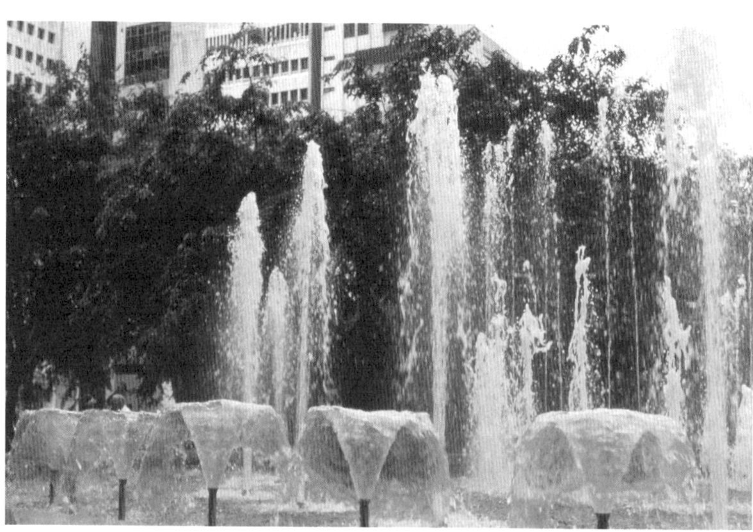

FIGURE 5
Wen-ying Tsai (b. 1928). *Cybernetic Water Sculpture, Shell Tower*, 1982. Water jets, submersible pumps, electronic audio feedback control system, and lights, 35 ft. (10.66 m) radius fan shape × 60 × 30 ft. (18.28 × 9.14 m). Commissioned by Singapore Land, Singapore

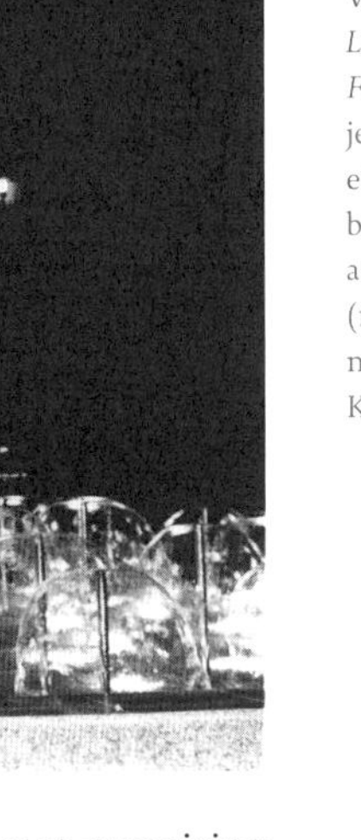

FIGURE 6
Wen-ying Tsai (b. 1928). Wing-ying Tsai and *Landmark Cybernetic Fountain*. 1980. Water jets, submersible pumps, electronic audio feedback control system, and lights, 34 × 50 ft. (10.36 × 15.24 m). Commissioned by Hong Kong Land, Hong Kong

later, they are transformed into *gongfu* performers. It is not surprising that Tsai's works have been used by choreographers and composers in theatrical performances.[12]

Nature is another source of inspiration for Tsai. He has remarked that he was inspired to create his vibrating sculptures by the sight of sunbeams shimmering through forest leaves at the Edward MacDowell Colony in New Hampshire.[13] Today, at the age of seventy-six, he still takes time to get close to nature. Many of his works evoke the movements of plants in nature. *Double Level Diffraction* (fig. 3) and *Suspended Cybernetic Sculpture* (fig. 4) are two such examples. Standing in front of these works, one can imagine bamboo waving in the wind, lotuses dancing in a pond, or irises swaying gently in the breeze. Unlike the living plants, Tsai's floral machines keep producing new blossoms, and the viewer is amazed at the magical wonder of Tsai's technological art and the nature it represents.

Movement alone cannot reproduce the wonders of life. Repeated mechanical movements will soon result in viewer expectations that will diminish interest. Tsai's works maintain continuous interest not only because they move gracefully, but also because the movements are unpredictable. For instance, in *Harmonic Sculpture* (see fig. 1) and *Cybernetic Sculpture Fiber Glass* (see fig. 2), we see the "dancers" performing various balancing movements in the air. Just when we think we know what they are going to do next, they make an unexpected movement, like an acrobat's breathtaking leap to another swinging rope or a circus rider's daring jumps on a galloping horse. Performances of such skilled movement are beyond the capability of ordinary people, so they surprise us and elicit admiration. Art becomes inspiring and exciting only when it reaches a level that we normally cannot ourselves reach; at that level, we are so filled with admiration of the dynamic presentation that we forget we are viewing a work of art, as we often forget that Tsai's works are made of lifeless rods. These rods become so full of life that they bring many familiar images to mind, and yet at the same time surpass our imagination and expectations.

Many of Wen-ying Tsai's works use water as a medium. Water is the most basic and ordinary element in nature, and yet it is one of the most symbolic and enchanting. In Daoism, water is associated with the Dao (the Way) because "water knows how to benefit all things without striving with them."[14] In Confucianism, water is a symbol of wisdom, virtue, and high moral character, for Confucius once said that "wisdom delights in water."[15] The natural characteristics of water—it can flow softly and gently, yet wear away the hardest of rocks; it is pure and cool and gives life to myriad things; it is forever in motion, like time—have made water one of the most often used motifs in poetry and painting. Water is a fitting motif for Tsai not only because of its rich symbolism, but also because it has been so closely associated with his own life. Tsai was born in Amoy

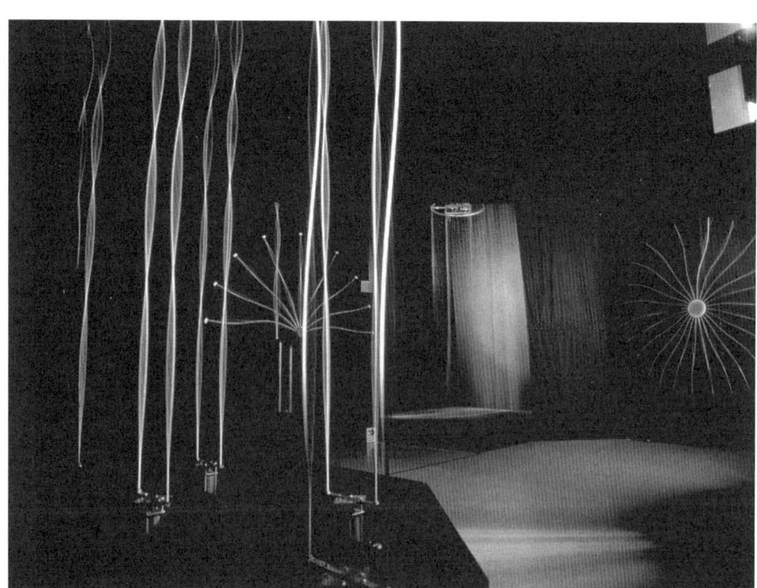

FIGURE 7
Wen-ying Tsai (b. 1928). *Desert Spring*, 1991. Mixed media installation, 18 × 25 × 30 ft. (5.48 × 7.62 × 9.14 m). Nagoya City Art Museum

(Xiamen), later moved to Shanghai, and eventually settled in New York, all seaside cities. He also lived and worked for several years in Paris, along the River Seine. Water is an inseparable part of Tsai's art, as seen in his *Cybernetic Water Sculpture, Shell Tower* (fig. 5), *Landmark Cybernetic Fountain* (fig. 6), and *Desert Spring* (fig. 7). In *Upward Falling Fountain* (fig. 8), the water and the strobe lights, and the various colors produced by their interaction, create an endless spiral of rainbows, much like twilight reflected on waves. Unlike in nature, however, Tsai's water responds directly to human action. If the viewer claps, shouts, or walks toward the work, the water forming the spiral rainbows will move upward. This interaction between the viewer and the work of art, made possible by sonic and light induction, explains why Tsai's works do not appear threatening as do some electronic devices. Its ability to respond to the audience is in fact the essence of Tsai's work.

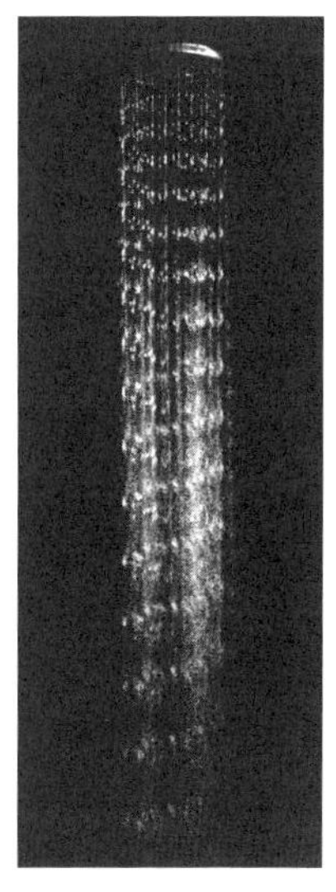

FIGURE 8
Wen-ying Tsai (b. 1928). *Upward Falling Fountain*, 1979. Recirculating water, electronic audio feedback control system and stroboscopic light, vibrators. Collection of the artist

Words cannot adequately convey the charm and beauty of Wen-ying Tsai's work. Nor can photographs, for just as one note of a symphony cannot convey the whole, photographs can capture only single moments of the infinite images Tsai's works generate. He has on occasion explained his works,[16] but for those of us who do not share his technological background, the explanations make little sense. The only way to know his work is to see it. Aware of the limitations of language and photography, Tsai has attempted through his numerous exhibitions to make his work accessible to a wide audience. He continues to create works, motivated by the desire to expand his vision and reach the ultimate goal of perfection.

NOTES

1. MacCurdy 1958, 57.

2. Sam Hunter wrote that Tsai's work "achieves a subtle amalgam of art and technology that makes the impossible not just convincing, but overwhelmingly seductive." See Hunter 1989, 59. Jonathan Benthall stated that Tsai operates "in the no-man's land between art and science." See Benthall 1989, 82.

3. Ruan Beikang and Ouyang Yingzhi 1980, 177. The interview with Wenying Tsai, on November 3, 1978, was first published in *South and North Poles* 107 (April 16, 1979). In this interview, Tsai articulates in detail his ideas on art and technology.

4. See Gombrich 1989, 1–4. The word "art," as in the "art of war," usually connotes skill. The meaning of "art" as something created for aesthetic purposes and basically without social functions came about with the rise of Romanticism in the eighteenth century; see Abrams 1953. In China, the word art (*yi*) usually means skill and aptitude. In Confucius' time, *yi* was considered as important as the Dao (Way) or Virtue or Benevolence. In the mid-nineteenth century *yi* came to include the Western notion of "fine art." The word "science" did not have an equivalent in ancient China. The Chinese borrowed the Western term from Japan after 1919.

5. It was due to this ambition that Leonardo devoted his life to the study of so many different subjects, including anatomy, physiology, optics, astrology, medicine, acoustics, botany, and hydraulics. This ambition seems to have been widespread among Renaissance masters. Donatello (1386–1466), for example, used to shout at his sculpture, "speak, speak, speak!" The human desire to endow man's creations with life can be traced back at least to the myth of Pygmalion.

6. For an analysis of Cubist art, see Rosenblum 1961. See also Golding 1988.

7. Ruan Beikang and Ouyang Yingzhi 1980, 172.

8. Kemp 1989, 12. Gombrich observed that in Leonardo's notes there is no clear distinction between "experience" and "experiment." See Gombrich 1989, 2.

9. These technologies include cybernetic principles, feedback theory, optical principles, and visual perceptual psychology.

10. Woodford 1987, 10.

11. Although he studied dance with a Western teacher, Tsai's art reflects the tradition of Chinese dance and the influence of his Oriental heritage.

12. In 1974 Tsai created a "cybernetic theater" in collaboration with the composer Chou Wen-chung and the choreographer Chiang Ching at Hunter Playhouse in New York, the first production of its kind. Later, Tsai created a group of sculptural works for the Chiang Ching Dance Company, with financial support from The National Endowment for the Arts.

13. Woodford 1987, 8.

14. Laozi, *Daode jing*, chap. 8.

15. Confucius, *Analects*, chap. 6: "The Master said: 'Wisdom delights in water. Benevolence delights in mountains. Wisdom is moving, benevolence is quiet. Wisdom enjoys life, benevolence enjoys longevity.'" The Neo-Confucian philosopher Zhu Xi (1130–1200) elaborated on this: "People of wisdom understand the principles of things and will not let themselves be limited in one place, just like water, so they delight in water. The benevolent people are at ease

with the principles and are not easily moved [persuaded], just like mountains, so they delight in mountains." Zhu Xi, *Si shu ji zhu*, chap. 6.

16. Tsai explained the technological principles of his works in his patent for "Invention of Upward Falling Fountain." See *Cybernetic Art of Tsai Wen Ying* 1989, 103 and Ruan Beikang and Ouyang Yingzhi 1980, 164–66.

REFERENCES

Abrams, M.H. 1953. *The Mirror and the Lamp: Romantic Theory and the Critical Tradition.* New York: Oxford University Press.

Benthall, Jonathan. 1989. Cybernetic Art of Tsai. In *Cybernetic Art of Tsai Wen Ying.* Taipei: National Museum of History.

Cybernetic Art of Tsai Wen Ying. 1989. Taipei: National Museum of History.

Golding, John. 1988. *Cubism: A History and an Analysis, 1907–1914.* 3rd edition. Cambridge: Harvard University Press.

Gombrich, E.H. 1989. Preface. In *Leonardo da Vinci.* New Haven: Yale University Press.

Hunter, Sam. 1989. The Cybernetic Sculpture of Wen-ying Tsai. In *Cybernetic Art of Tsai Wen Ying.* Taipei: National Museum of History.

Kemp, Martin. 1989. Disciple of Experience. In *Leonardo da Vinci.* New Haven: Yale University Press.

MacCurdy, Edward, ed. 1958. *The Notebooks of Leonardo da Vinci.* 2nd edition. New York: George Braziller.

Rosenblum, Robert. 1961. *Cubism and 20th-Century Art.* New York: Abrams.

Ruan Beikang and Ouyang Yingzhi. 1980. *Interviews with Scholars.* Hong Kong.

Woodford, John. 1987. The Electrifying Artist: Engineering Grad Wen-ying Tsai. *Michigan Today* 19, no. 1 (February).

STUDIES IN HONOR OF CHU-TSING LI

A Century of Change in Chinese Art

TSENG YUHO ECKE

Although we had known of each other long before, I first met Chu-tsing Li in the summer of 1970 in Taipei, where we were both speakers at the first major international symposium on Chinese painting. The 1960s had been exciting years in Chinese art studies; universities and museums outside mainland China were bursting then with exhibitions and research projects. This conference, sponsored by the National Palace Museum, Taipei, was the first to be held on Chinese soil, and was enriched by its participants' access to many of the finest masterpieces from the imperial collections that comprise the holdings of the National Palace Museum. The meeting was attended by the most noted international Chinese art historians and artists, young and old. Collegial spirit was high; participants were buoyed by the feeling that Chinese art scholarship had truly become international. Since that time, many more such conferences have been held and, with the end of the Cultural Revolution in 1976, art scholars from the People's Republic of China have joined the worldwide research community.

In the early part of the century, however, the situation was much different. China had failed to attain stability in the decades following the overthrow of the imperial system in 1912. The disorder of a long period of warlordism was followed by the eruption of war with Japan in 1937 and eight long years of Japanese aggression. When the war came to an end, in 1945, the country was divided by two implacable political rivals, resulting in the establishment of the Republic of China on Taiwan and the People's Republic of China on the mainland. The country endured, but peace seemed tenuous and prosperity elusive. For several decades, most mainland Chinese lived in poverty, and art was placed at the service of politics.

Chinese painting has always had, at least since the Song (960–1279) period, a close relationship with state authority. While the imperial court greatly influenced the painting tradition of China in its support of court and academy painters, most creative thinkers chose to withdraw from political engagement. This group of educated elite, who retreated from official life to pursue the study of art and moral self-cultivation, came to represent a mainstream component of the Chinese art tradition. When hostilities ceased between the "two Chinas" in the mid-twentieth century, art again was promoted by political authorities. On my first visit to Taiwan, in the 1960s, I met the Fifth Moon group of artists. They were boldly exploring new art forms and were indignant at being disapproved of and ignored by the authorities. They were not persecuted, however, as were their colleagues on the mainland who did not toe the correct ideological line.

The laments of the Fifth Moon artists brought to mind my years in Beijing in the 1930s. Cai Yuanpei (1868–1940) had been appointed Minister of Education in the newly established government and was advocating direct exchanges in the arts between East and West. Leading artists like Xu Beihong (1895–1953) and Lin Fengmian (1900–1991) returned to China after their studies abroad and established national art academies. They were young and compelling and emphatically denounced the deteriorated state of the Chinese painting tradition. Their criticism was tolerated and widely disseminated. Indeed, they were supported by the state; opposition to their views came overwhelmingly from the established art community. Especially in conservative Beijing, there were heated debates and open fights over the direction of Chinese art. Discussion focused on what was "Chinese" and what was "modern"; should the "classical" be preserved, or was an "infusion" of Western methods needed to revivify it? Could art employing such "new" techniques still be considered Chinese? Answers to these questions became a matter of national pride. That was the 1930s, but those debates continue today.

The years marched on, and with the prosperity of the 1970s and 1980s came advances in technology and communications. The political establishments, economies, educational systems, and lifestyles of nations worldwide were transformed, and the pace continues unabated. Cultural borders were breaking down; mass media continued its relentless creation of a mass culture. China, although initially hobbled by its allegiance to its glorious history and traditions, rushed to catch up. Looking back on a century of precarious existence and cultural deprivation, the younger generation had no time for the past; it looked only to the future.

The generational gap that had been created was great. Once restrictions on artistic activities were lifted inside China, tremendous change took place. In the second half of the twentieth century the artist population exploded; fueled by accumulated resentment, these artists energetically incorporated in their work messages of social protest. Their work began attracting interest in the worldwide art market, and, by the 1990s, commercial galleries were eagerly seeking new work from them.

But this was history repeating itself. Imperial China was as totalitarian as the nation was under Mao. There was no freedom of speech, so Chinese artists and writers developed a complex metaphorical system through which to communicate. Painters rarely showed their contempt openly, even though they loathed hypocrisy as much as the anti-establishment artists of today. Instead, they expressed themselves through the selection and juxtaposition of the subjects they portrayed as well as the techniques used to render them; using these devices, they accumulated and exploited a complex system of references that were transparent to the educated elite. In the tenth century, Chinese landscape painting had already begun evolving into a highly stylized form; calligraphy had moved toward abstraction with an advanced aesthetic as early as the fourth century. The nuances these forms made possible exceeded those of simple symbolism, and were able even to convey emotional and metaphysical experiences. When mastered by the literati, these were powerful tools. On one level, a work by Zhang Jizhi (1186–1266) or Hongren (1610–1664) might appear idyllic, even esoteric, while on another level it eloquently delivered a pointed message. A gifted master such as Huaisu (725–785) or Zhu Da (1626–1705) could be extremely evocative and powerful.

Inevitably, the international community "discovered" Eastern aesthetics. Japanese prints were a major influence on pictorial design in nineteenth-century France; the seemingly abstract forms of calligraphy and Zen ink painting were appropriated in support of new metaphysical and psychological theories of art. Painters such as Kandinsky and Klee found that line alone could embody and convey the emotional content of color and form. Pictorial representation gave way to enlightenment as a goal of art, and images were condensed to abstraction and preoccupied with suggestiveness. Along with a revival of Zen (Chan) art came an exaggeration in gesture and delivery, as in the art of Jackson Pollock and Pierre Soulages. While classic Zen art was an exercise in introspection, the acclaimed avant-garde chose to explode from the inside out, attacking the accepted with the abnormal and confronting the commonplace with the absurd. The presentation of art became an end in itself; by the late 1990s the cutting edge in most media was verging on performance art.

Was I surprised by the dramatic changes in China? Not really. I have lived for more than fifty years in the open society of the American art world. My professional activities have ranged from museum work to teaching art history at the university level. I have also continued to be active as a creative artist, thus keeping an open mind and remaining alert to current movements and innovations in the arts, in Europe and the Far East as well as in the United States. I am thus a part of the history of art in the last half century. This was a period during which the dissemination of visual images expanded exponentially, from stage to cinema, television, and personal video. Technology has made possible the ready manipulation of images, such as photographic prints, posters, computer-generated and -enhanced materials, for decorative, educational, or promotional use by anyone. Painting for painting's sake has been pushed into a corner and will be squeezed more so in the decades to come. Aside from the overwhelming commercialism of art, we will see more political and social messages. Art with a purely creative function will always be hanging precariously from the tail of more practical economic and political agendas.

During the critical period when artists in both Chinas were struggling for survival, Michael Sullivan was the first art historian to give serious consideration to the "new" Chinese painting. His *Chinese Art in the Twentieth Century*, published in 1959, gave the field a much-needed lift. Next to Professor Sullivan, I would say that Chu-tsing Li was the most vigorous supporter of contemporary Chinese painting. Professor Li and I are about the same age, and we both came to the United States from China and have taught in American universities. I have followed his academic career and noted that he has always rigorously maintained his academic objectivity and spoken from the perspective of a well-grounded art historian. He has readily supported grants for exchange scholarships and assisted artists in exhibiting. We have worked on many projects together, including the installation of the Fifth Moon exhibition at the Honolulu Academy of Arts, arranged for visiting lecturers at Hawaii, consulted on student theses, and introduced our art collections to graduate students. Like a father figure he gently chaperoned students engaged in field research, assigning them responsibilities and providing opportunities to gain practical experience.

Professor Li's former students now occupy positions in art centers in a number of countries, and many have maintained an interest in contemporary Chinese works. I have participated in several conferences in Hong Kong on contemporary Chinese painting for which Professor Li acted as a consultant, and another in Vancouver that was organized by his graduate students. All of these conferences have provided participating artists a chance for exposure as well as critical self-examination. Through all of these activities I have come to know Professor Li as a rare scholar of the highest integrity. His accomplishments as an earnest shepherd of Chinese art and art historical studies make him a major contributing figure to the growth and appreciation of Chinese painting in the twentieth century.

STUDIES IN HONOR OF CHU-TSING LI

A Case Study of Continuity in Buddhist Art: Origins of the *Attack of Mara* at Dunhuang

SARAH BLICK

Although it has lost esteem among art historians, pure visual analysis is still useful in calling attention to the larger issues of cultural influence and artistic exchange. This essay explores through visual analysis the remarkable continuity of a particular composition of the *Attack of Mara*, which originated in India, was developed further in Central Asia, and was later adapted in the cave temples of Dunhuang, in northwest China, during the Six Dynasties period (220–589). While Indian influence on Chinese Buddhist art has long been accepted, it has not been fully explored. Visual analysis of the *Attack of Mara* illustrates how a composition whose specific iconography and general meaning were created centuries before in India came to be used repeatedly thousands of miles away in the far western reaches of China. This composition not only established the formula for the placement of particular elements, but dictated what was to be emphasized or omitted from the narrative it depicted.

THE TEXTUAL BASIS

Images of the *Attack of Mara*—a visualization of all the fears and temptations which Shakyamuni, the historical Buddha, had to overcome to reach enlightenment—that spread from India to China might be said to have derived from common textual sources, but these sources, principally sutras, vary in their depiction of the story of the *Attack of Mara*, and even the most descriptive passages do not specify the placement of the participants.[1] The oldest surviving account of Buddha's life, in the *Pali Canon*,[2] describes the mortal Shakyamuni sitting alone under the bodhi tree. During the night he meditated, reaching higher and higher levels of understanding and enlightenment; by dawn, Shakyamuni, having reached enlightenment and become the Buddha, understood the Four Noble Truths and the Eightfold Path.[3] In this early account of his enlightenment, he confronted no physical demons, except those that dwelt within him.

Only in later texts, such as the *Buddhacarita*, *Mahavastu*, and *Lalitavistara*, does the *Attack* become a cacophonous battle[4]—not just a struggle by one man to overcome inner evil, but a struggle for the fate of the entire world (see Appendix). Mara,[5] who leads the attack, is a "personification of evil and death and of the whole Samsara"[6] and "thus a figure peculiar to Buddhism."[7] He is also seen as a lord of pleasure, in opposition to enlightenment.[8] Mara first tries unsuccessfully to dissuade Shakyamuni by soft words. He then sends out his lovely daughters to seduce the chaste

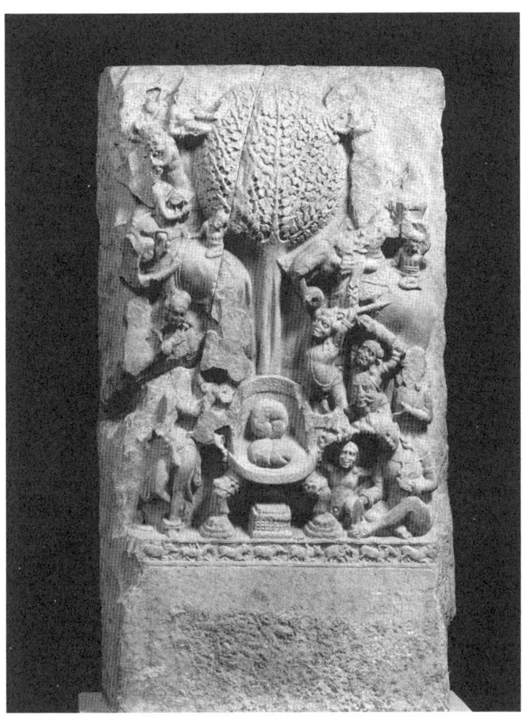

FIGURE 1
Cushioned Throne with the Assault of Mara. School of Amaravati, Andhra period, late 2nd century. Relief, marble. Musée Guimet, Paris

Shakyamuni, but Shakyamuni overcomes this temptation. Then, Mara calls on his host, or demon assistants, to help him destroy Shakyamuni.

Mara's host, demons who personify evil and are linked to demon spirits called *yaksas* (terrible spirits), *raksases* (animal-shaped goblins), and *pisacas* (cannibals),[9] have the ability to possess people, assume forms of animals or reptiles, and appear as human beings. They threaten Shakyamuni, throwing weapons and screaming, but he is unaffected.[10] He resists these enemies through "total passivity"[11] and becomes enlightened. Through enlightenment, the Buddha has conquered death (the literal meaning of Mara's name), the ultimate evil—for him and his followers no new death will follow upon this life's death. Touching the earth as a witness, Buddha says upon his enlightenment, "You are overcome, O death."

INDIAN DEPICTIONS

Inspired by these texts, Indian artists created a compelling composition[12] which conflated the separate stages of the *Attack*. This schema, once codified, would survive more than seven centuries and spread throughout Asia. The earliest extant example of the schema is a late second-century marble slab from Amaravati[13] in which the Buddha is represented as an aniconic throne under the bodhi tree. The throne is placed in the center of the composition, forming a focal point around which Mara's frenzied demon attendants move in diagonals (fig. 1). The artist, in an attempt to depict the figures receding into space, piles up the creatures vertically, filling the space around the central focal point. The attendants are *yaksas*-type creatures with sharp fangs and pointed ears; one is shown with a *udare-mukha* (face on the belly),[14] a supernatural trait that appears exclusively in *Attack* scenes. Mara's sensual daughters are shown dancing to the right of the bodhi tree, but the representation of Mara himself is unclear; he might be either the figure riding the elephant or the man seated at the lower left.[15] The schema focuses on the conflict between Shakyamuni and Mara's host, relegating the threat of Mara and his daughters to minor incidents.

What most captured Indian artists' imaginations, however, was the struggle between Shakyamuni and Mara's demon attendants. This is evident in the *Assault of Mara's Host*, a Gandharan relief from the second century (fig. 2).[16] Not only is it difficult to identify Mara, but Mara's daughters are eliminated altogether.[17] This relief copies the Amaravati composition (see fig. 1), except that here the figures are arrayed in horizontal rows, replacing the sense of active conflict with that of impending threat.

The Gandharan frieze adds narrative elements to the standard schema, aligning them along the top and the bottom. One creature at the top right prepares to hurl down an enormous rock on the meditating Shakyamuni,[18] while at the base of the throne sprawl defeated human soldiers.[19] The animal-headed monsters (described in later sutras) are also additions. Creatures with heads of boars, goats, and monkeys dominate the upper half of the composition, and human figures in battle dress are lined up across the bottom. These different narrative details increase the menace of the *Attack*, while simultaneously showing Buddha's triumph over his enemies. The two princely Indian figures flanking the Buddha probably represent the image of Mara; the figures dressed in Roman-style armor and tunics may be Mara's sons.[20]

The composition and its specific iconography were codified sometime during the fifth century. In a relief from Cave 26 in Ajanta, dated to the end

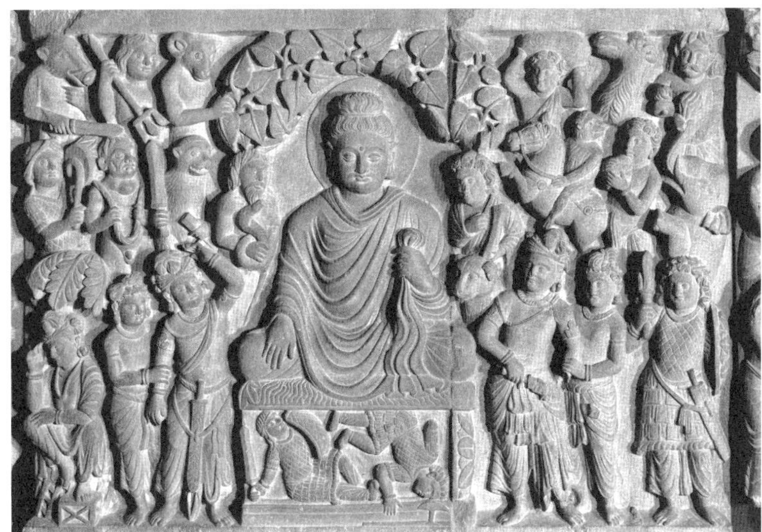

FIGURE 2
Assault of Mara's Host. Gandhara, 2nd century. Courtesy of the Freer Gallery of Art, Smithsonian Institution, Washington, D.C.

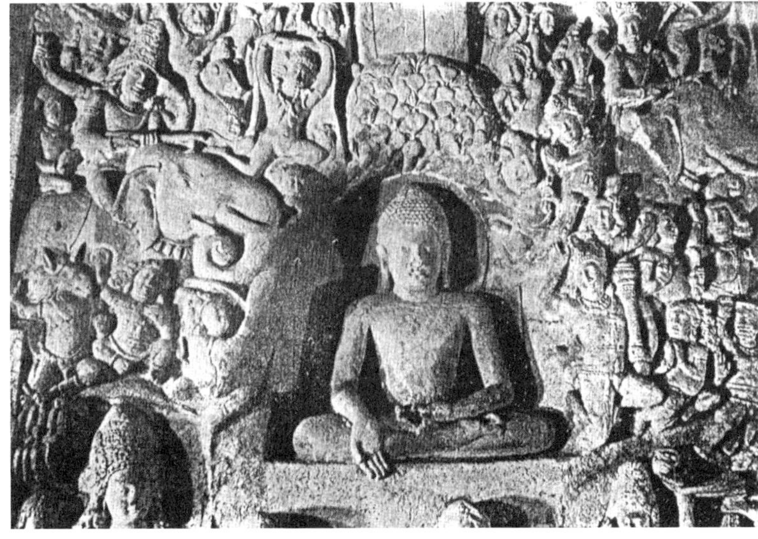

FIGURE 3
Maradharshana and Enlightenment. Ajanta, Cave 26, late 5th century. From Parimoo 1982, fig. 29

of the fifth century, Shakyamuni still sits in the center, safely ensconced within his cavelike niche made of leaves from the bodhi tree (fig. 3).[21] Surrounding him are a vast array of demons, some of which have recognizable animal heads, while others are hybrids of several animal species. The Ajanta artists use a more complete *udare-mukha*, with ears, eyebrows, and beard (as seen at the upper left). The relief shows two figures at the top of the composition preparing to hurl down huge rocks; at the base of the

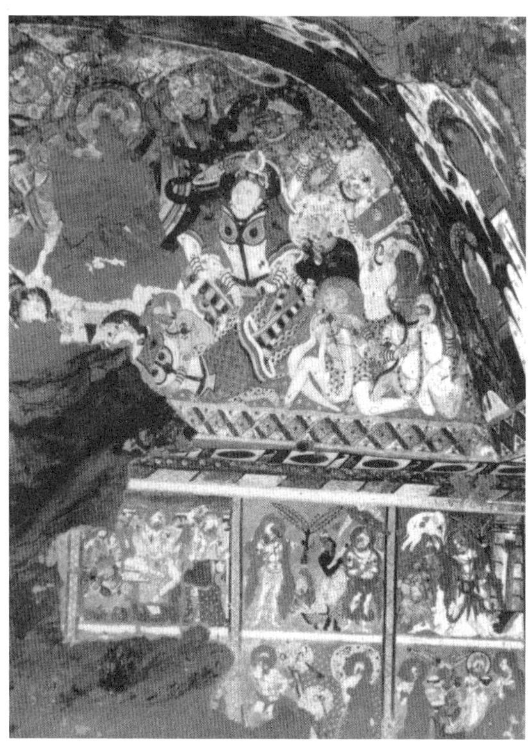

FIGURE 4
The Attack of Mara.
Kizil, Stairs Cave, 600–50. Staatliche Museen zu Berlin-Preussischer Kulturbesitz, Museum für Indische Kunst

dais, the human soldiers, who are depicted as demons, fall to their knees or flee in despair. Flanking Shakyamuni is Mara, depicted on one side riding a camel and on the other an elephant.

CENTRAL ASIAN VERSIONS

This powerful depiction of the *Attack of Mara* followed the spread of Buddhism east through Central Asia. Because much of the earlier Central Asian Buddhist art has been destroyed, one must look to the Stairs Cave at Kizil (fig. 4), dated to the first half of the seventh century,[22] to trace the composition's development. Here the artists generally followed Indian conventions, but added their own iconographic twists. Most remarkable is their depiction of Mara's host. Indian versions feature *yaksas* in human and animal-headed forms,[23] but in the Stairs Cave the demons are transformed into truly ferocious monsters. While *yaksas* also appear, the other creatures take on astonishing shapes, such as the six-faced, three-eyed, wild-haired running figure in the upper right.[24]

Unlike the earlier Indian renditions, the Kizil image depicts a more intense, physical attack, with the increased action and movement conveyed in the diagonal lines. The demons assault Shakyamuni, thrusting their arms up and jostling in the crowded, chaotic battle scene. Perhaps the Indian artists recognized that the attack was a metaphor rather than an actual physical assault, while the Central Asian artists wished to make the image more immediate and provocative.[25] (The abstract nature of a spiritual attack was possibly more difficult to understand.) The later sutras, particularly the *Lalitavistara*, discuss the attack in brutal, physical terms. These later sutras spread farther beyond India than the earlier ones, and thus exerted a stronger influence on artists.

In the Kizil painting Mara is depicted in military armor instead of a *dhoti*, emphasizing his preparedness for physical battle. One can make out Mara's armored form as he attacks from either side and finally lies defeated beneath the Buddha's dais. The image of Mara to the right of Shakyamuni has six arms. As usual, the schema varies most in the depiction of Mara and in the omission of his daughters.[26] With the addition of the sense of a physical attack, the now-familiar schema spread into China[27] with the steady traffic of merchants and pilgrims who brought with them knowledge of Indian and Central Asian Buddhist sites.[28]

THE ATTACK OF MARA AT DUNHUANG

Chinese artists revered the written descriptions, drawings, and eyewitness accounts by pilgrims of famous Indian and Central Asian Buddhist art works.[29] The *Attack of Mara* schema was transmitted in this manner because of the religious merit attached to copies of these works. Indeed, many believed that copies of paintings and sculptures at Indian holy sites contained the presence of the Buddha's body (*dharmakaya*).[30] The emphasis on the faithful rendering of the original compositions is probably due to this religious fervor, as seen at the cave temples at Dunhuang.[31] The *Wei Shu* notes that areas such as Dunhuang, "from its contacts with clerics and laity of the West, obtained ancient models to follow."[32]

The rendition of the *Attack of Mara* in Caves 254, 263, 260, and 428,[33] dating from the Northern Wei (386–534) and Northern Zhou (557–581) dynasties, reveals a consistent use of the schema.[34] Here again we see the centrally placed Shakyamuni,[35] the scary host, the ambiguous Mara, the fallen, remorseful soldiers lying prostrate below the dais, and the monsters who prepare to hurl down mountains on the meditating Shakyamuni. These images, however, display more narrative detail. In particular, the Dunhuang artists focused on the transformation of Mara's beautiful daughters into shriveled old women, who hobble away from the Buddha.[36] This ultimate punishment, never explicit in either the Indian or the Central Asian depictions, appears often at Dunhuang. Another addition (adopted from Central Asia) is that of Mara's son attempting to restrain his father by clutching his arm, as seen in Caves 254 and 263.[37] The schema's ultimate basis in the *Nidanakatha*, the *Buddhacarita*, and the *Lalitavistara* is evident.[38]

The most complete representation of the schema at Dunhuang, in Cave 254 of the Northern Wei period, is also the earliest (fig. 5). This detailed depiction, in turn, influenced the representation of the *Attack* scene in the later caves at Dunhuang. Here Shakyamuni sits peacefully in the center of a raging storm of horrific demons and alluring temptations. Depicted with elfin ears, bulging eyes, and long tongues lolling over brutish teeth, the demons aim a variety of weapons at Shakyamuni. Mara's three daughters, dressed in the fashionable Chinese court costume of the day, stand demurely to the left of Shakyamuni. Two confer quietly, while the third turns toward Shakyamuni with raised hands. They exhibit their beauty to him to no avail, for he overcomes all weakness and misery, reaching enlightenment before our very eyes. On the right, the daughters slowly sink to the ground with horrified expressions as Shakyamuni transforms them into old women.

The narrative continues as soldiers, who at first prepare to attack from either side, are overcome with remorse below; two kneel in prayer on the left and two more bow deeply in front of the Buddha's dais. To the immediate right of Shakyamuni stands a figure who appears to be praying in reverence, perhaps a misunderstanding of the repeated Mara figure.[39] The story and its particular details clearly engaged the artists, as all sense of setting is discarded in favor of the dramatic encounter. (The bodhi tree, for example, is only hinted at in the sketchy depiction of foliage at the top of the mandorla.) The painting's dark background not only provides a neutral background for the multicolored monsters, but iconographically alludes to nighttime, when the demons' power is greatest.[40]

What the Dunhuang artists truly excelled at was the depiction of the incredible variety of demons.[41] Animal-headed demons, such as the horse-headed figure in the lower left and the figure above him with stag horns,

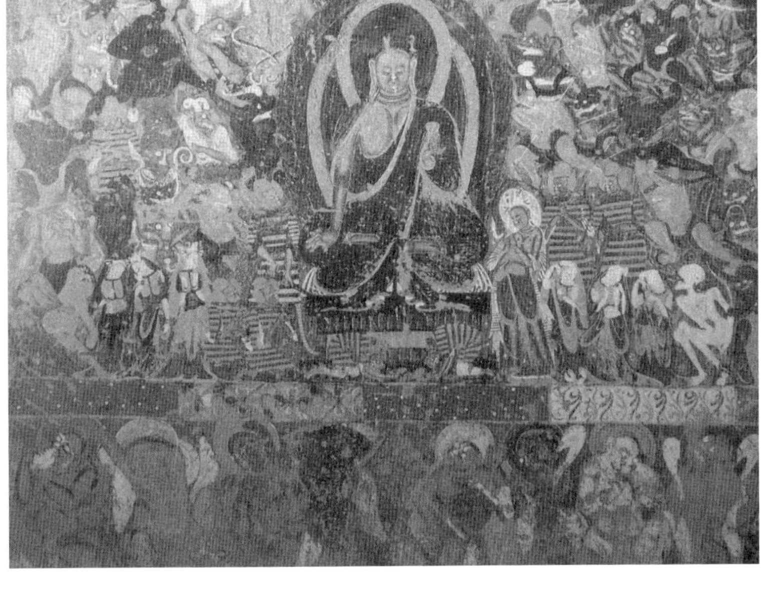

FIGURE 5
The Attack of Mara. Dunhuang, Cave 254, Northern Wei dynasty (386–534). From *Chūgoku Sekkutsu Tonkō Bakkōkutsu* (Tokyo: Heibonsha, 1980), pl. 33

play a conspicuous role. Nearby is a menacing ram-headed demon, while above charges a white elephant. None of these animal creatures bears the *udare-mukha*, a feature that can be seen on the composite-headed monsters, such as the figure whose pectoral muscles form a pair of worried eyebrows over wide eyes bridged by a large nose. The round navel forms a puckered mouth. Note also the creature to the left, which bears a facial stomach, curly ears that form a V, and an extraordinarily long tongue.

Yaksas, shown with their stomachs bulging over their loincloths and larger in size than the human members of Mara's army, also make their appearance in Cave 254. Although their bodies are human-like, their faces have supernatural features, such as bulging eyes and wide mouths filled with razor-sharp teeth.

Depicted in the *Attack* scenes in both Caves 254 and 263 is a mysterious figure wearing a loincloth who is shown pitching himself headlong, his legs kicking up behind, downward into the lower left corner. The presence of this enigmatic figure is explained by a ninth-century silk painting of the *Attack of Mara* from Dunhuang, now in the Musée Guimet (fig. 6), which employs the same model as the Northern Wei and Northern Zhou Dunhuang murals but is far more elaborate and complex in its rendition of the scene. In the lower left corner of the painting a wagon has been tipped

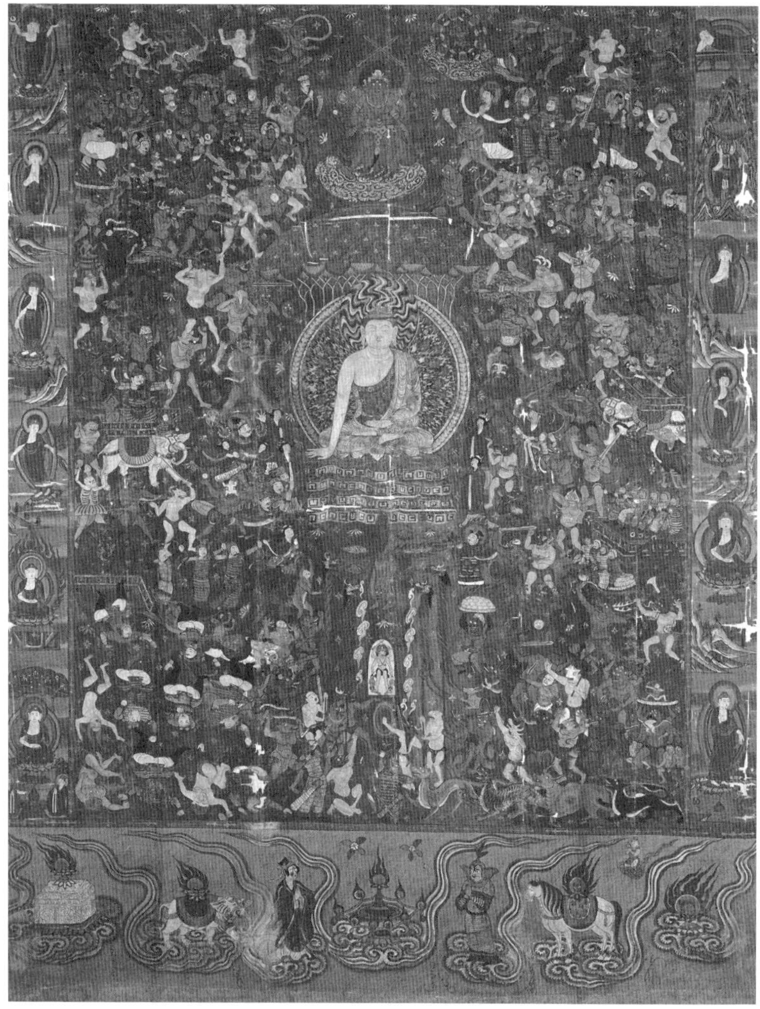

FIGURE 6
The Attack of Mara. Dunhuang. Painting on silk, 9th century. Musée Guimet, Paris

over, spilling out all of its occupants, including the figure seen in the earlier murals.

The detailed description of the demons in the Dunhuang paintings emphasizes the ferocity of the attack, provoking a dramatic response from the viewer. The demons are frightening, and their gruesome features and violent gestures evoke a feeling of impending doom. In sharp contrast, Shakyamuni sits in calm repose in the center of this chaotic scene, his sense of peace enveloping the viewer and inviting the viewer to become part of his world.

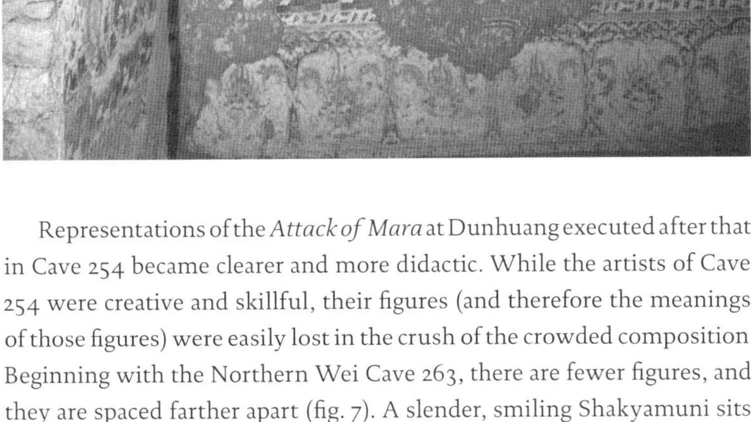

FIGURE 7
The Attack of Mara. Dunhuang, Cave 263, Northern Wei dynasty (386–534). From *Chūgoku Sekkutsu Tonkō Bakkōkutsu* (Tokyo: Heibonsha, 1980), pl. 51

Representations of the *Attack of Mara* at Dunhuang executed after that in Cave 254 became clearer and more didactic. While the artists of Cave 254 were creative and skillful, their figures (and therefore the meanings of those figures) were easily lost in the crush of the crowded composition. Beginning with the Northern Wei Cave 263, there are fewer figures, and they are spaced farther apart (fig. 7). A slender, smiling Shakyamuni sits atop an elaborate throne as demons move slowly about him. The demons' bodies are elongated, creating vertical axes which accentuate the languid quality of the demons' movements and displace entirely the earlier

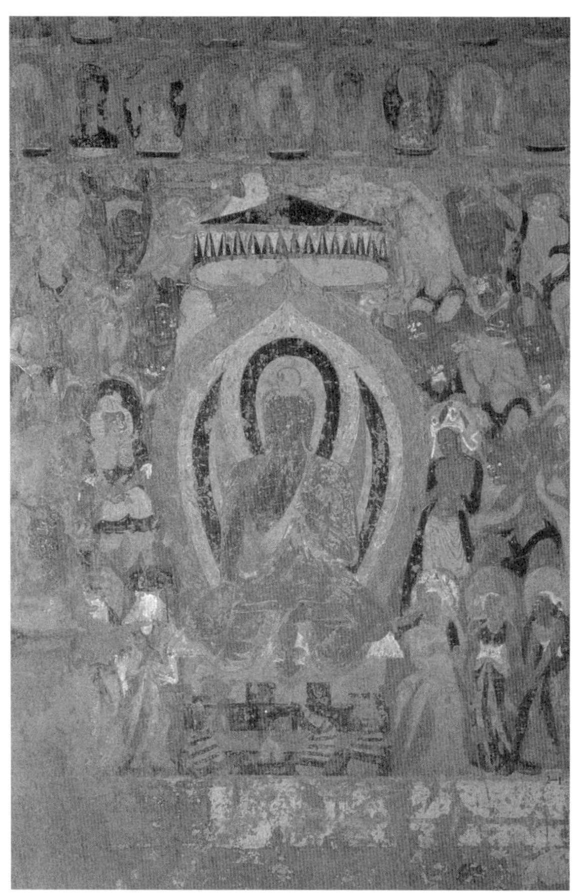

FIGURE 8
The Attack of Mara. Dunhuang, Cave 260, Northern Wei dynasty (386–534). From *Chūgoku Sekkutsu Tonkō Bakkōkutsu* (Tokyo: Heibonsha, 1980), pl. 61

impression of anger and excitement. The *Attack* becomes more symbolic and less literal, but much easier to read. For example, the representation of the *udare-mukha* in Cave 263 replicates the work of the artists of Cave 254. Again, Mara's daughters gaze up at the Buddha on the left and, after being punished, cringe on the right. Mara, shown on the left, is restrained from drawing his sword by a smaller male figure, perhaps his son.

In Cave 260 the composition is further simplified and flattened (fig. 8). The two monsters who threaten to hurl a mountain down on Shakyamuni are replaced by a single demon, while the *udare-mukhas*, with round white eyes, wedge-shaped noses, and trapezoid-shaped mouths, are rendered in a more simplified form. *Yaksas*-type creatures dominate the picture; only a few demons sport animal heads. The stiff, awkward-looking animal-headed figures menace the Buddha, but they are depicted in alter-

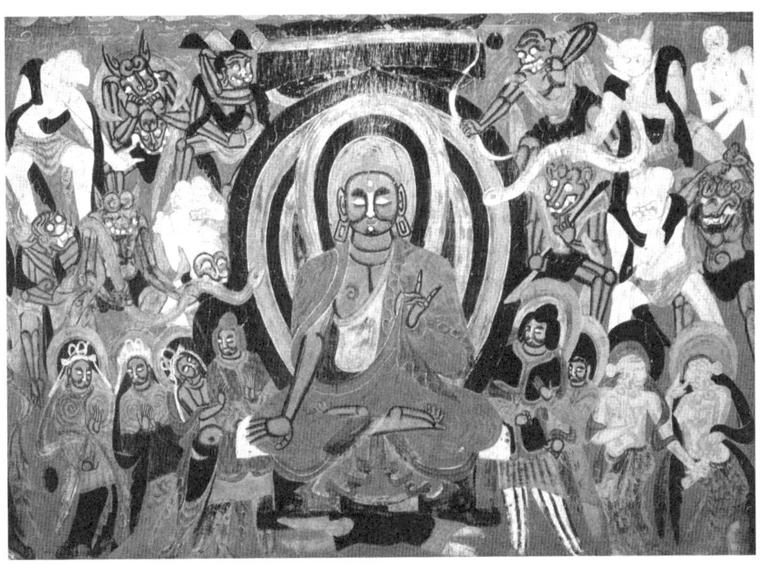

FIGURE 9
The Attack of Mara. Dunhuang, Cave 428, Northern Zhou dynasty (557–581). From *Chūgoku Sekkutsu Tonkō Bakkō-kutsu* (Tokyo: Heibonsha, 1980), pl. 163

nating colors of blue and brown, which gives the painting a patterned, abstract effect. Shakyamuni is flanked by Mara, on the left, and by a bodhisattva, on the right. Three soldiers in striped uniforms kneel below the Buddha's dais.

The simplification of the composition in Cave 260 is taken to its logical end in Cave 428 of the Northern Zhou period (fig. 9). The number of figures is radically reduced. While the composition is easier to read, almost all the terrifying emotion with which the viewer empathized is gone. The creatures move languidly, completely self-contained within their allotted space. There is no sense of impending movement, but rather an undulating linear rhythm throughout, with the creatures' black scarves and loincloths serving as accents and their white scarves turning into writhing snakes.

In this interpretation of the composition, all the pictorial elements are abbreviated. The color scheme of the entire cave, including the *Attack* mural, has been reduced to gray, black, red, and white. Only one figure (at the top left) hurls mountains down on Shakyamuni. All the demons look alike, displaying unvarying white, toothy grins. The sole *udare-mukha*, placed in the center of the top row, has curling tusks which extend out beyond its body. Even the representation of Mara's three daughters is reduced to two blank-eyed lovelies on the left who become half-naked crones on the right. Mara appears on either side of Shakyamuni, restrained by the boy, on the right, and by a bodhisattva, on the left. While the composition is quite easy to read, it conveys none of the heightened drama of earlier compositions.

The *Attack of Mara* scenes at Dunhuang represent the fruition of the development of a compositional schema based on the artists' fidelity to Indian and Central Asian prototypes. The specific iconographic details and placement of certain elements that were copied over centuries and across many thousands of miles went beyond the generalized descriptions found in the sutras. This powerful image resonated with artists and their audiences, and it was worthy of being repeated, especially when the act of copying the image accrued not only artistic but also spiritual merit. During the Northern Wei period, the Dunhuang artists maintained great fidelity to the original compositions. By the Northern Zhou period, however, interest in the historical Buddha had begun to fade in China with the growth in the popularity of Amitabha Buddha and the promise of salvation in the Pure Land.

The *Attack of Mara* composition is only one of many Buddhist compositions that were transmitted to China. The fundamental connection of Chinese Buddhist art to the art of India and Central Asia, as seen, for example, in the *Attack* paintings at the cave temples of Dunhuang, can be revealed by pure visual analysis. It is to the written documents that scholars must turn to place this connection in a wider context.

APPENDIX

Mara dreams of this occurrence, and gazing upon the prospect of losing his power, commands his followers to gather. Therefore do not hesitate to go there with our army, and reduce that monk who is going to become Buddha to nothing. Let us go!

When he [Mara] had spoken so, his son Savarthavaha tried to dissuade him, but to no avail. Mara would not listen to his words, but gathered all of the Simnus,

Who possessed the strength of foremost heroes,
who had ferocious faces such as never before were seen,
who were carrying swords, spears, and various knives,
who had never been seen before by gods or men;

Who had lumpy and bald foreheads,
who had large bellies and fat bodies,
who had mouths with thick lips,
whose faces were on their shoulder blades and chests;
who had protruding and high noses, and glowing eyes like fire ...

The creatures then, coming and doing all of this, above and below, in all the four cardinal points, for a distance of eighty miles, they circled and danced with no space between them.

"Seize him, bind him, chop him!"
With such evil shouts, would they frighten him.
Pointing with sharp knives,
They would terrify, shouting "Get up quickly."

They would frighten him by tearing their bellies open and showing [him] their intestines. They would extract snakes from the openings in their faces, they would roll their eyes and lips ...

All of this was for naught. When the weapons approached the Bodhisattva, they turned into flowers, falling into garlands and decorating the Bodhi tree.

The Bodhisattva enumerates the many sacrifices he has given for living beings in his previous lives. Mara responds by asking his retinue to witness his superior merit and says,

"My only witness to those alms void of evil is you. No matter how much you have done, what is the use of speaking about it? Who is the witness to all that? You are vanquished!"

The Bodhisattva, having no one to witness for him, touched the earth with his right hand and said, "This earth, the support of everything is my witness, which does not discriminate between those who act and those who do not act. If what I have said is true, you be my witness here!"

When he said this the great world shook in six different manners and a loud noise was heard. Emerging from the earth, showing half of her body the earth spoke, "That is exactly so! Great saint, that is exactly true! I am witness to that as you have said! ..."

Then, Mara, having failed to defeat the Bodhisattva by intimidation sent out his three daughters: Discontent, Delight, and Desire to seduce the Bodhisattva. He was impervious to all of their charms. As the sun set, in exhaustion and rage Mara and his hosts gave up and went away.

During the night the Bodhisattva went into deep meditation gaining six super knowledges and finally in the late night understanding the four noble truths. When dawn shone upon the face of the new Buddha, the world celebrated.

Source: Nicholas Poppe, *The Twelve Deeds of Buddha: A Mongolian Version of the* Lalitavistara (Wiesbaden: Otto Harrassowitz, 1967), 152–54.

NOTES

1. Malandra 1981, 122. Malandra found it impossible to prove which version of the *Attack* the artists or patrons had in mind in creating a specific image.

2. It dates from the first century B.C. For a translation of the original Pali text, see Hoppe 1973.

3. Ch'en 1968, 16, 22.

4. Other early sutras such as the *Padhana sutra* of the *Mahavagga* hint at the later drama, but the battle is not described. See Karetzky 1982, 80. See also Ling 1962, 96–163. Malandra 1981, 121–30, thoroughly reviews the literature connected with the *Attack* scene. See also David 1925, 190–97 (*Nidanakatha*); Johnson 1972, 188–202; Jones 1952, 310–15, 360–67; and Foucaux 1884, 258–86.

5. Mara is comparable in these accounts to Satan in Christianity. See Ling 1962, chap. 5, and Thomas 1927.

6. Windisch 1895, 197; Ling 1962, 46.

7. Ling 1962, 46. Ling also discusses his and other scholars' views on the conception of Mara that is exclusively Buddhist; see ibid., 46–47. See also Karetzky 1982, 75–92.

8. Karetsky 1982, 76.

9. Ling 1962, 44–46, and Karetzky 1982, 78.

10. The *yaksas* are representatives of traditional religion, so they, like Mara, fear the advent of the Buddha, who will destroy them.

11. Karetzky 1982, 81.

12. The earliest image of Mara and his daughters appears at Bharhut, but the earliest surviving image of the *Attack of Mara* comes from the Great Stupa at Sanchi (1st century B.C.). The Sanchi image is unique in its composition and iconography. The bodhi tree is placed at the left, next to Sujata, who proffers her offering. On the right, filling much of the space, is Mara's host; these figures are identifiable by their corpulent forms and wide, flat faces like those of the *yaksa* demons. Rather than attacking, the host sits in a circle, engaged in a dialogue. Strangely, for such an important figure, Mara is ill-defined. It appears that Mara, holding an umbrella symbolic of his royal stature, is the largest demon. The image seems to contradict the texts: there is no sense of actual conflict here, only the presence of these evil beings, which is sufficient to imply menace. This early image did not influence later works. Malandra 1981, 122, notes that this image cannot be connected with any specific text.

13. Williams 1975, 181, links the iconography at Amaravati to the *Lalitavistara*.

14. For a description of a *udare-mukha*, see the *Lalitavistara*, chap. 9, F55v. Hoppe 1973, 153. Malandra 1981, 124, relates the sculptures from Amaravati to the *Nidanakatha* or the *Mahavastu*.

15. Parimoo 1982, 18. Parimoo identifies both figures as possibly being Mara. The figure (now damaged) seated on the elephant can be read as a reference to the description of Mara in the *Nidanakatha* (190); the man in the lower left, according to Parimoo, is displaying a *vitarka* mudra, perhaps expounding. Mara is rarely depicted, or identifiable, in images of the *Attack*. It may be that images featuring an overwhelming army of attackers rather than a single leader were considered more effective, or that the power of Mara as an individual was intentionally downplayed.

Mara is mentioned as being mounted on an elephant in the *Padhana sutra* of the *Mahavagga*. See Karetzky 1982, 80.

Malandra 1981, 122, notes that portraying Mara twice might indicate a lapse of time in the episode.

16. A contemporary Mathuran example in the Lucknow Provincial Museum is illustrated in Rowland 1977, fig. 104.

17. Malandra 1981, 125–30, attributes this work to the descriptions in the *Buddhicarita*.

18. A passage in the *Mahavastu* (2nd century) talks of demons (*pisacas*) who carry mountaintops as they attack the sage. Karetzky 1982, 79.

19. Scholars differ about the interpretation of these fallen figures. Malandra (1981) believes that they have a literary source, playing the role of Mara's vanquished army as told in the *Buddhicarita* (197) and the *Mahavastu* (314, 366), whereas Karetzky (1982, 89), believes that they derive from Hellenistic sculptural traditions, not from Buddhist texts.

20. A son tries to dissuade his father from his evil deed. In the *Lalitavistara*, Mara has two thousand sons, half of whom are benevolent. The image of a son first appears at the Great Stupa at Sanchi. Mara's sons are discussed in Malandra 1981, 122; Karetzky 1982, 87; and Rosenfield 1967, 25.

21. An abbreviated version of the standard composition of the *Attack of Mara*, based on earlier Kushan prototypes, survives from Sarnath. The interest in epic narrative is dropped in favor of an easily read vignette. For example, a *Stele from the Life of the Buddha* (5th century) shows no sense of physical conflict. Williams 1975, 171, 179–81.

22. Two Kizil murals of the *Attack* survive: the earlier from the Stairs Cave and the later from the Cave of the Temptation. Härtel 1982, 92, 98.

23. These strongmen can also be found in the Hell scenes at Kizil.

24. Nagai 1977, 108. Nagai proposes that this image is perhaps a satirical representation of a form of Shiva. The Shivism cult was considered heretical to the Buddhists, so the hideous forms of Shiva would not be out of place amongst Mara's host.

25. This idea was suggested to me by Frederick Asher.

26. Nagai 1977, 26–35, lists the incredible variety of Buddhist texts found in the area of Kucha. It is difficult to pinpoint exactly which texts influenced the depiction of the *Attack of Mara*. An oral tradition, too, might account for the diversity of images. Although it is difficult to tell because of their poor condition, neither painting appears to illustrate the episode of Mara's daughters.

27. Buddhism in China developed into two regional forms, one in the north and the other in the south. In the south, centered on the native Chinese court at Nanjing, Buddhism reflected a continuation of the Han Confucian tradition that emphasized theory and discussion. This included public preaching, sermons, and lectures. The monastic practices emphasized the metaphysical "pure conversation." This point was suggested to me by Wai-Kam Ho. See also Ho 1968/69, 7. This less tangible approach to religious practices, combined with destructive civil wars, resulted in the survival of very few artworks from southern China in the Six Dynasties period (220–589). Consequently, it is necessary to look to the Northern Buddhists, centered at Ye, for physical evidence of Indian and Central Asian influences. Buddhism in the north emphasized practice and ritual over theory. While in the south Buddhism remained partially separate from the state, in the north it was strongly

supported by the government. See Soper 1959, 94.

28. See Zürcher 1959, for a thorough study of Buddhism's spread in China, as traced through literary sources, and Wu Hung 1986, 263–352. The political and social upheavals of this period were a miraculous boon to the spread of Buddhism, in which everything is considered to be an illusion. Davidson 1954, 13.

29. The most famous of these pilgrims were the monks Faxian (4th century) and Xuanzang (7th century). Faxian's *Records of Buddhistic Kingdoms*, widely available in China in the Northern Wei (386–534) period, exposed people to a greater knowledge of Indian Buddhism than ever before. For translated accounts of Faxian's trip to India, see Beal 1869.

30. Rowland 1947, 7–8, describes a silk banner from Dunhuang dated to the Tang dynasty that illustrates famous Indian statues as models for Chinese sculptors. However, the artist seemed more interested in the general proportions and attributes of the figures than their style, which also appears to be the case with the Dunhuang paintings of the *Attack of Mara*.

31. For a complete history of the Dunhuang area, see Huie 1980.

32. Soper 1958, 134. Soper 1959, 141, quotes the *Wei Shu*, cxiv, p. 4r.

33. It is difficult to assign this group of caves to specific reign dates. Huie 1980, for example, dates Caves 254, 263, and 260 to the pre-Northern Wei period, but based on stylistic analysis, I date them to the Northern Wei period.

34. The composition spread to other Chinese sites as well, including Cave 10 at Yungang (Mizuno and Nagahiro 1951, 132, point to a story of the restraining son in the *Sutra of Cause and Effects of the Past and Present*, quoting from Taishō-Daizōkyō III, 639, 640, chap. 3) and to stelae at Maijishan. See also *Maijishan shiku*, Beijing, 1954, and *Wenwu* nos. 2–6 (1954), which show Stele No. 10 from Cave 133 (second quarter of the 6th century). For further information on Maijishan, see Sullivan 1969.

35. Rowland 1947, 7. To the literal-minded Chinese, Shakyamuni was the most real of all the sacred Buddhist personages, because actual places associated with his life could be visited in India by Chinese pilgrims. In all the sutras, Shakyamuni was the most familiar figure as the "eternal preacher." As the source of all knowledge, he followed the Chinese concept of a living person becoming a deity—like Laozi and Confucius. See Soper 1959, 181.

Shakyamuni Buddha was also linked to the *Lotus Sutra* in the Six Dynasties period. The *Lotus Sutra* in part "redeems Shakyamuni from the position of relative insignificance" vis-à-vis popular cults devoted to Maitreya and Amitayus. In the *Lotus Sutra* Shakyamuni is the master of two realms of existence, earthly and spiritual. His short life on earth was just an illusion "suited to the special needs of the age." See Soper 1959, 182. His career as a savior spanned countless lifetimes. Although it was said that he appeared to enter Nirvana and disappear, that was simply a story preached by him to the faithful who were not ready to hear the full truth. Kern 1884, 299.

36. The narrative sequence is presented from left to right, rather than from right to left in the traditional Chinese manner. This seems to be an additional piece of evidence supporting the theory that this image of the *Attack of Mara* comes from Indian sources.

37. This image may also have been de-

picted originally in the painting in Cave 260, whose edges have worn away. It is seen in the versions of the *Attack of Mara* at Yungang as well.

38. Chinese translations of early sutras were available as early as the second century, but by the fifth century later sutras, with their vivid descriptions of Mara's host, became available. Karetzky 1982, 81, lists the following: *Xiu Xing Ben Qi Jing* (471), *Tai Ci Sui Ying Ben Qi Jing* (477).

The introduction of the *Lalitavistara* sutra into China can be dated as early as 70 A.D. See Beal 1871, 13. Numerous translations have survived from later centuries, including one that slightly predates the Northern Wei caves at Dunhuang. In 420 a translation was completed by the Indian priest Dharmaraksha.

39. This added figure appears in the later Caves 260 and 428.

40. One tradition of monsters that does not seem to have had an impact on the depictions of the *Attack* at Dunhuang is that of native Chinese demonology. While the Chinese monsters also sport immense, muscular physiques, instead of corpulent bellies and stocky legs, the monsters in the Dunhuang paintings display the exaggerated musculature of a weight lifter whose enormous chest, arms, and thighs dwarf his birdlike wrists and ankles, features that are emphasized by the pair of serrated wings growing out of the monsters' arms. While the demons in Dunhuang depictions of the *Attack* push toward the Buddha, their movements are less nervous and flighty. Unlike the demons found in the *Attack* scenes, the Chinese-style demons were thought to serve as guardians against evil forces.

Cave 254 seems to have some stylistic roots in the earlier Kuchan Central Asian school, particularly in the use of contrasting colors within stiff contour lines. One similarity between the styles is the use of bright greens and blues as skin and hair colors.

41. Some of the demons depicted in Cave 254 reappear in the same positions in Caves 260 and 263.

REFERENCES

Beal, Samuel. 1869. *Travels of Fa-hsian and Sung-yun, Buddhist Pilgrims from China to India (400 A.D. and 518 A.D.)*. London: Trubner and Co.; repr. 1964, London and Santiago de Compostela, Spain: Susil Gupta.

———. 1871. *A Catena of Buddhist Scriptures from the Chinese*. London: Trubner and Co.

Ch'en, Kenneth K.S. 1968. *Buddhism: The Light of Asia*. New York: Barron's Educational Series, Inc.

David, T.W. Rhys, trans. 1925. *Buddhist Birth Stories*. London.

Davidson, J. Leroy. 1954. *The Lotus Sutra in Chinese Art: A Study in Buddhist Art to the Year 1000*. New Haven: Yale University Press.

Foucaux, E., trans. 1884. *Le Lalitavistara. Annales du Musée Guimet*, vol. 6.

Härtel, Herbert. 1982. *Along the Silk Routes: Central Asian Art from the West Berlin State Museums*. New York: The Metropolitan Museum of Art.

Ho, Wai-Kam. 1968/69. Notes on Chinese Sculpture from Northern Ch'i to Sui. Part I: Two Seated Stone Buddhas in the Cleveland Museum. *Archives of Asian Art* 22.

Hoppe, Max. 1973. *Buddha, seine Lehre und sein Weg: Texte aus dem Pali-Kanon mit Erklärungen und Erläuterungen.* Vienna: Octopus Verl.

Huie, Chee Mee. 1980. A Study of the Chronology and Development of the Cave Temples at Tunhuang Excavated from Northern Liang to T'ang. PhD diss., New York University.

Johnson, E.H., trans. 1972. *The Buddhicarita or Acts of the Buddha.* New Delhi.

Jones, J. J., trans. 1952. *The Mahavastu*, vol. II. London.

Karetzky, Patricia. 1982. Mara, Buddhist Deity of Death and Desire. *East and West* (N.S.), 32, nos. 1–4 (December).

Kern, H., trans. 1884. *Saddharma-Pundarika or The Lotus of the True Law.* Repr. 1963. New York: Dover Publications, Inc.

Ling, Trevor Oswald. 1962. *Buddhism and the Mythology of Evil: A Study in Theravada Buddhism.* London: George Allen & Unwin Ltd.

Malandra, Geri Hockfield. 1981. Mara's Army: Text and Image in Early Indian Art. *East and West* (N.S.), 31, nos. 1–4 (December).

Mizuno, Seiichi and T. Nagahiro. 1951. *Yun-kang: The Buddhist Cave Temple of the Fifth Century A.D. in North China*, vol. 9. Kyoto.

Nagai, Evelyn H. 1977. *Iconographic Innovations in Kuchean Buddhist Art.* Ann Arbor: University Microfilms International.

Parimoo, Ratan. 1982. *Life of the Buddha in Indian Sculpture.* New Delhi: Kanak Publications.

Rosenfield, John. 1967. *The Dynastic Art of the Kushans.* Berkeley: University of California Press.

Rowland, Benjamin Jr. 1947. Indian Images in Chinese Sculpture. *Artibus Asiae* 10, no. 1.

———. 1977. *The Art and Architecture of India: Buddhism, Hindu, Jain.* Penguin Books.

Soper, Alexander. 1958. Northern Liang and Northern Wei in Kansu. *Artibus Asiae* 21.

———. 1959. *Literary Evidence for Early Buddhist Art in China.* Ascona, Switzerland: Artibus Asiae Supplementum 19.

Sullivan, Michael. 1969. *The Cave Temples of Maichishan.* Berkeley: University of California Press.

Thomas, E. J. 1927. *The Life of the Buddha as Legend and History.* London.

Williams, Joanna. 1975. Sarnath Gupta Steles of Buddha's Life. *Ars Orientalis* 10.

Windisch, E. 1895. *Mara und Buddha.* Leipzig.

Wu Hung. 1986. Buddhist Elements in Early Chinese Art (2nd and 3rd Centuries A.D.). *Artibus Asiae* 47, nos. 3, 4.

Zürcher, E. 1959. *The Buddhist Conquest of China: The Spread and Adaptation of Buddhism in Early Medieval China.* Leiden: E. J. Brill.

STUDIES IN HONOR OF CHU-TSING LI

Dunhuang Cave 427: Evidence of Imperial Iconography

JANET BAKER

The Sui dynasty (581–618) lasted fewer than forty years, yet its achievements and effects on later Chinese history were far reaching. The Sui reunified China politically after nearly three hundred years of disunion, reorganized and unified the economy, and made great strides toward cultural homogeneity. The founder and first emperor of the Sui dynasty, Sui Wendi (r. 581–604), chose certain Buddhist models of antiquity to forge his power and atone for the persecution that had occurred in the preceding Northern Zhou period (557–581). Sui Wendi established splendid imperial temples and stupas, which were intended to serve as tangible evidence of his secular and religious power. A series of edicts issued by the emperor between 601 and 604 called for the distribution of Buddhist relics and their enshrinement in stupas across the empire, recalling the achievements of the Buddhist emperor Ashoka (r. ca. 272–231 B.C.) of India.[1] Like Ashoka, Sui Wendi envisioned himself as a *cakravartin*, a universal monarch destined to fulfill the Buddha's prophecy of a sovereign who would bring all sentient creatures to abide in the *dharma* (law) during the period of moral decay.[2]

The imperial edict of 601 commissioning thirty stupas for the enshrinement of sacred Buddhist relics included a stupa at Guazhou, in present-day Gansu Province, which served as the administrative prefecture for the Dunhuang region. The large number of caves at Dunhuang ascribed to the Sui dynasty, estimated by the Dunhuang Academy to be more than eighty, is astounding in view of the relatively short period of time in which they were created and provides clear testimony to both the vigor of Sui Wendi's undertakings and the importance of Dunhuang as a major center of Buddhist artistic activity during his reign.[3]

One of the caves widely recognized as being attributable to the Sui period is Cave 427 (fig. 1). The uniqueness of this cave lies in its monumental scale and its inclusion of a central pillar at the rear of the main chamber and an antechamber. The main chamber, nearly 33 feet deep and 23 feet wide, is not equaled in size by any other cave at Dunhuang until well into the Tang dynasty (618–907). A central pillar is seen in earlier caves at the site dated to the Northern Wei (386–534), Western Wei (535–556), and Northern Zhou periods, but in Cave 427 it is relocated toward the rear of the chamber. On the west, north, and south sides of the pillar are sculptural niches; immediately in front of the east side of the pillar, which has no niches, stand three monumental sculpture triads, which are identical in the size, pose, costume, and style of the figures.[4] Each triad includes a Buddha, nearly 13 feet tall, flanked by two bodhisattvas. The triads are almost three-dimensional in conception, emphasizing the sheer mass of the figures. In contrast to the simple garments of the Buddha, those of the bodhisattvas are richly detailed with jewelry, scarves with double loops, and colorful textile patterns that include lozenge designs and medallions with pearl borders enclosing lions and phoenixes.

In the wooden antechamber are the figures of four Heavenly Kings and two warriors, which herald both a new subject and a new style in Sui-period sculpture. Inhabiting the four peaks of Mount Sumeru, the cosmic Buddhist mountain, Heavenly Kings serve to protect the law of the Buddha from evil spirits. Each king is shown crushing an earth demon with his feet. These sculptures are also of an unprecedented scale: each of the Heavenly Kings measures 11⅞ feet and each warrior 12⅛ feet in height. Both types are portrayed in a vividly realistic style, with the warriors exhibiting straining muscles and bulging eyes and the Heavenly Kings robust bodies. The earth demons show contorted postures and anguished expressions. These figures were repainted in the Song dynasty (960–1279), making it impossible to discern their original costume and ornamentation.[5]

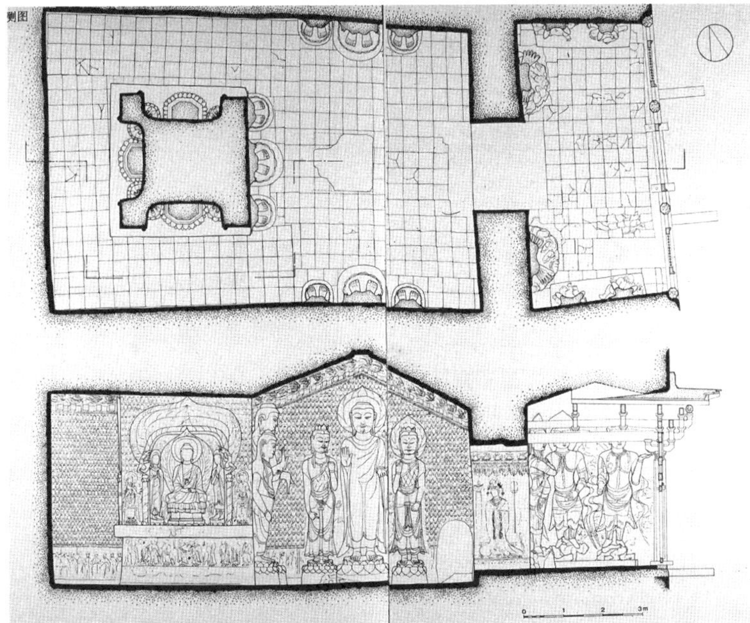

FIGURE 1
Diagram of Dunhuang Cave 427. From *Dunhuang Mogaoku II*. Beijing: Wenwu chubanshe, 1985, 228–29

The unusual features of Cave 427 raise many questions: Why was a central pillar included? Why is the scale of the sculptures so large? Why are the three triads identical? What is the significance of these iconographic choices and innovations? In order to answer these questions, it is necessary to discuss the significance of the central pillar and compare the design of Cave 427 with that of caves at other Buddhist sites.

The majority of Northern Wei, Western Wei, and Northern Zhou caves at Dunhuang are dominated by a central pillar. The front section of the rectangular chamber (roughly one-third of the total space) features a gabled roof that probably imitates the roofed corridor surrounding the pagoda in freestanding temple complexes of these three periods. The rear portion of the cave (roughly two-thirds of the total space) forms a perfect square, with the pillar situated at the center. The pillar features image niches on all four sides, with the largest group placed on the east side, greeting the worshipper upon entrance to the cave.[6] This plan allows for the practice of circumambulation of the central pillar, in the same manner as in an Indian *chaitya* hall (a building constructed with wooden pillars and a barrel-vaulted roof) with a stupa at the rear.

Circumambulation of a stupa is a traditional Buddhist practice in India. The presence of a pillar in the center of the early Dunhuang caves suggests this practice, although textual references are limited. One fifth-century Chinese text that gives instruction in the ritual is the *Tiwei boli jing* (Sutra of Trapusa and Bhallika), which emphasizes simple ritual practices suited for the common people, such as circumambulation and recitation of the names of the Buddhas (*foming*). That the ritual of *foming* was also carried out in the Dunhuang caves is evidenced by the countless number of small Buddha images affixed to the walls of the caves.

The prevalence of a central pillar and the Thousand Buddha motif in the pre-Tang caves at Dunhuang underscores an important aspect of the site. Unlike the cave-temple complexes of Yungang, near Datong, Shanxi Province, and Longmen, near Luoyang, Henan Province, Dunhuang was not located near an imperial capital city. It was most likely established as a monastic retreat, as were most Indian and Central Asian cave sites. The location of the Dunhuang caves combined the features of a remote spot conducive to meditation with the accessibility of a major populated area in order to draw upon the support of local Buddhists. While numerous inscriptions in the caves testify to the patronage of high-ranking Chinese court officials, it was the local elite whose influence and support was no doubt the strongest. The religious, political, and aesthetic programs of the early Dunhuang caves reflect the close relationship between the members of the local elite and the leaders of the small monastic community, who shared a common class background. The caves at Yungang and Longmen, in contrast, served as symbols of imperial political power, sanctioned by the court as sacred sites that manifested and reinforced the link between the Buddhist church and the Northern Wei court. Caves containing colossal images, such as the Tanyao caves at Yungang and the Binyang and Guyang caves at Longmen, served as memorials to the Northern Wei emperors. Monumental Buddha images, rather than a central pillar, dominate the interiors of those caves.[7]

Returning to the question of the design of Dunhuang Cave 427, it becomes clear that the presence of a central pillar and colossal triads in the same cave presents a logistical as well as an iconographical challenge. The answer may be that the cave was worked on at two different times during the Sui period. Initially, the cave was designed to be a central-pillar cave in which circumambulation could be practiced. However, the placement of the three large freestanding triads directly in front of the pillar creates a physical obstacle. In addition, a ledge along the lower third of the pillar protrudes in a visually incongruous manner from the north and south sides, interfering with one's view of the triads. All of this suggests that the original plan of the cave was later altered by the inclusion of the three triads and the addition of the wooden antechamber.

Why would a cave have been altered in such a fashion? What would have been the motive for or the meaning of this alteration? Significant clues can be found in the Binyang cave at Longmen, which was commissioned by the Northern Wei imperial family and completed between 505 and 523. As demonstrated by James O. Caswell, many of the caves previously thought to have been examples of imperial patronage at Longmen are most likely examples of non-imperial patronage. The Binyang cave, however, is still one of the few caves at Longmen that appears to have had connections with the imperial family, especially in view of the cave's processional scenes of the emperor and empress.[8]

The most imposing feature of the Binyang cave is the large-scale sculptural groups placed against three walls of the cave. The central group, on the west wall, is a pentad that consists of a seated image of the Buddha Shakyamuni, two bodhisattvas, and two monks. The groups on the north and south walls are triads consisting of a standing Buddha flanked by a pair of bodhisattvas. In this arrangement, the three groups represent the Buddhas of the Past, Present, and Future. The use of monumental sculpture as a visual symbol of homage to the imperial family first occurs in the Northern Wei Tanyao caves at Yungang and is continued in the Tang Fengxiansi cave at Longmen, produced under the sponsorship of Empress Wu Zetian (Wu Zhao; r. 690–705).

As mentioned above, the monumental figures in Cave 427 at Dunhuang constitute the first occurrence of such large-scale sculptures at the site. I propose that they also represent the first recognizable instance of direct imperial patronage at Dunhuang. What seems plausible is that Cave 427, a relatively large cave with a central pillar commissioned in the early Sui period, was transformed to fulfill an immediate need for an imperial iconic cave at Dunhuang—one that could have arisen due to the arrival of an imperial emissary or the emperor himself at Dunhuang. The pillar was retained either for structural stability or to symbolize the sacredness of the cave rather than to function as a point of circumambulation.

Further support for this idea of imperial homage can be found in an examination of the specific mode of representation of the three large Buddha figures in Cave 427, all of which are shown in Indian-style robes as opposed to Chinese-style robes. The earliest Buddha images produced in China, as exemplified by the five Tanyao caves of Yungang, portray the Buddha in Indian-style robes in adherence to the legend of King Udayana, king of Kausambi (present-day Kosam) and a patron of the Buddha, who created the first image of the historical Buddha as a visual replacement for his presence during his temporary absence from the physical world. The Udayana image found favor with the emperors of the Northern Wei because of its original royal association.[9]

Subsequently, upon the move of the dynasty's capital to Longmen in 486, the Northern Wei emperor Xiaowen (r. 471–99) decreed that the official court costume would be that of the Chinese aristocracy. This type of costume then made its appearance in Buddha figures at Yungang. At Longmen virtually all the Northern Wei Buddha figures, including those in the Binyang cave, are shown in Chinese costume. The notable exception is the Tang period Fengxiansi cave, where the colossal seated Buddha wears the Indian-style Udayana robe, which falls unencumbered from the neckline in stringlike folds. This implies a conscious archaistic choice of a formal mode associated with royalty in order to indicate the imperial homage represented by the Fengxiansi image in contrast to the other images at the site.

At Dunhuang, located far from the imperial capitals of Pingcheng (modern Datong) and Luoyang, the garments of the Northern Wei Buddha figures are primarily in the Udayana style. With the onset of the Western Wei period, however, this Indian-style garment is replaced by the Chinese mode of dress.[10] In this context the occurrence of the Udayana mode of costume on the three colossal standing Buddha images of Cave 427 at Dunhuang can similarly be viewed as a deliberate return to an archaistic mode to indicate the special imperial status of the cave.

The large-scale figures of the Heavenly Kings and warriors placed in the antechamber of Cave 427 also represent a new theme in Sui sculpture at Dunhuang. The initial appearance of these figures in Cave 427 is followed by numerous Tang and Song examples at Dunhuang and elsewhere. The most notable precedents are found at Yungang, in Caves 10 and 13, and at Longmen, in the Binyang cave.[11] In each case a pair of Heavenly Kings is carved in relief on the side walls of the entranceway to the cave. Unlike Dunhuang Cave 427, none of these caves has a separate antechamber for the display of three-dimensional figures. The separate chamber and the more fully plastic forms at Dunhuang seem to indicate the influence of freestanding wooden temple complexes in which a separate structure existed in front of the Buddha Hall, as evidenced by the later Fengxiansi caves at Longmen.

The first appearance of these guardian figures in the context of a Buddhist temple is difficult to ascertain, but the purpose of their placement at the entrance to the holy sector seems undisputed: they guard the four peaks of Mount Sumeru, the four quadrants of the Buddhist universe. The guardian figures in the Northern Wei caves at Yungang and Longmen were likely influenced by the use of such figures in a freestanding temple in the nearby metropolitan capital. The belated appearance of the guardian figures in Dunhuang Cave 427 similarly seems to indicate a new influence from the Sui capital. Their placement within a separate chamber reflects both an alteration to the original cave plan as well as an effort to elevate the status of Cave 427. Indeed, Cave 427 has the largest number of guardian figures of any of the other examples cited above. The monumental size and the splendor of the arrangement of these figures are not rivaled at Dunhuang until the mid-Tang period, nearly two centuries later.[12] For all of these reasons, it seems plausible that the sculptures in

Cave 427 may have been executed by cosmopolitan artists from the Sui capital, who introduced to Dunhuang a refined skill and a diversity of expression in large-scale sculpture.

Who would have implemented such a plan and for what reason? The answer to this question is most likely related to the second Sui emperor, Yangdi (r. 604–17), who, having allegedly conspired to murder his father, Wendi, ascended the throne in 604. Confucian historians have characterized Sui Yangdi as a selfish and extravagant ruler, yet he was also a follower and generous supporter of Buddhism and the arts. He ordered the repair of Buddhist sutras damaged in the fighting that attended the fall of the Chen dynasty (557–589) in southern China. In 607 he issued a decree calling upon all Buddhist monks to render homage to the emperor and imperial officials, terminating the tradition in south China of monks not honoring their earthly rulers. Yangdi's love of grandeur led to the establishment of two capitals, Chang'an and Luoyang, where he carried out large-scale palace construction. The building of a canal system linking the two capitals with the Yangzi River valley required huge amounts of labor and resources. Further economic burden was created by three unsuccessful expeditions against Korea, between 612 and 614, which lead to revolt and the assassination of Yangdi in 618.[13] In addition to his plans to expand his empire eastward, Yangdi was also concerned with securing the stability of China's western borders. The Sui histories record many emissaries who were sent from the Sui court to Dunhuang. Furthermore, a brother of the emperor served as an official in Dunhuang prefecture between 608 and 610. Most importantly, the emperor himself undertook personal tours of northwest China, in 607 and 608, as part of his frontier policy to ward off the threat posed by the eastern Turks. These imperial journeys, along with marriage diplomacy (the offering of Turkic girls to the imperial household), investiture, and barter, contributed to a major increase in the interaction of the people of the northwestern steppes and the cosmopolitan Chinese.[14]

In conclusion, it seems likely that Dunhuang Cave 427 underwent its transformation from a circumambulation cave with a central pillar as its focus to an imperial icon to honor the arrival of Sui Yangdi in the Dunhuang region in 607–8 and mark the acceptance of the 607 imperial decree that all monks render homage to the emperor. Prior to the emperor's arrival, court emissaries would have arranged for the transfer of cosmopolitan artists to Dunhuang to carry out the work at the site. The work was probably done in great haste, which would also explain why the artists chose to remodel an existing cave rather than undertake the construction of a new one. The emperor's love of the grandiose and the extravagant no doubt accounts for the large scale and superb quality of the sculpture and ornamentation found in Cave 427.

The most important achievement of the Sui dynasty was the reunification of the country under a single ruler who utilized Buddhism as a tool of imperial policy. Sui Wendi patronized Buddhism, sponsored pious works, and built and supported temples in the capitals and the provinces. He presented himself to the populace as a universal monarch, relying upon a foreign religion to validate himself as the legitimate Son of Heaven. The equation of the emperor and the Buddha was manifest in imperial commissions of Buddhist works and temples in the capital and in areas such as Dunhuang, which was thereby drawn into the cosmopolitan circle of Chinese culture, especially during the reign of Sui Yangdi. The most significant example of this accomplishment is Dunhuang Cave 427, which exhibits architecture and sculpture that can best be described as imperial in scale and grandeur. Comparisons with earlier examples of imperial Buddha icons at Yungang and Longmen confirm that the specific traits that characterize those images are found in those of Cave 427 as well. Therefore, it can be stated that Cave 427 represents a concrete example of the impact of the unification of China under the Sui empire at the beginning of the seventh century.

NOTES

1. Wright 1978, 134–36.
2. See ibid., 126–36. Wright's primary source is the *Suishu*, chaps. 38–45. See also Baker 1991, chap. 2.
3. Baker 1991, 111. The precise number of Sui caves at Dunhuang is still open to widely differing opinions due to the lack of clearly dated evidence.
4. Dunhuang Wenwu Yanjiusuo 1982, 156.
5. Ibid.
6. Xiao Xian 1985, 187–93.
7. See Longmen Wenwu Baoguansuo 1981, preface.
8. Caswell 1988, 121–24.
9. Ibid., chap. 5.
10. Based on this author's observations. Northern Wei examples are Caves 275, 259, 257, and 260; Western Wei examples are Caves 249, 285, and 432; Northern Zhou and Sui examples are Caves 296, 301, 423, 420, and 419; early Tang examples are Caves 244 and 57.
11. See Yungang Shiku Baoguansuo 1977, pls. 57, 72; and Longmen Wenwu Baoguansuo 1981, pl. 13.
12. Li Qiqiong 1985, 163–64.
13. Wright 1978, 192–94.
14. Shi Weixiang 1985, 230–32. The primary source is *Suishu*, chap. 28. See also Wright 1978, 188–91.

REFERENCES

Baker, Janet. 1991. The Art of the Sui Dynasty Caves at Dunhuang. University of Michigan Dissertation Information Service.

Caswell, James O. 1988. *Written and Unwritten: A New History of the Buddhist Caves at Yungang*. Vancouver: University of British Columbia Press.

Dunhuang Wenwu Yanjiusuo. 1982. *Dunhuang Mogaoku neirong zhonglu*. Beijing: Wenwu chubanshe.

Li Qiqiong. 1985. Suidaide Mogaoku yishu. In *Dunhuang Mogaoku II*. Beijing: Wenwu chubanshe.

Longmen Wenwu Baoguansuo. 1981. *Longmen shiku*. Beijing: Wenwu chubanshe.

Shi Weixiang. 1985. Dunhuang Mogaoku dashi nianbiao II. In *Dunhuang Mogaoku II*. Beijing: Wenwu chubanshe.

Wright, Arthur F. 1978. *The Sui Dynasty: The Unification of China, A.D. 581–617*. New York: Alfred A. Knopf.

Xiao Xian. 1985. Dunhuang Mogaoku dongku xingshi. In *Dunhuang Mogaoku II*. Beijing: Wenwu chubanshe.

Yungang Shiku Baoguansuo. 1977. *Yungang shiku*. Beijing: Wenwu chubanshe.

STUDIES IN HONOR OF CHU-TSING LI

The Development of Illustrations to Buddhist Sutras in the Sui and Tang Periods

JIN WEINUO

隋唐佛教經變的發展

金維諾

關於中國佛教壁畫，在隋唐時期最具有明顯特點的,是發展了具有民族特色的大型經變。[1] 這時出現的經變種類繁多,見於記載的有《西方變》、《藥師變》、《彌勒下生變》、《法華經變》、《華嚴經變》、《維摩變》、《金光明經變》、《除災患變》、《金剛經變》、《本行經變》、《降魔變》、《涅槃變》、《地獄變》、《日藏月藏經變》、《業報差別變》、《十輪經變》等。僅從敦煌莫高窟隋唐時期的壁畫來看，依據流行的佛經內容描繪的經變，又大大多於記載。敦煌經變不僅題材豐富，數量驚人，而且繪飾華麗，氣象恢宏。幾乎是取代了早期佛本生故事和佛傳故事畫而據有了寺院壁畫的主體位置，呈現出鮮明的時代特色。

關於佛教經變，從文獻記載可知在南北朝至隋已逐漸流行，如劉宋袁倩的《維摩經變》、梁張善果的《釋加會圖》、《贊績經變》、隋展子虔的《法華變》、董伯仁的《彌勒變》、楊契丹的《涅槃變》等都是多種情節組合在一起的大型構圖。而南朝遺存的佛教石刻圖像中《淨土變》、《維摩變》，以及麥積山窟西魏時期的《涅槃經變》、《西方淨土變》、《維摩詰經變》和《十善十惡圖》等，則是遺存到今天的早期經變圖像，構圖宏偉而富於變化，形象精麗而饒有生趣，是佛教藝術完全形成了本土樣式的里程碑。這種多情節有機組合在一起的經變的形成，為隋唐時期宏偉絢麗的大型經變的廣泛流行，開闢了途徑並積累了經驗。

《維摩詰經變》是流行最早，發展脈絡最清晰的一種經變。最初出現於東晉玄學風氣濃厚的南方，顧愷之首創的瓦官寺維摩詰形象，“有清羸示病之容，隱幾忘言之狀”，是士大夫好清談時尚影響下畫家對維摩詰人物民族化理解的體現。在他同時的張墨和其後的陸探微、張僧繇也都畫過同一題材，大致是取材《維摩詰經 · 問疾品》，主要著力於刻畫維摩詰的形象。陸探微的弟子袁倩又發展了這一經變的內容，《歷代名畫記》卷六說袁倩畫理的“維摩詰變一卷，百有餘事，運事高妙，六法備呈，置位無差。若神靈感會，精光指顧，得瞻仰威容，前使顧陸知慚，後得張閻駭歎。”袁倩的《維摩變》因是卷軸畫，畫面的處理方法要適應長卷畫的結構方式，與單幅構圖有所不同，但仍會是以維摩、文殊論辯為中心來展開全部經文內容。在遺存的南朝齊、梁石刻造像上的《維摩變》還可以看到這一特徵。

北方石窟中出現的維摩與文殊論辯的畫面，以炳靈寺169窟年代最早。在建弘元年(西元420年)的壁畫上，中為佛說法像，佛右側為文殊，左側為維摩，後來雲崗、龍門、麥積山、敦煌等北朝石窟中刻繪的《維摩變》數量逐漸增多，畫像也有所變化，出現了像敦煌 423 窟、雲崗第 6 窟將維摩和文殊論辯同置殿室內的畫面。在散藏於各地的北朝造像碑中，另見有一類情節較複雜的《維摩變》，如有‘大魏癸丑’(永熙二年)紀年的趙見禧造像碑上的《維摩變》，上下二層共刻繪八幅畫面，分別表現維摩與文殊論辯、維摩見舍利弗、國王聽法、天女散花等內容，不過主體畫面仍然是正中佛像，維摩、文殊分置左右，這種格局一直延襲下來，成為以後大型《維摩變》的主體規模。麥積山西魏早期第 127 窟以通壁巨幅的畫面圖繪《維摩詰經》內容，畫面的中心主體形象仍是文殊和維摩辯論的場面，同時加繪了四天王、阿修羅王、諸天菩薩以及各品的情節，畫面有主有從，這種以文殊和維摩為主體形象組合多種內容的構成方式也成為隋唐《維摩變》壁畫遵循的重要圖本。

敦煌莫高窟遺存的《維摩變》壁畫，隋代雖未完全擺脫前期的影響，文殊與維摩分別繪在佛龕的兩側，出主意人物形象地刻劃，環境的描繪更加生動。420 窟的《維摩變》除了在龕的兩側對稱畫出維摩、文殊論辯的場面外，還畫出堂前的碧水池、殿後的綠樹林、池中的鴛鴦紅蓮、樹上的白花翠鳥。

初唐，以文殊、維摩論辯相對的《維摩變》，開始由龕側壁面向更大的門壁空間發展，最大的壁畫面積達二十平米。220 窟《維摩變》畫在窟內門壁的兩側，南側的維摩居士手揮麈尾，撫膝帳內，身體前傾，畫家將維摩辯才無礙，咄咄逼人的表情作了出神入化的刻畫；帳下聽法的各國王子，在像貌、服飾以及神態上的描繪都十分精到。門北側，文殊菩薩從容而坐，神態自若。菩薩座下的禮法帝王及群臣，形象間流露出華貴之氣象可與傳世的初唐名作《古帝王圖》相毗美。在主體形象周圍，穿插繪出分屬方便品、不思議品、觀眾生品、香積佛品的情作。103 窟盛唐朝的《維摩變》，構圖宏麗，敷色簡淡，注重線條的表現力，另是一種別致的效果。敦煌大型完整的《維摩變》出現於武周時期，第 335、332 窟北壁《維摩變》和麥積山西魏第 127 窟《維摩變》一樣以通壁巨幅的畫面圖繪《維摩詰經》內容，這種以主體形象組合多種內容的構成方式為中晚唐《維摩變》遵循的主要圖本，在這以後的敦煌壁畫中幾乎都採用同一種形式，即使分繪在兩個壁面上，也不過是同一構圖的分拆而已。因此，麥積山西魏 127 窟的《維摩變》，實際上已成為大型《維摩變》的標準圖樣。

石窟中繪塑彌勒菩薩天宮說法的形象，年代大致在西元四世紀。新疆克孜爾石窟將交腳坐姿的彌勒菩薩及諸天伎樂畫在窟門的上方，間以天宮樓闕；敦煌莫高窟塑彌勒菩薩於窟內上層的闕形龕中，以示彌勒兜率天宮說法。圖像是依《彌勒上生經》所繪。這類圖本由南北朝傳到隋代，隋代畫家董伯仁所畫的《彌勒變》，即是在前代基礎上又有新的創造。敦煌莫高窟419窟後部平頂上為一鋪《彌勒上生經變》，彌勒端坐殿中，宮殿兩側有多層樓閣，閣中眾天女手執樂器，歌舞彈唱，渲染出彌勒淨土一派歌舞祥和的氣氛，大體是與董伯仁《彌勒變》相近似的作品。

《彌勒經變》在敦煌唐代的壁畫中出現了兩種圖本，一種仍延續著隋代的《彌勒上生經變》，沒有大的變化；另外新出現了以《彌勒下生經》為藍本的經變。《彌勒下生經變》畫的是彌勒菩薩下生成佛，說法度人的事蹟，壁畫的空間也由洞窟的上部移到大面積的壁面上，到盛唐時已發展成大型的《彌勒變》。第445窟《彌勒下生變》，居中畫彌勒佛倚坐說法，兩側脅侍為法華菩薩和大妙相菩薩等眾，靠畫面的左右兩邊，又各畫一鋪佛、弟子和菩薩。圖的下部畫穰佉王獻七寶臺，兩側畫剃度出家的穰佉王及王妃、太子、大臣、彩女等眾；翅頭城的羅刹鬼夜掃穢惡；閻浮提中自然樹上生衣；彌勒托生父母修梵摩；婆羅門拆毀樓閣等。上部則有兜率天宮和彌勒淨土一種七收的畫面。很明顯，這樣的《彌勒下生變》中同時包括了上生淨土，只不過是以下生的內容為主，早期上生兜率天宮的場景相應壓縮。148窟南壁的《彌勒變》畫得更加對稱規整，畫面上部採用透視法和濃重的色彩繪出重閣回廊，庭院深窅的"兜率陀天宮"，彌勒菩薩天宮說法的場面畫在庭院的中部，構圖呈俯瞰式。以下的彌勒下生成佛，初會說法及穰佉王供養，剃度出家等均平行描繪在畫面前部。兩重世界，兩種構圖，卻給人一種統一和諧的視覺效果，說明唐代的民間匠師已具備構造大場面的藝術才能。而透過剃度出家等場面，則生動表現了現實世俗生活中的人物情態。

隋唐《涅槃變》壁畫，佛典依據主要是《大磐涅槃經後分》，《大智度論》和《菩薩處胎經》等，畫面常見有雙林入滅、迦葉禮佛足、摩耶夫人下天、金棺出城、幢幡供養、梵棺、八王爭舍利和優波吉均分舍利等數種。通常是以佛涅槃圖為核心。文獻曾記載東晉畫家顧愷之作過《分舍利圖》，現存遺跡中，佛涅槃像及弟子舉哀。八王爭舍利的場面在克孜爾、庫木吐喇等早期石窟中是圍繞後室的涅槃像組成的《涅槃變》，可看作是內地《涅槃變》壁畫的早期樣式。繪於麥積山第127窟正壁的《涅槃圖》雖大部殘毀，但遺存部分所顯示的規模，仍大體反映了西魏《涅槃變》的宏偉面貌。莫高窟聖歷元年(西元698年)的332窟和大歷年間(西元766–779年)的148窟《涅槃變》壁畫，均是大場面的巨制。其中描繪分爭舍利，西域騎兵對陣鏖戰，弟子舉哀以及天王護持等等，形象刻畫極為生動，158窟以巨型彩塑涅磐像為主體，周圍以壁畫表現舉哀弟子與前來悼念的各族國王、邦長，佛涅槃像安祥恬靜，僧俗痛不欲生的情態，以及六師外道各各不同的表現，不失為《涅槃變》彩塑與壁畫結合的傳神佳作。

《西方淨土變》在南朝就開始流行。[2]在南北通道的麥積山127窟的《西方淨土變》，除畫西方三聖(阿彌陀、觀音、勢至)及羅漢弟子，聽法諸眾之外，畫面中已出現天宮臺榭、欄楯舞池、歌舞伎樂，從這鋪北朝晚期《西方淨土變》上也可窺見早期的基本形態。敦煌393窟的《西方淨土變》居中描繪坐出水蓮臺上的"西方三聖"，七寶池中蓮花盛開，化生童子合什供養，水中鴛鴦遊嬉，天際伎樂飛翔，後有寶樹華蓋，佛陀說法，是敦煌較早出現的隋代《西方淨土變》。隨著淨土信仰在民間的普及，唐代《西方淨土變》壁畫在寺廟石窟中大量出現。在敦煌石窟現存的經變畫中，數量最多，有唐一代《西方淨土變》(包括《觀無量壽經變》)不下百幅。表現《阿彌陀經》中有"七寶池，八功德水，金沙布地，金銀琉璃階道。……池中蓮花大如車輪，種種奇妙雜色之鳥，微風吹動寶樹出微妙音"、"無有眾苦，但受諸樂"的極樂世界圖景，在唐代貞觀年間更為完備起來。第220窟南壁貞觀十六年(西元624年)的一鋪《西方淨土變》，在原七寶池和西方三聖的主體圖像之上向四周擴展，在坐于寶池蓮台的阿彌陀、觀音、勢至前，勾勒欄楯，加繪供養菩薩。池前的琉璃地上，對稱畫出一班歌舞伎樂，兩位天女在管弦和鳴之下，相對而舞，動態激揚，天衣悄旋，真有滿壁風動之感。在畫面上方，是華殿寶幢、流雲飛花、散花天女、天鼓和鳴，形成天上地下一派歌舞昇平的祥和氣象。這鋪有紀年的初唐《淨土變》是莫高窟現存幅面最大的一壁，在構圖的完美和彩繪的精麗上，都具有代表性，可作為唐代《西方淨土變》的標準範式。

修習阿彌陀淨土法門，誦持《無量壽經》、《阿彌陀經》和《觀無量壽佛經》，這三部佛經通常稱作"淨土三經"。由唐初淨土大師道綽和善導極力推行。唐代有詮譯"淨土三經"的經疏和經變在民間流傳。依據這三部淨土經描繪的壁畫，最先完善的是《西方淨土經》。按《觀無量壽佛經》內容描繪的"未生怨""十六觀"以及"九品往生"的壁畫在敦煌初唐第431窟雖有表現，但還沒有形成完整統一的結構。敦煌《觀經變》的定型圖本在盛唐表現為"三聯式"構圖，即中間為大型的西方淨土，兩側是立軸式的長條畫面，分別畫十六觀和未生怨。第320窟北壁的《觀經變》中間的西方淨土為方型，畫面的格局與上流《西方淨土變》大體相同。在中部的大畫與左右長條幅畫面間隔以卷草花紋，以示畫面內容的區別。條幅中的十六觀和未生怨依上下結構展開故事情節，畫面構圖齊整。第172窟在南北兩壁各畫一舖《觀經變》，圖中亭臺樓閣錯落有致，宏敞壯麗。全壁設色富麗，人物造型極盡生動，呈現出盛唐壁畫藝術的輝煌氣象。

僧人信行創導的三階教主唱末法之說，勸導人們“廣施七法”立塔造象，作井架橋等七種施捨。因此依據《佛說諸種福田經》描繪的《福田經變》在莫高窟北周洞窟中開始出現。北周第296窟的《福田經變》畫出修福七法中的五事，形式還比較簡略。隋代第302窟的《福田經變》圖像內容較為豐富，計有伐木建塔、彩繪廟堂、廣施醫藥、道旁作井、修橋鋪路、植園開池等福田功德。不少畫面直接取自現實生活場景，對研究古代社會具有多方面的價值。三階教存世時間不長，在隋開皇二十年(公元600年)遭到禁止後，逐漸在民間失去影響，與此同時，和三階教主張相關的《福田經變》，在唐代莫高窟壁畫中也不再繼續。因此，這二舖《福田經變》是瞭解三階教歷史的珍貴的形象資料。

隋唐遺存的大型經變，一部份是在前代基礎上發展起來，另一部分則是隋唐時期新出現的經變。所占比例更多。以敦煌莫高窟現存情況來看，這一時期新出現的經變畫不下二十種，約二百舖，繪壁較多者如《法華變》、《東方藥師變》、《報恩經變》、《華嚴經變》、《金剛經變》、《天請問經變》、《金光明經變》、《勞度差鬥聖變》、《觀世音經變》等近十種。這些新出現的經變，或者是隋唐社會宗教生活的曲折反映，或者與某一佛教宗派的興起密切相關。因此，從這些新出現的經變中能看到更加鮮明的時代特色。

由隋代高僧智顗創立的天臺宗，採用大乘佛教的《法華經》作為開宗立派的理論依據，弘揚“三乘歸一”的“一佛乘”思想，遂使僧俗間唱誦《法華經》在隋唐之際成為一時風尚。於是依《法華經》內容描繪的《法華變》幾乎也於同時出現在寺廟石窟中。按唐裴孝源《貞觀公私畫史》、張彥遠《歷代名畫記》稱，隋代畫家展子虔畫有《法華變相》一卷，這是有關《法華變》最早的文獻記載。隋代的《法華變》遺跡在敦煌存有四窟，而以第420窟最為宏偉壯觀。420窟為覆斗頂方型窟，《法華變》畫在覆斗頂的四披：北披為序品、南披為譬喻品、東披為觀音普門品、西披為方便品。畫面分為三層，作長卷式的構圖，每段故事之間或以山林相隔，或由城廓貫通，大體沿襲著南北朝佛本生故事的結構方式。繪于南披的《譬喻品》在上部繪出滿載珍寶的牛車、鹿車和羊車，以喻佛教之三乘：下部則畫篷車一輛，載二童子離開火宅，用來比喻“三乘歸於一乘”的教旨，既生動又準確。東披的《觀音菩薩普門品》中繪觀音菩薩救難的生動場面，有滿載貨物的駱駝商隊，有攔路搶劫的群盜，有遇風履險的船隻……是當時社會生活的生動寫照。

敦煌隋代《法華變》壁畫採用的長卷式的構圖，仍在初唐的《法華變》中沿用了一段時間。第331窟東壁的法華變中層畫《序品》，上下兩層分別畫《見寶塔品》、《妙音菩薩品》、《從地踊出品》和《提婆達多品》。在圖像布排上以多寶塔和法華會為中心，五品的內容互有照應，畫面因此而收到統一的效果。已初見盛唐期大型《法華變》之端倪。盛唐時期的畫家從發展得已很完善的《西方淨土變》這樣一類巨構中得到啟發，將繪製大型經變的經驗用來構造大幅的《法華變》壁畫，出現了以佛及序品為中心，四周繪各品情節的較完備的《法華變》。第23窟為覆斗頂方形窟，窟內除佛和菩薩像外，主要是《法華變》壁畫，中心畫面與各品之間明顯表現出設計的整體性。

《妙法蓮華經》總共有二十八品，盛唐期的《法華變》已繪出十五品，其中以化城喻品、觀音菩薩普門品、法師品和比喻品表現得比較充分。中唐以後的《法華變》品目增加到二十品，經變的結構也根據窟內不同的壁面而發展出不同的形式，概括起來有三種：一種是按覆斗頂四披壁面的空間，構圖呈梯形。中心畫法華會，周圍繪各品故事，標明榜題。85窟窟頂南披的法華變即是這一形式的代表作。其餘兩種都是根據洞窟壁面而作方形或長方形畫面。畫面中央為序品法華會，左右環以《從地涌出品》及《提婆達多品》，往外的四周繪其他各品。138、144、472等窟屬於這種形式。在中晚唐觀音信仰興起之後，觀世音菩薩普門品有了特殊的地位，因此在《法華變》的方形構圖的下方，單辟出四條屏畫面，專門表現普門品的內容。敦煌159、231、12等窟均是以這種構圖形式來表現《法華經》各品豐富內容。上述三種形式的《法華變》作為固定的圖本樣式，一直流傳到宋代。

在大型《法華變》流行的同時，莫高窟出現了表現《法華經》單品的獨幅壁畫，繪於第45窟南壁的《觀音經變》是唐代最具代表性的作品之一。這幅壁畫居中畫觀世音菩薩立像，左右兩側作多層小畫，分別表現觀世音菩薩三十三現身和救苦救難的情節。其中表現念菩薩名號、商人遇賊脫險、枷鎖系身皆得解脫、船遇黑風化險為夷等畫面，不僅主題突出，而且人物刻畫極為傳神，是《法華經》單品變相中發展得最完備的一類作品。

在敦煌莫高窟，東方《藥師經變》現存有九十六壁之多，是隋唐新出經變畫中數量最大的一種。在隋唐以前，民間雖有《藥師經》的流傳，也偶有燃藥師燈，轉《藥師經》的法事活動(見《周書．張元傳》)，但未見取材《藥師經》的繪畫。大概東方藥師信仰還不很流行。入隋以後，敦煌始見有《藥師經變》壁畫，隋代大業年間，外域僧人達摩笈多譯出《藥師如來本願功德經》，唐代高僧玄奘、義淨又相繼譯出《藥師琉璃光如來本願功德經》和《藥師琉璃光七佛本願功德經》後，東方藥師信仰得以流行。隋代敦煌出現的《藥師變》構圖較為簡單。第417窟後部平頂上的一鋪藥師變，人物分作兩層。上層繪結跏趺坐的藥師佛和日光月光菩薩，下層繪十二藥叉大將合十跪拜七層燈輪。第433、436、394等隋窟的《藥師變》中，藥師佛、菩薩和藥叉神將均作對稱排列，人物前畫有供養藥師佛的七層燈輪和五色長幡。這些圖像在入唐以後便成為大型《藥師變》的主體圖像。

莫高窟唐代的《東方藥師變》，有表現"七佛本願功德"和"藥師佛本願功德"兩種形式。初唐220窟北壁為一鋪通壁巨制的《藥師變》，畫面中間的主體形象為七身藥師佛和脅侍菩薩，上有七寶華蓋，下有重瓣蓮臺，十二藥叉大將分立畫面兩側。在寶階圍欄之前，燈樓火木的燭照之下，笙歌管弦合鳴，舞者胡旋如風，一派東方琉璃淨土的歡樂景象。在畫面樂舞之間另畫有燃點七輪燈的菩薩，一蹲一立，神情十分專注，燃燈的細節繪畫面又增添了一種人間的情調。中間的燈樓座下，還題有墨書發願文，為貞觀十六年(西元642年)發願施繪，這也是敦煌初唐經變畫中最早紀年的壁畫。經藥師佛本願功德為依據的《東方藥師經變》，從盛唐天寶年間開始以三聯式的構圖出現，中間主畫面與《西方淨土變》相近，著力於極樂世界的渲染。左右兩側立幅中分別繪《藥師經》的十二大願和九橫死。單獨畫出這方面的內容，意在"致福消災"。第148窟東壁的《藥師變》即是這一形式的代表之作。從中晚唐時起，九橫死十二大願還以獨立的畫面描繪出來，從而發展和豐富了《東方藥師經變》的表現形式。

武則天重瑞應，好圖讖，當政期間因《大雲經》中有女王之文而頒行天下，詔各州建大雲寺。敦煌也於此時營建了大雲寺(即今第96窟)，並在321窟的南壁新繪出一鋪圖解武則天聖諱的《寶雨經變》壁畫。《寶雨經》(亦名《寶雲經》)先有蕭梁時扶南國三藏曼陀羅仙的譯本，大周長壽二年(西元693年)，南天竺沙門菩提流支宣釋梵本《寶雨經》，由白馬寺僧懷義監譯奉獻給武則天。在這個重譯本中，插入了佛與一位名日月光的東方天子解說因緣的情節。經文說這位日月光天子實是菩薩現女身，下凡到瞻部洲，化度東北方摩訶支那國眾生，為自在主。這實際是在稱喻武則天。第321窟《寶雨經變》即依此經內容而畫，在構圖的中央畫《序品》，表現薄伽梵在伽耶山頂說法時，漫天寶雨的場面。在寶雨的上方，畫一帶通壁的海水，海中出一雙大手，一手擎日，一手托月，圖像表面上是象徵日月光天子，實際上是武則天名'曌'字的圖解。在薄伽梵說法的下方還專畫有女王和二侍女禮佛的圖像，這也是以現女身于摩訶支那國的"日月光天子"來象徵武則天。像這樣直接為統治者歌功頌德的繪畫作品，在此前的寺院石窟中實屬罕見。

唐代初年，玄奘法師譯出了一部僅千餘字的短小佛經《天請問經》，經的內容是釋迦牟尼回答一位元天神所提的九個問題，如"無生為樂"，"佈施種福"，"解脫諸欲"等等。不料這一帶有較濃厚的人生哲理的佛經在吐蕃攻佔敦煌的前夕開始以經變畫的方式出現在莫高窟中，就現存的壁畫遺跡看，這一題材起自唐大歷年間，經五代到北宋，共有三十一舖之多。繪於第148窟北壁不空絹索龕上的天請問經變以佛說法的宏大場面為中心，下部和兩側共畫出九組天神面佛問法；上部繪象徵忉利天宮的樓閣庭院；背景處為重巒岩岫，蔥木翠喬。人物和景物相互映襯，顯示出民間畫師高度成熟的藝術技巧。

唐天寶末年，安祿山攻陷長安，玄宗幸蜀，隨之西遷的京師之民中有不少的僧人及畫師巧匠，他們給邊地帶來了中原流行的佛經論疏，俗講梵文以及變相圖本。畫史上記載吳道子、楊廷光、尹琳、李生、盧稜伽、陳靜眼、張法受、武靜藏等一代名手曾在兩京寺廟中畫過的《金剛經變》、《華嚴經變》、《金光明經變》、《報恩經變》等題材，也在安史之亂后流傳到敦煌。莫高窟的經變畫一時間增加了許多新內容，計有《金剛經變》、《金光明經變》、《楞伽經變》、《楞嚴經變》、《華嚴經變》、《報恩經變》、《報父母恩重經變》、《密嚴經變》、《思益梵天請問經變》、《勞度差鬥聖變》等十多種，一些經變由唐入宋反復繪製，多的竟至數十舖。例如《報恩經變》，莫高窟現存三十二舖，其中以第148和31窟年代最早。第148窟甬道盝形頂中央繪序品，南披為惡友品，北披殘存孝養品部份。人物活動依故事情節各有聚散，用色用線簡潔明快。第85窟南壁的《報恩經變》，構圖龐大，氣象恢宏，中央畫序品的大型法會，佛與脅侍菩薩安居高臺，菩薩天人等眾位列兩班，前有歌舞伎樂，旁有堂塔構欄，形勢曲折近似壇場。畫面四周以城廓山野為背景，分別畫出諸品，各有榜題標明內容。惡友品中表現善友太子園中彈琴自娛，遇利師跋王女，雙眼復明，結為夫婦一節，畫二人對坐柳下，撫琴交談，極富生活情趣。類似的畫面在婆羅門子孝養、金毛獅子堅誓等故事情節中都能看到，是這類大型經變畫中最有生趣的部分。

《報父母恩重經變》在內容主旨上與《報恩經變》有一定的聯

繫，原是依《報父母恩重經》而作的變相，內容與中國傳統的《孝經》頗多相近處，故《開元釋教錄》疑為偽經。依這部偽經作的經變在敦煌既有畫幀，也有壁畫。238窟是現存年代最早的一舖，從中可看到這一經變在敦煌的最初面貌。156窟同時畫有《報恩經變》和《報父母恩重經變》，這一方面反映了中國歷來"君君臣臣，父父子子"的儒家正統觀念的影響。另一方面也說明中晚唐儒、佛、道三教合流的時代風氣在藝術中的反映。

唐代經變畫的發展，與這一時期佛寺俗講風氣的盛行關係極大。當時佛教寺院為了爭取更多的信眾，使佛法由過去的偏走上層轉向普及下層氓庶，因而採用了類似民間講故事的口頭文學方式，向一般老百姓講說佛經內容，即是‘俗講’。根據唐代人有關俗講的記載和敦煌石室出的敦煌卷子紙背所書《俗講儀式》，至遲在唐代，佛寺俗講已有固定的講唱形式。九世紀上半葉來中國的日本僧人圓仁在《入唐求法巡禮行記》中說，當時長安有名的俗講法師，左街是海岸，體虛，齊高，光影四人，右街為文漵法師，他們都是名動一時的俗講大師，而文漵法師因"其聲宛暢，感動里人"令"聽者填咽寺舍"，被稱之為"京國第一人"。僧人俗稱，一般是有說有唱，同時還配合有與講唱內容相關的圖畫，以助講唱的效果。

唐代中晚期，寺院俗講的流行在一定程度上影響到石窟寺院壁畫的繪作，部份壁畫不是直接依據佛經，而是根據梵文來描繪。因此，這樣一類經變畫具有更強烈的世俗化和戲劇性色彩。如晚唐更加豐富起來的《勞度差門聖變》，就是其中的代表。巴黎藏P. 4524號敦煌《降魔變文》，卷子背面畫的就是勞度差門聖變，變文與變相合若符契。《勞度差門聖變》是由《賢愚經》卷十《須達起精舍品》改寫而成的變文，依此變文創作的變相，敦煌西千佛洞隋代及莫高窟初唐的洞窟中開始出現較為簡單的鬥法場面。真正形成大型的變相，是在張義潮收復河西之後。莫高窟第196窟和第9窟保存了兩舖完整的《勞度差門聖變》，壁畫也是根據變文所描繪，畫面以宏大的場面和戲劇性的手法生動地構畫出舍利弗同勞度差之間鬥法的種種神通變幻：勞度差化作大樹，舍利弗化作旋風，連根拔樹；勞度差作七寶池，舍利弗化作六牙白象，汲幹池水；勞度差化作龍，舍利弗化作金翅鳥王……六個回合，勞度差皆敗。在形象刻劃上，畫家選取旋風卷樹，草木披靡，烈火延燒，勞度差的寶座搖搖欲墜等情節，以勞度差的惶恐神態巧妙地映襯出舍利弗的神通力。這一鬥法場面以風為引子，展示了一個驚心動魄的時刻，具有引人入勝的藝術效果。

印度密宗自從開元三大士到長安譯經弘密之後，密像的繪塑逐漸在中土流傳開來，崇密風尚也由兩京地區傳到敦煌河西邊地。在莫高窟中晚唐的經變畫中，新出現了根據密宗經典描繪的《密嚴經變》、《佛頂尊勝陀羅尼經變》、《千手眼觀音菩薩經變》、《如意輪菩薩經變》和《不空絹索經變》。晚唐第85窟和第150窟的密嚴經變典出《大乘密嚴經》，是一部佛為金剛藏菩薩解答法性問題所說的經典，內容較為抽象。85窟的《密嚴經變》與《藥師經變》,《思益梵天問經變》同畫於北壁，構圖為方形，畫面著重於渲染大型說法場面的整體氣氛。像這類抽象內容的經變畫在中晚唐壁畫中數量不少，是隋唐新出經變畫中不可忽略的藝術品類。

注

李鑄晉教授於1979年6月作為美國第一位美術史交流學者來中國，我陪同他從敦煌開始了在中國有意義的學術考察；以後在1980年10月我得美中交流中心的邀請和李鑄晉教授的安排，得以訪問哥倫比亞大學、堪薩斯大學等十四所大學，從此中美美術史學者交流不斷，在李鑄晉教授的紀念文集編撰之際，特寄上有關敦煌藝術的論文以茲紀念。

1. 本來按佛教經文繪製的圖畫都可概稱為經變。但這裡所指為按某部佛典所繪整體圖像的大型經變。而個體圖像或單獨成幅的本生故事或佛傳圖像不包含在內。
2. 詳見拙著《中國美術史論集》中《西方淨土變的形成與發展》一文。

STUDIES IN HONOR OF CHU-TSING LI

The *Thousand-armed Avalokiteshvara* in the Birmingham Museum of Art

DONALD A. WOOD

Within the greater Buddhist pantheon the Thousand-armed Avalokiteshvara (*Sahasrabhuja Avalokiteshvara*) is one of the most beneficent and compassionate of deities. The multiple arms and heads represent the ability of the deity to see in all directions in every universe at any time and to assist all beings in trouble. First popularized in China during the Tang dynasty (618–907), images of this deity quickly proliferated throughout China, Japan, and the Himalayan region, and they remain immensely popular to this day.

In 1999 the Birmingham Museum of Art, Alabama, acquired an important eighteenth-century Sino-Tibetan gilt bronze statue of the Thousand-armed Avalokiteshvara (fig. 1). The image consists of two pieces, the body of the deity and the base, which together measure 22⅛ inches in height. The figure displays the traditional iconography of eleven heads and forty-two arms. It stands on a double-lotus throne, which in turn rests atop a trapezoid-shaped pierced base decorated with cascading drapery in the center, a lion and dragon to either side, and a single row of lotus petals below. The bottom of the base is sealed with a metal plate impressed with the design of a double *vajra*. The back of the base has two slots where the tenons of a mandorla (now missing) would have been inserted.

A rich diversity exists within the iconography of the Thousand-armed Avalokiteshvara. Images in wood, lacquer, and bronze range in size from diminutive works intended for private worship to colossal figures made for public display. Statues with nine, ten, eleven, or even twelve heads arranged in tiara- and coronet-crown configurations with benign, angry, tusked, and laughing faces in various numerical combinations are also found. The deity is most commonly shown with eight principal arms that hold a variety of attributes, such as a rosary, lotus, bow, and jewel. In the Birmingham statue thirty-four arms, each with an eye in the palm, surround the eight-armed image, adding to the all-seeing nature of the deity. The mandorla that originally backed the image was most likely comprised of hundreds of small arms that formed a halo around the figure and completed the thousand-armed iconography.[1] Nine heads with benign faces, arranged in three rows of three, are topped by the head of a wrathful *dharmapala*. The entire configuration is crowned by the head of Amitabha, the spiritual parent of the deity.

The Thousand-armed Avalokiteshvara appears to be an offspring of the basic cosmic form of Avalokiteshvara, the Eleven-headed Avalokiteshvara (*Ekadasamukha Avalokiteshvara*). According to Pratapaditya Pal, a

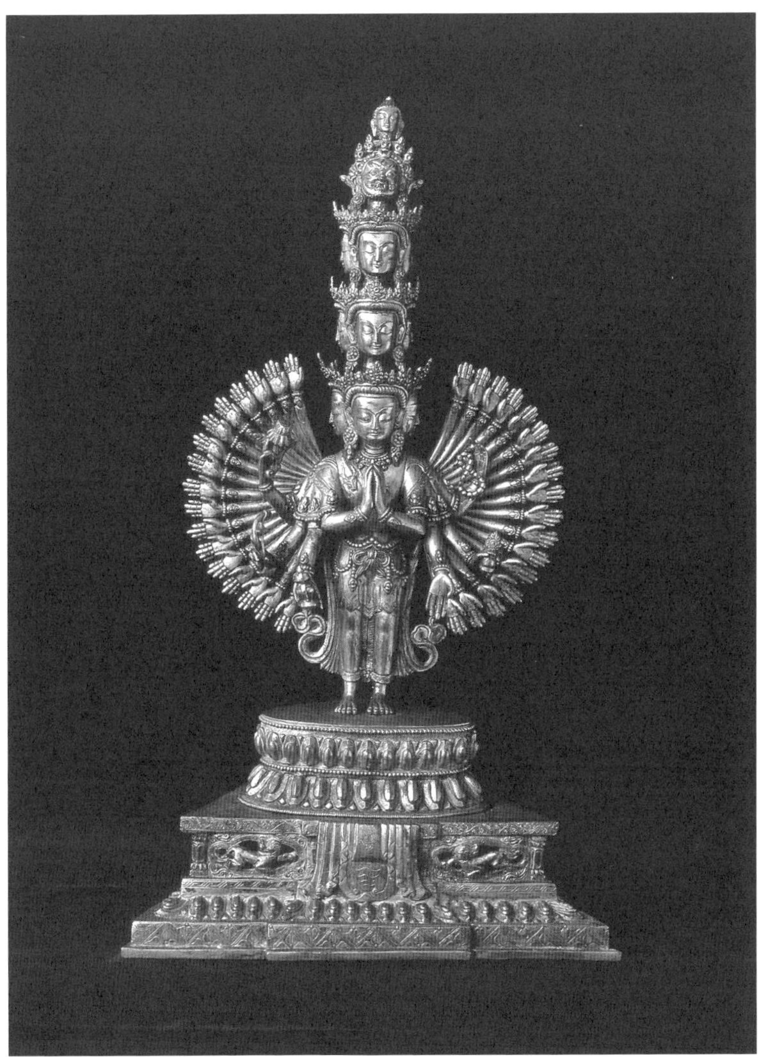

FIGURE 1
Thousand-armed Avalokiteshvara (*Sahasrabhuja Avalokiteshvara*), Sino-Tibetan, 18th century. Gilt bronze, h. 22 1/8 in. (56.2 cm). Museum purchase with funds provided by the 1998 Museum Dinner and Ball. Birmingham Museum of Art, Birmingham, Alabama (1999.9)

dhyana from the *Dharmakoshasamgraha* verifies this identification.[2] A visual comparison of the two deities also corroborates this, with the profusion of arms of the thousand-armed image being arranged like a halo around the basic eleven-headed deity.

The clearest description of the Thousand-armed Avalokiteshvara is found in the *Nilkathaka Sutra*, which was first translated into Chinese by the early-seventh-century monk Zhitong. Subsequent translations of this important text were also undertaken by the monks Bhagavaddharma (active mid-7th century), Bodhiruci (active 693–713), Subhakarasimha (637–735), Vajrabodhi (670–741), and Amoghvajra (704–770).[3] The credence accorded this sutra by the attention of these great masters of Tantric Buddhism is particularly important for the subsequent popularity of the deity. By the end of the ninth century, the Thousand-armed Avalokiteshvara was by far the most prevalent of the cosmic forms of Avalokiteshvara in China.[4] Due to the patronage of these masters, the cult of the Thousand-armed Avalokiteshvara spread far and wide, eventually being transported to Japan by the Chinese monk Jianzhen (J: Ganjin, 687–763), who propagated the cult in Japan after his arrival there in 754.

Tibet and China enjoyed a close relationship during the Qing dynasty (1644–1911). The Mongols were followers of Tibetan Buddhism, and monks and dignitaries frequently traveled between the two countries, exchanging gifts of texts, textiles, and sacred images. Tibetan craftsmen worked in both Beijing and Liaoning creating images specifically for this exchange. The Birmingham Museum statue most likely originated as part of the spiritual dialogue between these two countries.

On August 8, 1999, Tibetan monks associated with the Drepung Loseling Monastery in India performed the traditional *Zung bhul Rab gnes* ceremony at the Birmingham Museum for its newly acquired image. When images of Buddhist deities are first consecrated, the *Zung bhul Rab gnes* ceremony is held to empower and sanctify them. During the ceremony, prayers, charms, and drawings of various deities are inserted into chambers in the image or in the base. The various offerings in the chamber in the base of the Birmingham image were lost at some point in the history of the statue, and the monks reconsecrated the statue by filling the base with the appropriate sacred materials prepared especially for this occasion. The ceremony, rarely held in the United States, was performed at the Birmingham Museum to welcome the image to its new home.

NOTES

1. The mold for a votive plaque of this deity with the mandorla in place is in the collection of Jane B. Werner-Aye. The mold is illustrated in The Albuquerque Museum 1977, 176, pl. 88.
2. Pal 1982, 17.
3. Wood 1985, 148.
4. Ibid., 150.

REFERENCES

Pal, Pratapaditya. 1982. Cosmic Vision and Buddhist Images. *Art International* 25, nos. 1–2: 17.

The Albuquerque Museum. 1977. *Tibet: Tradition and Change.*

Wood, Donald A. 1985. *Eleven Faces of the Bodhisattva.* Ann Arbor: University of Michigan Press.

STUDIES IN HONOR OF CHU-TSING LI

Liu E and His Bronze Collection

THOMAS LAWTON

Liu E (1857–1909) was a remarkably resilient individual, intellectually and physically, who maintained his independent spirit and unrestrained curiosity in spite of many reversals throughout his life. His reputation as a writer, based on his novel *Laocan youji*, is secure.[1] His contribution to the study of *jiaguwen*, oracle bone inscriptions, together with his pioneering publication *Tieyun cang gui*, is recognized in every account of the subject.[2] His success in water conservation resulting from his accomplishments during the devastating floods of 1888 is recorded in official documents.[3] Oddly enough, Liu E's efforts as a collector of ancient bronze vessels remain relatively little known.

In his 1941 publication *Shang Zhou yiqi tongkao*, Rong Geng (1894–1983) assembled an impressive amount of information relating to virtually every aspect of early Chinese bronzes.[4] His biographical sketches of the people who studied and collected ancient ritual bronzes in themselves constitute a major contribution to the history of Chinese connoisseurship. Rong Geng's terse account of Liu E hints at his subject's flamboyant personality and his varied accomplishments.[5] He notes that Liu E's *zi* was Tieyun, and that he was a native of Dantu, Jiangsu Province. He also touches on Liu E's activities during the occupation of Peking (modern-day Beijing) by the Allied Relief Force following the 1900 Boxer Rebellion.

Since Liu E was living in the south at the time of the Boxer Rebellion, he was not involved in the fighting. When he learned that Peking was controlled by leaders of the foreign armies who defeated the Boxers and that many Chinese in the capital were starving as a result of the turmoil following the surrender, he determined to try and relieve the situation. Once he arrived in Peking, Liu E learned that the Russian troops, who controlled the area where the government granary was located, wanted to make use of the granary buildings and were planning to burn the rice, since they had no interest in eating it. Liu E negotiated with the Russians and, using relief funds contributed by a number of donors, he succeeded in purchasing the grain and selling it to the people of the capital.

Liu E is said to have used some of the relief funds to purchase antiquities, and he was subsequently charged with having profited from the purchase and sale of the grain. Those charges eventually resulted in his being exiled to Xinjiang in 1908. There is no question that many wealthy Chinese were forced to sell their art collections because of the economic instability in Peking after the Boxer Rebellion. Rare antiquities were offered at extremely low prices, and, whatever the source of his funds, Liu E began

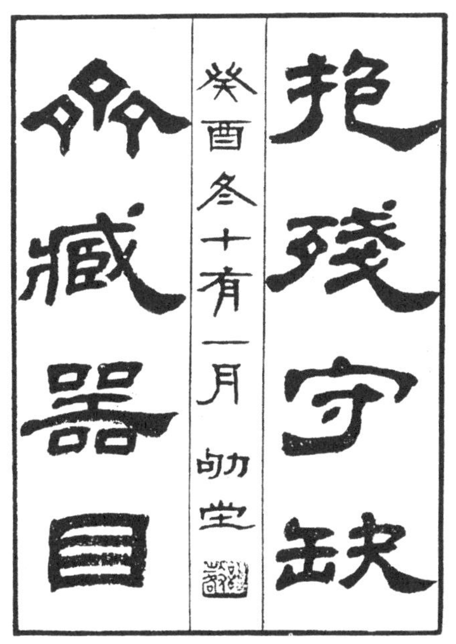

FIGURE 1
Title page of *Baocan shouquezhai cangqi mu*, 1933–34. Compiled by Bao Ding (b. 1899). Calligraphy by Liu Yizheng (1880–1956)

to collect Chinese ritual bronzes shortly after he arrived in the capital to carry out his humanitarian mission. Liu E's grandson, Liu Huisun, confirms that Liu E acquired most of his bronzes in Peking.[6]

In his diaries Liu E speaks of his fondness for antiquities.[7] Entries in those diaries record that in 1901 Liu E acquired Song and Yuan dynasty rare editions of books, as well as paintings and calligraphies, rubbings of stelae and texts, and some bronzes, including the Guo Wengong *ding*, Shinong *zhi*, Ju [?] Fugui *jue*, and the Fan zhong Wu sheng *ding*.[8]

An entry in Liu E's diary dated March 30, 1902, records how he purchased a bronze but could not decipher the inscription, even after having studied three imperial bronze catalogues—the Song dynasty *Bogu* and *Kaogutu* and the Qing dynasty *Xiqing gujian*—in an effort to find a corresponding inscription. The next day, March 31, 1902, Liu E reports the purchase of a small *ding* with the three-character inscription *zuolübao* that he acquired together with some pottery tiles, a Tang bronze mirror and two old jades. A rubbing of this inscription bearing one of Liu E's seals, *Tieyun cang jin*, appears in *Xiaojiaojingge jinwen tuoben*, 2.23b. Luo Zhenyu (1866–1940), a close friend of Liu E, includes a line drawing of the inscription in his *Zhengsongtang jijin tulu*, 2.18b, and notes that it appears in a bronze that had been in Liu's collection. Luo Zhenyu also

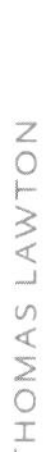

refers to Liu E's studio as the Shijutang, a name that he uses consistently when referring to Liu's bronzes, indicating that it was the name of the studio where Liu E kept his bronzes.

On April 15, 1902, Liu E records how delighted he was to have purchased several bronzes that were said to have come from the family of Shengyu (1850–1900). He describes nine of the bronzes as being of outstanding quality but does not identify them more specifically. Approximately two weeks later, on May 1, 1902, Liu E notes that he had acquired the Nie Bo *zuo fuyi zun*. Three days later, he mentions the *Fu jin yi*, a *gui* with a sixteen-character inscription that is more commonly referred to as the Guo Bo *gui*. This bronze is now in the Lüshun Museum, Dalian, Liaoning Province.[9]

Liu E died in exile in 1909 without having prepared a catalogue of his bronze collection. Several decades later Bao Ding (b. 1899) compiled *Baocan shouquezhai cangqi mu*,[10] a partial list of Liu E's bronzes that includes ninety-five Shang and Zhou dynasty vessels, nineteen bronze weapons, two Qin dynasty vessels, and thirty-one bronzes dating from the Han period and later (fig. 1). The calligraphy on the title page, written by Liu Yizheng (1880–1956), includes the lunar date *guiyin zhong shiyuyiyue*, which corresponds with the period from December 17, 1933, to January 14, 1934, in the Western calendar. According to his preface, Bao Ding had to compile the record of Liu E's bronze collection on the basis of rubbings of bronze inscriptions bearing Liu's seals because the bronzes themselves had already been dispersed. That method of compilation meant that Bao Ding did not include any bronzes that were not inscribed. Verification of Liu E's ownership of the bronzes listed in *Baocan shouquezhai cangqi mu* is also provided by references to specific bronzes in other Chinese records, including Luo Zhenyu's *Zhensongtang jijin tulu*.

There are one hundred forty-seven bronzes listed in *Baocan shouquezhai cangqi mu*. Bao Ding arranged the Shang and Zhou bronzes according to vessel type, beginning with three bells and ending with nineteen weapons; he further differentiated them on the basis of the number of characters in their inscriptions. The two Qin weights and thirty-one Han bronzes, which follow the Shang and Zhou pieces, are also arranged in the same way. Although Bao Ding includes a transcription of each inscription, he did not provide any annotation or illustrations. Had Bao Ding decided to include bronze mirrors, he could have expanded his list, since a number of rubbings of early mirrors also carry Liu E's seals.[11]

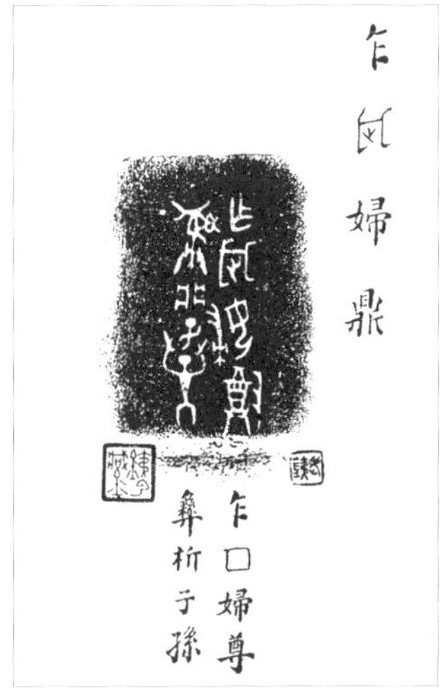

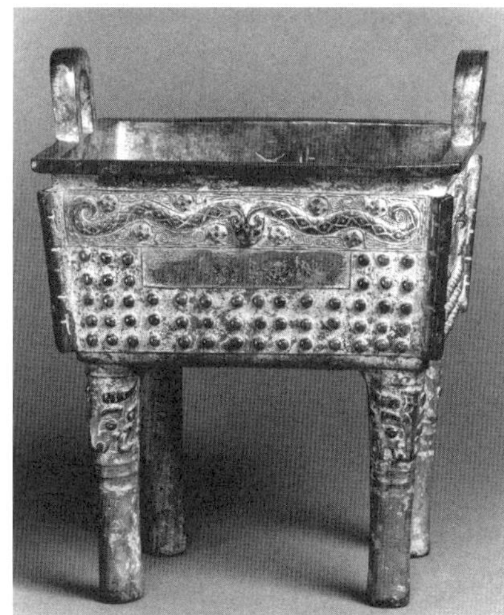

FIGURE 2
Xiaojiaojingge jinwen tuoben entry for Zuo X Fu *ding* with Liu E's seals, *Laotie* and *Tieyun cang jin*, 2.42b

FIGURE 3
Zuo X Fu *fangding*. Bronze, h. 6¾ in. (17.3 cm). The Art Museum, Princeton University. Museum purchase from the C. D. Carter Collection, by subscription. ©1965 Trustees of Princeton University

An example of the importance of Bao Ding's compilation is provided by the entry for the Zuo X Fu *ding*, which begins with the statement that the six-character inscription is arranged in two columns and that two of the characters, *Fu* and *zun*, are written in reverse (fig. 2). Bao Ding includes a drawing of the inscription. Rubbings of this inscription with two of Liu E's seals, *Laotie* and *Tieyun cang jin*, appear in *Sandai jijin wencun*, 3.7.3, *Xiaojiaojingge jinwen tuoben*, 2.42b, and *Kezhai jigulu*, 3.5. The bronze itself, a *fangding*, is now in the The Art Museum, Princeton University (fig. 3).[12]

Bao Ding's list offers a tantalizing glimpse of Liu E's bronze collection. Using *Baocan shouquezhai cangqi mu* as a starting point, it should be possible to reassemble most of the bronzes Liu E acquired during the last few years of his life and, thereby, enable Liu E's admirers to appreciate yet another of his accomplishments.

NOTES

1. Liu E began to write *Laocan youji* in Shanghai in 1904. The first eight chapters appeared in the Shanghai monthly *Xiuxiang xiaoshuo*, which was published by the Commercial Press. The remaining chapters of the novel were printed intermittently between 1904 and 1907 in the Tianjin *Riri xinwen*.

2. In 1903 Liu E selected 1,058 rubbings of inscriptions from the more than 5,000 oracle bones in his collection for publication in *Tieyun canggui*. It was the first publication of oracle bone inscriptions and helped to increase interest in those characters. Later scholars have pointed out that three of the rubbings

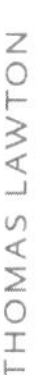

are duplicates and four of the inscriptions are spurious; hence there are only 1,051 rubbings of genuine inscriptions included in the catalogue. *Tieyun cang gui* includes prefaces by Luo Zhenyu (1866–1940), Wu Changshou (1844–1927), and Liu E.

3. From 1888 to 1893 Liu E was directly involved in formulating and implementing plans to regulate the Yellow River. After his success in ending the flooding in Henan Province in 1888, Liu E accepted an offer from Wu Dacheng (1835–1902) to serve as an Intendant (*Daotai*), and participated in the compilation of the *Yu Zhi Lu sansheng hedao quan tu*, an atlas of the Yellow River describing its course from Henan through Zhili and Shandong to the sea. As always, Liu E was an energetic participant; he was a surveyor and traveled extensively through those provinces along the route of the unpredictable Yellow River. The atlas, in five *ce*, was printed in 1890. Several months later, Zhang Yue (1832–1891), the governor of Shandong, invited Liu E to join his staff and assist in regulating the Yellow River in that northeastern province. While living in Shandong, Liu E set down his own theories about water conservancy in *Zhihe qishuo.*

4. Rong Geng devoted eight years of research to the subject, resulting in his magisterial 300,000-character, two-volume work *Shang Zhou yiqi tongkao*; see Rong Geng 1941. The book is noteworthy because of the breadth and depth of its coverage. In 1958 Rong Geng published another comprehensive study of Chinese bronzes in collaboration with Zhang Weichi, titled *Yin Zhou qingtongqi tonglun* (see Rong Geng and Zhang Weichi 1984), that is based extensively on material first discussed in *Shang Zhou yiqi tongkao.*

5. Rong Geng 1941, vol. 1, p. 255. The earliest account of Liu E's life was written by his friend Luo Zhenyu. See Luo Zhenyu 1915. Information about Liu E's career is also provided in Liu Delong, Zhu Xi, and Liu Deping 1985 and 1987; Jiang Yixue 1980. The most comprehensive study of Liu E was compiled by his grandson, Liu Huisun, who had access to Liu E's diaries, family papers, and the recollections of members of the Liu family; it provides a wealth of information and gossip. See Liu Huisun 1982. Among the English-language sources, Harold Shadick includes biographical information about Liu E in the introduction to *The Travels of Lao Ts'an*, first published by Cornell University Press in 1952, with subsequent reprints, including the Columbia University Press Morningside Edition in 1990; also see Fang Chaoying's entry in Hummel 1943, 516–18.

6. Liu Huisun 1982, 132.

7. Four volumes of Liu E's diaries, for the years 1902, 1905, and 1908, were published in 1985. See Liu Delong, Zhu Xi, and Liu Deping 1985, 143–289. Rong Geng believed the inscription on the Fan zhong Wu sheng *ding* was added by Zhang Fengyan, a well-known nineteenth-century forger. See Sun Zhichu 1981, 62, entry 1013; and his essay appended to volume three of *Sandai jijin wencun*, 18–19.

8. Liu Huisun 1982, 82–83.

9. For an illustration of the Guo Bo *gui*, see *Mengyicaotang jijin tu, shang*, 24a–b; and Shirakawa Shizuka 1962–84, 14.775.

10. Liu Huisun 1982, 111, states that as Liu E began to collect a few examples of pottery, he studied the inscriptions and determined some of them were pottery lamp bases made during the Sandai (i.e., Xia, Shang, and Zhou periods). Conse-

quently, Liu E named his studio Wushiwadengzhai (Fifty Tiles and Lamps Studio). As Liu E acquired more examples, he changed the name to Baiwadengzhai (One Hundred Tiles and Lamps Studio) and then to Erbaiwadengzhai (Two Hundred Tiles and Lamps Studio). Finally, in the face of his ever-increasing collection, Liu E settled on the name Baocan shouquezhai (Studio to Cherish the Damaged and Preserve the Broken).

11. For example, see Liu Tizhi 1935, *juan* 16:10a, 14b, 19b, 26a, and 28b.

12. See von Erdberg 1978, 28–29, entry 18, where the inscription is tentatively rendered by Noel Barnard and Chang Kwang-yue as "made for wife Wu [or Yüeh]. Hsi-tzu-sun [a compound clan sign?]."

REFERENCES

Hummel, Arthur W., ed. 1943. *Eminent Chinese of the Ch'ing Dynasty*. Washington, D.C.: Government Printing Office.

Jiang Yixue. 1980. *Liu E nianpu*. Jinan: Qin Lu shushe.

Kezhai jigulu. See Wu Dacheng 1896.

Liu Delong, Zhu Xi, and Liu Deping. 1985. *Liu E ji* Laocan youji *ziliao*. Chengdu: Sichuan renmin chubanshe.

———. 1987. *Liu E xiaojuan*. Tianjin: Tianjin renmin chubanshe.

Liu Huisun. 1982. *Tieyun xiansheng nianpu changbian*. Jinan: Qin Lu shushe.

Liu Tizhi 1935. *Xiaojiaojingge jinwen tuoben*. Shanghai: Zhongguo shudian.

Luo Zhenyu. 1915. *Liu Tieyun zhuan Wushiri menghenlu*. In *Xuetang congke*.

———. 1983. *Sandai jijin wencun*. Beijing: Zhonghua shuju.

Rong Geng. 1941. *Shang Zhou yiqi tongkao*. Peking: Harvard-Yenching Institute.

Rong Geng and Zhang Weichi. 1984. *Yin Zhou qingtongqi tonglun*. Beijing: Wenwu chubanshe.

Sandai jijin wencun. See Luo Zhenyu 1983.

Shirakawa Shizuka. 1962–84. *Kinbun tsūshaku*. Hakutsuru Bijutsukan-shi. Kyoto: Hakutsuru Bijutsukan.

Sun Zhichu. 1981. *Jinwen zhulu jianmu*. Beijing: Zhonghua shuju.

von Erdberg, Eleanor. 1978. *Chinese Bronzes from the Collection of Chester Dale and Dolly Carter*. Ascona: Artibus Asiae.

Wu Dacheng. 1896. *Kezhai jigulu*. Shanghai: Hanfenlou.

Xiaojiaojingge jinwen tuoben. See Liu Tizhi 1935.

STUDIES IN HONOR OF CHU-TSING LI

Notes on Chinese Ceramics Excavated in Japan

RICHARD L. WILSON

Japan's excavation industry, reduced from the high-growth period in the late 1980s to the early 1990s but still capitalized at about US$ 1 billion annually, is the largest in the world, and ceramics constitute the bulk of the finds. These excavated artifacts not only expand the historical knowledge constructed from documents and collected pieces, but open up alternative discourses about how objects are invested with value. An observer familiar only with collected pieces will feel a profound sense of disorientation on seeing the large groups of ceramics routinely excavated from consumer and trade sites. In addition to the sheer amount of material recovered, many of these excavations have revealed entire genres of ceramics that are not represented in major collections. Furthermore, it is clear that some of the ceramic types that are highly esteemed today were not always accorded such importance by their historical owners, who in some cases summarily discarded them.

The Chinese ceramics found at sites in Japan are accorded due attention as both art and text: they are clues to patterns of trade and exchange as well as to the aesthetic and social values of their purchasers and users. They also provide causal evidence for domestic production of ceramics based on Chinese models. Many of the excavated objects shed critical light on heirloom Chinese wares (*denseihin*) preserved in institutional and private collections. Unfortunately, archaeology in Japan is either grossly underreported or sensationalized; even the most general knowledge of systems of classification and models of interpretation is unknown outside a small circle of specialists. Since 1993 I have been fortunate to direct or otherwise participate in excavations of sites in Tokyo and Okinawa that have unearthed Chinese ceramics. In this essay I offer some observations on recent excavation work in Japan, drawing both on personal experience and on site reports and studies by Japanese colleagues, particularly those by Kamei Meitoku, Ueda Hideo, Ōno Masatoshi, and the late Mikami Tsugio and Morita Osamu.

RESEARCH

Art historical research often follows the market. The availability of fine Chinese ceramics in Japan after the collapse of the Qing dynasty (1644–1911) was the first major stimulus for art historical research on Chinese ceramics in Japan. In the 1920s and 1930s Okuda Seiichi, Ōtani Kōzui, Nakao Manzō, and Komori Shinobu emerged as researchers in the field, and collections of Chinese ceramics were established by Yokokawa Tamio, Iwasaki Koyata, and Hosokawa Moritate.[1] Japan's wartime aggression also rendered accessible Chinese sites and objects. The central figure in exploiting these new opportunities for field surveys and interaction with local specialists was the ceramics historian Koyama Fujio (1900–1975), whose 1943 publication *Shina seiji shi kō* (History of Chinese Celadon) stimulated the collecting and further research of Chinese ceramics in Japan and moreover helped to establish Chinese ceramics as a field of specialization.

In the immediate postwar period, the rebuilding of Japan's infrastructure determined the course of Chinese ceramics study. Especially important were excavations of sites from the historic period. Nara and Heian era sites included the capital cities of Heijō-kyō (in Nara) and Heian-kyō (in present-day Kyoto); the diplomatic center at Dazaifu (northern Kyushu); state Buddhist temples in the provinces (Kokubunji); and the regional government offices (*kokuga*). Kamakura and Muromachi sites of note are the medieval capital in Kamakura, Kusado Sengen-chō (a major entrepot in Hiroshima), the Asakura clan center in Ichijō-dani (present-day Fukui Prefecture), and a variety of early modern residence sites in Osaka and Tokyo.

At the same time, Japanese scholars were gaining access to the work of scholars in China, such as the preeminent ceramics specialists Zhen Wanli and Feng Xianming. Under the leadership of the Japanese scholar Mikami Tsugio, other zones of Chinese trade—the so-called ceramic road—were established as a conceptual framework following the Symposium on Excavated Ceramics at the Shimane Prefectural Museum in April 1979. This galvanized researchers in trade studies and led to the founding of the Trade Ceramics Association (Bōeki Tōji Kenkyūkai) in 1981. This movement was based in Japan, but it was a focal point for interaction with overseas researchers; excavations such as the Calatagan site in Luzon, the Butan site in Mindinao, Tuban in east Java, and Chaiya sites in the upper Maylay peninsula in Thailand brought researchers together, leading to the establishment of broad-based typologies and further understanding of maritime trade. The Sinan shipwreck excavation, carried out in Korean waters, was also a focal point for Japanese researchers. Initiated in 1976 and continuing for nine years, the excavation recovered more than 20,000 items. In addition to the load of Chinese celadon and white porcelain, the ship held twenty-eight tons of copper coins, peppers, and *shitan* wood. Wooden tallies indicated that the ship sank on the way to the Kyushu port city of Hakata from Ningbo, in southeast China, in 1323, with freight destined for Japanese consumers, particularly Tōfukuji, an important Zen temple in Kyoto.[2]

Today trade-ceramic research is a very active field and commands more attention than traditional art historical studies of Chinese ceramics. Complaints about this are frequently heard among the older generation of scholars and collectors who look back to the days when studies of tea ceremony heirlooms or imperial wares dominated discourse in the field.

NARA (710–794) TO EARLY HEIAN (794–CA. 900) PERIOD

As recently as two decades ago, the discovery of Chinese ceramics in sites dated to the Asuka (538–710) and Nara periods in eastern Japan was cause for astonishment, but excavations around the Tama River basin in Tokyo now regularly uncover such fragments, many associated with the establishment of the Kokubunji center in the ancient polity of Musashi. In 1993, when I lived alongside the Tama River, I joined Chōfu city archaeologists in several small digs and observed at those sites Chinese celadon shards along with the domestic Haji and Sue wares. Tang dynasty (618–907) *sancai* (three-color) pillow fragments dated to the eighth century have been discovered in neighboring Gunma, Saitama, and Chiba prefectures, and their Japanese derivatives—*sansai*, *nisai*, and *ryokuyū*—have been found as far northeast as Iwate Prefecture.

The scale of this first wholesale encounter with Chinese civilization, however, emerges elsewhere.[3] There are four areas of concentration: Okinoshima, a small island in the Genkai Sea; Fukuoka (Dazaifu-Kōrokan), the staging ground for the so-called *kentōshi*, or envoys, to Tang China; the Nara area (Heijō-kyō); and Tagajō, in Sendai Prefecture.[4] The two successive Kyoto-based capitals, Nagaoka (established in 784) and Heian-kyō (established in 794), and Hakata, developed by the government as an entry port for Dazaifu in Kyushu, yield many Chinese ceramic shards from this period as well. The major types of objects discovered at the above Nara and Heian era sites are Yue celadons (fig. 1.1), Tang white porcelains (fig. 1.2), Tongguan stonewares from Changsha (fig. 1.3), and Tang *sancai* wares (fig. 1.4).[5] The first three types are also found in Southeast Asia and West Asia in this period.

In the period 630–897 Chinese ceramics were imported to Japan primarily through the diplomatic missions (*kentōshi*). At the outset these

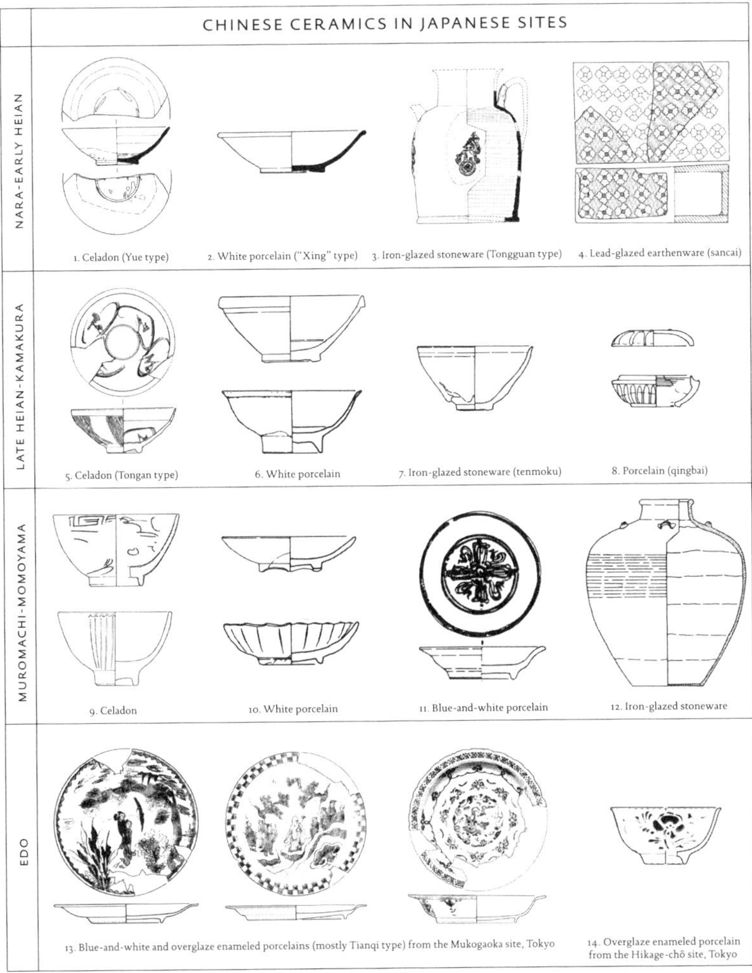

FIGURE 1
Chinese ceramics in Japanese sites (Note: Not intended as a statistical sampling. Objects not drawn to uniform scale.)

wares were intended mainly as gifts, not commodities, and only limited numbers are found in excavations. Finds are concentrated in sites related to diplomatic offices (*kōrokan*), located in Heian (Kyoto), Naniwa (Osaka), and Chikushi (Fukuoka). Among these, the Dazaifu *kōrokan*, in Chikushi (present-day Dazaifu City), which was built at the end of the seventh century, was the only diplomatic center with facilities for foreign delegations, which at that time consisted of envoys from the Chinese Tang dynasty and the Korean Unified Silla dynasty (668–935). In 1987 a survey was conducted at the site, near Heiwadai Stadium in Fukuoka. Nara-period layers yielded Tang *sancai* and Silla wares, and early Heian period layers yielded

Chinese Yue wares, white porcelains, and a smaller number of Tongguan wares. With the end of Japan's official relations with China, in the late ninth century, the *kōrokan* shifted from diplomatic to trade activities. The earliest trade vessel from China is recorded in 842.[6] The incidence of Yue wares and white porcelains dramatically increases in the ninth century; more than 2,500 Yue fragments have been found at the Dazaifu *kōrokan* alone. The general location of the Yue kilns in Zhejiang Province, in southeast China, is not disputed, but in Japan there is some disagreement about the source of the white porcelains from the period, especially the low bowls with a rolled rim and wide foot. Most scholars now favor the southeast coast over the old Xingzhou (present Hebei Province) attribution, although there is no evidence to suggest that both areas could not have been the source of such wares.

During the Nara and Early Heian periods, the consumers of imported Chinese ceramics were wealthy merchants, the court, and the Buddhist establishment. The latter two groups were consumers of Tang *sancai*, the first type of Chinese ceramics that directly influenced the Japanese ceramic industry; the wares preserved in the Shōsōin, Nara, are the best example of that stimulus. Fragments of Tang *sancai* wares have been discovered in some two dozen sites. The functions assigned to these wares in Japan, however, diverge from Chinese practice. First, almost all the *sancai* sites in Japan are connected with temples. Second, figurines, an important part of Chinese *sancai* production, are not found in Japan. Third, all the excavated ceramic objects, except for pillows, are vessels. The 1966 excavation of the Daianji temple in Nara (constructed in 744), where two hundred Tang *sancai* and marble wares were found, is noteworthy for the discovery of thirty such pillows.

The dating of Chinese ceramics found in pre-Heian sites is based on historical materials, such as the recorded founding of a temple or construction of a government office. The post-Nara dating system relies ultimately on such materials, but since many objects are found outside datable contexts, comparative chronologies based on indigenous earthenware types are very helpful. Earthenwares, which were used daily and replaced frequently, display conspicuous changes in shape and method of manufacture, and thus serve as a useful dating device. Also, the soil strata or the date of destruction of a certain building may help in dating.

Based on excavation finds, the number of Chinese ceramics entering Japan from the late tenth to the mid-eleventh century declined significantly. This contrasts with the large number of Chinese wares from this period discovered in Korea and Southeast Asia, where excavations have uncovered not only celadons but also Ding and Yaozhou wares. The decline in Japanese trade with China is attributed to internal factors. Production of domestic elite ceramics such as green-glazed (*ryokuyū*) and ash-glazed (*kaiyū*) wares also decreased, another indication of civil unrest and economic stagnation in Japan during this period.

LATE HEIAN (CA. 900–1185) TO KAMAKURA (1185–1333) PERIOD

Every year in May I take a group of students from International Christian University, Tokyo, to Kamakura, where we observe excavations in progress. Documentary research and archaeological finds have revealed Kamakura as a bustling new eastern capital in the late twelfth century, with a population of 50,000 to 100,000. In every site, from the most humble residence to the administrative and religious centers, it is impossible to overlook the emergence of a new era in ceramics trade, one that would have a great impact on domestic production. The picture is similar throughout the Japanese archipelago. In the late eleventh century, the beginning of Japan's medieval age, the number of Chinese ceramics imported to Japan dramatically increased. In addition to Kamakura, the major sites of the period include the Hakata port in Kyushu, an Inland Sea entrepot called Kusado-Sengen, and even the Tosa Minato outpost in Aomori.[7] Recent attention has focused on the Ōshū Fujiwara site, in Iwate, whose Chinese ceramics show similarites to those of Kyushu and Kamakura.

Surveys of Chinese ceramics excavated from sites of the Late Heian and Kamakura periods turn up two principal types of celadon, one from the southeastern coastal regions of China and the other from the Longquan kilns, in Zhejiang Province. The former are characterized by their incised patterns (fig. 1.5). Many bowls are distinguished by the "dotted-comb" patterns on the exterior. The glaze is characteristically transparent and glossy, and more brownish in color due to oxidation firing. The lower half of the bowls is often unglazed. These pieces are similar to the heirloom bowls called Shukō seiji in Japan and are attributed to the Tong-an Tingxi kilns in Fujian Province. This type is also found at other kiln sites in China, so Tongan should be regarded only as a classification, not a provenance. Longquan celadons, identifiable by their thicker, more bluish glazes, become dominant in the thirteenth century. The earliest types, from a century earlier, are bowls with lotus petals carved on the interior.

Large numbers of white porcelains have been unearthed. Early in this period, two types of bowls are ubiquitous, one with a rolled rim (fig. 1.6, above) and the other with a high foot ring (fig. 1.6, below). They are more roughly made than the ones of Tang origin, and the body is flecked with iron. The glazed surfaces are more gray than white in color. These wares are thought to have been made in Fujian or Guangdong provinces. Many of the white porcelain bowls dating to the twelfth century have stacking resist rings (*janome*) in the cavetto and frequently display rough underglaze iron brushwork. In the following century, most of the white porcelains have unglazed rims (*kuchihage*). Shard counts in major type-sites point to swings in popularity between celadons and white porcelains.

Substantial numbers of Chinese iron brown-glazed storage jars are attributed to this period. These have brown and yellowish glazes, with four or six lugs arrayed around the neck (see fig. 1.12 for a slightly later version). Many of these jars are found in Kyushu, used as sutra containers in burial mounds. They are attributed to kilns on the southeastern coast of China, but the exact location of these kilns is unclear. While not nearly as numerous as white porcelains or celadons, the iron-glazed bowls known as *tenmoku*, or Jian wares, appear in this period as well (fig. 1.7). In recent years the locations of the Fujian kilns that produced these wares have been reported. Drawing chiefly on excavated articles from Hakata, Morimoto Asako has studied the morphology of *tenmoku* bowls unearthed in Japan.[8] Four early phases, from the early twelfth century through the mid-fourteenth century, show the transition from a generic Chinese product to one of enduring Japanese preference that was copied in the Seto kilns.

A few northern Chinese wares, including Yaozhou celadons, Ding wares, and a handful of Cizhou and Jun wares, found their way into Japan at this time. A small number of Jizhou wares, from kilns in southern China, have been excavated as well. In May 2000 I observed the excavation of Kenchōji temple, a major ecclesiastical center in Kamakura, where thirteenth-century disposal pits yielded not only the conventional white porcelains and Longquan wares but a somewhat softer stoneware with a sandy body and devitrified green and brown glazes. These stonewares may be related to the sandy-bodied "yellow-glazed" Chinese jars and basins excavated in twelfth-century Kyushu sites, which are also thought to be from kilns on the southern coast.

Underlying the Late Heian–Kamakura revival were fundamental changes in the structure of Japan's trade with China.[9] First, as a result of the breakdown in central administration in the Late Heian, individual manors forged their own trading relationships with China. Second, in the eleventh century the port of Hakata began to flourish as an international trade center, replacing the *kōrokan*. During this period Chinese merchants stayed for extended periods in Hakata, where they built settlements (known as Daitō Gai, or Great Tang Quarters, and Sōjin Hyakudō, or Hundred Halls of the Song). Kamei Meitoku calls this phase in Japanese trade relations with China "residence-based trade," as opposed to the "coastal trade" of the earlier period. An example of the volume of trade in ceramics during this time is the massive deposits of porcelain shards excavated in Tenya-chō, near the Gion subway station in present-day Fukuoka. This site also revealed many shards painted with several recurring sets of characters, which may indicate the names of the Chinese commodities agents.[10]

Manorial trade grew exponentially as coastal port facilities were built throughout the archipelago. As a result, Chinese ceramics began to be widely used as daily wares, and examples of white porcelain and celadon can even be found in remote villages. The Kusado-Sengen site, located in Fukuyama City, Hiroshima Prefecture,[11] is one of the most important sites for understanding medieval manor trade. From the Kamakura through the Edo (1615–1868) period, it functioned as a port connecting the Ashida River and the Inland Sea maritime trade. Chinese ceramics unearthed at the site include Southern Song (1127–1279), Yuan (1272–1368), and Ming (1368–1644) dynasty wares, particularly celadon bowls with incised "thunder-pattern" rims and white porcelain dishes of the so-called *kuchihage* type.

The removal of the capital to Kamakura at the end of the twelfth century, in 1185, brought about an expansion of trade networks and nascent urbanization in the eastern part of the main island of Honshu. Chinese ceramics have now been found in medieval sites in the northeasternmost reaches of Honshu, and a small number have been recovered on the island of Hokkaido as well. The large share of Chinese ceramics among the artifacts found in Kamakura is evidence of the prosperity of the new military capital. By the late thirteenth century, when the Hōjō regime was established, the use of Chinese ceramics extended over the entire area of present-day Kamakura city. Celadon and white porcelain bowls are distributed widely, and a great many Longquan wares have been excavated. Small bluish-white porcelain dishes are found in staggering amounts, to the extent that they appear to have been discarded after a single use in the manner reserved for native earthenwares. Jingdezhen porcelain shards of the *qingbai* type (also considered white porcelain in Japanese taxonomies), especially the so-called *meiping* shape, are found in greater numbers in Kamakura than in other places, an indication of the use of these wares by the warrior class as both tableware and display objects.

The Sinan shipwreck excavations, carried out in waters off the southwestern coast of the Korean peninsula, have also furthered our knowledge of this period. The remains of an early-fourteenth-century Chinese merchant ship that sank near Sinan were first discovered in 1975 when a fisherman pulled up seven ceramics. The excavations began in October 1976 and by 1985 had produced some 22,000 salvaged articles, most of which were pottery objects. Among the finds were a bronze weight with an inscription reading "Qingyuan Route" and wooden tags inscribed "Tōfukuji" and the Yuan date of "Zhizhi 3" (1323). Thus it is thought that the vessel left the Chinese port of Qingyuan (Ningbo) in the third year of the Zhizhi reign carrying articles that were intended particularly for the Tōfukuji temple in Kyoto. Clog footwear (*geta*) and game pieces (for *sugoroku*) recovered in the excavations are regarded as evidence that there were Japanese among the ship's crew.

Longquan celadons constitute the largest percentage of the Sinan cargo, followed by white porcelains. Some of the wares are similar to those excavated in Heian-kyō and Kamakura. But the wreck also yielded wares that did not correspond to the then-standard schemes of classification: the Longquan celadon variety called Kinuta (formerly thought to be produced in the Southern Song), *tenmoku* bowls (also traditionally attributed to the Southern Song), and Korean celadons were all seen as anomalous.[12] The absence of Yuan blue-and-white porcelain is also noteworthy.

Reflecting a growing belief in an apocalyptic decline of the Buddhist law, Chinese ceramics were frequently used for sutra containers, interred in offertory "sutra mounds." Many of these mounds have dated material. Cylindrical and rounded jars constitute the principal finds, but smaller covered boxes (*gōsu*; fig.1. 8), small pots, and dishes occur as well. Most of the sutra jars have been found in Kyushu and include bluish-white porcelain (*qingbai*), celadon, and iron-glazed stoneware types. The porcelain version is rare, but the rougher celadon and iron-glazed jars were probably made in southern coastal kilns. The rounded jars were imitated in Japan at kilns in Seto.

Many of the *gōsu* boxes have been unearthed in small, isolated sites. All of these are of the *qingbai* type and were mass-produced in Jiangxi, Fujian, and Guangdong provinces.

GUSUKU PERIOD (1100–1609) ARCHAEOLOGY IN OKINAWA

The wealth of trade ceramic material in the Ryukyu Islands is staggering. The archaeology center at International Christian University has participated in several excavations on the small island of Izena, located off the west coast of the main island of Okinawa.[13] Izena is only fourteen kilometers in circumference, but the surface earth—much of it unfortunately disturbed by both natural events and human activities—is studded with ceramics from all over Asia. Most are of Chinese origin, but one can also find Thai, Vietnamese, Korean, and Japanese ceramics, as well as local products, including tiles, earthenware vessels, grayware, and stoneware, the latter produced in the Amami islands to the north of Okinawa.

In Japanese literature Okinawa is often represented as part of Japan, but that is more of a reflection of post-1609 power alignments than the situation that existed in the so-called Gusuku Period, when trade flourished in Okinawa. In this period, small castle-based groups gradually consolidated and rose to prominence through Pacific-Asia trade, finally forming a unified Ryukyu empire in the sixteenth century. The Gusuku fluorescence was due in large part to Okinawa's role as a trade intermediary. Almost two hundred castle sites (*gusuku*) have been identified, from the Amami islands in the north to the Miyako and Yaeyama islands in the south. With the excavation of major *gusuku*, notably Nakijin, Katsuren, and Shuri, all on the main island, typologies for ceramics and stone tools have been developed.

Chinese ceramics from the *gusuku* sites include celadons (mostly bowls), white porcelains (bowls and dishes), blue-and-white porcelains (mostly bowls and dishes), and iron-glazed stonewares (a few *tenmoku*-style teabowls and larger quantities of storage jars). Yuan blue-and-white porcelains attract the most attention since very few are found in the Japanese home islands. About two hundred fifty pieces of Yuan blue-and-white have been collected at Katsuren, a substantial quantity irrespective of location.[14]

Artifact assemblages from *gusuku* affirm the existence of two major trade zones, one dating from the late eleventh to the thirteenth century and another from the fourteenth through the sixteenth century.[15] In the former, Chinese wares exist as an assemblage with *kamuiyaki* (an unglazed gray stoneware made in Tokushima, an island in the Amami group, north of Okinawa) and a stone cooking pot originating in Kyushu called *kasseki-sei ishinabe*. It is noteworthy that both the *kamuiyaki* and *ishinabe* were made in the north and brought into Okinawa; it is speculated that the Chinese ceramics were brought into Okinawa along with these goods. The center for ceramic trade may well have been Hakata. The trade network shifts rapidly beginning in the fourteenth century, when the *gusuku* increase in size and fortification; the amount and types of trade ceramics show a dramatic increase. The *kamuiyaki* and *ishinabe* vanish, and instead one finds large amounts of Chinese, Korean, and Southeast Asian ceramics. The Chinese porcelains were employed as trade items, while the other wares were used and traded locally. The volume and the sources of the cargo are suggested by the presence of countless fragments of iron-glazed storage jars produced in Southeast Asia (especially Thailand) and southern China. The distribution patterns as a whole suggest a very different trade zone: Kyushu was no longer the center, with Okinawa on the periphery; rather both locations were important nodes in an extensive "down the line" network that also encompassed China, Korea, and Southeast Asia.

MUROMACHI (1392–1573) TO MOMOYAMA (1573–1615) PERIOD

Ichijodani, located in modern Fukui Prefecture, was the castle site of the powerful medieval warlord Asakura Yoshikage (1533–1573). Parts of the site are restored, and visitors will have no difficulty imagining an impregnable valley fortress, one that allowed Yoshikage to dominate the Hokuriku district. Yet the Asakura stronghold was totally destroyed by the forces of Oda Nobunaga (1534–1582) in 1573, a disaster for the clan but a boon for archaeologists who have a major medieval site with a *terminus ad quem*. The late medieval age in Japan was rife with warfare, and the sudden destruction of fortresses was not uncommon. The Negoro-dera site in Wakayama, devastated by Toyotomi Hideyoshi (1536–1598) in 1585, is another example. Natural disasters also created opportunities for excavators: the Tomitagawa Kashō site in Nogi-gun, Shimane, yielded rows of houses buried by flooding, and the Tomogashima-oki sites in Wakayama featured cargo-laden ships that sunk en route to the port of Sakai. Late medieval sites also have unprecedented distribution. Chinese Ming wares, for example, are found from the Okinawan *gusuku* sites, in the south, to sites in Hokkaido, in the north, such as the Ohamanaka port site in Yoichi-chō.

Up to the mid-fifteenth century the main type of imported wares continues to be celadon and white porcelain mass-produced by commercial kilns. The most popular shapes are bowls and dishes. The celadon glaze is more translucent and darker than that of the Longquan celadons of the Song or Yuan period. Kilns that produced these wares are located in and around the cities of Lonquan and Lishui in southern Zhejiang Province. Two major categories of celadon bowls found in Okinawa and western Japan have been identified by Ueda Hideo: one has a "thunder" pattern on the outer rim and a lotus-petal pattern incised into the body (fig. 1.9, above); the other is a fluted type (fig. 1.9, below). The former seems to date to the late fourteenth to fifteenth century, and the latter to the sixteenth century.[16] Celadon bowls and dishes decreased in number as blue-and-white porcelain became popular in the late fifteenth century.

New types of Chinese white porcelain also appeared in the late fourteenth century, some of them inspired by *qingbai* and *shufu* wares. In many fifteenth-century sites I have found small white porcelain dishes with four arches gouged out of the foot ring; stacking spur scars are found in the cavetto (fig. 1.10, above). Small cups with faceted sides, made of the same material, are also known. These wares seem to be a product of the coastal area, but the kiln site has not been identified. From the late fifteenth to the sixteenth century, many thinly formed white porcelain dishes with foliate rims appear; in the late sixteenth century, various body shapes, such as a foliate dish in a "chrysanthemum-flower" shape, became popular (fig. 1.10, below). The latter type carries over into domestic production at the Seto-Mino kilns.

Outside Okinawa there is very little evidence in Japan for early Ming dynasty underglaze decorated wares. For example, one sees very few examples of underglaze red of the so-called Hongwu reign period (1368–98) style. Blue-and-white wares from the Yongle (1403–24) and Xuande (1426–35) reign periods are virtually absent. But from the late fifteenth to sixteenth century, Chinese blue-and-white porcelains began to be exported vigorously to Japan. It is presumed that the image of Chinese ceramics in

Japan was very different from that in Southeast Asia or West Asia, where better quality imported Chinese wares are found. Nevertheless, it is still difficult to formulate a broad picture, especially prior to the mid-fifteenth century. This may reflect the priority that researchers give to Chinese ceramics from the Tang and Song periods. The major problem, however, is that Chinese ceramics chronologies from the Ming period are based on imperial wares from Jingdezhen, and hardly reflect commercial products.

Among the types of Chinese ceramics from the mid-fifteenth to mid-sixteenth century found in Japan are dishes with everted rims and simple painted designs (fig. 1.11), dishes with carved-out depressions in the cavetto, and rounded bowls with a simple profile. Beginning in the Momoyama period, excavated ceramics show greater uniformity in shape and design and frequently bear Ming reign marks or auspicious characters. There are also dishes with Japanese reign marks, such as "Tenbun nensei." Obviously the types of wares imported show some consideration of Japanese preferences, a trend that accelerates in the early decades of the seventeenth century.

Blue-and-white porcelain imports increase dramatically in the mid-fifteenth century, just before the Sengoku era. This was also the time when Seto and Mino kilns were changing from the simple tunnel kiln (*anagama*) to the more efficient above-ground kiln (*ōgama*), and domestic ceramics were undergoing a great change. Castle towns were developing, and the burgeoning of the market naturally affected the importation of blue-and-white wares.

Although they occur in limited numbers, the so-called "five-color" (*wucai*) overglaze enamelled wares are also found in Japan. Ming "three-color" (*sancai*) ware, however, was quite popular. The cloisonné type (*fahua*) and a type that features small molded wares with color zones bounded with incised lines or no lines at all (called *Kanan sansai* by archaeologists and *Kōchi* by collectors) were the main styles. A few *fahua* wares have been preserved in Japan as heirlooms, such as a pitcher in Rokuonji, Kyoto, but to my knowledge none have been excavated. *Kōchi* is preserved aboveground chiefly in incense containers popular among tea ceremony devotees. The kiln site in which these wares were produced, located in Nansheng, Pinghe county, Fujian Province, was excavated in 1997 and the finds exhibited in Japan in 1998.[17] Another type of *Kōchi*, a *ban*-type dish with a foliate rim, appears in a number of daimyo sites in Tokyo and other sites in the Kansai region, particularly Sakai.

Until quite recently, the discovery of Chinese ceramics in Japanese medieval sites was an occasion for quantitative analysis, the main activity being that of identifying and counting the articles uncovered. The focus has now turned to qualitative analysis, that is, a quest for the social meaning of the large number of Song and Yuan heirloom ceramics in sites associated with medieval warlords. Ōno Masatoshi has taken the lead in building a model for Chinese ceramics consumption during this period. Using evidence from medieval handscrolls, documents related to interior decoration of noble households (*kazari-ki*), and archaeological excavations, Ōno has identified discreet spaces for the use of Chinese ceramics based on the functional/spatial concepts of *hare* (formal and public) and *ke* (informal and private).

According to this research, the precedent for deployment of Chinese ceramics in official reception spaces was created by the Kamakura shogunate. These "official" wares, discerned from Kamakura city excavations, included Longquan celadon flower vases and incense burners and *tenmoku* teabowls. The wares used in "informal" spaces, as seen in the scroll paintings *Boki ekotoba* and *Matsuzaki tenjin engi*,[18] were white porcelain *meiping*, Longquan basins, and small numbers of Yuan blue-and-white and underglaze-red porcelains.

This practice was enthusiastically continued in the Muromachi period, inasmuch as the Ashikaga family had an interest in advocating an authentic "warrior" culture upon the return of the capital to Kyoto. Thus, fifteenth-century residences nationwide yield these pieces, but in the Muromachi the "informal" wares used for private consumption during the preceding Kamakura period migrate into the "formal" category. That is to say, white porcelain *meiping*, Longquan basins, and Yuan blue-and-white and underglaze-red porcelains are found in parts of sites thought to have been used for official receptions.[19] Ōno attributes this to the expansion of cultural activities in the late medieval period centered around the *kaisho*, a room used for intimate gatherings where various activities such as linked verse poetry and the tea ceremony were carried out.

In addition to patterns of consumption, medieval trade centers now receive due attention. In the late fifteenth century, Sakai, now located within the confines of Osaka Prefecture, began to prosper after receiving sanction as a port by the Hosokawa family. The city managers distanced themselves from the Muromachi shogunate and the Hosokawa family, and in this favorable climate Sakai eventually achieved a monopoly in trade with Ming China, Korea, and the Ryukyus. In 1469 Ming traders began to enter Sakai, followed by the Portuguese and Spanish. In the late sixteenth century, Sakai traders reached Luzon and Cham. Sites dating after the late fifteenth century—four datable strata, each created by a major conflagration, are known—have yielded many Chinese ceramics. Morimura Kenichi has studied extensively all the trade ceramics imported into Sakai, including what the Japanese call *gosu-de* and *gosu aka-e* wares. These are now firmly associated with the Zhangzhou kilns in Fujian, excavated in 1995.[20] In 1615 Sakai was burned by the Toyotomi during the Osaka summer campaign. With the subsequent promulgation of a seclusion policy in which Japanese were forbidden to leave Japan and outsiders (except for a select number of traders from China and the Netherlands) were forbidden to enter the country, Sakai's source of income was eliminated. Neighboring Osaka began to thrive as a commercial center, and by government mandate Nagasaki became the major gateway for foreign trade.

EDO PERIOD (1615–1868) URBAN ARCHAEOLOGY

Two excavations of premodern sites in Tokyo in 1974 were particularly important in demonstrating how archaeology might significantly augment conventional understanding of the history of the period between the seventeenth and the mid-nineteenth century. One was the excavation of the Hitotsubashi High School site in Chiyoda ward, which featured the remains of graves and commoners' residences. The other was the Dōzaka site in Bunkyo ward, which yielded the remains of a samurai residence. After decades of neglect, when Edo layers were simply disposed of as garbage, Edo suddenly became a "legitimate" period for archaeological study.[21] As budgets expanded during the high-growth era, it became economically feasible to excavate early modern sites, and at present nearly five hundred such sites have been excavated in Tokyo alone. Chinese ceramics, particularly decorated porcelains from Jingdezhen, principally those of the Tianqi reign period (1621–27), and from Zhangzhou (Swatow) are found in considerable numbers.

I had the good fortune to lead an excavation that unearthed one of the largest group of restorable Chinese ceramics discovered so far in Japan, the Mukogaoka High School site, located at 1–11–18 Mukogaoka, Bunkyō-ku, Tokyo. The excavation was carried out from March through September 1995. Analysis of the artifacts proceeded from October 1995 through

March 1996.[22] The site, measuring 2,500 square meters, is located between roads that were known historically as the Nakasendō and Iwatsuki Kaidō (Hongo-dori). According to historical documents, after 1683 the area was established as a barracks for two groups of lower-ranking samurai, the Osakitegumi and the Omochigumi. The Osakitegumi, which consisted of corps of bowmen and riflemen, served as an advance team during wartime; during peacetime they had the role of city gatekeepers. When the shogun traveled, the Osakitegumi acted as a kind of secret service and also investigated crimes such as arson and robbery. The Omochigumi had the job of protecting the shogun; in peacetime they guarded the inner gates of Edo castle. In the hierarchy of the Edo police corps, these two groups ranked below deputized personnel such as *shoshidai* (a kind of military commissioner) and *machi-bugyō* (precinct magistrates).

Special attention was given to a group of porcelain artifacts excavated from a layer of burnt soil deposited inside an underground storage chamber, designated as feature no. 199. The greater part of the shards from this feature, porcelain as well as other material, showed some evidence of having been in a fire. Among the sets of porcelain dishes excavated, almost all showed burn marks on the edges, but only a few were burned on the top or bottom, suggesting that the dishes were in stacks when the fire occurred. It would appear that these artifacts had been stored in one place and after the conflagration were discarded together with the burnt soil from the site. Other artifacts in the feature suggest disposal in the first quarter of the eighteenth century. Among the porcelains were considerable numbers of Hizen (Arita) wares dating through the first quarter of the eighteenth century and wares from late Ming dynasty China.

The Chinese porcelain shards from the Mukogaoka site are typical of seventeenth-century finds in urban sites, most of which are attributable to the late Tianqi and Chongzheng (1628–44) reign periods. But at Mukogaoka the shards were found in large numbers and in good condition, and were subsequently restored into one hundred twenty pieces representing twenty-eight varieties.[23] Among these were: one large dish, three octagonal dishes, and a dish with a monochrome blue glaze, all comparable to well-known collected specimens; and underglaze-blue and overglaze enamel dishes and small bowls, many of them in sets. In addition to the porcelains, the site also yielded a three-color earthenware dish and stoneware teabowls from kilns in Tsuishū (Tsushima). The ceramics from feature no. 199 also included a fragment of Ding ware from Song dynasty

China and a natural ash-glazed bowl of a type called *yamachawan* from medieval period kilns in Mino.

This type of material might be expected in an excavation of a daimyo mansion, such as that of the Maeda or Date family, but its presence in a single feature from a low-level samurai household is without precedent. Various interpretations have been offered: that the objects represent part of an antique collection; that they were merchandise for sale; and that they were the collective property of the "police" corps that occupied the site.[24] These theories will need to be examined after further study of the archaeological evidence from the site and related documents.

Neutron activation analysis was conducted on thirty-nine specimens of porcelain, mostly those found in feature no. 199. The data from the Mukogaoka tests were also clustered together with data from identical tests done on porcelain shards excavated from Tokyo Science Building no. 7 and the Fukiage Hama site in Kagoshima Prefecture. Two tightly sorted clusters were found to represent Hizen (Arita) porcelain and Chinese porcelain from Jingdezhen. A more loosely sorted cluster represented Chinese porcelain and stoneware from Fujian and Guangdong provinces.

The Archaeology Research Center at Tokyo National University has compiled an extensive chronology for Edo period domestic ceramics and imports. Their findings are based chiefly on excavations of the official residence of the wealthy Maeda clan, which lies underneath the university's present campus. Their findings suggest a dramatic decrease in Chinese ceramics at the site after about 1690. No Chinese wares at all are discovered with artifacts from the first half of the eighteenth century; the absence of these wares is generally attributed to Japan's national seclusion edicts and an increase in the local manufacture of fine porcelain.

But imports of Chinese wares did not completely vanish, and Qing dynasty wares used in the late Edo period are now found in increasing numbers. My research team, Excavation Group for Metropolitan Schools, found dozens of Qing porcelains in early-nineteenth-century pits and other features at the Hikage-chō site in Bunkyō-ku, Tokyo.[25] Among the new types is a small rounded bowl with a flaring rim, called *hazori-wan* in Japanese (fig. 1.14). It probably reflects the growing interest in steeped tea, or *sencha*; the *hazori* shape is also copied at every major production center in Japan. The most dramatic discovery, however, was the excavation of the Sumitomo family residence in Osaka, carried out between 1990 and 1992.[26] Remains of a Sumitomo house that was constructed after a fire in 1724 yielded a large number of Qing wares, more than the total number of such wares excavated elsewhere in Japan. Porcelains from this site include blue-and-white, overglaze enamel, and monochrome blue wares. The high quality of the finds is attributable to the income derived by the Sumitomo family from the export of copper (the Sumitomo family ran a copper refinery next to the residence, which was also thoroughly excavated).

The quantity of artifacts recovered from archaeological sites in Japan is overwhelming. Fortunately, the Research Association for Trade Ceramics has continued to publish both raw data and thematic overviews of the subject. There are also numerous local research groups, such as the Research Group for Castle Towns, based in Tokushima, Shikoku. In recent years Japanese specialists have begun to participate in conferences outside Japan, such as those organized by the Asian Ceramics Research Organization (ACRO), based in Chicago. The media also plays a role in disseminating information on new discoveries and research to the public, and some of these reports are both timely and responsibly produced. For example, on the Japanese national holiday called Marine Day, which occurs every July, there are television specials on sites whose ceramic artifacts point to the existence of maritime trade networks. Finally, there is a long history of good exhibitions of imported and domestic ceramics excavated from sites in Japan. The catalogue of the 1988 exhibition of lead-glazed ceramics at the Gotoh Museum, for instance, included an extensive bibliography relating in part to *sancai* finds in Japan.

Still, one yearns for at least three things in this field: more research questions that transcend chronology and individual sites, more extensive contact with overseas researchers, especially in China, and wider dissemination of research results. There are some encouraging signs amidst the ongoing insularity.

SELECTED LITERATURE

The major interpretive and taxonomic literature on Chinese ceramics found in Japan is listed below. Included are key articles from *Bōeki tōji kenkyū* (Journal of Trade Ceramics), but interested readers might profitably consult other articles that have appeared in this journal since its inception in 1981. The National Museum of History and Ethnology, in Sakura, Chiba Prefecture, also publishes a database of trade ceramics, which lists the major sites; see Kokuritsu Rekishi Minzoku Hakubutsukan, eds., *Nihon no bōeki tōji: Nishi Nihon hen* (Chinese ceramics excavated in Japan: Western Japan), vols. 1–3, 1993 and forthcoming volumes.

Gotoh Museum. 1998. *Nippon no sansai to ryokuyū* (Crucibles of the spirit: Lead-glazed ceramics from ancient Japan). Tokyo: Gotoh Museum.

Hasebe Gakuji and Imai Atsushi. 1995. *Nihon shutsudo no Chūgoku tōji* (Chinese ceramics excavated in Japan; Chūgoku no tōji series no. 12). Tokyo: Heibonsha.

Hasebe Gakuji et al., eds. 1975. *Nihon shutsudo Chūgoku tōji* (Chinese ceramics excavated in Japan). Tokyo: Tokyo Kokuritsu Hakubutsukan.

Kamei Meitoku. 1986. *Chūgoku bōeki tōji shi no kenkyū* (Research in the history of Chinese trade ceramics). Tokyo: Dōbōsha Shuppan.

———. 1997. Ryukyu bōeki tōji no kōzōteki rikai (A structural understanding of Ryukyu trade ceramics). *Senshū Jinbun Ronshū* 60.

Koyama Fujio. 1943. *Shina seiji shikō* (History of Chinese celadon). Tokyo: Bunchūdō.

Kyōbara Kōkogaku Kenkyūjo Fuzoku Hakubutsukan, ed. 1993. *Bōeki tōjiki* (Trade ceramics). Nara: Yura Yamato Kodai Bunka Kyōkai.

Mikami Tsugio. 1981. Tōjiki bōeki no kenkyū to sono igi (Research of ceramics trade and its significance). *Bōeki tōji kenkyū* 1.

Morita, Tsutomu. 1982. Jūyon-jūroku seiki no hakuji no bunrui to hennen (Classification and chronology of white porcelain from the fourteenth through the sixteenth century). *Bōeki tōji kenkyu* 2.

———. 1995. *Dazaifu tōjiki kenkyū* (Research on ceramics from Dazaifu). Fukuoka: Morita Tsutomu Ikōshū-Tsuitōshū Kankōkai.

Ōno Masatoshi. 1982. Jūgo-jūroku seiki sometsuke wan, sara no bunrui to hennen (Classification and chronology of fifteenth- and sixteenth-century blue-and white-porcelain bowls and dishes). *Bōeki tōji kenkyū* 2.

Ōno Masatoshi, ed. 2001. *Zukai–Nihon no chūsei iseki* (Atlas of archaeological sites in medieval Japan). Tokyo: Tokyo Daigaku Shuppankai.

Ueda Hideo. 1982. Jūyon-jūroku seiki no seiji wan no bunrui (Classification of celadon bowls from the fourteenth through the sixteenth century). *Bōeki tōji kenkyū* 2.

———. 1985. Jūyon-jūroku seiki no sometsuke, seiji, hakuji no hennen no jōken (State of the chronologies for blue-and-white porcelain, celadon, and white porcelain from the fourteenth through the sixteenth century). *Wakayama ken maizō bunkazai jōhō* 17.

Yokota Kanjirō. 1978. Dazaifu shutsudo no yūnyū Chūgoku tōjiki ni tsuite–keshiki bunrui to hennen wo chūshin ni shite (Imported Chinese ceramics excavated at Dazaifu: Focusing on stylistic classification and chronology). *Kyushu Rekishi Shiryōkan kenkyū ronshū* 4.

NOTES

When recalling my graduate student years at the University of Kansas I never fail to think of my first encounter with Chinese art under the guidance of Chu-tsing Li. Dr. Li made it possible for me to have wonderful opportunities to study Chinese art, a subject that I continue to teach at the undergraduate level. Moreover, sensing my interest in ceramics, he urged me to survey the fine collection at the Nelson-Atkins Museum of Art under Laurence Sickman. How well these experiences served me in later years! But that is not all: Chu-tsing and his wonderful wife, Yao-wen, were like warm and caring parents, helping all of us through the highs and lows of graduate school. This overview of recent decades of fieldwork in Japan with its implications for Chinese ceramics is respectfully and affectionately dedicated to Dr. Li.

1. For this research summary I have drawn extensively from Hasebe Gakuji and Imai Atsushi 1995.

2. *Kokusai shinpojūmu* 1984.

3. Early examples are known in collections, such as the well-known sixth-century Yue celadon jar from the Hōryūji Treasure Collection. Six Dynasties (220–589) Yue ware has been excavated in Korea, but not in Japan.

4. Tagajō Castle was built sometime before 737 as a provincial office and military headquarters. It served this function until it was burned down in a revolt in 780.

5. I translate the Japanese term *seiji* as celadon, *hakuji* as white porcelain (this conventionally encompasses *qingbai* as well as other white wares), and *seika* as blue-and-white porcelain.

6. Hasebe Gakuji and Imai Atsushi 1995, 103.

7. See <http://www.pref.aomori.jp/culture/tosaminato/0002-e.html>

8. See Morimoto Asako 1994, 194–200.

9. For an extensive study of these changes, see Kamei Meitoku 1986.

10. See ibid., 213.

11. See <http://www.mars.dti.ne.jp/~suzuki-y/what.html>

12. In the Sinan shipwreck, there were fifty Jian-type *tenmoku* bowls and two hundred seventy other black-glazed bowls. The former showed signs of use, but the latter did not. The Jian types were contained in a cylindrical-shaped wooden box; from this it is speculated that older Jian wares had been collected and shipped to Japan. This suggests that Jian ceramics were traded as antiques in the market and that production of Jian wares had ceased at the time of the wreck.

13. See Kishimoto Masahiko 2000.

14. However, the Chinese blue-and-white porcelains from the Yuan are noticeably fewer in number in Okinawa than in West or Southeast Asia. The small jars decorated with simple grasses or flowers frequently seen in Southeast Asian sites are seldom discovered in

Okinawa. Only about twenty such examples have been found on the Japanese mainland.

15. Tabata Yukitsugu 1999.

16. Ueda Hideo 1982.

17. See *Kōchi kōgō* 1998. Fujian Provincial Museum has also published a report in *Fujian Wenbo* (1998).

18. For an illustration of *Boki ekotoba*, see Komatsu Shigemi 1990. For an illustration of *Matsuzaki tenjin engi*, see Komatsu Shigemi 1992.

19. It should be mentioned that the reason we can be so sure about the original deployment is that so many medieval sites were burned in sieges and then totally abandoned. The situation is very different in the case of peacetime sites, such as those of the Edo period, where the sites are cleaned up and the pieces disposed in pits, intermingled with earlier and later artifacts.

20. See Fujian Xing Bowuguan 1997.

21. Regrettably the downturn of the Japanese economy has had a negative influence on Japanese archaeology; the Agency for Cultural Affairs argues that Edo sites should not be excavated, although compromises have been made for "important" sites. Recently, in Tokyo the term "important" has been interpreted to mean the residential sites of samurai whose domains produced more than 10,000 shares of rice income.

22. For the excavation report, see Wilson 1997. The title of the report, *Osakitegumi yashiki*, refers to the Edo period inhabitants of the site, the Osakitegumi.

23. Ibid., nos. 1–38.

24. The merchandise and collection theories are based on the assumption that the police corps, the nominal owners of the site, rented it out to wealthy merchants, a well-documented practice driven by the scarcity of non-samurai land in the city. The police would have gained custody of the goods as a result of their occasional role in confiscating property.

25. Wilson 2000. Readers interested in Qing pieces in Edo sites will also want to consult Horiuchi Hideki and Nagasako Shinya 1996, 99–118.

26. Suzuki Hidenori 1998.

REFERENCES

Fujian Xing Bowuguan. 1997. *Zhangzhou yao* (Zhangzhou kilns). Fuzhou.

Hasebe Gakuji and Imai Atsushi. 1995. *Nippon shutsudo no Chūgoku tōji* (Chinese ceramics excavated in Japan). Vol. 12, Chūgoku no tōji series. Tokyo.

Horiuchi Hideki and Nagasako Shinya. 1996. Edo iseki shutsudo 18–19 seiki yūnyū tōji (Imported ceramics of the eighteenth and nineteenth centuries found in Edo sites). *Tokyo kokō* 14.

Kamei Meitoku. 1986. *Chūgoku bōeki tōji shi no kenkyū* (Research in the history of Chinese trade ceramics). Tokyo: Dōbōsha Shuppan.

Kishimoto Masahiko et al. 2000. *Izena Motojima iseki* (The Izena Motojima site). Izena.

Kōchi kōgō: Fukkenshō shutsudo ibutsu to Nihon no denseihin (Kōchi-style incense cases: Artifacts excavated from Fujian Province and Japanese heirloom wares). 1998. Kyoto.

Kokusai shinpojūmu: Shinan kaitei hikiage bunbutsu (International symposium on artifacts excavated from the seabed at Sinan). 1984. Nagoya: Chunichi Shinbun.

Komatsu Shigemi, ed. 1990. *Boki ekotoba* (Zoku Nihon no emaki, vol. 9). Tokyo: Chūō Kōronsha.

———. 1992. *Matsuzaki tenjin engi* (Zoku Nihon no emaki, vol. 22). Tokyo: Chūō Kōronsha.

Morimoto Asako. 1994. Hakata isekigun shutsudo (Excavation of sites in Hakata County). In *Tokubetsu ten Karamono tenmoku—Fukkenshō kenyō shutsudo tenmoku to Nippon densei no tenmoku*, ed. Fujian Provincial Museum and Chadō Shiryōkan. Kyoto.

Suzuki Hidenori et al. 1998. *Sumitomo dōbukisho ato* (The site of the Sumitomo copper refinery). Osaka.

Tabata Yukitsugu. 1999. Okinawa hontō ni okeru bōeki tōjiki no shoyōsō: sanchi, keishiki, hensen no kentō (Trade ceramics excavated from Okinawa gusuku: Sources, types, and change). Master's thesis, International Christian University.

Ueda Hideo. 1982. Jūyon-jūroku seiki no seiji wan no bunrui (Classification of celadon bowls from the fourteenth through the sixteenth century). *Bōeki tōji kenkyū* 2.

Wilson, Richard L. et al. 1997. *Osakitegumi yashiki* (Residence of the Osakitegumi). Tokyo.

———. 2000. *Hikage-chō III-2* (Hikage-chō site, vol. III, pt. 2). Tokyo.

GLOSSARY

Abaoji (d. 926) 阿保機
An Qi (1683–ca. 1744) 安岐
Aoru 澈如

Bai Juyi (772–846) 白居易
Ban Weizhi (14th century) 班惟志
Bao Ding (b. 1899) 鮑鼎
Bao Shichen (1775–1855) 包世臣
bapo 八破
Beian 悲盦
Beian wei Jiasun zhi 悲盦為稼孫製
beibei 北碑
beixue 碑學
Benlu bingma fudujian 本路兵馬副都監
Bian Luan (ca. 785–802) 邊鸞
biankuan 邊款
bifa 筆法
biyi 筆意

Cai Han (1647–1686) 蔡含
Cai Yuanpei (1868–1940) 蔡元培
cainü 才女
caizi jiaren 才子佳人
Canjing yangnian 餐經養年
Cao Gemin (1800–ca. 1875) 曹葛民
Cao Xun (1098–1174) 曹勛
Chang Siyan (1031–1100) 常思言
Chen Banding (1876–1969) 陳半丁
Chen Chun (1483–1544) 陳淳
Chen Duxiu (1879–1942) 陳獨秀
Chen Guan (1563–ca. 1647) 陳祼
Chen Hengke (1876–1923) 陳衡恪
Chen Hongshou (1598–1652) 陳洪綬
Chen Jiru (1558–1639) 陳繼儒
Chen Juzhong (active 1201–30) 陳居中
Chen Sheng (active Liao Shengzong era, 982–1031) 陳升
Chen Shizeng (1876–1923) 陳師曾
Cheng Sui (1602–after 1690) 程邃
Cheru 澈如 see Wu Zhengzhi
Ch'oe Puk (1712–ca. 1786) 崔北
Chŏng Hwang (b. 1735) 鄭榥
Chŏng Sŏn (1676–1759) 鄭敾
Chŏng Su-yŏng (1743–1831) 鄭遂榮
Chunqiu gongyang xue 春秋公羊學
Cui Bo (active ca. 1060–85) 崔白

Dai Mingshuo (*jinshi* 1634) 戴明說
Dai Quheng (1755–1811) 戴衢亨
Dai Xi (1801–1860) 戴熙
daibi 代筆
Dan Zhongguang (1623–1692) 笪重光
Danxia (738–823) 丹霞
Dao buyongxiu 道不用修
Daoan (312 or 314–385) 道安
Daochuo (562–645) 道綽
Daoguang (Qing emperor, r. 1821–50) 道光
Daotong 道統
Daoxuan (596–667) 道宣
Daoxue 道學
Deng Chun (active ca. 1167) 鄧椿
Deng Shiru (1743–1805) 鄧石如
Deshou gong jin bingma qianxia 德壽宮進兵馬鈐轄
dian 點
ding 鼎
ding 定
Ding Jing (1695–1765) 丁敬
Dong Bai (1625–1651) 董白
Dong Bangda (1699–1769) 董邦達
Dong Gao (1740–1818) 董誥
Dong Qichang (1555–1636) 董其昌
Dong Yuan (active 930s–60s) 董源
Donggao 東皋
Donglin 東林
dongtian 洞天
Du Mu (1459–1525) 都穆
Du Qiong (1396–1474) 杜瓊

fahua 法華
Falin (572–640) 法琳

Fan Chengda (1126–1193) 范成大
Fan Jue 范珏
Fan Kuan (active ca. 990–1030) 范寬
Fan Xuan (active second half of the 4th century) 范宣
Fan Yunlin (*jinshi* 1595) 范允臨
Fan zhong Wu sheng *ding* 番中吳生鼎
fang 倣
Fang Shijie (b. 1697) 方士庶
Fang Shishu (1692–1752) 方士庶
Fang Yizhi (1611–1671) 方以智
Fang Zhenguan (1679–1747) 方貞觀
fangding 方鼎
fangzuo 倣作
Fanlong (active first half of the 12th century) 梵隆
Fei Changfang (Sui dynasty, 581–618) 費長房
Feixi (active mid-8th century) 飛錫
foming 佛名
Fu jin yi 孚金彝
Fu Shan (1607–1684/85) 傅山
Fu Yi (active 618–49) 傅奕
fupi 斧劈

gan 感
ganlei 感類
Gao Fenghan (1683–1748) 高鳳翰
Gao Kegong (1248–1310) 高克恭
Gao Qi (1336–1374) 高啟
Gao Shiqi (1645–1703) 高士奇
Gaozong (Song emperor, r. 1127–62) 高宗
Gong Kai (1222–1307) 龔開
Gong Xian (1619–1689) 龔賢
Gongan 公安
Gu Fu (17th century) 顧復
Gu Hongzhong (active ca. 943–60) 顧閎中
Gu Kaizhi (ca. 345–406) 顧愷之
Gu Ningyuan (late Ming dynasty, 1368–1644) 顧凝遠
Gu Yanwu (1613–1682) 顧炎武
Guan Tong (active ca. 907–23) 關同
guanji 官妓
Guanxiu (832–912) 貫休
guixiu 閨秀
Guo Bo *gui* 過伯簋
Guo Ruoxu (active 11th century) 郭若虛
Guo Wengong *ding* 虢文公鼎
Guo Xi (ca. 1000–ca. 1090) 郭熙
Guo Zhongshu (d. 977) 郭忠恕

Han Gan (active ca. 742–56) 韓幹
Han Huang (723–787) 韓滉
Han shijing shi 漢石經室
Han Xiaozhou (12th century) 韓肖胄
Han Xizai (907–970) 韓熙載
Han Yu (768–824) 韓愈
Han Zhuo (active ca. 1119–26) 韓拙
Hanlin yuan daizhao 翰林院待詔
Hang Zhiying (1900–1947) 杭穉英
He Cheng (1224–after 1315) 何澄
He Liangjun (1506–1573) 何良俊
He Shaoji (1799–1873) 何紹基
Heshen (1750–1799) 和珅
Hong Tae-yong (1731–1783) 洪大容
Hongren (1610–1664) 弘仁
Hongwu (Ming emperor, r. 1368–98) 洪武
Hongwu, prince (d. 1811) 弘旿
Hongzhou Chan 洪州禪
Hu Gui (active early 10th century) 胡瓌 (瑰)
Hu Peiheng (1891–1962) 胡佩衡
Hu Shi (1891–1962) 胡適
Hu Shu 胡澍
Hu Yinglin (1543–1581) 胡應麟
Hu Zuoqu (active mid- to late 18th century) 胡作渠
Huaisu (725–785) 懷素
Huang Binhong (1865–1955) 黃賓虹
Huang Ding (1660–1730) 黃鼎
Huang Gongwang (1269–1354) 黃公望
Huang Junbi (1898–1991) 黃君璧

Huang Tingjian (1045–1105) 黃庭堅
Huang Yi (1744–1802) 黃易
Huang Yuanjie (17th century) 黃媛介
Huang Zongxi (1610–1695) 黃宗羲
huazao 華藻
Hŭh Kyun (d. 1618) 許筠
Huijiao (497–554) 慧皎
Huiyuan (334–416) 慧遠
Huizong (Song emperor, r. 1101–25) 徽宗

Jia Shigu (active ca. 1130–60) 賈師古
Jiacai (8th century) 迦才
jiaguwen 甲骨文
Jiang Ren (1743–1795) 蔣仁
Jiang Shantang yin 蔣山堂印
Jiang Shen (ca. 1090–1138) 江參
Jiang Zhaoshen (1925–1996) 江兆申
Jiang Zhu (b. 1625) 江注
jiaolu zhai 醮錄齋
Jiaqing (Qing emperor, r. 1796–1820) 嘉慶
Jie Xisi (1274–1344) 揭傒斯
Jiefu (d. 1762) 介福
jietuo ren 解脫人
Jin Cheng (1877–1926) 金城
Jin Nong (1687–1763) 金農
Jin Yue (17th century) 金玥
Jing Hao (active ca. 870–ca. 930) 荊浩
jinggong 精工
Jingzong (Liao emperor, r. 969–82) 景宗
jinshi 進士
jinshi 金石
jinshi pi 金石癖
jinshixue 金石學
Jixi Hu Shu Chuansha Shen Shuyong Renhe Wei Xizeng Jiasun Kuaiji Zhao Zhiqian tongshi shending yin 績谿胡澍川沙沈樹鏞仁和魏錫曾稼孫會稽趙之謙同時審定印
Ju (?) Fugui *jue* 舉父癸爵
Juran (active ca. 960–95) 巨然
Jurchen (Nüzhen) 女真
juren 舉人

kaihe 開合
Kang Se-hwang (1713–1791) 姜世晃
Kang Youwei (1858–1927) 康有為
Kangxi (Qing emperor, r. 1662–1722) 康熙
kaojuxue 考據學
kaozheng 考證
Kim Hong-do (1745–1806) 金弘道
Kim Tŭk-sin (1754–1822) 金得臣
Kim Ŭng-hwan (1742–1789) 金應煥
Kim Yun-gyŏm (1711–1775) 金允謙
Kong Keqi (active 14th century) 孔克齊
konghou 箜篌
Kŏyon-dang (active late 18th century) 居然堂

Lan Ying (1585–ca. 1644) 藍瑛
langyou 浪游
Laocan youji 老殘遊記
Laotie 老鐵
Laozi 老子
lei 類
li 理
Li Anzhong (active second half of the 12th century) 李安忠
Li Bai (701–763) 李白
Li Cheng (919–967) 李成
Li Chi (late 11th–early 12th century) 李吉
Li Dou (active 18th century) 李斗
Li Gonglin (ca. 1041–1106) 李公麟
Li Guo 李郭
Li Jiancheng (589–626) 李建成
Li Keran (1907–1989) 李可染
Li Keyong (856–908) 李克用
Li Liufang (1575–1629) 李流芳
Li Peng 李彭
Li Shan (active early 13th century) 李山
Li Sixun (653–718) 李思訓
Li Song (active ca. 1190–1230) 李嵩
Li Tang (ca. 1070s–1150s) 李唐
Li Yu (1611–1680?) 李漁
Li Yu (Pingfu) 李遹 (平甫)

Li Yufen (19th century) 李玉棻
Li Zanhua 李贊華 see Yelü Bei
Li Zhaodao (active ca. 670–730) 李昭道
Li Zhi (1527–1602) 李贄
Li Zhongqing (early Tang dynasty, 618–907) 李重慶
Liang Qingbiao (1620–1691) 梁清標
Liang Shimin (active early 12th century) 梁師閔
Lienü 列女
lin 臨
Lin Fengmian (1900–1991) 林風眠
Lin Nuer (active Chenghua era, 1465–87) 林奴兒
Lin Zexu (1785–1850) 林則徐
Linji Yixuan (d. 867) 臨濟義玄
Liu E (1857–1909) 劉鶚
Liu Guosong (b. 1932) 劉國松
Liu Haisu (1896–1994) 劉海粟
Liu Huisun 劉蕙孫
Liu Yin (1618–1664) 柳隱
Liu Yiqing (402–444) 劉義慶
Liu Yizheng (1880–1956) 劉詒徵
Liu Yong (1720–1805) 劉墉
Liu Zongyuan (773–819) 柳宗元
liufenbanshu 六分半書
Lixue 理學
Loudong 婁東
Lu Fei 陸飛
Lü Fengzi (1885–1959) 呂鳳子
Lü Wenying (active late 15th century) 呂文英
Lu Xinzhong (13th century) 陸信忠
Lu Xiujing (406–477) 陸修靜
Lu Xun (1881–1936) 魯迅
Luo Pin (1733–1799) 羅聘
Luo Qinshun (1465–1544) 羅欽順
Luo Zhenyu (1866–1940) 羅振玉

Ma Hezhi (active ca. 1130–ca. 1170) 馬和之
Ma Kui (active late 12th–early 13th century) 馬逵
Ma Lin (ca. 1180–after 1256) 馬麟
Ma Shouzhen (1548–1604) 馬守真
Ma Yuan (active ca. 1190–1225) 馬遠
Ma Yueguan (1677–1755) 馬曰琯
Ma Yuelu (1697–after 1766) 馬曰璐
Maihua maishan 賣畫買山
Mao Xiang (1611–1693) 冒襄
Mazu Daoyi (709–788) 馬祖道一
Mei Qing (1623–1697) 梅清
meiren 美人
Mi Fu (1052–1107) 米芾
Mi Wanzhong (active 1595–1628) 米萬鍾
Mi Youren (1074–1151) 米友仁
Miankai, prince (1795–1839) 綿愷
Mianyi, prince (1764–1815) 綿億
Mingdi (Liu Song emperor, r. 465–72) 明帝
mingji 名妓
Mingjiao Qisong (1011–1072) 明教契嵩
Mingzong (Later Tang emperor, r. 926–34) 明宗
Minning (prince, 1782–1850) 旻寧
Mo Shilong (d. 1587) 莫是龍
mogu 沒骨
Mou Yan (1227–1311) 牟巘

Naner sheng bu chengming shen yilao 男兒生不成名身已老
neiren 內人
Ni Yagu (1579–1633) 倪雅谷
Ni Zan (1301–1374) 倪瓚
nianfo 念佛
nianzhang 年丈
Nie Bo *zuo fuyi zun* 矢白作父乙尊

Ŏ Yu-bong (1671–1744) 魚有鳳

Pak Chi-wŏn (1737–1805) 朴趾源
Pan Tianshou (1897–1971) 潘天壽
Pang Yuanji 龐元濟
Pei Kuan (ca. 700–60) 裴寬
piaoyi 飄逸
pingchangxin 平常心

Prince Gong (1932–1898) 恭親王
Pu Xinyu (1896–1963) 溥心畬

Qi Baishi (1864–1957) 齊白石
Qian Dong (1752–1817) 錢東
Qian Qianyi (1582–1664) 錢謙益
Qian Xuan (ca. 1235–before 1307) 錢選
Qianlong (Qing emperor, r. 1736–95) 乾隆
Qiao Zhongchang (active first half of the 12th century) 喬仲常
Qidan (Khitan) 契丹
qifu 起伏
Qin Bingwen (1803–1873) 秦炳文
qing 情
qingbai 青白
Qinjinguo fei Xiaoshi (1001–1069) 秦晉國妃蕭氏
qishu 漆書
Qiu Ying (ca. 1495–1552) 仇英
Qiu Yuan (1247–after 1327) 仇遠
qiyun 氣韻
quli 曲笠

Ren Chunqi (19th century) 任春琪
Renhe Wei Xizeng Jiasun zhi yin 仁和魏錫曾稼孫之印
renyun zizai 任運自在
Rong Geng (1894–1983) 容庚
Ruan Yuan (1764–1849) 阮元

sancai 三彩
Sandai jijin wencun 三代吉金文存
Sanshisi sui jiapo renwang nai hao Beian 三十四歲家破人亡乃號悲盦
Sengyou (445–518) 僧佑
Shang Zhou yiqi tongkao 商周彝器通考
Shangjing 上京
Shen Hao (1586–ca. 1661) 沈顥
Shen Shichong (active ca. 1607–40) 沈士充
Shen Shuyong (1832–1873) 沈樹鏞
Shen Zhou (1427–1509) 沈周
shendao bei 神道碑
Sheng feng Yao Shun jun buren bian yongjue 生逢堯舜君不忍便永訣
Shengyu (1850–1900) 盛昱
shengyuan 生員
Shengzong (Liao emperor, r. 982–1031) 聖宗
Shenqing (9th century) 神清
Shenshi jinshi 沈氏金石
shensi 神似
shengding 生定
shi 實
shi 師
Shi Ke (10th century) 石恪
Shinong *zhi* 史農觶
Shitao (Daoji; 1642–1707) 石濤 (道濟)
shiwu 石屋
Shizong (Liao emperor, r. 947–51) 世宗
Shizu (Kublai Khan; Yuan emperor, r. 1260–94) 世祖
Shou Shigong (1885–1950) 壽石工
shoushu li 受書禮
shuiguan 水關
shuque chu 疎闕處
Song Xu (1525–ca. 1607) 宋旭
Songshan shaoshi shique Han hua-xiang long 嵩山少室石闕漢畫象龍
Su Hanchen (active ca. 1120s–60s) 蘇漢臣
Su Shi (1037–1101) 蘇軾
Sun Chengze (1592–1676) 孫承澤
Sun Guoting (648?–703?) 孫過庭
Sun Hu (active Qianlong era, 1736–95) 孫祜
Sun Kehong (1533–1611) 孫克弘
Sun Zhiwei 孫知微
Susong 蘇松

tali 他力
Taigu Yimin (first half of the 13th century) 太古遺民
Taizong (Liao emperor, r. 927–47) 太宗

Taizong (Song emperor, r. 976–97) 太宗
Taizong (Tang emperor, r. 626–49) 太宗
Taizu (Liao emperor, r. 907–26) 太祖
Taizu (Song emperor, r. 960–76) 太祖
Tang Dingzhi (1878–1946) 湯定之
Tang Hou (active late 13th–early 14th century) 湯垕
Tang Souyu 湯漱玉
Tang Xianzu (1550–1616) 湯顯祖
Tang Yin (1470–1524) 唐寅
Tangdai (d. 1754) 唐岱
Tanluan (475–after 554) 曇鸞
Tanyao 曇曜
Tao Qian (Tao Yuanming; 365–427) 陶潛 (陶淵明)
taohuawu 桃花塢
ti 體
tianzhen ziran 天真自然
tie 帖
Tieyun 鐵雲
Tieyun cang gui 鐵雲藏龜
Tieyun cang jin 鐵雲藏金
tongnian 同年
Tongzhi (Qing emperor, r. 1862–74) 同治
Tu Long (1542–1605) 屠隆
tuoyou 托遊

Wan Lan (active early 19th century) 萬嵐
Wang Chuzhi (d. 924) 王處直
Wang Duo (1593–1652) 王鐸
Wang Fuzhi (1619–1692) 王夫之
Wang Hui (1632–1717) 王翬
Wang Jian (1598–1677) 王鑑
Wang Meng (ca. 1308–85) 王蒙
Wang Nanming 汪南溟
Wang Ruoxu (*jinshi* 1197) 王若虛
Wang Shen (ca. 1048–after 1104) 王詵
Wang Shimao (1536–1588) 王世懋
Wang Shimin (1592–1680) 王時敏
Wang Shipeng (1112–1171) 王十朋
Wang Shizhen (1526–1590) 王世貞
Wang Tingxiang (1474–1544) 王廷相
Wang Tingyun (1151–1202) 王庭筠
Wang Tingzhang 汪廷璋
Wang Wei (700–761) 王維
Wang Ximeng (1096–1119) 王希孟
Wang Xizhi (303–361) 王羲之
Wang Yangming (1472–1529) 王陽明
Wang Yuanqi (1642–1715) 王原祁
Wang Zhen (1867–1938) 王震
Wang Zhideng (1535–1612) 王穉登
Wang Zhirui (active mid-17th century) 汪之瑞
Wei Xizeng 魏錫曾
Wen Zhengming (1470–1559) 文徵明
Wendi (Sui emperor, r. 581–604) 文帝
Weng Fanggang (1733–1818) 翁方綱
Wenxuan (Northern Qi emperor, r. 550–60) 文宣
Wo shi rulai zuixiao zhi di 我是如來最小之弟
Wu Changshuo (1844–1927) 吳昌碩
Wu Dacheng (1835–1902) 吳大澂
Wu Daozi (ca. 650s–after 758) 吳道子
Wu Hufan (1894–1968) 吳湖帆
Wu Li (1632–1718) 吳歷
Wu Sheng (active ca. 1670–1713) 吳升
Wu Xizai (1799–1870) 吳熙載
Wu Yuanzhi (active late 12th–early 13th century) 武元直
Wu Yun (early Tang dynasty, 618–907) 吳蘊
Wu Zetian (Wu Zhao; Tang empress, r. 690–705) 武則天
Wu Zhen (1280–1354) 吳鎮
Wu Zhengzhi (d. ca. 1619) 吳正志
Wu Zuoren (1908–1997) 吳作人

wucai 五彩
Wudi (Liang emperor, r. 502–50) 武帝
Wuliu 五柳
wuran 污染

Xi Gang (1746–1803) 奚岡
Xia Gui (active ca. 1195–1230) 夏珪
Xia Wenyan (active mid–14th century) 夏文彥
Xianfeng (Qing emperor, r. 1851–61) 咸豐
Xiang Deming (probably active 1573–630) 項德明
Xiang Yuanbian (1525–1590) 項元汴
Xiao Rong (active mid–11th century) 蕭瀜
Xiao Sun (1883–1944) 蕭愻
Xiao Tong (Liang prince, 501–531) 蕭統
Xiao Yuncong (1596–1673) 蕭雲從
Xiaojiaojingge jinwen tuoben 小校經閣金文拓本
Xiaowen (Northern Wei emperor, r. 471–99) 孝文
Xiaozong (Song emperor, r. 1162–89) 孝宗
Xie An (320–385) 謝安
Xie He (active ca. 479–502) 謝赫
Xie Lingyun (385–433) 謝靈運
Xie Zhen (1495–1575) 謝榛
Xieli Kehan 頡利可汗
xieyi 寫意
Xiling 西泠
xin 心
Xin'an 新安
xing 興
xingling 性靈
xingsi 形似
Xingzong (Liao emperor, r. 1031–55) 興宗
Xinjing shixue 新經世學
xinxue 心學
xinza 心雜
Xiongnu 匈奴
xiuding 修定
xiyangjing 西洋鏡
xu 虛
Xu Bangda (b. 1911) 徐邦達
Xu Beihong (1895–1953) 徐悲鴻
Xu Daoning (ca. 1000–after 1066) 許道寧
Xu Wei (1521–1593) 徐渭
Xu Xiake (1586–1641) 徐霞客
Xu Yongqing (1880–1953) 徐詠青
Xu Zhengqing (1479–1511) 徐禎卿
Xuantong (Qing emperor, r. 1909–11) 宣統
Xuanwang (Zhou king, r. 827–782 B.C.) 宣王
Xue Wu (ca. 1573–1620) 薛五

Yan Ciping (active ca. 1162–89) 閻次平
Yan Ciyu (active ca. 1162–89) 閻次于
Yan Wengui (active ca. 970–1030) 燕文貴
Yang Meizi (1162–1232) 楊妹子
Yang Yunyi (1170–1228) 楊雲翼
Yangdi (Sui emperor, r. 604–17) 煬帝
Yao Shou (1423–1495) 姚綬
Yao Tingmei (14th century) 姚廷美
Ye Fanglin (active late 17th–early 18th century) 葉芳林
Yelü Bei (899–936) 耶律倍
Yelü Yuan (918–951) 耶律阮
Yi Bingshou (1754–1815) 伊秉綬
Yi Ik (1681–1763) 李瀷
Yi In-sang (1710–1760) 李麟祥
Yi Su-gwang (1563–1628) 李粹光
Yi Yun-yŏng (1714–1759) 李胤永
yimin 遺民
Yin Zhongkan (late 4th–early 5th century) 殷仲勘
yixing xieshen 移形寫神
Yonglin, prince (1766–1820) 永璘
Yongxing, prince (1752–1823) 永瑆
Yongxuan, prince (1746–1832) 永璇
You Wenhui (1575–1633) 游文輝

Yu Feian (1881–1959) 于非闇
Yu Huai (1616–1696) 余懷
Yu Shaosong (1882–1955) 余紹宋
Yu Zhiding (1647–after 1709) 禹之鼎
Yuan Haowen (1190–1257) 元好問
Yuan Hongdao (1568–1610) 袁宏道
Yuan Zhongdao (1570–1624) 袁中道
Yuan Zongdao (1560–1600) 袁宗道
Yun Shouping (1633–1690) 惲壽平
Yun Tu-sŏ (1668–1715) 尹斗緒
Yushan 虞山

Zha Shibiao (1615–1698) 查士標
Zhang Chongren (1907–1998) 張充仁
Zhang Chou (1577–1643) 張丑
Zhang Daqian (1899–1983) 張大千
Zhang Geng (1685–1760) 張庚
Zhang Huanzhen 張還真
Zhang Ji (active second half of the 11th century–first half of the 12th century) 張激
Zhang Jizhi (1186–1266) 張即之
Zhang Shen (early Ming dynasty, 1368–1644) 張紳
Zhang Weichi 張維持
Zhang Yanchang (1738–1814) 張燕昌
Zhang Yin (1761–1829) 張崟
Zhang Yu (1277–1348) 張雨
Zhang Yue (1832–1891) 張曜
Zhang Yuguang (1885–1966) 張聿光
Zhang Zai (1020–1077) 張載
Zhang Zhao (1691–1745) 張照
Zhang Zikun (1734–1791) 張自坤
Zhao Bingwen (1159–1232) 趙秉文
Zhao Boju (ca. 1120–1162) 趙伯駒
Zhao Bosu (1124–1182) 趙伯驌
Zhao Danian (Zhao Lingrang; active ca. 1080–1100) 趙大年 (趙令穰)
Zhao Fu (active Shaoxing era, 1131–62) 趙黻
Zhao Lingjun 趙令晙
Zhao Mengfu (1254–1322) 趙孟頫
Zhao Tingxi (active early to mid-19th century) 趙廷熙
Zhao Xigu (ca. 1190) 趙希鵠
Zhao Yong (1289–after 1360) 趙雍
Zhao Yuan (d. after 1373) 趙原
Zhao Zhicheng 趙志成
Zhao Zhiqian (1829–1884) 趙之謙
Zhao Zuo (ca. 1570–after 1633) 趙左
Zheng Chang (1894–1952) 鄭昶
Zheng Sixiao (1239–1316) 鄭思肖
Zheng Xie (1693–1765) 鄭燮
zhengli guoku 整理國庫
Zhengzhai jinshi 鄭齋金石
Zhenshui wuxiang 真水無香
Zhensongtang jijin tulu 貞松堂吉金圖錄
Zhipan (active 1258–1269) 志磐
Zhou Bida (1126–1204) 周必大
Zhou Hao (1685–1773) 周顥
Zhou Jichang (active late 12th century) 周季常
Zhou Mi (1232–1298) 周密
Zhou Tianqiu (1514–1595) 周天球
Zhou Wenju (active ca. 940–75) 周文矩
Zhou Xiang (1871–1933) 周湘
Zhou Zhaoxiang (1880–1953) 周肇祥
Zhu Da (1626–1705) 朱耷
Zhu Henian (1760–1834) 朱鶴年
Zhu Wenzhen (active ca. 1740–70) 朱文震
Zhu Xi (1130–1220) 朱熹
Zhu Yunming (1461–1527) 祝允明
Zhuang Su (active late 13th century) 莊肅
zili 自力
zongheng 縱橫
Zongmi (780–841) 宗密
Zou Yigui (1686–1772) 鄒一桂
Zou Zhilin (active early 17th century) 鄒之麟
zuolübao 作旅寶

Editor Judith G. Smith
Associate Editors Raymond Furse, Elizabeth Powers

Book design and production by Binocular, New York
Chinese characters typeset by Birdtrack Press, New Haven, CT
Printed and bound in Canada by Friesens

Jacket illustration: Zhao Mengfu (1254–1322), *Autumn Colors on the Que and Hua Mountains*, dated 1296. Handscroll, ink and color on paper, 11¼ × 36¾ in. (28.4 × 93.2 cm). National Palace Museum, Taipei. Detail

Library of Congress Cataloguing-in-Publication Data:
Tradition and transformation : studies in Chinese art in honor of Chu-tsing Li / edited by Judith G. Smith. — 1st ed.
p. cm.
Includes bibliographical references.
ISBN 0-295-98573-9 (hardback : alk. paper)
1. Art, Chinese. I. Smith, Judith G., 1941– . II. Li, Chu-tsing, 1920– . III. Helen Foresman Spencer Museum of Art. IV. Title: Studies in Chinese art in honor of Chu-tsing Li.
N7340.T69 2005
709.51—dc22 2005025948